AND DATA COMMUNICATIONS TE

COMPUTER SECURITY (with

A comprehensive treatment of computer security technology, including algorithms, protocols, and applications. Covers cryptography, authentication, access control, database security, intrusion detection and prevention, malicious software, denial of service, firewalls, software security, physical security, human factors, auditing, legal and ethical aspects, and trusted systems. **Received the 2008 Text and Academic Authors Association (TAA) award for the best Computer Science and Engineering Textbook of the year.** ISBN 0-13-600424-5

NETWORK SECURITY ESSENTIALS, THIRD EDITION

A tutorial and survey on network security technology. The book covers important network security tools and applications, including S/MIME, IP Security, Kerberos, SSL/TLS, SET, and X509v3. In addition, methods for countering hackers and viruses are explored. ISBN 0-13-238033-1

WIRELESS COMMUNICATIONS AND NETWORKS, SECOND EDITION

A comprehensive, state-of-the art survey. Covers fundamental wireless communications topics, including antennas and propagation, signal encoding techniques, spread spectrum, and error correction techniques. Examines satellite, cellular, wireless local loop networks and wireless LANs, including Bluetooth and 802.11. Covers Mobile IP and WAP. ISBN 0-13-191835-4

COMPUTER NETWORKS WITH INTERNET PROTOCOLS AND TECHNOLOGY

An up-to-date survey of developments in the area of Internet-based protocols and algorithms. Using a top-down approach, this book covers applications, transport layer, Internet QoS, Internet routing, data link layer and computer networks, security, and network management. ISBN 0-13141098-9

HIGH-SPEED NETWORKS AND INTERNETS, SECOND EDITION

A state-of-the art survey of high-speed networks. Topics covered include TCP congestion control, ATM traffic management, Internet traffic management, differentiated and integrated services, Internet routing protocols and multicast routing protocols, resource reservation and RSVP, and lossless and lossy compression. Examines important topic of self-similar data traffic. ISBN 0-13-03221-0

BUSINESS DATA COMMUNICATIONS

SIXTH EDITION

William Stallings

PEARSON
Prentice
Hall

Upper Saddle River, New Jersey 07458

Library of Congress Cataloging in Publication Data on File

Executive Editor: Tracy Dunkelberger
Editorial Director: Marcia J. Horton
Editorial Assistant: Melinda Haggerty
Marketing Manager: Erin Davis
Senior Managing Editor: Scott Disanno
Production Editor: Rose Kernan
Senior Operations Supervisor: Alexis Heydt-Long
Operations Specialist: Lisa McDowell
Design Manager: Kenny Beck
Cover Design: Kristine Carney
Director, Image Resource Center: Melinda Patelli
Manager, Rights and Permissions: Zina Arabia
Manager, Visual Research: Beth Brenzel
Manager, Cover Visual Research & Permissions: Karen Sanatar
Composition: Aptara
Printer/Binder: Edwards Brothers

Pearson Education LTD. London
Pearson Education Singapore, Pte. Ltd
Pearson Education, Canada, Ltd
Pearson Education–Japan
Pearson Education Australia PTY, Limited

Pearson Education North Asia Ltd
Pearson Educación de Mexico, S.A. de C.V.
Pearson Education Malaysia, Pte. Ltd
Pearson Education, Upper Saddle River, New Jersey

10 9 8 7 6 5 4 3 2 1
ISBN-13: 978-0-13-606745-0
ISBN-10:   0-13-606745-X

For my loving wife ATS, the best, the bravest, the kindest

CONTENTS

Preface xi

Chapter 0   Reader's Guide 1

   0.1   Outline of This Book 2
   0.2   Topic Ordering 2
   0.3   Internet and Web Resources 3
   0.4   Useful Publications 4

Chapter 1   Introduction 6

   1.1   Information and Communication 7
   1.2   Data Communications and Networking for Today's Enterprise 8
   1.3   Convergence and Unified Communications 10
   1.4   The Nature of Business Information Requirements 15
   1.5   Distributed Data Processing 17
   1.6   The Internet and Distributed Applications 17
   1.7   Networks 19
   1.8   The Transmission of Information 24
   1.9   Management Issues 26
   1.10   Standards 27
   1.11   Recommended Reading and Web Sites 28
   1.12   Key Terms and Review Questions 29
        Appendix 1A Prefixes for Numerical Units 29

PART ONE REQUIREMENTS 31

Chapter 2   Business Information 32

   2.1   Audio 33
   2.2   Data 36
   2.3   Image 37
   2.4   Video 40
   2.5   Performance Measures 42
        Application Note: File Sizes 47
   2.6   Summary 48
   2.7   Recommended Reading and Web Sites 48
   2.8   Key Terms, Review Questions, and Problems 48

Chapter 3   Distributed Data Processing 52

   3.1   Centralized Versus Distributed Processing 53
   3.2   Forms of Distributed Data Processing 62
   3.3   Distributed Data 65
   3.4   Networking Implications of DDP 71
        Application Note: Distributed Computing Support 73
   3.5   Summary 74
   3.6   Recommended Reading 74
   3.7   Key Terms, Review Questions, and Problems 75

Case Study I MasterCard International 78

PART TWO THE INTERNET AND DISTRIBUTED APPLICATIONS 81

Chapter 4   The Internet 83

    4.1   Internet History 84
    4.2   Internet Architecture 91
    4.3   Internet Domains 95
        Application Note: Fitting DNS into your organizational structure 101
    4.4   Summary 102
    4.5   Recommended Reading and Web Sites 103
    4.6   Key Terms, Review Questions, and Problems 103

Chapter 5   TCP/IP and OSI 106

    5.1   A Simple Protocol Architecture 107
    5.2   The TCP/IP Protocol Architecture 114
    5.3   Internetworking 121
    5.4   The OSI Protocol Architecture 125
    5.5   Virtual Private Networks and IP Security 130
        Application Note: Practical Guide to Networking 133
    5.6   Summary 134
    5.7   Recommended Reading and Web Sites 134
    5.8   Key Terms, Review Questions, and Problems 135
        Appendix 5A TCP UDP, and IP Details 138
        Appendix 5B The Trivial File Transfer Protocol 142

Case Study II Florida Department of Management Services—Part One 147

Chapter 6   Client/Server and Intranet Computing 152

    6.1   The Growth of Client/Server Computing 153
    6.2   Client/Server Applications 157
    6.3   Middleware 163
    6.4   Intranets 170
    6.5   Extranets 174
    6.6   Service Oriented Architecture 179
        Application Note: To Be Fat or Thin – That is the Question 179
    6.7   Summary 180
    6.8   Recommended Reading and Web Sites 181
    6.9   Key Terms, Review Questions, and Problems 182

Chapter 7   Internet-Based Applications 185

    7.1   Electronic Mail and SMTP 186
    7.2   Web Access and HTTP 200
    7.3   Web Security 205
    7.4   Internet Telephony and SIP 208
        Application Note: To Serve or Not to Serve 218
    7.5   Summary 219
    7.6   Recommended Reading and Web Sites 220
    7.7   Key Terms, Review Questions, and Problems 221

Case Study III ING Life 223

Chapter 8   Internet Operation 226

    8.1   Internet Addressing 227
    8.2   Internet Routing Protocols 230
    8.3   The Need for Speed and Quality of Service 237
    8.4   Differentiated Services 242

8.5   Service Level Agreements 249
8.6   IP Performance Metrics 250
            Application Note: Where Does My Network Address Come From? 253
8.7   Summary 255
8.8   Recommended Reading and Web Sites 255
8.9   Key Terms, Review Questions, and Problems 256

PART THREE LOCAL AREA NETWORKS 259

Chapter 9   LAN Architecture and Protocols 260

9.1   Background 261
9.2   LAN Configurations 265
9.3   Guided Transmission Media 267
9.4   LAN Protocol Architecture 276
            Application Note: Cabling Infrastructure 281
9.5   Summary 282
9.6   Recommended Reading and Web Sites 283
9.7   Key Terms, Review Questions, and Problems 283
            Appendix 9A Decibels and Signal Strength 285

Chapter 10   Ethernet 288

10.1   Traditional Ethernet 290
10.2   Bridges, Hubs, and Switches 294
10.3   High-Speed Ethernet 301
             Application Note: Networking with Ethernet 308
10.4   Summary 309
10.5   Recommended Reading and Web Sites 310
10.6   Key Terms, Review Questions, and Problems 311

Case Study IV Carlson Companies 313

Chapter 11   Wireless LANs 316

11.1   Overview 317
11.2   Wi-Fi Architecture and Services 322
11.3   IEEE 802.11 MAC and Physical Layer Standards 327
11.4   IEEE 802.11 Security Considerations 333
             Application Note: Deploying Wireless LANs 334
11.5   Summary 336
11.6   Recommended Reading and Web Sites 336
11.7   Key Terms, Review Questions, and Problems 337

Case Study V St. Luke's Episcopal Hospital 339

PART FOUR WIDE AREA NETWORKS 342

Chapter 12   Circuit Switching and Packet Switching 343

12.1   Switching Techniques 344
12.2   Circuit-Switching Networks 345
12.3   Packet-Switching Networks 354
12.4   Traditional Wide Area Network Alternatives 359
             Application Note: Switching 364
12.5   Summary 366
12.6   Recommended Reading and Web Sites 366
12.7   Key Terms, Review Questions, and Problems 367

Chapter 13   Frame Relay and ATM 369

  13.1   Wide Area Networking Alternatives 370
  13.2   Frame Relay 374
  13.3   Asynchronous Transfer Mode (ATM) 381
          Application Note: Offsite Connectivity Solutions 389
  13.4   Summary 391
  13.5   Recommended Reading and Web Sites 391
  13.6   Key Terms, Review Questions, and Problems 392

Case Study VI Florida Department of Management Services—Part Two 395

Case Study VII Guardian Life Insurance 400

Chapter 14   Wireless WANs 403

  14.1   Cellular Wireless Networks 404
  14.2   Multiple Access 412
  14.3   Third-Generation Wireless Communications 417
  14.4   Satellite Communications 420
          Application Note: PDAs, Cell Phones, and Laptops 426
  14.5   Summary 428
  14.6   Recommended Reading and Web Sites 428
  14.7   Key Terms, Review Questions, and Problems 429

Case Study VIII Choice Hotels International 432

PART FIVE DATA COMMUNICATIONS 435

Chapter 15   Data Transmission 437

  15.1   Signals for Conveying Information 438
  15.2   Transmission Impairments and Channel Capacity 447
          Application Note: Analog Signals 453
  15.3   Summary 455
  15.4   Recommended Reading and Web Sites 455
  15.5   Key Terms, Review Questions, and Problems 456

Chapter 16   Data Communication Fundamentals 458

  16.1   Analog and Digital Data Communications 459
  16.2   Data Encoding Techniques 463
  16.3   Asynchronous and Synchronous Transmission 472
  16.4   Error Detection 476
          Application Note: Devices, Encoding, Communication Parameters and Protocols 478
  16.5   Summary 479
  16.6   Recommended Reading and Web Sites 480
  16.7   Key Terms, Review Questions, and Problems 480

Chapter 17   Data Link Control and Multiplexing 483

  17.1   Flow Control and Error Control 484
  17.2   High-Level Data Link Control 486
  17.3   Motivation for Multiplexing 492
  17.4   Frequency Division Multiplexing 493
  17.5   Synchronous Time Division Multiplexing 500
          Application Note: Changing Communications 506
  17.6   Summary 507

17.7   Recommended Reading and Web Sites 508
17.8   Key Terms, Review Questions, and Problems 509

Case Study IX Haukeland University Hospital 511

PART SIX MANAGEMENT ISSUES 514

Chapter18   Computer and Network Security Threats 515

18.1   Computer Security Concepts 516
18.2   Threats, Attacks, and Assets 518
18.3   Intruders 523
18.4   Malicious Software Overview 527
18.5   Viruses, Worms, and Bots 531
18.6   Recommended Reading and Web Sites 541
18.7   Key Terms, Review Questions, and Problems 542

Chapter 19   Computer and Network Security Techniques 545

19.1   Virtual Private Networks and IPSec 546
19.2   SSL and TLS 548
19.3   Wi-Fi Protected Access 552
19.4   Intrusion Detection 555
19.5   Firewalls 558
19.6   Malware Defense 566
             Application Note: Security Layers 572
19.7   Recommended Reading 573
19.8   Key Terms, Review Questions, and Problems 574

Case Study X The Hacker in All of Us 577

Chapter 20   Network Management *(ONLINE)* 20-1

20.1   Network Management Requirements 20-2
20.2   Network Management Systems 20-6
20.3   Simple Network Management Protocol (SNMP) 20-8
             Application Note: How Much Management? 20-18
20.4   Recommended Reading and Web Sites 20-19
20.5   Key Terms, Review Questions, and Problems 20-20

Chapter 21   Network Planning and Design *(ONLINE)* 21-1

21.1   The Project Environment — The Big Picture 21-2
21.2   Planning 21-4
21.3   Design Techniques 21-9
21.4   Some Capacity Planning and Network Design Tools 21-11
             Appendix 21A Some Simple Design Algorithms 21-11
             Appendix 21B Selling Books Online — A Case Study 21-19

Appendix A   Business Data Communications Projects 581

A.1   Animation and Animation Projects 582
A.2   Practical Exercises 583
A.3   Ethereal Projects 584
A.4   Research Projects 584
A.5   Reading/Report Assignments 584
A.6   Writing Assignments 585

Glossary 586

References 593

Index 602

ONLINE APPENDICES   **William Stallings.com/BDC/BDC6e.html**

Appendix B   Standards Organizations

   B.1   The Importance of Standards
   B.2   Standards and Regulation
   B.3   Standards-Setting Organizations

Appendix C   Uniform Resource Locators (URLs) and Uniform Resource Identifiers (URIs)

   C.1   Uniform Resource Locator
   C.2   Uniform Resource Identifier
   C.3   To Learn More

Appendix D   The International Reference Alphabet

Appendix E   The TCP/IP Checksum

   E.1   Ones-Complement Addition
   E.2   Use in TCP and IP

Appendix F   IBM's System Network Architecture (SNA)

   F.1   Network Architecture
   F.2   Advanced Program-to-Program Communication
   F.3   Protocol Architecture

Appendix G   Fibre Channel

   G.1   Fibre Channel Elements
   G.2   Fibre Channel Protocol Architecture

Appendix H   Bluetooth

   H.1   Bluetooth Applications
   H.2   Bluetooth Standards Documents
   H.3   Protocol Architecture
   H.4   Usage Models
   H.5   Piconets and Scatternets

Appendix I   Multipath Interference and Orthogonal Frequency-Division Multiplexing (OFDM)

   I.1   Multipath Interference
   I.2   Orthogonal Frequency-Division Multiplexing

Appendix J   Cryptographic Algorithms

   J.1   Symmetric Encryption
   J.2   Public-Key Cryptography
   J.3   Message Authentication and Hash Functions
   J.4   Secure Hash Functions

Appendix K   Sliding-Window Flow Control and Error Control

   K.1   Flow Control
   K.2   Error Control

PREFACE

Over the past several decades, as data processing capability has been introduced into the office, data communications products and services have gradually assumed increasing importance. Now, technological developments and the widespread acceptance of standards are transforming the ways in which information is used to support the business function. In addition to the traditional communications requirements for voice and data (meaning text and numerical data), there is now the need to deal with pictorial images and video information. These four types of information (voice, data, image, and video) are essential to the survival of any business in today's competitive international environment. What is needed in a business data communications book is a treatment not just of **data communications** but also of **information communications** for the business environment.

Information communications and computer networking have become essential to the functioning of today's businesses, large and small. Furthermore, they have become a major and growing cost to organizations. Management and staff need a thorough understanding of information communications in order to assess needs; plan for the introduction of products, services, and systems; and manage the systems and technical personnel that operate them. This understanding must comprise the following:

- **Technology:** The underlying technology of information communications facilities, networking systems, and communications software
- **Architecture:** The way in which hardware, software, and services can be organized to provide computer and terminal interconnection
- **Applications:** How information communications and networking systems can meet the requirements of today's businesses

APPROACH

The purpose of this text is to present the concepts of information communications in a way that relates specifically to the business environment and to the concerns of business management and staff. To this end, the book takes an approach based on requirements, ingredients, and applications:

- **Requirements:** The need to provide services that enable businesses to utilize information is the driving force behind data and information communications technology. The text outlines the specific requirements that this technology is intended to address. This linkage between requirements and technology is essential to motivate a text of this nature.
- **Ingredients:** The technology of information communications includes the hardware, software, and communications services available to support distributed systems. An understanding of this technology is essential for a manager to make intelligent choices among the many alternatives.
- **Applications:** Management and staff must understand not only the technology but also the way in which that technology can be applied to satisfy business requirements.

These three concepts structure the presentation. They provide a way for the student to understand the context of what is being discussed at any point in the text, and they motivate the material. Thus, the student will gain a *practical* understanding of business information communications.

An important theme throughout the book is the essential role of standards. The proliferation of personal computers and other computer systems inevitably means that the manager will be faced with the need to integrate equipment from a variety of vendors. The only way to manage this requirement effectively is through standards. And, indeed, increasingly vendors are offering products and services that conform to international standards. This text addresses some of the key groupings of standards that are shaping the marketplace and that define the choices available to the decision maker.

INTENDED AUDIENCE

This book is addressed to students and professionals who now have or expect to have some information technology management responsibility. As a full-time job, some readers may have or plan to have responsibility for management of the company's telecommunications function. But virtually all managers and many staff personnel will need to have a basic understanding of business information communications to perform their tasks effectively.

For students, this text is intended as an introductory course in information communications for business and information management students. It does not assume any background in data communications but does assume a basic knowledge of data processing.

The book is also intended for self-study and is designed for use as both a tutorial and a reference book for those already involved in business information communications.

PLAN OF THE TEXT

This text is a survey of the broad and fast-changing field of information communications. It is organized in such a way that new material is seen to fit into the context of the material already presented. By emphasizing requirements and applications as well as technology, the student is provided with motivation and a means of assessing the importance of a particular topic with respect to the whole. The book is divided into six parts:

1. **Requirements:** Defines the needs for information communications in the business environment. It discusses the way in which various forms of information are used and the need for interconnection and networking facilities. An examination of the nature and role of distributed data processing is the highlight of this first part.

2. **The Internet and Distributed Applications:** Provides an overview of the Internet and the basic protocols that are the foundation of the Internet and also addresses the critical issue of quality of service. This part also deals with the specific business applications that require information communications facilities and networks. This part presents key applications, such as electronic mail and the World Wide Web, and includes a discussion of client/server computing and intranets.

3. **Local Area Networks:** Explores the technologies and architectures that have been developed for networking over shorter distances. The transmission media,

topologies, and medium access control protocols that are the key ingredients of a Local Area Network (LAN) design are explored and specific standardized LAN systems examined.

4. **Wide Area Networks:** Examines the internal mechanisms and user-network interfaces that have been developed to support voice, data, and multimedia communications over long-distance networks. The traditional technologies of packet switching and circuit switching are examined, as well as the more recent Asynchrous Transfer Mode (ATM) and wireless Wide Area Networks (WANs).

5. **Data Communications:** Deals with the basic technology of the communication of information. The emphasis is on digital communications techniques, since these are rapidly displacing analog techniques for all products and services related to information communications. Key topics include transmission media, data link control protocols, and multiplexing.

6. **Management Issues:** Deals with two key areas: network security and network management.

This ordering of topics represents a more-or-less **top-down approach**, with the early part of the book dealing with applications and upper level protocols. Some instructors may prefer a **bottom-up approach**, and the book is designed to accommodate that sequence as well. See Chapter 0 for a discussion.

In addition, the book includes an extensive glossary, a list of frequently used acronyms, and a bibliography. Each chapter includes review questions, problems and suggestions for further reading. Finally, a number of real-world cases studies are sprinkled throughout the book.

INSTRUCTOR SUPPORT MATERIALS

The major goal of this text is to make it as effective a teaching tool for this exciting and fast-moving subject as possible. This goal is reflected both in the structure of the book and in the supporting material.

The book contains a number of features that provide strong pedagogical support for the instructor. Each chapter begins with a list of chapter objectives, which provides, in effect, an outline of the chapter and alerts the student to look for certain key concepts as the chapter is read. Key terms are introduced in boldface in the chapter, and all of the new key terms for that chapter are listed at the end of the chapter. Acronyms are highlighted and listed on the back endpaper; this is important because the field of information communications is loaded with acronyms. A glossary at the end of the book provides a handy summary of key terms. The summary at the end of each chapter highlights the key concepts and places them in the context of the entire book. In addition, there are questions and homework problems to reinforce and extend what has been learned. The book is also liberally supplied with figures and tables to enhance points made in the text.

Throughout the book a number of case studies are presented. These are not "made-up" or "toy" cases but actual cases reported in the literature. Each case is chosen to reinforce or extend concepts introduced prior to the case study.

The text is also accompanied by the following supplementary material that will aid the instructor:

- **Solutions manual:** Solutions to end-of-chapter review questions and problems
- **Projects manual:** Suggested project assignments for all of the project categories listed later in this Preface, together with supporting materials
- **PowerPoint slides:** A set of slides covering all chapters, suitable for use in lecturing
- **PDF files:** Reproductions of all figures and tables from the book

All of these support materials are available at the Instructor Resource Center (IRC) for this textbook. To gain access to the IRC, please contact your local Prentice Hall sales representative via **pearsonhighered.com/educator/replocator** or call Prentice Hall Faculty Services at 1-800-526-0485.

In addition, the book's Web site at williamstallings.com/BDC/BDC6e supports instructors with

- Links to Web sites for other courses being taught using this book
- Sign-up information for an Internet mailing list for instructors

INTERNET SERVICES FOR INSTRUCTORS AND STUDENTS

There is a Web page for this book that provides support for students and instructors. The page includes links to relevant sites, transparency masters of figures in the book in PDF format, PowerPoint slides, and sign-up information for the book's Internet mailing list. The Web page is at **WilliamStallings.com/BDC/BDC6e.html**. An Internet mailing list has been set up so that instructors using this book can exchange information, suggestions, and questions with each other and with the author. As soon as typos or other errors are discovered, an errata list for this book will be available at **WilliamStallings.com**. Finally, I maintain the Computer Science Student Resource Site at **WilliamStallings.com/StudentSupport.html**.

PROJECTS AND OTHER STUDENT EXERCISES

For many instructors, an important component of a Business Data Communications course is a project or set of projects by which the student gets hands-on experience to reinforce concepts from the text. This book provides an unparalleled degree of support for including a projects component in the course. The instructor's support materials available through Prentice Hall not only includes guidance on how to assign and structure the projects but also includes a set of specific assignments written especially for this book. Instructors can assign work in the following areas:

- **Animation assignments:** Described in the following section.
- **Practical exercises:** Using network commands, the student gains experience in network connectivity.
- **Wireshark projects:** Wireshark, formerly known as Ethereal, is a protocol analyzer that enables students to study the behavior of protocols.
- **Research projects:** A series of research assignments that instruct the student to research a particular topic on the Internet and write a report.
- **Reading/report assignments:** A list of papers that can be assigned for reading and writing a report, plus suggested assignment wording.
- **Writing assignments:** A list of writing assignments to facilitate learning the material.

This diverse set of projects and other student exercises enables the instructor to use the book as one component in a rich and varied learning experience and to tailor a course plan to meet the specific needs of the instructor and students. See Appendix A in this book for details.

ANIMATIONS

New to this edition is the incorporation of animations. Animations provide a powerful tool for understanding the complex mechanisms of network protocols. A total of 12 Web-based animations are used to illustrate protocol behavior. At various points in the book, an icon indicates that a relevant animation is available online for student use. Each animation allows the users to step through the operation of the protocol by selecting the next step at each point in the protocol exchange. The entire protocol exchange is illustrated by an animated diagram as the exchange proceeds. The animations can be used in two ways. In a **passive mode**, the student can click more or less randomly on the next step at each point in the animation and watch as the given concept or principle is illustrated. In an **active mode**, the user can be given a specific set of steps to invoke and watch the animation, or be given a specific end point and devise a sequence of steps that achieve the desired result. Thus, the animations can serve as the basis for student assignments. The instructor's supplement includes a set of assignments for each of the animations, plus suggested solutions so that instructors can assess the student's work.

WHAT'S NEW IN THE SIXTH EDITION

In the five years since the fifth edition of this book was published, the field has seen continued innovations and improvements. In this new edition, we try to capture these changes while maintaining a broad and comprehensive coverage of the entire field. To begin the process of revision, the fifth edition of this book was extensively reviewed by a number of professors who teach the subject and by professionals working in the field. The result is that, in many places, the narrative has been clarified and tightened, and illustrations have been improved.

Beyond these refinements to improve pedagogy and user friendliness, there have been major substantive changes throughout the book. Highlights include the following:

- **Animations:** Animation provides a powerful tool for understanding the complex mechanisms of network protocols. The sixth edition incorporates 12 separate animations covering such protocols as HyperText Transfer Protocol (HTTP), Simple Mail Transfer Protocol (SMTP), and Transmission Control Protocol (TCP).
- **Updated coverage of WiFi/IEEE 802.11 wireless LANs:** IEEE 802.11 and the related WiFi specifications have continued to evolve. Expanded coverage includes 802.11n.
- **Updated coverage of Gigabit Ethernet, 10-Gbps Ethernet, and 100-Gbps Ethernet:** New details of these standards are provided.
- **New coverage of IP performance metrics and service level agreements (SLAs):** These aspects of quality of service (QoS) and performance monitoring are increasingly important.
- **New coverage of unified communications:** Coverage includes unified communications, convergence, and service-oriented architecture (SOA).

- **Expanded coverage of security:** The coverage of security, in Part Six, has been completely rewritten and expanded to two chapters. It is more detailed, covering a number of new topics. In addition, at key points in the book (Chapters 5, 7, and 11) there is an overview of security for the relevant topic.

With each new edition it is a struggle to maintain a reasonable page count while adding new material. In part this objective is realized by eliminating obsolete material and tightening the narrative. For this edition, chapters and appendices that are of less general interest have been moved online, as individual PDF files. This has allowed an expansion of material without the corresponding increase in size and price.

ACKNOWLEDGMENTS

This new edition has benefited from review by a number of people, who gave generously of their time and expertise. The following people reviewed all or a large part of the manuscript: Edwin Otto (Webster University, MO); Richard Macarthy (Charter Oak State College, CT); Samuel Yang (Fullerton State, CA); Dan Turk (Colorado State University); Sang-Baek Chris Kang (University of Missouri, St. Louis) Morgan Shepherd (University of Colorado, Colorado Springs); Jeff Zhang (CA State University, Northridge); John Rupf (Southern Polytechnic State, GA); Song Xing (CA State University, Los Angeles); D. Scott Weaver (Messiah College, PA); and Huei Lee (Eastern Michigan University).

Thanks also to the people who provided detailed technical reviews of a one or more chapters: Nikhil Bhargava (Hughes Systique, India), John South (University of Dallas), Paul Pot, Vance Shipley, Jennifer Jabbusch, and Peter Tregunno.

Bruce Hartpence (Department of Information Technology, Rochester Institute of Technology) authored the application notes at the end of each chapter and contributed a number of review questions and homework problems. Ric Heishman (Assistant Dean—Computer Science & Information Technology, Northern Virginia Community College) also contributed homework problems. Fernando Ariel Gont contributed a number of homework problems.

Larry Tan of the University of Stirling in Scotland developed the animation assignments. Michael Harris of Indiana University initially developed the Wireshark exercises and user's guide. Dave Bremer, a principal lecturer at Otago Polytechnic in New Zealand, updated the material for the most recent Wireshark release; he also developed an online video tutorial for using Wireshark.

Steven Kilby contributed the case study on ING Life, and he contributed part of Chapter 4. Professor Varadharajan Sridhar of the Indian Institute of Management contributed the case study on Staten Island University Hospital.

Richard Van Slyke of Brooklyn Polytechnic Institute made substantial contributions to earlier editions of this book and was listed as a coauthor. Much of his contribution has been retained and revised.

Finally, I would like to thank the many people responsible for the publication of the book, all of whom did their usual excellent job. This includes my editor Tracy Dunkelberger, her assistant Melinda Hagerty, production manager Rose Kernan, and supplements manager ReeAnne Davies. Also, Jake Warde of Warde Publishers managed the reviews; and Patricia M. Daly did the copy editing.

CHAPTER 0

READER'S GUIDE

0.1   **Outline of This Book**

0.2   **Topic Ordering**

0.3   **Internet and Web Resources**

Web Sites for This Book
Other Web Sites
USENET Newsgroups

0.4   **Useful Publications**

This book, with its accompanying Web site, covers a lot of material. In this chapter, we give the reader an overview.

0.1 OUTLINE OF THIS BOOK

Following an introductory chapter, the book is organized into six parts:

Part One Requirements: Defines the needs for information communications in the business environment. Discusses the way in which various forms of information are used and the need for interconnection and networking facilities. An examination of the nature and role of distributed data processing is the highlight of this first part.

Part Two The Internet and Distributed Applications: Provides an overview of the Internet and the basic protocols that are the foundation of the Internet and addresses the critical issue of quality of service (QoS). This part also deals with the specific business applications that require information communications facilities and networks. This part presents key applications, such as electronic mail and the World Wide Web, and includes a discussion of client/server computing and intranets.

Part Three Local Area Networks: Explores the technologies and architectures that have been developed for networking over shorter distances. The transmission media, topologies, and medium access control protocols that are the key ingredients of a local area network (LAN) design are explored and specific standardized LAN systems are examined.

Part Four Wide Area Networks: Examines the internal mechanisms and user–network interfaces that have been developed to support voice, data, and multimedia communications over long-distance networks. The traditional technologies of packet switching and circuit switching are examined, as well as the more recent Asynchronous Transfer Mode (ATM) and wireless wide area networks (WANs).

Part Five Data Communications: Deals with the basic technology of information communication. The emphasis is on digital communications techniques, since these are rapidly displacing analog techniques for all products and services related to information communications. Key topics include transmission media, data link control protocols, and multiplexing.

Part Six Management Issues: Deals with two key areas: network security and network management.

A number of online appendices at this book's Web site cover additional topics relevant to the book.

0.2 TOPIC ORDERING

The book is laid out to present the material in a top-down fashion. The business reader wants, and rightly so, to see the technical material in the context of the needs of the business and the ways in which communications and networking technology support desired business functions. Thus this book begins by defining the requirements for information communications in business. The types of information and their utility are examined first. This sets the stage to discuss the applications that can meet those requirements and the role of the Internet in supporting the applications. We are then in a position to examine the communications networks, both LANs and WANs, that form the infrastructure for distributed applications and the network. Continuing in this top-down fashion, the book then examines fundamental communications technologies. Finally, security and network management issues are discussed. It is hoped that this strategy will make the material more comprehensible and provide a structure that is more natural to a reader with a business orientation.

Some readers, and some instructors, are more comfortable with a bottom-up approach. With this approach, each part builds on the material in the previous part, so that it is always clear how a given layer of functionality is supported from below. Accordingly, the book is organized in a modular fashion. After reading Part One, the other parts can be read in a number of possible sequences.

0.3 INTERNET AND WEB RESOURCES

There are a number of resources available on the Internet and the Web that support this book and help readers keep up with developments in this field.

Web Sites for This Book

There is a Web page for this book at **WilliamStallings.com/BDC/BDC6e.html**. The site includes the following:

- **Useful Web sites:** There are links to other relevant Web sites, including the sites listed throughout this book.
- **Errata sheet:** An errata list for this book will be maintained and updated as needed. Errata sheets for my other books are at **WilliamStallings.com**.
- **Figures:** All of the figures in this book in PDF (Adobe Acrobat) format.
- **Tables:** All of the tables in this book in PDF format.
- **Slides:** A set of PowerPoint slides, organized by chapter.
- **Internet mailing list:** The site includes sign-up information for the book's Internet mailing list.
- **Business data communications courses:** There are links to home pages for courses based on this book; these pages may be useful to other instructors in providing ideas about how to structure their course.

I also maintain the Computer Science Student Resource Site, at **WilliamStallings. com/StudentSupport.html**. The purpose of this site is to provide documents, information, and links for computer science students and professionals. Links and documents are organized into six categories:

- **Math:** Includes a basic math refresher, a queuing analysis primer, a number system primer, and links to numerous math sites.

- **How-to:** Advice and guidance for solving homework problems, writing technical reports, and preparing technical presentations.
- **Research resources:** Links to important collections of papers, technical reports, and bibliographies.
- **Miscellaneous:** A variety of other useful documents and links.
- **Computer science careers:** Useful links and documents for those considering a career in computer science.
- **Humor and other diversions:** You have to take your mind off your work once in a while.

Other Web Sites

There are numerous Web sites that provide information related to the topics of this book. In subsequent chapters, pointers to specific Web sites can be found in the *Recommended Reading and Web Sites* section. Because the addresses for Web sites tend to change frequently, the book does not provide URLs. For all of the Web sites listed in the book, the appropriate link can be found at this book's Web site. Other links not mentioned in this book will be added to the Web site over time.

USENET Newsgroups

A number of USENET newsgroups are devoted to some aspect of data communications and networking. As with virtually all USENET groups, there is a high noise-to-signal ratio, but it is worth experimenting to see if any meet your needs. Here is a sample:

- **comp.dcom.lans, comp.dcom.lans.ethernet, and comp.dcom.lans.misc:** General discussions of LANs
- **comp.std.wireless:** General discussion of wireless networks including wireless LANs
- **comp.security.misc:** Computer security and encryption
- **comp.dcom.cell-relay:** Covers ATM and ATM LANs
- **comp.dcom.frame-relay:** Covers frame relay networks
- **comp.dcom.net-management:** Discussion of network management applications, protocols, and standards
- **comp.protocols.tcp-ip:** The TCP/IP protocol suite

0.4 USEFUL PUBLICATIONS

This book serves as a tutorial for learning about the field of business data communications and a reference that can be turned to for help on a specific topic. However, with the rapid changes taking place in this field, no book can hope to stand alone for very long. If you are truly interested in this field, you will need to invest some of your time keeping up with new developments, and the best way to do that is by reading a

Table 0.1 Useful Periodicals

Name	Web Site
Network World	The best Web site on this list. Contains a well-organized archive of the paper's contents. Also contains links to sites related to current news stories, sites related to various technical topics covered in the paper, and vendor information.
Network Computing	Articles from the magazine available plus pointers to advertisers. Site also includes a hypertext network design manual with useful practical tips for end-user network design.
Performance Edge Journal	Archive of all past issues.
Telecommunications	Articles and new product information from past issues, plus an extensive international listing of industry trade shows. Product listings include a brief description plus the ability to request product information from the vendor. A useful search capability can be used to search articles and product listing by keyword.
IT Professional	Includes career resources and links related to information technology.
ACM Networker	Includes online copies of magazine articles.

few relevant periodicals. The list of publications that could be recommended is huge. Included here is a small, select list of publications that will repay the time that you devote to them. All of these publications have Web sites (Table 0.1).

Network World, a weekly newsmagazine, is an excellent source of information about the industry and market for information communications products and services. The coverage is thorough and includes buyers' guides on products and services. Each week there are one or more in-depth articles that touch upon a single area, such as network management. The treatment is from a management rather than a technical orientation. The newsmagazine also provides product comparisons. **Network Computing** focuses on networking products but also has some technical articles. This magazine provides an excellent means for tracking new product releases and for obtaining comparative analyses of product offerings.

Performance Edge Journal focuses on network performance management issues. This is a free online magazine. **Telecommunications** is a monthly magazine that contains both industry-related and technical articles. The magazine concentrates heavily on long-distance networking topics, such as telephone, telecommunications, and regulatory issues.

IT Professional, published by IEEE (Institute of Electrical and Electronics Engineers), is intended for developers and managers of enterprise information systems. The magazine is good at explaining technology to help you build and manage your information systems today, and provides advance notice of trends that may shape your business in the next few years. **Networker**, published by ACM (Association for Computing Machinery), is another good source of information for developers and managers of enterprise information systems, but with more emphasis on networking and data communications than *IT Professional*.

CHAPTER 1

INTRODUCTION

1.1 Information and Communication

1.2 Data Communications and Networking for Today's Enterprise
Trends
Business Drivers

1.3 Convergence and Unified Communications
Convergence
Unified Communications

1.4 The Nature of Business Information Requirements

1.5 Distributed Data Processing

1.6 The Internet and Distributed Applications
The Internet
TCP/IP
Distributed Applications
Client/Server Architectures and Intranets

1.7 Networks
Wide Area Networks
Local Area Networks
Wireless Networks
Metropolitan Area Networks
An Example Configuration

1.8 The Transmission of Information
Transmission and Transmission Media
Communication Techniques
Transmission Efficiency

1.9 Managements Issues
Network Security
Network Management

1.10 Standards

1.11 Recommended Reading and Web Sites

1.12 Key Terms and Review Questions

APPENDIX 1A   Prefixes for Numerical Units

Chapter Objectives

After reading this chapter, you should be able to

♦ Understand the basic requirements for data communications and networking to support business information needs.

♦ See the "big picture" of the major topics discussed in the book.

♦ Appreciate the importance of the Internet and wireless communications in business planning.

♦ Understand the central role of standards in data communications and networking.

This introductory chapter begins with an overview of the role of data communications and networking in the enterprise. Then a brief discussion introduces each of the parts of this book.

1.1 INFORMATION AND COMMUNICATION

A confluence of computers, communication technologies, and demographics is transforming the way any enterprise conducts itself and carries out its organizational mandate. And it's happening fast. A business that ignores these changes will fall hopelessly to the rear in the global race for the competitive edge. At the heart of the transformation is information. No longer a byproduct and no longer, in many cases, a cost center, the generation, storage, and movement of information have been made profitable by companies that have taken up the technological challenge posed by the myriad machines that automate so much of our lives.

We are unquestionably dependent on computers and the communication devices and services that connect them. The number of computers and terminals at work in the world today is in the billions. The overwhelming need of organizations and their workers now is for connectivity, for integration, for ease of access to information. So fundamental is information communication technology to business success that it is emerging as the foundation of a strategy taking shape in American businesses: using management structures to gain a competitive advantage.

As businesses are challenged by such forces as global competition, mergers, and acquisitions, time-tested management structures are putting a strain on corporate bottom lines. In response, companies are breaking down divisional walls and flattening top-heavy management pyramids to create new corporate structures that help them to compete more effectively. The technology that is making much of this possible is *networking*.

Communication technology helps companies overcome three kinds of basic organizational difficulties: Good networks make geographically dispersed companies more manageable; they help top-heavy companies trim down middle management; and they help companies break down barriers between divisions. As we examine the technology and applications throughout this book, we will see the ways in which information communication technology solves these and other vital business problems.

1.2 DATA COMMUNICATIONS AND NETWORKING FOR TODAY'S ENTERPRISE

Effective and efficient data communication and networking facilities are vital to any enterprise. In this section, we first look at trends that are increasing the challenge for the business manager in planning and managing such facilities. Next we introduce the concept of business drivers that will guide the enterprise in developing an overall data communications and networking plan.

Trends

Three different forces have consistently driven the architecture and evolution of data communications and networking facilities: traffic growth, development of new services, and advances in technology.

Communication **traffic**, both local (within a building or building complex) and long distance, both voice and data, has been growing at a high and steady rate for decades. The increasing emphasis on office automation, remote access, online transactions, and other productivity measures means that this trend is likely to continue. Thus, managers are constantly struggling to maximize capacity and minimize transmission costs.

As businesses rely more and more on information technology, the range of **services** expands. This increases the demand for high-capacity networking and transmission facilities. In turn, the continuing growth in high-speed network offerings with the continuing drop in prices encourages the expansion of services. Thus, growth in services and growth in traffic capacity go hand in hand. Figure 1.1 gives some examples of information-based services and the data rates needed to support them [ELSA02].

Finally, trends in **technology** enable the provision of increasing traffic capacity and the support of a wide range of services. Four technology trends are particularly notable and need to be understood by the manager responsible for information technology:

1. The trend toward faster and cheaper, both in computing and communications, continues. In terms of computing, this means more powerful computers and clusters of computers capable of supporting more demanding applications, such as multimedia applications. In terms of communications, the increasing use of optical fiber and high-speed wireless has brought transmission prices down and greatly increased capacity. For example, for long-distance telecommunication and data network links, recent offerings of dense wavelength division multiplexing (DWDM) enable capacities of many terabits per second. For local area networks (LANs), many enterprises now have Gigabit Ethernet or 10-Gbps Ethernet backbone networks.[1] Further, the need for the next-generation 100-Gpbs is pressing, and products at this data rate should appear in the near future. Figure 1.2, based on [MELL07], indicates the Ethernet demand trend.

---

[1]See Appendix 1A for an explanation of numerical prefixes, such as *tera* and *giga*.

Figure 1.1   Services versus Throughput Rates

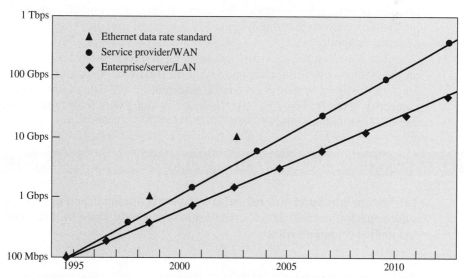

Figure 1.2   Past and Projected Growth in Ethernet Bandwidth Compared to Existing Ethernet Data Rates

2. Both voice-oriented telecommunications networks, such as the public switched telephone network (PSTN), and data networks, including the **Internet**, are more "intelligent" than ever. Two areas of intelligence are noteworthy. First, today's networks can offer differing levels of quality of service (QoS), which include specifications for maximum delay, minimum throughput, and so on. Second, today's networks provide a variety of customizable services in the areas of network management and security.

3. The Internet, the Web, and associated applications have emerged as dominant features of both the business and personal world, opening up many opportunities and challenges for managers. In addition to exploiting the Internet and the Web to reach customers, suppliers, and partners, enterprises have formed intranets and extranets[2] to isolate their proprietary information free from unwanted access.

4. There has been a trend toward ever-increasing mobility for decades, liberating workers from the confines of the physical enterprise. Innovations include voice mail, remote data access, pagers, fax, e-mail, cordless phones, cell phones and cellular networks, and Internet portals. The result is the ability of employees to take their business context with them as they move about. We are now seeing the growth of high-speed wireless access, which further enhances the ability to use enterprise information resources and services anywhere.

Business Drivers

The trends discussed in the preceding subsection are enabling the development of enterprise network and communications facilities that are increasingly better integrated with the information base, which the enterprise itself runs. Network management and operation depend on some key enterprise-specific information, such as names, network addresses, security capabilities, end-user groupings, priority designations, mailboxes, and application attributes. With the increasing capacity and functionality of enterprise networks, this information can be unified with the enterprise information base so that the information is correct, consistent, and available across all business applications.

The nature of the enterprise networking and communications facility depends on the business applications it must support. [MILO00] lists four main application areas that will serve as the drivers in determining the design and makeup of the enterprise network. Figure 1.3 lists these areas, along with their business motivators and the expected benefits.

1.3 CONVERGENCE AND UNIFIED COMMUNICATIONS

This section introduces two related concepts that are important determinants of requirements for business data communications and networking facilities: **convergence** and **unified communications**.

---

[2]Briefly, an intranet uses Internet and Web technology in an isolated facility internal to an enterprise; an extranet extends a company's intranet out onto the Internet to allow selected customers, suppliers, and mobile workers to access the company's private data and applications. See Chapter 6 for a discussion.

IP = Internet Protocol
e-Business = Enterprise activities based on mobile, global access to enterprise networks

Figure 1.3 Applications Driving Enterprise Networks

Convergence

Convergence refers to the merger of previously distinct telephony and information technologies and markets. We can think of this convergence in terms of a three-layer model of enterprise communications:

- **Applications:** These are seen by the end users of a business. Convergence integrates communications applications, such as voice calling (telephone), voice mail, e-mail, and instant messaging, with business applications, such as work-group collaboration, customer relationship management, and other back-office functions. With convergence, applications provide features that incorporate voice, data, and video in a seamless, organized, and value-added manner. One example is multimedia messaging, which enables a user to employ a single interface to access messages from a variety of sources (e.g., office voice mail, office e-mail, beeper, and fax).

- **Enterprise services:** At this level, the manager deals with the information network in terms of the services it supplies to support applications. The network manager needs design, maintenance, and support services related to the deployment of convergence-based facilities. Also at this level, network managers deal with the enterprise network as a function-providing system. Such management services may include setting up authentication schemes; capacity management for various users, groups, and applications; and QoS provision.

- **Infrastructure:** The infrastructure consists of the communication links, LANs, WANs, and Internet connections available to the enterprise. The key aspect of convergence at this level is the ability to carry voice and video over data networks, such as the Internet.

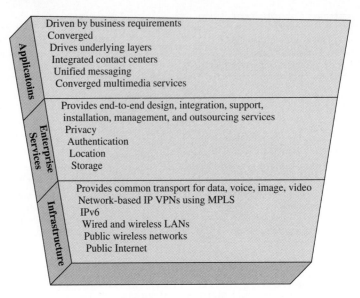

Figure 1.4   Business-Driven Congergence

Figure 1.4, based on [MILL05], illustrates the three layers and their associated convergence attributes. In simple terms, convergence involves moving voice into a data infrastructure, integrating all the voice and data networks inside a user organization into a single data network infrastructure, and then extending that into the wireless arena. The foundation of this convergence is packet-based transmission using the Internet Protocol (IP). Convergence increases the function and scope of both the infrastructure and the application base.

Convergence brings many benefits, including simplified network management, increased efficiency, and greater flexibility at the application level. For example, a converged network infrastructure makes it easier to add applications that combine video, data, and voice. [POL07] lists the following three key benefits of convergence:

- **Efficiency:** Provides a double-digit percent reduction in operating costs through the convergence of legacy networks onto a single global IP network, better use of and reduction in existing resources, and implementation of centralized capacity planning, asset management, and policy management.

- **Effectiveness:** The converged environment has the potential to provide users with great flexibility, irrespective of where they are. Such a company-wide environment provides for rapid standardized service deployment and enhanced remote connectivity and mobility.

- **Transformation:** Convergence also enables the enterprise-wide adoption of global standards and associated service levels, thus providing better data, enhanced real-time global decision-making processes, and improved execution in business planning and operations. This leads to greater agility for the enterprise in providing new services to its customers and employees.

Unified Communications

A concept related to that of convergence is unified communications (UC). Whereas convergence focuses on the merger of fundamental voice, video, and data communications facilities and the resulting ability to support multimedia applications, UC focuses on the user perspective to the broad spectrum of business applications. Key elements of UC include the following:

1. UC is based on an integrated set of user interfaces and backend connectivity for all communications services.

2. UC merges real-time communications services with non-real-time collaboration and business process applications.

Figure 1.5, based on [LAZA07], shows the typical components of a UC architecture and how they relate to one another. The key elements of this architecture are as follows:

- **Web 2.0:** Refers to a second generation of Web capability. Two prominent aspects of Web 2.0 are as follows: (1) Much of the content is user generated, including blogs, wikis, documents, images, and video clips; and (2) the user interface is rich, easy to use, and provides a desktop-like experience. Although Web 2.0 services and features are primarily associated with public Web use by the general population, Web 2.0 has become a significant element of corporate strategy [MURU07]. The term *Enterprise 2.0,* which is also becoming common, refers to the application of Web 2.0 technologies to workers using network software within an organization or business [MCAF06].

- **Real-time communications (RTC) dashboard:** May consist of both desktop and mobile software clients, though often with differing levels of functionality. RTC dashboards blend instant messaging, e-mail, audio-and videoconferencing,

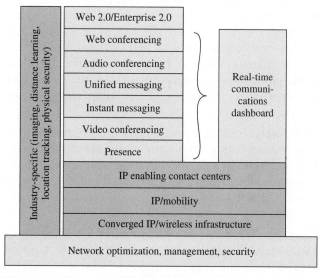

Figure 1.5   Elements of Unified Communications Architecture

whiteboarding, and file sharing into a unified view. An RTC dashboard enables a user to locate other users and invoke collaborative applications with those other uses. [GITT06] points out that the RTC dashboard has moved from the "nice to have" to "need to have" category for many businesses.

- **Web conferencing:** Refers to live meetings or presentations in which participants access the meeting or presentation via the Web, either over the Internet or a corporate intranet.

- **Audio conferencing:** Also called conference calling, refers to a live meeting in which participants are linked together for audio transmission and reception. A participant may be on a landline, mobile phone, or at a computer equipped with microphone and speaker.

- **Unified messaging:** Allows users to have access to e-mail, voice mail, and faxes via a common interface either on their computer or on their telephone. Computer users can select and play voice-mail recordings that appear in their inboxes. Telephone users can both retrieve voice mail and hear text-to-voice translations of e-mail messages. Messages of any type can be saved, answered, filed, sorted and forwarded.

- **Instant messaging:** Real-time messaging.

- **Desktop video:** Videoconferencing to the desktop.

- **Presence:** The ability to determine, in real time, where someone is, how he or she prefers to be reached, and even what he or she is doing. Presence was once considered simply an underlying technology to instant messaging. Presence has been broadened to encompass a user's status on phones, wireless devices, video conferencing, and other collaborative tools.

- **IP enabling contact centers:** Refers to the use of IP-based unified communications to enhance customer contact center functionality and performance. The unified communications infrastructure makes use of presence technology to enable customers and internal enterprise employees to be quickly connected to the required expert or support person. Additionally, this technology supports mobility, so that call center personnel need not be located at a particular office or remain in a particular place. Finally, the unified communications infrastructure enables the call center employee to quickly access other employees and information assets, including data, video, image, and audio.

- **IP/mobility:** Refers to the delivery of information to and collection of information from enterprise personnel who are usually mobile, using an IP network infrastructure. In a typical enterprise, upward of 30% of employees use some form of remote access technology in the performance of their jobs. Figure 1.6, from [SENS02], illustrates the typical breakdown of usage profiles for mobile employees.

- **Converged IP/wireless infrastructure:** A unified networking and communications base that relies on IP packet transfer to support voice, data, and video transmission and that is extended to include local and wide area wireless communications.

Employee Profiles	At desk	Somewhere on site	On the move
Desk soldier Accountant	90%	10%	
On-site rover Assistant	70%	30%	
Home worker Tele-agent	100% (Home)		
Road warrior Salesperson	10%	10%	80%
Off-site rover Consultant	30%		70%
Global hopper Corporate executive marketing, pre-sales	25%	25%	50%

Figure 1.6   Three Main Profiles for Mobile Employees

The importance of unified communications is not only that it integrates communication channels, within the enterprise and with key constituents, but also that it offers a way to integrate communication functions directly into business applications. [ELLI08] notes three functional levels of this integration:

- **Personal unified communications:** Intended to enhance individual productivity. This area includes smart phones, personal digital assistants (PDAs), and other personal devices that provide access to voice, instant messaging (IM), presence information, and business applications.

- **Workgroup unified communications:** Supports collaborative and team efforts to improve performance. Examples include the use of presence to speed identification of an available individual with the right skills to address a problem and automated business rules to route or escalate communications.

- **Enterprise unified communications:** Integrates communications with enterprise-wide and departmental-level applications, business processes, and workflows.

Enterprises are increasingly migrating to some form and level of commitment to unified communications. The unified communications architecture, together with a converged network approach, will drive requirements for business data communications from the fundamental transmission and networking level up though the applications and services upon which the enterprise depends.

1.4 THE NATURE OF BUSINESS INFORMATION REQUIREMENTS

A business survives and thrives on information: information within the organization and information exchanged with suppliers, customers, and regulators. Moreover, the information needs to be consistent, accessible, and at the right location. In Part One, Chapters 2 and 3, we consider information in four forms (voice, data, image, and video) and the implications of distributed data processing.

In this book, the term **voice communications** primarily refers to telephone-related communications. By far the most common form of communication in any organization and for most personnel is direct telephone conversation. The telephone has been a basic business tool for decades. Telephone communication has been enhanced by a variety of computer-based services, including voice mail and computerized telephone exchange systems. Voice mail provides the ability to send, forward, and reply to voice messages nonsimultaneously, and it has become a cost-efficient tool even for many small and midsize organizations. It provides savings on answering machines and services, as well as a more responsive service to customers and suppliers. Advances have also been made in computerized telephone exchange systems, including in-house digital private branch exchanges (PBX) and Centrex systems provided by the local telephone company. These new systems provide a host of features, including call forwarding, camp-on call waiting, least-cost routing of long-distance calls, and a variety of accounting and auditing features. More recently, the merger of voice and Internet technologies, based on the voice over IP (VoIP) protocol, has resulted in PBX and IP Centrex offerings that provide full Internet support.

The term **data communications** is sometimes used to refer to virtually any form of information transfer other than voice. It is sometimes convenient to limit this term to information in the form of text (such as reports, memos, and other documents) and numerical data (such as accounting files). The rapid changes in technology have created fresh challenges for management in making effective use of data communications. Later in this chapter we briefly outline the changes in technology in transmission, networks, and communications software that present the manager with new and powerful business tools but also the necessity of making choices among complex alternatives.

Image communications is now an important component of the office environment. The best-known example of this technology is facsimile (fax). Like the tortoise who surpasses the hare, facsimile machines have caught up with higher-tech alternatives and have achieved status over the past few years as the preferred method of sending documents over a long distance. With fax, the document can have any content, including text, graphics, signatures, and even photographs. Newer machines can transmit these documents over telephone networks in seconds, and low-cost hardware, including personal computer attachments, is now available. In addition, image communications is starting to play an important role within the office. The arrival of the optical disc, based on the same technology as that of the familiar compact disc of the music industry, allows massive amounts of information to be stored inexpensively. Thus, all sorts of images, including engineering and design specifications, mixed documents (text, graphs, signatures, etc.), presentation material, and so on, can be moved quickly around the office and displayed on user workstations. This new technology for storing and transmitting images creates a demand for high-capacity networks and is one of the driving forces in the development of networking technology.

Video communications is also becoming important in the office environment. Traditionally, this technology has been used as a one-way delivery system of entertainment programs. Now, with the availability of high-capacity transmission links and networks, it has an increasing business application, most notably videoconferencing. Videoconferencing allows the linkup of two or more remotely located conference rooms to conduct such meetings as planning sessions, contract negotiations, and project reviews. The time and money saved on travel, food, and lodging make videoconferencing a powerful tool for increasing efficiency and productivity.

All these forms of information communications play a key role in today's business. The manager responsible for them must understand the technology sufficiently to deal effectively with vendors of communications products and services and to make cost-effective choices among the growing array of options. Chapter 2 examines the business uses of these four classes of information and the communications requirements that they generate.

1.5   DISTRIBUTED DATA PROCESSING

The steady drop over many years in the cost of data processing equipment, coupled with an increase in the capability of such equipment, has led to the introduction of many small- and medium-size computers into the business environment. Traditionally, the data processing function was centrally organized around a mainframe computer. Today, however, it is much more common to find a distributed data processing configuration, one that consists of a number of computers and terminals linked together by networks. Chapter 3 examines the motivation for distributed data processing and discusses the various forms that it takes.

1.6   THE INTERNET AND DISTRIBUTED APPLICATIONS

A business needs to be concerned with two dimensions of computer communications software: the application software that is provided for a community of terminals and computers, and the underlying interconnection software that allows these terminals and computers to work together cooperatively.

The mere existence of a large population of computers and terminals creates the demand that these devices work together. For example, when most employees in an organization have access to a terminal or a personal computer (PC), one of the most effective means of communication within the organization is electronic mail (e-mail). If one employee needs to communicate with another, a message sent by e-mail can be far more effective than hit-or-miss attempts to reach the person by telephone. A detailed e-mail message can be left in the recipient's "electronic mailbox," to be read and answered when the recipient returns to the office. Other applications, such as the exchange of documents, the use of a database that is distributed among a number of computers, and the ability to access many different computers from a single terminal, can be provided by applications software that is geared for the networked environment.

The key to the success of these applications is that all the terminals and computers in the community "speak" the same language. This is the role of the underlying interconnection software. This software must ensure that all the devices transmit messages in such a way that they can be understood by the other computers and terminals in the community. With the introduction of the Systems Network Architecture (SNA) by IBM in the 1970s, this concept became a reality. However, SNA worked only with IBM equipment. Soon other vendors followed with their own proprietary communication architectures to tie together their equipment. Such an approach may be good business for the vendor, but it is bad business for the customer. Happily, that situation has changed radically with the adoption of standards for interconnection software. The manager needs to understand the scope and status of these standards to exploit them in building a multiple-vendor, tailored installation.

Modern data communications and microelectronics are radically changing the architecture of modern information systems. Most applications have evolved away from large, general-purpose mainframe computers to *distributed computing*. Instead of dumb terminals enslaved to mainframes, high-performance workstations and PCs provide, local to the user, powerful graphical interfaces and much of the application computing. The local workstations and PCs are supported by specialized servers specifically designed for a single function, such as printing, storing files, or supporting database activities. The workstations and PCs are often connected to the servers by high-speed LANs. This approach, called *client/server architecture,* requires sophisticated, reliable, and secure data communications, but its inherent flexibility and responsiveness make it an essential tool in the businessperson's information systems repertoire.

Part Two looks at a number of topics that deal with the infrastructure for supporting **distributed applications**.

The Internet

Virtually no business, and certainly no medium or large enterprise, can compete without exploiting the Internet and the Web. The Web provides a way to communicate with consumers and to publicize the company and can form the base for a number of e-commerce applications. Internet technology, in the form of intranets and extranets, enables secure communication both within an enterprise and with customers, suppliers, and partners. Chapter 4 provides important background on the Internet.

TCP/IP

One of the most difficult problems that has traditionally faced computer users is that different vendors have used different and incompatible architectures. Chapter 5 discusses the use of standardized communications protocols to integrate diverse equipment. The focus is on the **TCP/IP** (Transmission Control Protocol/Internet Protocol) protocol suite, which is now universally used for the communications software function across multiple-vendor equipment and is the basis for the operation of the Internet.

Chapter 5 also briefly reviews the Open System Interconnection (OSI) architecture developed by the International Organization for Standardization (ISO).

Client/Server Architectures and Intranets

A remarkable transformation is taking place in the architecture of today's commercial computers. The large mainframe, although still important, has been replaced or supplemented in many applications by networked PCs and workstations, as is illustrated by the increased manufacture of computers of different types. The number of PCs and workstations is growing at a much greater rate than that of mainframes and midrange computers, with the result that computing is being more widely distributed. Increasingly, computation is provided by the **client/server** model. Separate computers (servers) support database functions, store files, perform printing services, and provide other specialized functions on a shared basis for many users (clients). These servers, which can offer enhanced performance and cost savings through specialization, are accessed over LANs and other communications networks.

Even more recently, a new approach has gained widespread support within organizations: the intranet. An intranet provides the same sorts of applications and interfaces as found on the Internet, especially the World Wide Web. The difference is that an intranet is confined to use within the organization, with no access to outsiders. The intranet is a flexible, easy-to-use, and easy-to-implement approach to many business applications.

Chapter 6 looks at client/server computing, intranets, and extranets.

Distributed Applications

Distributed information processing is essential in virtually all businesses. There is a growing use of applications that are designed to work among a distributed set of computers for both intracompany and intercompany information exchange. Chapter 7 examines some of the key applications that are likely to be the most important to a business.

1.7   NETWORKS

The number of computers in use worldwide is in the billions. Moreover, the expanding memory and processing power of these computers means that users can put the machines to work on new kinds of applications and functions. Accordingly, the pressure from the users of these systems for ways to communicate among all these machines is irresistible. It is changing the way vendors think and the way all automation products and services are sold. This demand for connectivity is manifested in two specific requirements: the need for communications software, which is previewed in the next section, and the need for networks.

One type of network that has become increasingly common is the **local area network (LAN)**. Indeed, the LAN is to be found in virtually all medium- and large-size office buildings. As the number and power of computing devices have grown, so have the number and capacity of LANs to be found in an office. Although standards have been developed that reduce somewhat the number of types of LANs, there are still half a dozen general types of local area networks to choose from. Furthermore, many offices need more than one such network, with the attendant problems of interconnecting and managing a diverse collection of networks, computers, and terminals.

Beyond the confines of a single office building, networks for voice, data, image, and video are equally important to business. Here, too, there are rapid changes. Advances in technology have led to greatly increased capacity and the concept of integration. *Integration* means that the customer equipment and networks can deal simultaneously with voice, data, image, and even video. Thus, a memo or report can be accompanied by voice commentary, presentation graphics, and perhaps even a short video introduction or summary. Image and video services impose large demands on wide area network transmission. Moreover, as LANs become ubiquitous and as their transmission rates increase, the demands on the **wide area networks** to support LAN interconnection have increased the demands on wide area network capacity and switching. On the other hand, fortunately, the enormous and ever-increasing capacity of fiber optic and wireless transmission provides ample resources to meet these demands. However, developing switching systems with the capacity and rapid response to support these increased requirements is a challenge not yet conquered.

The opportunities for using networks as an aggressive competitive tool and as a means of enhancing productivity and slashing costs are great. The manager who understands the technology and can deal effectively with vendors of service and equipment is able to enhance a company's competitive position.

In the remainder of this section, we provide a brief overview of various networks. Parts Three and Four cover these topics in depth.

Wide Area Networks

Wide area networks generally cover a large geographical area, require the crossing of public right-of-ways, and rely at least in part on circuits provided by a common carrier. Typically, a WAN consists of a number of interconnected switching nodes. A transmission from any attached device is routed through these internal nodes to the specified destination device. These nodes (including the boundary nodes) are not concerned with the content of the data; rather, their purpose is to provide a switching facility that will move the data from node to node until they reach their destination.

Traditionally, WANs have been implemented using one of two technologies: **circuit switching** and **packet switching**. More recently, **frame relay** and ATM networks have assumed major roles. Chapter 13 looks at frame relay and ATM.

CIRCUIT SWITCHING   In a circuit-switching network, a dedicated communication path is established between two stations through the nodes of the network. That path is a connected sequence of physical links between nodes. On each link, a logical channel is dedicated to the connection. Data generated by the source station are transmitted along the dedicated path as rapidly as possible. At each node, incoming data are routed or switched to the appropriate outgoing channel without delay. The most common example of circuit switching is the telephone network.

PACKET SWITCHING   A different approach is used in a packet-switching network. In this case, it is not necessary to dedicate transmission capacity along a path through the network. Rather, data are sent out in a sequence of small chunks, called packets. Each packet is passed through the network from node to node along some path leading from source to destination. At each node, the entire packet is received, stored briefly, and then transmitted to the next node. Packet-switching networks are commonly used for terminal-to-computer and computer-to-computer communications.

FRAME RELAY   Packet switching was developed at a time when digital long-distance transmission facilities exhibited a relatively high error rate compared to today's facilities. As a result, there is a considerable amount of overhead built into packet-switching schemes to compensate for errors. The overhead includes additional bits added to each packet to introduce redundancy and additional processing at the end stations and the intermediate switching nodes to detect and recover from errors.

With modern high-speed telecommunications systems, this overhead is unnecessary and counterproductive. It is unnecessary because the rate of errors has been dramatically lowered and any remaining errors can easily be caught in the end systems by logic that operates above the level of the packet-switching logic. It is counterproductive because the overhead involved soaks up a significant fraction of the high capacity provided by the network.

Frame relay was developed to take advantage of these high data rates and low error rates. Whereas the original packet-switching networks were designed with a data rate to the end user of about 64 kbps, frame relay networks are designed to operate efficiently at user data rates of up to 2 Mbps. The key to achieving these high data rates is to strip out most of the overhead involved with error control.

ATM **Asynchronous transfer mode (ATM),** sometimes referred to as cell relay, is a culmination of developments in circuit switching and packet switching. ATM can be viewed as an evolution from frame relay. The most obvious difference between frame relay and ATM is that frame relay uses variable-length packets, called frames, and ATM uses fixed-length packets, called cells. As with frame relay, ATM provides little overhead for error control, depending on the inherent reliability of the transmission system and on higher layers of logic in the end systems to catch and correct errors. By using a fixed packet length, the processing overhead is reduced even further for ATM compared to frame relay. The result is that ATM is designed to work in the range of 10s and 100s of Mbps, and in the Gbps range.

ATM can also be viewed as an evolution from circuit switching. With circuit switching, only fixed-data-rate circuits are available to the end system. ATM allows the definition of multiple virtual channels with data rates that are dynamically defined at the time the virtual channel is created. By using small, fixed-size cells, ATM is so efficient that it can offer a constant-data-rate channel even though it is using a packet-switching technique. Thus, ATM extends circuit switching to allow multiple channels with the data rate on each channel dynamically set on demand.

Local Area Networks

As with WANs, a LAN is a communications network that interconnects a variety of devices and provides a means for information exchange among those devices. There are several key distinctions between LANs and WANs:

1. The scope of the LAN is small, typically a single building or a cluster of buildings. This difference in geographic scope leads to different technical solutions, as we shall see.

2. It is usually the case that the LAN is owned by the same organization that owns the attached devices. For WANs, this is less often the case, or at least a significant fraction of the network assets are not owned. This has two implications. First, care must be taken in the choice of LAN, because there may be a substantial capital investment (compared to dial-up or leased charges for WANs) for both purchase

and maintenance. Second, the network management responsibility for a LAN falls solely on the owner.

3. The internal data rates of LANs are typically much greater than those of WANs.

LANs come in a number of different configurations. The most common are switched LANs and wireless LANs. The most common switched LAN is a switched Ethernet LAN, which consists of a single switch with a number of attached devices, or a number of interconnected switches. Two other prominent examples are ATM LANs, which simply use an ATM network in a local area, and Fibre Channel. Wireless LANs use a variety of wireless transmission technologies and organizations.

Part Three covers LANs.

Wireless Networks

As was just mentioned, wireless LANs are common and are being widely used in business environments. Wireless technology is also common for both wide area voice and data networks. **Wireless networks** provide advantages in the areas of mobility and ease of installation and configuration. Chapter 14 covers wireless WANs.

Metropolitan Area Networks

As the name suggests, a **metropolitan area network (MAN)** occupies a middle ground between LANs and WANs. Interest in MANs has come about as a result of a recognition that the traditional point-to-point and switched network techniques used in WANs may be inadequate for the growing needs of organizations. While frame relay and ATM promise to meet a wide range of high-speed needs, there is a requirement now for both private and public networks that provide high capacity at low costs over a large area. A number of approaches have been implemented, including wireless networks and metropolitan extensions to Ethernet.

The primary market for MANs is the customer that has high capacity needs in a metropolitan area. A MAN is intended to provide the required capacity at lower cost and greater efficiency than obtaining an equivalent service from the local telephone company.

An Example Configuration

To give some feel for the scope of concerns of Parts Two through Four, Figure 1.7 illustrates some of the typical communications and network elements in use today. In the upper left-hand portion of the Figure 1.7, we see an individual residential user connected to an Internet service provider (ISP) through some sort of subscriber connection. Common examples of such a connection are the public switched telephone network, for which the user requires a dial-up modem (e.g., a 56-kbps modem); a digital subscriber line (DSL), which provides a high-speed link over telephone lines and requires a special DSL modem; and a cable TV facility, which requires a cable modem. In each case, there are separate issues concerning signal encoding, error control, and the internal structure of the subscriber network.

Figure 1.7 Networking Configuration

Typically, an ISP will consist of a number of interconnected servers (only a single server is shown) connected to the Internet through a high-speed link. One example of such a link is a SONET (synchronous optical network) line, described in Chapter 17. The Internet consists of a number of interconnected routers that span the globe. These routers forward packets of data from source to destination through the Internet.

The lower portion of Figure 1.7 shows a LAN implemented using a single Ethernet switch. This is a common configuration at small businesses and other small organizations. The LAN is connected to the Internet through a firewall host that provides security services. In this example the firewall connects to the Internet through an ATM network. There is also a router off of the LAN hooked into a private WAN, which might be a private ATM or frame relay network.

A variety of design issues, such as signal encoding and error control, relate to the links between adjacent elements. Examples are links between routers on the Internet, between switches in the ATM network, and between a subscriber and an ISP. The internal structure of the various networks (telephone, ATM, Ethernet) raises additional issues. We will be occupied in Parts Two through Four with the design features suggested by Figure 1.7.

1.8   THE TRANSMISSION OF INFORMATION

The basic building block of any communications facility is the transmission line. Much of the technical detail of how information is encoded and transmitted across a line is of no real interest to the business manager. The manager is concerned with whether the particular facility provides the required capacity, with acceptable reliability, at minimum cost. However, there are certain aspects of transmission technology that a manager must understand to ask the right questions and make informed decisions.

One of the basic choices facing a business user is the transmission medium. For use within the business premises, this choice is generally completely up to the business. For long-distance communications, the choice is generally but not always made by the long-distance carrier. In either case, changes in technology are rapidly changing the mix of media used. Of particular note are *fiber optic* transmission and *wireless* transmission (e.g., satellite and radio). These two media are now driving the evolution of data communications transmission.

The ever-increasing capacity of fiber optic channels is making channel capacity a virtually free resource. The growth of the market for optical fiber transmission systems since the beginning of the 1980s is without precedent. During the past 10 years, the cost of fiber optic transmission has dropped by more than an order of magnitude, and the capacity of such systems has grown at almost as rapid a rate. Long-distance telephone communications trunks within the United States will soon consist almost completely of fiber optic cable. Because of its high capacity and its security characteristics (fiber is difficult to tap), it is becoming increasingly used within office buildings to carry the growing load of business information. However, switching is now becoming the bottleneck. This problem is causing radical changes in communication architecture, including asynchronous transfer mode (ATM) switching, highly parallel processing in switches, and integrated network management schemes.

The second medium, wireless transmission, is a result of the trend toward universal personal telecommunications and universal access to communications. The first concept refers to the ability of a person to identify himself or herself easily and to use conveniently any communication system in a large area (e.g., globally, over a continent, or in an entire country) in terms of a single account. The second refers to the capability of using one's terminal in a wide variety of environments to connect to information services (e.g., to have a portable terminal that will work in the office, on the street, and on airplanes equally well). This revolution in personal computing obviously involves wireless communication in a fundamental way.

Despite the growth in the capacity and the drop in the cost of transmission facilities, transmission services remain the most costly component of a communications budget for most businesses. Thus, the manager needs to be aware of techniques that increase the efficiency of the use of these facilities. The two major approaches to greater efficiency are multiplexing and compression. *Multiplexing* refers to the ability of a number of devices to share a transmission facility. If each device needs the facility only a fraction of the time, then a sharing arrangement allows the cost of the facility to be spread over many users. *Compression,* as the name indicates, involves squeezing the data down so that a lower-capacity, cheaper transmission facility can be used to meet a given demand. These two techniques show up separately and in combination in a number of types of communications equipment. The manager needs to understand these technologies to assess the appropriateness and cost-effectiveness of the various products on the market.

Chapters 15 and 16, in Part Five, examine the key issues and technologies in the area of information transmission.

Transmission and Transmission Media

Information can be communicated by converting it into an electromagnetic signal and transmitting that signal over some medium, such as a twisted-pair telephone line. The most commonly used transmission media are twisted-pair lines, coaxial cable, optical fiber cable, and terrestrial and satellite microwave. The data rates that can be achieved and the rate at which errors can occur depend on the nature of the signal and the type of medium. Chapter 15 examines the significant properties of electromagnetic signals. Chapters 9, 11, and 14 discuss the various transmission media.

Communication Techniques

The transmission of information across a transmission medium involves more than simply inserting a signal on the medium. The technique used to encode the information into an electromagnetic signal must be determined. There are various ways in which the encoding can be done, and the choice affects performance and reliability. Furthermore, the successful transmission of information involves a high degree of cooperation. The interface between a device and the transmission medium must be agreed on. Some means of controlling the flow of information and recovering from its loss or corruption must be used. These latter functions may be performed by a data link control protocol. All these issues are examined in Chapters 16 and 17.

Transmission Efficiency

A major cost in any computer/communications facility is transmission cost. Because of this, it is important to maximize the amount of information that can be carried over a given resource or, alternatively, to minimize the transmission capacity needed to satisfy a given information communications requirement. The standard technique for achieving this objective is multiplexing. Chapter 17 examines both multiplexing frequency division, and synchronous time division.

1.9 MANAGEMENT ISSUES

Part Six concludes the book by examining key management issues related to business data communications.

Network Security

As companies rely increasingly on networks and as access by outsiders via the Internet and other links grows, the vexing question of security becomes ever more important. Companies are at risk for the disclosure of confidential information and for the unauthorized altering of corporate data. Chapters 18 and 19 look at the basic tools for achieving network security and discusses how they can be adapted to meet a company's needs.

Network Management

In the early years of data communications, in the 1970s, the key focus was the functionality and performance of the technology. The key questions were, What could the technology do? How fast? For how many transactions? As electronic information systems became part of the basic fabric of many businesses, managers discovered that the operation of their businesses had become dependent on their information systems and that the economic performance of their firms depended on the cost-effective use of the technology. That is, like any resource, information technology had to be managed. For example, managers of data communications are often most concerned today about network reliability. Many of the management functions required are common to other aspects of business management, but the following requirements are special to information technology:

- Networks have evolved from an easily controlled client/server (i.e., mainframe/dumb terminal) approach into peer-to-peer interconnections among highly distributed systems.
- Peer-to-peer networks have grown larger and larger—some have tens or hundreds of thousands of attached devices—so that managing, monitoring, and maintaining them has become very complex.
- In many business sectors, such as banking, retailing, and other service industries, networks of computing devices constitute a critical strategic resource that cannot be allowed to fail.
- Communications costs, meanwhile, are climbing, and there is a shortage of skilled personnel to staff network command centers and to handle network management.

Network management must provide global visibility on corporate information flow. Techniques of centralized, remote monitoring and control provide rapid notification of failures and automatic invocation of recovery measures. On-the-fly analysis of network performance and dynamic adjustment of network parameters provide adaptation to varying cycles of business activity. Network management is a complex discipline, particularly in a multivendor environment. The manager must understand the requirements for network management and the tools and technologies available to plan effectively for an automated network management strategy.

Chapters 20 and 21 focus on network management.

1.10 STANDARDS

Standards have come to play a dominant role in the information communications marketplace. Virtually all vendors of products and services are committed to supporting international standards. Throughout this book, we describe the most important standards in use or being developed for various aspects of data communications and networking. Various organizations have been involved in the development or promotion of these standards. The most important (in the current context) of these organizations are as follows:

- **Internet Society:** ISOC is a professional membership society with worldwide organizational and individual membership. It provides leadership in addressing issues that confront the future of the Internet and is the organization home for the groups responsible for Internet infrastructure standards, including the Internet Engineering Task Force (IETF) and the Internet Architecture Board (IAB). These organizations develop Internet standards and related specifications, all of which are published as Requests for Comments (RFCs).

- **ITU-T:** The International Telecommunication Union (ITU) is an international organization within the United Nations System in which governments and the private sector coordinate global telecom networks and services The ITU Telecommunication Standardization Sector (ITU-T) is one of the three sectors of the ITU. ITU-T's mission is the production of standards covering all fields of telecommunications. ITU-T standards are referred to as Recommendations.

- **ISO:** The International Organization for Standardization (ISO)[3] is a worldwide federation of national standards bodies from more than 140 countries, one from each country. ISO is a nongovernmental organization that promotes the development of standardization and related activities with a view to facilitating the international exchange of goods and services, and to developing cooperation in the spheres of intellectual, scientific, technological, and economic activity. ISO's work results in international agreements that are published as International Standards.

- **IEEE 802:** The IEEE (Institute of Electrical and Electronics Engineers) 802 LAN/MAN Standards Committee develops local area network standards and metropolitan area network standards. The most widely used standards are for

---

[3]ISO is not an acronym (in which case it would be IOS), but a word, derived from the Greek, meaning *equal*.

the Ethernet family, wireless LAN, bridging, and virtual bridged LANs. An individual working group provides the focus for each area.

- **National Institute of Standards and Technology:** NIST is a U.S. federal agency that deals with measurement science, standards, and technology related to U.S. government use and to the promotion of U.S. private-sector innovation. Despite its national scope, NIST Federal Information Processing Standards (FIPS) and Special Publications (SP) have a worldwide impact.

A more detailed discussion of these organizations is contained in Appendix B.

1.11 RECOMMENDED READING AND WEB SITES

Good overview articles on convergence include [AUDI04a], [HETT03], and [MILO00]. [MILL05] and [AUDI04b] look at the business implications of evolving toward a convergence architecture.

[LAZA07] is a good overview of unified communications. [TARL07] makes the business case for unified communications. [KERR06] compares the Microsoft and Cisco approaches to unified communications, from a Cisco perspective. [TURE04] provides a detailed discussion of presence.

AUDI04a Audin, G. "Architectures for Convergence." *Business Communications Review,* October 2004.

AUDI04b Audin, G. "A Roadmap to Convergence." *Business Communications Review,* October 2004.

HETT03 Hettick, L. "Building Blocks for Converged Applications." *Business Communications Review,* June 2003.

KERR06 Kerravala, Z. *The Impact of Microsoft's Unified Communications Launch.* White Paper, Yankee Group, August 2006.

LAZA07 Laxar, I. *"Unified Communications: What, Why, and How?"* Issue Paper, Nemertes Research, 2007.

MILL05 Miller, H.; Levine, H.; and Bates, S. "Welcome to Convergence." *IT Pro,* May/June 2005.

MILO00 Milonas, A. "Enterprise Networking for the New Millennium." *Bell Labs Technical Journal,* January–March 2000.

TARL07 Tarleja, M.; Chandra, S.; and Tantzen, B. "UC: Adding to the Bottom and Top Lines Today." *Business Communications Review,* November 2007.

TURE04 Turek, M. "The Future of Presence." *Business Communications Review,* May 2004.

Recommended Web sites:

- **IEEE Standards in Education:** A wealth of information on standards, including case studies, tutorials, news, and links to standards organizations.

- **No Jitter:** Oriented toward the business user, this site integrates data and voice communications topics well. The site focuses on unified communications, convergence, and IP communications.
- **ZDNet:** A rich collection of material on business and information technology, including white papers, computer magazine articles, news, blogs, and cases studies.

1.12 KEY TERMS AND REVIEW QUESTIONS

Key Terms

asynchronous transfer mode (ATM)	frame relay	TCP/IP
circuit switching	image communications	unified communications
client/server	Internet	video communications
convergence	local area network (LAN)	voice communications
data communications	metropolitan area network (MAN)	wide area network (WAN)
distributed applications	packet switching	wireless network

Review Questions

1.1 What three kinds of basic organizational difficulties can communications technology help companies overcome?

1.2 Name four types of information that are found on networks.

1.3 Briefly define *convergence* and *unified communications*.

1.4 How has the technology of the compact disc used in the music industry been used in image communications?

1.5 Why are the burdens on the manager greater today than in previous years when it comes to using new technology efficiently?

1.6 Why has optical fiber transmission become popular in the past few years?

1.7 What types of communications can be carried by satellite transmission?

1.8 Name two approaches that can be used for increasing the efficiency of transmission services.

1.9 Contrast the function of application software with that of interconnection software.

APPENDIX 1A PREFIXES FOR NUMERICAL UNITS

The **bit** (b) is the fundamental unit of discrete information. It represents the outcome of one choice: 1 or 0, yes or no, on or off. One bit represents two potential outcomes. So, for example, one bit can represent the on/off state of a switch. Two bits can represent four outcomes: 00, 01, 10, 11. Three bits represent eight outcomes: 000, 001, 010, 011, 100, 101, 110, 111. Each time another bit is added, the numbers of outcomes double (Table 1.1). A **byte** (or **octet**, usually abbreviated as B) is the name given to 8 bits (e.g., 8 b = 1 B). The number of potential outcomes a byte represents is $2 \times 2 \times 2 \times 2 \times 2 \times 2 \times 2 \times 2 = 2^8 = 256$. Bytes are usually used in representing quantities of storage in computers. Bits are traditionally used in describing communications rates.

Table 1.1 Bits and Outcomes

Number of Bits (x)	Number of Outcomes (2^x)	Typical Use
1	2	Basic unit of information
4	16	Hexadecimal digit
7	128	IRA (International Reference Alphabet) character without parity bit
8	256	Byte; character with parity bit
10	1,024	Number of bytes in a kilobyte of storage
13	8,192	Number of bits in a kilobyte of storage
16	65,536	Address size in older computers
20	1,048,576	Number of bytes in a megabyte of storage
23	8,388,608	Number of bits in a megabyte of storage
32	$4.3 + 10^9$	Common memory address size
64	$1.84 + 101^9$	Memory address size on newer computers

In the computer science literature, the prefixes kilo, mega, and so forth are often used on numerical units. These have two different interpretations (Table 1.2):

- **Data transmission:** For data transmission, the prefixes used are those defined for the International System of Units (SI), the international standard. In this scheme, prefixes are used as a shorthand method of expressing powers of 10. For example, one kilobit per second (1 kbps) = 10^3 bps = 1000 bps.

- **Computer storage:** The amount of data in computer memory, in a file, or a message that is transmitted is typically measured in bytes. Because memory is indicated by binary addresses, the size of memory is expressed as powers of 2. The same prefixes are used in a way that approximates their use in the SI scheme. For example, one kilobyte (1 kB) = 2^{10} bytes = 1024 bytes.

Table 1.2 Numerical Prefixes

Prefix Name	Prefix Symbol	Factor	
		SI	Computer Storage
tera	T	10^{12}	2^{40}
giga	G	10^9	$2^{30} = 1,073,741,824$
mega	M	10^6	$2^{20} = 1,048,576$
kilo	k	10^3	$2^{10} = 1024$
milli	m	10^{-3}	
micro	μ	10^{-6}	
nano	n	10^{-9}	

PART ONE

Requirements

Part One defines the needs for information communications in the business environment. It discusses the ways in which various forms of information are used and the need for interconnection and networking facilities.

ROAD MAP FOR PART ONE

Chapter 2 Business Information

The requirements for data communications and networking facilities in an organization are driven by the nature and volume of information that is handled. Chapter 2 provides an overview of the four basic categories of information used in any organization: audio, data, image, and video. The chapter discusses some of the salient characteristics of each type and looks at their networking implications.

Chapter 3 Distributed Data Processing

Chapter 3 describes the nature and role of distributed data processing (DDP) in an organization. Virtually all business information systems organizations are distributed, and the networking and communications requirements are driven by the way in which data and applications are distributed.

CHAPTER 2

BUSINESS INFORMATION

2.1 Audio
> Networking Implications

2.2 Data
> Networking Implications

2.3 Image
> Image Representation
> Image and Document Formats
> Networking Implications

2.4 Video
> Digital Video
> Networking Implications

2.5 Performance Measures
> Response Time
> Throughput

2.6 Summary

2.7 Recommended Reading and Web Sites

2.8 Key Terms, Review Questions, and Problems

Chapter Objectives

After reading this chapter, you should be able to

♦ Distinguish between digital and analog information sources.

♦ Characterize business information types into one of four categories: audio, data, image, and video.

♦ Estimate quantitatively the communication resources required by the four types of information sources.

♦ Explain why system response time is a critical factor in user productivity.

It is important to understand how information communication relates to business requirements. A first step in this understanding is to examine the various forms of business information. There is a wide variety of applications, each with its own information characteristics. For the analysis and design of information networks, however, the kinds of information usually can be categorized as requiring one of a small number of services: **audio**, **data**, **image**, and **video**.

Our examination covers the following topics:

• How the impact of information sources on communications systems is measured

• The nature of the four major forms of business information: audio, data, image, and video

• The types of business services that relate to each of these forms of information

• An introductory look at the implications of these services from the point of view of the communications requirements that they generate

Information sources can produce information in **digital** or **analog** form. *Digital information* is represented as a sequence of discrete symbols from a finite "alphabet." Examples are text, numerical data, and binary data. For digital communication, the information rate and the capacity of a digital channel are measured in bits per second (bps).

Analog information is a continuous signal (for example, a voltage) that can take on a continuum of values. An example is the electrical signal coming out of a microphone when someone speaks into it. In this case, the analog electrical signal represents the continuous acoustic changes in air pressure that make up sound. For analog communication, information rate and channel capacity are measured in hertz (Hz) of bandwidth (1 Hz = 1 cycle per second). Virtually any communication signal can be expressed as a combination of pure oscillations of various frequencies. The bandwidth measures the limits of these frequencies. The higher the frequencies allowed, the more accurately a complex signal can be represented.

2.1 AUDIO

The audio service supports applications based on sound, usually of the human **voice**. The primary application using audio service is telephone communication. Other applications include telemarketing, voice mail, audio teleconferencing, and entertainment

Figure 2.1 Signal Frequency and Bandwidth (Hz)

radio. The quality of sound is characterized mainly by the bandwidth used (Figure 2.1). Voice on a telephone is limited to about 3400 Hz of bandwidth, which is of moderate quality. Voice of teleconference quality requires about 7000 Hz of bandwidth. For high-fidelity sound of reasonable quality, about 15,000 Hz (approximately the range of the human ear) is needed. For compact discs, 20,000 Hz is supported for each of two channels for stereo.

Audio information can also be represented digitally. The details are given in Chapter 16. We give an abbreviated discussion here. To get a good representation of sound in digital format, we need to sample its amplitude at a rate (samples per second, or smp/s) equal to at least twice the maximum frequency (in Hz) of the analog signal. For voice of telephone quality, one usually samples at a rate of 8000 smp/s. For high-quality sound on compact discs, 44,100 smp/s is the rate used on each channel. After sampling, the signal amplitudes must be put in digital form, a process referred to as **quantization**. Eight bits per sample are usually used for telephone voice and 16 bits per sample for each channel for stereophonic compact disc. In the first case, 256 levels of amplitude can be distinguished, and in the second, 65,536 levels. Thus, without compression, digital voice requires 8 b/smp × 8,000 smp/s = 64,000 bps. In the case of CDs, a straightforward multiplication of the foregoing parameters leads to a data rate of about 1.41 Mbps for both channels. A CD is usually rated at a capacity of about 600 megabytes (MB). This leads to an audio capacity of about 1 hour of stereo sound.

Typical telephone conversations have an average length in the range of 1 to 5 min. For ordinary voice telephone communication, information in either direction is transmitted less than half the time; otherwise, the two parties would be talking at once [SRIR88].

Networking Implications

The requirements just discussed suggest the need for both a powerful and flexible intralocation facility plus access to a variety of outside telephone services. Outside services are provided by public telephone networks, including the local telephone company and long-distance carriers such as AT&T or a national PTT (postal, telegraph, and telephone) authority. In addition, various private networking facilities and leased line arrangements are possible. All of these are discussed in Chapter 12.

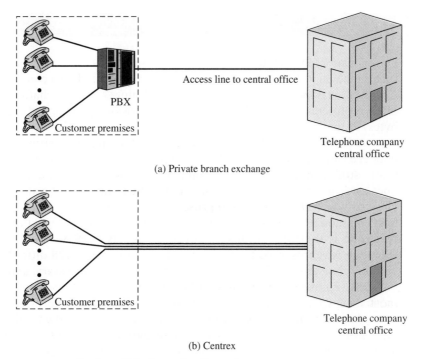

(a) Private branch exchange

(b) Centrex

Figure 2.2 Business Telephone Configurations

The most effective way of managing voice requirements is to tie all of the phones at a given site into a single system. There are two main alternatives for this: the private branch exchange and Centrex. The **private branch exchange (PBX)** is an on-premise switching facility, owned or leased by an organization, that interconnects the telephones within the facility and provides access to the public telephone system (Figure 2.2a). Typically, a telephone user on the premises dials a three- or four-digit number to call another subscriber on the premises and dials one digit (usually 8 or 9) to get a dial tone for an outside line, which allows the caller to dial a number in the same fashion as a residential user.

Centrex is a telephone company offering that provides the same sort of service as a PBX but performs the switching function in equipment located in the telephone company's central office as opposed to the customer's premises (Figure 2.2b). All telephone lines are routed from the customer site to the central switch. The user can still make local calls with a short extension number, giving the appearance of an on-premise switch.

Either a PBX or Centrex facility can support a wide variety of voice-related services. Both voice mail and audio teleconferencing can be supported by either approach.

A dramatic change in the way in which audio transmission is supported has been underway for some years. This is the increasing reliance on packet transmission using the Internet Protocol (IP), over both the Internet and private IP-based networks. In general, this type of transmission is referred to as voice over IP (VoIP). Both IP-based PBX and IP Centrex offerings are now common.

2.2 DATA

Data consist of information that can be represented by a finite alphabet of symbols, such as the digits 0 through 9 or the symbols represented on a computer keyboard. Common examples of data include text and numerical information. Symbols are often represented in computers or for transmission by groups of 8 bits (octets or bytes).

A familiar example of digital data is **text** or character strings. While textual data are most convenient for human beings, they cannot, in character form, be easily stored or transmitted by data processing and communications systems. Such systems are designed for binary data. Thus a number of codes have been devised by which characters are represented by a sequence of bits. Perhaps the earliest common example of this is the Morse code. Today, the most commonly used text code is the International Reference Alphabet (IRA). [1] Each character in this code is represented by a unique 7-bit pattern; thus 128 different characters can be represented. This is a larger number than is necessary, and some of the patterns represent invisible *control characters*. IRA-encoded characters are almost always stored and transmitted using 8 bits per character. The eighth bit is a parity bit used for error detection. This bit is set such that the total number of binary 1s in each octet is always odd (**odd parity**) or always even (**even parity**). Thus a transmission error that changes a single bit, or any odd number of bits, can be detected.

Text, numerical data, and other types of data are typically organized into a database. This topic is explored in Chapter 3.

To get some practice in using the concepts introduced so far, let us estimate approximately how many bits are required to transmit a page of text. Commonly, a letter of the alphabet or a typographical symbol is represented by a **byte**, or 8 bits. Let us consider an 8.5-by-11-in. sheet, with a 1-in. margin on all sides. This leaves a 6.5-by-9 in. message space. A double-spaced page ordinarily has 3 lines to the inch, or 27 lines for the page. In a common typeface, there are 10 characters per inch, or 65 characters per line. This gives us a total $8 \times 27 \times 65 = 14{,}040$ bits. This overstates the situation because contiguous spaces at the ends of lines are not ordinarily included, and some pages are not full. As a round number, 10,000 bits per page is probably a fair estimate. For a PC communicating with a server over a telephone line using a relatively slow modem, a typical channel capacity is 56,000 bps. Thus, it would take about 0.18 s to transmit a page.

This is by no means the whole story. For example, English text is very redundant. That is, the same information can be sent by using many fewer bits. In the experiment just described, we used a standard compression routine to reduce the file to less than 40% of its size, or 4098 bits per page. Another feature that characterizes

---

[1]IRA is defined in ITU-T Recommendation T.50 and was formerly known as International Alphabet Number 5 (IA5). The U.S. national version of IRA is referred to as the American Standard Code for Information Interchange (**ASCII**). A description and table of the IRA code is contained in Appendix D.

many data-oriented information sources is the **response time** required, discussed later in this chapter.

Networking Implications

The networking requirements for supporting data applications in an organization vary widely. We begin a consideration of these requirements in Chapter 3.

2.3 IMAGE

The image service supports the communication of individual pictures, charts, or drawings. Image-based applications include facsimile, computer-aided design (CAD), publishing, and medical imaging.

As an example of the types of demands that can be placed by imaging systems, consider medical image transmission requirements. Table 2.1 summarizes the communication impact of various medical image types [DWYE92]. As well as giving the bits per image and the number of images per exam, the table gives the transmission time per exam for three standard digital transmission rates: DS-0 = 56 kbps, DS-1 = 1.544 Mbps, and DS-3 = 44.736 Mbps.

Again, compression can be used. If we allow some barely perceivable loss of information, we can use "lossy" compression, which might reduce the data by factors

Table 2.1 Transfer Time for Digital Radiology Images

Image Type	Mbytes per Image	Images per Exam	DS-0 Time/Exam (seconds)	DS-1 Time/Exam (seconds)	DS-3 Time/Exam (seconds)
Computerized tomography (CT)	0.52	30	2247	81	3
Magnetic resonance imagery (MRI)	0.13	50	928	34	1
Digital angiography	1	20	2857	104	4
Digital fluorography	1	15	2142	78	3
Ultrasound	0.26	36	1337	48	2
Nuclear medicine	0.016	26	59	2	0.1
Computerized radiography	8	4	4571	166	6
Digitized film	8	4	4571	166	6

DS-0 = 56 kbps
DS-1 = 1.544 Mbps
DS-3 = 44.736 Mbps

of roughly 10 : 1 to 20 : 1. On the other hand, for medical imaging lossy compression usually is not acceptable. Using lossless compression, ratios for these applications run below 5 : 1.

Image Representation

There are a variety of techniques used to represent image information. These fall into two main categories:

- **Vector graphics:** An image is represented as a collection of straight and curved line segments. Simple objects, such as rectangles and ovals, and more complex objects are defined by the grouping of line segments.

- **Raster graphics:** An image is represented as a two-dimensional array of spots, called pixels.[2] In the simplest form, each pixel is either black or white. This approach is used not only for computer image processing but also for facsimile.

All of the figures in this book were prepared with a graphics package (Adobe Illustrator) that makes use of vector graphics. Vector graphics involves the use of binary codes to represent object type, size, and orientation. In all these cases, the image is represented and stored as a set of binary digits and can be transmitted using digital signals.

Figure 2.3 shows a simple 10×10 representation of an image using raster graphics. This could be a facsimile or raster-scan computer graphics image. The 10×10 representation is easily converted to a 100-bit code for the image. In this example, each pixel is represented by a single bit that indicates black or white. A **grayscale image** is produced if each pixel is defined by more than one bit, representing shades of gray. Figure 2.4 shows the use of a 3-bit grayscale to produce eight shades of gray, ranging from white to black. Grayscale can also be used in vector graphics to define the grayscale of line segments or the interior of closed objects such as rectangles.

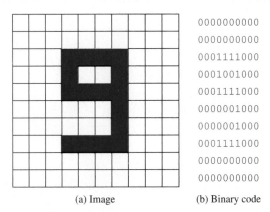

```
0000000000
0000000000
0001111000
0001001000
0001111000
0000001000
0000001000
0001111000
0000000000
0000000000
```

(a) Image   (b) Binary code

Figure 2.3   A 100-Pixel Image and Its Binary code

---

[2]A **pixel,** or picture element, is the smallest element of a digital image that can be assigned a gray level. Equivalently, a pixel is an individual dot in a dot-matrix representation of a picture.

Figure 2.4 An Eight-Level Grayscale

Images can also be defined in color. There are a number of schemes in use for this purpose. One example is the RGB (red-green-blue) scheme, in which each pixel or image area is defined by three values, one for each of the three colors. The RGB scheme exploits the fact that a large percentage of the visible spectrum can be represented by mixing red, green, and blue in various proportions and intensities. The relative magnitude of each color value determines the actual color.

Image and Document Formats

The most widely used format for raster-scan images is referred to as **JPEG**. The Joint Photographic Experts Group (JPEG) is a collaborative standards-making effort between ISO and ITU-T. JPEG has developed a set of standards for the compression of raster-scan images, both grayscale and color. The JPEG standard is designed to be general purpose, meeting a variety of needs in such areas as desktop publishing, graphic arts, newspaper wire photo transmission, and medical imaging. JPEG is appropriate for high-quality images, including photographs. Another format that is often seen on the Web is the Graphics Interchange Format (**GIF**). This is an 8-bit color format that can display up to 256 colors and is generally useful for nonphotographic images with a fairly narrow range of color, such as a company logo. Table 2.2 compares these and other popular formats.

There are also two popular document formats that are suitable for documents that include text and images. The Portable Document Format (**PDF**) is widely used on the Web, and PDF readers are available for virtually all operating systems.

Table 2.2 Comparison of Common Graphics File Formats

Type	File Extension	Compression Methods	Principal Application/Usage	Originated By
Graphics Interchange Format	.gif	Lempel-Ziv-Welch (LZW) algorithm	Flat-color graphics, animation	Compuserve
Joint Photographic Experts Group	.jpg	Various lossy	Photographic images	Joint Photographic Experts Group
Portable Network Graphics	.png	Lossless	Replacement for GIF	World Wide Web Consortium
Raw negative	Various	None	High-end digital camera	Individual equipment makers
Tagged Image File Format	.tif	Various or none	Document imaging, scanning	Adobe Systems, Inc.
Windows bit map	.bmp	None	On-screen display	Microsoft Corp.

Postscript is a page description language that is built into many desktop printers and virtually all high-end printing systems.

Networking Implications

The various configurations by which image information is used and communicated do not fundamentally differ from the configurations used for text and numerical data. The key difference is in the volume of data. As was mentioned, a page of text contains about 10,000 bits of 8-bit character data. The bit image of a good-quality personal computer screen requires over 2 million bits (i.e., for the $640 \times 480 \times 256$ video mode). A facsimile page with a resolution of 200 dots per inch (which is an adequate but not unnecessarily high resolution) would generate about 4 million bits for a simple black-and-white image and considerably more bits for grayscale or color images. Thus, for image information, a tremendous number of bits is needed for representation in the computer.

The number of bits needed to represent an image can be reduced by the use of image compression techniques. In a typical document, whether it contains text or pictorial information, the black and white areas of the image tend to cluster. This property can be exploited to describe the patterns of black and white in a manner that is more concise than simply providing a listing of black and white values, one for each point in the image. Compression ratios (the ratio of the size of the uncompressed image, in bits, to the size of the compressed image) of from 8 to 16 are readily achievable.

Even with compression, the number of bits to be transmitted for image information is large. As usual, there are two concerns: response time and throughput. In some cases, such as a CAD/CAM (computer-aided manufacturing) application, the user is interactively manipulating an image. If the user's terminal is separated from the application by a communications facility, then the communications capacity must be substantial to give adequate response time. In other cases, such as facsimile, a delay of a few seconds or even a few minutes is usually of no consequence. However, the communications facility must still have a capacity great enough to keep up with the average rate of facsimile transmission. Otherwise, delays on the facility will grow over time as a backlog develops.

2.4 VIDEO

The video service carries sequences of pictures in time. In essence, video makes use of a sequence of raster-scan images. Here it is easier to characterize the data in terms of the viewer (destination) of the TV screen rather than the original scene (source) that is recorded by the TV camera. To produce a picture on the screen, an electron beam scans across the surface of the screen from left to right and top to bottom. For black-and-white television, the amount of illumination produced (on a scale from black to white) at any point is proportional to the intensity of the beam as it passes that point. Thus at any instant in time the beam takes on an analog value of intensity to produce the desired brightness at that point on the screen. Further, as the beam scans, the analog value changes. Thus the video image can be thought of as a time-varying analog signal.

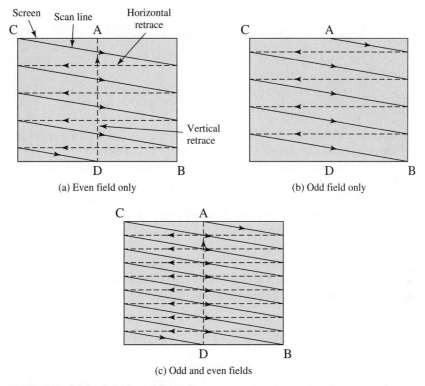

Figure 2.5 Video Interlaced Scanning

Figure 2.5 depicts the scanning process. At the end of each scan line, the beam is swept rapidly back to the left (horizontal retrace). When the beam reaches the bottom, it is swept rapidly back to the top (vertical retrace). The beam is turned off (blanked out) during the retrace intervals.

To achieve adequate resolution, the beam produces a total of 483 horizontal lines at a rate of 30 complete scans of the screen per second. Tests have shown that this rate will produce a sensation of flicker rather than smooth motion. To provide a flicker-free image without increasing the bandwidth requirement, a technique known as **interlacing** is used. As Figure 2.5 shows, the odd-numbered scan lines and the even numbered scan lines are scanned separately, with odd and even fields alternating on successive scans. The odd field is the scan from A to B and the even field is the scan from C to D. The beam reaches the middle of the screen's lowest line after 241.5 lines. At this point, the beam is quickly repositioned at the top of the screen and recommences in the middle of the screen's topmost visible line to produce an additional 241.5 lines interlaced with the original set. Thus the screen is refreshed 60 times per second rather than 30, and flicker is avoided.

Digital Video

The term *digital video* refers to the capture, manipulation, and storage of video in digital formats. If an analog video camera signal is digitized and then transmitted or stored in a digital format, either compressed or uncompressed, this could be

Table 2.3   Digital Television Formats

Format	Spatio-Temporal Resolution	Sampling Rate
CIF	$360 \times 288 \times 30$	3 MHz
CCIR	$720 \times 576 \times 30$	12 MHz
HDTV	$1280 \times 720 \times 60$	60 MHz

considered digital video. However, the term is more typically applied to video content that is initially captured with a digital video device.

Digital video cameras capture moving images digitally. In essence, this is done by taking a series of digital photographs, at a rate of at least 30 frames per second. Typically, the resolution is considerably less than that of a digital still camera, more in line with a typical PC screen. The low end of digital video cameras are Web cameras (Webcams). Their low resolution is tailored to match the needs of Webcasting and video messaging.

Digital video camera use either the interlaced technique discussed previously or progressive scan, in which all the lines of each frame are drawn in sequence. Progressive scan is used for computer monitors and most HDTV (high-definition television) schemes.

Networking Implications

Applications based on video include instructional and entertainment television, teleconferencing, closed circuit TV, and multimedia. For example, a black-and-white TV signal for video conferencing might have a frame resolution of 360 by 280 pixels sent every 1/30 s with an intensity ranging from black through gray to white represented by 8 bits. This would correspond to a raw data rate, without compression, of about 25 Mbps. To add color, the bit rate might go up by 50%. Table 2.3 gives the sampling rate for three common types of video. The table gives only the rates for luminance, because color is treated differently in the three formats. At the extreme, uncompressed high-definition color television would require more than a gigabit per second to transmit. As with images, lossy compression can be used. Moreover, use can be made of the fact that video scenes in adjacent frames are usually very similar. Reasonable quality can be achieved using compression ratios from about 20 : 1 to 100 : 1.

Increasingly important to the enterprise is the transmission of video over IP-based networks, including the Internet and private intranets. This type of transmission is known as video streaming or TVoIP (television over IP). TVoIP places substantial burdens on enterprise networks but brings substantial benefits. Thus, a key management concern is scaling up IP networks to effectively support video transmission while at the same time providing adequate quality of service to other business transmission requirements.

2.5 PERFORMANCE MEASURES

This section considers two key parameters related to performance requirements: response time and throughput.

Response Time

Response time is the time it takes a system to react to a given input. In an interactive transaction, it may be defined as the time between the last keystroke by the user and the beginning of the display of a result by the computer. For different types of applications, a slightly different definition is needed. In general, it is the time it takes for the system to respond to a request to perform a particular task.

Ideally, one would like the response time for any application to be short. However, it is almost invariably the case that shorter response time imposes greater cost. This cost comes from two sources:

- **Computer processing power:** The faster the computer, the shorter the response time. Of course, increased processing power means increased cost.
- **Competing requirements:** Providing rapid response time to some processes may penalize other processes.

Thus the value of a given level of response time must be assessed versus the cost of achieving that response time.

Table 2.4, based on [MART88], lists six general ranges of response times. Design difficulties are faced when a response time of less than 1 second is required.

Table 2.4   Response Time Ranges

Greater than 15 seconds
This rules out conversational interaction. For certain types of applications, certain types of users may be content to sit at a terminal for more than 15 seconds waiting for the answer to a single simple inquiry. However, for a busy person, captivity for more than 15 seconds seems intolerable. If such delays will occur, the system should be designed so that the user can turn to other activities and request the response at some later time.

Greater than 4 seconds
These are generally too long for a conversation requiring the operator to retain information in short-term memory (the operator's memory, not the computer's). Such delays would be very inhibiting in problem-solving activity and frustrating in data entry activity. However, after a major closure, delays from 4 to 15 seconds can be tolerated.

2 to 4 seconds
A delay longer than 2 seconds can be inhibiting to terminal operations demanding a high level of concentration. A wait of 2 to 4 seconds at a terminal can seem surprisingly long when the user is absorbed and emotionally committed to completing what he or she is doing. Again, a delay in this range may be acceptable after a minor closure has occurred.

Less than 2 seconds
When the terminal user has to remember information throughout several responses, the response time must be short. The more detailed the information remembered, the greater the need for responses of less than 2 seconds. For elaborate terminal activities, 2 seconds represents an important response-time limit.

Subsecond response time
Certain types of thought-intensive work, especially with graphics applications, require very short response times to maintain the user's interest and attention for long periods of time.

Decisecond response time
A response to pressing a key and seeing the character displayed on the screen or clicking a screen object with a mouse needs to be almost instantaneous—less than 0.1 second after the action. Interaction with a mouse requires extremely fast interaction if the designer is to avoid the use of alien syntax (one with commands, mnemonics, punctuation, etc.).

That rapid response time is the key to productivity in interactive applications has been confirmed in a number of studies [SHNE84; THAD81; GUYN88; SEVC03]. These studies show that when a computer and a user interact at a pace that ensures that neither has to wait on the other, productivity increases significantly, the cost of the work done on the computer therefore drops, and quality tends to improve. It used to be widely accepted that a relatively slow response, up to 2 seconds, was acceptable for most interactive applications because the person was thinking about the next task. However, it now appears that productivity increases as rapid response times are achieved.

The results reported on response time are based on an analysis of online transactions. A transaction consists of a user command from a terminal and the system's reply. It is the fundamental unit of work for online system users. It can be divided into two time sequences:

- **User response time:** The time span between the moment a user receives a complete reply to one command and enters the next command. People often refer to this as *think time*.

- **System response time:** The time span between the moment the user enters a command and the moment a complete response is displayed on the terminal.

As an example of the effect of reduced system response time, Figure 2.6 shows the results of a study carried out on engineers using a computer-aided design graphics program for the design of integrated circuit chips and boards [SMIT88]. Each transaction consists of a command by the engineer that alters in some way the graphic image being displayed on the screen. The results show that the rate of transactions increases

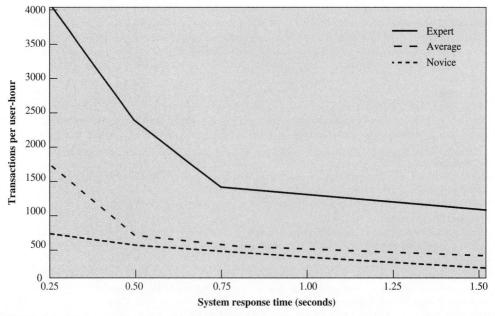

Figure 2.6   Response Time Results for High-Function Graphics

Figure 2.7   Response Time Requirements

as system response time falls and rises dramatically once system response time falls below 1 second. What is happening is that as the system response time falls, so does the user response time. This has to do with the effects of short-term memory and human attention span.

In terms of the types of computer-based information systems that we have been discussing, rapid response time is most critical for transaction processing systems. The output of management information systems and decision support systems is generally a report or the results of some modeling exercise. In these cases, rapid turnaround is not essential. For office automation applications, the need for rapid response time occurs when documents are being prepared or modified, but there is less urgency for things such as electronic mail and computer teleconferencing. The implication in terms of communications is this: If there is a communications facility between an interactive user and the application and a rapid response time is required, then the communications system must be designed so that its contribution to delay is compatible with that requirement. Thus, if a transaction processing application requires a response time of 1 s and the average time it takes the computer application to generate a response is 0.75 s, then the delay due to the communications facility must be no more than 0.25 s.

Another area where response time has become critical is the use of the World Wide Web, either over the Internet or over a corporate intranet.[3] The time it takes for a typical Web page to come up on the user's screen varies greatly. Response times can be gauged based on the level of user involvement in the session; in particular, systems with very fast response times tend to command more user attention.

As Figure 2.7 indicates, Web systems with a 3-second or better response time maintain a high level of user attention [SEVC96]. With a response time of between

---

[3]*Intranet* is a term used to refer to the implementation of Internet technologies within a corporate organization, rather than for external connection to the global Internet; this topic is explored in Chapter 6.

3 and 10 seconds, some user concentration is lost, and response times above 10 seconds discourage the user, who may simply abort the session. For an organization that maintains an Internet Web site, much of the response time is determined by forces beyond the organization's control, such as the Internet throughput, Internet congestion, and the end user's access speed. In such circumstances, the organization may consider keeping the image content of each page low and relying heavily on text, to promote rapid response time.

Throughput

The trend toward higher and higher transmission speed makes possible increased support for different services (e.g., broadband-based multimedia services) that once seemed too demanding for digital communications. To make effective use of these new capabilities, it is essential to have a sense of the demands each service puts on the storage and communications of integrated information systems. Services can be grouped into data, audio, image, and video, whose demands on information systems vary widely. Figure 2.8 gives an indication of the data rates required for various information types [TEGE95]. [4]

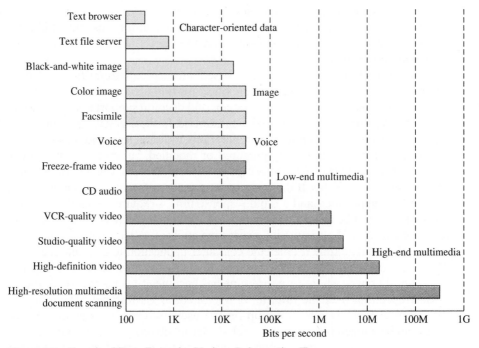

Figure 2.8 Required Data Rates for Various Information Types

---

[4] Note the use of a log scale for the *x*-axis. A basic review of log scales is in the math refresher document at the Computer Science Student Resource Site at WilliamStallings.com/StudentSupport.html.

APPLICATION NOTE

File Sizes

Image file sizes are based on the amount of information on the page and the color content. High-resolution color images can take up a very large amount of storage space. Sound and video files can be larger still. Though audio files do not contain data or color they extend over a period of time. The characteristics that change audio file sizes are length, sampling rate, and bits per sample. The better the sound quality, the larger the file and the greater the bandwidth required to transmit the sounds. For example, CD quality sound takes up much more space than a basic recording of the same music. Video is essentially a series of color pictures over time and so these files can be immense. Frame rate describes the number of times per second an image is sent and this value can drastically change the file size or bandwidth required for transmission.

The popularity of digital cameras has certainly increased and because they can take both pictures and record video, a little understanding of file sizes and types can help preserve hard drive and removable media storage space.

To start, we must decide on the quality required. Higher quality reduces our options for reducing file size. Next, we will select the appropriate file type. Depending on the application, this can be an important choice. For example, using very high quality, large images and video on a Web page can have a negative impact on the performance. It is for this reason that so much thought goes in to optimizing content for the web. By adjusting the image size, color content or file type we can dramatically reduce the file size and the page loading time.

As an example, the following is a table of various image file sizes based on the type of information.

As we can see, changing the file type used and the color content can have a tremendous affect on the size of the file. It is no wonder that a digital camera taking high-resolution pictures can run out of memory so quickly. The downside of modifying an image or stream in order to reduce the size is that you usually sacrifice some amount of quality. Once the quality is gone it cannot be recovered without the original file. For applications like spreadsheets and word processing, there is usually little to be done because organizations standardize on the programs and operating systems for use. Fortunately, files of this type, with text only, do not take up much room.

The network is often on the receiving end of this shift to digital images and video streams. As more information is sent via the network, links can become over utilized and response times can be slow. Voice over IP, streaming media, and video conferencing all contribute to

Information	File Type	Size
640 × 480 pixel picture	24 bit bitmap	900 KB
640 × 480 pixel picture	256 color (8 bit) bitmap	300 KB
640 × 480 pixel picture	16 color (4 bit) bitmap	150 KB
640 × 480 pixel picture	GIF	58 KB
640 × 480 pixel picture	JPEG	45 KB

(Continued)

performance problems. It is for this reason that we must now design for these changes and network administrators are under pressure to supply sufficient network storage and the bandwidth. However, an administrator is not able to change the information once it is sent. By optimizing the data before it is transmitted, we can often alleviate network utilization and storage problems before they even start.

2.6 SUMMARY

Business communications systems and networks must deal with a variety of information types, which can be conveniently categorized as voice, data, image, and video. Each type presents its own requirements in terms of throughput, response time, and demands on the networking facility.

2.7 RECOMMENDED READING AND WEB SITES

Three books that provide expanded coverage of the topics explored in this chapter are [LI04], [RAO02], and [STEI02].

LI04 Li, Z., and Drew, M. *Fundamentals of Multimedia.* Upper Saddle River, NJ: Prentice Hall, 2004.

RAO02 Rao, K.; Bojkovic, Z.; and Milovanovic, D. *Multimedia Communication Systems: Techniques, Standards, and Networks.* Upper Saddle River, NJ: Prentice Hall, 2002.

STEI02 Steinmetz, R., and Nahrstedt, K. *Multimedia Fundamentals, Volume 1: Media Coding and Content Processing.* Upper Saddle River, NJ: Prentice Hall, 2002.

Recommended Web sites:

- **Multimedia Communications Research Laboratory:** At Bell Labs. Good source of leading-edge research information.

2.8 KEY TERMS, REVIEW QUESTIONS, AND PROBLEMS

Key Terms

analog	grayscale	Private branch exchange
audio	image	(PBX)
ASCII	interlacing	quantization
byte	JPEG	raster graphics
Centrex	IRA	response time
digital	PDF	vector graphics
data	pixel	video
GIF	Postscript	voice

Review Questions

2.1 What are the two different interpretations of the prefixes *kilo, mega,* and *giga?* Define a context in which each interpretation is used.

2.2 What is the bandwidth of telephone voice?

2.3 The process that takes advantage of redundancy to reduce the number of bits sent for a given piece of data is called what?

2.4 What is the difference between Centrex and PBX?

2.5 What is the difference between a printable character and a control character?

2.6 Explain the basic principles of vector graphics and raster graphics.

2.7 List two common image formats.

2.8 List two common document formats.

2.9 Describe the process used to prevent flicker in a video screen.

2.10 Define response time.

2.11 What is considered an acceptable system response time for interactive applications and how does this response time relate to acceptable response times for Web sites?

Problems

2.1 How many CD-quality music channels can be transmitted simultaneously over a 10-Mbps Ethernet, assuming that no other traffic is carried on the same network and ignoring overhead?

2.2 The compact disc (CD) was originally designed to hold audio data. The information on the CD is arranged in a specific format that divides the data into segments. Hardware design considerations in effect at the time the CD was developed dictated that each second of audio would span exactly 75 sectors on the CD.
   a. Using stereo audio at a standard high-quality audio CD sample rate, what is the maximum number of bytes that can be stored in a single audio CD sector?
   b. How many minutes of CD quality audio can a 700-MB CD hold?
   c. How much storage is required to hold 5 minutes of CD-quality audio? What types of media are available to hold this amount of data?

2.3 A company's telephone exchange digitizes telephone channels at 8000 smp/s, using 8 bits for quantization. This telephone exchange must transmit simultaneously 24 of these telephone channels over a communications link.
   a. What's the required data rate?
   b. In order to provide answering-machine service, the telephone exchange can store 3-minute audio messages of the same quality as that of the telephone channels. How many megabytes of data storage space are needed to store each of these audio messages?

2.4 How many bits will it take to represent the following sets of outcomes?
   a. The uppercase alphabet A, B, . . . , Z
   b. The digits 0, 1, . . . , 9
   c. The seconds in a 24-hour day
   d. The people in the United States (about 300,000,000 of them)
   e. Population of the world (about 6 billion)

2.5 IRA is a 7-bit code that allows 128 characters to be defined. In the 1970s, many newspapers received stories from the wire services in a 6-bit code called TTS. This code carried upper and lowercase characters as well as many special characters and formatting commands. The typical TTS character set allowed over 100 characters to be defined. How do you think this could be accomplished?

2.6 Review the IRA code in the document at this book's Web site.
   a. Indicate the 7-bit code for the following letters: D, d, H, h.
   b. Repeat part (a), but this time show the 8-bit code that includes an odd parity bit.

2.7 In a document, what standard ASCII characters might fall into the category of invisible?

2.8 A primary primitive (due to its atomic nature) data type available to most programming languages is the character data type. This data type has traditionally been represented internally to the computer system using the ASCII (7-bit) or Extended Binary-Coded Decimal Interchange Code, EBCDIC (8-bit) encoding schemes. Programming languages such as Java use the Unicode (16-bit) encoding scheme to represent primitive character data elements (www.unicode.org). Discuss the implications, beneficial and detrimental, inherent in the decision process regarding the use of these various encoding schemes.

2.9 Base64 encoding allows arbitrary sequences of octets to be represented by printable characters. The encoding process represents 24-bit groups of input bits as strings of four encoded characters. The 24-bit groups are formed by concatenating three octets. These 24-bit groups are then treated as four concatenated 6-bit groups, each of which is translated to a character of the Base64 alphabet. The encoded output stream is represented by lines of no more than 76 printable characters, with line breaks being indicated by the "CR, LF" character sequence. How much will a file be expanded by encoding it with Base64?

2.10 The text of the *Encyclopaedia Britannica* is about 44 million words. For a sample of about 2000 words, the average word length was 5.1 characters per word.
   a. Approximately how many characters are there in the encyclopedia? (Be sure to allow for spaces and punctuation between words.)
   b. How long would it take to transmit the text over a T-1 line at 1.544 Mbps? On a fiber optic link at 2.488 Gbps?
   c. Could the text fit on a 600-MB CD?

2.11 A drawing in a 8.5-by-11-inch sheet is digitized by means of a 300 dpi (dots per inch) scanner.
   a. What is the visual resolution of the resulting image (number of dots in each dimension)?
   b. If 8 bits are used for the quantization of each pixel, how much data storage space is needed to store the image as raw data?

2.12 When examining X-rays, radiologists often deal with four to six images at a time. For a faithful digital representation of an X-ray photograph, a pixel array of 2048 by 2048 is typically used with a grayscale of intensity for each pixel of 12 bits. As you would hope, radiologists do not look kindly on compression that degrades quality.
   a. How many levels of grayscale are represented by 12 bits?
   b. How many bits does it take to represent an X-ray based on these parameters?
   c. Suppose five X-rays have to be sent to another site over a T-1 line (1.544 Mbps). How long would it take, at best—ignoring overhead?
   d. Suppose now that we wish to build a communications system that will provide the five X-rays of part (c) upon demand; that is, that from the time the X-rays are requested we want them available within 2 s. What is a lowest channel rate that can support this demand?
   e. The next generation of displays for X-rays is planned for 4096 by 4096 pixels with a 12-bit grayscale. What does the answer to part d become when using this resolution?

2.13 A multimedia version of a multivolume reference book is being prepared for storage on compact disc (CD-ROM). Each disc can store about 700 MB (megabytes). The input to each volume consists of 1000 pages of text typed 10 characters to the inch, 6 lines to the inch, on 8.5-by-11-in. paper with 1-in. margins on each side. Each volume also has about 100 pictures, which will be displayed in color at Super VGA resolution (1024×768 pixel, 8 b/pixel). Moreover, each volume is enhanced for the CD version with 30 min of audio of teleconferencing quality (16,000 smp/s, 6 b/smp).
   a. How many bits are there on a 700-megabyte CD (1 megabyte = 2^{20} bytes)?
   b. Without compression and ignoring overhead, how many volumes can be put on one CD?

    c. Suppose the material is to be transmitted over a T-1 facility (1.544 Mbps). How long will it take, exclusive of overhead, to transmit a volume?

    d. Suppose the text can be compressed at a 3 : 1 rate, the pictures at 10 : 1, and the audio at 2 : 1. How many volumes, exclusive of overhead, will fit on a CD? How long will it take to transmit a compressed volume on a T-1 channel?

2.14 Commonly, medical digital radiology ultrasound studies consist of about 25 images extracted from a full-motion ultrasound examination. Each image consists of 512 by 512 pixels, each with 8 b of intensity information.

    a. How many bits are there in the 25 images?

    b. Ideally, however, doctors would like to use $512 \times 512 \times 8$ bit frames at 30 fps (frames per second). Ignoring possible compression and overhead factors, what is the minimum channel capacity required to sustain this full-motion ultrasound?

    c. Suppose each full-motion study consists of 25 s of frames. How many such studies could fit on a 600-MB CD-ROM?

2.15 An 800×600 image with 24-bit color depth needs to be stored on disc. Even though the image might contain 224 different colors, only 256 colors are actually present. This image could be encoded by means of a table (palette) of 256 24-bit elements and, for each pixel, an index of its RGB value in the table. This type of encoding is usually called Color Look-Up Table (CLUT) encoding.

    a. How many bytes are needed to store the image raw information?

    b. How many bytes are needed to store the image using CLUT encoding?

    c. What's the compression ratio achieved by using this simple encoding method?

2.16 A digital video camera provides an uncompressed output video stream with a resolution of 320×240 pixels, a frame rate of 30 fps, and 8 bits for quantization of each pixel.

    a. What's the required bandwidth for the transmission of the uncompressed video stream?

    b. How much data storage space is needed to record two minutes of the video stream?

2.17 An MPEG-encoded video stream with a resolution of 720×480 pixels and a frame rate of 30 fps is transmitted over a network. An old workstation is meant to receive and display the video stream. It takes 56 milliseconds for the workstation to decode each received frame and display it on the screen. Will this workstation display the video stream successfully? Why or why not?

2.18 Refer to Table 2.4 for a list and description of general system response time categories. Assume you are providing five computer systems for video game developer and the budget for hardware (e.g., CPU clock speed, RAM, bus data rate, disc I/O data rate, etc.) is limited by the consumer. The base price of a system is $1.5K (providing basic >15 s response time for all application scenarios) and each increase in response time range adds $0.5K to the cost of the system hardware. Make a case for the classification of each of the systems running the application scenarios listed that will keep the customer's total cost for the five systems below $15K.

    a. System 1—word-processing application and basic Internet access

    b. System 2—skateboard equipment checkout terminal (for gamer recreation)

    c. System 3—graphic design and basic Internet access

    d. System 4—programming and basic Internet access

    e. System 5—video game testing

Note: There is no unique solution. In your answer, each lettered response should provide some rationalization as to why each category was selected, to show that you have given some thought to the impact on productivity that choices such as these can affect.

CHAPTER 3

DISTRIBUTED DATA PROCESSING

3.1 Centralized Versus Distributed Processing

Centralized and Distributed Organization

Technical Trends Leading to Distributed Data Processing

Management and Organizational Considerations

Client/Server Architecture

Intranets

Extranets

3.2 Forms of Distributed Data Processing

Distributed Applications

Other Forms of DDP

3.3 Distributed Data

Database Management Systems

Centralized Database

Replicated Database

Partitioned Database

3.4 Networking Implications of DDP

3.5 Summary

3.6 Recommended Reading

3.7 Key Terms, Review Questions, and Problems

Chapter Objectives

After reading this chapter, you should be able to

♦ Describe the difference between centralized and distributed data processing and discuss the pros and cons of each approach.

♦ Explain why a distributed data processing system needs to be interconnected with some sort of data communications or networking facility.

♦ Describe the different forms of distributed data processing for applications.

♦ Describe the different forms of distributed databases.

♦ Discuss the implications of distributed data processing in terms of the requirements for data communications and networking facilities.

♦ Understand the motivation behind the trend to client/server architectures.

In Chapter 2 we looked at the overall requirements for information in an organization and found that four types of information are vital to the competitive health of any business: data, voice, image, and video. In terms of data communications and networking facilities, it is the first of these types of information, data, that has shaped corporate strategy. Until recently, voice was treated as an entirely separate requirement, and indeed it still is treated that way in many organizations. As we shall see as the text progresses, the advent of digital transmission and networking facilities, plus the use of flexible transmission protocols such as IP (Internet Protocol) and ATM (asynchronous transfer mode), makes it feasible for businesses to integrate voice, data, image, and in some cases video to provide cost-effective networking solutions.

Voice, image, and video have each produced separate communications technologies and what must be considered relatively straightforward solutions from the user's point of view. The situation with respect to data is much more complex, both because the variety of data processing facilities is wide and because the range of approaches to support the business data communications function is large. Therefore, so that the various approaches to business data communications and networking can be seen in context, we devote this chapter to looking at the types of data processing systems that are typical in organizations. We begin with a look at the two extremes in organization of the computing function: centralized and distributed data processing. The computing function in most organizations is implemented somewhere along a spectrum between these two extremes. By examining this spectrum, we can see the nature of the communications and networking requirements for business begin to emerge. We then focus on distributed data processing, examine various approaches, and look at the communications implications of these approaches. In particular, we examine the client/server architectures as one approach to achieving the best of centralized and decentralized architectures.

3.1 CENTRALIZED VERSUS DISTRIBUTED PROCESSING

Centralized and Distributed Organization

Traditionally, the data processing function was organized in a centralized fashion. In a **centralized data processing** architecture, data processing support is provided by one or a cluster of computers, generally large computers, located in a central data processing facility. Many of the tasks performed by such a facility are initiated at the center with the results produced at the center. An example is a payroll application. Other tasks may require interactive access by personnel who are not physically located in the data processing center. For example, a data entry function, such as inventory update, may be performed by personnel at sites throughout the organization. In a centralized architecture, each person is provided with a local terminal that is connected by a communications facility to the central data processing facility.

A fully centralized data processing facility is centralized in many senses of the word:

- **Centralized computers:** One or more computers are located in a central facility. In many cases, there are one or more large mainframe computers, which require special facilities such as air conditioning and a raised floor. In a smaller organization, the central computer or computers are high-performance servers or midrange systems. The iSeries from IBM is an example of a midrange system.

- **Centralized processing:** All applications are run on the central data processing facility. This includes applications that are clearly central or organization-wide in nature, such as payroll, as well as applications that support the needs of users in a particular organizational unit. As an example of the latter, a product design department may make use of a computer-aided design (CAD) graphics package that runs on the central facility.

- **Centralized data:** Most data are stored in files and databases at the central facility and are controlled by and accessible by the central computer or computers. This includes data that are of use to many units in the organization, such as inventory figures, as well as data that support the needs of, and should be used by, only one organizational unit. As an example of the latter, the marketing organization may maintain a database with information derived from customer surveys.

- **Centralized control:** A data processing or information systems manager has responsibility for the centralized data processing facility. Depending on the size and importance of the facility, control may be exercised at the middle-management level or may be very high in the organization. It is quite common to have control exercised at the vice-presidential level, and a number of organizations have the equivalent of a corporate chief information officer (CIO) who has authority at the board level. In the case of very senior management, a subordinate generally has control of the centralized data processing facility, whereas the top data processing (DP) or information officer has broader authority in matters related to corporate acquisition, use, and protection of information.

- **Centralized support staff:** A centralized data processing facility must include a technical support staff to operate and maintain the data processing equipment. In addition, some (and in many cases all) programming is done by a central staff.

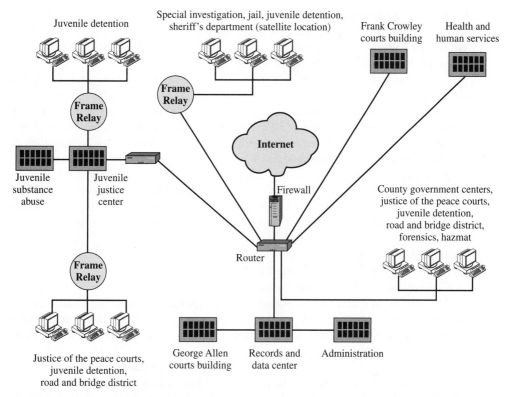

Figure 3.1   Dallas County Information Systems Architecture

Such a centralized organization has a number of attractive aspects. There may be economies of scale in the purchase and operation of equipment and software. A large central DP shop can afford to have professional programmers on staff to meet the needs of the various departments. Management can maintain control over data processing procurement, enforce standards for programming and data file structure, and design and implement a security policy.

An example of a centralized data processing facility is that of Dallas County [CLAR03], shown in general terms in Figure 3.1. The county's information technology (IT) infrastructure is fairly typical of government entitles of its size. The bulk of the applications and databases are housed in the data center. The data center includes several mainframes and a number of high-end servers. The mainframe runs customized applications that support the court and justice system requirements. The servers support a variety of database applications to support the countywide user population.

The networking architecture is a hub-and-spoke configuration. Some sites have direct high-speed leased lines connecting to the base router. Other sites are connected by means of private frame relay wide-area network offerings. This arrangement minimizes transmission costs and the amount of network equipment needed to handle the traffic. Prior to the installation of this networking architecture, the network architecture was the result of natural growth of demand over the years. The old architecture involved a number of cascaded switches, with some traffic going through multiple hops to reach the data center. Finally, the data center provides an Internet connection protected by a firewall.

This centralized configuration meets a number of objectives for Dallas County. To meet security and privacy requirements, Dallas County has found that the centralized database and application resources are more easily protected than if these resources were geographically distributed. Dallas County has seen performance gains with the new architecture. The simplified networking architecture has also simplified network management.

A data processing facility may depart in varying degrees from the centralized data processing organization by implementing a **distributed data processing (DDP) strategy**. A distributed data processing facility is one in which computers, usually smaller computers, are dispersed throughout an organization. The objective of such dispersion is to process information in a way that is most effective based on operational, economic, and/or geographic considerations, or all three. A DDP facility may include a central facility plus satellite facilities, or it may more nearly resemble a community of peer computing facilities. In either case, some form of interconnection is usually needed; that is, the various computers in the system must be connected to one another. As may be expected, given the characterization of centralized data processing provided here, a DDP facility involves the distribution of computers, processing, and data.

A simple example of a distributed data processing facility is that implemented on the cruise ship *Carnival Valor,* owned by Florida based Carnival Cruise Lines [KNAU05]. The facility (Figure 3.2) is a wireless local area network (WLAN) that supports both data traffic and voice over IP (VoIP). The WLAN connects to the outside world via a satellite link that connects to the Internet, to Carnivals private wide area network (WAN) and to the public switched telephone network (PSTN) in the U.S.

Although not germane to our discussion, the voice network is of some interest. There is a private branch exchange (PBX) that connects to the PSTN. The PBX supports a number of business telephones directly connected to it and supports a voice mail facility for Carnival employees. Passengers and crew may also use cell phones that are connected into the WLAN via wireless access point (WAP) equipment. The WAP routes cell phone traffic over the WLAN to the PBX using the VoIP protocol. Routers that function as VoIP gateways convert between VoIP traffic and voice signals for connection to the PBX.

On the data side, the WLAN supports a distributed data processing configuration based on application. Separate servers handle call management, network management and access control/security applications. These servers have direct wired links into the WLAN. A number of applications specific to the operation of the ship are managed from enterprise data servers that have wireless access to the WLAN via the WAPs. Both passenger and crew may use wireless laptops for Internet access, again via the WAPs. Finally, the LAN services modules act both as LAN switches and as network management control points.

This distributed architecture provides great flexibility. Ship-related applications, such as those rotated to personnel, entertainment scheduling, food services,

Figure 3.2 Carnival Valor Wireless LAN

engineering and maintenance, and so on, are maintained on individual servers, allowing for easy upgrade. Servers are not tied to a centralized computer room but can be sited at the most convenient location. Because all of the servers have wireless access to the WLAN, they are mobile and can be moved if conditions warrant. At the same time, because all communications and networking, including voice, Internet access, and shipboard applications, are tied into a single LAN, network management and network security are more easily managed.

Technical Trends Leading to Distributed Data Processing

Until the early 1970s, the centralized data processing approach enjoyed near-universal use in businesses. Since that time, there has been a steady evolution to distributed processing. We can address this trend from two points of view: means and motive. First, let us look at the changes in the data processing industry that have given companies the means to choose distributed processing. We then turn to the question of why distributed data processing is coming to be preferred to centralized data processing.

Table 3.1   Requirements for the Corporate Computing Function

1. Provide computing capability to all organizational units that legitimately require it.
2. Contain the capital and operations cost in provision of computing services within the organization.
3. Satisfy special computing needs of user departments.
4. Maintain organizational integrity in operations that are dependent on computing (i.e., avoid mismatches in operation among departments).
5. Meet information requirements of management.
6. Provide computing services in a reliable, professional, and technically competent manner.
7. Allow organizational units sufficient autonomy in the conduct of their tasks to optimize creativity and performance at the unit level.
8. Preserve autonomy among organizational units and, if possible, increase their importance and influence within the larger organization.
9. Make the work of employees enjoyable as well as productive.

The key factor that has made DDP possible is the dramatic and continuing decrease in cost of computer hardware, accompanied by an increase in its capabilities. Today's personal computers have speeds, instruction sets, and memory capacities comparable to those of minicomputers and even mainframes of just a few years ago. Equally important, today's personal computers boast graphical user interfaces (GUIs) that provide unprecedented ease of use and responsiveness.

Management and Organizational Considerations

The increasing availability of inexpensive yet powerful systems with a growing repertoire of applications software has made it possible for organizations to disperse computing capability throughout the organization rather than to continue to rely on a centralized facility with, at most, distributed terminals for access. However, the centralized option is still very much available to the organization. As with other types of computers, the powerful mainframes that are the heart of a centralized facility have also dropped in price and increased in power.

To begin, let us consider the requirements for the corporate computing function, that is, those needs that the computing facility must fulfill. Table 3.1 suggests nine specific requirements for the computing facility. A case can clearly be made that requirements 1, 3, 7, 8, and 9 can be satisfied with a distributed arrangement of low-cost servers, workstations, and personal computers. Widespread use of small computers can provide highly individualistic service to all the departments needing computing, allow users to establish and maintain autonomy in their operations using their own equipment, and provide users with hands-on opportunity to enjoy computing use while improving departmental productivity.

Two aspects of the needs of users demonstrate the truth of the preceding statement: the need for new applications and the need for short response time. First, consider the need for new applications. For any organization to remain competitive, each department within the organization must continually strive to improve productivity and effectiveness. A major source of such improvement is increasing reliance on data processing and computers. The result is that in most well managed organizations, the demand for new applications is rising faster than the central data processing service can develop them. There are a variety of reasons for this, including the inadequacy of techniques for communicating requirements from users to professional programmers and the fact that much of the time of programmers in any mature data processing facility is taken up with software maintenance. For these reasons, the backlog of needed applications is growing. Indeed, a waiting time of from two to seven years for new user applications on central computer systems is not uncommon. A way around this dilemma is to make use of distributed servers, workstations, and personal computers. If end users have access to such machines, the application logjam can be broken in two ways:

- **Off-the-shelf applications:** There is a long list of applications software for common machines, such as UNIX-based and Linux-based servers and workstations, and for Windows-based and Macintosh personal computers.
- **End-user programming:** Many tools are available on small systems that allow users to construct modest applications without needing to use a traditional programming language. Examples are spreadsheet programs and project management tools.

The second need mentioned earlier is for short response time. As described in Chapter 2, in many applications it is critical to productivity that response time be short. On a mainframe computer with a complex operating system that is being time-shared by many users, it is often difficult to achieve reasonable response times, but a user on a dedicated personal computer or workstation or a user who is one of only a few sharing a powerful minicomputer can often experience extremely short response times.

We can see, then, that with distributed small systems that are both physically closer to the user and more dedicated to the user's particular applications, user productivity and computing effectiveness may be improved. However, the manager must exercise caution in adopting a distributed strategy. The lack of centralized computing may result in the loss of centralized control. Individual departments may adopt incompatible systems, making interdepartmental cooperation difficult. Procurement decisions may be made without systematic forecasts of requirements and cost and with no enforcement of standards for hardware, software, or departmental programming practices. These effects jeopardize objectives 4 and 6 of Table 3.1. Equally important, the devolvement of data processing activities to the departmental level can increase the difficulty of obtaining data for use by top management (objective 5). The adoption of differing departmental standards and means of summarizing data makes uniform collection of data for upward reporting more difficult.

Tables 3.2 and 3.3 summarize some of the key potential benefits and potential drawbacks of distributed data processing.

Client/Server Architecture

The widely used client/server architecture is intended to provide the best aspects of both distributed and centralized computing. Users work on powerful workstations or PCs, which supports the end-user programming, provides the ability to use off-the-shelf software, and gives the immediate response inherent in distributed architecture. These workstations, or *clients,* are supported by specialized *servers.*

Table 3.2 Potential Benefits of Distributed Data Processing

Responsiveness
Local computing facilities can be managed in such a way that they can more directly satisfy the needs of local organizational management than one located in a central facility and intended to satisfy the needs of the total organization.

Availability
With multiple interconnected systems, the loss of any one system should have minimal impact. Key systems and components (e.g., computers with critical applications, printers, mass storage devices) can be replicated so that a backup system can quickly take up the load after a failure.

Correspondence to Organizational Patterns
Many organizations employ a decentralized structure with corresponding policies and operational procedures. Requirements for data files and other automated resources tend to reflect these organizational patterns.

Resource Sharing
Expensive hardware, such as a laser printer, can be shared among users. Data files can be centrally managed and maintained, but with organization-wide access. Staff services, programs, and databases can be developed on an organization-wide basis and distributed to the dispersed facilities.

Incremental Growth
In a centralized facility, an increased workload or the need for a new set of applications usually involves a major equipment purchase or a major software upgrade. This involves significant expenditure. In addition, a major change may require conversion or reprogramming of existing applications, with the risk of error and degraded performance. With a distributed system, it is possible to gradually replace applications or systems, avoiding the "all-or-nothing" approach. In addition, old equipment can be left in the facility to run a single application if the cost of moving the application to a new machine is not justified.

Increased User Involvement and Control
With smaller, more manageable equipment physically located close to the user, the user has greater opportunity to affect system design and operation, either by direct interaction with technical personnel or through the user's immediate superior.

Decentralized Operation and Centralized Control
Decentralized applications and facilities can be tailored to the individual organizational unit's requirements and be enhanced by centralized services and databases with varying degrees of centralized control.

End-User Productivity
Distributed systems tend to give more rapid response time to the user, since each piece of equipment is attempting a smaller job. Also, the applications and interfaces of the facility can be optimized to the needs of the organizational unit. Unit managers are in a position to assess the effectiveness of the local portion of the facility and to make the appropriate changes.

Distance and Location Independence
Distributed systems introduce interfaces and access methods for utilizing computing services. These interfaces and access methods become independent of location or distance. Hence the user has access to organization-wide facilities with little or no additional training.

Privacy and Security
With a distributed system, it is easier to assign responsibility for security of data files and other resources to the owners and users of those resources. Physical and software means can be employed to prevent unauthorized access to data and resources.

Vendor Independence
Properly implemented, a distributed system will accommodate equipment and software from a variety of suppliers. This provides greater competition and enhanced bargaining power on the part of the buyer. The organization is less likely to become dependent on a single vendor with the risks that that position entails.

Flexibility
Users may be in a position to adapt their application software to changing circumstances if they have control over program maintenance and day-to-day running. Because their equipment is not used by other users, they are able to change the configuration if they need to with little trouble.

Table 3.3   Potential Drawbacks of Distributed Data Processing

More Difficult Test and Failure Diagnosis
Particularly when there is a high degree of interaction between elements of a distributed system, it is difficult to determine the cause of failure or performance degradation.

More Dependence on Communications Technology
To be effective, a distributed system must be interconnected by communication and networking facilities. These facilities become critical to the day-to-day operation of the organization.

Incompatibility among Equipment
Equipment from different vendors may not easily connect and communicate. To guarantee avoidance of this problem, the user must restrict applications and resources to those for which standards exist.

Incompatibility among Data
Similarly, data generated by one application may not be usable in the generated form by another application. Again, the user may need to restrict applications to those that are standardized.

Network Management and Control
Because equipment is physically dispersed, may involve multiple vendors, and may be controlled by various organizational units, it is difficult to provide overall management, to enforce standards for software and data, and to control the information available through the network. Thus, data processing facilities and services may evolve in an uncontrolled fashion.

Difficulty in Control of Corporate Information Resources
Data may be dispersed or, if not, at least access to data is dispersed. If distributed users can perform the update function (essential in many applications), it becomes difficult for a central authority to control the integrity and security of the data needed at the corporate level. In some cases, it may even be difficult to gather required management information from the dispersed and dissimilar detailed databases.

Suboptimization
With the dispersal of computer equipment and the ease of incrementally adding equipment and applications, it becomes easier for managers of suborganizations to justify procurement for their unit. Although each procurement may be individually justifiable, the totality of procurements throughout an organization may well exceed the total requirement.

Duplication of Effort
Technical personnel in various units may individually develop similar applications or data files, resulting in unnecessary and costly duplication of effort.

Data Integrity
With distributed access to distributed data, it is more difficult to ensure that overlapping requests do not corrupt databases. If data files are duplicated for more efficient access, this requirement is even more difficult to satisfy.

Security
Enforcing security policies and authenticating users is more complex in a distributed environment.

Examples of servers are specialized computers for providing database services, printing and fax services, file storage, and communications front ends, gateways, and bridges. This architecture has been made possible by the advent of high-speed local area networks (LANs) and LAN interconnections, along with more sophisticated systems software to provide intermachine processing.

Client/server architecture is attractive for several reasons. First, it is cost-effective and achieves economies of scale by centralizing support for specialized functions. File servers and database servers also make it easier to provide universal access to information by authorized users and to maintain consistency and security of files and data. The physical architecture of the computers used can be designed especially to support their service function. Finally, this architecture is very flexible. One reason is that functional services are not necessarily in a one-to-one relation with physical computers. That is, file service and database services can be on the same computer, or, for an example at the other extreme, database services can be provided by several geographically dispersed machines. Services can share processors for smaller information systems, and they can be split among processors in larger systems to increase availability, capacity, and responsiveness. This popular approach is examined in more detail in Chapter 6.

An example of a client/server architecture is that used by MasterCard International, described in the case study following this chapter.

Intranets

One of the latest developments in the ongoing evolution of distributed data processing is the intranet. In essence, an intranet provides users the features and applications of the Internet but isolated within the organization. Key features of an intranet are as follows:

- Uses Internet-based standards, such as the HyperText Markup Language (HTML) and the Simple Mail Transfer Protocol (SMTP)
- Uses the TCP/IP protocol suite for local and wide area networking
- Comprises wholly owned content not accessible to the public Internet even though the corporation has Internet connections and runs a Web server on the Internet
- Can be managed, unlike the Internet

In general terms, an intranet can be considered as a form of client/server architecture. The advantages of the intranet approach include ease of implementation and ease of use. Intranets are examined in detail in Chapter 6.

Extranets

Another recent development is that of the extranet. Like the intranet, the extranet makes use of TCP/IP protocols and applications, especially the Web. The distinguishing feature of the extranet is that it provides access to corporate resources by outside clients, typically suppliers and customers of the organization. This outside access can be through the Internet or through other data communications networks. An extranet provides more than the simple Web access for the public that virtually all companies now provide. Instead, the extranet provides more extensive access to corporate resources, usually in a fashion that enforces a security policy. As with the intranet, the typical model of operation for the extranet is client/server.

Extranets are examined in detail in Chapter 6.

3.2 FORMS OF DISTRIBUTED DATA PROCESSING

We have defined a DDP system as a computing facility in which computers are dispersed within an organization with some means of interconnection among them. DDP systems have been implemented in a wide variety of forms that conform to this general definition. One way to gain an appreciation of this variety is to consider in more detail the following functions or objects that are supported by distributed processors:

- Applications
- Device controllers
- Control
- Data

It is often the case that more than one of these functions or objects is distributed in a DDP system. For our purposes, it is sufficient to examine them one at a time to gain insight into the configurations that are implemented in DDP. We examine the first three topics in this section and the last topic in the next section.

Distributed Applications

Two dimensions characterize the distribution of applications. First, there is the allocation of application functions:

- One application split up into components that are dispersed among a number of machines
- One application replicated on a number of machines
- A number of different applications distributed among a number of machines

Distributed application processing can also be characterized by whether the distribution is vertical or horizontal. In general, vertical partitioning involves one application split up into components that are dispersed among a number of machines, whereas horizontal partitioning involves either one application replicated on a number of machines or a number of different applications distributed among a number of machines.

With **vertical partitioning**, data processing is distributed in a hierarchical fashion. This distribution may reflect organizational structure, or it may simply be the most appropriate for the application. Examples include the following:

- **Insurance:** Data processing distribution is often a two-level hierarchy. Each branch has a computer system that it uses for preparing new contracts and for processing claims. In most cases, these transactions can be handled directly by the local office. Summary information is sent to a head office. The head office uses contract and claim information to perform risk analysis and actuarial calculations. On the basis of the company's financial position and current exposure, the head office can adjust rates and communicate the changes to the branches.

- **Retail chain:** Each retail store includes point-of-sale terminals and terminals for use by sales and office personnel. A convenient arrangement is a single powerful workstation or server that houses all the information used at the store. An interconnected set of personal computers is also possible, but the nature of the application lends itself more readily to a single site for storing all branch information. Point-of-sale terminals make use of pricing information from the computer system. Sales transactions record sales and changes in inventory and accounts receivable. Sales and office personnel can use terminals to display summary sales information, inventory, accounts receivable, and customer statements. Store management can display information on sales performance, goods aging, and other analyses. Periodically, perhaps once a day, sales and inventory information is transmitted to the head office system.

- **Process control:** The process-control function in a factory adapts readily to a vertical DDP system. Each major operational area is controlled by a workstation, which is fed information from individual process-control microprocessors. These microprocessors are responsible for the automated control of sensors and effector devices on the shop floor. The operations workstation scans sensor readings, looking for exceptions or analyzing trends. It may also control part of the operation to vary the rate or mix of production. These distributed workstations ensure rapid response to conditions at the process level. All the workstations are linked to a higher-level computer concerned with operations planning, optimization, provision of management information, and general corporate data processing.

As these examples illustrate, a vertically partitioned DDP system generally consists of a central computer system with one or more levels of satellite systems. The nature of the partition reflects organizational structure or the structure of the task to be performed, or both. The objective is to assign processing load to the level of the hierarchy at which it is most cost-effective. Such an arrangement combines some of the best features of both centralized and distributed data processing.

With **horizontal partitioning**, data processing is distributed among a number of computers that have a peer relationship. That is, there is no concept of client/server. Computers in a horizontal configuration normally operate autonomously, although in some cases this configuration is used for load balancing. In many cases, horizontal partitioning reflects organizational decentralization. Two examples follow:

- **Office automation support system:** Typically, secretarial staff and other personnel are equipped with personal computers linked together by a network. Each user's personal computer contains software packages useful to that user (e.g., word processing, spreadsheet). The systems are linked together so that users may exchange messages, files, and other information.

- **Air traffic control system:** Each regional center for air traffic control operates autonomously of the other centers, performing the same set of applications. Within the center, several computers are used to process radar and radio data and to provide a visual status to the air traffic controllers.

It is more often the case that an organization's computing function will include both horizontal and vertical partitioning. Corporate headquarters may maintain a mainframe computer facility with a corporate management information system and a decision support system. Central staff functions, such as public relations, strategic planning, and corporate finance and accounting, may be supported here. A vertical partition is created by providing subordinate computing facilities at branch offices. Within each branch office, a horizontal partition will provide office automation support.

Other Forms of DDP

In addition to, or instead of, the distribution of applications or data, a DDP system may involve the distribution of device controllers, or network management. Let us briefly examine each of these possibilities.

DISTRIBUTED DEVICES   One natural use of DDP is to support a distributed set of devices that can be controlled by processors, such as automatic teller machines or laboratory interface equipment. One common application of this approach is in factory automation. A factory may contain a number of sensors, programmable controllers, microprocessors, and even robots that are involved in the automation of the manufacturing process. Such a system involves the distribution of processing technology to the various locations of the manufacturing process.

NETWORK MANAGEMENT   Any distributed system requires some form of management and control, including control of access to some of the facilities in the distributed system, monitoring of the status of various components of the distributed system, and management of the communications facility to ensure availability and responsiveness. In most cases, some sort of central network management system is required. However, such a system needs to obtain status information from the various computers in the distributed system and to issue commands to those computers. Thus, each computer in the distributed system must include some management and control logic to be able to interact with the central network management system. A more detailed look at these issues can be found in Chapter 19.

3.3   DISTRIBUTED DATA

Before beginning our discussion of distributed data, it is necessary to say something about the nature of the organization of data in a computer system. We first provide a brief overview of the concepts of database and database management system, and then look at the various ways in which an enterprise might organize data.

Database Management Systems

In some cases, an organization can function with a relatively simple collection of files of data. Each file may contain text (e.g., copies of memos and reports) or numerical data (e.g., spreadsheets). A more complex file consists of a set of records. However, for an organization of any appreciable size, a more complex organization known as a database is required. A **database** is a structured collection of data stored for use in one or more applications. In addition to data, a database contains the relationships between data items and groups of data items. As an example of the distinction between data files and a database, consider the following. A simple personnel file might consist of a set of records, one for each employee. Each record gives the employee's name, address, date of birth, position, salary, and other details needed by the personnel department. A personnel database includes a personnel file, as just described. It may also include a time and attendance file, showing for each week the hours worked by each employee. With a database organization, these two files are

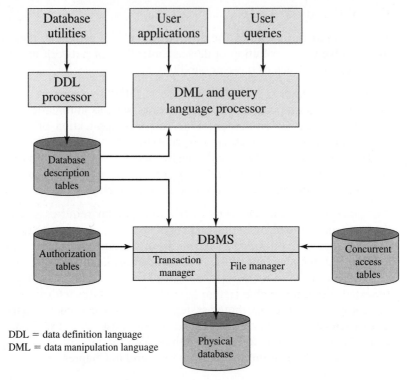

Figure 3.3 DBMS Architecture

tied together so that a payroll program can extract the information about time worked and salary for each employee to generate paychecks.

Accompanying the database is a **database management system (DBMS)**, which is a suite of programs for constructing and maintaining the database and for offering ad hoc query facilities to multiple users and applications. A **query language** provides a uniform interface to the database for users and applications.

Figure 3.3 provides a simplified block diagram of a DBMS architecture. Developers make use of a data definition language (DDL) to define the database logical structure and procedural properties, which are represented by a set of database description tables. A data manipulation language (DML) provides a powerful set of tools for application developers. Query languages are declarative languages designed to support end users. The database management system makes use of the database description tables to manage the physical database. The interface to the database is through a file manager module and a transaction manager module. In addition to the database description table, two other tables support the DBMS. The DBMS uses authorization tables to ensure the user has permission to execute the query language statement on the database. The concurrent access table prevents conflicts when simultaneous, conflicting commands are executed.

Database systems provide efficient access to large volumes of data and are vital to the operation of many organizations.

A **distributed database** is a collection of several different databases, distributed among multiple computers, that looks like a single database to the user. The DBMS controls access to the distributed database and enables the user to treat the distributed database as a single database. The DBMS must include a directory that identifies the physical location of each data element in the database.

In general terms, we can distinguish three ways of organizing data for use by an organization: centralized, replicated, and partitioned.

Centralized Database

A centralized database is housed in a central computer facility. If the computing function is distributed, then users and application programs at remote locations may have access to the centralized database. A centralized database is often used with a vertical DDP organization. It is desirable when the security and integrity of the data are paramount, because the central facility is more easily controlled than is a dispersed collection of data. On the other hand, there are a number of reasons why a distributed data organization might be attractive, including the following:

1. A distributed design can reflect an organization's structure or function. This makes the design of the data organization and the use of the data more understandable and easier to implement and maintain.

2. Data can be stored locally, under local control. Local storage decreases response times and communications costs and increases data availability.

3. Distributing data across multiple autonomous sites confines the effects of a computer breakdown to its point of occurrence; the data on the surviving computers can still be processed.

4. The size of the total collection of data and the number of users of those data need not be limited by a computer's size and processing power.

Replicated Database

When data are distributed, one of two overall strategies may be adopted: replicated or partitioned. In a **replicated database**, all or part of the database is copied at two or more computers. Before looking at the general principles of this important strategy, we briefly describe two examples from [CONN99].

The first example is Golden Gate Financial Group, which makes about $1 billion in trades per month. The trades are recorded at their system in San Francisco and, as each trade is made, it is also recorded in a remote office in San Jose. Golden Gate makes use of a leased line to transfer about 6.6 GBytes of data each month to achieve replication. The company recouped its investment in replication software and line charges for the year when San Francisco was hit by a daylong power outage. Employees traveled to San Jose, set up shop, and used current replicated data to do their work. As a result, trading was down only for half an hour.

A different strategy is used by Merrill Lynch, which must distribute 2 GBytes of critical financial information to three remote offices daily for use by staff. Previously, information systems (IS) staff copied the entire database to remote offices once per week by manual command. Now, data are updated twice per day to servers in each

Table 3.4   Replication Strategy Variants

	Real Time	**Near Real Time**	**Deferred**
Design Architecture	Two-phase commit	Cascade or broadcast distribution	Messaging and queuing
Benefits	Tight data synchronization Distributed transactions Data currency	Data consolidation Data distribution Improved response time Less WAN loading	Heterogeneous database updates Guaranteed delivery across any network Multiple network protocol support
Drawbacks	Longer response time Difficult to implement Two-phase commit does not always work	Lack of data currency Single-vendor solution	Time delay in updates More programming work required

remote location. Only changed data, amounting to about 200 Mbytes, is sent, thus saving bandwidth and time. Now users have access to the latest data, and the data are local, avoiding the need to use long-distance hookups.

Data replication has become increasingly popular. Numerous vendors offer data replication technology for Windows and UNIX platforms for backing up mainframe-based data. Its use is virtually mandated in the banking industry. The key advantage of data replication is that it provides backup and recovery from both network and server failure.

Three variants of data replication are in common use: real time, near real time, and deferred, as shown in Table 3.4 (based on [GOLI99]). **Real-time replication** is often used in transactional systems, such as order entry, where all copies of data must be synchronized immediately. Updates involve the use of an algorithm called the two-phase commit, which attempts to avoid inconsistencies in the two databases (primary and backup) by adding a confirmation step to each update. This operation doubles the response time and may not always succeed, however.

Near-real-time replication is more commonly used. In this case backups occur in batches, with a small amount of lag time (e.g., 30 minutes). This is adequate for most applications.

Deferred replication involves bulk transfer of a large number of changes at infrequent intervals, such as once or twice a day. The transfer is in the nature of a message or bulk file transfer, which may involve a large amount of data. This approach minimizes network resource requirements but does not provide current data.

Partitioned Database

In a partitioned database, the database exists as distinct and nonoverlapping segments that are dispersed among multiple computer systems. In general, there is no duplication of data among the segments of a partitioned database. This strategy can be used with either a horizontal or vertical DDP organization.

Table 3.5 Advantages and Disadvantages of Database Distribution Methods

Type of Distribution	Advantages	Disadvantages
Common database accessed by all processors. **(Centralized)**	No duplication of data, little reorganization required.	Contention among multiple processors attempting to access data simultaneously. Database is large, so response time is slow. During disc failures, all processors lose access to data.
Copy of the common central database stored at each processor. **(Replicated)**	Each processor has access to database without contention. Short response time. During failure, new copy can be obtained.	High storage cost due to extensive duplication of data. Updates of one copy must subsequently be made on all other copies. High database reorganization costs.
Individual database for each processor. **(Partitioned)**	No duplication of data minimizes storage cost. Size of database determined by application of node, not total corporate requirement. Short response time.	Ad hoc or management reports must be obtained from different databases.

The main advantage of this approach is that it disperses the load and it eliminates a single point of failure. This approach can be counterproductive if the typical database request will involve data from multiple partitions.

Table 3.5 provides a simplified comparison of these three approaches to database organization. In practice, a mixture of strategies will be used. A more detailed look at strategies for database organization is provided in Table 3.6 (based on [HOFF02]). For replicated databases, two strategies are possible. First, a central database is maintained, and copies of portions of the database may be extracted for local use. Typically, such systems lock the affected portion of the central database if the satellite computer has the authority to update. If this is the case, then the remote computer transmits the updates back to the central database upon completion of the task. Alternatively, a more elaborate synchronization technique can be employed so that updates to one copy of a replicated database are automatically propagated throughout the DDP system to update all copies. This strategy requires considerably more software and communications load but provides the user with a more flexible system.

The simplest partitioned strategy is one in which there are a number of independently operated databases with remote access allowed. In effect, we have a collection of centralized databases, with more than one center. A more complex system is one in which the databases are integrated so that a single query by the user may require access to any of the databases. In a sophisticated system, this access is invisible to the user, who need not specify where the data are located and who need not use a different command style for different portions of the distributed database.

Thus, we can see that a variety of strategies is possible. In designing a distributed database, two sets of objectives are paramount: database objectives and communications objectives. *Database objectives* include accessibility of the data, security and privacy, and completeness and integrity of the data. *Communications objectives* are to minimize the communications load and the delays imposed by the use of communications facilities.

Table 3.6   Strategies for Database Organization

Strategy	Reliability	Expandability	Communications Overhead	Manageability	Data Consistency or Integrity
Centralized					
Centralized database Database resides in one location on host; data values may be distributed to geographically dispersed users for local processing	**Poor** Highly dependent on central server	**Poor** Limitations are barriers to performance	**Very high** High traffic to one site	**Very good** One monolithic site requires little coordination	**Excellent** All users always have same data
Replicated					
Distributed snapshot databases Copy of portion of the central database created by extraction and replication for use at remote sites	**Good** Redundancy and tolerated delays	**Very good** Cost of additional copies may be less than linear	**Low to medium** Periodic snapshots can cause bursts of network traffic	**Very good** All copies are identical	**Medium** Fine as long as delays are tolerated by business needs
Replicated, distributed database Data are replicated and synchronized at multiple sites	**Excellent** Redundancy and minimal delays	**Very good** Cost of additional copies may be low	**Medium** Messages are constant, but some delays are tolerated	**Medium** Collisions add some complexity to manageability	**Medium to very good** Close to precise consistency
Partitioned					
Distributed, nonintegrated databases Independent databases that can be accessed by applications on remote computers	**Good** Depends on local database availability	**Good** New sites independent of existing ones	**Low** Little if any need to pass data or queries across a network	**Very good** Easy for each site, until there is a need to share data across sites	**Low** No guarantees of consistency
Distributed, integrated database Data span multiple computers and software	**Very good** Effective use of partitioning	**Very good** New nodes get only data they need without changes in overall database design	**Low to medium** Most queries are local but queries that require data from multiple sites can cause a temporary load	**Difficult** Especially difficult for queries that need data from distributed tables, and updates must be tightly coordinated	**Very poor** Considerable effort and inconsistencies not tolerated

70

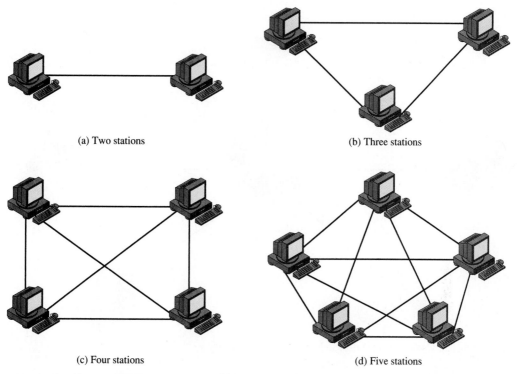

(a) Two stations

(b) Three stations

(c) Four stations

(d) Five stations

Figure 3.4 Full Connectivity Using Direct Links

3.4 NETWORKING IMPLICATIONS OF DDP

We can characterize the requirements for communications and networking generated by the use of distributed data processing as falling into three key areas: connectivity, availability, and performance.

The **connectivity** of a distributed system refers to the ability of components in the system to exchange data. In a vertically partitioned DDP system, components of the system generally need links only to components above and below them in the hierarchical structure. Such a requirement can often be met with simple direct links between systems. In a horizontally partitioned system, it may be necessary to allow data exchange between any two systems. For example, in an office automation system, any user should be able to exchange electronic mail and files with any other user, subject to any security policy. In a system requiring high connectivity, some sort of network may be preferable to a large number of direct links. To see this, consider Figure 3.4. If we have a distributed system requiring full connectivity and use a direct link between each pair of systems, the number of links and the communication interfaces needed grows rapidly with the number of systems. With four computers, six links are required; with five computers, ten links are required. Instead, suppose we create a network by providing a central switch and connecting each computer system to that switch. The results are shown in Figure 3.5. In this case, with four computers, four links are required, and with five computers, five links are required.

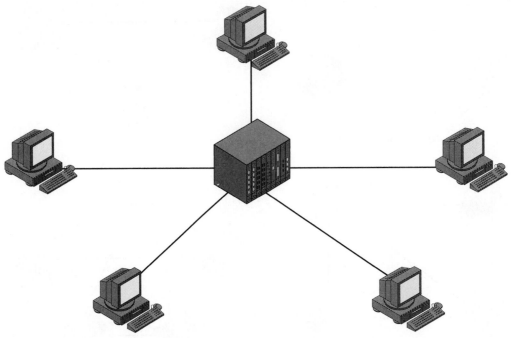

Figure 3.5 The Use of a Central Switch for Full Connectivity

If the components of a distributed system are geographically dispersed, the requirement for connectivity dictates that some method of transmitting data over long distances is needed. This involves the use of public telecommunications facilities or some private installation.

Availability refers to the percentage of time that a particular function or application is available for users. Depending on the application, availability may be merely desirable or it may be essential. For example, in an air traffic control system, the availability of the computer system that supports the air traffic controllers is critical. High availability requirements mean that the distributed system must be designed in such a way that the failure of a single computer or other device will not deny access to the application. For example, backup processors can be employed. High availability requirements also mean that the communications facility must be highly available. Thus, some form of redundancy and backup in the communications facility is needed.

Finally, the **performance** of the communications facility can be assessed, given the nature of the DDP system and the applications that it supports. In a highly interactive system, such as a data entry system or a graphics design application, we have seen that response time is critically important. Thus, not only must the processors that execute the applications respond rapidly but also, if the interaction involves transmission across a network, the network must have sufficient capacity and flexibility to provide the required response time. If the system is used instead to move a lot of data around but without the time being critical, the concern may be more one of throughput. That is, the communications facility must be designed to handle large volumes of data.

Once we have examined the details of the available data communications techniques and facilities, we will return to this topic and examine strategies for communications and network planning.

APPLICATION NOTE

Distributed Computing Support

It is difficult to imagine running a business without a large number of desktop computers. Today, the same can be said for laptop computers and handheld devices. Supporting such a collection of powerful appliances, some of which are mobile, can present an organization with unprecedented challenges. Using the appropriate strategy can be the difference between an efficiently run shop and one that is not only less efficient, but much more costly.

One of the largest of these challenges is the maintenance demands on an already overworked support staff. Perhaps the single most important approach that a business can take in order to save money, time and energy when dealing with computers and data networks is to standardize on a set of applications, computing platforms and networking hardware. While there are always a few exceptions, where possible, the choices should be minimal. By selecting a single set of applications for desktop and laptop use, licensing and software fees can be reduced by buying in bulk. Licenses can be very expensive on a per seat basis but site licensing can be much more cost effective. In addition, the maintenance of the software becomes easier as technicians have fewer variables to contend with in their troubleshooting and updates.

The same is true of hardware. With a single manufacturer to deal with, fewer spares need to be kept on hand, technicians become very familiar with the equipment and the vendors are known and have a vested interest in keeping their customer happy. It can be a troubleshooting nightmare moving from one machine equipped with Windows to an Apple computer or a Linux machine.

Security has become one of the primary concerns for network and systems administrators, particularly when dealing with so many machines. In addition to patches, spyware, adware, and viruses, we must battle regular attacks from outside. In many cases, an attack can have consequences beyond the initial problem. As an example, when a virus is downloaded, it is often shared between users. Most viruses come through e-mail downloads, but today we can add USB memory sticks as an ideal way to spread viruses between autonomous systems. In the case of a fully distributed environment, the best cure for this eventuality is prevention. A good antivirus package on all machines and the server is critical.

Once the virus has been contracted by the network and by the machines, a virus removal process must be initiated immediately. Standard scans may not be enough to eradicate the virus. In some cases, scanning from removable media and an inoculation procedure must be followed to remove the virus. Worse yet, the infected machine(s) may be backed up to the network resulting in infected servers and potential large-scale loss of the organizations' data. If this occurs, it is possible that the data cannot be recovered. Any removable media that was in use at the time of the infection must also be considered at risk.

Understanding all of the security measures necessary to protect a modern communications network is a difficult, full-time job. If we add the mobile and handheld devices, we can see what a truly daunting task security can become, so training is very important. It must also be continuing, for administrators and end users alike, as the environment is constantly changing.

(*Continued*)

Many problems like this can be resolved quickly and easily if the computing staff is skilled and has a solid support structure. Often, IT departments are not considered part of the core business and so receive secondary consideration for budgets, personnel and equipment. There are dozens of stories in which computing departments receive little support but all of the blame for problems. Because personal computers are inexpensive and have a reduced complexity when compared to mainframes, organizations may staff themselves with personnel having a corresponding level of training and skill. While this may be an attempt at cost effectiveness, it is inappropriate long-range planning.

Often underestimated is the helpdesk or trouble call center. Staffing and reliability are important aspects of this particular area. For large organizations, the number of trouble calls can be staggering. An ineffective or understaffed group answering the telephones or handling the troubleshooting can slow the primary business functions down and have a significant effect on the bottom line due to excessive man-hours spent and downtime. Additionally, the software used to support such a system should be simple but also have functions such as trend analysis, searching, categorizing and various reporting capabilities.

Decentralized or distributed systems can pose a unique problems not experienced by fully centralized systems. With large numbers of autonomous nodes, an understanding of the issues, proper training and appropriate resources can minimize the financial impact of problems and reduce downtime of the communications system.

3.5 SUMMARY

With the increasing availability of inexpensive yet powerful personal computers and workstations, there has been an increasing trend toward distributed data processing (DDP). With DDP, processors, data, and other aspects of a data processing system may be dispersed within an organization. This provides a system that is more responsive to user needs, is able to provide better response times, and may minimize communications costs compared to a centralized approach. A DDP system involves either the horizontal or vertical partitioning of the computing function and may also involve a distributed organization of databases, device control, and interaction (network) control. This trend has been facilitated by the advent of client/server architectures.

At this stage, we are not yet ready to translate our description of DDP characteristics into an analysis of the needed data communications and networking facilities. In general terms, we can say that a DDP system involves requirements in the areas of connectivity, availability, and performance. These requirements, in turn, dictate the type of data communications or networking approach that is appropriate for a given DDP system.

3.6 RECOMMENDED READING

One of the best treatments of distributed data processing is [COUL05]. This book is a broad survey of the issues involved, including networking, file and database design, protocols, transaction issues, and security. Another excellent broad survey is

[TANE07]. A worthwhile and thorough discussion of distributed databases is found in [OZSU99].

COUL05 Coulouris, G.; Dollimore, J.; and Kindberg, T. *Distributed Systems: Concepts and Design.* Reading, MA: Addison-Wesley, 2005.

OZSU99 Ozsu, M., and Valduriez, P. *Principles of Distributed Database Systems.* Upper Saddle River, NJ: Prentice Hall, 1999.

TANE07 Tanenbaum, A., and Steen, M. *Distributed Systems: Principles and Paradigms.* Upper Saddle River, NJ: Prentice Hall, 2007.

3.7 KEY TERMS, REVIEW QUESTIONS, AND PROBLEMS

Key Terms

availability	database	Intranet
centralized database	distributed database	partitioned database
centralized data processing	distributed data processing (DDP)	performance
client/server architecture	extranet	replicated database
connectivity	horizontal partitioning	vertical partitioning

Review Questions

3.1 What are some functions that are centralized in a fully centralized data processing facility?

3.2 What are some advantages of a centralized data processing facility?

3.3 Based on your reading of the chapter, name five components that might be part of a fully centralized system.

3.4 What is a distributed data processing (DDP) strategy?

3.5 Applications for the distributed environment are available much sooner than those in the centralized environment. What are the main sources of these applications?

3.6 Describe three ways that an application can be allocated in a distributed environment

3.7 What major problems for the data processing manager result from distributed small systems?

3.8 What are some reasons for wanting to interconnect distributed data processing systems?

3.9 Distinguish between horizontal and vertical partitioning of applications.

3.10 Why would a company want a distributed database?

3.11 In designing a distributed database, database objectives and communications objectives are not always the same. Distinguish between these two sets of objectives.

3.12 How does a factory often reflect the use of distributed devices?

3.13 Name three types of communications and networking requirements generated by the use of distributed data processing.

3.14 Why do we still need mainframe computers even though personal computers and workstations have become so much more powerful?

Problems

3.1 The new corporate CIO (chief information officer) has devised a nine-point mission statement for the company's Information Technology division (refer to Table 3.1). As one of the operations managers in the department, you have received a memo on the new policy and an associated task. The CIO wants to address the new strategy in a three-phase rollout plan and wants your feedback on which three of the nine points are of highest importance and therefore should be the focus for the initial rollout phase. Select the three you feel meet this criteria and prepare a case for each of your selections.

3.2 You have just accepted the position as CIO for Holiday Inn. As your first official act, the CEO has asked you to assess the corporation's computer operations (refer to Figure 3.1) and report back to her with your recommendation on whether to remain with the status quo (i.e., a centralized IS architecture), migrate to a distributed architecture, or create a hybrid solution using aspects from both general architectures. Choose your position and prepare a case for presentation at the next staff meeting.

3.3 The Internet, if viewed from a global client/server perspective, generally consists of Web servers and their associated databases and other data repositories on the server side and various Web browser applications and associated plug-ins on the client side. Is a system of this sort best described as vertically distributed application processing, horizontally distributed application processing, or some hybrid of these two characterizations?

3.4 How many direct connections does it take to connect n computers together? (*Hint:* Count the number of "ends" of connections and divide by 2.) Suppose you have a computer in each of the 50 states in the United States; how many direct connections would you need?

3.5 While many systems are considered centralized such as a company mainframe performing financial functions, there are fewer and fewer "dumb terminals" accessing the mainframe. Instead, terminal emulation programs that simulate the terminal environment are used. The Windows operating system family has a program like this built in. What is it called?

3.6 This chapter describes several components and advantages of a fully centralized system. What might be some of the major drawbacks of a system like this?

3.7 This chapter describes both "off the shelf" and "end user programming" as types of applications. Discuss what is meant by these terms and provide some examples of each.

3.8 In the client/server architecture, what in meant by the term *server*?

3.9 Two data centers used for retail credit authorization are located in two different major population centers, which are separated from each other by a large zone of very little population. Each data center is intended to cover a particular geographical area and thus contains data that reflect the account status of the cardholders in that area (only). Terminals for each area are connected to the corresponding data center. Communication between both data centers occurs only in case a cardholder from one geographical area shops in a retail credit establishment of the geographical area covered by the other data center.

    a. Classify the relationship between each terminal and the corresponding data center as either client/server or peer-to-peer.

    b. Classify the relationship between both data centers as either client/server or peer-to-peer.

    c. Classify the database of the retail credit system as either partitioned or replicated.

    d. Is this approach to distributed data processing suitable for the scenario described? Why or why not?

    e. Would this approach be suitable if the two major population centers were close to each other? Why or why not?

3.10. An online terminal system implemented on one computer is being used to service four cities. Discuss how the overall system availability could be increased by
    a. reducing the scope of failures
    b. reducing the impact of failures GONT

3.11. Retail is one of the first areas in adopting distributed data processing. Instead of centralizing the POS (point-of-sale) systems, retailers deploy distributed databases, so all of their POS systems are local, but linked to a central system. Prices for all merchandise are determined and maintained at the central system. Each day, before trading starts, relevant prices are downloaded to the POS system at each store, replicating the data of the central system. Analyze the economic advantages of the adoption of distributed data processing in the retail area.

3.12. Napster was a famous music exchange system that additionally offered many add-on services. It was sentenced to go out of business due to copyright infringement. The system worked as follows. The Napster server held a database of all music files offered by the participating users. Users had to login to the Napster server, and send the list of files they offered. Each user could then send search requests to the Napster server, in order to receive a list of the users that offered files that matched the query. The requester could then choose a user from that list, establish a direct connection with him, and request a download of the file.
    a. Categorize the relationship between the Napster server and the users of the system as either client/server or peer-to-peer.
    b. Categorize the relationship between the users of the system as either client/server or peer-to-peer.
    c. Categorize the database of music files as centralized, decentralized, or distributed, and analyze the economic implications on the system.
    d. Categorize the database containing the list available music files as either centralized or distributed, and analyze its technical implications.
    e. Analyze the relationship between the Napster system architecture and the vulnerability of Napster against legal actions.

3.13. A company will deploy a credit sales system that will provide service to ten large population centers. A database will be used to store user information and record credit transactions. The IT department is considering two choices:
    a. A centralized database, where a single copy of the data is stored in one datacenter and used from all population centers
    b. A replicated database, where one copy of the data is stored at multiple datacenters (one in each population center) and all copies of the data are synchronized
    Give some criteria for deciding which type of database should be used for this project.

MASTERCARD INTERNATIONAL

An example of a client/server architecture is that used by MasterCard International [HIGG03, STEI02b]. The company's computer facility authorizes, clears, and settles each credit card transaction in real time as a cardholder's credit card is swiped. The client/server system ties together 25,000 member banks with MasterCard's massive data warehouse, which helps the credit card giant and its bank clients make more effective business decisions. MasterCard has converted the 50 terabytes (TB)[1] of transactional and financial data into a business-intelligence engine for use by banks and MasterCard employees.

Planning for the data warehouse began in the mid-1990s. Interestingly, the IT (information technology) staff did not feel the need to present a detailed business case to upper management for this major project. Rather, the data warehouse was presented as a strategic move to give MasterCard a competitive edge. Specifically, MasterCard wanted to improve market share. At the time, MasterCard accounted for only about 25% of charges for goods sold worldwide using credit cards, with Visa accounting for 50%. Today, that market share is closer to one-third and growing.

Financial institutions that use MasterCard rely on the history of credit card transactions to provide information for targeted marketing and business planning. For example, a bank that issues credit cards might notice a large volume of charges to flights from a specific airline. The bank can use this information to negotiate a deal with the airline to provide special offers and incentives to cardholders.

The company runs a combination of homegrown and off-the-shelf analytic tools to identify buying trends, credit card fraud, and other useful information. The company can correlate and analyze transactions to determine a consumer's interest or detect anomalies that suggest a card has been stolen. MasterCard offers bank clients access to these tools, as well as custom reports.

Among the signature applications provided by MasterCard is the Business Performance Intelligence suite of operational reporting tools. This suite includes about 70 standard reports that let members analyze transactions every day, week, or month and compare the results to different parts of the country, other parts of the world, or predefined groups of similar banks. For example, one member bank found that it had a disproportionally high rate of turning down transactions. It was not because of any analysis of the cardholder's creditworthiness; instead, the bank's systems simply timed out.

Another popular tool is MarketScope, which helps banks monitor, analyze, and develop campaigns to increase use of their cards. For example, a card issuer in New York might use the data to see how many cardholders spent $25 or more in January and February on sporting goods at Wal-Mart stores. Then it might propose

---

[1]See Appendix 1A for an explanation of numerical prefixes, such as *tera* and *giga*.

Figure I.1   MasterCard Client/Server Architecture

to Wal-Mart a mail marketing campaign before the opening of baseball season, tied
to heavy spenders with an affinity to the New York Mets or Yankees.

The configuration is shown in general terms in Figure I.1. A client/server transaction proceeds in the following way:

1. Member bank connects to MasterCard facility, known as MasterCard Online.
This could be by Internet, by means of a private dial-up access service, or by
means of a private wide area network, such as a frame relay network. In the
case of Internet access, all traffic must go through a firewall, which assures that
unwanted traffic is blocked.

2. User authenticates to MasterCard Online. A dedicated group of servers is assigned the task of authenticating all incoming transaction requests to assure
that the user has permission to use the facility and to specify the user's level of
privilege.

3. MasterCard Online verifies user product licensing. This has to do with which
business enterprise software tools the bank client is able to use.

4. User request is forwarded to a transaction server, which invokes the appropriate
application software for this transaction. The application translates the request
into the corresponding database requests and updates.

5. The transaction server forwards a transaction request to the data warehouse,
which processes the request and returns a response to the member user.

MasterCard continues to expand the size of the database and the tool set. The goal is to include every transaction handled by members over a three-year period, capturing the dollar amount, the card number, the location, and the merchant in each instant. But it is the set of applications provided to members that is crucial in gaining competitive edge. MasterCard aims to gain favor with portfolio managers and member banks, who decide whether to push Visa or MasterCard. If the online tools help those managers analyze the profitability of the cards in their portfolio better or gain more customers and transaction volume faster, then MasterCard benefits. To keep ahead of Visa, the MasterCard IT shop has 35 full-time developers tasked to come up with new tools to put in the hands of the banks. The developers also work with banks to create repeatable custom reports that can focus on any aspect of authorizing a card or transaction, including charge backs for disputed amounts and fraud.

Discussion Points

1. The IT managers responsible for selling the data warehouse concept to upper management say that it would be much harder to make the case in today's climate of shrinking IT budgets, because most organizations are trying to cut costs rather than launch new initiatives. Discuss the approach that the IT shop would need to take in presenting a business case for a data warehouse with application tools such as that of MasterCard International.

2. MasterCard makes its tools available to all of its member banks. [STEI02b] states that these tools are more likely to be attractive to state and regional banks. Big national and international banks are likely to have developed and use their own analytical tools. Discuss the implications of this in terms of the marketing of MasterCard's IT services. Include in your discussion a consideration of what MasterCard can offer the big banks.

3. Suggest applications or tools that MasterCard could provide that would be attractive to member banks.

PART TWO

The Internet and Distributed Applications

Part Two provides an overview of the Internet and the basic protocols that are the foundation of the Internet. This part then looks at the services perceived by end users, including Internet-based distributed applications and client/server support. Finally, Part Two looks at some of the details of Internet operation.

ROAD MAP FOR PART TWO

Chapter 4 Internet History and Architecture

Chapter 4 provides an overview of the Internet. The chapter begins with a brief history of the Internet, and then looks at the principal components of the Internet and the way they are organized and interact. The chapter also discusses the important concept of Internet domains.

Chapter 5 TCP/IP and OSI

Data network communication and distributed applications rely on underlying communications software that is independent of applications and relieves the application of much of the burden of reliably exchanging data. This communications software is organized into a protocol architecture, the most important incarnation of which is the TCP/IP protocol suite. Chapter 5 introduces the concept of a protocol architecture and provides an overview of TCP/IP. Then the concept of internetworking and the use of TCP/IP to achieve internetworking are discussed.

Chapter 6 Client/Server and Intranet Computing

A more general treatment of distributed applications is provided in Chapter 6, which deals with client/server computing and with intranets. The client/server approach provides an architecture to support distributed applications that is an ideal match for today's PC-dominated business environment. An intranet is an Internet-style facility that makes use of Internet technologies to provide a client/server base. An extranet extends these Internet-based facilities to business partners, such as customers and suppliers.

Chapter 7 Internet-Based Applications

The range of applications supported by data communications facilities is broad. In Chapter 7, we examine some distributed applications that are widely used in business. These include electronic mail, Web access using HTTP, and Internet telephony using SIP. All of these areas require the use of communications and networking technologies, and each is important in improving the performance, efficiency, and competitiveness of a company.

Chapter 8 Internet Operation

Chapter 8 continues the discussion of TCP/IP technology begun in Chapters 4 and 5 by looking at the critical issue of addressing on the Internet and the related issues of routing. The remainder of the chapter looks at recent efforts to provide a given level of quality of service (QoS) to various applications, with emphasis on the area of differentiated services.

CHAPTER 4

THE INTERNET

4.1 Internet History
Beginnings
National Science Foundation Takes on a Role
Internet Interconnection Points
The World Wide Web

4.2 Internet Architecture
What the Internet Looks Like Today
Commercial Use of the Internet

4.3 Internet Domains
Internet Names and Addresses
Domain Name System

4.4 Summary

4.5 Recommended Reading and Web Sites

4.6 Key Terms, Review Questions, and Problems

Chapter Objectives

After reading this chapter, you should be able to

♦ Discuss the history of the Internet and explain its explosive growth.

♦ Describe the overall Internet architecture and its key components, including ISPs, POPs, and NAPs.

♦ Explain Internet domains and domain names.

♦ Discuss the operation of the Domain Name System.

4.1 INTERNET HISTORY

Beginnings

The Internet evolved from the ARPANET, which was developed in 1969 by the Advanced Research Projects Agency (ARPA) of the U.S. Department of Defense. It was the first operational packet-switching network. ARPANET began operations in four locations. Today the number of hosts is in the hundreds of millions, the number of users is in the billions, and the number of countries participating is around 250. The number of connections to the Internet continues to grow exponentially (Figure 4.1).

ARPANET made use of the new technology of packet switching, which offered advantages over circuit switching, both of which were briefly introduced in Section 1.7.

Traditionally, the two primary paradigms for electronic communications were circuit switching (essentially, voice communication; see Chapter 12), and message switching (telegraph and Telex). In **circuit switching** (Figure 4.2), when source S communicates with destination T through a network, a dedicated path of transmission facilities is established (e.g., S, A, C, E, T) connecting S to T. All of these facilities are held for the duration of the "call." In particular, if there were lulls in the conversation, the transmission path would remain unused during these periods. On the other hand, after the connection is established there is minimal delay through the network. Moreover, once the "call" was set up, the network could basically be passive. Because switching was often electromechanical, this was a big plus.

In **message switching** (Figure 4.2), a message is sent from S to T in stages. First the transmission facility from S to A might be seized and the message is transmitted from S to A, where it is temporarily stored. At this point the S to A channel is released. Then a channel from A to C is accessed and the message is sent to C, and so on. In this case the transmission channels are only used when they are needed, and not wasted when they are not needed. In exchange for this more efficient transmission, the delay can be substantial and quite variable. The messages were frequently stored at each intermediate location on slow peripheral processors such as discs, magnetic drums, or, in the early days, on punched paper tapes. These peripherals are slow. Moreover, each time the message is transmitted, a transmission time equal to the length of the message divided by the channel's data rate was incurred. Very long messages would incur very long delays on each hop. There would be one such delay

Figure 4.1 Internet Domain Survey Host Count
Source: Internet Software Consortium (http://www.isc.org)

for each hop on the path connecting the source to the destination. So the delay due to transmissions would vary widely depending on the length of the message and the number of hops on the path connecting source to destination.

    Packet switching is a special case of message switching, with substantially different properties. First the transmitted data unit, the packet, is limited in length. If a message is bigger than the maximum packet size, it is broken up into a number of packets. Second, when packets are passed from switch to switch they are stored in high-speed random access memory (RAM) rather than in the slower peripherals ordinarily used in message switching systems. Packet switching has several obvious advantages compared to message switching: The delay is much shorter. The delay of the first packet to arrive is only the transmission time of the first packet times the number of hops on the path used. Subsequent packets follow in sequence immediately

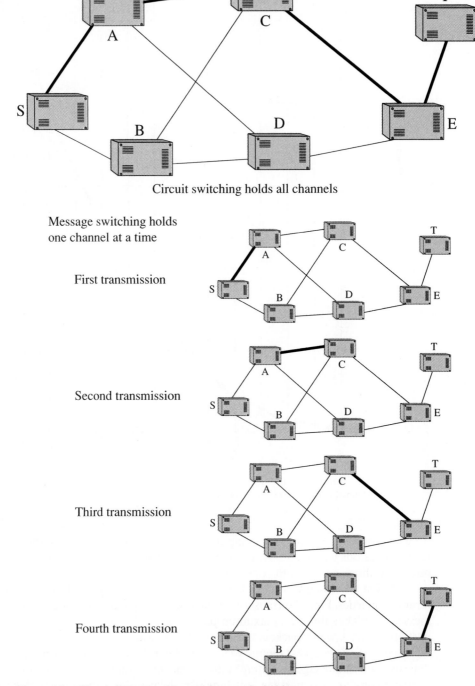

Figure 4.2   Circuit Switching Versus Message Switching

behind. If high-speed channels are used, the delay, even across the United States, is a few hundred milliseconds. The ARPANET used 50-kbps links. Thus for a path with 5 or less hops and a packet length of less than 1000 bytes, the transmission time is less than $1000 \times 8/50,000 = 0.16$ second. At the same time, the channels are used as efficiently as for message switching.

The ARPANET technology offered other new advantages, as discussed in the following paragraphs.

When circuit switching is used for data transmission, the data rates of the transmitting device and the receiving device must be the same. With packet switching, this is not necessary. A packet can be sent at the data rate of the transmitting device into the network; travel through the network at a variety of different data rates, usually higher than the transmitter's rate; and then be metered out at the data rate that the receiver was expecting. The packet-switching network and its interfaces can buffer backed-up data to make speed conversion from a higher rate to a lower one possible. It was not just differing data rates that made interconnections difficult at the time of ARPANET's invention; the complete lack of open communication standards made it very difficult for a computer made by one manufacturer to communicate electronically with a computer made by another. Therefore, a key part of the ARPANET effort was the development of standardized communication and application protocols, as discussed subsequently. Of particular interest to its military sponsors, ARPANET also offered adaptive routing. Each packet, individually, was routed to its destination by whatever route seemed fastest at the time of its transmission. Thus, if parts of the network got congested or failed, packets would automatically be routed around the obstacles.

Some of the early applications developed for the ARPANET also offered new functionality. The first two important applications were Telnet and FTP. Telnet provided a universal language for remote computer terminals. When the ARPANET was introduced, each different computer system supported a different terminal. The Telnet application provided a common denominator terminal. If software was written for each type of computer to support the "Telnet terminal," then one terminal could interact with all computer types. The File Transfer Protocol (FTP) offered a similar open functionality. FTP allowed the transparent transfer of files from one computer to another over the network. This is not as trivial as it may sound because various computers had different word sizes, stored their bits in different orders, and used different word formats. However, the first "killer app" for the ARPANET was electronic mail. Before ARPANET there were electronic mail systems, but they were all single-computer systems. In 1972, Ray Tomlinson of Bolt Beranek and Newman (BBN) wrote the first system to provide distributed mail service across a computer network using multiple computers. By 1973, an ARPA study had found that three-quarters of all ARPANET traffic was e-mail [HAFN96].

The network was so successful that ARPA applied the same packet-switching technology to tactical radio communication (packet radio) and to satellite communication (SATNET). Because the three networks operated in very different communication environments, the appropriate values for certain parameters, such as maximum packet size, were different in each case. Faced with the dilemma of integrating these networks, Vint Cerf and Bob Kahn of ARPA started to develop methods and protocols for *internetworking;* that is, communicating across arbitrary, multiple, packet-switched networks. They published an influential paper in May of

1974 [CERF74] outlining their approach to a Transmission Control Protocol (TCP). The proposal was refined and details filled in by the ARPANET community, with major contributions from participants from European networks, such as Cyclades (France), and EIN, eventually leading to the TCP and IP (Internet Protocol) specifications, which, in turn, formed the basis for what eventually became the TCP/IP protocol suite. This provided the foundation for the Internet. In 1982–1983, ARPANET converted from the original NCP (Network Control Protocol) to TCP/IP. Many networks then were connected using this technology throughout the world. Nevertheless, use of the ARPANET was generally restricted to ARPA contractors.

The 1980s saw the widespread deployment of local area networks (LANs), personal computers (PC), and workstations. Many of these were connected to the Internet, resulting in large-scale expansion. As the scale of the Internet increased, new innovations were required to meet new challenges. Originally, hosts were given numeric addresses, but these quickly became cumbersome. The Domain Name System (DNS) was invented so hosts could be assigned names that were easier to remember, with DNS providing a translation from the domain names to numeric addresses. New routing algorithms were also invented to handle the ever-increasing complexity of the many connected networks.

Figure 4.3 illustrates the key elements that comprise the Internet. The purpose of the Internet, of course, is to interconnect end systems, called **hosts**; these include

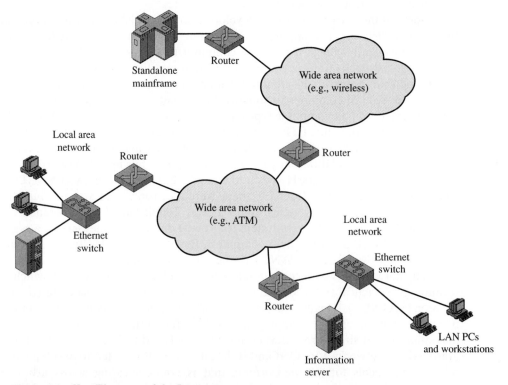

Figure 4.3   Key Elements of the Internet

PCs, workstations, servers, mainframes, and so on. Most hosts that use the Internet are connected to a **network**, such as a local area network (LAN) or a wide area network (WAN). These networks are in turn connected by **routers**. Each router attaches to two or more networks. Some hosts, such as mainframes or servers, connect directly to a router rather than through a network.

In essence, the Internet operates as follows. A host may send data to another host anywhere on the Internet. The source host breaks the data to be sent into a sequence of packets, called **IP datagrams** or **IP packets**. Each packet includes a unique numeric address of the destination host. This address is referred to as an **IP address**, because the address is carried in an IP packet. Based on this destination address, each packet travels through a series of routers and networks from source to destination. Each router, as it receives a packet, makes a routing decision and forwards the packet along its way to the destination. We have more to say about this process in Chapter 5.

National Science Foundation Takes on a Role

In 1985 the U.S. National Science Foundation (NSF) announced plans to establish NSFNET to serve U.S. universities. The NSF also agreed to provide the backbone for the U.S. Internet service. Within three years the NSFNET backbone was implemented and servicing traffic at T-1 speed (1.544 Mbps). This version of the Internet, however, excluded "purposes not in support of research and education"; this purpose was codified in an *acceptable use policy,* which limited commercial exploitation of the Internet. Eventually, NSF offered interconnection through its backbone to regional packet-switching networks across the country.

The NSF extended support to other computer science research groups with CSNET in 1980–1981; in 1986, NSF extended Internet support to all the disciplines of the general research community with the NSFNET backbone. In 1990 the ARPANET was shut down.

The NSF was responsible for many of the policy decisions that led to the modern Internet. One of the primary goals of the foundation was to establish a wide area networking infrastructure that was not directly funded by the federal government. To this end, the foundation encouraged regional networks that were part of NSFNET to expand their facilities to commercial customers. The NSF also helped standardize the use of many technologies we are familiar with today, such as TCP/IP. The foundation also standardized the requirements for routers (called Internet gateways in many of the early documents) to ensure interoperability between the pieces of the Internet.

NSF policies deliberately fostered competition, and in 1995 the Internet went "private" as the role of the NSFNET backbone was taken over by private long-haul networks. From this point onward the Internet became open to virtually unlimited commercial activity.

Internet Interconnection Points

In 1991, General Atomics, which operated CERFnet (a California regional network); Performance Systems International operating PSINet (a commercial spin-off from New York's regional network, NYSERnet); and UUNET Technologies, a commercial Internet service provider that owned Alternet, provided nearly all the commercial

TCP/IP services in the United States. On their own networks, because they did not use the NSF backbone, they were not subject to NSF's acceptable use policy. However, to communicate among their networks, they had been using the NSF backbone, which brought them under the policy. To get around this problem they formed the Commercial Information Interchange (CIX). Originally, it was a mechanism for the networks of the three founders to interchange traffic carried on their networks at a West Coast router so that each network's customers would have access to customers on others' networks at no extra charge. As other providers entered the market, they too found the concept useful and joined the exchange. By 1996, CIX had 147 member networks. One feature of the CIX is that there are no *settlements*, that is, no traffic-based fees for use of the interchange. A similar interconnection point was formed in 1994 in England, the London Internet Exchange (LINX); in 1996, it had 24 member networks. Also in 1991, the U.S. government announced that it would no longer subsidize the Internet after 1995. As part of the privatization plan, the government mandated interconnection points called network access points (NAPs). There are also metropolitan area exchanges, MAE East and MAE West. The MAEs are a special version of the NAPs that are implemented as metropolitan area networks. Basically, the MAE network connect with major providers in the service area it covers. After the U.S. government privatized the national backbone in 1995, commercial activity began to dominate.

The World Wide Web

In the spring of 1989, at CERN (the European Laboratory for Particle Physics), Tim Berners–Lee proposed the idea of a distributed hypermedia technology to facilitate the international exchange of research findings using the Internet. Two years later, a prototype **World Wide Web** (WWW, or the Web for short) was developed at CERN using the NeXT computer as a platform. By the end of 1991, CERN released a line-oriented *browser* or reader to a limited population. The explosive growth of the technology came with the development of the first graphically oriented browser, *Mosaic*, developed at the NCSA Center at the University of Illinois by Mark Andreasson and others in 1993. Two million copies of Mosaic were delivered over the Internet. Today, the characteristic Web addresses, the URLs (uniform resource locators), are ubiquitous. One cannot read a newspaper or watch TV without seeing the addresses everywhere.

The Web is a system consisting of an internationally distributed collection of *multimedia files* supported by clients (users) and servers (information providers). Each file is addressed in a consistent manner using its URL. The files from the providers are viewed by the clients using *browsers* such as Firefox or Microsoft's Internet Explorer. Most browsers have graphical display and support multimedia—text, audio, image, video. The user can move from file to file by clicking with a mouse or other pointing device on specially highlighted text or image elements on the browser display; the transfer from one file to the next is called a *hyperlink*. The layout of the browser display is controlled by the *HyperText Markup Language* (HTML) standard, which defines embedded commands in text files that specify features of the browser display, such as the fonts, colors, images and their placement on the display, and the location of the locations where the user can invoke the hyperlinks and their targets. Another important feature of the Web is the Hypertext Transfer Protocol (HTTP), which is a communications protocol for use in TCP/IP networks for fetching the files from the appropriate servers as specified by the hyperlinks.

4.2 INTERNET ARCHITECTURE

What the Internet Looks Like Today

The Internet today is made up of thousands of overlapping hierarchical networks. Because of this, it is not practical to attempt a detailed description of the exact architecture or topology of the Internet. However, an overview of the common, general characteristics can be made. Figure 4.4 illustrates the discussion and Table 4.1 summarizes the terminology.

A key element of the Internet is the set of hosts attached to it. Simply put, a host is a computer. Today, computers come in many forms, including mobile phones and even cars. All of these forms can be hosts on the Internet. Hosts are sometimes grouped together in a LAN. This is the typical configuration in a corporate environment. Individual hosts and LANs are connected to an **Internet service provider (ISP)** through a **point of presence (POP)**. The connection is made in a series of steps starting with the **customer premises equipment (CPE)**. The CPE is the communications equipment located onsite with the host.

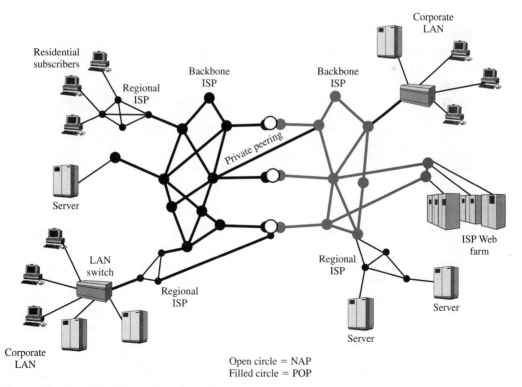

Figure 4.4   Simplified View of Portion of Internet

Table 4.1 Internet Terminology

Central Office (CO)

The place where telephone companies terminate customer lines and locate switching equipment to interconnect those lines with other networks.

Customer Premises Equipment (CPE)

Telecommunications equipment that is located on the customer's premises (physical location) rather than on the provider's premises or in between. Telephone handsets, modems, cable TV set-top boxes, and digital subscriber line routers are examples. Historically, this term referred to equipment placed at the customer's end of the telephone line and usually owned by the telephone company. Today, almost any end-user equipment can be called customer premises equipment, and it can be owned by the customer or by the provider.

Internet Service Provider (ISP)

A company that provides other companies or individuals with access to, or presence on, the Internet. An ISP has the equipment and the telecommunication line access required to have a POP on the Internet for the geographic area served. The larger ISPs have their own high-speed leased lines so that they are less dependent on the telecommunication providers and can provide better service to their customers.

Network Access Point (NAP)

In the United States, a NAP is one of several major Internet interconnection points that serve to tie all the ISPs together. Originally, four NAPs—in New York, Washington, D.C., Chicago, and San Francisco—were created and supported by the National Science Foundation as part of the transition from the original U.S. government-financed Internet to a commercially operated Internet. Since that time, several new NAPs have arrived, including WorldCom's "MAE West" site in San Jose, California, and ICS Network Systems' "Big East."

The NAPs provide major switching facilities that serve the public in general. Companies apply to use the NAP facilities. Much Internet traffic is handled without involving NAPs, using peering arrangements and interconnections within geographic regions.

Network Service Provider (NSP)

A company that provides backbone services to an ISP. Typically, an ISP connects at a point called an Internet exchange (IX) to a regional ISP that in turn connects to an NSP backbone.

Point of Presence (POP)

A site that has a collection of telecommunications equipment; usually refers to an (ISP) or telephone company sites. An ISP POP is the edge of the ISP's network; connections from users are accepted and authenticated here. An Internet access provider may operate several POPs distributed throughout its area of operation to increase the chance that their subscribers will be able to reach one with a local telephone call. The largest national ISPs have POPs all over the country.

For a number of home users, the CPE is a 56K modem. This is perfectly adequate for e-mail and related services but marginal for graphics-intensive Web surfing. Newer CPE offerings provide greater capacity and guaranteed service in some cases. A sample of these new access technologies includes DSL, cable modem, terrestrial wireless, and satellite. Users who connect to the Internet through their work often use workstations or PCs connected to their employer-owned LANs, which in turn connect through shared organizational trunks to an ISP. In these cases the shared circuit is often a T-1 connection (1.544 Mbps), while for very large organizations T-3 connections (44.736 Mbps) are sometimes found. Alternatively, an organization's LAN may be hooked to a wide area network (WAN), such as a frame relay network, which in turn connects to an ISP.

The CPE is physically attached to the "local loop" or "last mile." This is the infrastructure between a provider's installation and the site where the host is located. For example, a home user with a 56K modem attaches the modem to the telephone line. The telephone line is typically a pair of copper wires that runs from the house to a **central office (CO)** owned and operated by the telephone company. In this instance the local loop is the pair of copper wires running between the home and the CO. If the home user has a cable modem, the local loop is the coaxial cable that runs from the home to the cable company facilities. The preceding examples are a bit of an oversimplification but they suffice for this discussion. In many cases the wires that leave a home are aggregated with wires from other homes and then converted to a different media such as fiber. In these cases the term *local loop* still refers to the path from the home to the CO or cable facility. The local loop provider is not necessarily the ISP. In many cases the local loop provider is the telephone company and the ISP is a large, national service organization. Often, however, the local loop provider is also the ISP.

Other forms of CPE-ISP connection do not go through a telephone company CO. For example, a cable link would connect the local user to the cable company site, which would include or link to an ISP. Mobile users can take advantage of a wireless link to a WiFi that provides access to the Internet. And corporate access to an ISP may be by dedicated high-speed links or through a wide area network, such as an ATM (asynchronous transfer mode) or frame relay network.

The ISP provides access to its larger network through a POP. A POP is simply a facility where customers can connect to the ISP network. The facility is sometimes owned by the ISP, but often the ISP leases space from the local loop carrier. A POP can be as simple as a bank of modems and an access server installed in a rack at the CO. The POPs are usually spread out over the geographic area where the provider offers service. The ISP acts as a gateway to the Internet, providing many important services. For most home users, the ISP provides the unique numeric IP address needed to communicate with other Internet hosts. Most ISPs also provide name resolution and other essential network services. The most important service an ISP provides, though, is access to other ISP networks. Access is facilitated by formal peering agreements between providers. Physical access can be implemented by connecting POPs from different ISPs. This can be done directly with a local connection if the POPs are collocated or with leased lines when the POPs are not collocated. A more commonly used mechanism is the **network access point (NAP)**.

A NAP is a physical facility that provides the infrastructure to move data between connected networks. In the United States, the NSF privatization plan called for the creation of four NAPs. The NAPs were built and are operated by the private sector. The number of NAPs has grown significantly over the years, and the technology employed has shifted from Fiber Distributed Data Interface (FDDI) and Ethernet to ATM and Gigabit Ethernet. Most NAPs today have an ATM core. The networks connected at a NAP are owned and operated by **network service providers (NSPs)**. A NSP can also be an ISP but this is not always the case. Peering agreements are between NSPs and do not include the NAP operator. The NSPs install routers at the NAP and connect them to the NAP infrastructure. The NSP equipment is responsible for routing, and the NAP infrastructure provides the physical access paths between routers.

A small hypothetical example can help make the picture clearer. In this example there are two companies, one named A, Inc. and the other B, Inc. and they are both NSPs. A, Inc. and B, Inc. have a peering agreement and they both install routers in two NAPs, one located on the east coast of the United States and the other on the west coast. There are also two other companies known as Y, Inc. and Z, Inc. and they are both ISPs. Finally, there is a home user named Bob and a small company named Small, Inc.

Small, Inc. has four hosts connected together into a LAN. Each of the four hosts can communicate and share resources with the other three. Small, Inc. would like access to a broader set of services so they contract with ISP Y, Inc. for a connection. Small, Inc. installs a CPE to drive a leased T-1 line into a Y, Inc. POP. Once the CPE is connected, software automatically assigns a numeric address to each Small, Inc. host. The Small, Inc. hosts can now communicate and share resources with any other host connected to the larger ISP network. On the other side of the country, Bob decides to contract with ISP Z, Inc. He installs a modem on his phone line to dial into a Z, Inc. POP. Once the modem connects, a numeric address is automatically assigned to his home computer. His computer can now communicate and share resources with any other computer connected to the larger ISP network.

Bob's home machine and the hosts owned by Small, Inc. cannot yet communicate. This becomes possible when their respective ISPs contract with NSPs that have a peering agreement. In this example, the ISP Y, Inc. decides to expand its service coverage to the opposite coast and contracts with the NSP A, Inc. A, Inc. sells bandwidth on its high speed coast-to-coast network. The ISP Z, Inc. also wishes to expand its service coverage and contracts with the NSP B, Inc. Like A, Inc., B, Inc. also sells bandwidth on a high speed coast-to-coast network. Because A, Inc. and B, Inc. have a peering agreement and have implemented the agreement at two NAPs, Bob's home machine and the hosts of Small, Inc. can now communicate and share resources. Although this example is contrived, in principle this is what the Internet is. The differences are that the Internet has many millions of hosts and many thousands of networks using dozens of access technologies, including satellite, radio, leased T-1, and DSL.

Commercial Use of the Internet

The commercial uses of the Internet came in stages. In the early days, limited by the access rules of the ARPANET and, later, by the Acceptable Use Policy, commercial use was limited to research and development (R&D) or other technical units using the Net for research and educational uses, although some informational activities that could be considered marketing were carried on under the name of research and education. When the Internet was privatized in 1995, the first new applications were mainly informational ones for sales and marketing information and public relations. Electronic data interchange (EDI) transactions for intercompany invoices, billing, and the like, which were originally designed for use on dedicated wide area networks and commercial public networks began to be carried on the Internet. Commercial networks, especially America Online, have long played a customer service role by providing bulletin board type services dealing with technical and usage problems. These activities were gradually extended to the Internet as well. However, the most significant activity is direct sales to the tens of millions of Internet users throughout the world. The initial infrastructure of the Internet did not support online transactions well. There were three limitations: lack of an easy-to-use graphical user interface, lack of security, and lack of effective payment systems. The most popular and easy-to-use interface, the World Wide Web and its browsers, did not become commonly available until the early 1990s. In its early incarnations there was very little support to allow the client browser to submit information (forms) to the server. Moreover, there were not many options for payment for online ordering, and all the options were insecure. One obvious payment method is to use credit card accounts. However, many people are uncomfortable about sending credit card numbers over the Internet, with good reason, because of the lack of security. For example, if the credit card information is not encrypted, it is very easy to "listen in" on Internet communications. Moreover, several files of customers' credit card numbers on merchants' computers have been compromised. The ease of collecting and integrating information on customer transactions when they are in electronic form also raises privacy concerns for customers. One of the hottest application areas in financial information systems is "data mining," which often involves collecting large amounts of customer transaction information to improve the targeting of marketing efforts. These limitations have been addressed. Today's browsers support secure communication with the server for filling out forms and providing credit card information.

4.3 INTERNET DOMAINS

Internet Names and Addresses

Boot Protocol Simulator

Recall from Section 4.1 that data traverse the Internet in the form of packets, with each packet including a numeric destination address. These addresses are 32-bit binary numbers. The 32-bit IP address provides a way of uniquely identifying devices attached to the Internet. This address is interpreted as having two components: a network number, which identifies a network on the Internet, and a host address, which identifies a unique host on that network. The use of IP addresses presents two problems:

1. Routers devise a path through the Internet on the basis of the network number. If each router needed to keep a master table that listed every network and the preferred path to that network, the management of the tables would be cumbersome and time consuming. It would be better to group the networks in such a way as to simplify the routing function.

2. The 32-bit address is usually written as four decimal numbers, corresponding to the four octets of the address. This number scheme is effective for computer processing but is not convenient for users, who can more easily remember names than numeric addresses.

These problems are addressed by the concept of **domain** and the use of **domain names**. In general terms, a domain refers to a group of hosts that are under the administrative control of a single entity, such as a company or government agency. Domains are organized hierarchically, so that a given domain may consist of

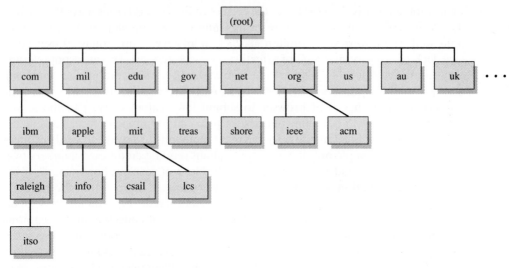

Figure 4.5 Portion of Internet Domain Tree

a number of subordinate domains. Names are assigned to domains and reflect this hierarchical organization.

Figure 4.5 shows a portion of the domain naming tree. At the very top level are a small number of domains that encompass the entire Internet. Table 4.2 lists the currently defined top-level domains. These top-level domains are assigned by the Internet Assigned Numbers Authority (IANA). Each subordinate level is named by prefixing a subordinate name to the name at the next highest level. For example,

- edu is the domain of college-level educational institutions.
- mit.edu is the domain for the Massachusetts Institute of Technology (MIT).
- csail.mit.edu is the domain for the MIT Computer Science and Artificial Intelligence Laboratory.

As you move down the naming tree, you eventually get to leaf nodes that identify specific hosts on the Internet. These hosts are assigned Internet addresses. Domain names are assigned hierarchically in such a way that every domain name is unique. At a top level, the creation of new top-level names and the assignment of names and addresses is administered by the Internet Corporation for Assigned Names and Numbers (ICANN). The actual assignment of addresses is delegated down the hierarchy. Thus, the mil domain is assigned a large group of addresses. The U.S. Department of Defense (DoD) then allocates portions of this address space to various DoD organizations for eventual assignment to hosts.

For example, the main host at MIT, with a domain name of mit.edu, has the IP address 18.7.22.69. The subordinate domain csail.mit.edu has the IP address 128.30.2.121. [1]

---

[1] You should be able to demonstrate the name/address function by connecting your Web browser to your local ISP. The ISP should provide a ping or nslookup tool that allows you to enter a domain name and retrieve an IP address. Such a tool is typically available on user operating systems as well.

Table 4.2 Top-Level Internet Domains

Domain	Contents
com	Commercial organizations
edu	Educational institutions
gov	U.S. federal government agencies
mil	U.S. military
net	Network support centers, Internet service providers, and other network-related organizations
org	Nonprofit organizations
us	U.S. state and local government agencies, schools, libraries, and museums
country code	ISO standard 2-letter identifier for country-specific domains (e.g., au, ca, uk)
biz	Dedicated exclusively for private businesses
info	Unrestricted use
name	Individuals, for e-mail addresses and personalized domain names
museum	Restricted to museums, museum organizations, and individual members of the museum profession
coop	Member-owned cooperative organizations, such as credit unions
aero	Aviation community
pro	Medical, legal, and accounting professions
arpa	Temporary ARPA domain (still used)
int	International organizations
jobs	Human resource managers
mobi	Consumers and providers of mobile products and services
tel	For businesses and individuals to publish their contact data
travel	Entities whose primary area of activity is in the travel industry

Domain Name System

The Domain Name System (DNS) is a directory lookup service that provides a mapping between the name of a host on the Internet and its numeric address. DNS is essential to the functioning of the Internet.

Four elements comprise the DNS:

- **Domain name space:** DNS uses a tree-structured name space to identify resources on the Internet.
- **DNS database:** Conceptually, each node and leaf in the name space tree structure names a set of information (e.g., IP address, name server for this domain name, etc.) that is contained in resource record (RRs). The collection of all RRs is organized into a distributed database.
- **Name servers:** These are server programs that hold information about a portion of the domain name tree structure and the associated RRs.
- **Resolvers:** These are programs that extract information from name servers in response to client requests. A typical client request is for an IP address corresponding to a given domain name.

We have already looked at domain names. The remaining DNS elements are discussed in the remainder of this subsection.

THE DNS DATABASE   DNS is based on a hierarchical database containing **resource records (RRs)** that include the name, IP address, and other information about hosts. The key features of the database are:

- **Variable-depth hierarchy for names:** DNS allows essentially unlimited levels and uses the period (.) as the level delimiter in printed names, as described earlier.
- **Distributed database:** The database resides in DNS servers scattered throughout the Internet.
- **Distribution controlled by the database:** The DNS database is divided into thousands of separately managed zones, which are managed by separate administrators. Distribution and update of records is controlled by the database software.

Using this database, DNS servers provide a name-to-address directory service for network applications that need to locate specific servers. For example, every time an e-mail message is sent or a Web page is accessed, there must be a DNS name lookup to determine the IP address of the e-mail server or Web server.

DNS OPERATION   DNS operation typically includes the following steps (Figure 4.6):

1. A user program requests an IP address for a domain name.
2. A resolver module in the local host or local ISP queries a local name server in the same domain as the resolver.
3. The local name server checks to see if the name is in its local database or cache, and, if so, returns the IP address to the requestor. Otherwise, the name server

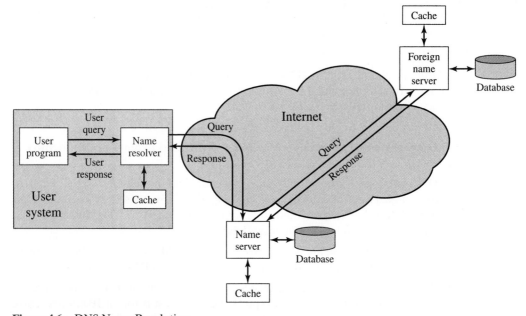

Figure 4.6   DNS Name Resolution

queries other available name servers, if necessary going to the root server, as explained subsequently.

4. When a response is received at the local name server, it stores the name/address mapping in its local cache and may maintain this entry for the amount of time specified in the time to live field of the retrieved RR.

5. The user program is given the IP address or an error message.

The distributed DNS database that supports the DNS functionality must be updated frequently because of the rapid and continued growth of the Internet. Further, the DNS must cope with dynamic assignment of IP addresses, such as is done for home DSL users by their ISP. Accordingly, dynamic updating functions for DNS have been defined. In essence, DNS name servers automatically send out updates to other relevant name servers as conditions warrant.

THE SERVER HIERARCHY   The DNS database is distributed hierarchically, residing in DNS name servers scattered throughout the Internet. Name servers can be operated by any organization that owns a domain; that is, any organization that has responsibility for a subtree of the hierarchical domain name space. Each name server is configured with a subset of the domain name space, known as a **zone**, which is a collection of one or more (or all) subdomains within a domain, along with the associated RRs. This set of data is called authoritative, because this name server is responsible for maintaining an accurate set of RRs for this portion of the domain name space. The hierarchical structure can extend to virtually any depth. Thus, a portion of the name space assigned to an authoritative name server can be delegated to a subordinate name server in a way that corresponds to the structure of the domain name tree. For example, a name server is authoritative for the domain ibm.com. A portion of that domain is defined by the name watson.ibm.com, which corresponds to the node watson.ibm.com and all of the branches and leaf nodes underneath the node watson.ibm.com.

At the top of the server hierarchy are 13 **root name servers** that share responsibility for the top-level zones (Table 4.3). This replication is to prevent the root server from becoming a bottleneck, and for reliability. Even so, each individual root server is quite busy. For example, the Internet Software Consortium reports that its server (F) answers almost 300 million DNS requests daily (www.isc.org/services/public/ F-root-server.html). Note that some of the root servers exist as multiple servers that are geographically distributed. When there are multiple root servers with the same name, each has an identical copy of the database for that server and the same IP address. When a query is made to that root server, the IP routing protocol and algorithm directs the query to the most convenient server, which is generally the nearest server physically. Figure 4.7 shows the geographical distribution of the root servers.

Consider a query by a program on a user host for watson.ibm.com. This query is sent to the local name server, and the following steps occur:

1. If the local server already has the IP address for watson.ibm.com in its local cache, it returns the IP address.

2. If the name is not in the local name server's cache, it sends the query to a root server. The root server returns the names and addresses of the domain name servers that contain information for ibm.com.

Table 4.3 Internet Root Servers

Server	Operator	Cities	IP Addr
A	VeriSign Global Registry Services	Herndon, VA, U.S.	198.41.0.4
B	Information Sciences Institute	Marina Del Rey, CA, U.S.	IPv4: 192.228.79.201 IPv6: 2001:478:65::53
C	Cogent Communications	Herndon, VA; Los Angeles; New York City; Chicago	192.33.4.12
D	University of Maryland	College Park, MD, U.S.	128.8.10.90
E	NASA Ames Research Center	Mountain View, CA, U.S.	192.203.230.10
F	Internet Software Consortium	43 sites	IPv4: 192.5.5.241 IPv6: 2001:500::1035
G	U.S. DOD Network Information Center	Columbus, Ohio, U.S.	192.112.36.4
H	U.S. Army Research Lab	Aberdeen, MD, U.S.	IPv4: 128.63.2.53 IPv6: 2001:500:1::803f:235
I	Autonomica	31 sites	192.36.148.17
J	VeriSign Global Registry Services	37 sites	192.58.128.30
K	Reseaux IP Europeens - Network Coordination Centre	17 sites	IPv4: 193.0.14.129 IPv6: 2001:7fd::1
L	Internet Corporation for Assigned Names and Numbers	Los Angeles, CA, U.S.	198.32.64.12
M	WIDE Project	4 sites	IPv4: 202.12.27.33 IPv6: 2001:dc3::35

3. If there is a delegated name server just for watson.ibm.com, then the ibm.com name server forwards the request to the watson.ibm.com name server, which returns the IP address.

NAME RESOLUTION As Figure 4.6 indicates, each query begins at a name resolver located in the user host system (e.g., gethostbyname in UNIX). Each resolver is configured to know the IP address of a local DNS name server. If the resolver does not have the requested name in its cache, it sends a DNS query to the local DNS server, which either returns an address immediately or does so after querying one or more other servers.

There are two methods by which queries are forwarded and results returned. Suppose a resolver issues a request to local name server (A). If A has the name/address in its local cache or local database, it can return the IP address to the resolver. If not, then A can do either of the following:

1. Query another name server for the desired result and then send the result back to the resolver. This is known as a **recursive** technique.

2. Return to the resolver the address of the next server (B) to whom the request should be sent. The resolver then sends out a new DNS request to B. This is known as the **iterative** technique.

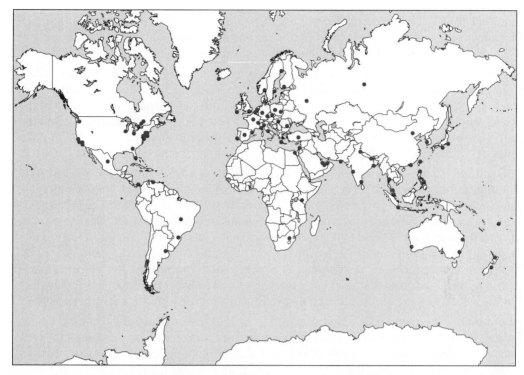

Figure 4.7 Geographical Distribution of DNS Root Servers (January 2008)

APPLICATION NOTE

Fitting DNS into Your Organizational Structure

The Domain Name System (DNS) is an integral part of communicating over your local area network and the Internet. Every time a name or uniform resource locator (URL) is entered into a program that runs over a network, the name must be converted to the Internet Protocol (IP) address. The best example is a Web browser. The DNS allows us to dispense with difficult to remember IP addresses like 207.42.16.185, in favor of easier "human readable" names like www.yahoo.com. The Yahoo Web site is actually comprised of servers accessed by their IP addresses after the name has been converted to these numbers.

DNS is also used for services other than those used to access Web sites. E-mail, network shares, and FTP are a few of the network resources to which we connect using names. End users typically contact all of the company servers by name rather than by IP address. For example, the command "ftp www.georgia.com" uses a name that must first be resolved to a numerical address for the server.

At the beginning of almost any network transaction, a computer (host) must contact the DNS in order to complete that transaction. So where is the DNS that is providing this service? An organization can either have this service provided by an outside entity or it can run its own DNS that connects to the rest of the DNS system. The size of your organizational

(Continued)

network usually determines the choice. Small networks usually have no need or desire to maintain their own DNS server. It is only when you have large number of servers and services running internally that you might opt to run your own.

When the service is provided to you, it is usually by your Internet service provider or ISP. The ISP may also automatically provide other services like the IP addresses for the organizations computers and email. If you receive an IP address automatically, the address of the DNS server can be provided at the same time. Another option is to manually configure the DNS server address on the individual computers. An institution may decide to do this if the network is configured with private IP addresses that do not come from the ISP.

Should the institution decide that it is time to run its own DNS server, there are several configurations possible. DNS is actually a huge collection of servers working together in a hierarchy. These servers will be both on site (your local DNS) and off site. The off-site systems are those servers used by everyone else connected to the Internet. This means that unless the server is designed to be isolated, it will have to communicate with DNS servers external to and upstream of the local network. Operationally, when the DNS system receives a request for name resolution, the closest server attempts to provide the answer (that is, the IP address that goes with the name in the request). If that server does not know the answer, the request is passed upward and a server with the answer responds.

Just about any computer can be configured as a DNS server. While the technical details are beyond the scope of this text, running your own server adds an additional layer of complexity and management. The DNS server must be kept up to date and have a backup system. Should the local DNS server be off line, all the machines depending on it may have difficulty connecting. To mitigate this, companies running their own DNS server usually will run a secondary server for redundancy.

One consideration may be how much a company depends on Windows Active Directory. Active Directory is a repository or database of organization objects. These objects can describe people, groups, services and many others. Previously, Windows networks were supported by domain controllers, NetBIOS, and DNS. Active Directory modifies this by increased reliance on DNS. Thus, the Windows system is even more dependent on the proper operation of DNS. In this case, it may be best to run a local DNS server because of all of the organization specific information that must be stored there and on the Active Directory systems.

DNS is an integral and critical part of any data communications network. The decision to implement your own or rely on services provided from an external organization must be given a good deal of thought as it is a significant investment in time and management resources.

4.4 SUMMARY

The most important networking facility available to organizations is the Internet. The Internet can be used to link to customers and suppliers and can function as a portion of the wide area networking strategy for linking corporate facilities. The Internet is an unusual corporate tool in that it is not owned or managed by a single entity. Instead, each organization that uses the Internet must understand and deploy the standardized protocols necessary for communication across the Internet.

The Internet, and any private intranet, consists of multiple separate networks that are interconnected by routers. Data are transmitted in packets from a source system to a destination across a path involving multiple networks and routers. A router accepts packets and relays them on toward their destination and is responsible for determining the route, much the same way as packet-switching nodes operate.

An essential element of the Internet is its addressing scheme. It is necessary that each attached host have a unique address to make routing and delivery possible. Internet standards define a 32-bit addressing scheme for this purpose. The Domain Name System provides a means of translating host names to Internet addresses, making it easier for users to identify Internet resources.

4.5 RECOMMENDED READING AND WEB SITES

[COME07] is an excellent in-depth discussion of the topics covered in this chapter. [KLEI08] is a good overview history of the Internet.

COME07 Comer, D. *The Internet Book*. Upper Saddle River, NJ: Prentice Hall, 2007.
KLEI08 Kleinrock, L. "History of the Internet and Its Flexible Future." *IEEE Wireless Communications*, February 2008.

Recommended Web site:

- **The Living Internet:** Provides comprehensive and in-depth information about the history of the Internet, plus links to numerous other relevant sites
- **CAIDA:** The Cooperative Association for Internet Data Analysis, provides tools and analyses promoting the engineering and maintenance of a robust, scalable global Internet infrastructure

4.6 KEY TERMS, REVIEW QUESTIONS, AND PROBLEMS

Key Terms

ARPANET	Internet service provider (ISP)	network service provider (NSP)
central office	IP address	
customer premises equipment (CPE)	IP datagram	point of presence (POP)
	IP packet	root name server
domain	message switching	router
domain name system (DNS)	network	Transmission Control Protocol (TCP)
host	network access point (NAP)	
Internet Protocol (IP)		World Wide Web (WWW)

Review Questions

4.1 What is the difference between ARPANET and the Internet?

4.2 What two protocols form the foundation of and govern the way we communicate on the Internet?

4.3 What are the roles of host, network, and routers in the Internet?

4.4 What were two of the first applications developed for use over a network?

4.5 What is an IP address?

4.6 What is Mosaic?

4.7 What are two applications programs that have taken the place of Mosaic?

4.8 What is the programming language used to display Web pages?

4.9 What is the difference between an ISP and a POP?

4.10 What is the difference between an NAP and an NSP?

4.11 What is an Internet domain?

4.12 What is DNS?

4.13 Name the four major components of the domain name system.

4.14 What is the difference between a name server and a resolver in DNS?

4.15 What is a DNS resource record?

4.16 Give a brief description of DNS operation.

4.17 What is a root name server?

4.18 Explain the difference between the recursive technique and the iterative technique in DNS.

Problems

4.1 Compare and contrast circuit switching and packet switching. Describe the tradeoffs between the two technologies. Why is packet switching the more appropriate mechanism for the operation of the Internet?

4.2 Two seemingly unrelated events took place in late 1992 and early 1993 that together seeded the explosive growth of the Internet that is rooted in the early 1990s. One was a piece of legislation authored by Congressman Rick Boucher and the other was a piece of software authored by Marc Andreessen. Explain how and why these two events were major contributors to the state of the Internet as we know it today. References: http://www.house.gov/boucher/docs/boucherinfotech.htm http://www.webhistory.org/www.lists/www-talk.1993q1/0262.html

4.3 The dig tool provides easy interactive access to the DNS. The dig tool is available for UNIX and Windows operating systems. It can also be used from the Web. Here are three sites that, at the time of this writing, provided free access to dig:

http://www.gont.com.ar/tools/dig

http://www.webmaster-toolkit.com/dig.shtml

http://www.webhostselect.com/whs/dig-tool.jsp

Use the dig tool to get the list of root servers.

4.4 Choose a root server, and use the dig tool to send it a query for the IP address of www.example.com, with the RD (Recursion Desired) bit set. Does it support recursive lookups? Why or why not?

4.5 A user on the host 170.210.17.145 is using a Web browser to visit www.example.com. In order to resolve the www.example.com domain to an IP address, a query is sent to an authoritative name server for the 'example.com' domain. In response, the name server returns a list of four IP addresses, in the following order: {192.168.0.1, 128.0.0.1, 200.47.57.1, 170.210.10.130}. Even though it is the last IP address in the list returned by the name server, the Web browser creates a connection to 170.210.17.130. Why?

4.6 Before the deployment of the Domain Name System, a simple text file ('HOSTS.TXT') centrally maintained at the SRI Network Information Center was used to enable mapping between host names and addresses. Each host connected to the Internet had to have an updated local copy of it to be able to use host names instead of having to cope directly with their IP addresses. Discuss the main advantages of the DNS over the old centralized HOSTS.TXT system.

4.7 Every machine connected to a network should have an IP address. This is true whether the address comes from a server or is manually configured. Use the following tools to determine your IP address. To use each one, you must first open up either a DOS shell (for Windows) or a Bourne shell (most often used Linux shell). These shells are sometimes called command windows. In Windows operating systems, the shell can be accessed by typing "command" in the Start/Run box. For Linux, the shell may be the default or can be accessed by the shell icon on the task bar.

Windows 98/2000/XP—Type "ipconfig" in the shell window then press "Enter"

Linux—Type "ifconfig eth0" in the shell window then press "Enter"

4.8 What is the name of the protocol used to provide your IP address automatically?

4.9 In this same, you can interact with the server providing the IP address for your computer. For Linux you can use the command ifdown eth0 followed by the command ifup eth0. This will send a series of requests to the server. On the Windows 98/2000/XP machine, type the command ipconfig /? which will display a series of options. Release and renew your IP address using these options. Did you get the same IP address?

4.10 Windows 2000/XP and Linux have a program built in that will allow you to interact with the DNS server. This program is called "nslookup". Type this name into the command windows and press "Enter". What is the automatic feedback you receive and what does it mean? Typing "exit" will close the program.

4.11 In the previous problem you learned your IP address. Type the command nslookup and use your IP as an argument. For example, nslookup 10.20.30.40. This will look up your IP address with the DNS system. What does the server return?

4.12 What kind of lookup did you perform in the preceding problem?

CHAPTER 5

TCP/IP AND OSI

5.1 A Simple Protocol Architecture
The Need for a Protocol Architecture
A Three-Layer Model
Standardized Protocol Architectures

5.2 The TCP/IP Protocol Architecture
TCP/IP Layers
Operation of TCP/IP
TCP and UDP
IP and IPv6
TCP/IP Applications
Protocol Interfaces

5.3 Internetworking
Routers
Internetworking Example

5.4 The OSI Protocol Architecture

5.5 Virtual Private Networks and IP Security
IPSec
Applications of IPSec
Benefits of IPSec
IPSec Functions

5.6 Summary

5.7 Recommended Reading and Web Sites

5.8 Key Terms, Review Questions, and Problems

APPENDIX 5A TCP, UDP, and IP Details

APPENDIX 5B The Trivial File Transfer Protocol

Chapter Objectives

After reading this chapter, you should be able to

♦ Define the term *protocol architecture* and explain the need for and benefits of a communications architecture.

♦ Describe the TCP/IP protocol architecture and explain the functioning of each layer.

♦ Explain the motivation for the development of a standardized architecture and the reasons why a customer should use products based on a protocol architecture standard in preference to products based on a proprietary architecture.

♦ Explain the need for internetworking.

♦ Describe the operation of a router within the context of TCP/IP to provide internetworking.

♦ Give a brief description of the OSI architecture and each of its constituent layers.

This chapter examines the underlying communications software required to support distributed applications. We will see that the required software is substantial. To make the task of implementing this communications software manageable, a modular structure known as a protocol architecture is used.

We begin this chapter by introducing a simple protocol architecture consisting of just three modules, or layers. This will allow us to present the key characteristics and design features of a protocol architecture without getting bogged down in details. With this background, we are then ready to examine the most important such architecture: TCP/IP (Transmission Control Protocol/Internet Protocol). TCP/IP is an Internet-based standard and is the framework for developing a complete range of computer communications standards. Virtually all computer vendors now provide support for this architecture. Open Systems Interconnection (OSI) is another standardized architecture that is often used to describe communications functions but that is now rarely implemented. For the interested reader, OSI is covered at the end of this chapter.

Following a discussion of TCP/IP, the important concept of internetworking is examined. Inevitably, a business will require the use of more than one communications network. Some means of interconnecting these networks is required, and this raises issues that relate to the protocol architecture.

5.1 A SIMPLE PROTOCOL ARCHITECTURE

The Need for a Protocol Architecture

When computers, terminals, and/or other data processing devices exchange data, the procedures involved can be quite complex. Consider, for example, the transfer of a file between two computers. There must be a data path between the two computers, either directly or via a communication network. But more is needed. Typical tasks to be performed include the following:

1. The source system must either activate the direct data communication path or inform the communication network of the identity of the desired destination system.

2. The source system must ascertain that the destination system is prepared to receive data.

3. The file transfer application on the source system must ascertain that the file management program on the destination system is prepared to accept and store the file for this particular user.

4. If the file formats or data representations used on the two systems are incompatible, one or the other system must perform a format translation function.

The exchange of information between computers for the purpose of cooperative action is generally referred to as *computer communications*. Similarly, when two or more computers are interconnected via a communication network, the set of computer stations is referred to as a *computer network*. Because a similar level of cooperation is required between a terminal and a computer, these terms are often used when some of the communicating entities are terminals.

In discussing computer communications and computer networks, two concepts are paramount:

- Protocols
- Computer communications architecture, or protocol architecture

A protocol is used for communication between entities in different systems. The terms *entity* and *system* are used in a very general sense. Examples of entities are user application programs, file transfer packages, database management systems, electronic mail facilities, and terminals. Examples of systems are computers, terminals, and remote sensors. Note that in some cases the entity and the system in which it resides are coextensive (e.g., terminals). In general, an entity is anything capable of sending or receiving information, and a system is a physically distinct object that contains one or more entities. For two entities to communicate successfully, they must "speak the same language." What is communicated, how it is communicated, and when it is communicated must conform to mutually agreed conventions among the entities involved. The conventions are referred to as a **protocol**, which may be defined as a set of rules governing the exchange of data between two entities. The key elements of a protocol are as follows:

- **Syntax:** Includes such things as data format and signal levels
- **Semantics:** Includes control information for coordination and error handling
- **Timing:** Includes speed matching and sequencing

Appendix 5B provides a specific example of a protocol, the Internet standard Trivial File Transfer Protocol (TFTP).

Having introduced the concept of a protocol, we can now introduce the concept of a **protocol architecture**. It is clear that there must be a high degree of cooperation between the two computer systems engaged in a coooperative application. Instead of implementing the logic for this as a single module, the task is broken up into subtasks, each of which is implemented separately. The result is a layered

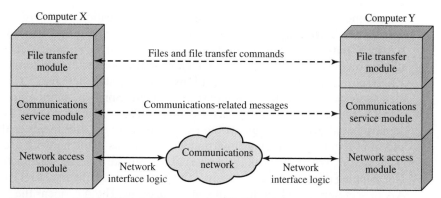

Figure 5.1 A Simplified Architecture for File Transfer

architecture, with **peer entities** at each layer performing subtasks appropriate to the layer. As an example, Figure 5.1 suggests the way in which a file transfer facility could be implemented between two computer systems connected by a network. Three modules are used. Tasks 3 and 4 in the preceding list could be performed by a *file transfer module*. The two modules on the two systems exchange files and commands. However, rather than requiring the file transfer module to deal with the details of actually transferring data and commands, the file transfer modules each rely on a *communications service module*. This module is responsible for making sure that the file transfer commands and data are reliably exchanged between systems. The manner in which a communications service module functions is explored subsequently. Among other things, this module would perform task 2. Finally, the nature of the exchange between the two communications service modules is independent of the nature of the network that interconnects them. Therefore, rather than building details of the network interface into the communications service module, it makes sense to have a third module, a *network access module*, that performs task 1 by interacting with the network.

To summarize, the file transfer module contains all the logic that is unique to the file transfer application, such as transmitting passwords, file commands, and file records. These files and commands must be transmitted reliably. However, the same sorts of reliability requirements are relevant to a variety of applications (e.g., electronic mail, document transfer). Therefore, these requirements are met by a separate communications service module that can be used by a variety of applications. The communications service module is concerned with assuring that the two computer systems are active and ready for data transfer and for keeping track of the data that are being exchanged to assure delivery. However, these tasks are independent of the type of network that is being used. Therefore, the logic for actually dealing with the network is put into a separate network access module. If the network to be used is changed, only the network access module is affected.

Thus, instead of a single module for performing communications, there is a structured set of modules that implements the communications function. That structure is referred to as a **protocol architecture**. An analogy might be useful at this point. Suppose an executive in office X wishes to send a document to an executive in office Y. The executive in X prepares the document and perhaps attaches a note. This corresponds to the actions of the file transfer application in Figure 5.1. Then the executive in X hands the document to a secretary or administrative assistant (AA). The AA in X puts the document in an envelope and puts Y's address and X's return address on the outside. Perhaps the envelope is also marked "confidential." The AA's actions correspond to the communications service module in Figure 5.1. The AA in X then gives the package to the shipping department. Someone in the shipping department decides how to send the package: mail, UPS, or express courier. The shipping department attaches the appropriate postage or shipping documents to the package and ships it out. The shipping department corresponds to the network access module of Figure 5.1. When the package arrives at Y, a similar layered set of actions occurs. The shipping department at Y receives the package and delivers it to the appropriate AA or secretary based on the name on the package. The AA opens the package and hands the enclosed document to the executive to whom it is addressed.

Another important aspect of a protocol architecture is that modules in different systems communicate with peer modules on the same level. Thus, the file transfer module can focus on what it wants to communicate to a peer file transfer module on the other system (represented by the dotted line between the two modules in Figure 5.1).

In the remainder of this section, we generalize the example of Figure 5.1 to present a simplified protocol architecture. Following that, we look at the real-world example of TCP/IP.

A Three-Layer Model

In very general terms, distributed data communications can be said to involve three agents: applications, computers, and networks. In Chapter 7, we look at several applications; examples include file transfer and electronic mail. These applications execute on computers that typically support multiple simultaneous applications. Computers are connected to networks, and the data to be exchanged are transferred by the network from one computer to another. Thus, the transfer of data from one application to another involves first getting the data to the computer in which the application resides and then getting it to the intended application within the computer.

With these concepts in mind, it appears natural to organize the communication task into three relatively independent layers: network access layer, transport layer, and application layer.

The **network access layer** is concerned with the exchange of data between a computer and the network to which it is attached. The sending computer must provide the network with the address of the destination computer, so that the network may route the data to the appropriate destination. The sending computer may wish to invoke certain services, such as priority, that might be provided by the network. The specific software used at this layer depends on the type of network to be used; different standards have been developed for circuit switching, packet switching, local area networks (LANs), and others. For example, IEEE 802 is a standard that specifies the access to a LAN; this standard is described in Part Three. It makes sense to put those functions having to do with network access into a separate layer. By doing this, the remainder of the communications software, above the network access layer, need not be concerned about the specifics of the network to be used. The same higher-layer software should function properly regardless of the particular network to which the computer is attached.

Regardless of the nature of the applications that are exchanging data, there is usually a requirement that data be exchanged reliably. That is, we would like to be assured that all of the data arrive at the destination application and that the data arrive in the same order in which they were sent. As we shall see, the mechanisms for providing reliability are essentially independent of the nature of the applications. Thus, it makes sense to collect those mechanisms in a common layer shared by all applications; this is referred to as the **transport layer**.

Finally, the **application layer** contains the logic needed to support the various user applications. For each different type of application, such as file transfer, a separate module is needed that is peculiar to that application.

Figures 5.2 and 5.3 illustrate this simple architecture. Figure 5.2 shows three computers connected to a network. Each computer contains software at the network access and transport layers and software at the application layer for one or more applications. For successful communication, every entity in the overall system must have a unique address. In our three-layer model, two levels of addressing are needed. Each computer on the network has a unique network address; this allows the network to deliver data to the proper computer. Each application on a computer has an address that is unique within that computer; this allows the transport layer to support multiple applications at each computer. These latter addresses are known as **service access points** (SAPs), or **ports**, connoting the fact that each application is individually accessing the services of the transport layer.

Figure 5.2 indicates that modules at the same level (peers) on different computers communicate with each other by means of a protocol. An application entity (e.g., a file transfer application) in one computer communicates with an application

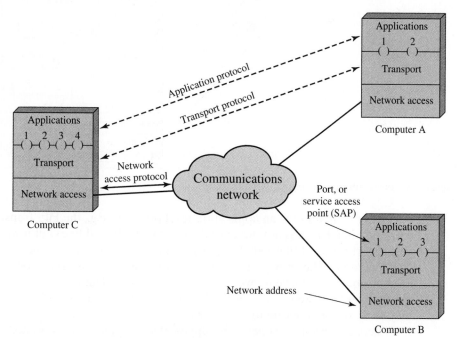

Figure 5.2   Protocol Architectures and Networks

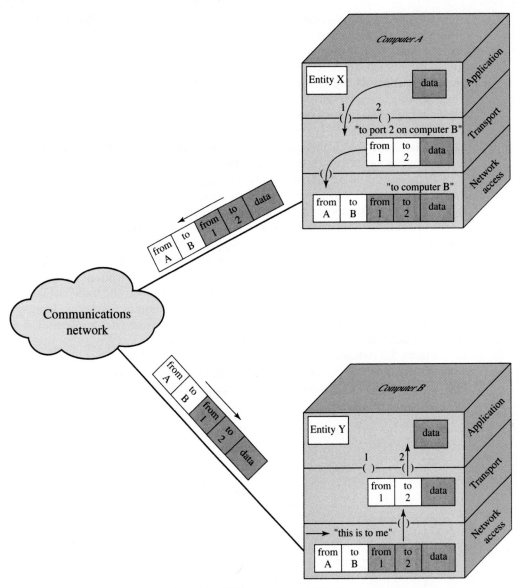

Figure 5.3 Protocols in a Simplified Architecture

in another computer via an application-level protocol (e.g., the File Transfer Protocol). The interchange is not direct (indicated by the dashed line) but is mediated by a transport protocol that handles many of the details of transferring data between two computers. The transport protocol is also not direct but relies on a network-level protocol to achieve network access and to route data through the network to the destination system. At each level, the cooperating peer entities focus on what they need to communicate to each other.

Let us trace a simple operation. Suppose that an application, associated with port 1 at computer A, wishes to send a message to another application, associated with port 2 at computer B. The application at A hands the message over to its transport layer with instructions to send it to port 2 on computer B. The transport layer hands the message over to the network access layer, which instructs the network to send the message to computer B. Note that the network need not be told the identity of the destination port. All that it needs to know is that the data are intended for computer B.

To control this operation, control information, as well as user data, must be transmitted, as suggested in Figure 5.3. Let us say that the sending application generates a block of data and passes this to the transport layer. The transport layer may break this block into two smaller pieces for convenience, as discussed subsequently. To each of these pieces the transport layer appends a transport **header**, containing protocol control information. The combination of data from the next higher layer and control information is known as a **protocol data unit** (PDU); in this case, it is referred to as a transport PDU. Transport PDUs are typically called **segments**. The header in each segment contains control information to be used by the peer transport protocol at computer B. Examples of items that may be stored in this header include the following:

- **Source port:** This indicates that application that sent the data.
- **Destination port:** When the destination transport layer receives the segment, it must know to which application the data are to be delivered.
- **Sequence number:** Because the transport protocol is sending a sequence of segments, it numbers them sequentially so that if they arrive out of order, the destination transport entity may reorder them.
- **Error-detection code:** The sending transport entity may include a code that is a function of the contents of the segment. The receiving transport protocol performs the same calculation and compares the result with the incoming code. A discrepancy results if there has been some error in transmission. In that case, the receiver can discard the segment and take corrective action. This code is also referred to as a **checksum** or **frame check sequence**.

The next step is for the transport layer to hand each segment over to the **network layer**, with instructions to transmit it to the destination computer. To satisfy this request, the network access protocol must present the data to the network with a request for transmission. As before, this operation requires the use of control information. In this case, the network access protocol appends a network access header to the data it receives from the transport layer, creating a network access PDU, typically called a **packet**. Examples of the items that may be stored in the header include the following:

- **Source computer address:** Indicates the source of this packet.
- **Destination computer address:** The network must know to which computer on the network the data are to be delivered.
- **Facilities requests:** The network access protocol might want the network to make use of certain facilities, such as priority.

Note that the transport header is not "visible" at the network access layer; the network access layer is not concerned with the contents of the transport segment.

The network accepts the network packet from A and delivers it to B. The network access module in B receives the packet, strips off the packet header, and transfers the enclosed transport segment to B's transport layer module. The transport layer examines the segment header and, on the basis of the port field in the header, delivers the enclosed record to the appropriate application, in this case the file transfer module in B.

Standardized Protocol Architectures

When communication is desired among computers from different vendors, the software development effort can be a nightmare. Different vendors use different data formats and data exchange protocols. Even within one vendor's product line, different model computers may communicate in unique ways.

Now that computer communications and computer networking are ubiquitous, a one-at-a-time special-purpose approach to communications software development is too costly to be acceptable. The only alternative is for computer vendors to adopt and implement a common set of conventions. For this to happen, standards are needed. Such standards would have two benefits:

- Vendors feel encouraged to implement the standards because of an expectation that, because of wide usage of the standards, their products would be less marketable without them.

- Customers are in a position to require that the standards be implemented by any vendor wishing to propose equipment to them.

Two protocol architectures have served as the basis for the development of interoperable protocol standards: the TCP/IP protocol suite and the OSI reference model. TCP/IP is by far the most widely used interoperable architecture. OSI, though well known, has never lived up to its early promise. There is also a widely used proprietary scheme: IBM's Systems Network Architecture (SNA). Although IBM provides support for TCP/IP, it continues to use SNA, and this latter architecture will remain important for some years to come. The remainder of the chapter looks in some detail at TCP/IP and introduces OSI. SNA is summarized in Appendix F.

5.2   THE TCP/IP PROTOCOL ARCHITECTURE

TCP/IP is a result of protocol research and development conducted on the experimental packet-switched network, ARPANET, funded by the Defense Advanced Research Projects Agency (DARPA), and is generally referred to as the TCP/IP protocol suite. This protocol suite consists of a large collection of protocols that have been issued as Internet standards by the Internet Activities Board (IAB). Appendix B provides a discussion of Internet standards.

TCP/IP Layers

There is no official TCP/IP protocol model as there is in the case of OSI. However, based on the protocol standards that have been developed, we can organize the communication task for TCP/IP into five relatively independent layers:

- Application layer
- Host-to-host, or transport layer

- Internet layer
- Network access layer
- Physical layer

The **application layer** and **transport layer** correspond to the top two layers described in the three-layer model of Section 5.1. At the transport layer, the Transmission Control Protocol (TCP) is the most commonly used protocol.

In those cases where two devices are attached to different networks, procedures are needed to allow data to traverse multiple interconnected networks. This is the function of the internet layer. The **Internet Protocol** (IP) is used at this layer to provide the routing function across multiple networks. This protocol is implemented not only in the end systems but also in routers. A **router** is a device that connects two networks and whose primary function is to relay data from one network to the other on a route from the source to the destination end system.

The **network access layer** was also discussed in our three-layer model. Let us consider the case in which two computers that wish to communicate are both connected to the same network, such as the same local area network (LAN) or the same wide area network (WAN). The sending computer must provide the network with the address of the destination computer, so that the network may route the data to the appropriate destination. In the case in which the two communicating computers are not connected to the same network, the data transfer must occur as a sequence of hops across multiple networks. In this latter case, the network access layer is concerned with access to one network along the route. Thus, from the source computer, the network access layer provides the attached network with the information needed to reach a router that connects this network to the next network on the route to the destination.

The **physical layer** covers the physical interface between a data transmission device (e.g., workstation, computer) and a transmission medium or network. This layer is concerned with specifying the characteristics of the transmission medium, the nature of the signals, the data rate, and related matters.

Operation of TCP/IP

Figure 5.4 indicates how the TCP/IP architecture is configured for communications. Compare this with Figure 5.2. The architectural difference is the inclusion of the internet layer, which allows for multiple networks connected by routers. Some sort of network access protocol, such as the Ethernet protocol, is used to connect a computer to a network. This protocol enables the host to send data across the network to another host or, in the case of a host on another network, to a router. IP is implemented in all end systems and routers. It acts as a relay to move a block of data from one host, through one or more routers, to another host. TCP is implemented only in the end systems; it keeps track of the blocks of data being transferred to assure that all are delivered reliably to the appropriate application.

The figure highlights the levels of addressing of the TCP/IP architecture. Each host on a network must have a unique network address that identifies the host on that network. In addition, each host has a unique global internet address; this allows the data to be delivered to the proper host. This address is used by IP for routing and delivery. Each application within a host must have port number that is unique within the host; this allows the host-to-host protocol (TCP) to deliver data to the proper process.

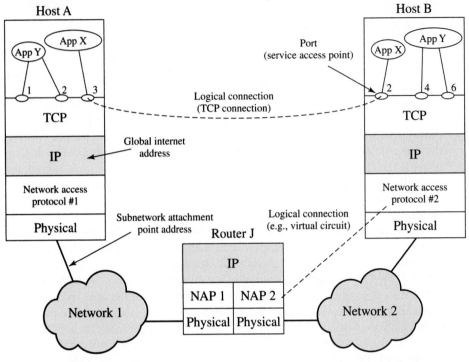

Figure 5.4 TCP\IP Concepts

As was shown in Figure 5.3 for a three-layer architecture, it is relatively easy to trace the operation of the four-layer TCP/IP model. For a transfer between applications in Hosts A and B, control information as well as user data must be transmitted, as suggested in Figure 5.5. Let us say that the sending process generates a block of data and passes this to TCP. TCP appends control information known as the TCP

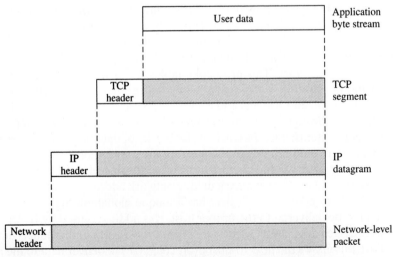

Figure 5.5 Protocol Data Units (PDUs) in the TCP\IP Architecture

header, forming a TCP segment. The control information is to be used by the peer TCP protocol entity at host B.

Next, TCP hands each segment over to IP, with instructions to transmit it to B. These segments must be transmitted across one or more networks and relayed through one or more intermediate routers. This operation, too, requires the use of control information. Thus IP appends a header of control information to each segment to form an **IP datagram**. An example of an item stored in the IP header is the destination host address (in this example, B).

Finally, each IP datagram is presented to the network access layer for transmission across the first network in its journey to the destination. The network access layer appends its own header, creating a packet, or frame. The packet is transmitted across the network to router J. The packet header contains the information that the network needs in order to transfer the data across the network.

At router J, the packet header is stripped off and the IP header examined. On the basis of the destination address information in the IP header, the IP module in the router directs the datagram out across network 2 to B. To do this, the datagram is again augmented with a network access header.

When the data are received at B, the reverse process occurs. At each layer, the corresponding header is removed, and the remainder is passed on to the next higher layer, until the original user data are delivered to the destination process.

TCP and UDP

For most applications running as part of the TCP/IP protocol architecture, the transport layer protocol is TCP. TCP provides a reliable connection for the transfer of data between applications. A connection is simply a temporary logical association between two processes in different systems. For the duration of the connection each process keeps track of segments coming from and going to the other process, in order to regulate the flow of segments and to recover from lost or damaged segments.

Figure 5.6a shows the header format for TCP, which is a minimum of 20 octets, or 160 bits. The Source Port and Destination Port fields identify the applications at the source and destination systems that are using this connection. The Sequence Number, Acknowledgment Number, and Window fields provide flow control and error control. The checksum is a 16-bit frame check sequence used to detect errors in the TCP segment. For the interested reader, Appendix 5A provides more detail.

In addition to TCP, there is one other transport-level protocol that is in common use as part of the TCP/IP protocol suite: the User Datagram Protocol (UDP). UDP does not guarantee delivery, preservation of sequence, or protection against duplication. UDP enables a process to send messages to other processes with a minimum of protocol mechanism. Some transaction-oriented applications make use of UDP; one example is SNMP (Simple Network Management Protocol), the standard network management protocol for TCP/IP networks. Because it is connectionless, UDP has very little to do. Essentially, it adds a port addressing capability to IP. This is best seen by examining the UDP header, shown in Figure 5.6b.

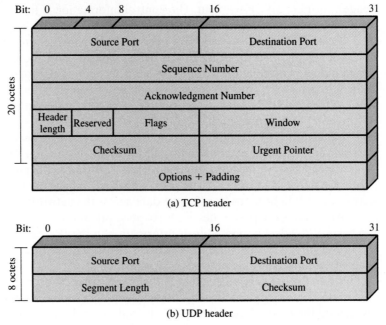

(a) TCP header

(b) UDP header

Figure 5.6 TCP and UDP Headers

IP and IPv6

For decades, the keystone of the TCP/IP protocol architecture has been IP. Figure 5.7a shows the IP header format, which is a minimum of 20 octets, or 160 bits. The header, together with the segment from the transport layer, forms an IP-level PDU referred to as an IP datagram or an IP packet. The header includes 32-bit source and destination addresses. The Header Checksum field is used to detect errors in the header to avoid misdelivery. The Protocol field indicates which higher-layer protocol is using IP, such as TCP or UDP. The ID, Flags, and Fragment Offset fields are used in the fragmentation and reassembly process. For the interested reader, Section 5.4 provides more detail.

In 1995, the Internet Engineering Task Force (IETF), which develops protocol standards for the Internet, issued a specification for a next-generation IP, known then as IPng. This specification was turned into a standard in 1996 known as **IPv6**. IPv6 provides a number of functional enhancements over the existing IP. It is designed to accommodate the higher speeds of today's networks and the mix of data streams, including graphic and video, that are becoming more prevalent. But the driving force behind the development of the new protocol was the need for more addresses. The current IP uses a 32-bit address to specify a source or destination. With the explosive growth of the Internet and of private networks attached to the Internet, this address length became insufficient to accommodate all systems needing addresses. As Figure 5.7b shows, IPv6 includes 128-bit source and destination address fields.

Ultimately, all installations using TCP/IP are expected to migrate from the current IP to IPv6, but this process will take many years, if not decades.

For more detail, see Appendix 5A.

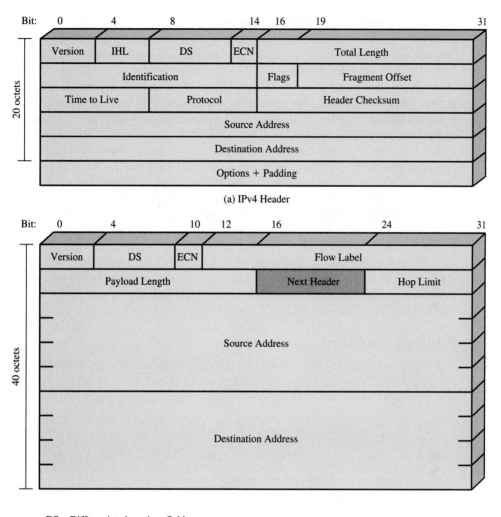

DS = Differentiated services field
ECN = Explicit congestion notification field

Figure 5.7   IP Headers

TCP/IP Applications

A number of applications have been standardized to operate on top of TCP. We mention three of the most common here.

The **Simple Mail Transfer Protocol** (SMTP) supports a basic electronic mail facility, by providing a mechanism for transferring messages among separate hosts. Features of SMTP include mailing lists, return receipts, and forwarding. The SMTP protocol does not specify the way in which messages are to be created; some local editing or native electronic mail facility is required. Once a message is created, SMTP accepts the message and makes use of TCP to send it to an SMTP module on another host. The target SMTP module will make use of a local electronic mail package to store the incoming message in a user's mailbox. SMTP is examined in more detail in Chapter 7

The **File Transfer Protocol** (FTP) is used to send files from one system to another under user command. Both text and binary files are accommodated, and the protocol provides features for controlling user access. When a user wishes to engage in file transfer, FTP sets up a TCP connection to the target system for the exchange of control messages. This connection allows user ID and password to be transmitted and allows the user to specify the file and file actions desired. Once a file transfer is approved, a second TCP connection is set up for the data transfer. The file is transferred over the data connection, without the overhead of any headers or control information at the application level. When the transfer is complete, the control connection is used to signal the completion and to accept new file transfer commands.

SSH (Secure Shell) provides a secure remote logon capability, which enables a user at a terminal or personal computer to logon to a remote computer and function as if directly connected to that computer. SSH also supports file transfer between the local host and a remote server. SSH enables the user and the remote server to authenticate each other; it also encrypts all traffic in both directions. SSH traffic is carried on a TCP connection.

Protocol Interfaces

Each layer in the TCP/IP protocol suite interacts with its immediate adjacent layers. At the source, the application layer makes use of the services of the transport layer and provides data down to that layer. A similar relationship exists at the interface

BGP = Border Gateway Protocol
FTP = File Transfer Protocol
HTTP = Hypertext Transfer Protocol
ICMP = Internet Control Message Protocol
IGMP = Internet Group Management Protocol
IP = Internet Protocol
MIME = Multipurpose Internet Mail Extension

OSPF = Open Shortest Path First
RSVP = Resource ReSerVation Protocol
SMTP = Simple Mail Transfer Protocol
SNMP = Simple Network Management Protocol
SSH = Secure Shell
TCP = Transmission Control Protocol
UDP = User Datagram Protocol

Figure 5.8 Some Protocols in the TCP/IP Protocol Suite

between the transport and internet layers and at the interface of the internet and network access layers. At the destination, each layer delivers data up to the next higher layer.

This use of each individual layer is not required by the architecture. As Figure 5.8 suggests, it is possible to develop protocols that directly invoke the services of any one of the layers. Most applications require a reliable transport protocol and thus make use of TCP. Some special-purpose applications do not need the services of TCP. Some of these applications, such as the Simple Network Management Protocol (SNMP), use another transport protocol known as the User Datagram Protocol (UDP); others may make use of IP directly. Applications or other protocols that do not involve internetworking and that do not need TCP have been developed to invoke the network access layer directly.

5.3 INTERNETWORKING

In most cases, a LAN or WAN is not an isolated entity. An organization may have more than one type of LAN at a given site to satisfy a spectrum of needs. An organization may have multiple LANs of the same type at a given site to accommodate performance or security requirements. And an organization may have LANs at various sites and need them to be interconnected via WANs for central control of distributed information exchange.

Table 5.1 lists some commonly used terms relating to the interconnection of networks, or internetworking. An interconnected set of networks, from a user's point of view, may appear simply as a larger network. However, if each of the constituent networks retains its identity, and special mechanisms are needed for communicating across multiple networks, then the entire configuration is often referred to as an **internet**, and each of the constituent networks as a **subnetwork**. The most important example of an internet is referred to simply as the Internet. As the Internet has evolved from its modest beginnings as a research-oriented packet-switching network, it has served as the basis for the development of internetworking technology and as the model for private internets within organizations. These latter are also referred to as **intranets**. If an organization extends access to its intranet, over the Internet, to selected customers and suppliers, then the resulting configuration is often referred to as an **extranet**.

Each constituent subnetwork in an internet supports communication among the devices attached to that subnetwork; these devices are referred to as **end systems** (ESs). In addition, subnetworks are connected by devices referred to in the ISO documents as **intermediate systems** (ISs). ISs provide a communications path and perform the necessary relaying and routing functions so that data can be exchanged between devices attached to different subnetworks in the internet.

Two types of ISs of particular interest are **bridges** and **routers**. The differences between them have to do with the types of protocols used for the internetworking logic. We look at the role and functions of bridges in Chapter 10. The role and functions of routers were introduced in the context of IP earlier in this chapter. However, because of the importance of routers in the overall networking scheme, it is worth providing additional comment in this section.

Table 5.1 Internetworking Terms

Communication Network
A facility that provides a data transfer service among devices attached to the network.

Internet
A collection of communication networks interconnected by bridges and/or routers.

Intranet
An internet used by a single organization that provides the key Internet applications, especially the World Wide Web. An intranet operates within the organization for internal purposes and can exist as an isolated, self-contained internet, or may have links to the Internet.

Extranet
The extension of a company's intranet out onto the Internet to allow selected customers, suppliers, and mobile workers to access the company's private data and applications via the World Wide Web.

Subnetwork
Refers to a constituent network of an internet. This avoids ambiguity because the entire internet, from a user's point of view, is a single network.

End System (ES)
A device attached to one of the networks of an internet that is used to support end-user applications or services.

Intermediate System (IS)
A device used to connect two networks and permit communication between end systems attached to different networks.

Bridge
An IS used to connect two LANs that use similar LAN protocols. The bridge acts as an address filter, picking up packets from one LAN that are intended for a destination on another LAN and passing those packets on. The bridge does not modify the contents of the packets and does not add anything to the packet. The bridge operates at layer 2 of the OSI model.

Router
An IS used to connect two networks that may or may not be similar. The router employs an internet protocol present in each router and each end system of the network. The router operates at layer 3 of the OSI model.

Routers

Internetworking is achieved by using intermediate systems, or routers, to interconnect a number of independent networks. Essential functions that the router must perform include the following:

1. Provide a link between networks.
2. Provide for the routing and delivery of data between end systems attached to different networks.
3. Provide these functions in such a way as to not require modifications of the networking architecture of any of the attached networks.

Point 3 means that the router must accommodate a number of differences among networks, such as the following:

- **Addressing schemes:** The networks may use different schemes for assigning addresses to devices. For example, an IEEE 802 LAN uses 48-bit binary addresses for each attached device; an ATM network typically uses 15-digit decimal addresses (encoded as 4 bits per digit for a 60-bit address). Some form of global network addressing must be provided, as well as a directory service.

- **Maximum packet sizes:** Packets from one network may have to be broken into smaller pieces to be transmitted on another network, a process known as **fragmentation**. For example, Ethernet imposes a maximum packet size of 1500 bytes; a maximum packet size of 1600 bytes is common on frame relay networks. A packet that is transmitted on a frame relay network and picked up by a router for forwarding on an Ethernet LAN may have to be fragmented into two smaller ones.

- **Interfaces:** The hardware and software interfaces to various networks differ. The concept of a router must be independent of these differences.

- **Reliability:** Various network services may provide anything from a reliable end-to-end virtual circuit to an unreliable service. The operation of the routers should not depend on an assumption of network reliability.

The preceding requirements are best satisfied by an internetworking protocol, such as IP, that is implemented in all end systems and routers.

Internetworking Example

Figure 5.9 depicts a configuration that we will use to illustrate the interactions among protocols for internetworking. In this case, we focus on a server attached to a frame relay WAN and a workstation attached to an IEEE 802 LAN such as Ethernet, with a router connecting the two networks. The router provides a link between the server and the workstation that enables these end systems to ignore the details of the intervening networks. For the frame relay network, what we have referred to as the network access layer consists of a single frame relay protocol. In the case of the IEEE 802 LAN, the network access layer consists of two sublayers: the logical link control (LLC) layer and the medium access control (MAC) layer. For purposes

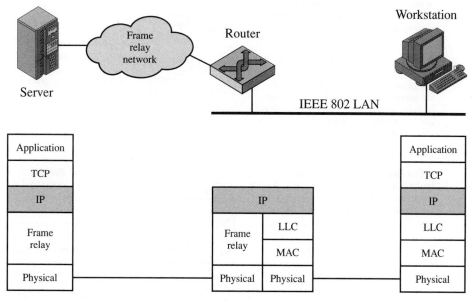

Figure 5.9   Configuration for TCP/IP Example

of this discussion, we need not describe these layers in any detail, but they are explored in subsequent chapters.

Figures 5.10 through 5.12 outline typical steps in the transfer of a block of data, such as a file or a Web page, from the server, through an internet, and ultimately to an application in the workstation. In this example, the message passes through just one router. Before data can be transmitted, the application and transport layers in the server establish, with the corresponding layers in the workstation, the applicable ground rules for a communication session. These include character code to be used, error-checking method, and the like. The protocol at each layer is used for this purpose and then is used in the transmission of the message.

1. Preparing the data. The application protocol prepares a block of data for transmission. For example, an email message (SMTP), a file (FTP), or a block of user input (TELNET).

2. Using a common syntax. If necessary, the data are converted to a form expected by the destination. This may include a different character code, the use of encryption, and/or compression.

3. Segmenting the data. TCP may break the data block into a number of segments, keeping track of their sequence. Each TCP segment includes a header containing a sequence number and a frame check sequence to detect errors.

4. Duplicating segments. A copy is made of each TCP segment, in case the loss or damage of a segment necessitates retransmission. When an acknowledgment is received from the other TCP entity, a segment is erased.

5. Fragmenting the segments. IP may break a TCP segment into a number of datagrams to meet size requirements of the intervening networks. Each datagram includes a header containing a destination address, a frame check sequence, and other control information.

6. Framing. A frame relay header and trailer is added to each IP datagram. The header contains a connection identifier and the trailer contains a frame check sequence.

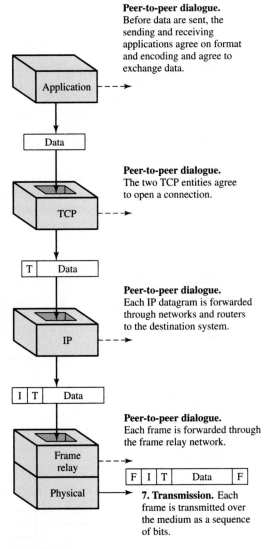

Peer-to-peer dialogue. Before data are sent, the sending and receiving applications agree on format and encoding and agree to exchange data.

Peer-to-peer dialogue. The two TCP entities agree to open a connection.

Peer-to-peer dialogue. Each IP datagram is forwarded through networks and routers to the destination system.

Peer-to-peer dialogue. Each frame is forwarded through the frame relay network.

7. Transmission. Each frame is transmitted over the medium as a sequence of bits.

Figure 5.10   Operation of TCP/IP: Action at Sender

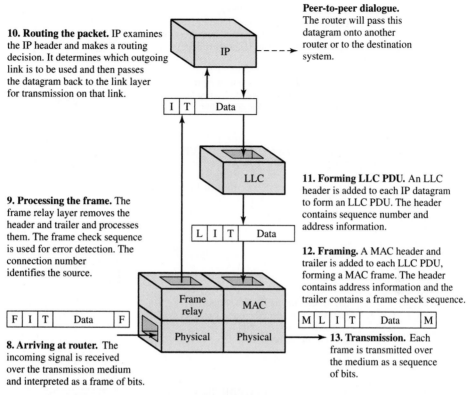

10. Routing the packet. IP examines the IP header and makes a routing decision. It determines which outgoing link is to be used and then passes the datagram back to the link layer for transmission on that link.

Peer-to-peer dialogue. The router will pass this datagram onto another router or to the destination system.

9. Processing the frame. The frame relay layer removes the header and trailer and processes them. The frame check sequence is used for error detection. The connection number identifies the source.

11. Forming LLC PDU. An LLC header is added to each IP datagram to form an LLC PDU. The header contains sequence number and address information.

12. Framing. A MAC header and trailer is added to each LLC PDU, forming a MAC frame. The header contains address information and the trailer contains a frame check sequence.

8. Arriving at router. The incoming signal is received over the transmission medium and interpreted as a frame of bits.

13. Transmission. Each frame is transmitted over the medium as a sequence of bits.

Figure 5.11 Operation of TCP/IP: Action at Router

5.4 THE OSI PROTOCOL ARCHITECTURE

The **Open Systems Interconnection (OSI) reference model** was developed by the International Organization for Standardization (ISO) as a model for a computer protocol architecture and as a framework for developing protocol standards. As with TCP, the OSI model uses the structuring technique known as layering. The communications functions are partitioned into a hierarchical set of layers. Each layer performs a related subset of the functions required to communicate with another system. It relies on the next lower layer to perform more primitive functions and to conceal the details of those functions. It provides services to the next higher layer. Ideally, the layers should be defined so that changes in one layer do not require changes in the other layers. Thus, we have decomposed one problem into a number of more manageable subproblems.

The task of ISO was to define a set of layers and the services performed by each layer. The partitioning should group functions logically and should have enough layers to make each layer manageably small but should not have so many layers that the processing overhead imposed by the collection of layers is burdensome. The resulting reference model has seven layers, which are listed with a brief

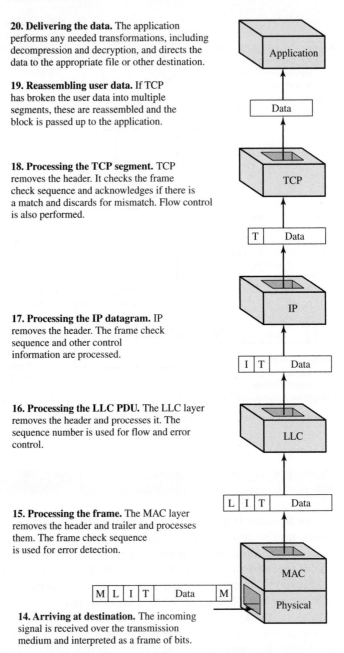

20. Delivering the data. The application performs any needed transformations, including decompression and decryption, and directs the data to the appropriate file or other destination.

19. Reassembling user data. If TCP has broken the user data into multiple segments, these are reassembled and the block is passed up to the application.

18. Processing the TCP segment. TCP removes the header. It checks the frame check sequence and acknowledges if there is a match and discards for mismatch. Flow control is also performed.

17. Processing the IP datagram. IP removes the header. The frame check sequence and other control information are processed.

16. Processing the LLC PDU. The LLC layer removes the header and processes it. The sequence number is used for flow and error control.

15. Processing the frame. The MAC layer removes the header and trailer and processes them. The frame check sequence is used for error detection.

14. Arriving at destination. The incoming signal is received over the transmission medium and interpreted as a frame of bits.

Figure 5.12   Operation of TCP/IP: Action at Receiver

definition in Figure 5.13. The intent of the OSI model is that protocols be developed to perform the functions of each layer.

The designers of OSI assumed that this model and the protocols developed within this model would come to dominate computer communications, eventually replacing proprietary protocol implementations and rival multivendor models such

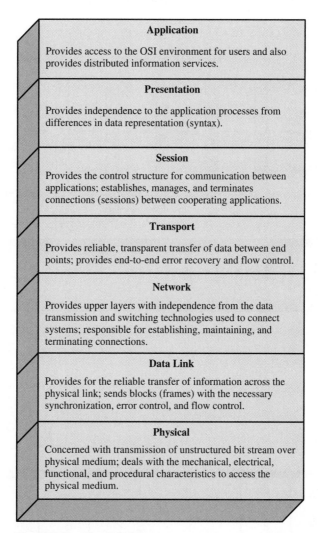

Figure 5.13   The OSI Layers

as TCP/IP. This did not happen. Although many useful protocols have been developed in the context of OSI, the overall seven-layer model has not flourished. Instead, the TCP/IP architecture has come to dominate. There are a number of reasons for this outcome. Perhaps the most important is that the key TCP/IP protocols were mature and well tested at a time when similar OSI protocols were in the development stage. When businesses began to recognize the need for interoperability across networks, only TCP/IP was available and ready to go. Another reason is that the OSI model is unnecessarily complex, with seven layers to accomplish what TCP/IP does with fewer layers.

Figure 5.14 illustrates the OSI architecture. Each system contains the seven layers. Communication is between applications in the two computers, labeled application X

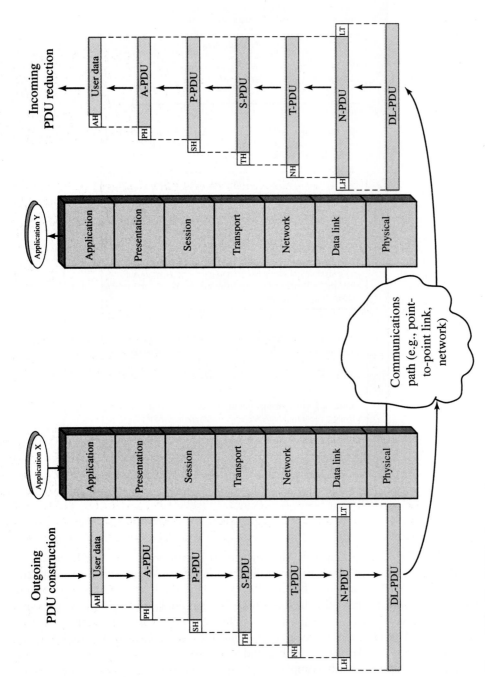

Figure 5.14   The OSI Environment

and application Y in the figure. If application X wishes to send a message to application Y, it invokes the application layer (layer 7). Layer 7 establishes a peer relationship with layer 7 of the target computer, using a layer 7 protocol (application protocol). This protocol requires services from layer 6, so the two layer 6 entities use a protocol of their own, and so on down to the physical layer, which actually transmits bits over a transmission medium.

Note that there is no direct communication between peer layers except at the physical layer. That is, above the physical layer, each protocol entity sends data down to the next lower layer to get the data across to its peer entity. Even at the physical layer, the OSI model does not stipulate that two systems be directly connected. For example, a packet-switched or circuit-switched network may be used to provide the communication link.

Figure 5.14 also highlights the use of PDUs within the OSI architecture. First, consider the most common way in which protocols are realized. When application X has a message to send to application Y, it transfers those data to an application entity in the application layer. A header is appended to the data that contains the required information for the peer layer 7 protocol (encapsulation). The original data, plus the header, are now passed as a unit to layer 6. The presentation entity treats the whole unit as data and appends its own header (a second encapsulation). This process continues down through layer 2, which generally adds both a header and a trailer (e.g., HDLC). This layer 2 unit, called a frame, is then passed by the physical layer onto the transmission medium. When the frame is received by the target system, the reverse process occurs. As the data ascend, each layer strips off the outermost header, acts on the protocol information contained therein, and passes the remainder up to the next layer.

OSI	TCP/IP
Application	Application
Presentation	
Session	
Transport	Transport (host-to-host)
Network	Internet
Data link	Network access
Physical	Physical

Figure 5.15   A Comparison of the OSI and TCP/IP Protocol Architectures

At each stage of the process, a layer may fragment the data unit it receives from the next higher layer into several parts, to accommodate its own requirements. These data units must then be reassembled by the corresponding peer layer before being passed up.

Figure 5.15 shows roughly the correspondence in functionality of the layers of the TCP/IP and OSI architectures.

5.5   VIRTUAL PRIVATE NETWORKS AND IP SECURITY

In today's distributed computing environment, the **virtual private network** (VPN) offers an attractive solution to network managers. In essence, a VPN consists of a set of computers that interconnect by means of a relatively unsecure network and that make use of encryption and special protocols to provide security. At each corporate site, workstations, servers, and databases are linked by one or more local area networks (LANs). The LANs are under the control of the network manager and can be configured and tuned for cost-effective performance. The Internet or some other public network can be used to interconnect sites, providing a cost savings over the use of a private network and offloading the wide area network management task to the public network provider. That same public network provides an access path for telecommuters and other mobile employees to log on to corporate systems from remote sites.

But the manager faces a fundamental requirement: security. Use of a public network exposes corporate traffic to eavesdropping and provides an entry point for unauthorized users. To counter this problem, the manager may choose from a variety of encryption and authentication packages and products. Proprietary solutions raise a number of problems. First, how secure is the solution? If proprietary encryption or authentication schemes are used, there may be little reassurance in the technical literature as to the level of security provided. Second is the question of compatibility. No manager wants to be limited in the choice of workstations, servers, routers, firewalls, and so on by a need for compatibility with the security facility. This is the motivation for the IP Security (IPSec) set of Internet standards.

IPSec

In 1994, the Internet Architecture Board (IAB) issued a report titled "Security in the Internet Architecture" (RFC 1636). The report stated the general consensus that the Internet needs more and better security and identified key areas for security mechanisms. Among these were the need to secure the network infrastructure from unauthorized monitoring and control of network traffic and the need to secure end-user-to-end-user traffic using authentication and encryption mechanisms.

To provide security, the IAB included authentication and encryption as necessary security features in the next-generation IP, which has been issued as IPv6. Fortunately, these security capabilities were designed to be usable both with the current IPv4 and the future IPv6. This means that vendors can begin offering these features now, and many vendors do now have some IPSec capability in their products. The IPSec specification now exists as a set of Internet standards.

Applications of IPSec

IPSec provides the capability to secure communications across a LAN, across private and public WANs, and across the Internet. Examples of its use include the following:

- **Secure branch office connectivity over the Internet:** A company can build a secure virtual private network over the Internet or over a public WAN. This enables a business to rely heavily on the Internet and reduce its need for private networks, saving costs and network management overhead.
- **Secure remote access over the Internet:** An end user whose system is equipped with IP security protocols can make a local call to an Internet service provider (ISP) and gain secure access to a company network. This reduces the cost of toll charges for traveling employees and telecommuters.
- **Establishing extranet and intranet connectivity with partners:** IPSec can be used to secure communication with other organizations, ensuring authentication and confidentiality and providing a key exchange mechanism.
- **Enhancing electronic commerce security:** Even though some Web and electronic commerce applications have built-in security protocols, the use of IPSec enhances that security. IPSec guarantees that all traffic designated by the network administrator is both encrypted and authenticated, adding an additional layer of security to whatever is provided at the application layer.

The principal feature of IPSec that enables it to support these varied applications is that it can encrypt and/or authenticate *all* traffic at the IP level. Thus, all distributed applications, including remote logon, client/server, e-mail, file transfer, Web access, and so on, can be secured.

Figure 5.16 is a typical scenario of IPSec usage. An organization maintains LANs at dispersed locations. Nonsecure IP traffic is conducted on each LAN. For traffic off-site, through some sort of private or public WAN, IPSec protocols are used. These protocols operate in networking devices, such as a router or firewall, that connect each LAN to the outside world. The IPSec networking device will typically encrypt and compress all traffic going into the WAN, and decrypt and decompress traffic coming from the WAN; these operations are transparent to workstations and servers on the LAN. Secure transmission is also possible with individual users who dial into the WAN. Such user workstations must implement the IPSec protocols to provide security.

Benefits of IPSec

Some of the benefits of IPSec are as follows:

- When IPSec is implemented in a firewall or router, it provides strong security that can be applied to all traffic crossing the perimeter. Traffic within a company or workgroup does not incur the overhead of security-related processing.
- IPSec in a firewall is resistant to bypass if all traffic from the outside must use IP and the firewall is the only means of entrance from the Internet into the organization.
- IPSec is below the transport layer (TCP, UDP) and so is transparent to applications. There is no need to change software on a user or server system when

Figure 5.16 An IP Security Scenario

IPSec is implemented in the firewall or router. Even if IPSec is implemented in end systems, upper-layer software, including applications, is not affected.

- IPSec can be transparent to end users. There is no need to train users on security mechanisms, issue keying material on a per-user basis, or revoke keying material when users leave the organization.

- IPSec can provide security for individual users if needed. This is useful for off-site workers and for setting up a secure virtual subnetwork within an organization for sensitive applications.

IPSec Functions

IPSec provides three main facilities: an authentication-only function referred to as Authentication Header (AH), a combined authentication/encryption function called Encapsulating Security Payload (ESP), and a key exchange function. For VPNs, both authentication and encryption are generally desired, because it is important both to (1) assure that unauthorized users do not penetrate the virtual private network and (2) assure that eavesdroppers on the Internet cannot read messages sent over the virtual private network. Because both features are generally desirable, most implementations are likely to use ESP rather than AH. The key exchange function allows for manual exchange of keys as well as an automated scheme.

IPSec is explored in Chapter 19.

APPLICATION NOTE

Practical Guide to Networking

A couple of years ago, an article describing the choices regarding networking protocols would have been markedly different from one written today. There were several models with competing protocol stacks, each of them claiming advantages over the others. While many of these protocols enjoyed some measure of popularity, TCP/IP as the language of the Internet, finally won out. Currently networking architectures are very nearly standardized—at least in terms of the protocols used.

Gone are the days of choosing between various local area network transport mechanisms. Token Ring, FDDI, and LocalTalk have all been supplanted by the different forms of Ethernet. Gone too are the transport protocols that competed with TCP and UDP. Novell protocols (IPX and SPX), Appletalk, and the SNA architectures have all been replaced. At the center of it all we have the Internet Protocol (IP) as king of the hill with IPv6 on the remote horizon. While all of the core protocols may have been chosen for us, we still have plenty of decisions to make. New architectures and methodologies always seem to introduce their own rules and operations. Two of the most significant changes are 802.11 wireless networking and Voice over IP (VoIP).

Wireless networking brings with it the advantages of connectivity without being tethered, faster/lower cost deployment and the connection of geographically remote sites. On the downside, it also brings increased security risks, management headaches, and increased demands on the support staff. That said, before selecting a wireless technology, an organization must first decide whether or not it wants to support a wireless network. Even if the decision is against a WLAN, administrators still have to worry about wireless connections because they are built into so many devices. It turns out that wireless networks are often deployed with or without the aid of the network administrators.

Once the decision to adopt 802.11 is made, we must now decide on which version to use. 802.11b made WLANs popular but it doesn't really stand up to the rigors of a production network. As a result, two new standards; 802.11g and 802.11a, were developed. While they have similar top speeds, they are fundamentally different in their operational frequencies, range, coverage, and design parameters. On paper, 802.11a seems to have all of the advantages because it runs in the less populated 5GHz portion of the spectrum. In fact, 802.11g has enjoyed much more popularity because it has a similar footprint when compared to 802.11b. Yet no matter how popular the WLAN standards get, they have not been designed to replace Ethernet, only supplement it. However, recent developments with the 802.11n version promise speeds that rival the wired infrastructure and, in fact, could supplant end node Ethernet connections.

Previously we mentioned that IP was "king" and nowhere is this more apparent than in VoIP. It turns out that while IP is the language of the Internet, it is also becoming the language of the telephone system. This technology is becoming so cost effective that almost any company can be presented with a viable business case for switching to VoIP. So additional decisions now have to be made regarding the protocols to use when deploying voice on a data network. Once again we have several competing solutions including Session Initiation Protocol (SIP), H.323, and SKINNY. As VoIP gains more and more acceptance we are beginning to see that SIP is enjoying an increasing amount of support from

(Continued)

the communication industry. However, there is a tremendous install base of H.323 and Cisco SKINNY VoIP phones, with more still being deployed. However, each of these has its difficulties; H.323 is an older standard and SKINNY is a Cisco proprietary product.

Even though most vendors and manufacturers have standardized on the TCP/IP networking model, there are still many protocols and technologies to select from when building an entire communication system. Many times, the right choice emerges as more and more organizations adopt a particular set of standards, but we will have to decide for ourselves if it is the right time to jump and which way.

5.6 SUMMARY

The communication functionality required for distributed applications is quite complex. This functionality is generally implemented as a structured set of modules. The modules are arranged in a vertical, layered fashion, with each layer providing a particular portion of the needed functionality and relying on the next lower layer for more primitive functions. Such a structure is referred to as a protocol architecture.

One motivation for the use of this type of structure is that it eases the task of design and implementation. It is standard practice for any large software package to break the functions up into modules that can be designed and implemented separately. After each module is designed and implemented, it can be tested. Then the modules can be combined and tested together. This motivation has led computer vendors to develop proprietary layered protocol architectures. An example of this is the Systems Network Architecture (SNA) of IBM.

A layered architecture can also be used to construct a standardized set of communication protocols. In this case, the advantages of modular design remain. But, in addition, a layered architecture is particularly well suited to the development of standards. Standards can be developed simultaneously for protocols at each layer of the architecture. This breaks down the work to make it more manageable and speeds up the standards-development process. The TCP/IP protocol architecture is the standard architecture used for this purpose. This architecture contains five layers. Each layer provides a portion of the total communications function required for distributed applications. Standards have been developed for each layer. Development work still continues, particularly at the top (application) layer, where new distributed applications are still being defined.

Another standardized architecture is the Open Systems Interconnection (OSI) model. This seven-layer model was intended to be the international standard that would govern all protocol design. However, OSI never achieved market acceptance and has yielded to TCP/IP.

5.7 RECOMMENDED READING AND WEB SITES

[STAL07] provides a detailed description of the TCP/IP model and of the standards at each layer of the model. A very useful reference work on TCP/IP is [PARZ06], which covers the spectrum of TCP/IP-related protocols in a technically concise but thorough fashion (1000 pages).

PARZ06	Parziale, L., et al. *TCP/IP Tutorial and Technical Overview.* IBM Redbook GG24-3376-07, 2006. http://www.redbooks.ibm.com/abstracts/gg243376.html
STAL07	Stallings, W. *Data and Computer Communications, Seventh Edition.* Upper Saddle River, NJ: Prentice Hall, 2004.

Recommended Web sites:

- **Networking Links:** Excellent collection of links related to TCP/IP
- **IPv6 page:** Information about IPv6 and related topics

5.8 KEY TERMS, REVIEW QUESTIONS, AND PROBLEMS

Key Terms

application layer	IP datagram	protocol data unit (PDU)
checksum	IPv4	router
end system	IPv6	service access point (SAP)
extranet	network layer	subnetwork
frame check sequence (FCS)	Open Systems Interconnection	Transmission Control Protocol
header	(OSI)	(TCP)
intermediate system	packet	TCP segment
Internet	physical layer	transport layer
Internet Protocol (IP)	port	User Datagram Protocol
Internetworking	protocol	(UDP)
Intranet	protocol architecture	

Review Questions

5.1 What is the major function of the network access layer?

5.2 What tasks are performed by the transport layer?

5.3 What is a protocol?

5.4 What is a protocol data unit (PDU)?

5.5 What is a protocol architecture?

5.6 What is TCP/IP?

5.7 There are several protocol models that have been developed. Examples of these include SNA, Appletalk, OSI, and TCP/IP as well as more general models such as three-layer models. What model is actually used for communications that travel over the Internet?

5.8 What are some advantages of layering as seen in the TCP/IP architecture?

5.9 Which version of IP is the most prevalent today?

5.10 Does all traffic running on the Internet use TCP?

5.11 Compare the address space between IPv4 and IPv6. How many bits are used in each?

5.12 Large files sent over the network must be broken up into smaller packets. How does the IP layer keep the packets from getting misplaced or collected out of order?

5.13 What is a router?

5.14 Does a router require that all attached layer 2 protocols are the same?

Problems

5.1 Using the layer models in Figure 5.17, describe the ordering and delivery of a pizza, indicating the interactions at each level.

5.2 **a.** The French and Chinese prime ministers need to come to an agreement by telephone, but neither speaks the other's language. Further, neither has on hand a translator that can translate to the language of the other. However, both prime ministers have English translators on their staffs. Draw a diagram similar to Figure 5.17 to depict the situation, and describe the interaction at each layer.

 b. Now suppose that the Chinese prime minister's translator can translate only into Japanese and that the French prime minister has a German translator available. A translator between German and Japanese is available in Germany. Draw a new diagram that reflects this arrangement and describe the hypothetical phone conversation.

5.3 List the major disadvantages of the layered approach to protocols.

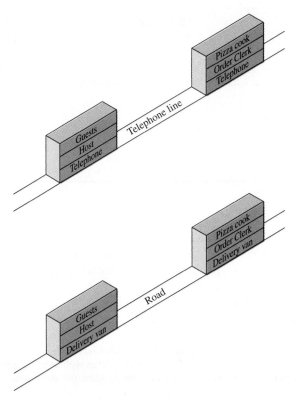

Figure 5.17 Architecture for Problem 5.1

5.4   Assume you have two machines on separate networks that are communicating via e-mail. Machine A is attached to a frame relay network and Machine B is attached to an Ethernet network. For a given set of network conditions (i.e., congestion, path selection, etc.), will an e-mail message transmitted from A to B take the same amount of time and effort as an identical message transmitted from B to A?

5.5   A TCP segment consisting of 1500 bits of data and 160 bits of header is sent to the IP layer, which appends another 160 bits of header. This is then transmitted through two networks, each of which uses a 24-bit packet header. The destination network has a maximum packet size of 800 bits. How many bits, including headers, are delivered to the network layer protocol at the destination?

5.6   Why is UDP needed? Why can't a user program directly access IP?

5.7   IP, TCP, and UDP all discard a packet that arrives with a checksum error and do not attempt to notify the source. Why?

5.8   Why does the TCP header have a header length field while the UDP header does not?

5.9   OSI has seven layers. Design an architecture with eight layers and make a case for it. Design one with six layers and make a case for that.

5.10 The previous version of the TFTP specification, RFC 783, included the following statement:

> All packets other than those used for termination are acknowledged individually unless a timeout occurs.

> The new specification revises this as follows:

> All packets other than duplicate ACKs and those used for termination are acknowledged unless a timeout occurs.

The change was made to fix a problem referred to as the "Sorcerer's Apprentice." Deduce and explain the problem.

5.11 What is the limiting factor in the time required to transfer a file using TFTP?

5.12 This chapter mentions the use of Frame Relay as a specific protocol or system used to connect to a wide area network. Each organization will have a certain collection of services available (like Frame Relay), but this is dependent upon provider provisioning, cost, and customer premises equipment. What are some of the services available to you in your area?

5.13 Ethereal is a free packet sniffer that allows you to capture traffic on a local area network. It can be used on a variety of operating systems and is available at www.ethereal.com. You must also install the WinPcap packet capture driver, which can be obtained from http://winpcap.mirror.ethereal.com/.

After starting a capture from Ethereal, start a TCP-based application like telnet, FTP, or http (Web browser). Can you determine the following from your capture?
  a. Source and destination layer 2 addresses (MAC)
  b. Source and destination layer 3 addresses (IP)
  c. Source and destination layer 4 addresses (port numbers)

5.14 Packet capture software or sniffers can be powerful management and security tools. By using the filtering capability that is built in, you can trace traffic based on several different criteria and eliminate everything else. Use the filtering capability built into Ethereal to do the following;
  a. Capture only traffic coming from your computer's MAC address.
  b. Capture only traffic coming from your computer's IP address.
  c. Capture only UDP-based transmissions.

5.15 Figure 5.8 shows the protocols the operate directly on top of IP. Ping is a program used to test connectivity between machines and is available on all operating systems. Which of the built-in protocols does Ping use and what does the payload data consist of? *Hint:* You can use Ethereal to help you determine the answers.

5.16 What other programs are built into your operating system to help you troubleshoot or provide feedback about your connectivity?

APPENDIX 5A TCP, UDP, AND IP DETAILS

Having looked at the TCP/IP architecture and the basic functionality of internetworking, we can now return to TCP and IP and look at a few details.

Transmission Control Protocol Client-Server Simulator
Transmission Control Protocol Peer-Peer Simulator

TCP

TCP uses only a single type of segment. The header is shown in Figure 5.6a. Because one header must serve to perform all protocol mechanisms, it is rather large, with a minimum length of 20 octets. The fields are as follows:

- **Source Port (16 bits):** Source TCP user.
- **Destination Port (16 bits):** Destination TCP user.
- **Sequence Number (32 bits):** Sequence number of the first data octet in this segment except when the SYN flag is set. If SYN is set, this field contains the initial sequence number (ISN) and the first data octet in this segment has sequence number ISN + 1.
- **Acknowledgment Number (32 bits):** Contains the sequence number of the next data octet that the TCP entity expects to receive from the other TCP entity.
- **Header Length (4 bits):** Number of 32-bit words in the header.
- **Reserved (4 bits):** Reserved for future use.
- **Flags (8 bits):** For each flag, if set to 1, the meaning is as follows:
  CWR: congestion window reduced.
  ECE: ECN-Echo; the CWR and ECE bits, defined in RFC 3168, are used for the explicit congestion notification function,
  URG: urgent pointer field significant.
  ACK: acknowledgment field significant.
  PSH: push function.
  RST: reset the connection.
  SYN: synchronize the sequence numbers.
  FIN: no more data from sender.
- **Window (16 bits):** Flow control credit allocation, in octets. Contains the number of data octets, beginning with the sequence number indicated in the acknowledgment field that the sender is willing to accept.
- **Checksum (16 bits):** The ones complement of the ones complement sum modulo of all the 16-bit words in the segment plus a pseudoheader, described subsequently.[1]

---

[1]Appendix E describes this checksum.

Table 5.2 Some Assigned Port Numbers

5	Remote Job Entry	79	Finger
7	Echo	80	World Wide Web (HTTP)
20	FTP (Default Data)	88	Kerberos
21	FTP (Control)	119	Network News Transfer Protocol
23	TELNET	161	SNMP Agent Port
25	SMTP	162	SNMP Manager Port
43	WhoIs	179	Border Gateway Protocol
53	Domain Name Server	194	Internet Relay Chat Protocol
69	TFTP	389	Lightweight Directory Access Protocol

- **Urgent Pointer (16 bits):** This value, when added to the segment sequence number, contains the sequence number of the last octet in a sequence of urgent data. This allows the receiver to know how much urgent data are coming.
- **Options (Variable):** Zero or more options may be included.

The Source Port and Destination Port specify the sending and receiving users of TCP. There are a number of common users of TCP that have been assigned fixed numbers; some examples are shown in Table 5.2. These numbers should be reserved for that purpose in any implementation. Other port numbers must be arranged by agreement between the two communicating parties.

The Sequence Number and Acknowledgment Number are bound to octets rather than to entire segments. For example, if a segment contains Sequence Number 1001 and includes 600 octets of data, the Sequence Number refers to the first octet in the data field; the next segment in logical order will have Sequence Number 1601. Thus, TCP is logically stream oriented: It accepts a stream of octets from the user, groups them into segments as it sees fit, and numbers each octet in the stream. These numbers are used for flow control, together with the Window field. The scheme works as follows, for a TCP segment traveling from X to Y: The Acknowledgment Number is the number of the next octet expected by X; that is, X has already received data octets up to this number. The Window indicates how many additional octets X is prepared to receive from Y. By limiting the value of Window, X can limit the rate at which data arrive from Y.

The Checksum field is used to detect errors. This field is calculated based on the bits in the entire segment plus a pseudoheader prefixed to the header at the time of calculation (at both transmission and reception). The sender calculates this Checksum and adds it to the segment. The receiver performs the same calculation on the incoming segment and compares that calculation to the Checksum field in that incoming segment. If the two values don't match, then one or more bits have been accidentally altered in transit. The pseudoheader includes the following fields from the IP header: Source and Destination Address and Protocol, plus a segment length field. By including the pseudoheader, TCP protects itself from misdelivery by IP. That is, if IP delivers a segment to the wrong host, even if the segment contains no bit errors, the receiving TCP entity will detect the delivery error.

User Datagram Protocol Simulator

UDP

UDP uses only a single type of segment, shown in Figure 5.6b. The header includes a source port and destination port. The Length field contains the length of the entire UDP segment, including header and data. The checksum is the same algorithm used for TCP and IP. For UDP, the checksum applies to the entire UDP segment plus a pseudoheader prefixed to the UDP header at the time of calculation and which is the same pseudoheader used for TCP. If an error is detected, the segment is discarded and no further action is taken.

The Checksum field in UDP is optional. If it is not used, it is set to zero. However, it should be pointed out that the IP checksum applies only to the IP header and not to the data field, which in this case consists of the UDP header and the user data. Thus, if no checksum calculation is performed by UDP, then no check is made on the user data at either the transport or internet protocol layers.

Internet Protocol Simulator

IPv4

Figure 5.7a shows the IP header format, which is a minimum of 20 octets, or 160 bits. The fields are as follows:

- **Version (4 bits):** Indicates version number, to allow evolution of the protocol; the value is 4.
- **Internet Header Length (IHL) (4 bits):** Length of header in 32-bit words. The minimum value is five, for a minimum header length of 20 octets.
- **DS/ECN (8 bits):** Prior to the introduction of differentiated services, this field was referred to as the **Type of Service** field and specified reliability, precedence, delay, and throughput parameters. This interpretation has now been superseded. The first 6 bits of the TOS field are now referred to as the DS (differentiated services) field, discussed in Chapter 8.
- **Total Length (16 bits):** Total datagram length, including header plus data, in octets.
- **Identification (16 bits):** A sequence number that, together with the source address, destination address, and user protocol, is intended to identify a datagram uniquely. Thus, this number should be unique for the datagram's source address, destination address, and user protocol for the time during which the datagram will remain in the internet.
- **Flags (3 bits):** Only two of the bits are currently defined. The More bit is used for fragmentation and reassembly, as previously explained. The Don't Fragment bit prohibits fragmentation when set. This bit may be useful if it is known that the destination does not have the capability to reassemble fragments. However, if this bit is set, the datagram will be discarded if it exceeds the maximum size of an en route network. Therefore, if the bit is set, it may be advisable to use source routing to avoid networks with small maximum packet size.

Table 5.3 Some Assigned Protocol Numbers

1	Internet Control Message Protocol	17	User Datagram Protocol
2	Internet Group Management Protocol	46	Reservation Protocol (RSVP)
6	Transmission Control Protocol	89	Open Shortest Path First (OSPF)
8	Exterior Gateway Protocol		

- **Fragment Offset (13 bits):** Indicates where in the original datagram this fragment belongs, measured in 64-bit units. This implies that fragments other than the last fragment must contain a data field that is a multiple of 64 bits in length.

- **Time to Live (8 bits):** Specifies how long, in seconds, a datagram is allowed to remain in the internet. Every router that processes a datagram must decrease the TTL by at least one, so the TTL is somewhat similar to a hop count.

- **Protocol (8 bits):** Indicates the next-higher-level protocol that is to receive the data field at the destination; thus, this field identifies the type of the next header in the packet after the IP header.

- **Header Checksum (16 bits):** An error-detecting code applied to the header only. Because some header fields may change during transit (e.g., time to live, fragmentation-related fields), this is reverified and recomputed at each router. The checksum is formed by taking the ones complement of the 16-bit ones complement addition of all 16-bit words in the header. For purposes of computation, the checksum field is itself initialized to a value of zero.[2]

- **Source Address (32 bits):** Coded to allow a variable allocation of bits to specify the network and the end system attached to the specified network, as discussed subsequently.

- **Destination Address (32 bits):** Same characteristics as source address.

- **Options (variable):** Encodes the options requested by the sending user.

- **Padding (variable):** Used to ensure that the datagram header is a multiple of 32 bits in length.

- **Data (variable):** The data field must be an integer multiple of 8 bits in length. The maximum length of the datagram (data field plus header) is 65,535 octets.

The protocol field indicates to which IP user the data in this IP datagram are to be delivered. Although TCP is the most common user of IP, other protocols can access IP. For common protocols that use IP, specific protocol numbers have been assigned and should be used. Table 5.3 lists some of these assignments.

IPv6

The IPv6 header has a fixed length of 40 octets, consisting of the following fields (Figure 5.7b):

- **Version (4 bits):** Internet protocol version number; the value is 6.

- **DS/ECN (8 bits):** Available for use by originating nodes and/or forwarding routers for differentiated services and congestion functions, as described for the IPv4 DS/ECN field.

---

[2]Appendix D describes this checksum.

- **Flow Label (20 bits):** May be used by a host to label those packets for which it is requesting special handling by routers within a network; discussed subsequently.
- **Payload Length (16 bits):** Length of the remainder of the IPv6 packet following the header, in octets. In other words, this is the total length of all of the extension headers plus the transport-level PDU.
- **Next Header (8 bits):** Identifies the type of header immediately following the IPv6 header; this will either be an IPv6 extension header or a higher-layer header, such as TCP or UDP.
- **Hop Limit (8 bits):** The remaining number of allowable hops for this packet. The hop limit is set to some desired maximum value by the source and decremented by 1 by each node that forwards the packet. The packet is discarded if Hop Limit is decremented to zero. This is a simplification over the processing required for the Time to Live field of IPv4. The consensus was that the extra effort in accounting for time intervals in IPv4 added no significant value to the protocol. In fact, IPv4 routers, as a general rule, treat the Time to Live field as a hop limit field.
- **Source Address (128 bits):** The address of the originator of the packet.
- **Destination Address (128 bits):** The address of the intended recipient of the packet. This may not in fact be the intended ultimate destination if a Routing header is present, as explained subsequently.

Although the IPv6 header is longer than the mandatory portion of the IPv4 header (40 octets versus 20 octets), it contains fewer fields (8 versus 12). Thus, routers have less processing to do per header, which should speed up routing.

APPENDIX 5B THE TRIVIAL FILE TRANSFER PROTOCOL

This appendix provides an overview of the Internet standard Trivial File Transfer Protocol (TFTP). Our purpose is to give the reader some flavor for the elements of a protocol.

Trivial File Transfer Protocol Simulator

Introduction to TFTP

TFTP is far simpler than the Internet standard File Transfer Protocol (FTP). There are no provisions for access control or user identification, so TFTP is only suitable for public access file directories. Because of its simplicity, TFTP is easily and compactly implemented. For example, some diskless devices use TFTP to download their firmware at boot time.

TFTP runs on top of UDP. The TFTP entity that initiates the transfer does so by sending a read or write request in a UDP segment with a destination port of 69 to the target system. This port is recognized by the target UDP module as the identifier

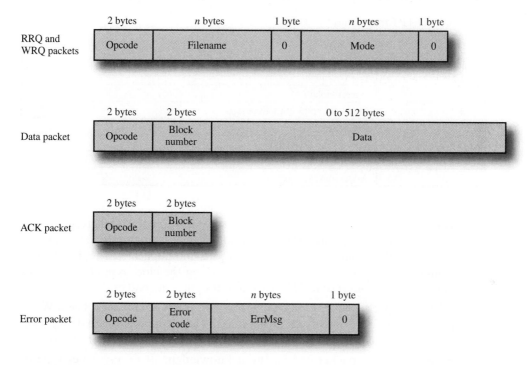

Figure 5.18 TFTP Packet Formats

of the TFTP module. For the duration of the transfer, each side uses a transfer identifier (TID) as its port number.

TFTP Packets

TFTP entities exchange commands, responses, and file data in the form of packets, each of which is carried in the body of a UDP segment. TFTP supports five types of packets (Figure 5.18); the first two bytes contain an opcode that identifies the packet type:

- **RRQ:** The read request packet requests permission to transfer a file from the other system. The packet includes a file name, which is a sequence of ASCII[3] bytes terminated by a zero byte. The zero byte is the means by which the receiving TFTP entity knows when the file name is terminated. The packet also includes a mode field, which indicates whether the data file is to be interpreted as a string of ASCII bytes or as raw 8-bit bytes of data.

- **WRQ:** The write request packet requests permission to transfer a file to the other system.

---

[3]ASCII is the American Standard Code for Information Interchange, a standard of the American National Standards Institute. It designates a unique 7-bit pattern for each letter, with an eighth bit used for parity. ASCII is equivalent to the International Reference Alphabet (IRA), defined in ITU-T Recommendation T.50. Appendix D provides a description and table of the IRA code.

Table 5.4   TFTP Error Codes

Value	Meaning
0	Not defined, see error message (if any)
1	File not found
2	Access violation
3	Disc full or allocation exceeded
4	Illegal TFTP operation
5	Unknown transfer ID
6	File already exists
7	No such user

- **Data:** The block numbers on data packets begin with one and increase by one for each new block of data. This convention enables the program to use a single number to discriminate between new packets and duplicates. The data field is from zero to 512 bytes long. If it is 512 bytes long, the block is not the last block of data; if it is from zero to 511 bytes long, it signals the end of the transfer.

- **ACK:** This packet is used to acknowledge receipt of a data packet or a WRQ packet. An ACK of a data packet contains the block number of the data packet being acknowledged. An ACK of a WRQ contains a block number of zero.

- **Error:** An error packet can be the acknowledgment of any other type of packet. The error code is an integer indicating the nature of the error (Table 5.4). The error message is intended for human consumption, and should be in ASCII. Like all other strings, it is terminated with a zero byte.

All packets other than duplicate ACKs (explained subsequently) and those used for termination are to be acknowledged. Any packet can be acknowledged by an error packet. If there are no errors, then the following conventions apply: A WRQ or a data packet is acknowledged by an ACK packet. When a RRQ is sent, the other side responds (in the absence of error) by beginning to transfer the file; thus, the first data block serves as an acknowledgment of the RRQ packet. Unless a file transfer is complete, each ACK packet from one side is followed by a data packet from the other, so that the data packet functions as an acknowledgment. An error packet can be acknowledged by any other kind of packet, depending on the circumstance.

Figure 5.19 shows a TFTP data packet in context. When such a packet is handed down to UDP, UDP adds a header to form a UDP segment. This is then passed to IP, which adds an IP header to form an IP datagram.

Overview of a Transfer

The example illustrated in Figure 5.20 is of a simple file transfer operation from A to B. No errors occur and the details of the option specification are not explored.

The operation begins when the TFTP module in system A sends a write request (WRQ) to the TFTP module in system B. The WRQ packet is carried as the body of a UDP segment. The write request includes the name of the file (in this case, XXX) and a mode of octet, or raw data. In the UDP header, the destination port number is 69, which alerts the receiving UDP entity that this message is intended for

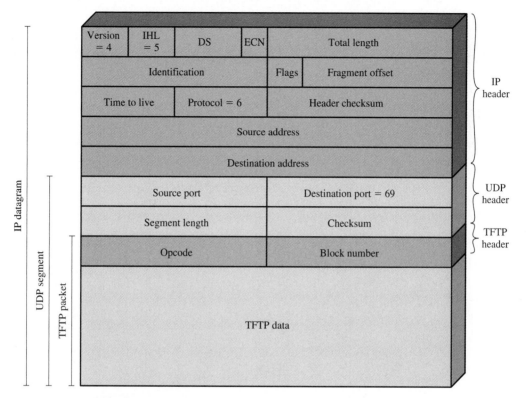

Figure 5.19 A TFTP Packet in Context

the TFTP application. The source port number is a TID selected by A, in this case 1511. System B is prepared to accept the file and so responds with an ACK with a block number of 0. In the UDP header, the destination port is 1511, which enables the UDP entity at A to route the incoming packet to the TFTP module, which can match this TID with the TID in the WRQ. The source port is a TID selected by B for this file transfer, in this case 1660.

Following this initial exchange, the file transfer proceeds. The transfer consists of one or more data packets from A, each of which is acknowledged by B. The final data packet contains less than 512 bytes of data, which signals the end of the transfer.

Errors and Delays

If TFTP operates over a network or internet (as opposed to a direct data link), it is possible for packets to be lost. Because TFTP operates over UDP, which does not provide a reliable delivery service, there needs to be some mechanism in TFTP to deal with lost packets. TFTP uses the common technique of a timeout mechanism. Suppose that A sends a packet to B that requires an acknowledgment (i.e., any packet other than duplicate ACKs and those used for termination). When A has transmitted the packet, it starts a timer. If the timer expires before the acknowledgment is received from B, A retransmits the same packet. If in fact the original packet

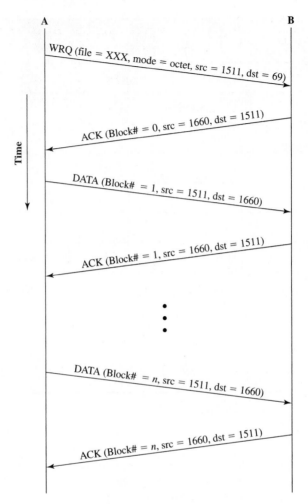

Figure 5.20 Example TFTP Operation

was lost, then the retransmission will be the first copy of this packet received by B. If the original packet was not lost but the acknowledgment from B was lost, then B will receive two copies of the same packet from A and simply acknowledges both copies. Because of the use of block numbers, this causes no confusion. The only exception to this rule is for duplicate ACK packets. The second ACK is ignored.

Syntax, Semantics, and Timing

In Section 5.1, it was mentioned that the key features of a protocol can be classified as syntax, semantics, and timing. These categories are easily seen in TFTP. The formats of the various TFTP packets form the **syntax** of the protocol. The **semantics** of the protocol are shown in the definitions of each of the packet types and the error codes. Finally, the sequence in which packets are exchanged, the use of block numbers, and the use of timers are all aspects of the **timing** of TFTP.

CASE STUDY

FLORIDA DEPARTMENT OF MANAGEMENT SERVICES— PART ONE

By the early 1990s, the Florida Department of Management Service (DMS) had built up a large information systems network that served state government agencies in 10 regional sites and connected these to the data center in Tallahassee. The network was based on the use of the proprietary Systems Network Architecture (SNA) from IBM and a mainframe at the data center that housed most of the applications.

Although relatively happy with the SNA operation, DMS saw a need to expand applications and services by providing TCP/IP capability and Internet access. The goal was met in a remarkably short time. Over the course of 30 months, DMS built a statewide TCP/IP network, began offering Internet services to local and state agencies, and created a suite of Internet applications that will ultimately move personnel, accounting, and billing systems online [JOHN96]. To complete the success story, DMS managed to accomplish all that while saving the state of Florida more than $4 million. The breakdown is shown in Table II.1.

The aim of this upgrade was to exploit the Internet. Internet connectivity, together with key Internet applications such as the Web, could make it easier for agencies across the state to communicate with each other, with suppliers, and with users, thereby improving employee productivity.

THE IP INFRASTRUCTURE

The first step was to build an IP infrastructure. The then-current configuration, based on SNA, made heavy use of telephone company (telco)–supplied equipment and services. DMS considered the possibility of outsourcing the IP capability but rejected this for the following reasons:

1. None of the telcos had a router-based service at that time, which meant DMS would have to wait for the carrier to build its own network.

2. DMS wanted to select the routers. The telcos wouldn't purchase the products picked by DMS because they did not fit in with their plans. Finally, a regulatory prohibition against colocation meant that user-owned equipment couldn't be installed at telco central offices.

3. The existing SNA network could easily be adapted to TCP/IP.

Table II.1 DMS Cost Breakdown

What Was Spent		What Was Not Spent	
Personnel	$450,000	Terminal upgrades	$150,000
Application development	$300,000	Mainframe application development	$1,000,000
Software (including Web software, databases, and development tools)	$850,000	Mainframe hardware upgrades	$6,000,000
		Mainframe software upgrades	$600,000
Hardware (servers, routers, telco services)	$1,525,000		
Maintenance	$450,000		
TOTAL	**$3,575,000**	**TOTAL**	**$7,750,000**

The existing configuration had been put in place to allow some 6000 users throughout the state to access mainframe application in Tallahassee. SNA network control processors (NCPs) in 10 cities were linked via T-1 (1.544 Mbps) and T-3 (45 Mbps) lines to a communications controller on a token ring LAN in the DMS data center. The communications controller handled SNA traffic into and out of the mainframe. The token ring also supported SNA terminals, personal computers, and other equipment.

To transform the SNA backbone into a router network, all DMS had to do, in essence, was deploy routers at each site, connect the boxes, and link them to a central-site router at the data center (Figure II.1). Put that way, it sounds easy, and in fact the installation and startup went remarkably smoothly.

DMS chose the Cisco 7000 as its backbone router, with one deployed at each of the 10 regional sites. The Cisco gear came with strong network management and could be booted and configured centrally. At each site the Cisco router and the NCP are hooked to a digital access cross-connect switch (DACS). This switch segregates SNA from TCP/IP traffic and directs it accordingly. The DACS now provides the T-1/T-3 link to the SNA communications controller at the data center. In addition, each DACS is connected to the DACS at each of the nine other regional centers to create a mesh for IP traffic. Finally, there is a link from each DACS to a router at the data center.

At the regional center, SNA traffic is handled as before from IBM 3270 terminals. This traffic only goes from the regional center to the mainframe at the data center. For connection to the IP backbone and the Internet applications, each regional center is equipped with Cisco 2000 routers to connect workstations, personal computers, and servers via LANs.

At the data center, there is a high-capacity Cisco 2000 router that has a direct leased link to each of the 10 regional centers. This router is also connected to the Internet and provides the entry point for the entire far-flung DMS network into the Internet. Finally, there are several Network Systems Corp. routers that connect the data center to the Tallahassee MAN, which is an FDDI ring owned and operated by Sprint Corporation. The MAN gives agencies located throughout Tallahassee access to the data center and to each other.

Figure II.1 Network Configurations for Florida Department of Management Services

THE APPLICATIONS

Once the IP infrastructure was in place, DMS began to add applications. The first, and still the most popular, application was a client/server employment system. The original system stored information about some 125,000 state employees on the mainframe. About 1200 users throughout the state accessed it over the SNA network. Although the system was secure and reliable, services were slow and the interface clumsy. The applications around the database had been developed and installed in the early 1980s and were batch-mode with fixed-transaction access. Users couldn't configure their own requests and searches on the fly. If they wanted anything out of the ordinary, they had to contact mainframe programmers, who might take days or weeks to develop what was needed. The new application makes use of a UNIX server at the data center that is hooked to the mainframe and downloads the employee database at least weekly to store in its own server database. Users at workstations at the various agencies and centers access the server over the IP network running an application called Copesview.

Another client/server application that generates a lot of traffic over the IP network is Spursview, a purchasing application. Like Copesview, it was adapted from a mainframe application, SPURS (Statewide Purchasing System). SPURS, which was used by roughly 4000 employees, stored information on the mainframe about products purchased by the site, including vendor, model number, and price. Here again, users were limited as to the type of searches they could perform. With Spursview, users gained a variety of new capabilities, such as wild-card searches on any parameters (data of purchase, vendor, type of product, etc.). They also can create graphs and bar charts and import data directly into PC-based spreadsheets.

INTRANET AND INTERNET APPLICATIONS

The data center maintains a link to the Internet through which all traffic between the data center's IP network and the Internet pass. This link is equipped with a firewall that prevents unauthorized access.

With the Internet link and the IP network up, DMS was in a position to offer Internet access to state employees as well as to set up Web services for both intranet and Internet access. Like the servers in the client/server configuration, the Web server has a link to the mainframe and is able to construct databases accessible from Web browsers.

One of the most popular Web-based applications is a job-posting service that lets users search for vacancies within the state system by location, salary ranges, and type of work. The state has about 8000 job vacancies on any given day. Applicants can fill out an online job application and store it for multiple submissions. This application averages about 100,000 hits per week.

Another well-used site eliminates the need for state employees to process information regarding government contracts and suppliers. Previously, when a vendor won a bid, it submitted pricing and product data on floppy discs. The DMS employed several people full time just to review that information, format it, and enter it onto the mainframe. That information is now available on the Web. Users can access this information on the DMS Web server and on Web servers at vendor sites. For example, users can search for contracted suppliers that offer computers priced below $2000. The search generates a list of names, each of which is a Web link. Because the data reside on the vendors' Web servers, it is up to the suppliers, not the DMS, to make sure all data are accurate and up to date.

DMS is also working on an online purchasing system running over the Web. Users not only would be able to view vendor information but also could order products online. This application will take a lot of coordination, because it involves the purchasing department, comptroller's office, and accounting. It also involves authenticating users to ensure they are authorized to make purchases.

DMS has not neglected those who pay state employees' salaries: the citizens of Florida. The Web service available to the public is called the Florida Community Network (FCN), and it has been a success story and a model for other states [REGE96]. The FCN is currently averaging a million hits per month. Online access to information can in many cases eliminate two or three layers of bureaucracy and provide a self-service connection to the government. For example, one of the projects under development is automatic fishing and gaming licensing. Mrs. X in Palm Beach wants to go fishing but knows she needs a license. She logs on to the FCN site, chooses the search option, and types "fishing." Within seconds, a form appears that lets Mrs. X apply and pay for a license from the comfort of her home. She fills out the form, submits it, and moments later a license is e-mailed to her. No clerks, no lines, no trips to the Office of the Tax Collector or a sporting goods store.

Yet another popular Web service is the Statewide Telephone Directory, which includes listings for state and local government, universities, community colleges, and school boards. DMS has also worked with the state Board of Regents to set up a distance learning service, which makes use of the DMS networking facilities [MADA98].

In 2007, the DMS network went through another major overhaul and was re-named MyFloridaNet. This new network retains the fundamental TCP/IP and net-working architecture with many upgrades. We examine MyFloridaNet in Case Study VI.

The DMS Web site is undergoing constant evolution and refinement. It is located at http://dms.myflorida.com.

Discussion Points

1. What security mechanisms are needed to protect the DMS systems from both state employees and users accessing over the Internet?

2. Visit the DMS Web site and list the major services found there. Discuss the relative merits of each.

3. Suggest improvements to existing services and suggest new services that should be added.

CHAPTER 6

CLIENT/SERVER AND INTRANET COMPUTING

6.1 The Growth of Client/Server Computing
What Is Client/Server Computing?
The Evolution of Client/Server Computing

6.2 Client/Server Applications
Database Applications
Classes of Client/Server Applications
Three-Tier Client/Server Architecture

6.3 Middleware
Middleware Architecture
Message Passing
Remote Procedure Calls
Object-Oriented Mechanisms

6.4 Intranets
Intranet Web
Other Intranet Technologies

6.5 Extranets

6.6 Service-Oriented Architecture

6.7 Summary

6.8 Recommended Reading and Web Sites

6.9 Key Terms, Review Questions, and Problems

Chapter Objectives

After reading this chapter, you should be able to

♦ Discuss the reasons for the growing interest in and availability of client/server computing systems.

♦ Describe the features and characteristics of client/server computing.

♦ Describe the architecture of client/server applications.

♦ Explain the role of middleware in client/server systems.

♦ Assess the networking requirements and implications of client/server computing.

♦ Define *intranet* and contrast it with *Internet*.

♦ Compare client/server and intranet approaches to distributed computing.

♦ List the benefits of and communications options for extranets.

Most distributed applications in a business environment involve a style of distributed computing known as client/server computing. We begin this chapter with a general description of the client/server philosophy and the implications for businesses. Next, we examine the nature of the application support provided by the client/server architecture. Then we look at the rather fuzzy but very important concept of middleware.

Following this survey of client/server computing, we examine a more recent approach referred to as an intranet. An intranet uses Internet technology and applications (especially Web-based applications) to provide in-house support for distributed applications. Next, this chapter covers the concept of the extranet. Finally, we examine the increasingly important service oriented architecture (SOA).

6.1 THE GROWTH OF CLIENT/SERVER COMPUTING

The concept of client/server computing, and related concepts, has become increasingly important in information technology systems. This section begins with a description of the general nature of client/server computing and then looks at how it has evolved.

What Is Client/Server Computing?

As with other new waves in the computer field, client/server computing comes with its own set of jargon words. Table 6.1 lists some of the terms that are commonly found in descriptions of client/server products and applications.

Figure 6.1 attempts to capture the essence of these themes. **Client** machines are typically single-user PCs or workstations that provide a highly user-friendly interface to the end user. The client-based station generally presents the type of graphical interface that is most comfortable to users, including the use of windows and a mouse. Common examples of such interfaces are provided by Microsoft Windows and Macintosh OS X. Client-based applications are tailored for ease of use and include such familiar tools as the spreadsheet.

Table 6.1 Client/Server Terminology

Application Programming Interface (API) A set of function and call programs that allow clients and servers to intercommunicate.
Client A networked information requester, usually a PC or workstation, that can query database and/or other information from a server.
Middleware A set of drivers, APIs, or other software that improves connectivity between a client application and a server.
Relational Database A database in which information access is limited to the selection of rows that satisfy all search criteria.
Server A computer, usually a high-powered workstation or a mainframe, that houses information for manipulation by networked clients.
Structured Query Language (SQL) A language developed by IBM and standardized by ANSI for addressing, creating, updating, or querying relational databases.

Each **server** in the client/server environment provides a set of shared user services to the clients. The most common type of server is the database server, usually controlling a relational database. The server enables many clients to share access to the same database and enables the use of a high-performance computer system to manage the database.

In addition to clients and servers, the third essential ingredient of the client/server environment is the **network**. Client/server computing is distributed computing. Users,

LAN or WAN
or Internet

Server

Workstation
(client)

Figure 6.1 Generic Client/Server Environment

applications, and resources are distributed in response to business requirements and linked by a single LAN or WAN or by an internet.

There are a number of characteristics that together make client/server distinct from ordinary distributed processing:

- There is a heavy reliance on bringing user-friendly applications to the user on his or her system. This gives the user a great deal of control over the timing and style of computer usage and gives department-level managers the ability to be responsive to their local needs.

- Although the applications are dispersed, there is an emphasis on centralizing corporate databases and many network management and utility functions. This enables corporate management to maintain overall control of the total capital investment in computing and information systems and enables corporate management to provide interoperability so that systems are tied together. At the same time, it relieves individual departments and divisions of much of the overhead of maintaining sophisticated computer-based facilities but enables them to choose just about any type of machine and interface they need to access data and information.

- There is an emphasis on open and modular systems. This means that the user has greater choice in selecting products and in mixing equipment from a number of vendors.

- Networking is fundamental to the operation. Thus, network management and network security have a high priority in organizing and operating information systems.

Client/server computing is, on the one hand, a natural solution from the product point of view, because it exploits the declining cost of microcomputers and networks. On the other hand, client/server computing may be the ideal choice to support the direction that business is taking in the organization of work.

This latter point deserves elaboration. The success of client/server computing in the marketplace is not just a matter of new jargon on top of old solutions. Client/server computing is indeed a relatively new technical approach to distributed computing. But beyond that, client/server computing is responsive to, and indeed creates the conditions for, new ways of organizing business. Let us consider two significant trends in industry that illustrate the point.

The first of these is the permanent shedding of jobs by companies in an effort to downsize and streamline for success in a fiercely competitive market. Why have companies needed to shed jobs to remain competitive and how have they managed to increase productivity so fast as to have sales growth without payroll growth? The cost per employee is rising rapidly, with wage increases coupled to mandated benefits increases. At the same time, business equipment, especially computer and network equipment and services, has suffered only modest cost increases. This has led, as one might expect, to substantial increases in investment in computers and other information technology in an effort to compensate for a smaller employee base.

This trend occurs in small as well as large businesses and is affecting middle managers as well as clerical staff. What client/server computing provides is a way of automating tasks and eliminating barriers to information, which allows companies to eliminate layers of management and to add work without adding workers.

Another trend that illustrates the effectiveness of client/server computing is the so-called internal market. This is a business strategy that affects primarily large businesses, which seek to combine entrepreneurial zeal with corporate might to have the best of both worlds: the economies of scale of a large business with the agility of a small business. In an era of rapid technological and market changes, many large companies are tearing down traditional functional hierarchies and replacing them with collections of relatively independent business units. These units must then compete with external companies for business from other units. In an internal market, every business unit operates as an independent company. Each one decides to buy its inputs from internal sources (other units of the corporation) or from outside suppliers. Even traditional "overhead" departments, such as information systems, accounting, and legal, must sell their services to other units and compete with outside providers.

This dose of internal competition is designed to correct the flaws of the traditional way of doing business. As Jay Forrester of MIT observes [ROTH93], "American corporations are some of the largest socialist bureaucracies in the world. They have central planning, central ownership of capital, central allocation of resources, subjective evaluation of people, lack of internal competition, and decisions made at the top in response to political pressures."

Internal markets have already transformed some companies and promise to have a major impact on others. But, until recently, there has been a formidable obstacle to implementing such a scheme. In a large company, the use of an internal market can result in thousands of teams making agreements among themselves and with outsiders. Somehow, the ledgers for all the resulting transactions have to be reconciled. Analyses of this situation have suggested that the cost and complexity of bookkeeping would overwhelm the benefits of an internal market. The evolution of computing technology has overcome this obstacle. Today, a number of multinationals are using the latest database software running on client/server networks to set up internal markets.

The Evolution of Client/Server Computing

The way in which client/server computing has evolved is worth noting. This style of organizing computer resources began at the workgroup and departmental level. Departmental managers found that relying on central, mainframe-based applications hindered their ability to respond rapidly to business demands. Application development time within the central IS shop was too slow, and the results were not tailored to the specific needs of the department. The deployment of PCs enabled workers to have computing power and data at their command and enabled department-level managers to select needed applications quickly.

However, in a pure PC environment, cooperation among users was difficult. Even within the department, there needed to be a departmental-level database and departmental formatting and data usage standards. The solution to these requirements is a departmental-level client/server architecture. Typically, such an architecture involves a single LAN, a number of PCs, and one or two servers.

The success of departmental-level client/server systems paved the way for the introduction of enterprise-wide client/server computing. Ideally, such an architecture enables the integration of departmental and IS organization resources, allowing for applications that give individual users ready but controlled access to corporate databases. The dominant theme of such architectures is the reestablishment of control over data by the central IS organization but in the context of a distributed computing system.

6.2   CLIENT/SERVER APPLICATIONS

The central feature of a client/server architecture is the allocation of application-level tasks between clients and servers. Figure 6.2 illustrates the general case. In both client and server, the basic software is an operating system running on the hardware platform. The platforms and the operating systems of client and server may differ. Indeed, there may be a number of different types of client platforms and operating systems and a number of different types of server platforms and operating systems in a single environment. As long as a particular client and server share the same communications protocols and support the same applications, these lower-level differences are irrelevant.

It is the communications software that enables client and server to interoperate. The principal example of such software is TCP/IP. Of course, the point of all this support software (communications and operating system) is to provide a base for distributed applications. Ideally, the actual functions performed by the application can be split up between client and server in a way that optimizes platform and network resources and that optimizes the ability of users to perform various tasks and to cooperate with one another in using shared resources. In some cases, these requirements dictate that the bulk of the applications software executes at the server, while in other cases, most of the application logic is located at the client.

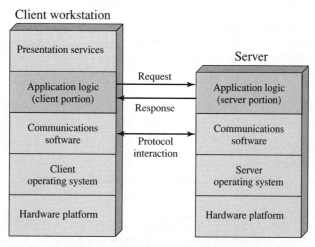

Figure 6.2   Generic Client/Server Architecture

An essential factor in the success of a client/server environment is the way in which the user interacts with the system as a whole. Thus, the design of the user interface to the client machine is critical. In most client/server systems, there is heavy emphasis on providing a **graphical user interface (GUI)** that is easy to use, easy to learn, yet powerful and flexible. Thus, we can think of a presentation services module[1] in the client workstation that is responsible for providing a user-friendly interface to the distributed applications available in the environment.

Database Applications

As an example that illustrates the concept of splitting application logic between client and server, let us consider the most common family of client/server applications: those that make use of relational databases. In this environment, the server is essentially a database server. Interaction between client and server is in the form of transactions in which the client makes a database request and receives a database response.

Figure 6.3 illustrates, in general terms, the architecture of such a system. The server is responsible for maintaining the database, for which purpose a complex database management system software module is required. A variety of applications that make use of the database can be housed on client machines. The "glue" that ties client and server together is software that enables the client to make requests for access to the server's database. A popular example of such logic is the Structured Query Language (SQL).

Figure 6.3 suggests that all of the application logic—the software for "number crunching" or other types of data analysis—is on the client side, while the server is only

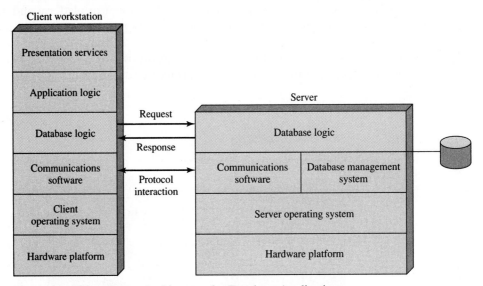

Figure 6.3   Client/Server Architecture for Database Applications

---

[1]Not to be confused with the presentation layer of the OSI model. The presentation layer is concerned with the formatting of data so that they can be properly interpreted by the two communicating machines. A presentation services module is concerned with the way in which the user interacts with an application and with the layout and functionality of what is presented to the user on the screen.

Client

Initial query →

← 100,000 possible records

Next query →

← 1000 possible records

Final query →

← One record returned

Server

1,000,000-record database

(a) Desirable client/server use

Server

Client

Query →

← 300,000 records returned

1,000,000-record database

(b) Misused client/server

Figure 6.4 Client/Server Database Usage

concerned with managing the database. Whether such a configuration is appropriate depends on the style and intent of the application. For example, suppose that the primary purpose is to provide online access for record lookup. Figure 6.4a suggests how this might work. Suppose that the server is maintaining a database of one million records (called rows in relational database jargon), and the user wants to perform a lookup that should result in zero, one, or at most a few records. The user could search for these records using a number of search criteria (e.g., records older than 1992; records referring to individuals in Ohio; records referring to a specific event or characteristic, etc.). An initial client query may yield a server response that there are 100,000 records that satisfy the search criteria. The user then adds additional qualifiers and issues a new query. This time, a response indicating that there are 1000 possible records is returned. Finally, the client issues a third request with additional qualifiers. The resulting search criteria yield a single match, and the record is returned to the client.

The preceding application is well suited to a client/server architecture for two reasons:

1. There is a massive job of sorting and searching the database. This requires a large disc or bank of discs, a high-speed processor, and a high-speed I/O architecture. Such capacity and power is not needed and is too expensive for a single-user workstation or PC.

2. It would place too great a traffic burden on the network to move the entire one-million-record file to the client for searching. Therefore, it is not enough for the server to just be able to retrieve records on behalf of a client; the server needs to have database logic that enables it to perform searches on behalf of a client.

Now consider the scenario of Figure 6.4b, which has the same one-million-record database. In this case, a single query results in the transmission of 300,000 records over the network. This might happen if, for example, the user wishes to find the grand total or mean value of some field across many records or even the entire database.

Clearly, this latter scenario is unacceptable. One solution to this problem, which maintains the client/server architecture with all its benefits, is to move part of the application logic over to the server. That is, the server can be equipped with application logic for performing data analysis as well as data retrieval and data searching.

Classes of Client/Server Applications

Within the general framework of client/server, there is a spectrum of implementations that divide the work between client and server differently. The exact distribution of data and application processing depends on the nature of the database information, the types of applications supported, the availability of interoperable vendor equipment, and the usage patterns within an organization.

Figure 6.5 illustrates some of the major options for database applications. Other splits are possible, and the options may have a different characterization for other types of applications. In any case, it is useful to examine this figure to get a feel for the kind of trade-offs possible.

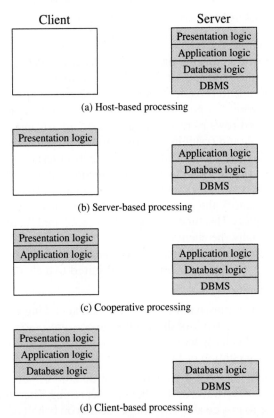

Figure 6.5 Classes of Client/Server Applications

The figure depicts four classes:

- **Host-based processing:** Host-based processing is not true client/server computing as the term is generally used. Rather, host-based processing refers to the traditional mainframe environment in which all or virtually all of the processing is done on a central host. Often the user interface is via a dumb terminal. Even if the user is employing a microcomputer, the user's station is generally limited to the role of a terminal emulator.

- **Server-based processing:** The simplest class of client/server configuration is one in which the client is principally responsible for providing a graphical user interface, while virtually all of the processing is done on the server.

- **Client-based processing:** At the other extreme, virtually all application processing may be done at the client, with the exception of data validation routines and other database logic functions that are best performed at the server. Generally, some of the more sophisticated database logic functions are housed on the client side. This architecture is perhaps the most common client/server approach in current use. It enables the user to employ applications tailored to local needs.

- **Cooperative processing:** In a cooperative processing configuration, the application processing is performed in an optimized fashion, taking advantage of the strengths of both client and server machines and of the distribution of data. Such a configuration is more complex to set up and maintain but, in the long run, this type of configuration may offer greater user productivity gains and greater network efficiency than other client/server approaches.

Figures 6.5c and d correspond to configurations in which a considerable fraction of the load is on the client. This so-called **thick client** model has been popularized by application development tools such as Powersoft Corp.'s Power-Builder. Applications developed with these tools are typically departmental in scope, supporting between 25 and 150 users [ECKE95]. The main benefit of the thick client model is that it takes advantage of desktop power, off-loading application processing from servers and making them more efficient and less likely to be bottlenecks.

There are, however, several disadvantages to the thick client strategy. The addition of more functions rapidly overloads the capacity of desktop machines, forcing companies to upgrade. If the model extends beyond the department to incorporate many users, the company must install high-capacity LANs to support the large volumes of transmission between the thin servers and the thick clients. Finally, it is difficult to maintain, upgrade, or replace applications distributed across tens or hundreds of desktops.

Figure 6.5b is representative of a **thin client**, or fat server, approach. This approach more nearly mimics the traditional host-centered approach and is often the migration path for evolving corporate-wide applications from the mainframe to a distributed environment.

Figure 6.6, based on [MCFA08], illustrates five client/server categories based on the distribution of computational services between the client process and the server process. Each category is defined by the client-side functionality.

	Thin client				Thick client
	←				→
Computational services	Distributed presentation	Local presentation	Distributed appication logic	Local application logic	
Presentation services	Shared	Client	Client	Client	Client
Application services	Server	Server	Shared	Client	Client
Data services	Server	Server	Server	Server	Shared

Figure 6.6 Three-Level Architectural Client/Server Framework

Three-Tier Client/Server Architecture

The traditional client/server architecture involves two levels, or tiers: a client tier and a server tier. In recent years, a three-tier architecture has become increasingly common (Figure 6.7). In this architecture, the application software is distributed among three types of machines: a user machine, a middle-tier server, and a backend server. The user machine is the client machine we have been discussing and, in the three-tier model, is typically a thin client. The middle-tier machines are essentially gateways between the thin user clients and a variety of backend database servers. The middle-tier machines can convert protocols and map from one type of database query to another. In addition, the middle-tier machine can merge/integrate results from different data sources. Finally, the middle-tier machine can serve as a gateway between the desktop applications and the backend legacy applications by mediating between the two worlds.

The interaction between the middle-tier server and the backend server also follows the client/server model. Thus, the middle tier system acts as both a client and a server.

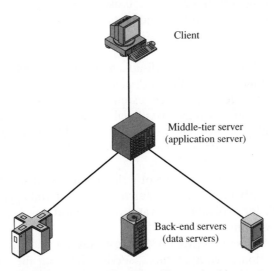

Client

Middle-tier server (application server)

Back-end servers (data servers)

Figure 6.7 Three-Tier Client/Server Architecture

6.3 MIDDLEWARE

The development and deployment of client/server products has far outstripped efforts to standardize all aspects of distributed computing, from the physical layer up to the application layer. This lack of standards makes it difficult to implement an integrated, multivendor, enterprise-wide client/server configuration. Because much of the benefit of the client/server approach is tied up with its modularity and the ability to mix and match platforms and applications to provide a business solution, this interoperability problem must be solved.

To achieve the true benefits of the client/server approach, developers need tools that provide a uniform means and style of access to system resources across all platforms. This will enable programmers to build applications that not only look and feel the same on various PCs and workstations but that use the same method to access data regardless of the location of that data.

The most common way to meet this requirement is by the use of standard programming interfaces and protocols that sit between the application above and communications software and operating system below. Such standardized interfaces and protocols have come to be referred to as **middleware**. With standard programming interfaces, it is easy to implement the same application on a variety of server types and workstation types. This obviously benefits the customer, but vendors are also motivated to provide such interfaces. The reason is that customers buy applications, not servers; customers will only choose among those server products that run the applications they want. The standardized protocols are needed to link these various server interfaces back to the clients that need access to them.

There is a variety of middleware packages ranging from the very simple to the very complex. What they all have in common is the capability to hide the complexities and disparities of different network protocols and operating systems. Client and server vendors generally provide a number of the more popular middleware packages as options. Thus, a user can settle on a particular middleware strategy and then assemble equipment from various vendors that support that strategy.

Middleware Architecture

Figure 6.8 suggests the role of middleware in a client/server architecture. The exact role of the middleware component will depend on the style of client/server computing being used. Referring back to Figure 6.5, recall that there are a number of different client/server approaches, depending on the way in which application functions are split up. In any case, Figure 6.8 gives a good general idea of the architecture involved.

Note that there is both a client and server component of middleware. The basic purpose of middleware is to enable an application or user at a client to access a variety of services on servers without being concerned about differences among servers. To look at one specific application area, the Structured Query Language (SQL) is supposed to provide a standardized means for access to a relational database by either a local or remote user or application. However, many relational database vendors, although they support SQL, have added their own proprietary extensions to SQL. This enables vendors to differentiate their products but also creates potential incompatibilities.

Client workstation

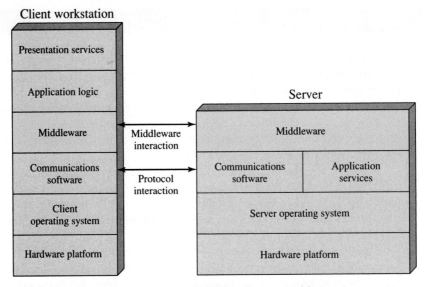

Figure 6.8 The Role of Middleware in Client/Server Architecture

As an example, consider a distributed system used to support, among other things, the personnel department. The basic employee data, such as employee name and address, might be stored on a Gupta database, whereas salary information might be contained on an Oracle database. When a user in the personnel department requires access to particular records, that user does not want to be concerned with which vendor's database contains the records needed. Middleware provides a layer of software that enables uniform access to these differing systems.

It is instructive to look at the role of middleware from a logical, rather than an implementation, point of view. This viewpoint is illustrated in Figure 6.9 [BERN96].

Figure 6.9 Logical View of Middleware

Middleware enables the realization of the promise of distributed client/server computing. The entire distributed system can be viewed as a set of applications and resources available to users. Users need not be concerned with the location of data or indeed the location of applications. All applications operate over a uniform **application programming interface (API)**. The middleware, which cuts across all client and server platforms, is responsible for routing client requests to the appropriate server.

Although there is a wide variety of middleware products, these products are typically based on one of three underlying mechanisms: message passing, remote procedure calls, and object-oriented mechanisms. The remainder of this section provides an overview of these mechanisms.

Message Passing

Figure 6.10a shows the use of distributed message passing to implement client/server functionality. A client process requires some service (e.g., read a file, print) and sends

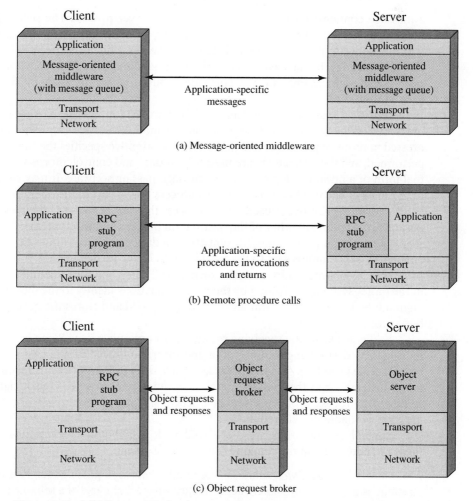

(a) Message-oriented middleware

(b) Remote procedure calls

(c) Object request broker

Figure 6.10 Middleware Mechanisms

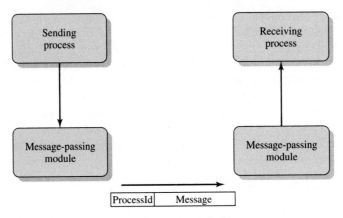

Figure 6.11 Basic Message-Passing Primitives

a message containing a request for service to a server process. The server process honors the request and sends a message containing a reply. In its simplest form, only two functions are needed: Send and Receive. The Send function specifies a destination and includes the message content. The Receive function tells from whom a message is desired (including "all") and provides a buffer where the incoming message is to be stored.

Figure 6.11 suggests an implementation approach for message passing. Processes make use of the services of a message-passing module. Service requests can be expressed in terms of primitives and parameters. A primitive specifies the function to be performed, and the parameters are used to pass data and control information. The actual form of a primitive depends on the message-passing software. It may be a procedure call or it may itself be a message to a process that is part of the operating system.

The Send primitive is used by the process that desires to send the message. Its parameters are the identifier of the destination process and the contents of the message. The message-passing module constructs a data unit that includes these two elements. This data unit is sent to the machine that hosts the destination process, using some sort of communications facility, such as TCP/IP. When the data unit is received in the target system, it is routed by the communications facility to the message-passing module. This module examines the processId field and stores the message in the buffer for that process.

In this scenario, the receiving process must announce its willingness to receive messages by designating a buffer area and informing the message-passing module by a Receive primitive. An alternative approach does not require such an announcement. Instead, when the message-passing module receives a message, it signals the destination process with some sort of Receive signal and then makes the received message available in a shared buffer.

Several design issues are associated with distributed message passing, and these are addressed in the remainder of this subsection.

RELIABILITY VERSUS UNRELIABILITY   A reliable message-passing facility is one that guarantees delivery if possible. Such a facility would make use of a reliable transport protocol or similar logic to perform error checking, acknowledgment, retransmission, and reordering of misordered messages. Because delivery is guaranteed, it is not necessary to let the sending process know that the message was delivered. However, it might be useful to provide an acknowledgment back to the sending process so that it knows that delivery has already taken place. In either case, if the facility fails to achieve delivery (e.g., persistent network failure, crash of destination system), the sending process is notified of the failure.

At the other extreme, the message-passing facility may simply send the message out into the communications network but will report neither success nor failure. This alternative greatly reduces the processing and communications overhead of the message-passing facility. For those applications that require confirmation that a message has been delivered, the applications themselves may use request and reply messages to satisfy the requirement.

BLOCKING VERSUS NONBLOCKING With nonblocking, or asynchronous, primitives, a process is not suspended as a result of issuing a Send or Receive. Thus, when a process issues a Send primitive, the operating system returns control to the process as soon as the message has been queued for transmission or a copy has been made. If no copy is made, any changes made to the message by the sending process before or even while it is being transmitted are made at the risk of the process. When the message has been transmitted, or copied to a safe place for subsequent transmission, the sending process is interrupted to be informed that the message buffer may be reused. Similarly, a nonblocking Receive is issued by a process that then proceeds to run. When a message arrives, the process is informed by interrupt, or it can poll for status periodically.

Nonblocking primitives provide for efficient, flexible use of the message-passing facility by processes. The disadvantage of this approach is that it is difficult to test and debug programs that use these primitives. Irreproducible, timing-dependent sequences can create subtle and difficult problems.

The alternative is to use blocking, or synchronous, primitives. A blocking Send does not return control to the sending process until the message has been transmitted (unreliable service) or until the message has been sent and an acknowledgment received (reliable service). A blocking Receive does not return control until a message has been placed in the allocated buffer.

Remote Procedure Calls

A variation on the basic message-passing model is the remote procedure call, which is a common method for encapsulating communication in a distributed system. The essence of the technique is to allow programs on different machines to interact using simple procedure call/return semantics, just as if the two programs were on the same machine. That is, the procedure call is used for access to remote services. The popularity of this approach is due to the following advantages:

1. The procedure call is a widely accepted, used, and understood abstraction.
2. The use of remote procedure calls enables remote interfaces to be specified as a set of named operations with designated types. Thus, the interface can be clearly documented and distributed programs can be statically checked for type errors.

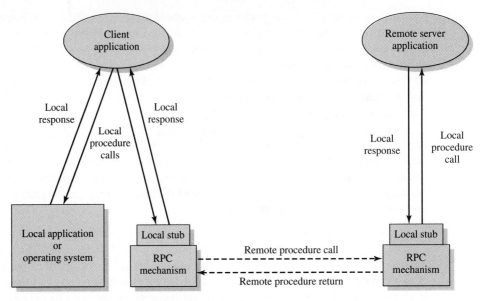

Figure 6.12 Remote Procedure Call Mechanism

3. Because a standardized and precisely defined interface is specified, the communication code for an application can be generated automatically.

4. Because a standardized and precisely defined interface is specified, developers can write client and server modules that can be moved among computers and operating systems with little modification and recoding.

The remote procedure call mechanism can be viewed as a refinement of reliable, blocking message passing. Figure 6.10b illustrates the general architecture, and Figure 6.12 provides a more detailed look. The calling program makes a normal procedure call with parameters on its machine. For example,

$$\text{CALL P (X, Y)}$$

where

    P = procedure name
    X = passed arguments
    Y = returned values

It may or may not be transparent to the user that the intention is to invoke a remote procedure on some other machine. A dummy or stub procedure P must be included in the caller's address space or be dynamically linked to it at call time. This procedure creates a message that identifies the procedure being called and includes the parameters. It then sends this message to a remote system and waits for a reply. When a reply is received, the stub procedure returns to the calling program, providing the returned values.

At the remote machine, another stub program is associated with the called procedure. When a message comes in, it is examined and a local CALL P (X,Y) is generated. This remote procedure is thus called locally, so its normal assumptions

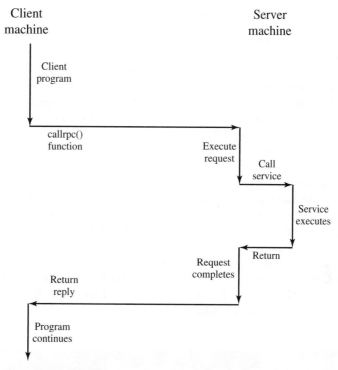

Figure 6.13 RPC Flow

about where to find parameters, the state of the stack, and so on, are identical to the case of a purely local procedure call.

Figure 6.13 illustrates the flow of control for an RPC operation.

CLIENT/SERVER BINDING   Binding specifies how the relationship between a remote procedure and the calling program will be established. A binding is formed when two applications have made a logical connection and are prepared to exchange commands and data.

Nonpersistent binding means that a logical connection is established between the two processes at the time of the remote procedure call and that as soon as the values are returned, the connection is dismantled. Because a connection requires the maintenance of state information on both ends, it consumes resources. The nonpersistent style is used to conserve those resources. On the other hand, the overhead involved in establishing connections makes nonpersistent binding inappropriate for remote procedures that are called frequently by the same caller.

With **persistent binding**, a connection that is set up for a remote procedure call is sustained after the procedure return. The connection can then be used for future remote procedure calls. If a specified period of time passes with no activity on the connection, the connection is terminated. For applications that make many repeated calls to remote procedures, persistent binding maintains the logical connection and allows a sequence of calls and returns to use the same connection.

Object-Oriented Mechanisms

As object-oriented technology becomes more prevalent in operating system design, client/server designers have begun to embrace this approach. In this approach, clients and servers ship messages back and forth between objects. Object communications may rely on an underlying message or RPC structure or be developed directly on top of object-oriented capabilities in the operating system.

A client that needs a service sends a request to an object request broker, which acts as a directory of all the remote services available on the network (Figure 6.10c). The broker calls the appropriate object and passes along any relevant data. Then the remote object services the request and replies to the broker, which returns the response to the client.

The success of the object-oriented approach depends on standardization of the object mechanism. Unfortunately, there are several competing designs in this area. One is Microsoft's Component Object Model (COM), the basis for Object Linking and Embedding (OLE). COM is used on Windows and has also been implemented by a number of vendors for UNIX. A competing approach, developed by the Object Management Group, is the Common Object Request Broker Architecture (CORBA), which has wide industry backing. IBM, Apple, Sun, and many other vendors support the CORBA approach.

6.4 INTRANETS

Intranet is a term used to refer to the implementation of Internet technologies within a corporate organization rather than for external connection to the global Internet. This concept has resulted in the most rapid change of direction in the history of business data communications. By any measure, including product announcements by vendors, statements of intent by customers, actual deployment of products, and even books on the shelves of bookstores, intranets have enjoyed a more rapid penetration of the corporate consciousness than personal computers, client/server computing, or even the Internet and the World Wide Web.

What accounts for this growth is a long list of attractive features and advantages of an intranet-based approach to corporate computing, including the following:

- Rapid prototyping and deployment of new services (can be measured in hours or days)
- Scales effectively (start small, build as needed)
- Virtually no training required on the part of users and little training required of developers, because the services and user interfaces are familiar from the Internet
- Can be implemented on virtually all platforms with complete interoperability
- Open architecture means a large and growing number of add-on applications is available across many platforms
- Supports a range of distributed computing architectures (few central servers or many distributed servers)

- Structured to support integration of "legacy" information sources (databases, existing word processing documents, groupware databases)
- Supports a range of media types (audio, video, interactive applications)
- Inexpensive to start, requires little investment either in new software or infrastructure

The enabling technologies for the intranet are the high processing speed and storage capacity of personal computers together with the high data rates of LANs.

Although the term *intranet* refers to the whole range of Internet-based applications, including network news, e-mail, and FTP, Web technology is responsible for the almost instant acceptance of intranets. Thus, the bulk of this section is devoted to a discussion of Web systems. At the close of the section, we briefly mention other intranet applications.

Intranet Web

The Web browser has become the universal information interface. An increasing number of employees have had experience using the Internet Web and are comfortable with the access model it provides. The intranet Web takes advantage of this experience base.

WEB CONTENT An organization can use the intranet Web to enhance management-employee communication and to provide job-related information easily and quickly. Figure 6.14 suggests, at a top level, the kinds of information that can be provided by a

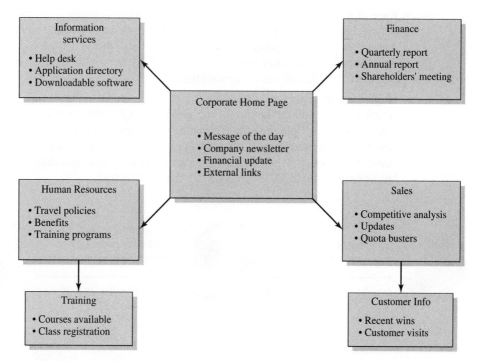

Figure 6.14 Example Corporate Web Page Structure

corporate Web. Typically, there is an internal corporate home page that serves as an entry point for employees into the corporate intranet. From this home page, there are links to areas of interest company-wide or to large groups of employees, including human resources, finance, and information system service. Other links are to areas of interest to groups of employees, such as sales and manufacturing.

Beyond these broad-based Web services, an intranet Web is ideal for providing departmental- and project-level information and services. A group can set up its own Web pages to disseminate information and to maintain project data. With the widespread availability of easy-to-use WYSIWYG Web authoring tools, such as Adobe Dreamweaver, it is relatively easy for employees outside the information services group to develop their own Web pages for specific needs.

WEB/DATABASE APPLICATIONS   Although the Web is a powerful and flexible tool for supporting corporate requirements, the HTML used to construct Web pages provides a limited capability for maintaining a large, changing base of data. For an intranet to be truly effective, many organizations will want to connect the Web service to a database with its own database management system.

Figure 6.15 illustrates a general strategy for Web/database integration in simple terms. To begin, a client machine (running a Web browser) issues a request for information in the form of a URL reference. This reference triggers a program at the Web server that issues the correct database command to a database server. The output returned to the Web server is converted into HTML format and returned to the Web browser.

[WHET96] lists the following advantages of a Web/database system compared to a more traditional database approach:

- **Ease of administration:** The only connection to the database server is the Web server. The addition of a new type of database server does not require configuration of all the requisite drivers and interfaces at each type of client machine. Instead, it is only necessary for the Web server to be able to convert between HTML and the database interface.

- **Deployment:** Browsers are already available across almost all platforms, which relieves the developer of the need to implement graphical user interfaces across multiple customer machines and operating systems. In addition, developers can assume that customers already have and will be able to use browsers as soon as the intranet Web server is available, avoiding deployment issues such as installation and synchronized activation.

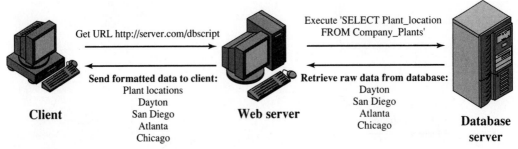

Figure 6.15   Web/Database Connectivity

- **Development speed:** Large portions of the normal development cycle, such as deployment and client design, do not apply to Web-based projects. In addition, the text-based tags of HTML allow for rapid modification, making it easy to continually improve the look and feel of the application based on user feedback. By contrast, changing form or content of a typical graphical-based application can be a substantial task.

- **Flexible information presentation:** The hypermedia base of the Web enables the application developer to employ whatever information structure is best for a given application, including the use of hierarchical formats in which progressive levels of detail are available to the user.

These advantages are compelling in the decision to deploy a Web-based database interface. However, managers need to be aware of potential disadvantages, also listed in [WHET96]:

- **Functionality:** Compared to the functionality available with a sophisticated graphical user interface (GUI), a typical Web browser interface may be more limited.

- **Stateless operation:** The nature of HTTP is such that each interaction between a browser and a server is a separate transaction, independent of prior or future exchanges. Typically, the Web server keeps no information between transactions to track the state of the user. Such history information can be important. For example, consider an application that allows the user to query a database of parts for cars and trucks. Once the user has indicated that he or she is looking for a specific truck part, subsequent menus should show only parts that pertain to trucks. It is possible to work around this difficulty, but it is awkward.

INTRANET WEBS VERSUS TRADITIONAL CLIENT/SERVER Although traditional client/server systems have become increasingly widespread and popular, displacing older corporate computing models, their use is not without problems, including the following:

- Long development cycles
- Difficulty of partitioning applications into client and server modules and the even greater difficulty of modifying the partition in response to user feedback
- Effort involved in distributing upgrades to clients
- Difficulty of scaling the servers to respond to increased load in a distributed environment
- Continuous requirement for increasingly powerful desktop machines

Much of this difficulty can be traced to the typical client/server design, which puts much of the load on the client; this thick client strategy corresponds to Figures 6.5c and 6.5d. As was mentioned earlier, this strategy may not scale well to corporate-wide applications. Thus, many companies opt for a fat server approach. An intranet Web can be viewed as one realization of the fat server.

Viewed as an alternative to other fat server schemes, the intranet Web has the advantages of ease of deployment, use of a small number of widely accepted standards, and integration with other TCP/IP-based applications. However, it is unlikely that the intranet Web will kill or even slow down traditional client/server deployment, at least in the near term. Longer term, the intranet Web may come to dominate corporate computing or it may simply be a widely used alternative to other client/server strategies that also flourish.

Other Intranet Technologies

The centerpiece of any intranet strategy is the intranet Web. However, other Internet technologies can also play a key role in the success of an intranet. Perhaps the two most important, after the Web, are electronic mail and network news.

ELECTRONIC MAIL   Electronic mail is already the most heavily used network application in the corporate world. However, traditional e-mail is generally limited and inflexible. Intranet mail products provide standard, simple methods for attaching documents, sound, images, and other multimedia to mail messages.

In addition to supporting multimedia, intranet mail systems generally make it easy to create and manage an **electronic mailing list**. A mailing list is really nothing more than an alias that has multiple destinations. Mailing lists are usually created to discuss specific topics. Anyone interested in that topic may join that list. Once a user has been added to a list, he or she receives a copy of every message posted to the list. A user can ask a question or respond to someone else's question by sending a message to the list address. The mailing list is thus an effective way of supporting project-level communication.

NETWORK NEWS   Most readers of this book are familiar with **USENET**, otherwise known as network news. USENET is a collection of electronic bulletin boards that work in much the same way as the Internet mailing lists. If you subscribe to a particular news group, you receive all messages posted to that group, and you may post a message that is available to all subscribers. One difference between USENET and Internet mailing lists has to do with the mechanics of the systems. USENET is actually a distributed network of sites that collect and broadcast news group entries. To access a news group, for read or write, one must have access to a USENET node. Another, more significant, difference is the way in which messages are organized. With an electronic mailing list, each subscriber receives messages one at a time, as they are sent. With USENET, the messages are archived at each news site and organized by subject matter. Thus, it is easier to follow the thread of a particular discussion with USENET. This ability to organize and store messages in threads makes USENET ideal for collaborative work.

As with other Internet technologies, USENET is readily adapted to form an intranet news service. The news messages can be stored on a single news server, or multiple servers within the organization can act as news repositories. New groups are created as needed by departments and projects.

6.5   EXTRANETS

A concept similar to that of the intranet is the **extranet**. Like the intranet, the extranet makes use of TCP/IP protocols and applications, especially the Web. The distinguishing feature of the extranet is that it provides access to corporate resources by outside clients, typically suppliers and customers of the organization. This outside access can be through the Internet or through other data communications networks. An extranet provides more than the simple Web access for the public that virtually all companies now provide. Instead, the extranet provides more extensive access to corporate resources, usually in a fashion that enforces a security policy. As with the intranet, the typical model of operation for the extranet is client/server.

The essential feature of an extranet is that it enables the sharing of information among companies. [BIDG08b] lists the following benefits of extranets:

- **Reduced costs:** Information sharing is done in a highly automated fashion, with minimized paperwork and human involvement.

- **Coordination:** Critical information from one partner can be made available so that another partner can quickly make decisions. For example, a manufacturer can coordinate its production by checking the inventory status of a customer.

- **Customer satisfaction:** By linking the customer to an organization, an extranet provides more information about the current status of products and services of the vendor.

- **Expedited communications:** Extranets increase the efficiency and effectiveness of communication among business partners by linking intranets for immediate access to critical information.

An important consideration with extranets is security. Because corporate Web resources and database resources are made available to outside parties and transactions against these resources are allowed, privacy and authentication concerns must be addressed. This is typically done with the use of a virtual private network, which is discussed in Chapter 19. Here, we can simply list some of the communications options available for opening up the corporate intranet to outsiders to create an extranet:

- **Long-distance dial-up access:** This enables outsiders to access the intranet directly, using a logon procedure to authenticate the user. This approach may provide the weakest security because of the risk of impersonation, with few tools to counteract such risks.

- **Internet access to intranet with security:** Authentication of users and encryption of communications between user and intranet provide enhanced security. The encryption prevents eavesdropping, and authentication is intended to prevent unauthorized access. However, as with dial-up access, if a hacker is able to defeat the authentication mechanism, then the entire resources of the intranet become vulnerable.

- **Internet access to an external server that duplicates some of a company's intranet data:** This approach reduces the risk of hacker penetration but may also reduce the value of the extranet to external partners.

- **Internet access to an external server that originates database queries to internal servers:** The external server acts as a firewall to enforce the company's security policy. The firewall may employ encryption in communicating to external users, will authenticate external users, and filters the information flow to restrict access on the basis of user. If the firewall is itself secure from hacker attacks, this is a powerful approach.

- **Virtual private network:** The VPN in effect is a generalization of the firewall approach and takes advantage of IP security capabilities to allow secure communications between external users and the company's intranet. VPNs are discussed in Chapter 19.

6.6   SERVICE-ORIENTED ARCHITECTURE

The service-oriented architecture (SOA) is a form of client/server architecture that now enjoys widespread use in enterprise systems. An SOA organizes business functions into a modular structure rather than as monolithic applications for each department. As a result, common functions can be used by different departments internally and by external business partners as well. The more fine-grained the modules, the more they can be reused. In general, a SOA consists of a set of services and a set of client applications that use these services. A client request may involve a single service or may involve two or more services to coordinating some activity, requiring communication of services with each other. The services are available through published and discoverable interfaces.

Standardized interfaces are used to enable service modules to communicate with one another and to enable client applications to communicate with service modules. The most popular interface is the use of XML (Extensible Markup Language) over HTTP (Hypertext Transfer Protocol), known as *Web services*. SOAs are also implemented using other standards, such as CORBA (Common Object Request Broker Architecture).

At a top level, an SOA contains three types of architectural elements [BIH06], illustrated in Figure 6.16:

- **Service provider:** A network node that provides a service interface for a software asset that manages a specific set of tasks. A service provider node can

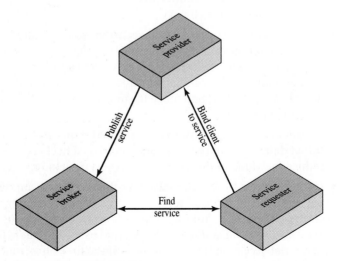

Figure 6.16   SOA Model

represent the services of a business entity or it can simply represent the service interface for a reusable subsystem.

- **Service requestor:** A network node that discovers and invokes other software services to provide a business solution. Service requestor nodes will often represent a business application component that performs remote procedure calls to a distributed object, the service provider. In some cases, the provider node may reside locally within an intranet or in other cases it could reside remotely over the Internet. The conceptual nature of SOA leaves the networking, transport protocol, and security details to the specific implementation.

- **Service broker:** A specific kind of service provider that acts as a registry and allows for the lookup of service provider interfaces and service locations. The service broker can pass on service requests to one or more additional service providers.

[BROW03] lists the following as key characteristics for effective use of services:

- **Coarse-grained:** Operations on services are frequently implemented to encompass more functionality and operate on larger data sets, compared with component-interface design.

- **Interface-based design:** Services implement separately defined interfaces. The benefit of this is that multiple services can implement a common interface and a service can implement multiple interfaces.

- **Discoverable:** Services need to be found at both design time and run time, not only by unique identity but also by interface identity and by service kind.

- **Single instance:** Unlike component-based development, which instantiates components as needed, each service is a single, always running instance that a number of clients communicate with.

- **Loosely coupled:** Services are connected to other services and clients using standard, dependency-reducing, decoupled message-based methods such as XML document exchanges.

- **Asynchronous:** In general, services use an asynchronous message-passing approach; however, this is not required. In fact, many services will use synchronous message passing at times.

To give the reader some feel for the use of SOA, we look at an example from [SECR06]. Figure 6.17a shows a common approach to building applications targeted at specific user categories. For each specific application, a single self-contained application module is built. What ties together the various applications in the enterprise is an application-independent database management system that supports a number of databases. Multiple applications may have access to a single database. For example, in this configuration all three applications require access to a customer information database. The advantages of this arrangement are clear. By separating the data from the applications and providing a uniform database interface, multiple applications can be developed and revised independently from one another.

This typical approach, of a variety of applications using a common set of databases, has some drawbacks. The addition of a new feature or user service, such as ATM (automatic teller machine), generally requires building a new application independent

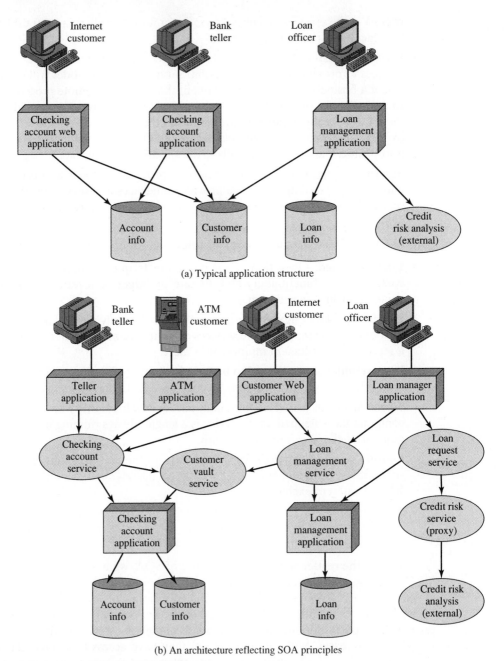

(a) Typical application structure

(b) An architecture reflecting SOA principles

Figure 6.17   Example Use of SOA

of existing applications—this despite the fact that much of the necessary logic has already been implemented in related applications.

We can achieve greater efficiency and flexibility by migrating to an SOA, as shown in Figure 6.17b. Here, the strategy is to isolate services that may be of common use to multiple applications and implement these as separate service modules.

In this particular example of the SOA, there are some core applications that deal with the functionality of individual databases. These applications are accessible by application programming interfaces (APIs) by service modules that implement common services. Finally, the specific applications visible to users deal primarily with presentation issues and with specific business logic.

APPLICATION NOTE

To Be Fat or Thin—That Is the Question

One of the most popular communications architectures is the client/server model. Figure 6.2 illustrates this relationship. In a nutshell, the client computer has a small program that makes specific requests of the server. For example, when you access a Web page on a Web server, you are making the requests through a Web browser. The browser is your client application. The usual configuration for a computer is to have its own hard drive, processing power, memory, a collection of programs for doing work (e.g., Microsoft Office), and a collection of programs that are used to connect to other machines or resources. These last are called client applications or simply "clients." This configuration is also true of network components. With the exception of the hard drive, routers, switches, and access points all have processors, memory, and software. In most cases the hard drive has simply been replaced by flash memory. Computers and devices built in this fashion are considered "fat" because they have everything that they need built in.

However, this is not the only way to configure computers or the other machines in a network. There are many products that sacrifice one or more of these parts in order to reduce cost or to fit a particular use. The following examples show how the configuration of the network and systems can be modified.

When you set up a printer for your home, it is dedicated to the computer directly attached. Even for a small company, individual printers for everyone may be appropriate. This is certainly something that becomes less feasible as the number of users increases. In this case, it is far more likely that the printers will be shared and that one of the servers will be operating as a print server, handling all of the printing requests from the clients.

Inventory software is an application that will run on the server or mainframe. Clients may work via serial or network connections, but very little processing or storage will occur on the clients. This is to ensure that the database information is accurate and up to date. The user keystrokes are passed to the mainframe or server and the information is sent back to the user after the "number crunching" has been completed. With respect to this application, the clients may be considered "thin." The user cannot work with these applications unless they are connected and possibly authenticated. This type of installation allows controlled use of the program and the software licenses.

Software licenses can cost a great deal of money, and there is always the possibility of fines if licenses are improperly administered. The server can act to control the number of users using the applications at any one time. This can also create problems if the number of licenses is not updated when new users are added. More than one user has been locked out of a network application because there were too many people already logged in.

(Continued)

Applications such as word processors and spreadsheets typically reside in full on computers. Again, clients configured in this way are considered fat. In a fully distributed environment with fat clients, the users will have a complete set of applications whose operation does not require any network connectivity.

It is also possible that the word processor exists entirely or in part on the server. In fact, the computer itself may be configured to be thin, in which case there are very few resources on the computer itself. The hard drive is only large enough to store essential operating system components and all of the applications are stored on, and run from, the server out in the network. In this case, the installation potentially saves space on the client machines. Thin clients also have the advantage of being less expensive and easier to use. They are also less at risk for data corruption and theft. The downside is that the devices are now heavily dependent on the network. One can expect an increase of network traffic and, in the case of a loss of network access, a decrease in productivity.

Network devices can also be configured as fat or thin depending on their use. In the case of a wireless network for a large company, there can be dozens of deployed access points. The usual way of managing all of these is to configure each one individually and allow it to handle security and forwarding for that area—in other words, "fat" access points. This approach can be very time consuming, especially with the threats leveled against wireless networks today. An alternative would be to connect all of the access points back to a network controller and have all of the decisions made at this central location. The access points only have enough processing capability to provide feedback to the controller. All of the operational decisions are made in the central location. While this does make management easier, the controller is a single point of failure. Even if the failure is short in duration, the entire wireless network may be down completely.

There are some significant choices to be made when deciding on fat versus thin servers and clients. The choices made can have a significant effect on cost, security, performance, and impact on end users. Both fat and thin clients have particular areas to which they are well suited, and every installation is different from the next. It is important to understand the capabilities of the installed system, the services required, and the use of the client machines.

6.7   SUMMARY

Client/server computing is the key to realizing the potential of information systems and networks to significantly improve productivity in organizations. With client/server computing, applications are distributed to users on single-user workstations and personal computers. At the same time, resources that can and should be shared are maintained on server systems that are available to all clients. Thus, the client/server architecture is a blend of decentralized and centralized computing.

Typically, the client system provides a graphical user interface (GUI) that enables a user to exploit a variety of applications with minimal training and relative ease. Servers support shared utilities, such as database management systems. The actual application is divided between client and server in a way intended to optimize ease of use and performance.

Because there are no generally accepted standards for client/server networking, a number of products have been developed to bridge the gap between client and server and to enable users to develop multivendor configurations. Such products generally are referred to as middleware. Middleware products are based on either a message-passing or a remote-procedure-call mechanism.

A more recent organizational model that competes with the client/server model is the intranet. An intranet leverages existing Internet applications, especially the Web, to provide an internal suite of applications suited to the needs of an organization. Intranets are easy to set up, involve standardized software, can be deployed on multiple platforms, and require virtually no user training.

6.8 RECOMMENDED READING AND WEB SITES

[BERS96] provides a good technical discussion of the design issues involved in allocating applications to client and server and in middleware approaches; the book also discusses products and standardization efforts. [RENA96] is oriented toward the management aspects of installing client/server systems and selecting applications for that environment. [SIMO95] describes the principles and mechanisms of client/server computing and middleware in the context of two detailed case studies, one for Windows and one for UNIX. [REAG00a] and [REAG00b] are more recent treatments of client/server computing and network design approaches for supporting client/server computing. A good short overview of middleware is [CAMP99].

[EVAN96] provides a practical, detailed how-to manual on setting up a corporate intranet; the book covers a wide spectrum of applications and gives concrete guidance for implementation. [ECKE96] is another good treatment, although somewhat less detailed. A more informal but very enlightening treatment is [BERN98]; this book provides a management-level discussion of the advantages of Web intranets and strategies for building and exploiting them. [PFAF98] is a thorough treatment of extranets.

A good overview of middleware technology and products is [BRIT04]. [MENA05] provides a performance comparison of remote procedure calls and distributed message passing.

Two worthwhile surveys of SOA are [BROW03] and [BIH06]. [CHER05] and [BIEB05] analyze the impact of migrating to a SOA. [HUTC08] discusses strategies for migrating to an SOA. [CARE08] looks at the role of data services in an SOA.

BERN98 Bernard, R. *The Corporate Intranet.* New York: Wiley, 1998.

BERS96 Berson, A. *Client/Server Architecture.* New York: McGraw-Hill, 1996.

BIEB05 Bieberstein, N., et al. "Impact of Service-Oriented Architecture on Enterprise Systems, Organizational Structures, and Individuals." *IBM Systems Journal*, Vol. 44, No. 4, 2005.

BIH06 Bih, J. "Service Oriented Architecture (SOA): A New Paradigm to Implement Dynamic E-Business Solutions." *ACM Ubiquity*, August 2006; acm.org/ubiquity/views/v7i30_soa.html

BRIT04 Britton, C. *IT Architectures and Middleware.* Reading, MA: Addison-Wesley, 2004.

BROW03 Brown, A.; Johnston, S.; and Kelly, K. *Using Service-Oriented Architecture and Component-Based Development to Build Web Service Applications.* IBM Rational Software Technical Report, 2003; ibm.com/developerworks/rational/library/510.html

CAMP99 Campbell, A.; Coulson, G.; and Kounavis, M. "Managing Complexity: Middleware Explained." *IT Pro,* October 1999.

CARE08 Carey, M. "SOA What?" *IEEE Computer,* March 2008.

CHER05 Cherbacko, L., et al. "Impact of Service Orientation at the Business Level." *IBM Systems Journal,* Vol. 44., No. 4, 2005.

ECKE96 Eckel, G. *Intranet Working.* Indianapolis, IN: New Riders, 1996.

EVAN96 Evans, T. *Building an Intranet.* Indianapolis, IN: Sams, 1996.

HUTC08 Hutchinson, J., et al. "Migrating to SOAs by Way of Hybrid Systems." IT Pro, January/February 2008.

MENA05 Menasce, D. "MOM vs. RPC: Communication Models for Distributed Applications." *IEEE Internet Computing,* March/April 2005.

PFAF98 Pfaffenberger, B. *Building a Strategic Extranet.* Foster City, CA: IDG Books, 1998.

REAG00a Reagan, P. *Client/Server Computing.* Upper Saddle River, NJ: Prentice Hall, 2000.

REAG00b Reagan, P. *Client/Server Network: Design, Operation, and Management.* Upper Saddle River, NJ: Prentice Hall, 2000.

RENA96 Renaud, P. *An Introduction to Client/Server Systems.* New York: Wiley, 1996.

SIMO95 Simon, A., and Wheeler, T. *Open Client/Server Computing and Middleware.* Chestnut Hill, MA: AP Professional Books, 1995.

Useful Web sites:

- **Complete Intranet Resource Site:** Wide range of resources useful in research, planning, design, and implementation of intranets
- **Intranet Journal:** Includes news and features, as well as links to intranet vendors and other intranet-related sites
- **SQL Standards:** A central source of information about the SQL standards process and its current documents

6.9 KEY TERMS, REVIEW QUESTIONS, AND PROBLEMS

Key Terms

application programming interface (API)	graphical user interface (GUI)	object-oriented middleware remote procedure call (RPC)
client	intranet	server
client/server	message	service-oriented architecture (SOA)
electronic mailing list	middleware	
extranet	network news	USENET

Review Questions

6.1   What is client/server computing?

6.2   What distinguishes client/server computing from any other form of distributed data processing?

6.3   Discuss the rationale for locating applications on the client, the server, or split between client and server.

6.4   What are four different ways processing can be divided between machines communicating with each other?

6.5   How are machines interacting in client/server-based systems different from a typical laptop or desktop computer?

6.6   What are thick clients and thick servers, and what are the differences in philosophy of the two approaches?

6.7   Suggest pros and cons for thick client and thick server strategies.

6.8   What is middleware?

6.9   Middleware is often required for clients accessing data in different locations. Are telnet and ftp examples of applications requiring middleware?

6.10   Because we have standards such as TCP/IP and OSI, why is middleware needed?

6.11   What is an intranet?

6.12   What is the distinction between client/server and intranet?

6.13   What is an extranet?

6.14   List some benefits of the information sharing provided by an extranet.

6.15   What are the communications options available for converting an intranet into an extranet?

Problems

6.1   You have just been hired as the CIO of an organization that has been in business for a while and has recently acquired another smaller organizations in order to increase market share. The original organization operated a fleet of buses that conducted tours and travel packages along the northern portion of the U.S. eastern coast. All of its computer applications existed on a central mainframe at company headquarters in Baltimore, Maryland. The acquired organization conducted helicopter tours around New York City and Washington, DC. All of its systems were C/S based (primarily thick clients accessing thin DB servers) and they were based outside Baltimore, near the BWI airport. Due to the mergers, the organization's IT architecture is now a disparate combination of computer systems and manual procedures. Given the general description of the stakeholder groups below and using the general C/S classes defined in Figure 6.5, prepare a cohesive IT architectural plan for the new organization and present it to the CEO for approval. Address all potential advantages and disadvantages of the plan from the perspectives of the various groups of stakeholders.

- bus/helicopter maintenance workers and mechanics (10 employees)
  - system for ordering parts/supplies
- drivers/pilots (20 employees)
  - logs and route/schedule information
- administration/HR (5 employees)
  - employee records
  - financial records
- marketing (8 employees)
  - marketing activities
  - customer interactions (CRM)

- management (9 employees)
  - reports RIC

6.2   The Java programming language is referred to by some as the language of the Web due to its platform independent nature. Java uses a hybrid form of RPC and CORBA called RMI (Remote Method Invocation). How does RMI differ from these two technologies and for what type of environment might RMI be an acceptable (or even optimal) solution? Reference: http://www.25hoursaday.com/DistributedComputingTechnologiesExplained.html

6.3   A relatively new term that has been introduced to the Web environment is that of the Web service. What is a Web service and how does it differ from the concept of a Web application? Reference: http://www.w3.org/TR/2003/WD-ws-gloss-20030514/

6.4   What are the client/server-based applications that are part of your operating system?

6.5   What are some of the servers on your local network operating within the client/server paradigm? Where are these servers located? What are the IP addresses of the servers? What are the names of the servers?

6.6   This chapter discusses thick clients. There has been a good deal of work, past and present, in the area of thin clients. How would you characterize a thin client?

6.7   This chapter introduced the term *intranet*. Previously the term *Internet* was introduced. Based on your understanding of these terms, draw a diagram depicting your local intranet (school network) and your organization's (school's) connection to the Internet.

- How big is your network?
- Who is your Internet Service Provider?
- How many networks comprise your school network?
- How many users does the network serve?
- What kind of network performance have you received?

CHAPTER 7

INTERNET-BASED APPLICATIONS

7.1 Electronic Mail and SMTP
Single-Computer versus Multiple-Computer Electronic Mail
Simple Mail Transfer Protocol
Multipurpose Internet Mail Extensions (MIME)

7.2 Web Access and HTTP
HTTP Overview
Messages

7.3 Web Security
Web Traffic Security Approaches
Secure Sockets Layer
HTTPS

7.4 Internet Telephony and SIP
SIP Components and Protocols
SIP Uniform Resource Identifier
Examples of Operation
SIP Messages
Session Description Protocol

7.5 Summary

7.6 Recommended Reading and Web Sites

7.7 Key Terms, Review Questions, and Problems

Chapter Objectives

After reading this chapter, you should be able to

♦ Discuss the applications for electronic mail.

♦ Explain that basic functionality of SMTP.

♦ Explain the need for MIME as an enhancement to ordinary e-mail.

♦ Describe the key elements of MIME.

♦ Explain the role of HTTP in the operation of the Web.

♦ Describe the functions of proxies, gateways, and tunnels in HTTP.

♦ Explain Web caching.

♦ Discuss the role of SIP.

♦ Explain the relationship between SIP and SDP.

As we discussed in Chapters 2 and 3, distributed information processing is essential in virtually all businesses. Much of the distributed processing is tailored to specific types of data and is supported by proprietary vendor software. However, there is a growing use of distributed applications for both intracompany and intercompany exchange that are general purpose in nature and that are defined by international standards or by industry de facto standards. These applications can have a direct impact on the efficiency and competitiveness of a business. In this chapter, we look at three of the most important and widespread of these distributed applications: electronic mail (e-mail), Web access, and multimedia support including voice over IP. In each case, international standards have been developed. As these standards become more widely implemented by computer vendors and software houses, these applications become increasingly important and useful in the business environment.

7.1 ELECTRONIC MAIL AND SMTP

Electronic mail is a facility that allows users at workstations and terminals to compose and exchange messages. The messages need never exist on paper unless the user (sender or recipient) desires a paper copy of the message. Some e-mail systems only serve users on a single computer; others provide service across a network of computers. Table 7.1 lists some of the common features provided by an e-mail facility.

In this section, we look at the basic functioning of e-mail, its use in a distributed environment, and finally the international standards for e-mail.

Single-Computer versus Multiple-Computer Electronic Mail

The simplest form of e-mail is the single-system facility (Figure 7.1a). This facility allows all the users of a shared computer system to exchange messages. Such a facility might be used in a mainframe environment in which multiple users share the same

Table 7.1   Typical Electronic Mail Facilities

Message Preparation

Word Processing
Facilities for the creation and editing of messages. Usually these need not be as powerful as a full word processor, since electronic mail documents tend to be simple. However, most electronic mail packages allow "off-line" access to word processors: the user creates a message using the computer's word processor, stores the message as a file, and then uses the file as input to the message preparation function of the email facility.

Annotation
Messages often require some sort of short reply. A simple technique is to allow the recipient to attach annotation to an incoming message and send it back to the originator or on to a third party.

Message Sending

User Directory
Used by the system. May also be accessible to users to be able to look up addresses.

Timed Delivery
Allows the sender to specify that a message be delivered before, at, or after a specified date/time. A message is considered delivered when it is placed in the recipient's mailbox.

Multiple Addressing
Copies of a message are sent to multiple addressees. The recipients are designated by listing each in the header of the message or by the use of a distribution list. The latter is a file containing a list of users. Distribution lists can be created by the user and by central administrative functions.

Message Priority
A message may be labeled at a given priority level. Higher-priority messages will be delivered more rapidly, if that is possible. Also, the recipient will be notified or receive some indication of the arrival of high-priority messages.

Status Information
A user may request notification of delivery or of actual retrieval by the recipient. A user may also be able to query the current status of a message (e.g., queued for transmission, transmitted but receipt confirmation not yet received).

Interface to Other Facilities
These would include other electronic systems, such as telex, and physical distribution facilities, such as couriers and the public mail service (e.g., U.S. postal service).

Message Receiving

Mailbox Scanning
Allows the user to scan the current contents of mailbox. Each message may be indicated by subject, author, date, priority, and so on.

Message Selection
The user may select individual messages from the mailbox for display, printing, storing in a separate file, or deletion.

Message Notification
Many systems notify an online user of the arrival of a new message and indicate to a user during log on that there are messages in his or her mailbox.

Message Reply
A user may reply immediately to a selected message, avoiding the necessity of keying in the recipient's name and address.

Message Rerouting
A user who has moved, either temporarily or permanently, may reroute incoming messages. An enhancement is to allow the user to specify different forwarding addresses for different categories of messages.

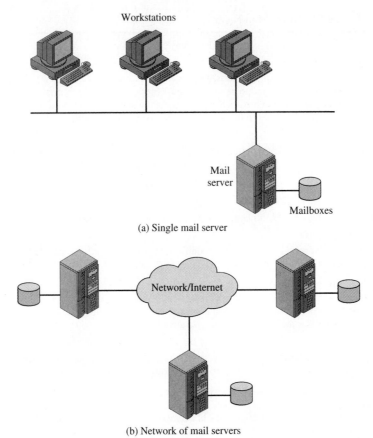

(a) Single mail server

(b) Network of mail servers

Figure 7.1 Electronic Mail Configurations

system. Each user is registered on the system and has a unique identifier, usually the person's last name. Associated with each user is a mailbox. The e-mail facility is an application program available to any user logged onto the system. A user may invoke the e-mail facility, prepare a message, and "send" it to any other user on the system. The act of sending simply involves putting the message in the recipient's mailbox. The mailbox is actually an entity maintained by the file management system and is in the nature of a file directory. One mailbox is associated with each user. Any "incoming" mail is simply stored as a file under that user's mailbox directory. The user may later go and fetch that file to read the message. The user reads messages by invoking the mail facility and "reading" rather than "sending." In most systems, when the user logs on, he or she is informed if there is any new mail in that user's mailbox.

In a LAN configuration, the central mail system is a dedicated mail server or a mail facility on a multipurpose server. In this latter case, the software for preparing and processing mail may be on each individual's workstation, while the mailboxes themselves are on the server.

With a single-system e-mail facility, messages can only be exchanged among users of that particular system. Clearly, this is too limited. In a distributed environment, we would like to be able to exchange messages with users attached to other systems. Thus, we would like to treat e-mail as a distributed application.

For a distributed mail system, a number of mail handlers (e.g., mail servers) connect over a network facility (e.g., public or private WAN or the Internet) and exchange mail (Figure 7.1b). With this configuration, it is useful to group e-mail functions into two distinct categories: user agent and message transfer agent.

The **user agent** (UA) functions are visible to the e-mail user. These include facilities for preparing and submitting messages for routing to the destination(s), as well as utility functions to assist the user in filing, retrieving, replying, and forwarding. The **message transfer agent** (MTA) accepts messages from the user agent for transmission across a network or internetwork. The message transfer agent is concerned with the protocol operation needed to transmit and deliver messages.

The user does not directly interact with the message transfer agent. If the user designates a local recipient for a message, the user agent stores the message in the local recipient's mailbox. If a remote recipient is designated, the user agent passes the message to the message transfer agent for transmission to a remote message transfer agent and ultimately to a remote mailbox.

A number of vendors offer a distributed e-mail facility. Examples include IBM's Lotus Notes and Novell Groupwise. These software packages provide a rich set of e-mail functionality for a community of users all using the same package. However, this will only allow the user to send mail to users on systems of the same vendor. Several forms of interconnection are needed. It is most desirable to provide an interconnection between a private e-mail network and a public e-mail service. Also desirable is the ability to interconnect private systems based on computers from different vendors. To provide these interconnections, a set of standards is needed. Four standards are noteworthy:

- **Post Office Protocol (POP3):** POP3 allows an e-mail client (user agent) to download an e-mail from an e-mail server (message transfer agent). POP3 UAs connect via TCP/IP to the server (typically port 110). The UA enters a username and password (either stored internally for convenience or entered each time by the user for stronger security). After authorized, the UA can issue POP3 commands to retrieve and delete mail.

- **Internet Mail Access Protocol (IMAP):** As with POP3, IMAP also enables an e-mail client to access mail on an e-mail server. IMAP also uses TCP/IP, with server TCP port 143. IMAP is more complex than POP3. IMAP provides stronger authentication than POP3 and provides other functions not supported by POP3.

- **Simple Mail Transfer Protocol (SMTP):** This protocol is used for transfer of mail from a UA to and MTA and from one MTA to another.

- **Multipurpose Internet Mail Extensions (MIME):** Supplements SMTP and allows the encapsulation of multimedia (nontext) messages inside of a standard SMTP message.

In the remainder of this section, we elaborate on SMTP and MIME.

Simple Mail Transfer Protocol

SMTP is the standard protocol for transferring mail between hosts in the TCP/IP protocol suite; it is defined in RFC 821.

Although messages transferred by SMTP usually follow the format defined in RFC 822, described later, SMTP is not concerned with the format or content of messages themselves, with two exceptions. This concept is often expressed by saying that SMTP uses information written on the envelope of the mail (message header) but does not look at the contents (message body) of the envelope. The two exceptions are as follows:

1. SMTP standardizes the message character set as 7-bit ASCII.[1]

2. SMTP adds log information to the start of the delivered message that indicates the path the message took.

BASIC E-MAIL OPERATION Figure 7.2 illustrates the overall flow of mail in a typical distributed system. Although much of this activity is outside the scope of SMTP, the figure illustrates the context within which SMTP typically operates.

To begin, mail is created by a user agent program in response to user input. Each created message consists of a header that includes the recipient's e-mail address and other information, and a body containing the message to be sent. These messages are then queued in some fashion and provided as input to an SMTP Sender program, which is typically an always-present server program on the host.

Although the structure of the outgoing mail queue will differ depending on the host's operating system, each queued message conceptually has two parts:

1. The message text, consisting of
   - The 822 header: This constitutes the message envelope and includes an indication of the intended recipient or recipients.
   - The body of the message, composed by the user.

2. A list of mail destinations.

The list of mail destinations for the message is derived by the user agent from the message header. In some cases, the destination or destinations are literally specified in the message header. In other cases, the user agent may need to expand mailing list names, remove duplicates, and replace mnemonic names with actual mailbox names. If any blind carbon copies (BCCs) are indicated, the user agent needs to prepare messages that conform to this requirement. The basic idea is that the multiple formats and styles preferred by humans in the user interface are replaced by a standardized list suitable for the SMTP send program.

The **SMTP sender** takes messages from the outgoing mail queue and transmits them to the proper destination host via SMTP transactions over one or more TCP connections to port 25 on the target hosts. A host may have multiple SMTP senders

---

[1]The American Standard Code for Information Interchange is described in Appendix D.

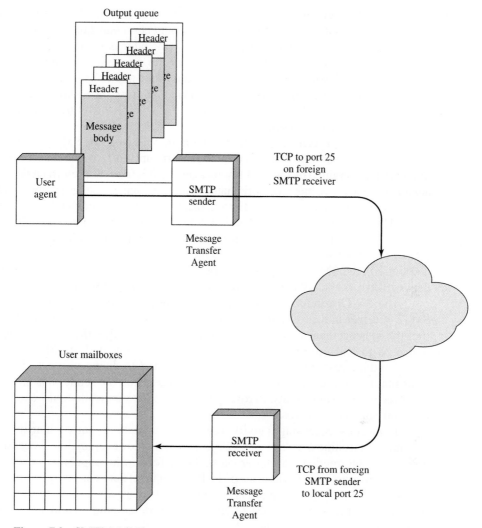

Figure 7.2 SMTP Mail Flow

active simultaneously if it has a large volume of outgoing mail and should also have the capability of creating SMTP receivers on demand so that mail from one host cannot delay mail from another.

Whenever the SMTP sender completes delivery of a particular message to one or more users on a specific host, it deletes the corresponding destinations from that message's destination list. When all destinations for a particular message are processed, the message is deleted from the queue. In processing a queue, the SMTP sender can perform a variety of optimizations. If a particular message is sent to multiple users on a single host, the message text needs to be sent only once. If multiple messages are ready to send to the same host, the SMTP sender can open a TCP connection, transfer the multiple messages, and then close the connection, rather than opening and closing a connection for each message.

The SMTP sender must deal with a variety of errors. The destination host may be unreachable, out of operation, or the TCP connection may fail while mail is being transferred. The sender can requeue the mail for later delivery but give up after some period rather than keep the message in the queue indefinitely. A common error is a faulty destination address, which can occur due to user input error or because the intended destination user has a new address on a different host. The SMTP sender must either redirect the message if possible or return an error notification to the message's originator.

The **SMTP protocol** is used to transfer a message from the SMTP sender to the SMTP receiver over a TCP connection. SMTP attempts to provide reliable operation but does not guarantee recovery of lost messages. SMTP does not return an end-to-end acknowledgment to a message's originator to indicate that a message is successfully delivered to the message's recipient. Error indications are not guaranteed to be returned either. However, the SMTP-based mail system is generally considered reliable.

The **SMTP receiver** accepts each arriving message and either places it in the appropriate user mailbox or copies it to the local outgoing mail queue if forwarding is required. The SMTP receiver must be able to verify local mail destinations and deal with errors, including transmission errors and lack of disc file capacity.

The SMTP sender is responsible for a message up to the point where the SMTP receiver indicates that the transfer is complete; however, this simply means that the message has arrived at the SMTP receiver, not that the message has been delivered to and retrieved by the intended final recipient. The SMTP receiver's error-handling responsibilities are generally limited to giving up on TCP connections that fail or are inactive for very long periods. Thus, the sender has most of the error recovery responsibility. Errors during completion indication may cause duplicate, but not lost, messages.

In most cases, messages go directly from the mail originator's machine to the destination machine over a single TCP connection. However, mail will occasionally go through intermediate machines via an SMTP forwarding capability, in which case the message must traverse a series of TCP connections between source and destination. One way for this to happen is for the sender to specify a route to the destination in the form of a sequence of servers. A more common event is forwarding required because a user has moved.

It is important to note that the SMTP protocol is limited to the conversation that takes place between the SMTP sender and the SMTP receiver. SMTP's main function is the transfer of messages, although there are some ancillary functions dealing with mail destination verification and handling. The rest of the mail-handling functionality depicted in Figure 7.2 is beyond the scope of SMTP and may differ from one system to another. As was mentioned, there are a number of enterprise-level applications, such as Lotus Notes and Novell Groupwise, that provide the end-user e-mail functionality. There are also a number of single-user e-mail client packages popular on personal computers, such as Microsoft Entourage.

We now turn to a discussion of the main elements of SMTP.

SMTP OVERVIEW The operation of SMTP consists of a series of commands and responses exchanged between the SMTP sender and receiver. The initiative is with the SMTP sender, which establishes the TCP connection. Once the connection is established, the SMTP sender sends commands over the connection to the receiver. Each command generates exactly one reply from the SMTP receiver.

Basic SMTP operation occurs in three phases: connection setup, exchange of one or more command-response pairs, and connection termination. We examine each phase in turn.

CONNECTION SETUP   An SMTP sender will attempt to set up a TCP connection with a target host when it has one or more mail messages to deliver to that host. The sequence is quite simple:

1. The sender opens a TCP connection with the receiver.
2. Once the connection is established, the receiver identifies itself with "220 Service Ready".
3. The sender identifies itself with the HELO command.
4. The receiver accepts the sender's identification with "250 OK".

If the mail service on the destination is unavailable, the destination host returns a "421 Service Not Available" reply in step 2 and the process is terminated.

MAIL TRANSFER   Once a connection has been established, the SMTP sender may send one or more messages to the SMTP receiver. There are three logical phases in the transfer of a message:

1. A MAIL command identifies the originator of the message.
2. One or more RCPT commands identify the recipients for this message.
3. A DATA command transfers the message text.

The **MAIL command** gives the reverse path, which can be used to report errors. If the receiver is prepared to accept messages from this originator, it returns a "250 OK" reply. Otherwise the receiver returns a reply indicating failure to execute the command or an error in the command.

The **RCPT command** identifies an individual recipient of the mail data; multiple recipients are specified by multiple use of this command. A separate reply is returned for each RCPT command, with one of the following possibilities:

1. The receiver accepts the destination with a 250 reply; this indicates that the designated mailbox is on the receiver's system.
2. The destination will require forwarding and the receiver will forward.
3. The destination requires forwarding but the receiver will not forward; the sender must resend to the forwarding address.
4. A mailbox does not exist for this recipient at this host.
5. The destination is rejected due to some other failure to execute or an error in the command.

The advantage of using a separate RCPT phase is that the sender will not send the message until it is assured that the receiver is prepared to receive the message for at least one recipient, thereby avoiding the overhead of sending an entire message only to learn that the destination is unknown. Once the SMTP receiver has agreed to receive the mail message for at least one recipient, the SMTP sender uses the DATA command to initiate the transfer of the message. If the SMTP receiver is still prepared to receive the message, it returns a Start message; otherwise the receiver returns a reply indicating failure to execute the command or an error in the command. If the Start reply is returned, the SMTP sender proceeds to send the message over the TCP connection as a sequence of ASCII lines. The end of the message is indicated by a line containing only a period. The SMTP receiver responds with an OK reply if the message is accepted or with the appropriate error code.

An example, taken from RFC 821, illustrates the process:

```
S: MAIL FROM:<Smith@Alpha.com>
R: 250 OK

S: RCPT TO:<Jones@Beta.com>
R: 250 OK

S: RCPT TO:<Green@Beta.com>
R: 550 No such user here

S: RCPT TO:<Brown@Beta.com>
R: 250 OK

S: DATA
R: 354 Start mail input; end with <CRLF>.<CRLF>
S: Blah blah blah...
S: ...etc. etc. etc.
S: <CRLF>.<CRLF>
R: 250 OK
```

The SMTP sender is transmitting mail that originates with the user Smith@Alpha.com. The message is addressed to three users on machine Beta.com, namely, Jones, Green, and Brown. The SMTP receiver indicates that it has mailboxes for Jones and Brown but does not have information on Green. Because at least one of the intended recipients has been verified, the sender proceeds to send the text message.

CONNECTION CLOSING The SMTP sender closes the connection in two steps. First, the sender sends a QUIT command and waits for a reply. The second step is to initiate a TCP close operation for the TCP connection. The receiver initiates its TCP close after sending its reply to the QUIT command.

RFC 822 RFC 822 defines a format for text messages that are sent using e-mail. The SMTP standard adopts RFC 822 as the format for use in constructing messages for transmission via SMTP. In the RFC 822 context, messages are viewed as having an envelope and contents. The envelope contains whatever information is needed to accomplish transmission and delivery. The contents compose the object to be delivered to the recipient. The RFC 822 standard applies only to the contents. However, the content standard includes a set of header fields that may be used by the mail system to create the envelope, and the standard is intended to facilitate the acquisition of such information by programs.

An RFC 822 message consists of a sequence of lines of text and uses a general "memo" framework. That is, a message consists of some number of header lines, which follow a rigid format, followed by a body portion consisting of arbitrary text.

A header line usually consists of a keyword, followed by a colon, followed by the keyword's arguments; the format allows a long line to be broken up into several lines. The most frequently used keywords are From, To, Subject, and Date. Here is an example message:

```
Date: Mon, 10 Mar 2008 10:37:17 (EDT)
From: "William Stallings" <ws@host.com>
Subject: The Syntax in RFC 822
To: Smith@Other-host.com
Cc: Jones@Yet-Another-Host.com

Hello. This section begins the actual message body, which
is delimited from the message heading by a blank line.
```

Another field that is commonly found in RFC 822 headers is Message-ID. This field contains a unique identifier associated with this message.

Multipurpose Internet Mail Extensions (MIME)

MIME is an extension to the RFC 822 framework that is intended to address some of the problems and limitations of the use of SMTP and RFC 822 for e-mail. [PARZ06] lists the following limitations of the SMTP/822 scheme:

1. SMTP cannot transmit executable files or other binary objects. A number of schemes are in use for converting binary files into a text form that can be used by SMTP mail systems, including the popular UNIX uuencode/uudecode scheme. However, none of these is a standard or even a de facto standard.

2. SMTP cannot transmit text data that include national language characters because these are represented by 8-bit codes with values of 128 decimal or higher, and SMTP is limited to 7-bit ASCII.

3. SMTP servers may reject mail message over a certain size.

4. SMTP gateways that translate between ASCII and the character code EBCDIC do not use a consistent set of mappings, resulting in translation problems.

5. SMTP gateways to X.400 e-mail networks cannot handle nontextual data included in X.400 messages.

6. Some SMTP implementations do not adhere completely to the SMTP standards defined in RFC 821. Common problems include the following:

   • Deletion, addition, or reordering of carriage return and linefeed

   • Truncating or wrapping lines longer than 76 characters

   • Removal of trailing white space (tab and space characters)

   • Padding of lines in a message to the same length

   • Conversion of tab characters into multiple space characters

These limitations make it difficult to use encryption with electron mail and to use SMTP to carry multimedia objects and electronic data interchange (EDI) messages. MIME is intended to resolve these problems in a manner that is compatible with existing RFC 822 implementations.

OVERVIEW The MIME specification includes the following elements:

1. Five new message header fields are defined, which may be included in an RFC 822 header. These fields provide information about the body of the message.
2. A number of content formats are defined, thus standardizing representations that support multimedia e-mail.
3. Transfer encodings are defined that enable the conversion of any content format into a form that is protected from alteration by the mail system.

In this subsection, we introduce the five message header fields. The next two subsections deal with content formats and transfer encodings.

The five header fields defined in MIME are as follows:

- **MIME-Version:** Must have the parameter value 1.0. This field indicates that the message conforms to the RFCs.
- **Content-Type:** Describes the data contained in the body with sufficient detail that the receiving user agent can pick an appropriate agent or mechanism to represent the data to the user or otherwise deal with the data in an appropriate manner.
- **Content-Transfer-Encoding:** Indicates the type of transformation that has been used to represent the body of the message in a way that is acceptable for mail transport.
- **Content-ID:** Used to uniquely identify MIME entities in multiple contexts.
- **Content-Description:** A plain text description of the object with the body; this is useful when the object is not readable (e.g., audio data).

Any or all of these fields may appear in a normal RFC 822 header. A compliant implementation must support the MIME-Version, Content-Type, and Content-Transfer-Encoding fields; the Content-ID and Content-Description fields are optional and may be ignored by the recipient implementation.

MIME CONTENT TYPES The bulk of the MIME specification is concerned with the definition of a variety of content types. This reflects the need to provide standardized ways of dealing with a wide variety of information representations in a multimedia environment.

Table 7.2 lists the MIME content types. There are seven different major types of content and a total of 14 subtypes. In general, a content type declares the general type of data, and the subtype specifies a particular format for that type of data.

For the **text type** of body, no special software is required to get the full meaning of the text, aside from support of the indicated character set. The only defined subtype is plain text, which is simply a string of ASCII characters.

The **multipart type** indicates that the body contains multiple, independent parts. The Content-Type header field includes a parameter, called boundary, that

Table 7.2 MIME Content Types

Type	Subtype	Description
Text	Plain	Unformatted text; may be ASCII or ISO 8859.
Multipart	Mixed	The different parts are independent but are to be transmitted together. They should be presented to the receiver in the order that they appear in the mail message.
	Parallel	Differs from Mixed only in that no order is defined for delivering the parts to the receiver.
	Alternative	The different parts are alternative versions of the same information. They are ordered in increasing faithfulness to the original and the recipient's mail system should display the "best" version to the user.
	Digest	Similar to Mixed, but the default type/subtype of each part is message/rfc822.
Message	rfc822	The body is itself an encapsulated message that conforms to RFC 822.
	Partial	Used to allow fragmentation of large mail items, in a way that is transparent to the recipient.
	External-body	Contains a pointer to an object that exists elsewhere.
Image	jpeg	The image is in JPEG format, JFIF encoding.
	gif	The image is in GIF format.
Video	mpeg	MPEG format.
Audio	Basic	Single-channel 8-bit ISDN mu-law encoding at a sample rate of 8 kHz.
Application	PostScript	Adobe Postscript.
	octet-stream	General binary data consisting of 8-bit bytes.

defines the delimiter between body parts. This boundary should not appear in any parts of the message. Each boundary starts on a new line and consists of two hyphens followed by the boundary value. The final boundary, which indicates the end of the last part, also has a suffix of two hyphens. Within each part, there may be an optional ordinary MIME header.

Here is a simple example of a multipart message, containing two parts both consisting of simple text:

```
From: John Smith <js@company.com>
To: Ned Jones <ned@soft.com>
Subject: Sample message
MIME-Version: 1.0
Content-type: multipart/mixed; boundary="simple boundary"

This is the preamble. It is to be ignored, though it is a
handy place for mail composers to include an explanatory
note to non-MIME conformant readers.
-simple boundary

This is implicitly typed plain ASCII text. It does NOT
end with a linebreak.
-simple boundary
Content-type: text/plain; charset=us-ascii
```

```
This is explicitly typed plain ASCII text. It DOES end with
a linebreak.

-simple boundary-
This is the epilogue. It is also to be ignored.
```

There are four subtypes of the multipart type, all of which have the same overall syntax. The **multipart/mixed subtype** is used when there are multiple independent body parts that need to be bundled in a particular order. For the **multipart/parallel subtype**, the order of the parts is not significant. If the recipient's system is appropriate, the multiple parts can be presented in parallel. For example, a picture or text part could be accompanied by a voice commentary that is played while the picture or text is displayed.

For the **multipart/alternative subtype**, the various parts are different representations of the same information. The following is an example:

```
From: John Smith <js@company.com>
To: Ned Jones <ned@soft.com>
Subject: Formatted text mail
MIME-Version: 1.0
Content-Type: multipart/alternative; boundary=boundary42

-boundary42

Content-Type: text/plain; charset=us-ascii

  ...plain text version of message goes here....
-boundary42
Content-Type: text/richtext

.... RFC 1341 richtext version of same message goes here ...
-boundary42-
```

In this subtype, the body parts are ordered in terms of increasing preference. For this example, if the recipient system is capable of displaying the message in the richtext format, this is done; otherwise, the plain text format is used.

The **multipart/digest subtype** is used when each of the body parts is interpreted as an RFC 822 message with headers. This subtype enables the construction of a message whose parts are individual messages. For example, the moderator of a group might collect e-mail messages from participants, bundle these messages, and send them out in one encapsulating MIME message.

The **message type** provides a number of important capabilities in MIME. The **message/rfc822 subtype** indicates that the body is an entire message, including header and body. Despite the name of this subtype, the encapsulated message may be not only a simple RFC 822 message, but also any MIME message.

The **message/partial subtype** enables fragmentation of a large message into a number of parts, which must be reassembled at the destination. For this subtype, three parameters are specified in the Content-Type: Message/Partial field:

- **id:** A value that is common to each fragment of the same message, so that the fragments can be identified at the recipient for reassembly, but unique across different messages.

- **number:** A sequence number that indicates the position of this fragment in the original message. The first fragment is numbered 1, the second 2, and so on.
- **total:** The total number of parts. The last fragment is identified by having the same value for the *number* and *total* parameters.

The **message/external-body subtype** indicates that the actual data to be conveyed in this message are not contained in the body. Instead, the body contains the information needed to access the data. As with the other message types, the message/external-body subtype has an outer header and an encapsulated message with its own header. The only necessary field in the outer header is the Content-type field, which identifies this as a message/external-body subtype. The inner header is the message header for the encapsulated message.

The Content-Type field in the outer header must include an access-type parameter, which has one of the following values:

- **FTP:** The message body is accessible as a file using the File Transfer Protocol (FTP). For this access type, the following additional parameters are mandatory: name, the name of the file; and site, the domain name of the host where the file resides. Optional parameters are as follows: directory, the directory in which the file is located; and mode, which indicates how FTP should retrieve the file (e.g., ASCII, image). Before the file transfer can take place, the user will need to provide a used id and password. These are not transmitted with the message for security reasons.
- **TFTP:** The message body is accessible as a file using the Trivial File Transfer Protocol (TFTP). The same parameters as for FTP are used.
- **Anon-FTP:** Identical to FTP, except that the user is not asked to supply a user id and password. The parameter name supplies the name of the file.
- **local-file:** The message body is accessible as a file on the recipient's machine.
- **AFS:** The message body is accessible as a file via the global AFS (Andrew File System). The parameter name supplies the name of the file.
- **mail-server:** The message body is accessible by sending an e-mail message to a mail server. A *server* parameter must be included that gives the e-mail address of the server. The body of the original message, known as the phantom body, should contain the exact command to be sent to the mail server.

The **image type** indicates that the body contains a displayable image. The subtype, jpeg or gif, specifies the image format. In the future, more subtypes will be added to this list.

The **video type** indicates that the body contains a time-varying picture image, possibly with color and coordinated sound. The only subtype so far specified is mpeg.

The **audio type** indicates that the body contains audio data. The only subtype, basic, conforms to an ISDN service known as "64-kbps, 8-kHz Structured, Usable for Speech Information," with a digitized speech algorithm referred to as μ-law PCM (pulse code modulation). This general type is the typical way of transmitting speech signals over a digital network. The term μ-*law* refers to the specific encoding technique; it is the standard technique used in North America and Japan. A competing system, known as A-law, is standard in Europe.

The **application type** refers to other kinds of data, typically either uninterpreted binary data or information to be processed by a mail-based application. The **application/octet-stream subtype** indicates general binary data in a sequence of octets. RFC 1521 recommends that the receiving implementation should offer to put the data in a file or use the data as input to a program.

The **application/Postscript subtype** indicates the use of Adobe Postscript.

7.2 WEB ACCESS AND HTTP

The Hypertext Transfer Protocol (HTTP) is the foundation protocol of the World Wide Web (WWW) and can be used in any client/server application involving hypertext. The name is somewhat misleading in that HTTP is not a protocol for transferring hypertext; rather it is a protocol for transmitting information with the efficiency necessary for making hypertext jumps. The data transferred by the protocol can be plaintext, hypertext, audio, images, or any Internet-accessible information.

We begin with an overview of HTTP concepts and operation and then look at some of the details, basing our discussion on the most recent version to be put on the Internet standards track, HTTP 1.1. A number of important terms defined in the HTTP specification are summarized in Table 7.3; these will be introduced as the discussion proceeds.

HyperText Transfer Protocol Simulator

HTTP Overview

HTTP is a transaction-oriented client/server protocol. The most typical use of HTTP is between a Web browser and a Web server. To provide reliability, HTTP makes use of TCP. Nevertheless, HTTP is a **stateless protocol**: Each transaction is treated independently. Accordingly, a typical implementation will create a new TCP connection between client and server for each transaction and then terminate the connection as soon as the transaction completes, although the specification does not dictate this one-to-one relationship between transaction and connection lifetimes.

The stateless nature of HTTP is well suited to its typical application. A normal session of a user with a Web browser involves retrieving a sequence of Web pages and documents. The sequence is, ideally, performed rapidly, and the locations of the various pages and documents may be a number of widely distributed servers.

Another important feature of HTTP is that it is flexible in the formats that it can handle. When a client issues a request to a server, it may include a prioritized list of formats that it can handle, and the server replies with the appropriate format. For example, a lynx browser cannot handle images, so a Web server need not transmit any images on Web pages. This arrangement prevents the transmission of unnecessary information and provides the basis for extending the set of formats with new standardized and proprietary specifications.

Figure 7.3 illustrates three examples of HTTP operation. The simplest case is one in which a user agent establishes a direct connection with an origin server. The **user agent** is the client that initiates the request, such as a Web browser being run on behalf of an end user. The **origin server** is the server on which a resource of interest resides; an example is a Web server at which a desired Web home page resides. For

Table 7.3   Key Terms Related to HTTP

Cache A program's local store of response messages and the subsystem that controls its message storage, retrieval, and deletion. A cache stores cacheable responses in order to reduce the response time and network band-width consumption on future, equivalent requests. Any client or server may include a cache, though a cache cannot be used by a server while it is acting as a tunnel.	**Origin Server** The server on which a given resource resides or is to be created.
Client An application program that establishes connections for the purpose of sending requests.	**Proxy** An intermediary program that acts as both a server and a client for the purpose of making requests on behalf of other clients. Requests are serviced internally or by passing them, with possible translation, on to other servers. A proxy must interpret and, if necessary, rewrite a request message before forwarding it. Proxies are often used as client-side portals through network fire-walls and as helper applications for handling requests via protocols not implemented by the user agent.
Connection A transport layer virtual circuit established between two application programs for the purposes of com-munication.	
Entity A particular representation or rendition of a data re-source, or reply from a service resource, that may be enclosed within a request or response message. An entity consists of entity headers and an entity body.	**Resource** A network data object or service that can be identified by a URI.
	Server An application program that accepts connections in order to service requests by sending back responses.
Gateway A server that acts as an intermediary for some other server. Unlike a proxy, a gateway receives requests as if it were the original server for the requested re-source; the requesting client may not be aware that it is communicating with a gateway. Gateways are often used as server-side portals through network firewalls and as protocol translators for access to resources stored on non-HTTP systems.	**Tunnel** An intermediary program that is acting as a blind relay between two connections. Once active, a tunnel is not considered a party to the HTTP communication, though the tunnel may have been initiated by an HTTP request. A tunnel ceases to exist when both ends of the relayed connections are closed. Tunnels are used when a portal is necessary and the interme-diary cannot, or should not, interpret the relayed communication.
Message The basic unit of HTTP communication, consisting of a structured sequence of octets transmitted via the connection.	**User Agent** The client that initiates a request. These are often browsers, editors, spiders, or other end-user tools.

this case, the client opens a TCP connection that is end-to-end between the client and the server. The client then issues an HTTP request. The request consists of a specific command, referred to as a method, an address [referred to as a Uniform Re-source Locator[2] (URL)], and a MIME-like message containing request parameters, information about the client, and perhaps some additional content information.

When the server receives the request, it attempts to perform the requested ac-tion and then returns an HTTP response. The response includes status information, a success/error code, and a MIME-like message containing information about the server, information about the response itself, and possible body content. The TCP connection is then closed.

The middle part of Figure 7.3 shows a case in which there is not an end-to-end TCP connection between the user agent and the origin server. Instead, there are one or more intermediate systems with TCP connections between logically adjacent

---

[2]Appendix C provides a discussion of URLs.

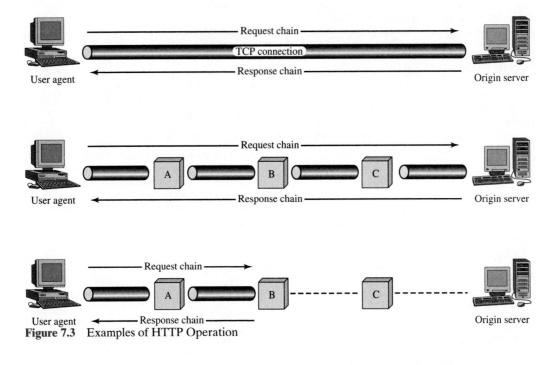

Figure 7.3 Examples of HTTP Operation

systems. Each intermediate system acts as a relay, so that a request initiated by the client is relayed through the intermediate systems to the server, and the response from the server is relayed back to the client.

Three forms of intermediate system are defined in the HTTP specification: proxy, gateway, and tunnel, all of which are illustrated in Figure 7.4.

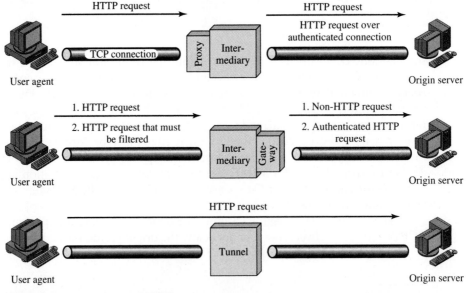

Figure 7.4 Intermediate HTTP Systems

PROXY   A proxy acts on behalf of other clients and presents requests from other clients to a server. The proxy acts as a server in interacting with a client and as a client in interacting with a server. There are two scenarios that call for the use of a proxy:

- **Security intermediary:** The client and server may be separated by a security intermediary such as a firewall, with the proxy on the client side of the firewall. Typically, the client is part of a network secured by a firewall and the server is external to the secured network. In this case, the server must authenticate itself to the firewall to set up a connection with the proxy. The proxy accepts responses after they have passed through the firewall.
- **Different versions of HTTP:** If the client and server are running different versions of HTTP, then the proxy can implement both versions and perform the required mapping.

In summary, a proxy is a forwarding agent, receiving a request for a URL object, modifying the request, and forwarding the request toward the server identified in the URL.

GATEWAY   A gateway is a server that appears to the client as if it were an origin server. It acts on behalf of other servers that may not be able to communicate directly with a client. There are two scenarios in which gateways can be used.

- **Security intermediary:** The client and server may be separated by a security intermediary such as a firewall, with the gateway on the server side of the firewall. Typically, the server is connected to a network protected by a firewall, with the client external to the network. In this case the client must authenticate itself to the gateway, which can then pass the request on to the server.
- **Non-HTTP server:** Web browsers have built into them the capability to contact servers for protocols other than HTTP, such as FTP and Gopher servers. This capability can also be provided by a gateway. The client makes an HTTP request to a gateway server. The gateway server then contacts the relevant FTP or Gopher server to obtain the desired result. This result is then converted into a form suitable for HTTP and transmitted back to the client.

TUNNEL   Unlike the proxy and the gateway, the tunnel performs no operations on HTTP requests and responses. Instead, a tunnel is simply a relay point between two TCP connections, and the HTTP messages are passed unchanged as if there were a single HTTP connection between user agent and origin server. Tunnels are used when there must be an intermediary system between client and server but it is not necessary for that system to understand the contents of messages. An example is a firewall in which a client or server external to a protected network can establish an authenticated connection and then maintain that connection for purposes of HTTP transactions.

CACHE   Returning to Figure 7.3, the lowest portion of the figure shows an example of a cache. A cache is a facility that may store previous requests and responses for handling new requests. If a new request arrives that is the same as a stored request, then the cache can supply the stored response rather than accessing the resource indicated in the URL. The cache can operate on a client or server or on an intermediate system other than a tunnel. In the figure, intermediary B has cached a request/response transaction, so that a corresponding new request from the client need not travel the entire chain to the origin server but is handled by B.

Not all transactions can be cached, and a client or server can dictate that a certain transaction may be cached only for a given time limit.

Messages

The best way to describe the functionality of HTTP is to describe the individual elements of the HTTP message. HTTP consists of two types of messages: **requests** from clients to servers, and **responses** from servers to clients. Figure 7.5 provides an example.

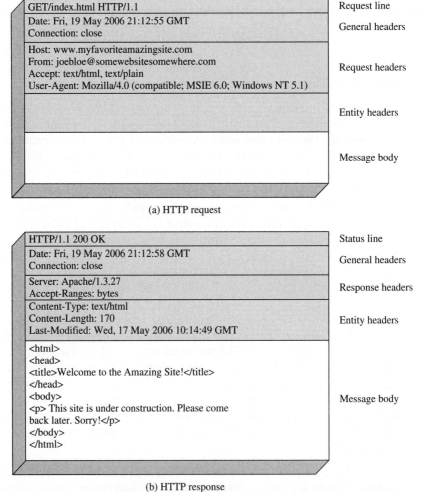

(a) HTTP request

(b) HTTP response

Figure 7.5   Examples of HTTP Message Format

The Simple-Request and Simple-Response messages were defined in HTTP/0.9. The request is a simple GET command with the requested URL; the response is simply a block containing the information identified in the URL. In HTTP/1.1, the use of these simple forms is discouraged because it prevents the client from using content negotiation and the server from identifying the media type of the returned entity.

All of the HTTP headers consist of a sequence of fields, following the same generic format as RFC 822 (described in Section 7.1). Each field begins on a new line and consists of the field name followed by a colon and the field value.

A full request uses the following fields:

- **Request-Line:** Indicates the requested action, the resource on which the action is to be performed, and the version of HTTP used in this message
- **General-Headers:** Contains fields that are applicable to the request message but that do not apply to the entity being transferred
- **Request-Headers:** Contains information about the request and the client. For example, a request may be conditional, specifying under what conditions the requested action is to be determined. A field in this header may also indicate which formats and encodings the client is able to handle.
- **Entity-Header:** Contains information about the resource identified by the request and information about the entity body, if any
- **Entity-Body:** The body of the message

A response message has the same structure as a request message, but substitutes the following headers for the request line and the request headers:

- **Status-Line:** Indicates the version of HTTP used in this message and provides status information about this response. For example, "OK" means that the request was successfully completed.
- **Response-Headers:** Provides additional data that expand on the status information in the status line.

7.3 WEB SECURITY

The World Wide Web is fundamentally a client/server application running over the Internet and TCP/IP intranets. [GARF02] points out the following security challenges presented by the use of the Web:

- The Web is vulnerable to attacks on the Web servers over the Internet.
- The Web is a highly visible outlet for corporate and product information and as the platform for business transactions. Reputations can be damaged and money can be lost if the Web servers are subverted.
- Web browsers are very easy to use, Web servers are relatively easy to configure and manage, and Web content is increasingly easy to develop, but the underlying software is extraordinarily complex. This complex software may hide many potential security flaws. The short history of the Web is filled with examples of

new and upgraded systems, properly installed, that are vulnerable to a variety of security attacks.

- A Web server can be exploited as a launching pad into the corporation's or agency's entire computer complex. Once the Web server is subverted, an attacker may be able to gain access to data and systems not part of the Web itself but connected to the server at the local site.

- Casual and untrained (in security matters) users are common clients for Web-based services. Such users are not necessarily aware of the security risks that exist and do not have the tools or knowledge to take effective countermeasures.

One way to classify Web security threats is in terms of the location of the threat: Web server, Web browser, and network traffic between browser and server. Issues of server and browser security fall into the category of computer system security; Part Six of this book addresses the issue of system security in general but is also applicable to Web system security. Issues of traffic security fall into the category of network security and are addressed in this section.

Web Traffic Security Approaches

A number of approaches to providing Web security are possible. The various approaches that have been considered are similar in the services they provide and, to some extent, in the mechanisms that they use, but they differ with respect to their scope of applicability and their relative location within the TCP/IP protocol stack.

One way to provide Web security is to use IP Security, described in Chapter 5. The advantage of using IPSec is that it is transparent to end users and applications and provides a general-purpose solution. Further, IPSec includes a filtering capability so that only selected traffic need incur the overhead of IPSec processing. The disadvantage of IPSec is the need to configure a relatively complex security architecture on all of the systems supporting both Web browsers and Web servers. An enterprise network that allows access from both enterprise systems and partner (vendor, customer) systems may not be a good candidate for such a configuration.

Another relatively general-purpose solution is to implement security just above TCP. This is the approach defined by the Secure Sockets Layer (SSL) and the follow-on Internet standard known as Transport Layer Security (TLS). At this level, there are two implementation choices. For full generality, SSL (or TLS) could be provided as part of the underlying protocol suite and therefore be transparent to applications. Alternatively, SSL can be embedded in specific packages. In the case of the Web, virtually all browsers and Web servers incorporate SSL.

The remainder of this chapter is devoted to a discussion of SSL/TLS the related concept of HTTPS.

Secure Sockets Layer

Figure 7.6 illustrates the position of SSL in the TCP/IP protocol architecture. Before discussing this architecture, we need to define the term *socket*. In essence, a socket is a method of directing data to the appropriate application in a TCP/IP network. The combination of the IP address of the host and a TCP port number make up a socket address. From the application point of view, a socket interface in

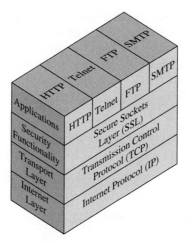

Figure 7.6 The Role of SSL in the TCP/IP Architecture

an application-programming interface (API). The socket interface is a generic communication programming interface implemented on UNIX and many other systems. Two applications communicate through TCP sockets. An application connects to TCP through a socket address and tells TCP what remote application is requested by means of the remote application's socket address.

With SSL in place, an application has an SSL socket address and communicates to the SSL socket of the remote application. The security functions provided by SSL are transparent to the application and also to TCP. Thus, neither TCP nor the application needs to be modified to invoke the security features of SSL. As shown in Figure 7.6, SSL supports not only HTTP, but also any other application that uses TCP.

SSL provides three categories of security:

- **Confidentiality:** All data that passes between the two applications (e.g., the two HTTP modules) are encrypted so that they cannot be eavesdropped on the Internet.

- **Message integrity:** SSL assures that the message is not altered or substituted for en route.

- **Authentication:** SSL can validate the identity of one or both partners to the exchange.

SSL consists of two phases: handshake and data transfer. During handshake, the two sides perform an authentication function and establish an encryption key to be used for data transfer. During data transfer, the two sides use the encryption key to encrypt all transmitted data.

HTTPS

HTTPS (HTTP over SSL) refers to the combination of HTTP and SSL to implement secure communication between a Web browser and a Web server. The HTTPS capability is built into all modern Web browsers. Its use depends on the Web server supporting HTTPS communication. For example, search engines do not support HTTPS.

The principal difference seen by a user of a web browser is that URL (uniform resource locator) addresses begin with https:// rather than http://. A normal HTTP connection uses port 80. If HTTPS is specified, port 443 is specified, which invokes SSL.

When HTTPS is used, the following elements of the communication are encrypted:

- URL of the requested document
- Contents of the document
- Contents of browser forms (filled in by browser user)
- Cookies sent from browser to server and from server to browser
- Contents of HTTP header

7.4 INTERNET TELEPHONY AND SIP

The Session Initiation Protocol (SIP), defined in RFC 3261, is an application-level control protocol for setting up, modifying, and terminating real-time sessions between participants over an IP data network. SIP can support any type of single media or multimedia session, including teleconferencing.

SIP is just one component in the set of protocols and services needed to support multimedia exchanges over the Internet. SIP is the signaling protocol that enables one party to place a call to another party and to negotiate the parameters of a multimedia session. The actual audio, video, or other multimedia content is exchanged between session participants using an appropriate transport protocol. In many cases, the transport protocol to use is the Real-Time Transport Protocol (RTP). Directory access and lookup protocols are also needed.

The key driving force behind SIP is to enable Internet telephony, also referred to as voice over IP (VoIP). There is wide industry acceptance that SIP will be the standard IP signaling mechanism for voice and multimedia calling services. Further, as older PBXs and network switches are phased out, industry is moving toward a voice networking model that is SIP signaled, IP based, and packet switched, not only in the wide area but also on the customer premises [BORT02, BORT03].

SIP supports five facets of establishing and terminating multimedia communications:

- **User location:** Users can move to other locations and access their telephony or other application features from remote locations.
- **User availability:** Determination of the willingness of the called party to engage in communications.
- **User capabilities:** Determination of the media and media parameters to be used.
- **Session setup:** Setup up point-to-point and multiparty calls, with agreed session parameters.
- **Session management:** Including transfer and termination of sessions, modifying session parameters, and invoking services.

SIP employs design elements developed for earlier protocols. SIP is based on an HTTP-like request/response transaction model. Each transaction consists of a client request that invokes a particular method, or function, on the server and at least one response. SIP uses most of the header fields, encoding rules, and status codes of HTTP. This provides a readable text-based format for displaying information. SIP incorporates the use of a Session Description Protocol (SDP), which defines session content using a set of types similar to those used in MIME.

SIP Components and Protocols

An SIP network can be viewed of consisting of components defined on two dimensions: client/server and individual network elements. RFC 3261 defines **client** and **server** as follows:

- **Client:** A client is any network element that sends SIP requests and receives SIP responses. Clients may or may not interact directly with a human user. User agent clients and proxies are clients.

- **Server:** A server is a network element that receives requests in order to service them and sends back responses to those requests. Examples of servers are proxies, user agent servers, redirect servers, and registrars.

The individual elements of a standard SIP network are:

- **User Agent:** Resides in every SIP end station. It acts in two roles:
  - **User Agent Client (UAC):** Issues SIP requests.
  - **User Agent Server (UAS):** Receives SIP requests and generates a response that accepts, rejects, or redirects the request.

- **Redirect Server:** Used during session initiation to determine the address of the called device. The redirect server returns this information to the calling device, directing the UAC to contact an alternate URI.[3]

- **Proxy Server:** An intermediary entity that acts as both a server and a client for the purpose of making requests on behalf of other clients. A proxy server primarily plays the role of routing, which means its job is to ensure that a request is sent to another entity closer to the targeted user. Proxies are also useful for enforcing policy (for example, making sure a user is allowed to make a call). A proxy interprets, and, if necessary, rewrites specific parts of a request message before forwarding it.

- **Registrar:** A server that accepts REGISTER requests and places the information it receives (the SIP address and associated IP address of the registering device) in those requests into the location service for the domain it handles.

- **Location Service:** A location service is used by a SIP redirect or proxy server to obtain information about a callee's possible location(s). For this purpose, the location service maintains a database of SIP-address/IP-address mappings.

---

[3]A URI is a generic identifier used to name any resource on the Internet. The URL, used for Web addresses is a type of URI. See RFC 2396 or Appendix C for more detail.

Figure 7.7 SIP Components and Protocols

- **Presence Server:** Accepts, stores, and distributes presence information[4]. The presence server has two distinct sets of clients:
  - —Presentities (producers of information) provide presence information to the server to be stored and distributed.
  - —Watchers (consumers of information) receive presence information from the server.

The various servers are defined in RFC 3261 as logical devices. They may be implemented as separate servers configured on the Internet or they may be combined into a single application that resides in a physical server.

Figure 7.7 shows how some of the SIP components relate to one another and the protocols that are employed. A user agent acting as a client (in this case UAC alice) uses SIP to set up a session with a user agent that will act as a server (in this case UAS bob). The session initiation dialogue uses SIP and involves one or more proxy servers to forward requests and responses between the two user agents. The

---

[4]The concept of presence is discussed in Chapter 1

user agents also make use of the Session Description Protocol (SDP), which is used to describe the media session.

The proxy servers may also act as redirect servers as needed. If redirection is done, a proxy server will need to consult the location service database, which may be colocated with a proxy server or not. The communication between the proxy server and the location service is beyond the scope of the SIP standard. The Domain Name Service (DNS), described in Chapter 4, is also an important part of SIP operation. Typically, a UAC will make a request using the domain name of the UAS, rather than an IP address. A proxy server will need to consult a DNS server to find a proxy server for the target domain.

SIP typically runs on top of UDP for performance reasons and provides its own reliability mechanisms but may also use TCP. If a secure, encrypted transport mechanism is desired, SIP messages may alternatively be carried over the Transport Layer Security (TLS) protocol, which provides a secure transport-level protocol.

Associated with SIP is the Session Description Protocol (SDP), defined in RFC 2327. SIP is used to invite one or more participants to a session, while the SDP-encoded body of the SIP message contains information about what media encodings (e.g., voice, video) the parties can and will use. Once this information is exchanged and acknowledged, all participants are aware of the participants' IP addresses, available transmission capacity, and media type. Then data transmission begins, using an appropriate transport protocol. Typically, the Real-Time Transport Protocol (RTP) is used. RTP is a transport protocol that provides direct support for real-time traffic, unlike TCP. Throughout the session, participants can make changes to session parameters, such as new media types or new parties to the session, using SIP messages.

SIP Uniform Resource Identifier

A resource within a SIP network is identified by a **Uniform Resource Identifier (URI)**. Examples of communications resources include the following:

- A user of an online service
- An appearance on a multiline phone
- A mailbox on a messaging system
- A telephone number at a gateway service
- A group (such as "sales" or "helpdesk") in an organization

SIP URIs have a format based on e-mail address formats, namely user@domain. There are two common schemes. An ordinary SIP URI is of the form:

sip:bob@biloxi.com

The URI may also include a password, port number, and related parameters. If secure transmission is required, "sip:" is replaced by "sips:". In the latter case, SIP messages are transported over TLS.

Examples of Operation

The SIP specification is quite complex; the main document, RFC 3261, is 269 pages long. To give some feel for its operation, we present a few examples.

Figure 7.8 SIP Successful Call Setup

Figure 7.8 shows a successful attempt by user Alice to establish a session with user Bob, whose URI is bob@biloxi.com. [5] Alice's UAC is configured to communicate with a proxy server (the outbound server) in its domain and begins by sending an INVITE message to the proxy server that indicates its desire to invite Bob's UAS into a session (1); the server acknowledges the request (2). Although Bob's UAS is identified by its URI, the outbound proxy server needs to take into account the possibility that Bob is not currently available or that Bob has moved. Accordingly, the outbound proxy server should forward the INVITE request to the proxy server that is responsible for the domain biloxi.com. The outbound

---

[5]Figures 7.7 through 7.9 are adapted from ones developed by Professor H. Charles Baker of Southern Methodist University.

proxy thus consults a local DNS server to obtain the IP address of the biloxi.com proxy server (3), by asking for the resource record that contains information on the proxy server for biloxi.com.

The DNS server responds (4) with the IP address of the biloxi.com proxy server (the inbound server). Alice's proxy server can now forward the INVITE message to the inbound proxy server (5), which acknowledges the message (6). The inbound proxy server now consults a location server to determine the location of Bob (7), and the location server responds with Bob's location, indicating that Bob is signed in, and therefore available for SIP messages (8). The proxy server can now send the INVITE message on to Bob (9). A ringing response is sent from Bob back to A (10, 11, 12) while the UAS at Bob is alerting the local media application (e.g., telephony). When the media application accepts the call, Bob's UAS sends back an OK response to Alice (13, 14, 15).

Finally, Alice's UAC sends an acknowledgement message to Bob's UAS to confirm the reception of the final response (16). In this example, the ACK is sent directly from Alice to Bob, bypassing the two proxies. This occurs because the endpoints have learned each other's address from the INVITE/200 (OK) exchange, which was not known when the initial INVITE was sent. The media session has now begun, and Alice and Bob can exchange data over one or more RTP connections.

The next example (Figure 7.9) makes use of two message types that are not yet part of the SIP standard but that are documented in RFC 2848 and are likely to be incorporated in a later revision of SIP. These message types support telephony applications. Suppose that in the preceding example, Alice was informed that Bob was not available. Alice's UAC can then issue a SUBSCRIBE message (1), indicating that it wants to be informed when Bob is available. This request is forwarded through the two proxies in our example to a PINT (PSTN-Internet Networking) server (2, 3). A PINT server acts as a gateway between an IP network from which comes a request to place a telephone call and a telephone network that executes the call by connecting to the destination telephone. In this example, we assume that the PINT server logic is colocated with the location service. It could also be the case that Bob is attached to the Internet rather than a PSTN, in which case, the equivalent of PINT logic is needed to handle SUBSCRIBE requests. In this example, we assume that latter and assume that the PINT functionality is implemented in the location service. In any case, the location service authorizes subscription by returning an OK message (4), which is passed back to Alice (5, 6). The location service then immediately sends a NOTIFY message with Bob's current status of not signed in (7, 8, 9), which Alice's UAC acknowledges (10, 11, 12).

Figure 7.10 continues the example of Figure 7.9. Bob signs on by sending a REGISTER message to the proxy in its domain (1). The proxy updates the database at the location service to reflect registration (2). The update is confirmed to the proxy (3), which confirms the registration to Bob (4). The PINT functionality learns of Bob's new status from the location server (here we assume that they are colocated) and sends a NOTIFY message containing the new status of Bob (5), which is forwarded to Alice (6, 7). Alice's UAC acknowledges receipt of the notification (8, 9, 10).

Figure 7.9 SIP Presence Example

SIP Messages

As was mentioned, SIP is a text-based protocol with a syntax similar to that of HTTP. There are two different types of SIP messages, requests and responses. The format difference between the two types of messages is seen in the first line. The first line of a request has a **method**, defining the nature of the request, and a Request-URI, indicating where the request should be sent. The first line of a response has a **response code**. All messages include a header, consisting of a number of lines, each line beginning with a header label. A message can also contain a body such as an SDP media description.

For **SIP requests**, RFC 3261 defines the following methods:

- **REGISTER:** Used by a user agent to notify a SIP configuration of its current IP address and the URLs for which it would like to receive calls
- **INVITE:** Used to establish a media session between user agents.

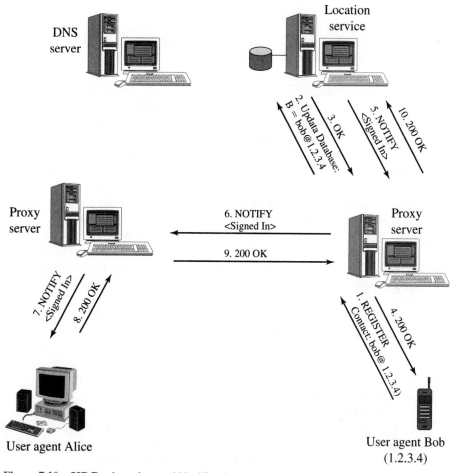

Figure 7.10   SIP Registration and Notification Example

- **ACK:** Confirms reliable message exchanges
- **CANCEL:** Terminates a pending request but does not undo a completed call
- **BYE:** - Terminates a session between two users in a conference
- **OPTIONS:** Solicits information about the capabilities of the callee but does not set up a call.

For example, the header of message (1) in Figure 7.8 might look like this:

```
INVITE sip:bob@biloxi.com SIP/2.0
Via: SIP/2.0/UDP 12.26.17.91:5060
Max-Forwards: 70
To: Bob <sip:bob@biloxi.com>
From: Alice <sip:alice@atlanta.com>;tag=1928301774
Call-ID: a84b4c76e66710@12.26.17.91
```

```
CSeq: 314159 INVITE
Contact: <sip:alice@atlanta.com>
Content-Type: application/sdp
Content-Length: 142
```

The boldface type used for header labels is not typical but is used here for clarity. The first line contains the method name (**INVITE**), a SIP URI, and the version number of SIP that is used. The lines that follow are a list of header fields. This example contains the minimum required set.

The **Via** headers show the path the request has taken in the SIP configuration (source and intervening proxies) and are used to route responses back along the same path. As the INVITE message leaves, there is only the header inserted by Alice. The line contains the IP address (12.26.17.91), port number (5060), and transport protocol (UDP) that Alice wants Bob to use in his response.

Max-Forwards serves to limit the number of hops a request can make on the way to its destination. It consists of an integer that is decremented by one by each proxy that forwards the request. If the Max-Forwards value reaches 0 before the request reaches its destination, it will be rejected with a 483 (Too Many Hops) error response.

To contains a display name (Bob) and a SIP or SIPS URI (sip:bob@biloxi.com) toward which the request was originally directed. **From** also contains a display name (Alice) and a SIP or SIPS URI (sip:alice@atlanta.com) that indicate the originator of the request. This header field also has a tag parameter containing a random string (1928301774) that was added to the URI by the UAC. It is used to identify the session.

Call-ID contains a globally unique identifier for this call, generated by the combination of a random string and the host name or IP address. The combination of the To tag, From tag, and Call-ID completely defines a peer-to-peer SIP relationship between Alice and Bob and is referred to as a dialog.

CSeq or Command Sequence contains an integer and a method name. The CSeq number is initialized at the start of a call (314159 in this example), incremented for each new request within a dialog, and is a traditional sequence number. The CSeq is used to distinguish a retransmission from a new request.

The **Contact** header contains a SIP URI for direct communication between UAs. While the Via header field tells other elements where to send the response, the Contact header field tells other elements where to send future requests for this dialog.

The **Content-Type** indicates the type of the message body. **Content-Length** gives the length in octets of the message body.

The **SIP response** types defined in RFC 3261 are in the following categories:

- **Provisional (1xx):** Request received and being processed.

- **Success (2xx):** The action was successfully received, understood, and accepted.

- **Redirection (3xx):** Further action needs to be taken in order to complete the request.

- **Client Error (4xx):** The request contains bad syntax or cannot be fulfilled at this server.

- **Server Error (5xx):** The server failed to fulfill an apparently valid request.
- **Global Failure (6xx):** The request cannot be fulfilled at any server.

For example, the header of message (13) in Figure 7.8 might look like this:

```
SIP/2.0 200 OK
Via: SIP/2.0/UDP server10.biloxi.com
Via: SIP/2.0/UDP bigbox3.site3.atlanta.com
Via: SIP/2.0/UDP 12.26.17.91:5060
To: Bob <sip:bob@biloxi.com>;tag=a6c85cf
From: Alice <sip:alice@atlanta.com>;tag=1928301774
Call-ID: a84b4c76e66710@12.26.17.91
CSeq: 314159 INVITE
Contact: <sip:bob@biloxi.com>
Content-Type: application/sdp
Content-Length: 131
```

The first line contains the version number of SIP that is used and the response code and name. The lines that follow are a list of header fields. The Via, To, From, Call-ID, and CSeq header fields are copied from the INVITE request. (There are three Via header field values - one added by Alice's SIP UAC, one added by the atlanta.com proxy, and one added by the biloxi.com proxy.) Bob's SIP phone has added a tag parameter to the To header field. This tag will be incorporated by both endpoints into the dialog and will be included in all future requests and responses in this call.

Session Description Protocol

The Session Description Protocol (SDP), defined in RFC 2327, describes the content of sessions, including telephony, Internet radio, and multimedia applications. SDP includes information about [SCHU99]:

- **Media streams:** A session can include multiple streams of differing content. SDP currently defines audio, video, data, control, and application as stream types, similar to the MIME types used for Internet mail (Table 7.2).
- **Addresses:** Indicates the destination addresses, which may be a multicast address, for a media stream.
- **Ports:** For each stream, the UDP port numbers for sending and receiving are specified.
- **Payload types:** For each media stream type in use (e.g., telephony), the payload type indicates the media formats that can be used during the session.
- **Start and stop times:** These apply to broadcast sessions, like a television or radio program. The start, stop, and repeat times of the session are indicated.
- **Originator:** For broadcast sessions, the originator is specified, with contact information. This may be useful if a receiver encounters technical difficulties.

APPLICATION NOTE

To Serve or Not to Serve

Web servers and mail servers are possibly the most difficult kinds of systems to manage. They are constantly barraged with requests from valid users and assailed by attacks from not so valid users. Before deciding to deploy either of these, there are some questions that an organization should ask itself. Very often, there is no need to manage these types of services internally.

Perhaps the best place to start is determining what the system will be required to do. In other words – what do you need and want? For mail servers, questions such as the number of accounts needed, security required and internal vs. external mail should be answered. Small companies or individuals running their own companies may be able to take advantage free mail services such as gmail. This does not provide a real identity for the organization but does facilitate communication.

Groups falling into the small office home office (SOHO) category often have their web pages hosted by their Internet Service Provider (ISP) or a specialized hosting firm. This allows them to have a web presence without the need to run a web server. In addition, web hosting services or ISPs will often register a domain name with the DNS for you. At a small cost (typically less than \$100/yr) this provides an identity to the group and often includes several e-mail accounts, some security/logging tools and management services.

Using web hosting and mail services from an ISP or hosting company can serve companies with several employees. For a few extra dollars the number of accounts can be increased and the space or scripting required by the web site can be expanded. However, there is a point at which the outside services become less attractive. For large organizations with dozens or hundreds of people, complex human resources or internal communication demands and a fully staffed IT department, it may be much more attractive to run your own services.

Setting up e-mail or web servers internally can be a daunting task for the unprepared. Like most installations, it is not difficult to put the software on a machine or set up a few accounts. It is the maintenance and security of the systems that can be a struggle. In addition, installing services internally can affect other systems. For example, if you are running your own web site that generates sales or provides support, what is the response if it goes down? How many hits does the site get? What is the network utilization? It is important to understand the operation and requirements of such a system before it is installed.

When running a web or mail server that is to be accessed from outside the company network, any firewalls that have been configured need to be updated to allow this sort of traffic. This is directly related to the ports used by these applications. The firewall rules may also be written based on other criterion such as IP address. In addition, the type of client software must be considered as not all external systems will have is required. Are the users carrying their laptops around with them? If so, they may need additional support and a full suite of applications. Do they access the corporate resources from outside? Do they need virtual private network (VPN) access? What about the additional security necessary when accessing information from a restaurant wireless hotspot?

Allowing access from outside can be tricky if the organization regularly handles sensitive data or has to contend with compliance issues. If this is the case, security will be a top priority with encryption and firewalls main focal points. A security policy should be established and careful consideration given to the personnel allowed external access to internal systems. Often companies will have two sets of servers running. These will be for internal or external use exclusively. For example, employee information and benefits may be run on an internal server while the company website and contact information may be on the external one. Often, authentication servers are deployed in conjunction with certain website features.

For the staff running the servers, the never-ending tasks of security patching and virus protection take up a good deal of time. Exploits for security installations pop up as fast as older holes can be closed and new viruses arrive as we are filtering out the existing ones. Viruses are a particularly tricky problem and this has led many administrators to do a good amount of mail filtering on the server itself. This means that many messages will arrive to the end user with a note describing how a potentially dangerous file was automatically removed from the original message. This is especially true of executable files. End users should also be running virus protection software that examines incoming mail and the local computer. In the end, the real problem with viruses is that the end users often download them to a computer either by going around the installed security or because the security measures didn't catch it. The answer here is training for everyone.

There are advantages and disadvantages to running your own services. On one hand local configuration permits tailored security changes, rapid account creation and content modification. On the other hand, server management headaches, costs and man hours can make external provisioning attractive.

7.5 SUMMARY

Standardized distributed applications are becoming increasingly important to businesses, for three main reasons:

- Standardized applications are more readily acquired and used than special-purpose software, which may have inadequate support and is accompanied by inadequate training.
- Standardized software allows the user to procure computers from a variety of vendors and yet have those computers work together.
- Standards promote the ability for different companies to exchange data.

This chapter examines three important distributed applications. Standards have been developed for these applications, and their use continues to grow.

A general-purpose e-mail facility provides a means of exchanging unstructured messages, usually text messages. E-mail is a rapid and convenient method for communication, supplementing, and, in many instances, replacing telephone and paper communications. Because e-mail is so general purpose in nature, it is perhaps the most popular distributed application and can have the most widespread benefits.

The most widely used protocol for the transmission of e-mail is SMTP. SMTP assumes that the content of the message is a simple text block. The recent MIME standard expands SMTP to support transmission of multimedia information.

The rapid growth in the use of the Web is due to the standardization of all the elements that support Web applications. A key element is HTTP, which is the protocol for the exchange of Web-based information between Web browsers and Web servers. Three types of intermediate devices can be used in an HTTP networks: proxies, gateways, and tunnels. HTTP uses a request/response style of communication.

The Session Initiation Protocol (SIP) is an application-level control protocol for setting up, modifying, and terminating real-time sessions between participants over an IP data network. One important use for SIP is to support telephony over the Internet, known as voice over IP. SIP uses the Session Description Protocol (SDP) to describe the media content to be used during a session.

7.6 RECOMMENDED READING AND WEB SITES

[KHAR98] provides a concise overview of SMTP. [HOFF00] is a good overview of SMTP and related e-mail standards. [KANE98] is a comprehensive look at SMTP and related mail standards, plus a comparison with proprietary schemes. [ROSE98] provides a book-length treatment of e-mail, including some coverage of SMTP and MIME.

[GOUR02] provides comprehensive coverage of HTTP. Another good treatment is [KRIS01]. [BISE07], [WEAV06], and [CHOU02] are good overview articles on SSL.

[SPAR07] and [SCHU98] are good overviews of SIP. [GOOD02] and [SCHU99] discuss SIP in the context of VoIP. [DIAN02] looks at SIP in the context of the support of multimedia services over the Internet. [SHER04] provides a readable overview of VoIP.

BISE07 Bisel, L. "The Role of SSL in Cybersecurity." *IT Pro*, March/April 2002.

CHOU02 Chou, W. "Inside SSL: The Secure Sockets Layer Protocol." *IT Pro*, July/August 2002.

DIAN02 Dianda, J.; Gurbani, V.; and Jones, M. "Session Initiation Protocol Services Architecture." *Bell Labs Technical Journal*, Volume 7, Number 1, 2002.

GOOD02 Goode, B. "Voice Over Internet Protocol (VoIP)." *Proceedings of the IEEE*, September 2002.

GOUR02 Gourley, D., et al. *HTTP: The Definitive Guide*. Sebastopol, CA: O'Reilly, 2002.

HOFF00 Hoffman, P. "Overview of Internet Mail Standards." *The Internet Protocol Journal*, June 2000 (www.cisco.com/warp/public/759)

KANE98 Kanel, J.; Givler, J.; Leiba, B.; and Segmuller, W. "Internet Messaging Frameworks." *IBM Systems Journal*, No. 1, 1998.

KHAR98 Khare, R. "The Spec's in the Mail." *IEEE Internet Computing*, September/October 1998.

KRIS01 Krishnamurthy, B., and Rexford, J. *Web Protocols and Practice: HTTP/1.1, Networking Protocols, Caching, and Traffic Measurement*. Upper Saddle River, NJ: Prentice Hall, 2001.

ROSE98 Rose, M., and Strom, D. *Internet Messaging: From the Desktop to the Enterprise.* Upper Saddle River, NJ: Prentice Hall, 1998.

SCHU98 Schulzrinne, H. and Rosenberg, J. "The Session Initiation Protocol: Providing Advanced Telephony Access Across the Internet." *Bell Labs Technical Journal*, October-December 1998.

SCHU99 Schulzrinne, H., and Rosenberg, J. "The IETF Internet Telephony Architecture and Protocols." *IEEE Network*, May/June 1999.

SHER04 Sherburne, P., and Fitzgerald, C. "You Don't Know Jack About VoIP." *ACM Queue*, September 2004.

SPAR07 Sparks, R., and Systems, E. "SIP – Basics and Beyond." *ACM Queue*, March 2007.

WEAV06 Weaver, A. "Secure Sockets Layer." *Computer*, April 2006.

Recommended Web sites:

- **WWW consortium:** Contains up-to-date information on HTTP and related topics.
- **SIP Forum:** Nonprofit organization to promote SIP. Site contains product information, white papers, and other useful information and links.
- **SIP working group:** Chartered by IETF to develop standards related to SIP. The Web site includes all relevant RFCs and Internet drafts.

7.7 KEY TERMS, REVIEW QUESTIONS, AND PROBLEMS

Key Terms

Electronic mail	RFC 822	SIP proxy server
HTTP gateway	Session Description Protocol	SIP redirect server
HTTP method	(SDP)	SIP registrar
HTTP proxy	Session Initiation Protocol	Uniform Resource Identifier
HTTP tunnel	(SIP)	(URI)
Hypertext Transfer Protocol	Simple Mail Transfer Protocol	Uniform Resource Locator
(HTTP)	(SMTP)	(URL)
Multipurpose Internet Mail	SIP location service	voice over IP (VoIP)
Extensions (MIME)	SIP method	

Review Questions

7.1 With a single-system mail facility or native mail facility, what major elements are needed?

7.2 By installing a mail client on your computer, are you storing your unread e-mail on your system?

7.3 In extending a single-system mail system to a distributed mail system, what key additions must be included?

7.4 What is the port used by SMTP?

7.5 What is the difference between the RFC 821 and RFC 822?

7.6 What are the SMTP and MIME standards?

7.7 What are some of the limitations of SMTP that MIME was intended to address?

7.8 What is meant by saying that HTTP is a stateless protocol?

7.9 Explain the differences among HTTP proxy, gateway, and tunnel.

7.10 What is the function of the cache in HTTP?

7.11 What port is used by HTTP?

7.12 What are the five key services provided by SIP?

7.13 List and briefly define the major components in an SIP network.

7.14 Provide an example of a transport protocol used to convey audio or video content during a SIP based transmission.

7.15 What is the Session Description Protocol?

Problems

7.1 E-mail systems differ in the manner in which multiple recipients are handled. In some systems, the originating user agent or mail sender makes all the necessary copies and these are sent out independently. An alternative approach is to determine the route for each destination first. Then a single message is sent out on a common portion of the route and copies are only made when the routes diverge; this process is referred to as mail bagging. Discuss the relative advantages and disadvantages of the two methods.

7.2 Excluding the connection establishment and termination, what is the minimum number of network round trips to send a small e-mail message using SMTP?

7.3 Suppose you need to send one message to three different users: user1@example.com, user2@example.com and user3@example.com. Is there any difference between sending one separate message per user and sending only one message with multiple (three) recipients? Explain.

7.4 Users are free to define and use additional header fields other than the ones defined in RFC 87. Such header fields must begin with the string "X-". Why?

7.5 Suppose you find some technical problems with the mail account user@example.com. Who should you try to contact in order to solve them?

7.6 HTTP caching is an operation that can be controlled at the originating server, an intermediate node, or at the client browser application. What are the potential benefits and detriments associated with this mechanism (from the perspective of both the originator and client) as it is implemented?

7.7 RFC 3298 describes the Spirits protocol requirements. What is Sprits and how might it be relative to a discussion of SIP and PINT?

7.8 Many mail clients allow you to view the mail header that will display the path that the message traveled. Does your mail client or program have this option? If so, can you trace the message from source to destination?

7.9 What TCP port does your mail system use?

7.10 In discovering the port your mail system uses, what port is your machine using?

7.11 Why is it important for the local systems administrator to understand what ports are being used by applications?

7.12 What are POP3 and IMAP?

7.13 What is HTTPS?

7.14 Netmeeting is a video conferencing program built into the Windows family of operating systems. It allows video, audio or video/audio combined communications. Using Netmeeting and some basic communications gear (microphone, speakers, camera), establish communication between two stations. What protocols and codecs are being used?

ING LIFE

ING Life (formerly NN Financial) is a leading provider of life insurance products in Canada. The company is based in Ontario and operates out of three regional offices. Over 2000 brokerage partners market its products [BRUN99, IBM00]. In 1997 most of the brokers relied on fax, phone, and postal services to request policy information. Response times could sometimes be measured in hours. The company did have a 56-kbps frame relay wide area network, but that only connected the Ontario headquarters to 70 managing general agent offices (Figure III.1). The systems in Ontario converted the frame relay requests to SNA from TCP/IP and routed them to the corporate mainframe in Connecticut.

In December of 1997, ING decided it had to reduce response times to remain competitive and attract new brokers. The company wanted a cost-effective solution that could provide its brokers fast access to mainframe data and scale to accommodate new partners. ING investigated extending the existing frame relay network and

Figure III.1   ING Life Network before Using Internet

Figure III.2 ING Life Network with Extranet

estimated the cost at a prohibitive $3.3 million. Instead, the company decided to build an extranet and offer a Web-to-host service that would allow partners to access mainframe data directly via the Internet. ING estimated the annual cost of extranet services for 2000 brokers at $70,000. The annual cost of maintaining the existing WAN for 70 brokers was $750,000.

Besides reducing maintenance costs, the Web-to-host solution offered other benefits. The client software installed automatically as a browser applet, thereby reducing administrative costs. Also, using a browser as an interface meant that brokers were no longer tied to a specific workstation or PC.

The new solution would include two NT servers, a new SNA gateway (to translate between SNA and IP), and a Cisco Pix firewall connected to the Internet via a leased T-1 line (Figure III.2). The NT servers would run Lotus Notes, IBM Host on Demand (Web-to-host software), and Web server software. Because this service would send private data over the public Internet, security was a concern. The Pix firewall would prevent unauthorized access to the data. In addition, the Web-to-host software used an SSL (secure sockets layer) connection (described in Chapter 18). Before bringing the service on line, ING had security consultants probe the system for vulnerabilities.

By July of 1999, ING had 350 brokers connected to the extranet and plans to connect the remaining brokers by sometime in 2000. To use the new service, brokers connect to the Internet using dial-up and point their browser at the Web server. The Host on Demand client loads automatically as a browser applet. The applet provides

TN3270 emulation services. After the applet has loaded, the broker can access the corporate mainframe as if he is using a directly connected TN3270 terminal. Response times for extranet requests are less than one minute.

Discussion Questions

1. What are the probable difficulties and risk associated with using public infrastructure, such as the Internet, as part of a private business solution?
2. Discuss the precautions taken by ING to ensure security. Were the measures adequate?
3. Comment on the extranet topology. Are there any potential bottlenecks?

CHAPTER 8

INTERNET OPERATION

8.1 Internet Addressing
Network Classes
Subnets and Subnet Masks

8.2 Internet Routing Protocols
Autonomous Systems
Border Gateway Protocol
Open Shortest Path First (OSPF) Protocol

8.3 The Need for Speed and Quality of Service
The Emergence of High-Speed LANs
Corporate Wide Area Networking Needs
Digital Electronics
QoS on the Internet

8.4 Differentiated Services
Services
DS Field
DS Configuration and Operation

8.5 Service Level Agreements

8.6 IP Performance Metrics

8.7 Summary

8.8 Recommended Reading and Web Sites

8.9 KEY Terms, Review Questions, and Problems

Chapter Objectives

After reading this chapter, you should be able to

♦ Describe Internet addressing and appreciate the key issues involved in address assignment.

♦ Understand the difference between an interior routing protocol and an exterior routing protocol.

♦ Explain the basic mechanisms in a routing protocol.

♦ Understand the concept of quality of service.

♦ Explain the difference between elastic traffic and inelastic traffic.

♦ Discuss the services provided by a differentiated services facility.

This chapter looks at some of the details "under the hood" of the Internet. We begin by examining the rather complicated issue of addressing in such a far-flung, massive, and dynamic configuration. Next, we provide an overview of routing protocols, by which routers cooperate to design routes, or paths, through the Internet from source to destination. Then we introduce the issue of quality of service. Next, we look at the most important approach to providing quality of service on the Internet, known as differentiated services. Finally, we introduce the topics of service level agreements and IP performance metrics.

8.1 INTERNET ADDRESSING

The source and destination address fields in the IP header each contain a 32-bit global Internet address, generally consisting of a network identifier and a host identifier.

Network Classes

The IP address is coded to allow a variable allocation of bits to specify network and host, as depicted in Figure 8.1 This encoding provides flexibility in assigning addresses to hosts and allows a mix of network sizes on an internet. The three principal network classes are best suited to the following conditions:

- **Class A:** Few networks, each with many hosts
- **Class B:** Medium number of networks, each with a medium number of hosts
- **Class C:** Many networks, each with a few hosts

In a particular environment, it may be best to use addresses all from one class. For example, a corporate internetwork that consists of a large number of departmental local area networks may need to use Class C addresses exclusively. However, the format of the addresses is such that it is possible to mix all three classes of addresses on the same internetwork; this is what is done in the case of the Internet itself. A mixture of classes is appropriate for an internetwork consisting of a few large networks, many small networks, plus some medium-sized networks.

Figure 8.1 IPv4 Address Formats

IP addresses are usually written in what is called **dotted decimal notation**, with a decimal number representing each of the octets of the 32-bit address. For example, the IP address 11000000 11100100 00010001 00111001 is written as 192.228.17.57.

Note that all Class A network addresses begin with a binary 0. Network addresses with a first octet of 0 (binary 00000000) and 127 (binary 01111111) are reserved, so there are 126 potential Class A network numbers, which have a first dotted decimal number in the range 1 to 126. Class B network addresses begin with a binary 10, so that the range of the first decimal number in a Class B address is 128 to 191 (binary 10000000 to 10111111). The second octet is also part of the Class B address, so that there are 2^{14} = 16,384 Class B addresses. For Class C addresses, the first decimal number ranges from 192 to 223 (11000000 to 11011111). The total number of Class C addresses is 2^{21} = 2,097,152.

Subnets and Subnet Masks

The concept of subnet was introduced to address the following requirement. Consider an internet that includes one or more WANs and a number of sites, each of which has a number of LANs. We would like to allow arbitrary complexity of interconnected LAN structures within an organization while insulating the overall internet against explosive growth in network numbers and routing complexity. One approach to this problem is to assign a single network number to all of the LANs at a site. From the point of view of the rest of the internet, there is a single network at that site, which simplifies addressing and routing. To allow the routers within the site to function properly, each LAN is assigned a subnet number. The *host* portion of the internet address is partitioned into a subnet number and a host number to accommodate this new level of addressing.

Table 8.1 IP Addresses and Subnet Masks
(a) Dotted decimal and binary representations of IP address and subnet masks

	Binary Representation	Dotted Decimal
IP address	11000000.11100100.00010001.00111001	192.228.17.57
Subnet mask	11111111.11111111.11111111.11100000	255.255.255.224
Bitwise AND of address and mask (resultant network/subnet number)	11000000.11100100.00010001.00100000	192.228.17.32
Subnet number	11000000.11100100.00010001.001	1
Host number	00000000.00000000.00000000.00011001	25

(b) Default subnet masks

	Binary Representation	Dotted Decimal
Class A default mask	11111111.00000000.00000000.00000000	255.0.0.0
Example class A mask	11111111.11000000.00000000.00000000	255.192.0.0
Class B default mask	11111111.11111111.00000000.00000000	255.255.0.0
Example class B mask	11111111.11111111.11111000.00000000	255.255.248.0
Class C default mask	11111111.11111111.11111111.00000000	255.255.255.0
Example class C mask	11111111.11111111.11111111.11111100	255.255.255.252

Within the subnetted network, the local routers must route on the basis of an extended network number consisting of the *network* portion of the IP address and the subnet number. The address mask indicates the bit positions containing this extended network number. The use of the address mask allows the host to determine whether an outgoing datagram is destined for a host on the same LAN (send directly) or another LAN (send datagram to router). It is assumed that some other means (e.g., manual configuration) are used to create address masks and make them known to the local routers.

Table 8.1a shows the calculations involved in the use of a subnet mask. Note that the effect of the subnet mask is to erase the portion of the host field that refers to an actual host on a subnet. What remain are the network number and the subnet number. Figure 8.2 shows an example of the use of subnetting. The figure shows a local complex consisting of three LANs and two routers. To the rest of the Internet, this complex is a single network with a Class C address of the form 192.228.17.x, where the leftmost three octets are the network number and the rightmost octet contains a host number x. Both routers R1 and R2 are configured with a subnet mask with the value 255.255.255.224 (see Table 8.1a). For example, if a datagram with the destination address 192.228.17.57 arrives at R1 from either the rest of the Internet or from LAN Y, R1 applies the subnet mask to determine that this address refers to subnet 1, which is LAN X, and so forwards the datagram to LAN X. Similarly, if a datagram with that destination address arrives at R2 from LAN Z, R2 applies the mask and then determines from its forwarding database that datagrams destined for subnet 1 should be forwarded to R1. Hosts must also employ a subnet mask to make routing decisions.

The default subnet mask for a given class of addresses is a null mask (Table 8.1b), which yields the same network and host number as the non-subnetted address.

Figure 8.2 Example of Subnetworking

8.2 INTERNET ROUTING PROTOCOLS

The routers in an internet are responsible for receiving and forwarding packets through the interconnected set of networks. Each router makes routing decisions based on knowledge of the topology and traffic/delay conditions of the internet. In a simple internet, a fixed routing scheme is possible, in which a single, permanent route is configured for each source-destination pair of nodes in the network. The routes are fixed, or at most only change when there is a change in the topology of the network. Thus, the link costs used in designing routes cannot be based on any dynamic variable such as traffic. They could, however, be based on estimated traffic volumes between various source-destination pairs or the capacity of each link.

In more complex internets, a degree of dynamic cooperation is needed among routers. In particular, routers must avoid portions of the network that have failed and should avoid portions of the network that are congested. To make such dynamic routing decisions, routers exchange routing information using a special routing protocol for that purpose. Information is needed about the status of the internet, in terms of which networks can be reached by which routes, and the delay characteristics of various routes.

In considering the routing function, it is important to distinguish two concepts:

- **Routing information:** Information about the topology and delays of the internet
- **Routing algorithm:** The algorithm used to make a routing decision for a particular datagram, based on current routing information

Autonomous Systems

To proceed with our discussion of routing protocols, we need to introduce the concept of **an autonomous system**. An autonomous system (AS) exhibits the following characteristics:

1. An AS is a set of routers and networks managed by a single organization.
2. An AS consists of a group of routers exchanging information via a common routing protocol.
3. Except in times of failure, an AS is connected (in a graph-theoretic sense); that is, there is a path between any pair of nodes.

A shared routing protocol, which we shall refer to as an **interior router protocol** (IRP), passes routing information between routers within an AS. The protocol used within the AS does not need to be implemented outside of the system. This flexibility allows IRPs to be custom tailored to specific applications and requirements.

It may happen, however, that an internet will be constructed of more than one AS. For example, all of the LANs at a site, such as an office complex or campus, could be linked by routers to form an AS. This system might be linked through a wide area network to other ASs. The situation is illustrated in Figure 8.3 In this case, the routing algorithms and information in routing tables used by routers in different ASs may differ. Nevertheless, the routers in one AS need at least a minimal level of information concerning networks outside the system that can be reached. We refer to the protocol used to pass routing information between routers in different ASs as an **exterior router protocol (ERP).**[1]

In general terms, IRPs and ERPs have a somewhat different flavor. An IRP needs to build up a rather detailed model of the interconnection of routers within an AS in order to calculate the least-cost path from a given router to any network within the AS. An ERP supports the exchange of summary reachability information between separately administered ASs. Typically, this use of summary information means that an ERP is simpler and uses less detailed information than an IRP.

In the remainder of this section, we look at what are perhaps the most important examples of these two types of routing protocols: BGP and OSPF.

Border Gateway Protocol

The Border Gateway Protocol (BGP) was developed for use in conjunction with internets that employ the TCP/IP suite, although the concepts are applicable to

---

[1]In the literature, the terms *interior gateway protocol* (IGP) and *exterior gateway protocol* (EGP) are often used for what are referred to here as IRP and ERP. However, because the terms *IGP* and *EGP* also refer to specific protocols, we avoid their use to define the general concepts.

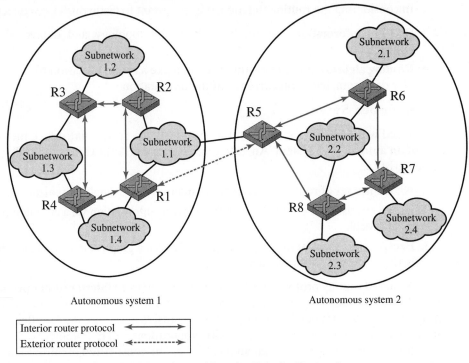

Figure 8.3   Application of Exterior and Interior Routing Protocols

any internet. BGP has become the preferred exterior router protocol for the Internet.

BGP was designed to allow routers, called gateways in the standard, in different ASs to cooperate in the exchange of routing information. The protocol operates in terms of messages, which are sent over TCP connections. The current version of BGP is known as BGP-4.

Three functional procedures are involved in BGP:

- Neighbor acquisition
- Neighbor reachability
- Network reachability

Two routers are considered to be neighbors if they are attached to the same network. If the two routers are in different autonomous systems, they may wish to exchange routing information. For this purpose, it is necessary first to perform **neighbor acquisition**. The term *neighbor* refers to two routers that share the same network. In essence, neighbor acquisition occurs when two neighboring routers in different autonomous systems agree to exchange routing information regularly. A formal acquisition procedure is needed because one of the routers may not wish to participate. For example, the router may be overburdened and may not want to be responsible for traffic coming in from outside the AS. In the neighbor acquisition process, one router sends a request message to the other, which may either accept or refuse the offer. The protocol does not address the issue of how one router knows the address or even the existence of another router, nor how it decides that it needs to exchange routing information with that particular router. These issues must be dealt with at configuration time or by active intervention of a network manager.

To perform neighbor acquisition, one router sends an Open message to another. If the target router accepts the request, it returns a Keepalive message in response.

Once a neighbor relationship is established, the **neighbor reachability** procedure is used to maintain the relationship. Each partner needs to be assured that the other partner still exists and is still engaged in the neighbor relationship. For this purpose, the two routers periodically issue Keepalive messages to each other.

The final procedure specified by BGP is **network reachability**. Each router maintains a database of the networks that it can reach and the preferred route for reaching each network. Whenever a change is made to this database, the router issues an Update message that is broadcast to all other routers for which it has a neighbor relationship. Because the Update message is broadcast, all BGP routers can build up and maintain their routing information.

Open Shortest Path First (OSPF) Protocol

The OSPF protocol is widely used as an interior router protocol in TCP/IP networks. OSPF uses what is known as a link state routing algorithm. Each router maintains descriptions of the state of its local links to networks, and from time to time transmits updated state information to all of the routers of which it is aware. Every router receiving an update packet must acknowledge it to the sender. Such updates produce a minimum of routing traffic because the link descriptions are small and rarely need to be sent.

OSPF computes a route through the internet that incurs the least cost based on a user-configurable metric of cost. The user can configure the cost to express a function of delay, data rate, dollar cost, or other factors. OSPF is able to equalize loads over multiple equal-cost paths.

Each router maintains a database that reflects the known topology of the autonomous system of which it is a part. The topology is expressed as a directed graph. The graph consists of the following:

- Vertices, or nodes, of two types:
  - Router
  - Network, which is in turn of two types:
    - Transit, if it can carry data the neither originates nor terminates on an end system attached to this network
    - Stub, if it is not a transit network
- Edges, of two types:
  - A graph edge that connects two router vertices when the corresponding routers are connected to each other by a direct point-to-point link

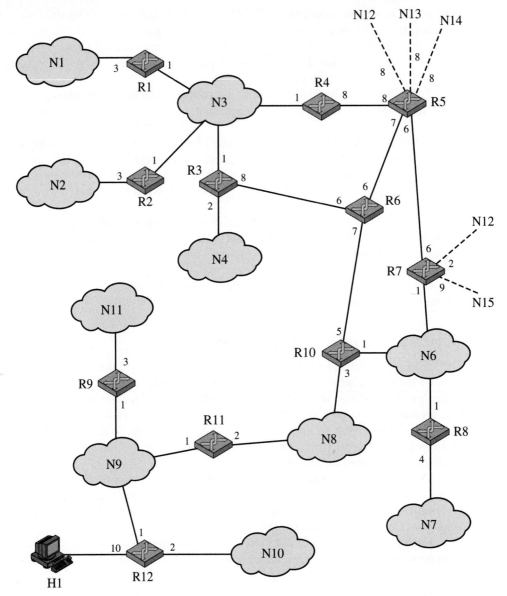

Figure 8.4 A Sample Autonomous System

—A graph edge that connects a router vertex to a network vertex when the router is directly connected to the network

Figure 8.4 shows an example of an autonomous system, and Figure 8.5 is the resulting directed graph. The mapping is straightforward:

- Two routers joined by a point-to-point link are represented in the graph as being directly connected by a pair of edges, one in each direction (e.g., routers 6 and 10).

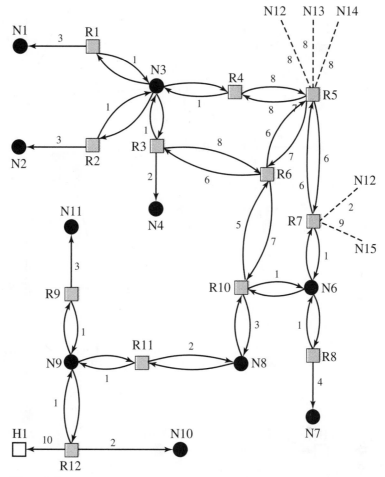

Figure 8.5 Directed Graph of Autonomous System of Figure 8.4

- When multiple routers are attached to a network (such as a LAN or packet-switching network), the directed graph shows all routers bidirectionally connected to the network vertex (e.g., routers 1, 2, 3, and 4 all connect to network 3).
- If a single router is attached to a network, the network will appear in the graph as a stub connection (e.g., network 7).
- An end system, called a host, can be directly connected to a router, in which case it is depicted in the corresponding graph (e.g., host 1).
- If a router is connected to other autonomous systems, then the path cost to each network in the other system must be obtained by some exterior routing protocol (ERP). Each such network is represented on the graph by a stub and an edge to the router with the known path cost (e.g., networks 12 through 15).

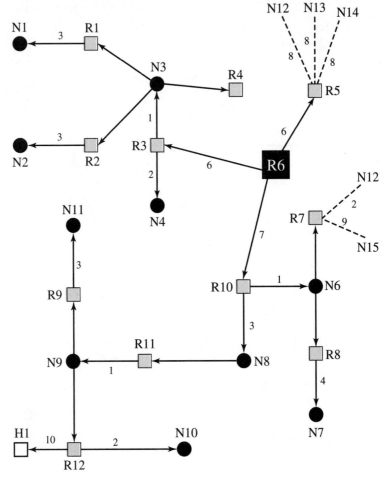

Figure 8.6 The SPF Tree for Router R6

A cost is associated with the output side of each router interface. This cost is configurable by the system administrator. Arcs on the graph are labeled with the cost of the corresponding router output interface. Arcs having no labeled cost have a cost of 0. Note that arcs leading from networks to routers always have a cost of 0.

A database corresponding to the directed graph is maintained by each router. It is pieced together from link state messages from other routers in the internet. Using an algorithm explained in the next subsection, a router calculates the least-cost path to all destination networks. The results for router 6 of Figure 8.4 are shown as a tree in Figure 8.6, with R6 as the root of the tree. The tree gives the entire route to any destination network or host. However, only the next hop to the destination is used in the forwarding process. The resulting routing table for router 6 is shown in Table 8.2 The table includes entries for routers advertising external routes (routers 5 and 7). For external networks whose identity is known, entries are also provided.

Table 8.2   Routing Table for R6

Destination	Next Hop	Distance
N1	R3	10
N2	R3	10
N3	R3	7
N4	R3	8
N6	R10	8
N7	R10	12
N8	R10	10
N9	R10	11
N10	R10	13
N11	R10	14
H1	R10	21
R5	R5	6
R7	R10	8
N12	R10	10
N13	R5	14
N14	R5	14
N15	R10	17

8.3   THE NEED FOR SPEED AND QUALITY OF SERVICE

Momentous changes in the way corporations do business and process information have been driven by changes in networking technology and at the same time have driven those changes. It is hard to separate chicken and egg in this field. Similarly, the use of the Internet by both businesses and individuals reflects this cyclic dependency: the availability of new image-based services on the Internet (i.e., the Web) has resulted in an increase in the total number of users and the traffic volume generated by each user. This, in turn, has resulted in a need to increase the speed and efficiency of the Internet. On the other hand, it is only such increased speed that makes the use of Web-based applications palatable to the end user.

In this section, we survey some of the end-user factors that fit into this equation. We begin with the need for high-speed LANs in the business environment, because this need has appeared first and has forced the pace of networking development. Then we look at business WAN requirements. Then we offer a few words about the effect of changes in commercial electronics on network requirements. Finally, we relate the requirements for quality of service (QoS) to the Internet.

The Emergence of High-Speed LANs

Personal computers and microcomputer workstations began to achieve widespread acceptance in business computing in the early 1980s and have now achieved virtually the status of the telephone: an essential tool for office workers. Traditionally, office LANs provided basic connectivity services—connecting personal computers and terminals to mainframes and midrange systems that ran corporate applications and providing workgroup connectivity at the departmental or divisional level. In both cases, traffic patterns were relatively light, with an emphasis on file transfer and electronic mail. The LANs that were available for this type of workload, primarily Ethernet and token ring, were well suited to this environment.

In recent years, two significant trends altered the role of the personal computer and therefore the requirements on the LAN:

1. The speed and computing power of personal computers continued to enjoy explosive growth. These more powerful platforms support graphics-intensive applications and ever more elaborate graphical user interfaces to the operating system.

2. IT (information technology) organizations have recognized the LAN as a viable and essential computing platform, resulting in the focus on network computing. This trend began with client/server computing, which has become a dominant architecture in the business environment and the more recent Web-focused intranet trend. Both of these approaches involve the frequent transfer of potentially large volumes of data in a transaction-oriented environment.

The effect of these trends has been to increase the volume of data to be handled over LANs and, because applications are more interactive, to reduce the acceptable delay on data transfers. The earlier generation of 10-Mbps Ethernets and 16-Mbps token rings is simply not up to the job of supporting these requirements.

The following are examples of requirements that call for higher-speed LANs:

- **Centralized server farms:** In many applications, there is a need for user, or client, systems to be able to draw huge amounts of data from multiple centralized servers, called server farms. An example is a color publishing operation, in which servers typically contain tens of gigabytes of image data that must be downloaded to imaging workstations. As the performance of the servers themselves has increased, the bottleneck has shifted to the network.

- **Power workgroups:** These groups typically consist of a small number of cooperating users who need to draw massive data files across the network. Examples are a software development group that runs tests on a new software version, or a computer-aided design (CAD) company that regularly runs simulations of new designs. In such cases, large amounts of data are distributed to several workstations, processed, and updated at very high speed for multiple iterations.

- **High-speed local backbone:** As processing demand grows, LANs proliferate at a site, and high-speed interconnection of these LANs is necessary.

- **Convergence and unified communications:** The increasing reliance on the LAN for voice and video traffic, plus the increasing use of collaborative applications have enormously increased the LAN traffic burden.

Corporate Wide Area Networking Needs

As recently as the early 1990s, there was an emphasis in many organizations on a centralized data processing model. In a typical environment, there might be significant computing facilities at a few regional offices, consisting of mainframes or well-equipped midrange systems. These centralized facilities could handle most corporate applications, including basic finance, accounting, and personnel programs, as well as many of the business-specific applications. Smaller, outlying offices (e.g., a bank branch) could be equipped with terminals or basic personal computers linked to one of the regional centers in a transaction-oriented environment.

This model began to change in the early 1990s, and the change accelerated through the mid-1990s. Many organizations have dispersed their employees into multiple smaller offices. There is a growing use of telecommuting. Most significant, the nature of the application structure has changed. First client/server computing and, more recently, intranet computing have fundamentally restructured the organizational data processing environment. There is now much more reliance on personal computers, workstations, and servers and much less use of centralized mainframe and midrange systems. Furthermore, the virtually universal deployment of graphical user interfaces to the desktop enables the end user to exploit graphic applications, multimedia, and other data-intensive applications. In addition, most organizations require access to the Internet. Because a few clicks of the mouse can trigger huge volumes of data, traffic patterns have become more unpredictable while the average load has risen.

All of these trends mean that more data must be transported off premises and onto WANs. It has long been accepted that in the typical business environment, about 80% of the traffic remains local and about 20% traverses wide area links. But this rule no longer applies to most companies, with a greater percentage of the traffic going into the WAN environment [COHE96]. This traffic flow shift places a greater burden on LAN backbones and, of course, on the WAN facilities used by a corporation. Thus, just as for LANs, changes in corporate data traffic patterns are driving the creation of high-speed WANs.

Digital Electronics

The rapid conversion of consumer electronics to digital technology is having an impact on both the Internet and corporate intranets. As these new gadgets come into view and proliferate, they dramatically increase the amount of image and video traffic carried by networks.

Two noteworthy examples of this trend are digital versatile discs and digital still cameras.

DIGITAL VERSATILE DISC (DVD)   With the capacious DVD, the electronics industry has at last found an acceptable replacement for the analog VHS videotape. The DVD has replaced the videotape used in videocassette recorders (VCRs) and, more important for this discussion, replaced the CD-ROM in personal computers and servers. The DVD takes video into the digital age. It delivers movies with picture quality that outshines laser discs, and it can be randomly accessed like audio CDs, which DVD machines can also play. Vast volumes of data can be crammed onto the disc. With DVD's huge storage capacity and vivid quality, PC games have become more realistic and educational software incorporates more video. The increasing acceptance of the Blu-Ray DVD just adds to the volume of data generated and stored on computers. Following in the wake of these developments is a new crest of traffic over the Internet and corporate intranets, as this material is incorporated into Web sites.

DIGITAL CAMERAS   The digital still camera is now widely used in both the home and office environments. An individual can take a picture of a loved one or pet and transfer it to a Web page. Companies can quickly develop online product catalogs with full-color pictures of every product. Thus, there has been a dramatic growth in the amount of online image traffic in recent years.

A related product development is the digital camcorder. This product makes it easier for individuals and companies to make digital video files to be placed on corporate and Internet Web sites, again adding to the traffic burden.

QoS on the Internet

As the Internet and private internets grow in scale, a host of new demands march steadily into view. Low-volume TELNET conversations are leapfrogged by high-volume client/server applications. To this has been added more recently the tremendous volume of Web traffic, which is increasingly graphics intensive. Real-time voice and video applications add to the burden.

To cope with these demands, it is not enough to increase internet capacity. Sensible and effective methods for managing the traffic and controlling congestion are needed.

The Internet and the Internet Protocol (IP) were designed to provide a **best-effort**, fair delivery service. Under a best-effort scheme, the Internet (or a private intranet) treats all packets equally. As the level of traffic on the network grows, and congestion occurs, all packet delivery is slowed down. If congestion becomes severe, packets are dropped more or less at random to ease the congestion. No distinction is made in terms of the relative importance of any traffic or of the timeliness requirements of any of the traffic.

With the tremendous increase in traffic volume and the introduction of new real-time, multimedia, and multicasting applications, the traditional Internet protocols and services are woefully inadequate. But the needs of users have changed. A company may have spent millions of dollars installing an IP-based internet designed to transport data among LANs but now finds that new real-time, multimedia, and multicasting applications are not well supported by such a configuration. The only networking scheme designed from day one to support both traditional TCP and UDP traffic and real-time traffic is ATM. However, reliance on ATM means either constructing a second networking infrastructure for real-time traffic or replacing the existing IP-based configuration with ATM, both of which are costly alternatives.

Traffic on a network or internet can be divided into two broad categories: elastic and inelastic. A consideration of their differing requirements clarifies the need for an enhanced internet architecture.

Elastic traffic can adjust, over wide ranges, to changes in delay and throughput across an internet and still meet the needs of its applications. This is the traditional type of traffic supported on TCP/IP-based internets and is the type of traffic for which internets were designed. With TCP, traffic on individual connections adjusts to congestion by reducing the rate at which data are presented to the network.

Elastic applications include common Internet-based applications, such as file transfer, electronic mail, remote logon, network management, and Web access. But there are differences among the requirements of these applications. For example,

- E-mail is generally quite insensitive to changes in delay.
- When file transfer is done online, as it frequently is, the user expects the delay to be proportional to the file size and so is sensitive to changes in throughput.
- With network management, delay is generally not a serious concern. However, if failures in an internet are the cause of congestion, then the need for network management messages to get through with minimum delay increases with increased congestion.
- Interactive applications, such as remote logon and Web access, are quite sensitive to delay.

So, even if we confine our attention to elastic traffic, a QoS-based internet service could be of benefit. Without such a service, routers are dealing evenhandedly with arriving IP packets, with no concern for the type of application and whether this packet is part of a large transfer or a small one. Under such circumstances, and if congestion develops, it is unlikely that resources will be allocated in such a way as to meet the needs of all applications fairly. When inelastic traffic is added to the mix, matters are even more unsatisfactory.

Inelastic traffic does not easily adapt, if at all, to changes in delay and throughput across an internet. The prime example is real-time traffic, such as voice and video. The requirements for inelastic traffic may include the following:

- **Throughput:** A minimum throughput value may be required. Unlike most elastic traffic, which can continue to deliver data with perhaps degraded service, many inelastic applications require a firm minimum throughput.
- **Delay:** An example of a delay-sensitive application is stock trading; someone who consistently receives later service will consistently act later, and with greater disadvantage.
- **Delay variation:** The larger the allowable delay, the longer the real delay in delivering the data and the greater the size of the delay buffer required at receivers. Real-time interactive applications, such as teleconferencing, may require a reasonable upper bound on delay variation.
- **Packet loss:** Real-time applications vary in the amount of packet loss, if any, that they can sustain.

These requirements are difficult to meet in an environment with variable queuing delays and congestion losses. Accordingly, inelastic traffic introduces two new requirements into the internet architecture. First, some means is needed to give preferential treatment to applications with more demanding requirements. Applications need to be able to state their requirements, either ahead of time in some sort of service request function, or on the fly, by means of fields in the IP packet header.

A second requirement in supporting inelastic traffic in an internet architecture is that elastic traffic must still be supported. Inelastic applications typically do not back off and reduce demand in the face of congestion, in contrast to TCP-based

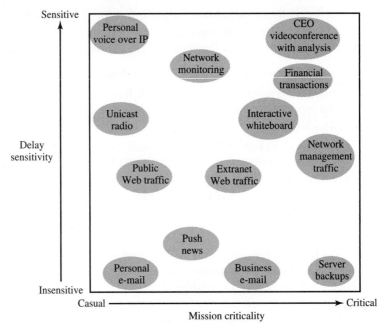

Figure 8.7 A Comparison of Application Delay Sensitivity and Criticality in an Enterprise

applications. Therefore, unless some control is imposed, in times of congestion in-elastic traffic will continue to supply a high load and elastic traffic will be crowded off the internet.

Another way to look at the traffic requirements of an organization is shown in Figure 8.7 [CROL00]. Applications can be characterized by two broad categories. The requirement of delay sensitivity can be satisfied by a QoS that emphasizes timely delivery and/or provides a high data rate. The requirement of criticality can be satisfied by a QoS that emphasizes reliability.

Several mechanisms for providing QoS services on the Internet have been proposed. The one that has received the broadest acceptance is known as differenti-ated services. We turn to this topic next.

8.4 DIFFERENTIATED SERVICES

As the burden on the Internet grows, and as the variety of applications grows, there is an immediate need to provide differing levels of QoS to different users. The dif-ferentiated services (DS) architecture is designed to provide a simple, easy-to-implement, low-overhead tool to support a range of network services that are differentiated on the basis of performance. In essence, **differentiated services** do not provide QoS on the basis of flows but rather on the basis of the needs of different groups of users. This means that all the traffic on the Internet is split into groups with different QoS requirements and that routers recognize different groups on the basis of a label in the IP header.

Several key characteristics of DS contribute to its efficiency and ease of deployment:

- IP packets are labeled for differing QoS treatment using the 6-bit DS field in the IPv4 and IPv6 headers (Figure 5.7). No change is required to IP.
- A service level agreement (SLA) is established between the service provider (internet domain) and the customer prior to the use of DS. This avoids the need to incorporate DS mechanisms in applications. Thus, existing applications need not be modified to use DS.
- DS provides a built-in aggregation mechanism. All traffic with the same DS octet is treated the same by the network service. For example, multiple voice connections are not handled individually but in the aggregate. This provides for good scaling to larger networks and traffic loads.
- DS is implemented in individual routers by queuing and forwarding packets based on the DS octet. Routers deal with each packet individually and do not have to save state information on packet flows.

Today, DS is the most widely accepted QoS mechanism in enterprise networks.

Services

The DS type of service is provided within a DS domain, which is defined as a contiguous portion of the Internet over which a consistent set of DS policies are administered. Typically, a DS domain would be under the control of one administrative entity. The services provided across a DS domain are defined in a service level agreement (SLA), which is a service contract between a customer and the service provider that specifies the forwarding service that the customer should receive for various classes of packets. A customer may be a user organization or another DS domain. Once the SLA is established, the customer submits packets with the DS octet marked to indicate the packet class. The service provider must assure that the customer gets at least the agreed QoS for each packet class. To provide that QoS, the service provider must configure the appropriate forwarding policies at each router (based on DS octet value) and must measure the performance being provided to each class on an ongoing basis.

If a customer submits packets intended for destinations within the DS domain, then the DS domain is expected to provide the agreed service. If the destination is beyond the customer's DS domain, then the DS domain will attempt to forward the packets through other domains, requesting the most appropriate service to match the requested service.

A DS framework document lists the following detailed performance parameters that might be included in an SLA:

- Service performance parameters, such as expected throughput, drop probability, and latency
- Constraints on the ingress and egress points at which the service is provided, indicating the scope of the service
- Traffic profiles that must be adhered to for the requested service to be provided
- Disposition of traffic submitted in excess of the specified profile

The framework document also gives some examples of services that might be provided:

1. Traffic offered at service level A will be delivered with low latency.

2. Traffic offered at service level B will be delivered with low loss.

3. Ninety percent of in-profile traffic delivered at service level C will experience no more than 50 ms latency.

4. Ninety-five percent of in-profile traffic delivered at service level D will be delivered.

5. Traffic offered at service level E will be allotted twice the bandwidth of traffic delivered at service level F.

6. Traffic with drop precedence X has a higher probability of delivery than traffic with drop precedence Y.

The first two examples are qualitative and are valid only in comparison to other traffic, such as default traffic that gets a best-effort service. The next two examples are quantitative and provide a specific guarantee that can be verified by measurement on the actual service without comparison to any other services offered at the same time. The final two examples are a mixture of quantitative and qualitative.

DS Field

Packets are labeled for service handling by means of the 6-bit DS field in the IPv4 header or the IPv6 header (Figure 5.7). The value of the DS field, referred to as the **DS codepoint**, is the label used to classify packets for differentiated services.

With a 6-bit codepoint, there are, in principle, 64 different classes of traffic that could be defined. These 64 codepoints are allocated across three pools of codepoints, as follows:

- Codepoints of the form xxxxx0, where x is either 0 or 1, are reserved for assignment as standards.

- Codepoints of the form xxxx11 are reserved for experimental or local use.

- Codepoints of the form xxxx01 are also reserved for experimental or local use but may be allocated for future standards action as needed.

Within the first pool, the codepoint 000000 is the default packet class. The default class is the best-effort forwarding behavior in existing routers. Such packets are forwarded in the order that they are received as soon as link capacity becomes available. If other higher-priority packets in other DS classes are available for transmission, these are given preference over default best-effort packets.

Codepoints of the form xxx000 are reserved to provide backward compatibility with the IPv4 precedence service. To explain this requirement, we need to digress to an explanation of the IPv4 precedence service. The original IPv4 type of service (TOS) field includes two subfields: a 3-bit precedence subfield and a 4-bit TOS subfield. These subfields serve complementary functions. The TOS subfield provides guidance to the IP entity (in the source or router) on selecting the next hop for this datagram, and the precedence subfield provides guidance about the relative allocation of router resources for this datagram.

The precedence field is set to indicate the degree of urgency or priority to be associated with a datagram. If a router supports the precedence subfield, there are three approaches to responding:

- **Route selection:** A particular route may be selected if the router has a smaller queue for that route or if the next hop on that route supports network precedence or priority (e.g., a token ring network supports priority).

- **Network service:** If the network on the next hop supports precedence, then that service is invoked.

- **Queuing discipline:** A router may use precedence to affect how queues are handled. For example, a router may give preferential treatment in queues to datagrams with higher precedence.

RFC 1812, *Requirements for IP Version 4 Routers*, provides recommendations for queuing discipline that fall into two categories:

- **Queue service**

  a. Routers SHOULD implement precedence-ordered queue service. Precedence-ordered queue service means that when a packet is selected for output on a (logical) link, the packet of highest precedence that has been queued for that link is sent.

  b. Any router MAY implement other policy-based throughput management procedures that result in other than strict precedence ordering, but it MUST be configurable to suppress them (i.e., use strict ordering).

- **Congestion control.** When a router receives a packet beyond its storage capacity, it must discard it or some other packet or packets.

  a. A router MAY discard the packet it has just received; this is the simplest but not the best policy.

  b. Ideally, the router should select a packet from one of the sessions most heavily abusing the link, given that the applicable QoS policy permits this. A recommended policy in datagram environments using FIFO queues is to discard a packet randomly selected from the queue. An equivalent algorithm in routers using fair queues is to discard from the longest queue. A router MAY use these algorithms to determine which packet to discard.

  c. If precedence-ordered queue service is implemented and enabled, the router MUST NOT discard a packet whose IP precedence is higher than that of a packet that is not discarded.

  d. A router MAY protect packets whose IP headers request the maximize reliability TOS, except where doing so would be in violation of the previous rule.

  e. A router MAY protect fragmented IP packets, on the theory that dropping a fragment of a datagram may increase congestion by causing all fragments of the datagram to be retransmitted by the source.

  f. To help prevent routing perturbations or disruption of management functions, the router MAY protect packets used for routing control, link control, or network management from being discarded. Dedicated routers (i.e.,

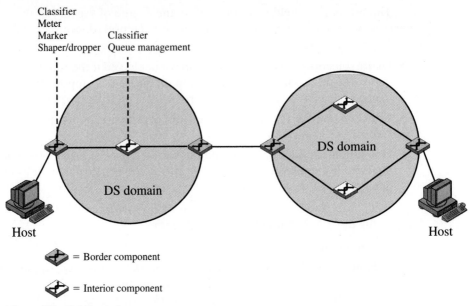

Figure 8.8 DS Domains

routers that are not also general purpose hosts, terminal servers, etc.) can achieve an approximation of this rule by protecting packets whose source or destination is the router itself.

The DS codepoints of the form xxx000 should provide a service that at minimum is equivalent to that of the IPv4 precedence functionality.

DS Configuration and Operation

Figure 8.8 illustrates the type of configuration envisioned in the DS documents. A DS domain consists of a set of contiguous routers; that is, it is possible to get from any router in the domain to any other router in the domain by a path that does not include routers outside the domain. Within a domain, the interpretation of DS codepoints is uniform, so that a uniform, consistent service is provided.

Routers in a DS domain are either boundary nodes or interior nodes. Typically, the interior nodes implement simple mechanisms for handling packets based on their DS codepoint values. This includes a queuing discipline to give preferential treatment depending on codepoint value, and packet-dropping rules to dictate which packets should be dropped first in the event of buffer saturation. The DS specifications refer to the forwarding treatment provided at a router as per-hop behavior (PHB). This PHB must be available at all routers, and typically PHB is the only part of DS implemented in interior routers.

The boundary nodes include PHB mechanisms but also more sophisticated traffic conditioning mechanisms required to provide the desired service. Thus, interior routers have minimal functionality and minimal overhead in providing the DS service, while most of the complexity is in the boundary nodes. The boundary node function can also be provided by a host system attached to the domain, on behalf of the applications at that host system.

The traffic conditioning function consists of five elements:

- **Classifier:** Separates submitted packets into different classes. This is the foundation of providing differentiated services. A classifier may separate traffic only on the basis of the DS codepoint (behavior aggregate classifier) or based on multiple fields within the packet header or even the packet payload (multifield classifier).

- **Meter:** Measures submitted traffic for conformance to a profile. The meter determines whether a given packet stream class is within or exceeds the service level guaranteed for that class.

- **Marker:** Re-marks packets with a different codepoint as needed. This may be done for packets that exceed the profile; for example, if a given throughput is guaranteed for a particular service class, any packets in that class that exceed the throughput in some defined time interval may be re-marked for best effort handling. Also, re-marking may be required at the boundary between two DS domains. For example, if a given traffic class is to receive the highest supported priority, and this is a value of 3 in one domain and 7 in the next domain, then packets with a priority 3 value traversing the first domain are remarked as priority 7 when entering the second domain.

- **Shaper:** Delays packets as necessary so that the packet stream in a given class does not exceed the traffic rate specified in the profile for that class.

- **Dropper:** Drops packets when the rate of packets of a given class exceeds that specified in the profile for that class.

Figure 8.9 illustrates the relationship between the elements of traffic conditioning. After a flow is classified, its resource consumption must be measured. The metering function measures the volume of packets over a particular time interval to determine a flow's compliance with the traffic agreement. If the host is bursty, a simple

Figure 8.9   DS Functions

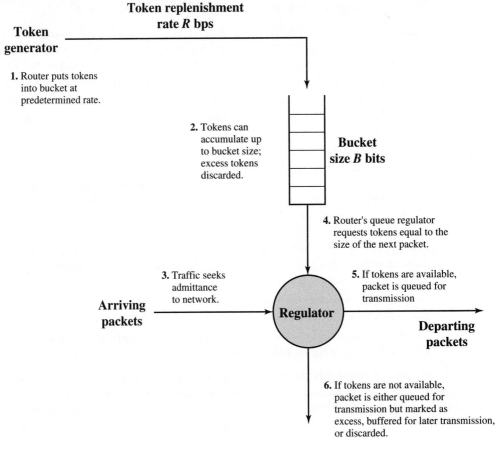

Figure 8.10   Token Bucket Scheme

data rate or packet rate may not be sufficient to capture the desired traffic characteristics. A token bucket scheme is an example of a way to define a traffic profile to take into account both packet rate and burstiness.

A token bucket traffic specification consists of two parameters: a token replenishment rate R and a bucket size B. The token rate R specifies the continually sustainable data rate; that is, over a relatively long period of time, the average data rate to be supported for this flow is R. The bucket size B specifies the amount by which the data rate can exceed R for short periods of time. The exact condition is as follows: during any time period T, the amount of data sent cannot exceed $RT + B$.

Figure 8.10 illustrates this scheme and explains the use of the term *bucket*. The bucket represents a counter that indicates the allowable number of octets of IP data that can be sent at any time. The bucket fills with *octet tokens* at the rate of R (i.e., the counter is incremented R times per second), up to the bucket capacity (up to the maximum counter value). IP packets arrive and are queued for processing. An IP packet may be processed if there are sufficient octet tokens to match the IP data size. If so, the packet is processed and the bucket is drained of the corresponding number of tokens. If a packet arrives and there are insufficient tokens available, then the packet exceeds the limit for this flow.

Over the long run, the rate of IP data allowed by the token bucket is R. However, if there is an idle or relatively slow period, the bucket capacity builds up, so that at most an additional B octets above the stated rate can be accepted. Thus, B is a measure of the degree of burstiness of the data flow that is allowed.

If a traffic flow exceeds some profile, several approaches can be taken. Individual packets in excess of the profile may be re-marked for lower-quality handling and allowed to pass into the DS domain. A traffic shaper may absorb a burst of packets in a buffer and pace the packets over a longer period of time. A dropper may drop packets if the buffer used for pacing becomes saturated.

8.5 SERVICE LEVEL AGREEMENTS

A service level agreement (SLA) is a contract between a network provider and a customer that defines specific aspects of the service that is to be provided. The definition is formal and typically defines quantitative thresholds that must be met. An SLA typically includes the following information:

- **A description of the nature of service to be provided:** A basic service would be IP-based network connectivity of enterprise locations plus access to the Internet. The service may include additional functions such as Web hosting, maintenance of domain name servers, and operation and maintenance tasks.

- **The expected performance level of the service:** The SLA defines a number of metrics, such as delay, reliability, and availability, with numerical thresholds.

- **The process for monitoring and reporting the service level:** This describes how performance levels are measured and reported.

Figure 8.11 shows a typical configuration that lends itself to an SLA. In this case, a network service provider maintains an IP-based network. A customer has a number of private networks (e.g., LANs) at various sites. Customer networks are connected to the provider via access routers at the access points. The SLA dictates service and performance levels for traffic between access routers across the provider network. In addition, the provider network links to the Internet and thus provides Internet access for the enterprise. For example, for the Internet Dedicated Service provided by MCI (http://global.mci.com/terms/us/products/dsl), the SLA includes the following items:

- **Availability:** 100% availability.

- **Latency (delay):** Average round-trip transmissions of ≤ 45 ms between access routers in the contiguous United States. Average round-trip transmissions of ≤ 90 ms between an access router in the New York metropolitan area and an access router in the London metropolitan area. Latency is calculated by averaging sample measurements taken during a calendar month between routers.

- **Network packet delivery (reliability):** Successful packet delivery rate of $\geq 99.5\%$.

- **Denial of service (DoS):** Responds to DoS attacks reported by customer within 15 minutes of customer opening a complete trouble ticket. MCI defines a DoS attack as more than 95% bandwidth utilization.

Figure 8.11 Typical Framework for Service Level Agreement

- **Network jitter:** Jitter is defined as the variation or difference in the end-to-end delay between received packets of an IP or packet stream. Jitter performance will not exceed 1 ms between access routers.

An SLA can be defined for the overall network service. In addition, SLAs can be defined for specific end-to-end services available across the carrier's network, such as a virtual private network, or differentiated services.

8.6 IP PERFORMANCE METRICS

The IPPM Performance Metrics Working Group (IPPM) is chartered by IETF to develop standard metrics that relate to the quality, performance, and reliability of Internet data delivery. Two trends dictate the need for such a standardized measurement scheme:

1. The Internet has grown and continues to grow at a dramatic rate. Its topology is increasingly complex. As its capacity has grown, the load on the Internet has grown at an even faster rate. Similarly, private internets, such as corporate intranets and extranets, have exhibited similar growth in complexity, capacity, and load. The sheer scale of these networks makes it difficult to determine quality, performance, and reliability characteristics.

2. The Internet serves a large and growing number of commercial and personal users across an expanding spectrum of applications. Similarly, private networks are growing in terms of user base and range of applications. Some of these applications are sensitive to particular QoS parameters, leading users to require accurate and understandable performance metrics.

A standardized and effective set of metrics enables users and service providers to have an accurate common understanding of the performance of the Internet and private internets. Measurement data is useful for a variety of purposes, including

- Supporting capacity planning and troubleshooting of large complex internets
- Encouraging competition by providing uniform comparison metrics across service providers
- Supporting Internet research in such areas as protocol design, congestion control, and quality of service
- Verification of service level agreements

Table 8.3 lists the metrics that have been defined in RFCs at the time of this writing. Table 8.3a lists those metrics which result in a value estimated based on a sampling technique. The metrics are defined in three stages:

- **Singleton metric:** The most elementary, or atomic, quantity that can be measured for a given performance metric. For example, for a delay metric, a singleton metric is the delay experienced by a single packet.
- **Sample metric:** A collection of singleton measurements taken during a given time period. For example, for a delay metric, a sample metric is the set of delay values for all of the measurements taken during a one-hour period.

Table 8.3 IP Performance Metrics
(a) Sampled metrics

Metric Name	Singleton Definition	Statistical Definitions
One-Way Delay	Delay = dT, where Src transmits first bit of packet at T and Dst received last bit of packet at T + dT	Percentile, median, minimum, inverse percentile
Round-Trip Delay	Delay = dT, where Src transmits first bit of packet at T and Src received last bit of packet immediately returned by Dst at T + dT	Percentile, median, minimum, inverse percentile
One-Way Loss	Packet loss = 0 (signifying successful transmission and reception of packet); = 1 (signifying packet loss)	Average
One-Way Loss Pattern	Loss distance: Pattern showing the distance between successive packet losses in terms of the sequence of packets Loss period: Pattern showing the number of bursty losses (losses involving consecutive packets)	Number or rate of loss distances below a defined threshold, number of loss periods, pattern of period lengths, pattern of inter-loss period lengths.
Packet Delay Variation	Packet delay variation (pdv) for a pair of packets with a stream of packets = difference between the one-way-delay of the selected packets	Percentile, inverse percentile, jitter, peak-to-peak pdv

Src = IP address of a host
Dst = IP address of a host

Table (b) Other metrics

Metric Name	General Definition	Metrics
Connectivity	Ability to deliver a packet over a transport connection.	One-way instantaneous connectivity, two-way instantaneous connectivity, one-way interval connectivity, two-way interval connectivity, two-way temporal connectivity
Bulk Transfer Capacity	Long-term average data rate (bps) over a single congestion-aware transport connection.	BTC = (data sent)/(elapsed time)

- **Statistical metric:** A value derived from a given sample metric by computing some statistic of the values defined by the singleton metric on the sample. For example, the mean of all the one-way delay values on a sample might be defined as a statistical metric

The measurement technique can be either active or passive. **Active techniques** require injecting packets into the network for the sole purpose of measurement. There are several drawbacks to this approach. The load on the network is increased. This in turn can affect the desired result. For example, on a heavily loaded network, the injection of measurement packets can increase network delay, so that the measured delay is greater than it would be without the measurement traffic. In addition, an active measurement policy can be abused for denial-of-service attacks disguised as legitimate measurement activity. **Passive techniques** observe and extract metrics from existing traffic. This approach can expose the contents of Internet traffic to unintended recipients, creating security and privacy concerns. So far, the metrics defined by the IPPM working group are all active.

For the sample metrics, the simplest technique is to take measurements at fixed time intervals, known as periodic sampling. There are several problems with this approach. First, if the traffic on the network exhibits periodic behavior, with a period that is an integer multiple of the sampling period (or vice versa), correlation effects may result in inaccurate values. Also, the act of measurement can perturb what is being measured (for example, injecting measurement traffic into a network alters the congestion level of the network), and repeated periodic perturbations can drive a network into a state of synchronization (e.g., [FLOY94]), greatly magnifying what might individually be minor effects. Accordingly, RFC 2330 (*Framework for IP Performance Metrics*) recommends Poisson sampling. This method uses a Poisson distribution to generate random time intervals with the desired mean value.

Most of the statistical metrics listed in Table 8.3a are self-explanatory. The percentile metric is defined as follows: The xth percentile is a value y such that $x\%$ of measurements $\geq y$. The inverse percentile of x for a set of measurements is the percentage of all values $\leq x$.

Figure 8.12 illustrates the packet delay variation metric. This metric is used to measure jitter, or variability, in the delay of packets traversing the network. The singleton metric is defined by selecting two packet measurements and measuring the difference in the two delays. The statistical measures make use of the absolute values of the delays.

Table 8.3b lists two metrics that are not defined statistically. Connectivity deals with the issue of whether a transport-level connection is maintained by the network.

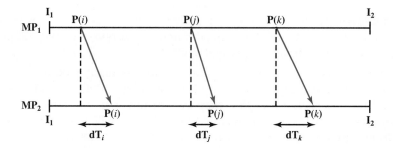

I_1, I_2 = times that mark that beginning and ending of the interval
in which the packet stream from which the singleton
measurement is taken occurs
MP_1, MP_2 = source and destination measurement points
$P(i)$ = ith measured packet in a stream of packets
dT_i = one-way delay for $P(i)$

Figure 8.12   Model for Defining Packet Delay Variation

APPLICATION NOTE
Where Does My Network Address Come From?

All computers connecting to a network must get a network address. This address is an IP (Internet Protocol) address. If your network connects to the Internet, then at least one node must have an address that is valid for use on the public net. This address usually is assigned by an Internet service provider or ISP. The approach used to assign the addresses for the internal network and the network nodes is usually based on the number of computers that will have globally unique Internet addresses.

Globally unique addresses are those that can only be used by one computer in the public Internet space. All communication interfaces connected to the Internet have globally unique addresses. These computers or interfaces are sometimes referred to as the "visible" machines. Visible means that these computers are directly attached to the public Internet. Being visible also implies that the machines are more exposed to attack from hackers; this is true.

An organization may decide to have all of their machines use these globally unique addresses and be visible. In this case, the ISP must assign many addresses to the organization by assigning a full or partial class address. The Internet address space is organized by classes A, B, and C, with class A networks being very large and class C's being much smaller. ISPs often control large chunks of address space that they can parcel out to their customers. For example, a company having 200 nodes may request that a class C network address be assigned to them.

Large ISPs can control millions of IP addresses and, using the subnet mask, can assign a slice of this address space to their clients. The subnet mask is used to determine what network a host is on and the size of that network. For example, an ISP like Time Warner may control a portion of the address space within a class A network. A small percentage of

(Continued)

these addresses can be provided to an individual company. When this is done, it is also common to see the ISP handling a good number of services for the company like DNS, domain name registration, security, and mail.

Another option is to have a small number of globally unique addresses assigned by the ISP and use these addresses as the outside connection to the company firewalls. It is possible to "hide" some or all of the computers behind a router running network address translation or NAT. The computers using the NAT box will all use the same global Internet address, effectively making them invisible. This does not mean that "invisible" machines are barred from communicating over the Internet or that they are immune from attack.

However, this presents the problem of addressing for the inside nodes. These addresses are not coming from the ISP and so must be assigned by the local network administrator, either by static configuration or by DHCP. Care must be taken to avoid using standard Internet addressing internally. If internal machines are assigned the same addresses as external visible machines, the routers on the Internet will not be able to route traffic back to the internal company machines. For this reason, private IP addressing has been established. The following Internet addresses have been reserved for organizations wishing to deploy networks in this manner:

10.0.0.0–10.255.255.255
172.16.0.0–172.31.255.255
192.168.0.0–192.168.255.255

Private addressing is described in detail in RFC 1918. Aside from the benefit of security for the internal machines, this scheme was introduced to alleviate the problem of increasing numbers of users on the Internet. With this tremendous growth, the number of globally unique addresses in IPv4 is insufficient for everyone to have their own unique public address.

There are benefits and drawbacks to each of the methods outlined above. Private addressing usually requires more management, but it does provide increased security and a reduction in the public address space used. Using public addressing throughout does ease the management and has the potential for easing connectivity concerns. However, it can make the organization dependent on the ISP for a large number of its concerns, including security.

The current specification (RFC 2678) does not detail specific sample and statistical metrics but provides a framework within which such metrics could be defined. Connectivity is determined by the ability to deliver a packet across a connection within a specified time limit. The other metric, bulk transfer capacity, is similarly specified (RFC 3148) without sample and statistical metrics but begins to address the issue of measuring the transfer capacity of a network service with the implementation of various congestion control mechanisms.

SUMMARY

An essential element of the Internet is its addressing scheme. It is necessary that each attached host have a unique address to make routing and delivery possible. Internet standards define a 32-bit addressing scheme for this purpose.

An Internet routing protocol is used to exchange information about reachability and traffic delays, allowing each router to construct a next-hop routing table for paths through the internet. Typically, relatively simple routing protocols are used between autonomous systems within a larger internet and more complex routing protocols are used within each autonomous system.

The increasing data rate (capacity) requirements of applications have spurred the development of higher speeds in data networks and the Internet. The higher available capacity has in turn encouraged ever more data-intensive applications. To cope with the varying demands on the Internet, the concept of quality of service has been introduced. A QoS facility allows the Internet to treat different classes of traffic differently in order to optimize the service to all customers.

The differentiated services architecture is designed to provide a simple, easy-to-implement, low-overhead tool to support a range of network services that are differentiated on the basis of performance. Differentiated services are provided on the basis of a 6-bit label in the IP header, which classifies traffic in terms of the type of service to be given by routers for that traffic.

8.8 RECOMMENDED READING AND WEB SITES

For the reader interested in a more in-depth discussion of IP addressing, [SPOR03] offers a wealth of detail. An excellent treatment of QoS is [CROL00].

[HUIT00], [BLAC00], and [PERL00] provide detailed coverage of various routing algorithms. [KESH98] provides an instructive look at present and future router functionality.

Perhaps the clearest and most comprehensive book-length treatment of Internet QoS is [ARMI00]. [XIAO99] provides an overview and overall framework for Internet QoS as well as integrated and differentiated services. [SHEN95] is a masterful analysis of the rationale for a QoS-based internet architecture.

[VERM04] is an excellent surveys of service level agreements for IP networks. [BOUI02] covers the more general case of data networks. [MART02] examines limitations of IP network SLAs compared to data networks such as frame relay.

[CHEN02] is a useful survey of Internet performance measurement issues. [PAXS96] provides an overview of the framework of the IPPM effort.

ARMI00 Armitage, G. *Quality of Service in IP Networks.* Indianapolis, IN: Macmillan Technical Publishing, 2000.

BLAC00 Black, U. *IP Routing Protocols: RIP, OSPF, BGP, PNNI & Cisco Routing Protocols.* Upper Saddle River, NJ: Prentice Hall, 2000.

BOUI02 Bouillet, E.; Mitra, D.; and Ramakrishnan, K. "The Structure and Management of Service Level Agreements in Networks." *IEEE Journal on Selected Areas in Communications*, May 2002.

CHEN02 Chen, T. "Internet Performance Monitoring." *Proceedings of the IEEE*, September 2002.

CROL00 Croll, A., and Packman, E. *Managing Bandwidth: Deploying QoS in Enterprise Networks.* Upper Saddle River, NJ: Prentice Hall, 2000.

HUIT00 Huitema, C. *Routing in the Internet.* Upper Saddle River, NJ: Prentice Hall, 2000.

KESH98 Keshav, S., and Sharma, R. "Issues and Trends in Router Design." *IEEE Communications Magazine*, May 1998.

MART02 Martin, J., and Nilsson, A. "On Service Level Agreements for IP Networks." *Proceedings, IEEE INFOCOMM '02*, 2002.

PAXS96 Paxson, V. "Toward a Framework for Defining Internet Performance Metrics." *Proceedings, INET '96*, 1996. http://www-nrg.ee.lbl.gov

PERL00 Perlman, R. *Interconnections: Bridges, Routers, Switches, and Internetworking Protocols.* Reading, MA: Addison-Wesley, 2000.

SHEN95 Shenker, S. "Fundamental Design Issues for the Future Internet." *IEEE Journal on Selected Areas in Communications*, September 1995.

SPOR03 Sportack, M. *IP Addressing Fundamentals.* Indianapolis, IN: Cisco Press, 2003.

VERM04 Verma, D. "Service Level Agreements on IP Networks." *Proceedings of the IEEE*, September 2004.

XIAO99 Xiao, X., and Ni, L. "Internet QoS: A Big Picture." *IEEE Network*, March/April 1999.

Recommended Web sites:

- **Inter-Domain Routing working group:** Chartered by IETF to revise BGP and related standards. The Web site includes all relevant RFCs and Internet drafts.
- **OSPF working group:** Chartered by IETF to develop OSPF and related standards. The Web site includes all relevant RFCs and Internet drafts.
- **IP Performance Metrics working group:** Chartered by IETF to develop a set of standard metrics that can be applied to the quality, performance, and reliability of Internet data delivery services. The Web site includes all relevant RFCs and Internet drafts.

8.9 KEY TERMS, REVIEW QUESTIONS, AND PROBLEMS

Key Terms

autonomous system (AS)	exterior routing protocol	routing
best effort	inelastic traffic	routing algorithm
Border Gateway Protocol (BGP)	interior routing protocol	routing protocol
	neighbor	subnet
differentiated services	Open Shortest Path First (OSPF)	subnet mask
dotted decimal notation		token bucket
elastic traffic	quality of service (QoS)	

Review Questions

8.1 Describe the five classes of Internet addresses.

8.2 What is a subnet?

8.3 What is the purpose of the subnet mask?

8.4 What is an autonomous system?

8.5 What is the difference between an interior router protocol and an exterior router protocol?

8.6 List and briefly explain the three main functions of BGP.

8.7 OSPF uses what type of routing algorithm?

8.8 OSPF is designed as what type of routing protocol?

8.9 Define quality of service (QoS).

8.10 Explain the difference between elastic and inelastic traffic.

8.11 What are the four possible requirements for inelastic traffic?

8.12 What is the purpose of a DS codepoint?

8.13 List and briefly explain the five main functions of DS traffic conditioning.

8.14 What is a token bucket and how does it work?

Problems

8.1 Provide the following parameter values for each of the network classes A, B, and C. Be sure to consider any special or reserved addresses in your calculations.

 a. Number of bits in network portion of address
 b. Number of bits in host portion of address
 c. Number of distinct networks allowed
 d. Number of distinct hosts per network allowed
 e. Integer range of first octet

8.2 What percentage of the total IP address space does each of the network classes represent?

8.3 What is the difference between the subnet mask for a Class A address with 16 bits for the subnet ID and a class B address with 8 bits for the subnet ID?

8.4 Is the subnet mask 255.255.0.255 valid for a Class A address?

8.5 Given a network address of 192.168.100.0 and a subnet mask of 255.255.255.192,

 a. How many subnets are created?
 b. How many hosts are there per subnet?

8.6 Given a company with six individual departments and each department having ten computers or networked devices, what mask could be applied to the company network to provide the subnetting necessary to divide up the network equally?

8.7 In contemporary routing and addressing, the notation commonly used is called classless interdomain routing or CIDR. With CIDR, the number of bits in the mask is indicated in the following fashion: 192.168.100.0/24. This corresponds to a mask of 255.255.255.0. If this example would provide for 256 host addresses on the network, how many addresses are provided with the following?

 a. 192.168.100.0/23
 b. 192.168.100.0/25

8.8 If an IPv4 address is given out every tenth of a second, how many years until all the IPv4 addresses are exhausted? If an IPv6 address is given out every second, how many years until all the IPv6 addresses are exhausted? Assume that, for practical purposes, 2125 IPv6 addresses are available.

8.9 Find out about your network. Using the command "ipconfig", "ifconfig", or "winipcfg", we can learn not only our IP address but other network parameters as well. Can you determine your mask, gateway, and the number of addresses available on your network?

8.10   Using your IP address and your mask, what is your network address? This is determined by converting the IP address and the mask to binary and then proceeding with a bitwise logical AND operation. For example, given the address 172.16.45.0 and the mask 255.255.224.0, we would discover that the network address would be 172.16.32.0.

8.11   Provide three examples (each) of elastic and inelastic Internet traffic. Justify each example's inclusion in their respective category.

8.12   Why does a differentiated services (DS) domain consist of a set of contiguous routers? How are the boundary node routers different from the interior node routers in a DS domain?

PART THREE

Local Area Networks

The trend in local area networks (LANs) involves the use of shared transmission media or shared switching capacity to achieve high data rates over relatively short distances. Several key issues present themselves. One is the choice of transmission medium. Whereas coaxial cable was commonly used in traditional LANs, contemporary LAN installations emphasize the use of twisted pair, optical fiber, or wireless. In the case of twisted pair, efficient encoding schemes are needed to enable high data rates over the medium. Wireless LANs have also assumed increased importance. Another design issue is that of access control.

ROAD MAP FOR PART THREE

Chapter 9 LAN Architecture and Protocols

An essential element of any organization's data processing operation is a LAN. A LAN is needed to interconnect equipment on the user's premises and to provide a means to efficiently connect to outside services and other corporate sites. Chapter 9 provides an overview of LAN technology and standards, including a discussion of transmission media, medium access control, and standards.

Chapter 10 Ethernet

Chapter 10 looks in detail at the transmission media and MAC protocols of the most widely used LAN system, Ethernet. Ethernet has been deployed in versions at 10 Mbps, 100 Mbps, 1 Gbps, and 10 Gbps.

Chapter 11 Wireless LANs

Wireless LANs use one of three transmission techniques: spread spectrum, narrowband microwave, and infrared. Chapter 11 provides an overview of wireless LAN technology and applications. The most significant set of standards defining wireless LANs, known as WiFi, are those defined by the IEEE 802.11 committee.

259

CHAPTER 9

LAN ARCHITECTURE AND PROTOCOLS

9.1 Background
Personal Computer LANs
Backend Networks and Storage Area Networks
High-Speed Office Networks
Backbone LANs
Factory LANs

9.2 LAN Configuration
Tiered LANs
Evolution Scenario

9.3 Guided Transmission Media
Twisted Pair
Coaxial Cable
Optical Fiber
Structured Cabling

9.4 LAN Protocol Architecture
IEEE 802 Reference Model
Logical Link Control
Medium Access Control

9.5 Summary

9.6 Recommended Reading and Web Sites

9.7 Key Terms, Review Questions, and Problems

Appendix 9A Decibels and Signal Strength

Chapter Objectives

After reading this chapter, you should be able to

♦ Define the various types of local area networks (LANs) and list the requirements that each is intended to satisfy.

♦ Give some representative examples of LAN applications.

♦ Discuss the transmission media commonly used for LANs.

♦ List the various options provided in current LAN standards, and explain why the customer should limit purchase consideration to those standards.

Recent years have seen rapid changes in the technology, design, and commercial applications for local area network LANs. A major feature of this evolution is the introduction of a variety of new schemes for high-speed local networking. In this chapter we look at the underlying technology of LANs. Chapters 10 and 11 are devoted to a discussion of specific LAN systems.

This chapter begins with a discussion of various types of LANS and various LAN configuration options. Next we look at alternatives for wired transmission media, putting off a discussion of wireless transmission until Chapter 11. This is followed by a discussion of LAN protocol architecture.

9.1 BACKGROUND

The variety of applications for LANs is wide. To provide some insight into the types of requirements that LANs are intended to meet, this section discusses some of the most important general application areas for these networks. In the next section, we look at the implications for LAN configuration.

Personal Computer LANs

A common LAN configuration is one that supports personal computers. With the relatively low cost of PCs, managers within organizations often independently procure personal computers for departmental applications, such as collaboration and project management tools, and Internet access.

But a collection of department-level processors will not meet all of an organization's needs; central processing facilities are still required. Some programs, such as econometric forecasting models, are too big to run on a small computer. Corporate-wide data files, such as accounting and payroll, require a centralized facility but should be accessible to a number of users. In addition, there are other kinds of files that, although specialized, must be shared by a number of users. Further, there are sound reasons for connecting individual intelligent workstations not only to a central facility but to each other as well. Members of a project or organization team need to share work and information. By far the most efficient way to do so is digitally.

Certain expensive resources, such as a large disc system or a laser printer, can be shared by all users of the departmental LAN. In addition, the network can tie into larger corporate network facilities. For example, the corporation may have a building-wide LAN and a wide area private network. A communications server can provide controlled access to these resources.

LANs for the support of personal computers and workstations have become nearly universal in organizations of all sizes. Even those sites that still depend heavily on the mainframe have transferred much of the processing load to networks of personal computers. Perhaps the prime example of the way in which personal computers are being used is to implement client/server applications.

Backend Networks and Storage Area Networks

Backend networks are used to interconnect large systems such as mainframes, supercomputers, and mass storage devices. The key requirement here is for bulk data transfer among a limited number of devices in a small area. High reliability is generally also a requirement. Typical characteristics include the following:

- **High data rate:** To satisfy the high-volume demand, data rates of 100 Mbps or more are required.
- **High-speed interface:** Data transfer operations between a large host system and a mass storage device are typically performed through high-speed parallel I/O interfaces, rather than slower communications interfaces. Thus, the physical link between station and network must be high speed.
- **Distributed access:** Some sort of distributed medium access control (MAC) technique is needed to enable a number of devices to share the LAN with efficient and reliable access.
- **Limited distance:** Typically, a **backend network** will be employed in a computer room or a small number of contiguous rooms.
- **Limited number of devices:** The number of expensive mainframes and mass storage devices found in the computer room generally is in the tens of devices.

Typically, backend networks are found at sites of large companies or research installations with large data processing budgets. Because of the scale involved, a small difference in productivity can mean millions of dollars.

Consider a site that uses a dedicated mainframe computer. This implies a fairly large application or set of applications. As the load at the site grows, the existing mainframe may be replaced by a more powerful one, perhaps a multiprocessor system. At some sites, a single-system replacement will not be able to keep up; equipment performance growth rates will be exceeded by demand growth rates. The facility will eventually require multiple independent computers. Again, there are compelling reasons for interconnecting these systems. The cost of system interrupt is high, so it should be possible, easily and quickly, to shift applications to backup systems. It must be possible to test new procedures and applications without degrading the production system. Large bulk storage files must be accessible from more than one computer. Load leveling should be possible to maximize utilization and performance.

It can be seen that some key requirements for backend networks differ from those for personal computer LANs. High data rates are required to keep up with the work, which typically involves the transfer of large blocks of data. The equipment for achieving high speeds is expensive. Fortunately, given the much higher cost of the attached devices, such costs are reasonable.

A concept related to that of the backend network is the **storage area network (SAN)**. A SAN is a separate network to handle storage needs. The SAN decouples storage tasks from specific servers and creates a shared storage facility across a high-speed network. The collection of networked storage devices can include hard discs, tape libraries, and CD arrays. Most SANs use Fibre Channel, which is described in Appendix G. In a typical large LAN installation, a number of servers and perhaps mainframes each has its own dedicated storage devices. If a client needs access to a particular storage device, it must go through the server that controls that device. In a SAN, no server sits between the storage devices and the network; instead, the storage devices and servers are linked directly to the network. The SAN arrangement improves client-to-storage access efficiency, as well as direct storage-to-storage communications for backup and replication functions.

Figure 9.1 suggests a typical SAN configuration. Users attached to the Internet send file requests (store, retrieve) to a bank of servers. These servers do not maintain the files locally but are connected to a SAN, which supports a number of mass storage devices. The SAN includes network devices optimized to handle storage tasks.

High-Speed Office Networks

Traditionally, the office environment has included a variety of devices with low- to medium-speed data transfer requirements. However, for newer applications in the office environment, the limited speeds (up to 10 Mbps) of the traditional LAN are inadequate. Desktop image processors have increased network data flow by an unprecedented amount. Examples of these applications include fax machines,

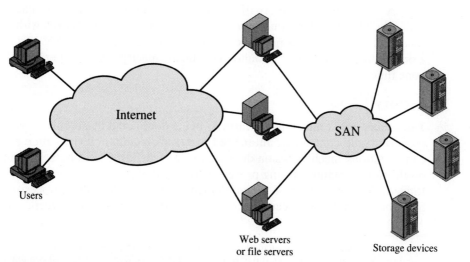

Figure 9.1 Storage Area Network Configuration

document image processors, and graphics programs on personal computers and workstations. Consider that a typical page with 200 picture elements, or pels[1] (black or white points), per inch resolution (which is adequate but not high resolution) generates 3,740,000 bits (8.5 inches × 11 inches × 40,000 pels per square inch). Even with compression techniques, this will generate a tremendous load. In addition, disc technology and price/performance have evolved so that desktop storage capacities of a few gigabytes are common. These new demands require LANs with high speed that can support the larger numbers and greater geographic extent of office systems as compared to backend systems.

Backbone LANs

The increasing use of distributed processing applications and personal computers has led to a need for a flexible strategy for local networking. Support of premises-wide data communications requires a networking service that is capable of spanning the distances involved and that interconnects equipment in a single (perhaps large) building or a cluster of buildings. Although it is possible to develop a single LAN to interconnect all the data processing equipment of a premises, this is probably not a practical alternative in most cases. There are several drawbacks to a single-LAN strategy:

- **Reliability:** With a single LAN, a service interruption, even of short duration, could result in a major disruption for users.
- **Capacity:** A single LAN could be saturated as the number of devices attached to the network grows over time.
- **Cost:** A single LAN technology is not optimized for the diverse requirements of interconnection and communication. The presence of large numbers of low-cost microcomputers dictates that network support for these devices be provided at low cost. LANs that support very low cost attachment will not be suitable for meeting the overall requirement.

A more attractive alternative is to employ lower-cost, lower-capacity LANs within buildings or departments and to interconnect these networks with a higher-capacity LAN. This latter network is referred to as a backbone LAN. If confined to a single building or cluster of buildings, a high-capacity LAN can perform the backbone function.

Factory LANs

The factory environment is increasingly being dominated by automated equipment: programmable controllers, automated materials handling devices, time and attendance stations, machine vision devices, and various forms of robots. To manage the production or manufacturing process, it is essential to tie this equipment together. Indeed, the very nature of the equipment facilitates this. Microprocessor devices have the potential to collect information from the shop floor and accept commands.

---

[1] A *picture element*, or *pel*, is the smallest discrete scanning-line sample of a facsimile system, which contains only black-white information (no gray scales). A *pixel* is a picture element that contains gray scale information.

With the proper use of the information and commands, it is possible to improve the manufacturing process and to provide detailed machine control.

The more that a factory is automated, the greater is the need for communications. Only by interconnecting all of the devices and by providing mechanisms for their cooperation can the automated factory be work effectively. The means for interconnection is the factory LAN. Key characteristics of a factory LAN include the following:

- High capacity
- Ability to handle a variety of data traffic
- Large geographic extent
- High reliability
- Ability to specify and control transmission delays

Factory LANs are a niche market requiring, in general, more flexible and reliable LANs than are found in the typical office environment.

9.2 LAN CONFIGURATION

Tiered LANs

Consider the kinds of data processing equipment to be supported in a typical organization. In rough terms, we can group this equipment into three categories:

- **Personal computers and workstations:** The workhorse in most office environments is the microcomputer, including personal computers and workstations. Most of this equipment is found at the departmental level, used by individual professionals and secretarial personnel. When used for network applications, the load generated tends to be rather modest.
- **Server farms**: Servers, used within a department or shared by users in a number of departments, can perform a variety of functions. Generic examples include supporting expensive peripherals such as mass storage devices, providing applications that require large amounts of processor resources, and maintaining databases accessible by many users. Because of this shared use, these machines may generate substantial traffic.
- **Mainframes:** For large database and scientific applications, the mainframe is often the machine of choice. When the machines are networked, bulk data transfers dictate that a high-capacity network be used.

The requirements indicated by this spectrum suggest that a single LAN will not, in many cases, be the most cost-effective solution. A single network would have to be rather high speed to support the aggregate demand. However, the cost of attachment to a LAN tends to increase as a function of the network data rate. Accordingly, a high-speed LAN would be very expensive for attachment of low-cost personal computers.

An alternative approach, which is becoming increasingly common, is to employ two or three tiers of LANs (Figure 9.2). Within a department, a low-cost, moderate-

Figure 9.2 Tiered Local Area Networks

speed LAN supports a cluster of personal computers and workstations. These departmental LANs are lashed together with a backbone LAN of higher capacity. In addition, shared systems are also supported off of this backbone. If mainframes are also part of the office equipment suite, then a separate high-speed LAN supports these devices and may be linked, as a whole, to the backbone LAN to support a traffic between the mainframes and other office equipment. We will see that LAN standards and products address the need for all three types of LANs.

Evolution Scenario

One final aspect of the tiered architecture should be mentioned: the way in which such a networking implementation comes about in an organization. This will vary widely from one organization to the next, but two general scenarios can be defined. It is useful to be aware of these scenarios because of their implications for the selection and management of LANs.

In the first scenario, the LAN decisions are made from the bottom up, with each department making decisions more or less in isolation. In this scenario, the particular application requirements of a department are typically well known. For example, an engineering department has very high data rate requirements to support its CAD environment, whereas the sale department has low data rate requirements for its order entry and order inquiry needs. Because the applications are well known, a decision can be made quickly on which network to purchase. Departmental budgets usually can cover the costs of these networks, so approval of a higher authority is not required. The result is that each department will develop its own cluster network (tier 3). In the meantime, if this is a large organization, the central data processing organization may acquire a high-speed (tier 1) LAN to interconnect mainframes.

Over time, many departments will develop their own cluster tier; each department will realize it has a need to interconnect. For example, the marketing department may have to access cost information from the finance department as well as last month's order rate from sales. When cluster-to-cluster communication requirements become important, the company will make a conscious decision to provide interconnect capability. This interconnect capability is realized through the LAN backbone (tier 2).

The advantage of this scenario is that, since the department manager is closest to the department's needs, local interconnect strategies can be responsive to the specific applications of the department, and acquisition can be timely. There are several disadvantages to this approach. First, there is the problem of suboptimization. If procurement is made on a company-wide basis, perhaps less total equipment will be acquired to satisfy the total need. In addition, larger-volume purchases may result in more favorable terms. Second, the company is eventually faced with the need to interconnect all of these departmental LANs. If there are a wide variety of such LANs from many different vendors, the interconnection problem becomes more difficult.

For these reasons, an alternative scenario is becoming increasingly common: a top-down design of a LAN strategy. In this case, the company decides to map out a total local networking strategy. The decision is centralized because it impacts the entire operation or company. The advantage of this approach is built-in compatibility to interconnect the users. The difficulty with this approach is, of course, the need to be responsive and timely in meeting needs at the departmental level.

9.3 GUIDED TRANSMISSION MEDIA

In a data transmission system, the **transmission medium** is the physical path between transmitter and receiver. Transmission media can be classified as guided or unguided. In both cases, communication is in the form of electromagnetic waves. With **guided media**, the waves are guided along a solid medium, such as copper twisted pair, copper coaxial cable, or optical fiber. The atmosphere and outer space are examples of **unguided media**, which provide a means of transmitting electromagnetic signals but do not guide them; this form of transmission is usually referred to as **wireless transmission**.

The characteristics and quality of a data transmission system are determined both by the characteristics of the medium and the characteristics of the signal. In the case of guided media, the medium itself is more important in determining the limitations of transmission. For unguided media, the bandwidth of the signal produced by the transmitting antenna is more important than the medium in determining transmission characteristics. One key property of signals transmitted by antenna is directionality. In general, signals at lower frequencies are omnidirectional; that is, the signal propagates in all directions from the antenna. At higher frequencies, it is possible to focus the signal into a directional beam.

In considering the design of data transmission systems, key concerns are data rate and distance: the greater the data rate and distance capability the better. A number of design factors relating to the transmission medium and the signal determine the data rate and distance:

- **Bandwidth:** All other factors remaining constant, the wider the bandwidth of a signal, the higher the data rate that can be achieved.

- **Transmission impairments:** Impairments, such as attenuation, limit effective distance. For guided media, twisted pair generally suffers more impairment than coaxial cable, which in turn suffers more than optical fiber.

- **Interference:** Interference from competing signals in overlapping frequency bands can distort or wipe out a signal. Interference is of particular concern for unguided media but is also a problem with guided media. For guided media, interference can be caused by emanations from nearby cables. For example, twisted pairs are often bundled together and conduits often carry multiple cables. Interference can also be experienced from unguided transmissions. Proper shielding of a guided medium can minimize this problem.

- **Number of receivers:** A guided medium can be used to construct a point-to-point link or a shared link with multiple attachments. In the latter case, each attachment introduces some attenuation and distortion on the line, limiting distance and/or data rate.

Figure 9.3 depicts the electromagnetic spectrum and indicates the frequencies at which various guided media and unguided transmission techniques operate. In

Figure 9.3   Electromagnetic Spectrum for Telecommunications

this section, we look at the guided media alternatives for LANs; a discussion of wireless media alternatives for LANs is deferred to Chapter 11.

Twisted Pair

A twisted pair consists of two insulated copper wires arranged in a regular spiral pattern (Figure 9.4). A wire pair acts as a single communication link. Typically, a number of these pairs are bundled together into a cable by wrapping them in a tough protective sheath. Over longer distances, cables may contain hundreds of pairs.

—Separately insulated
—Twisted together
—Often "bundled" into cables
—Usually installed in building
  during construction

Twist
length

(a) Twisted pair

Outer conductor

Outer sheath

Insulation

Inner
conductor

—Outer conductor is braided shield
—Inner conductor is solid metal
—Separated by insulating material
—Covered by padding

(b) Coaxial cable

Jacket

Core

Cladding

—Glass or plastic core
—Laser or light emitting diode
—Specially designed jacket
—Small size and weight

Light at less than
critical angle is
absorbed in jacket

Angle of
incidence

Angle of
reflection

(c) Optical fiber

Figure 9.4   Guided Transmission Media

Twisted pair is much less expensive than the other commonly used guided transmission media (coaxial cable, optical fiber) and is easier to work with. Compared to other transmission media, twisted pair is limited in distance, bandwidth, and data rate. The medium is quite susceptible to interference and noise because of its potential for coupling with electromagnetic fields. For example, a wire run parallel to an ac power line will pick up 60-Hz energy. Impulse noise also easily intrudes into twisted pair. Several measures are taken to reduce impairments. Shielding the wire with metallic braid or sheathing reduces interference. The twisting of the wire reduces low-frequency interference, and the use of different twist lengths in adjacent pairs reduces crosstalk.

UNSHIELDED AND SHIELDED TWISTED PAIR Twisted pair comes in two varieties: unshielded and shielded. **Unshielded twisted pair** (UTP) is ordinary telephone wire. Office buildings, by universal practice, are prewired with excess unshielded twisted pair, more than is needed for simple telephone support. This is the least expensive of all the transmission media commonly used for LANs and is easy to work with and easy to install.

Unshielded twisted pair is subject to external electromagnetic interference, including interference from nearby twisted pair and from noise generated in the environment. A way to improve the characteristics of this medium is to shield the twisted pair with a metallic braid or sheathing that reduces interference. This **shielded twisted pair** (STP) provides better performance at lower data rates. However, it is more expensive and more difficult to work with than unshielded twisted pair.

CATEGORY 3 AND CATEGORY 5 UTP Most office buildings are prewired with a type of twisted pair cable commonly referred to as voice grade. Because voice-grade twisted pair is already installed, it is an attractive alternative for use as a LAN medium. Unfortunately, the data rates and distances achievable with voice-grade twisted pair are limited.

In 1991, the Electronic Industries Association published standard EIA-568, *Commercial Building Telecommunications Cabling Standard*, which specifies the use of voice-grade unshielded twisted pair as well as shielded twisted pair for in-building data applications. At that time, the specification was felt to be adequate for the range of frequencies and data rates found in office environments. Up to that time, the principle interest for LAN designs was in the range of data rates from 1 Mbps to 16 Mbps. Subsequently, as users migrated to higher-performance workstations and applications, there was increasing interest in providing LANs that could operate up to 100 Mbps over inexpensive cable. In response to this need, EIA-568-A was issued in 1995. The new standard reflects advances in cable and connector design and test methods. It covers shielded twisted pair and unshielded twisted pair.

EIA-568-A recognizes three categories of UTP cabling:

- **Category 3:** UTP cables and associated connecting hardware whose transmission characteristics are specified up to 16 MHz
- **Category 4:** UTP cables and associated connecting hardware whose transmission characteristics are specified up to 20 MHz
- **Category 5:** UTP cables and associated connecting hardware whose transmission characteristics are specified up to 100 MHz

Of these, Category 3 and Category 5 cable have received the most attention for LAN applications. Category 3 corresponds to the voice-grade cable found in abundance in most office buildings. Over limited distances, and with proper design, data rates of up to 16 Mbps should be achievable with Category 3. Category 5 is a data-grade cable that is becoming increasingly common for preinstallation in new office buildings. Over limited distances, and with proper design, data rates of up to 100 Mbps should be achievable with Category 5.

A key difference between Category 3 and Category 5 cable is the number of twists in the cable per unit distance. Category 5 is much more tightly twisted, with a typical twist length of 0.6 to 0.85 cm, compared to 7.5 to 10 cm for Category 3. The tighter twisting of Category 5 is more expensive but provides much better performance than Category 3.

Table 9.1 summarizes the performance of Category 3 and Category 5 UTP, as well as the STP specified in EIA-568-A. The first parameter used for comparison, attenuation, is fairly straightforward. The strength of a signal falls off with distance over any transmission medium. For guided media attenuation is generally exponential and therefore is typically expressed as a constant number of decibels per unit distance (see Appendix 9A). Attenuation introduces three considerations for the designer. First, a received signal must have sufficient magnitude so that the electronic circuitry in the receiver can detect and interpret the signal. Second, the signal must maintain a level sufficiently higher than noise to be received without error. Third, attenuation is an increasing function of frequency.

Near-end crosstalk as it applies to twisted pair wiring systems is the coupling of the signal from one pair of conductors to another pair. These conductors may be the metal pins in a connector or wire pairs in a cable. The near end refers to coupling that takes place when the transmit signal entering the link couples back to the receive conductor pair at that same end of the link (i.e., the near transmitted signal is picked up by the near receive pair).

Since the publication of EIA-568-A, there has been ongoing work on the development of standards for premises cabling. These are being driven by two issues. First, the Gigabit Ethernet specification requires the definition of parameters that are not specified completely in any published cabling standard. Second, there is a desire to specify cabling performance to higher levels, namely Enhanced Category 5

Table 9.1 Comparison of Shielded and Unshielded Twisted Pair

Frequency (MHz)	Attenuation (dB per 100 m)			Near-end Crosstalk (dB)		
	Category 3 UTP	Category 5 UTP	STP	Category 3 UTP	Category 5 UTP	STP
1	2.6	2.0	1.1	41	62	58
4	5.6	4.1	2.2	32	53	58
16	13.1	8.2	4.4	23	44	50.4
25	–	10.4	6.2	–	41	47.5
100	–	22.0	12.3	–	32	38.5
300	–	–	21.4	–	–	31.3

Table 9.2   Twisted Pair Categories and Classes

	Category 3 Class C	Category 5 Class D	Category 5E	Category 6 Class E	Category 7 Class F
Bandwidth	16 MHz	100 MHz	100 MHz	200 MHz	600 MHz
Cable Type	UTP	UTP/FTP	UTP/FTP	UTP/FTP	SSTP
	0.7	1	1.2	1.5	2.2

UTP = Unshielded twisted pair
FTP = Foil twisted pair
SSTP = Shielded screen twisted pair

(Cat 5E), Category 6, and Category 7. Table 9.2 compares these schemes to the existing standards.

Coaxial Cable

Coaxial cable, like twisted pair, consists of two conductors but is constructed differently to permit it to operate over a wider range of frequencies. It consists of a hollow outer cylindrical conductor that surrounds a single inner wire conductor (Figure 9.4b). The inner conductor is held in place by either regularly spaced insulating rings or a solid dielectric material. The outer conductor is covered with a jacket or shield. A single coaxial cable has a diameter of from 1 to 2.5 cm. Because of its shielded, concentric construction, coaxial cable is much less susceptible to interference and crosstalk than is twisted pair. Coaxial cable can be used over longer distances and support more stations on a shared line than twisted pair.

Coaxial cable, like shielded twisted pair, provides good immunity from electromagnetic interference. Coaxial cable is more expensive than shielded twisted pair but provides greater capacity.

Traditionally, coaxial cable has been an important transmission medium for LANs, beginning with the early popularity of Ethernet. However, in recent years, the emphasis has been on low-cost limited distance LANs using twisted pair, and high-performance LANs using optical fiber. The effect is the gradual but steady decline in the use of coaxial cable for LAN implementation, to the point that it is rarely used today except in legacy LANs.

Optical Fiber

An optical fiber is a thin (2 to 125 μm), flexible medium capable of conducting an optical ray. Various glasses and plastics can be used to make optical fibers. The lowest losses have been obtained using fibers of ultrapure fused silica. Ultrapure fiber is difficult to manufacture; higher-loss multicomponent glass fibers are more economical and still provide good performance. Plastic fiber is even less costly and can be used for short-haul links, for which moderately high losses are acceptable.

An optical fiber has a cylindrical shape and consists of three concentric sections (Figure 9.4c). The two innermost are two types of glass with different indexes of refraction. The center one is called the core, and the next layer the cladding. These two sections of glass are covered by a protective, light-absorbing jacket. Optical fibers are grouped together into optical cables.

One of the most significant technological breakthroughs in information transmission has been the development of practical fiber optic communications systems. Optical fiber already enjoys considerable use in long-distance telecommunications, and its use in military applications is growing. The continuing improvements in performance and decline in prices, together with the inherent advantages of optical fiber, have made it increasingly attractive for local area networking. The following characteristics distinguish optical fiber from twisted pair or coaxial cable:

- **Greater capacity:** The potential bandwidth, and hence data rate, of optical fiber is immense; data rates of hundreds of Gbps over tens of kilometers have been demonstrated. Compare this to the practical maximum of hundreds of Mbps over about 1 km for coaxial cable and just a few Mbps over 1 km or up to 100 Mbps over a few tens of meters for twisted pair.

- **Smaller size and lighter weight:** Optical fibers are considerably thinner than coaxial cable or bundled twisted pair cable—at least an order of magnitude thinner for comparable information transmission capacity. For cramped conduits in buildings and underground along public rights-of-way, the advantage of small size is considerable. The corresponding reduction in weight reduces structural support requirements.

- **Lower attenuation:** Attenuation is significantly lower for optical fiber than for coaxial cable or twisted pair and is constant over a wide frequency range.

- **Electromagnetic isolation:** Optical fiber systems are not affected by external electromagnetic fields. Thus the system is not vulnerable to interference, impulse noise, or crosstalk. By the same token, fibers do not radiate energy, causing little interference with other equipment and providing a high degree of security from eavesdropping. In addition, fiber is inherently difficult to tap.

Optical fiber systems operate in the range of about 10^{14} to 10^{15} Hz; this covers portions of the infrared and visible spectrums. The principle of optical fiber transmission is as follows. Light from a source enters the cylindrical glass or plastic core. Rays at shallow angles are reflected and propagated along the fiber; other rays are absorbed by the surrounding material. This form of propagation is called **step-index multimode**, referring to the variety of angles that will reflect. With multimode transmission, multiple propagation paths exist, each with a different path length and hence time to traverse the fiber. This causes signal elements (light pulses) to spread out in time, which limits the rate at which data can be accurately received. Put another way, the need to leave spacing between the pulses limits data rate. This type of fiber is best suited for transmission over very short distances. When the fiber core radius is reduced, fewer angles will reflect. By reducing the radius of the core to the order of a wavelength, only a single angle or mode can pass: the axial ray. This **single-mode** propagation provides superior performance for the following reason. Because there is a single transmission path with single-mode transmission, the distortion found in multimode cannot occur. Single-mode is typically used for long-distance applications, including telephone and cable television. Finally, by varying the index of refraction of the core, a third type of transmission, known as **graded-index multimode**, is possible. This type is intermediate between the other two in characteristics. The higher refractive index at the center makes the light rays moving down the axis advance more slowly than those near the cladding. Rather than zigzagging off the cladding, light in the core curves helically because of the graded index, reducing its travel distance. The shortened path and higher speed allows light at the periphery to arrive at a receiver at about the same time as the straight rays in the core axis. Graded-index fibers are often used in LANs.

Two different types of light source are used in fiber optic systems: the light-emitting diode (LED) and the injection laser diode (ILD). Both are semiconductor devices that emit a beam of light when a voltage is applied. The LED is less costly, operates over a greater temperature range, and has a longer operational life. The ILD, which operates on the laser principle, is more efficient and can sustain greater data rates.

There is a relationship among the wavelength employed, the type of transmission, and the achievable data rate. Both single mode and multimode can support several different wavelengths of light and can employ laser or LED light source. In optical fiber, light propagates best in three distinct wavelength "windows," centered on 850, 1300, and 1550 nanometers (nm). These are all in the infrared portion of the frequency spectrum, below the visible-light portion, which is 400 to 700 nm. The loss is lower at higher wavelengths, allowing greater data rates over longer distances. Most local applications today use 850-nm LED light sources. Although this combination is relatively inexpensive, it is generally limited to data rates under 100 Mbps and distances of a few kilometers. To achieve higher data rates and longer distances, a 1300-nm LED or laser source is needed. The highest data rates and longest distances require 1500-nm laser sources.

Structured Cabling

As a practical matter, the network manager needs a cabling plan that deals with the selection of cable and the layout of the cable in a building. The cabling plan should be easy to implement and accommodate future growth.

To aid in the development of cabling plans, standards have been issued that specify the cabling types and layout for commercial buildings. These standards are referred to as *structured cabling systems*. A **structured cabling** system is a generic wiring scheme with the following characteristics:

- The scheme refers to the wiring within a commercial building.
- The scope of the system includes cabling to support all types of information transfer, including voice, LANs, video and image transmission, and other forms of data transmission.
- The cabling layout and cable selection is independent of vendor and end-user equipment.
- The cable layout is designed to encompass distribution to all work areas within the building, so that relocation of equipment does not require rewiring but simply requires plugging the equipment into a preexisting outlet in the new location.

One advantage of such standards is that they provide guidance for preinstallation of cable in new buildings so that future voice and data networking needs can be met without the need to rewire the building. The standards also simplify cable layout design for network managers. Two standards for structured cabling systems have

Figure 9.5   Elements of a Structured Cabling Layout

been issued: EIA/TIA-568, issued jointly by the Electronic Industries Association and the Telecommunications Industry Association, and ISO 11801, issued by the International Organization for Standardization. The two standards are quite similar; the details in this section are from the EIA/TIA-568 document.

A structured cabling strategy is based on the use of a hierarchical, star-wired cable layout. Figure 9.5 illustrates the key elements for a typical commercial building. External cables, from the local telephone company and from wide area networks, terminate in an equipment room that is generally on the ground floor or a basement level. Patch panel and cross-connect equipment in the equipment room connect the external cables to internal distribution cable. Typically, the first level of distribution consists of backbone cables. In the simplest implementation, a single backbone cable or set of cables run from the equipment room to telecommunications closets (called *wiring closets*) on each floor. A telecommunications closet differs from the equipment room only in that it is less complex; the telecommunications closet generally contains cross-connect equipment for interconnecting cable on a single floor to the backbone. The cables distributed on a single floor are referred to as *horizontal cabling*. This cabling connects the backbone to wall outlets that service individual telephone and data equipment.

The use of a structured cabling plan enables an enterprise to use the transmission media appropriate for its requirements in a systematic and standardized fashion. Figure 9.6 indicates the recommended media for each portion of the structured cabling hierarchy. For horizontal cabling, a maximum distance of 90 m is recommended independent of media type. This distance is adequate to

Media type	A	B	C	D
UTP (voice transmission)	800 m	500 m	300 m	90 m
Category 3 UTP up to 16 MHz	90 m	90 m	90 m	90 m
Category 5 UTP up to 100 Mbps	90 m	90 m	90 m	90 m
STP up to 300 MHz	90 m	90 m	90 m	90 m
62.5-μm optical fiber	2000 m	500 m	1500 m	90 m
Single-mode optical fiber	3000 m	500 m	2500 m	90 m

Figure 9.6   Cable Distances Specified in EIA-568-A

provide coverage for an entire floor for many commercial buildings. For build-ings with very large floor space, backbone cable may be required to interconnect multiple telecommunications closets on a single floor. For backbone cabling, dis-tances range from 90 m to 3000 m, depending on cable type and position in the hierarchy.

9.4   LAN PROTOCOL ARCHITECTURE

The architecture of a LAN is best described in terms of a layering of protocols that organize the basic functions of a LAN. This section opens with a description of the standardized protocol architecture for LANs, which encompasses physical, medium access control (MAC), and logical link control (LLC) layers. This section then pro-vides an overview of the MAC and LLC layers.

IEEE 802 Reference Model

Protocols defined specifically for LAN and MAN transmission address issues relat-ing to the transmission of blocks of data over the network. In OSI terms, higher-layer protocols (layer 3 or 4 and above) are independent of network architecture and are applicable to LANs, MANs, and WANs. Thus, a discussion of LAN protocols is concerned principally with lower layers of the OSI model.

Figure 9.7 relates the LAN protocols to the OSI architecture (Figure 5.15). This architecture was developed by the IEEE 802 committee and has been adopted by all organizations working on the specification of LAN standards. It is generally referred to as the IEEE 802 reference model.

Working from the bottom up, the lowest layer of the IEEE 802 reference model corresponds to the **physical layer** of the OSI model and includes such functions

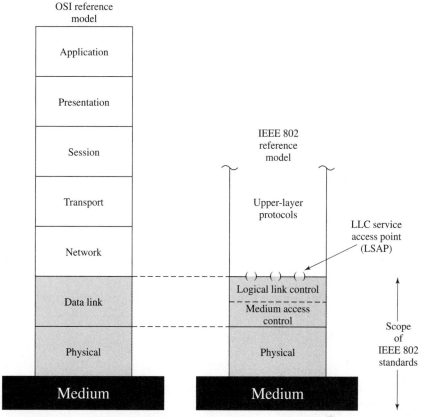

Figure 9.7 IEEE 802 Protocol Layers Compared to OSI Model

as encoding/decoding of signals and bit transmission/reception. In addition, the physical layer includes a specification of the transmission medium. Generally, the transmission medium is considered "below" the lowest layer of the OSI model. However, the choice of transmission medium is critical in LAN design, and so a specification of the medium is included.

Above the physical layer are the functions associated with providing service to LAN users. These include the following:

- On transmission, assemble data into a frame with address and error-detection fields.
- On reception, disassemble frame, and perform address recognition and error detection.
- Govern access to the LAN transmission medium.
- Provide an interface to higher layers and perform flow and error control.

These are functions typically associated with OSI layer 2. The functions in the last bullet item are grouped into a **Logical Link Control** (LLC) layer. The functions

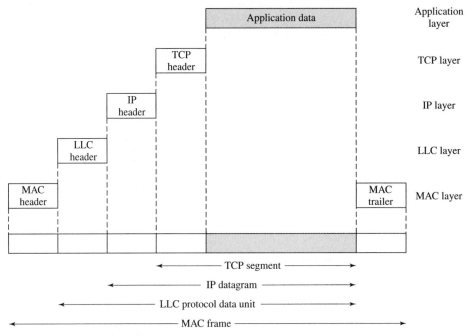

Figure 9.8 LAN Protocols in Context

in the first three bullet items are treated as a separate layer, called **Medium Access Control** (MAC). The separation is done for the following reasons:

- The logic required to manage access to a shared-access medium is not found in traditional layer 2 data link control.
- For the same LLC, several MAC options may be provided.

Figure 9.8 illustrates the relationship between the layers of the architecture (compare Figure 5.8). Higher-level data, such as an IP datagram, are passed down to LLC, which appends control information as a header, creating an **LLC protocol data unit** (PDU). This control information is used in the operation of the LLC protocol. The entire LLC PDU is then passed down to the MAC layer, which appends control information at the front and back of the packet, forming a **MAC frame**. Again, control information in the frame is needed for the operation of the MAC protocol. For context, the figure also shows the use of TCP/IP and an application layer above the LAN protocols.

Logical Link Control

Logical link control (LLC) is a common link protocol for all the LANs. LLC specifies the mechanisms for addressing stations across the medium and for controlling the exchange of data between two users. Three services are provided as alternatives for attached devices using LLC:

- **Unacknowledged connectionless service:** This service is a datagram-style service. It is a very simple service that does not involve any of the flow control and error control mechanisms. Thus, the delivery of data is not guaranteed. However, in most devices there will be some higher layer of software that deals with reliability issues.

- **Connection-mode service:** This service is similar to that offered by typical data link control protocols, such as HDLC (see Chapter 17). A logical connection is set up between two users exchanging data, and flow control and error control are provided.

- **Acknowledged connectionless service:** This is a cross between the previous two services. It provides that datagrams are to be acknowledged, but no prior logical connection is set up.

Typically, a vendor will provide these services as options that the customer can select when purchasing the equipment. Alternatively, the customer can purchase equipment that provides two or all three services and select a specific service based on application.

The **unacknowledged connectionless service** requires minimum logic and is useful in two contexts. First, it will often be the case that higher layers of software will provide the necessary reliability and flow-control mechanism, and it is efficient to avoid duplicating them. For example, TCP provides the mechanisms needed to ensure that data are delivered reliably. Second, there are instances in which the overhead of connection establishment and maintenance is unjustified or even counterproductive. One example is data collection activity that involves the periodic sampling of data sources, such as sensors and automatic self-test reports from security equipment or network components. In a monitoring application, the loss of an occasional data unit would not cause distress, as the next report should arrive shortly. Thus, in most cases, the unacknowledged connectionless service is the preferred option.

The **connection-mode service** could be used in very simple devices, such as terminal controllers, that have little software operating above this level. In these cases, it would provide the flow control and reliability mechanisms normally implemented at higher layers of the communications software.

The **acknowledged connectionless service** is useful in several contexts. With connection-mode service, the logical link control software must maintain some sort of table for each active connection, to keep track of the status of that connection. If the user needs guaranteed delivery but there are a large number of destinations for data, connection-mode service may be impractical because of the large number of tables required. An example is a process control or automated factory environment where a central site may need to communicate with a large number of processors and programmable controllers. Another use of this is the handling of important and time-critical alarm or emergency control signals in a factory. Because of their importance, an acknowledgment is needed so that the sender can be assured that the signal got through. Because of the urgency of the signal, the user might not want to take the time to first establish a logical connection and then send the data.

The LLC PDU includes destination and source service access point (DSAP, SSAP) addresses. These refer to the next higher layer protocol that uses LLC (typically IP). The LLC PDU also includes a control field that provides a sequencing and flow control mechanism. Such a control field is typical for data link control protocols and is described in Chapter 17.

Medium Access Control

All LANs and MANs (metropolitan area networks) consist of collections of devices that must share the network's transmission capacity. Some means of controlling access to the transmission medium is needed to provide an orderly and efficient use of that capacity. This is the function of a **medium access control** (MAC) protocol.

The relationship between LLC and the MAC protocol can be seen by considering the transmission formats involved. User data are passed down to the LLC layer, which prepares a link-level frame, known as an LLC protocol data unit (PDU). This PDU is then passed down to the MAC layer. where it is enclosed in a MAC frame.

The exact format of the MAC frame differs somewhat for the various MAC protocols in use. In general, all of the MAC frames have a format similar to that of Figure 9.9. The fields of this frame are as follows:

- **MAC Control:** This field contains any protocol control information needed for the functioning of the MAC protocol. For example, a priority level could be indicated here.

- **Destination MAC Address:** The destination physical attachment point on the LAN for this frame.

- **Source MAC Address:** The source physical attachment point on the LAN for this frame.

- **LLC PDU:** The LLC data from the next higher layer. This includes the user data plus the source and destination service access point (SAPs), which indicate the user of LLC.

- **CRC:** The cyclic redundancy check field (also known as the Frame Check Sequence, FCS, field). This is an error-detecting code, such as is used in other data

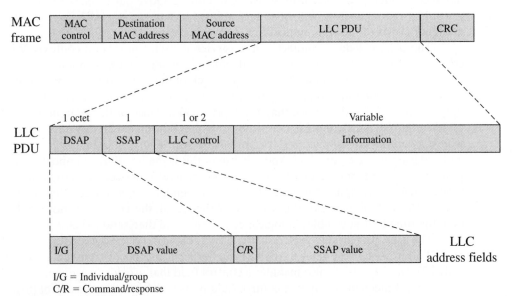

I/G = Individual/group
C/R = Command/response

Figure 9.9 LLC PDU in a Generic MAC Frame Format

link control protocols (Chapter 17). The CRC operates in the same fashion as the checksum described for TCP in Chapter 5. The CRC is calculated based on the bits in the entire frame. The sender calculates the CRC and adds it to the frame. The receiver performs the same calculation on the incoming frame and compares that calculation to the CRC field in that incoming frame. If the two values don't match, then one or more bits have been accidentally altered in transit.

In most data link control protocols, the data link protocol entity is responsible not only for detecting errors using the CRC, but for recovering from those errors by retransmitting damaged frames. In the LAN protocol architecture, these two functions are split between the MAC and LLC layers. The MAC layer is responsible for detecting errors and discarding any frames that contain errors. The LLC layer optionally keeps track of which frames have been successfully received and retransmits unsuccessful frames.

APPLICATION NOTE

Cabling Infrastructure

A solid cabling infrastructure is the basis for all reliable communications. On a new installation, proper procedures must be followed to ensure that the network will perform as expected and that the job will adhere to the budget. On older systems, a good understanding of the cable plant can help us understand the limitations of the system and to troubleshoot bottlenecks. Even with tremendous growth in the use of wireless communications, the cable plant is extremely important because wireless equipment is eventually connected to the wired backbone.

There are several important components to the cabling infrastructure, of which cabling is only a part. The network will be an integral part of the building systems and so space must be allocated for the wiring closets and consideration given for the location of the data cables. This is similar in scope to the attention given to the electrical system. Wiring closets are the termination points for all of the cabling and where the networking equipment will be located. Wiring closets also include connections to the data center or the backbone, and eventually lead to the Internet. Adequate space, cooling, drainage and cleanliness should be provided to ensure long life of the equipment and dependable connectivity. Often wiring closets are seen as a painful necessity and are relegated to the most inhospitable locations within the building. This can result in poor network performance as corrosion, heat, dirt, and interference all serve to degrade communications capability.

The wiring closet should also be located where distance limitations will not be violated. Every communication standard has its own maximum range. For example, Ethernet requires that each segment be no more than 100 meters in length for 10Mbps and 100Mbps transmissions. The 100 meters includes the installed cabling and patch cables at either end. While many building are not 100 meters in length or width, going through floors, through ceilings, and around obstacles can add distance quickly.

(Continued)

The quality of the cabling can make a big difference as well. There is saying that goes, "Communication can be done over barbed wire; it's just not high quality." While there can be a cost savings between CAT 5, CAT 5e, and CAT 6 cable, investment should be in the best available wiring. This provides some longevity to the network and the best possible transmission rates. It will usually save money in the long run as upgrades are less frequent.

Other cable installation issues include but are not limited to the following; proximity to power wiring, equipment installed near cable runs (motors, vent ducts, etc.), management of the cable in the run (cable trays, tie wraps, cable rings), proper cable used, spares, damage during and after installation, enough cable pulled to allow modification of termination locations (office occupant desires a jack to be moved) and labels. All cabling should be labeled on both ends, at the jack and in the wiring closet, to facilitate troubleshooting and modification.

Termination quality is very important. Increasingly, modular equipment is being used on new networks. This means that connections can be easily moved and terminations completed quickly but care must be taken to ensure that the correct components are purchased. Every type of cable and every type of application has a separate type of terminator. For example, a cat 6 solid cable will use a different jack than a cat 5 stranded cable. All terminations should be checked with the proper network test equipment such as a Fluke cable meter. This device will test the cable for crosstalk, return, attenuation and wire mapping to ensure that all runs are within specification.

Inside the wiring closet a suitable amount of wire management should be used. Wire management is used to organize and "tidy up" installations. Without it, a wiring closet can be an absolute mess that can make troubleshooting, maintenance or additions all but impossible. Wire management includes items such as vertical and horizontal management, front/back pieces, covers, guides and cable rings for bundling.

Finally, the entire cable installation should be clean and neat. No one wants cables hanging out of the wall or a crooked wall plate in their office. No network technician wants to work in a closet that looks like a bad day at the spaghetti factory. A clean, professional installation allows for faster troubleshooting, easier maintenance, facilitates future modifications and does not take up unnecessary room in the floor, ceiling or closet.

Most companies will use contractors for the installation because they do not have the manpower or expertise. In this case, having a local supervisor that understands the issues can mean the difference between a well-built installation and a poor one. Organizations should develop their own standards for the installation and ensure that these standards are met before payment is made.

9.5 SUMMARY

The requirement for networking capability within the individual building is just as strong as the requirement for wide area networking. Every business environment is populated with a large and growing collection of data processing equipment. Local area networks are needed to tie this equipment together, both for intraoffice communications and to provide a cost-effective link to wide area networks.

A LAN consists of a shared transmission medium and a set of hardware and software for interfacing devices to the medium and regulating the orderly access to the medium.

The transmission media that are used to convey information can be classified as guided or unguided. Guided media provide a physical path along which the signals are propagated; these include twisted pair, coaxial cable, and optical fiber. Unguided media employ an antenna for transmitting through air, vacuum, or water. Traditionally, twisted pair has been the workhorse for communications of all sorts. More recently, optical fiber has come to play a dominant role and has displaced other media in many applications. Of these two, optical fiber has the most promising future for the widest range of applications.

A set of standards has been defined for LANs that specifies a range of data rates and a variety of transmission media. These standards are widely accepted, and most of the products on the market conform to one of these standards.

9.6   RECOMMENDED READING AND WEB SITES

The material in this chapter is covered in much more depth in [STAL00]. [REGA04] also provides extensive coverage. [BARN04] provides extensive coverage of wired transmission media technology and standards.

BARN04 Barnett, D.; Groth, D.; and McBee, J. *Cabling: The Complete Guide to Network Wiring.* San Francisco: Sybex, 2004.

REGA04 Regan, P. *Local Area Networks.* Upper Saddle River, NJ: Prentice Hall, 2004.

STAL00 Stallings, W. *Local and Metropolitan Area Networks, Sixth Edition.* Upper Saddle River, NJ: Prentice Hall, 2000.

Recommended Web site:

- **IEEE 802 LAN/MAN Standards Committee:** Status and documents for all of the working groups.

9.7   KEY TERMS, REVIEW QUESTIONS, AND PROBLEMS

Key Terms

backend network	guided media	Medium access control
backbone LAN	IEEE 802	(MAC)
coaxial cable	local area network (LAN)	optical fiber
decibel (dB)	Logical link control (LLC)	server farm

shielded twisted pair (STP)	tiered LAN	unguided media
storage area network (SAN)	transmission medium	unshielded twisted pair (UTP)
structured cabling	twisted pair	wireless transmission

Review Questions

9.1 How do the key requirements for computer room networks differ from those for personal computer local networks?

9.2 What are the differences among backend LANs, SANs, and backbone LANs?

9.3 Other than large storage capacity, what other advantage does a SAN provide?

9.4 What is the protocol typically used in storage area networks?

9.5 Differentiate between guided media and unguided media.

9.6 Why are the wires twisted in twisted-pair copper wire?

9.7 What are some major limitations of twisted-pair wire?

9.8 What is the difference between unshielded twisted pair and shielded twisted pair?

9.9 Describe the components of optical fiber cable.

9.10 What are the wavelengths used in fiber optic communication?

9.11 Arrange the following in order from highest to lowest regarding bandwidth: UTP, fiber, and coaxial cable.

9.12 Arrange the following in order from highest to lowest regarding cost: UTP, fiber, and coaxial cable.

9.13 What is the purpose of the IEEE 802 committee?

9.14 Why are there multiple LAN standards?

9.15 List and briefly define the services provided by LLC.

9.16 List and briefly define the types of operation provided by the LLC protocol.

9.17 List some basic functions performed at the MAC layer.

Problems

9.1 The semiconductor industry requires a large degree of automation in the processing of microelectronics devices. This is primarily due to the fact that extremely small tolerances are required in the manufacturing process of most semiconductor devices and therefore semiconductor fabrication plants must be many times "cleaner" than the average hospital surgical facility. For example, the conducting channel of a MOSFET (Metal Oxide Semiconductor Field Effect Transistor) is typically < 1 micron in length. Conversely, a human hair is approximately 50 microns in diameter. Thus, seemingly minute biological contaminants (e.g., a single skin flake) can potentially render numerous transistors inoperable. Since the human process operator can be detrimental to the semiconductor fabrication process, robotics and automation must be instituted wherever possible. To facilitate this automation, the SEMI organization developed the SECS/GEM (Semiconductor Equipment Communication Standard/Generic Equipment Model) Protocol. Provide a basic overview of this standard and discuss the associated benefits relative to the design and operation of a factory LAN and its impact on general fabrication communications. Could this concept be useful in other scenarios outside the semiconductor industry?

9.2 Obtain a piece of Category 3 and a piece of category 5 wiring. Strip back the outer insulation and count the number of twists. You should be able to observe three characteristics of twisted pair wiring. Discuss.

9.3 Develop, in general terms, a cost-effective cable plan (meeting minimal data integrity requirements) for a scientific R&D organization that is building a new five-story research facility. The first floor will contain the lobby and administrative offices. The second and third floors will contain labs that utilize fairly large pieces of heavy-power-consumption equipment (e.g., small linear accelerators and reactive ion chambers). Numerous technicians and scientists will be working on this floor and data requirements include high-speed transmission of high bandwidth data (e.g., color video). The fourth floor will contain offices for the lab personnel and the fifth floor will contain executive offices.

9.4 Some organizations are implementing wide area networks as a high-speed backbone in order to increase communication efficiency and effectiveness of services throughout a particular region. One such example of this is Network Virginia, which delivers Internet and intranet services to organizations throughout the state of Virginia. Network Virginia also provides a regional interconnection point for Internet 2 members. Develop an overview of Network Virginia and discuss the importance of this concept in the evolution of networking strategy, with particular reference to LAN support.

9.5 Fill in the missing elements in the following table of approximate power ratios for various dB levels.

Decibels	1	2	3	4	5	6	7	8	9	10
Losses			0.5							0.1
Gains			2							10

9.6 If an amplifier has a 30-dB voltage gain, what voltage ratio does the gain represent?

9.7 Given a transmit power (P_{in}) of 5 watts and a received power (P_{out}) of 2.5 watts, what is the calculated loss in dB?

APPENDIX 9A   DECIBELS AND SIGNAL STRENGTH

An important parameter in any transmission system is the signal strength. As a signal propagates along a transmission medium, there will be a loss, or *attenuation*, of signal strength. To compensate, amplifiers may be inserted at various points to impart a gain in signal strength.

It is customary to express gains, losses, and relative levels in decibels because

- Signal strength often falls off exponentially, so loss is easily expressed in terms of the decibel, which is a logarithmic unit.

- The net gain or loss in a cascaded transmission path can be calculated with simple addition and subtraction.

The decibel is a measure of the ratio between two signal levels. The decibel gain is given by

$$G_{dB} = 10\log_{10}\frac{P_{out}}{P_{in}}$$

where

G_{dB} = gain, in decibels
P_{in} = input power level
P_{out} = output power level
$\log_{10}$ = logarithm to the base 10

Table 9.3 Decibel Values

Power Ratio	dB	Power Ratio	dB
10^1	10	10^{-1}	−10
10^2	20	10^{-2}	−20
10^3	30	10^{-3}	−30
10^4	40	10^{-4}	−40
10^5	50	10^{-5}	−50
10^6	60	10^{-6}	−60

Table 9.3 shows the relationship between decibel values and powers of 10.

There is some inconsistency in the literature over the use of the terms *gain* and *loss*. If the value of G_{dB} is positive, this represents an actual gain in power. For example, a gain of 3 dB means that the power has doubled. If the value of G_{dB} is negative, this represents an actual loss in power. For example a gain of −3 dB means that the power has halved, and this is a loss of power. Normally, this is expressed by saying there is a loss of 3 dB. However, some of the literature would say that this is a loss of −3 dB. It makes more sense to say that a negative gain corresponds to a positive loss. Therefore, we define a decibel loss as

$$L_{dB} = -10 \log_{10} \frac{P_{out}}{P_{in}} = 10 \log_{10} \frac{P_{in}}{P_{out}}$$

Example If a signal with a power level of 10 mW is inserted onto a transmission line and the measured power some distance away is 5 mW, the loss can be expressed as $L_{dB} = 10 \log(10/5) = 10(0.3) = 3$ dB.

Note that the decibel is a measure of relative, not absolute, difference. A loss from 1000 mW to 500 mW is also a loss of 3 dB. Thus, a loss of 3 dB halves the power level; a gain of 3 dB doubles the power.

The decibel is also used to measure the difference in voltage, taking into account that power is proportional to the square of the voltage:

$$P = \frac{V^2}{R}$$

where

P = power dissipated across resistance R
V = voltage across resistance R

Thus

$$L_{dB} = 10 \log \frac{P_{in}}{P_{out}} = 10 \log \frac{V_{in}^2/R}{V_{out}^2/R} = 20 \log \frac{V_{in}}{V_{out}}$$

Example Decibels are useful in determining the gain or loss over a series of transmission elements. Consider a series in which the input is at a power level of 4 mW, the first element is a transmission line with a 12-dB loss (–12-dB gain), the second element is an amplifier with a 35-dB gain, and the third element is a transmission line with a 10-dB loss. The net gain is (–12 + 35 – 10) = 13 dB. To calculate the output power P_{out},

$$G_{dB} = 13 = 10\log(P_{out}/4\text{mW})$$

$$P_{out} = 4 \times 10^{1.3}\text{mW} = 79.8\text{mW}$$

CHAPTER 10

ETHERNET

10.1 Traditional Ethernet
Bus Topology LAN
Medium Access Control
MAC Frame
IEEE 802.3 Medium Options at 10 Mbps

10.2 Bridges, Hubs, and Switches
Bridges
Hubs
Layer 2 Switches
Layer 3 Switches

10.3 High-Speed Ethernet
Fast Ethernet
Gigabit Ethernet
10-Gbps Ethernet
100-Gbps Ethernet

10.4 Summary

10.5 Recommended Reading and Web Sites

10.6 Key Terms, Review Questions, and Problems

Chapter Objectives

After reading this chapter, you should be able to

♦ Explain the continued interest in Ethernet-type systems at higher and higher data rates.

♦ Describe the various Ethernet alternatives.

♦ Explain the functions of, and need for, bridges.

♦ Explain the differences among bridges, hubs, layer 2 switches, and layer 3 switches.

Recent years have seen rapid changes in the technology, design, and commercial applications for local area networks (LANs). A major feature of this evolution is the introduction of a variety of new schemes for high-speed local area networking. To keep pace with the changing local networking needs of business, a number of approaches to high speed LAN design have become commercial products. The most important of these are as follows:

• **Fast Ethernet and Gigabit Ethernet:** The extension of 10-Mbps CSMA/CD (carrier sense multiple access with collision detection) to higher speeds is a logical strategy, because it tends to preserve the investment in existing systems.

• **Fibre Channel:** This standard provides a low-cost, easily scalable approach to achieving very high data rates in local areas.

• **High-speed wireless LANs:** Wireless LAN technology and standards have at last come of age, and high-speed standards and products have been introduced.

Table 10.1 lists characteristics of these approaches. The remainder of this chapter is devoted to Ethernet. Chapter 11 covers wireless LANs. Appendix G covers Fibre Channel.

Table 10.1 Characteristics of Some High-Speed LANs

	Fast Ethernet	**Gigabit Ethernet**	**Fibre Channel**	**Wireless LAN**
Data Rate	100 Mbps	1 Gbps, 10 Gbps, 100 Gbps	100 Mbps–3.2 Gbps	1 Mbps–54 Mbps
Transmission Media	UTP, STP, optical fiber	UTP, shielded cable, optical fiber	Optical fiber, coaxial cable, STP	2.4-GHz, 5-GHz microwave
Access Method	CSMA/CD	Switched	Switched	CSMA/Polling
Supporting Standard	IEEE 802.3	IEEE 802.3	Fibre Channel Association	IEEE 802.11

10.1 TRADITIONAL ETHERNET

The most widely used high-speed LANs today are referred to as Ethernet and were developed by the IEEE 802.3 standards committee. Collectively, the Ethernet-like LANs are the dominant force in the wired LAN market. As with other LAN standards, there is both a medium access control layer and a physical layer, which are considered in turn in what follows.

The original commercial Ethernet, as well as the original IEEE 802.3 standard, operated at 10 Mbps. Subsequently, standards were developed for 802.3 systems operating at 100 Mbps, 1Gbps, and 10 Gbps. Before looking at these high-speed LANs, we provide a brief overview of the original 10-Mbps Ethernet and introduce the concept of switched LANs.

Classical Ethernet operates at 10 Mbps over a bus topology LAN using the CSMA/CD (carrier sense multiple access with collision detection) medium access control protocol. In this section, we introduce the concepts of bus LANs and CSMA/CD operation, and then briefly discuss transmission medium options

Bus Topology LAN

In a bus topology LAN, all stations attach, through appropriate hardware interfacing known as a tap, directly to a linear transmission medium, or bus. Full-duplex operation between the station and the tap allows data to be transmitted onto the bus and received from the bus. A transmission from any station propagates the length of the medium in both directions and can be received by all other stations. At each end of the bus is a terminator, which absorbs any signal, removing it from the bus.

Two problems present themselves in this arrangement. First, because a transmission from any one station can be received by all other stations, there needs to be some way of indicating for whom the transmission is intended. Second, a mechanism is needed to regulate transmission. To see the reason for this, consider that if two stations on the bus attempt to transmit at the same time, their signals will overlap and become garbled. Or consider that one station decides to transmit continuously for a long period of time, blocking the access of other users.

To solve these problems, stations transmit data in small blocks, known as **frames**. Each frame consists of a portion of the data that a station wishes to transmit, plus a frame header that contains control information. Each station on the bus is assigned a unique address, or identifier, and the destination address for a frame is included in its header.

Figure 10.1 illustrates the scheme. In this example, station C wishes to transmit a frame of data to A. The frame header includes A's address. As the frame propagates along the bus, it passes B. B observes the address and ignores the frame. A, on the other hand, sees that the frame is addressed to itself and therefore copies the data from the frame as it goes by.

So the frame structure solves the first problem mentioned previously: It provides a mechanism for indicating the intended recipient of the data. It also provides the basic tool for solving the second problem, the regulation of access. In particular, the stations take turns sending frames in some cooperative fashion, as explained in the next subsection.

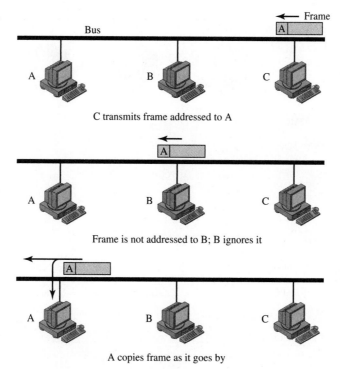

Figure 10.1 Frame Transmission on a Bus LAN

Medium Access Control

For CSMA/CD, a station wishing to transmit first listens to the medium to determine if another transmission is in progress (carrier sense). If the medium is idle, the station may transmit. It may happen that two or more stations attempt to transmit at about the same time. If this happens, there will be a **collision**; the data from both transmissions will be garbled and not received successfully. The following procedure specifies what a station should do if the medium is found busy and what it should do if a collision occurs:

1. If the medium is idle, transmit; otherwise, go to step 2.
2. If the medium is busy, continue to listen until it is idle, then transmit immediately.
3. If a collision is detected during transmission, transmit a brief jamming signal to assure that all stations know that there has been a collision and then cease transmission.
4. After transmitting the jamming signal, wait a random amount of time, referred to as the **backoff**, then attempt to transmit again (repeat from step 1).

Figure 10.2 illustrates the technique. The upper part of the figure shows a bus LAN layout. The remainder of the figure depicts activity on the bus at four successive

Figure 10.2 CSMA/CD Operation

instants in time. At time t_0, station A begins transmitting a packet addressed to D. At t_1, both B and C are ready to transmit. B senses a transmission and so defers. C, however, is still unaware of A's transmission and begins its own transmission. When A's transmission reaches C, at t_2, C detects the collision and ceases transmission. The effect of the collision propagates back to A, where it is detected some time later, t_3, at which time A ceases transmission.

The advantage of CSMA/CD is its simplicity. It is easy to implement the logic required for this protocol. Furthermore, there is little to go wrong in the execution of the protocol. For example, if for some reason a station fails to detect a collision, the worst that can happen is that it continues to transmit its frame, wasting some time on the medium. Once the transmission is over, the algorithm continues to function as before.

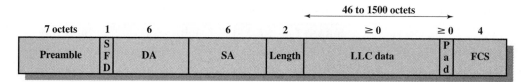

SFD = Start of frame delimiter
DA = Destination address
SA = Source address
FCS = Frame check sequence

Figure 10.3 IEEE 802.3 Frame Format

MAC Frame

Figure 10.3 depicts the frame format for the 802.3 protocol. It consists of the following fields:

- **Preamble:** A 7-octet pattern of alternating 0s and 1s used by the receiver to establish bit synchronization.
- **Start Frame Delimiter (SFD):** The sequence 10101011, which indicates the actual start of the frame and enables the receiver to locate the first bit of the rest of the frame.
- **Destination Address (DA):** Specifies the station(s) for which the frame is intended. It may be a unique physical address, a group address, or a global address.
- **Source Address (SA):** Specifies the station that sent the frame.
- **Length:** Length of LLC data field in octets. The maximum frame size, excluding the Preamble and SFD, is 1518 octets.
- **LLC Data:** Data unit supplied by LLC.
- **Pad:** Octets added to ensure that the frame is long enough for proper CD operation.
- **Frame Check Sequence (FCS):** A 32-bit CRC, based on all fields except preamble, SFD, and FCS.

IEEE 802.3 Medium Options at 10 Mbps

The IEEE 802.3 committee has defined a number of alternative physical configurations. This is both good and bad. On the good side, the standard has been responsive to evolving technology. On the bad side, the customer, not to mention the potential vendor, is faced with a bewildering array of options. However, the committee has been at pains to ensure that the various options can be easily integrated into a configuration that satisfies a variety of needs. Thus, the user who has a complex set of requirements may find the flexibility and variety of the 802.3 standard to be an asset.

Table 10.2 IEEE 802.3 10-Mbps Physical Layer Medium Alternatives

	10BASE5	10BASE2	10BASE-T	10BASE-F
Transmission Medium	Coaxial cable	Coaxial cable	Unshielded twisted pair	850-nm optical fiber pair
Topology	Bus	Bus	Star	Star
Maximum Segment Length (m)	500	185	100	500
Nodes per Segment	100	30	—	33
Cable Diameter	10 mm	5 mm	0.4 to 0.6 mm	62.5/125 μm

To distinguish the various implementations that are available, the committee has developed a concise notation:

<data rate in Mbps> <signaling method><maximum segment length in hundreds of meters>

Table 10.2 summarizes these options. Note that 10BASE-T and 10BASE-F do not quite follow the notation: "T" stands for twisted pair and "F" stands for optical fiber.

10.2 BRIDGES, HUBS, AND SWITCHES

Before continuing our discussion of Ethernet, we need to take a detour and examine the concepts of bridges, hubs, and switches.

Bridges

In virtually all cases, there is a need to expand beyond the confines of a single LAN, to provide interconnection to other LANs and to wide area networks. Two general approaches are used for this purpose: bridges and routers. The **bridge** is the simpler of the two devices and provides a means of interconnecting similar LANs. The router is a more general-purpose device, capable of interconnecting a variety of LANs and WANs. We explore bridges in this section; routers are discussed in Part Two.

The bridge is designed for use between local area networks (LANs) that use identical protocols for the physical and link layers (e.g., all conforming to IEEE 802.3). Because the devices all use the same protocols, the amount of processing required at the bridge is minimal. More sophisticated bridges are capable of mapping from one MAC format to another (e.g., to interconnect an Ethernet and a Fibre Channel LAN).

Because the bridge is used in a situation in which all the LANs have the same characteristics, the reader may ask, why not simply have one large LAN? Depending on circumstance, there are several reasons for the use of multiple LANs connected by bridges:

- **Reliability:** The danger in connecting all data processing devices in an organization to one network is that a fault on the network may disable communication for all devices. By using bridges, the network can be partitioned into self-contained units.

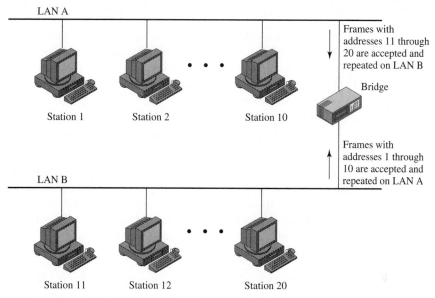

Figure 10.4 Bridge Operation

- **Performance:** In general, performance on a LAN declines with an increase in the number of devices or the length of the wire. A number of smaller LANs will often give improved performance if devices can be clustered so that intranetwork traffic significantly exceeds internetwork traffic.

- **Security:** The establishment of multiple LANs may improve security of communications. It is desirable to keep different types of traffic (e.g., accounting, personnel, strategic planning) that have different security needs on physically separate media. At the same time, the different types of users with different levels of security need to communicate through controlled and monitored mechanisms.

- **Geography:** Clearly, two separate LANs are needed to support devices clustered in two geographically distant locations. Even in the case of two buildings separated by a highway, it may be far easier to use a microwave bridge link than to attempt to string coaxial cable between the two buildings.

Figure 10.4 shows the action of a bridge connecting two LANs, A and B, using the same MAC protocol. In this example, a single bridge attaches to both LANs; frequently, the bridge function is performed by two "half-bridges," one on each LAN. The functions of the bridge are few and simple:

- Read all frames transmitted on A and accept those addressed to any station on B.
- Using the medium access control protocol for B, retransmit each frame on B.
- Do the same for B-to-A traffic.

Several design aspects of a bridge are worth highlighting:

- The bridge makes no modification to the content or format of the frames it receives, nor does it encapsulate them with an additional header. Each frame to be transferred is simply copied from one LAN and repeated with exactly the same bit pattern on the other LAN. Because the two LANs use the same LAN protocols, it is permissible to do this.
- The bridge should contain enough buffer space to meet peak demands. Over a short period of time, frames may arrive faster than they can be retransmitted.
- The bridge must contain addressing and routing intelligence. At a minimum, the bridge must know which addresses are on each network to know which frames to pass. Further, there may be more than two LANs interconnected by a number of bridges. In that case, a frame may have to be routed through several bridges in its journey from source to destination.
- A bridge may connect more than two LANs.

In summary, the bridge provides an extension to the LAN that requires no modification to the communications software in the stations attached to the LANs. It appears to all stations on the two (or more) LANs that there is a single LAN on which each station has a unique address. The station uses that unique address and need not explicitly discriminate between stations on the same LAN and stations on other LANs; the bridge takes care of that.

Hubs

In recent years, there has been a proliferation of types of devices for interconnecting LANs that goes beyond bridges and the routers. These devices can conveniently be grouped into the categories of layer 2 switches and layer 3 switches. We begin with a discussion of hubs and then explore these two concepts.

A hub is an alternative to the bus topology. Each station is connected to the hub by two lines (transmit and receive). The hub acts as a repeater: When a single station transmits, the hub repeats the signal on the outgoing line to each station. Ordinarily, the line consists of two unshielded twisted pairs. Because of the high data rate and the poor transmission qualities of unshielded twisted pair, the length of a line is limited to about 100 m. As an alternative, an optical fiber link may be used. In this case, the maximum length is about 500 m.

Note that although this scheme is physically a star, it is logically a bus: A transmission from any one station is received by all other stations, and if two stations transmit at the same time there will be a collision.

Multiple levels of hubs can be cascaded in a hierarchical configuration. Figure 10.5 depicts a two-level configuration. There is one **header hub** (HHUB) and one or more **intermediate hubs** (IHUBs). Each hub may have a mixture of stations and other hubs attached to it from below. This layout fits well with building wiring practices. Typically, there is a wiring closet on each floor of an office building, and a hub can be placed in each one. Each hub could service the stations on its floor.

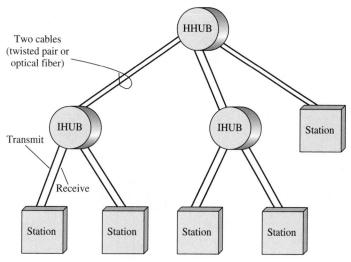

Figure 10.5 Two-Level Star Topology

Layer 2 Switches

In recent years, the layer 2 switch, has replaced the hub in popularity, particularly for high-speed LANs. The layer 2 switch is also sometimes referred to as a switching hub.

To clarify the distinction between hubs and switches, Figure 10.6 shows a typical bus layout of a traditional 10-Mbps LAN. A bus is installed that is laid out so that all the devices to be attached are in reasonable proximity to a point on the bus. In the figure, station B is transmitting. This transmission goes from B, across the link from B to the bus, along the bus in both directions, and along the access lines of each of the other attached stations. In this configuration, all the stations must share the total capacity of the bus, which is 10 Mbps.

A hub, often in a building wiring closet, uses a star wiring arrangement to attach stations to the hub. In this arrangement, a transmission from any one station is received by the hub and retransmitted on all of the outgoing lines. Therefore, to avoid collisions, only one station should transmit at a time. Again, the total capacity of the LAN is 10 Mbps. The hub has several advantages over the simple bus arrangement. It exploits standard building wiring practices in the layout of cable. In addition, the hub can be configured to recognize a malfunctioning station that is jamming the network and to cut that station out of the network. Figure 10.6b illustrates the operation of a hub. Here again, station B is transmitting. This transmission goes from B, across the transmit line from B to the hub, and from the hub along the receive lines of each of the other attached stations.

We can achieve greater performance with a layer 2 switch. In this case, the central hub acts as a switch, similar to a packet switch. An incoming frame from a particular station is switched to the appropriate output line to be delivered to the intended destination. At the same time, other unused lines can be used for switching

Figure 10.6 LAN Hubs and Switches

other traffic. Figure 10.6c shows an example in which B is transmitting a frame to A and at the same time C is transmitting a frame to D. So, in this example, the current throughput on the LAN is 20 Mbps, although each individual device is limited to 10 Mbps. The layer 2 switch has several attractive features:

1. No change is required to the software or hardware of the attached devices to convert a bus LAN or a hub LAN to a switched LAN. In the case of an Ethernet LAN, each attached device continues to use the Ethernet medium access control protocol to access the LAN. From the point of view of the attached devices, nothing has changed in the access logic.

2. Each attached device has a dedicated capacity equal to that of the entire original LAN, assuming that the layer 2 switch has sufficient capacity to keep up with all attached devices. For example, in Figure 10.6c, if the layer 2 switch can sustain a

throughput of 20 Mbps, each attached device appears to have a dedicated capacity for either input or output of 10 Mbps.

3. The layer 2 switch scales easily. Additional devices can be attached to the layer 2 switch by increasing the capacity of the layer 2 switch correspondingly.

Two types of layer 2 switches are available as commercial products:

- **Store-and-forward switch:** The layer 2 switch accepts a frame on an input line, buffers it briefly, and then routes it to the appropriate output line.

- **Cut-through switch:** The layer 2 switch takes advantage of the fact that the destination address appears at the beginning of the MAC (medium access control) frame. The layer 2 switch begins repeating the incoming frame onto the appropriate output line as soon as the layer 2 switch recognizes the destination address.

The cut-through switch yields the highest possible throughput but at some risk of propagating bad frames, because the switch is not able to check the cyclic redundancy check (CRC, described in Chapter 9) prior to retransmission. The store-and-forward switch involves a delay between sender and receiver but boosts the overall integrity of the network.

A layer 2 switch can be viewed as a full-duplex version of the hub. It can also incorporate logic that allows it to function as a multiport bridge. [BREY99] lists the following differences between layer 2 switches and bridges:

- Bridge frame handling is done in software. A layer 2 switch performs the address recognition and frame forwarding functions in hardware.

- A bridge can typically only analyze and forward one frame at a time, whereas a layer 2 switch has multiple parallel data paths and can handle multiple frames at a time.

- A bridge uses store-and-forward operation. With a layer 2 switch, it is possible to have cut-through instead of store-and-forward operation.

Because a layer 2 switch has higher performance and can incorporate the functions of a bridge, the bridge has suffered commercially. New installations typically include layer 2 switches with bridge functionality rather than bridges.

Layer 3 Switches

Layer 2 switches provide increased performance to meet the needs of high-volume traffic generated by personal computers, workstations, and servers. However, as the number of devices in a building or complex of buildings grows, layer 2 switches reveal some inadequacies. Two problems in particular present themselves: broadcast overload and the lack of multiple links.

A set of devices and LANs connected by layer 2 switches is considered to have a flat address space. The term *flat* means that all users share a common MAC broadcast address. Thus, if any device issues a MAC frame with a broadcast address, that frame is to be delivered to all devices attached to the overall network connected by layer 2 switches and/or bridges. In a large network, frequent transmission of broadcast frames can create tremendous overhead. Worse, a malfunctioning device can create a *broadcast storm,* in which numerous broadcast frames clog the network and crowd out legitimate traffic.

A second performance-related problem with the use of bridges and/or layer 2 switches is that the current standards for bridge protocols dictate that there be no closed loops in the network. That is, there can only be one path between any two devices. Thus, it is impossible, in a standards-based implementation, to provide multiple paths through multiple switches between devices. This restriction limits both performance and reliability.

To overcome these problems, it seems logical to break up a large local network into a number of **subnetworks** connected by routers. A MAC broadcast frame is then limited to only the devices and switches contained in a single subnetwork. Furthermore, IP-based routers employ sophisticated routing algorithms that allow the use of multiple paths between subnetworks going through different routers.

However, the problem with using routers to overcome some of the inadequacies of bridges and layer 2 switches is that routers typically do all of the IP-level processing involved in the forwarding of IP traffic in software. High-speed LANs and high-performance layer 2 switches may pump millions of packets per second whereas a software-based router may only be able to handle well under a million packets per second. To accommodate such a load, a number of vendors have developed layer 3 switches, which implement the packet-forwarding logic of the router in hardware.

There are various layer 3 schemes on the market, but fundamentally they fall into two categories: packet by packet and flow based. The packet-by-packet switch operates in the identical fashion as a traditional router. Because the forwarding logic is in hardware, the packet-by-packet switch can achieve an order of magnitude increase in performance compared to the software-based router. A flow-based switch tries to enhance performance by identifying flows of IP packets that have the same source and destination. This can be done by observing ongoing traffic or by using a special flow label in the packet header (allowed in IPv6 but not in IPv4; see Figure 5.7). Once a flow is identified, a predefined route can be established through the network to speed up the forwarding process. Again, huge performance increases over a pure software-based router are achieved.

Figure 10.7 is a typical example of the approach taken to local networking in an organization with a large number of PCs and workstations (thousands to tens of thousands). Desktop systems have links of 10 Mbps to 100 Mbps into a LAN controlled by a layer 2 switch. Wireless LAN connectivity is also likely to be available for mobile users. Layer 3 switches are at the local network's core, forming a local backbone. Typically, these switches are interconnected at 1 Gbps and connect to layer 2 switches at from 100 Mbps to 1 Gbps. Servers connect directly to layer 2 or layer 3 switches at 1 Gbps or possibly 100 Mbps. A lower-cost software-based router provides WAN connection. The circles in the figure identify separate LAN subnetworks; a MAC broadcast frame is limited to its own subnetwork.

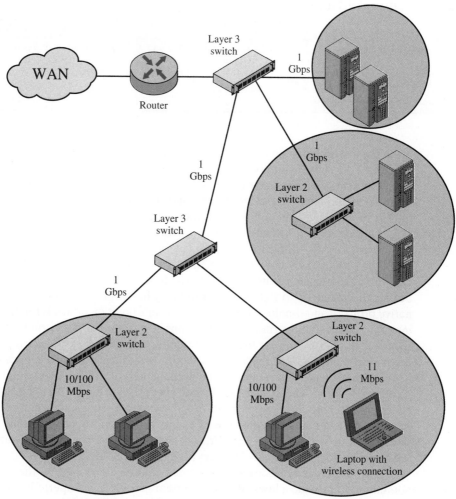

Figure 10.7 Typical Premises Network Configuration

10.3 HIGH-SPEED ETHERNET

Fast Ethernet

If one were to design a high-speed (100 Mbps or more) LAN from scratch, one would not choose CSMA/CD as the basis for the design. CSMA/CD is simple to implement and robust in the face of faults. However, it does not scale well. As the load on a bus increases, the number of collisions increases, degrading performance. Furthermore, as the data rate for a given system increases, performance also decreases. The reason for this is that at a higher data rate, a station can transmit more bits before it recognizes a collision, and therefore more wasted bits are transmitted.

Table 10.3 IEEE 802.3 100-Mbps Physical Layer Medium Alternatives

	100BASE-TX		100BASE-FX	100BASE-T4
Transmission medium	2 pair, STP	2 pair, Category 5 UTP	2 optical fibers	4 pair, Category 3, 4, or 5 UTP
Maximum segment length	100 m	100 m	100 m	100 m
Network span	200 m	200 m	400 m	200 m

These problems can be overcome. To accommodate higher loads, a system can be designed to have a number of different segments, interconnected with hubs. The hubs can act as barriers, separating the LAN into collision domains, so that a collision in one domain does not spread to other domains. The use of switched Ethernet hubs in effect eliminates collisions, further increasing efficiency.

Despite some drawbacks to its use, Ethernet-style LANs have been developed that operate at 100 Mbps, 1 Gbps, and 10 Gbps. The reasons for this are instructive. From the vendor's point of view, the CSMA/CD protocol is well understood and vendors have experience building the hardware, firmware, and software for such systems. Scaling the system up to 100 Mbps or more may be easier than implementing an alternative protocol and topology. From the customer's point of view, it is relatively easy to integrate older systems running at 10 Mbps with newer systems running at higher speeds if all the systems use the same frame format and the same access protocol. In other words, the continued use of Ethernet-style systems is attractive because Ethernet is already there. This same situation is encountered in other areas of data communications. Vendors and customers do not always, or even in the majority of cases, choose the technically superior solution. Cost, ease of management, and other factors relating to the already-existing base of equipment are more important factors in the selection. This is the reason that Ethernet-style systems continue to dominate the LAN market long after most observers predicted the demise of Ethernet.

Fast Ethernet refers to a set of specifications developed by the IEEE 802.3 committee to provide a low-cost, Ethernet-compatible LAN operating at 100 Mbps. The blanket designation for these standards is 100BASE-T. The committee defined a number of alternatives to be used with different transmission media.

Table 10.3 summarizes key characteristics of the 100BASE-T options. All of the 100BASE-T options use the IEEE 802.3 MAC protocol and frame format. 100BASE-X refers to a set of options that use the physical medium specifications. All of the 100BASE-X schemes use two physical links between nodes; one for transmission and one for reception. 100BASE-TX makes use of shielded twisted pair (STP) or high-quality (Category 5) unshielded twisted pair (UTP).[1] 100BASE-FX uses optical fiber.

In many buildings, any of the 100BASE-X options requires the installation of new cable. For such cases, 100BASE-T4 defines a lower-cost alternative that can use Category 3, voice-grade UTP in addition to the higher-quality Category 5 UTP. To achieve the 100-Mbps data rate over lower-quality cable, 100BASE-T4 dictates the

---

[1]See Chapter 9 for a discussion of Category 3 and Category 5 cable.

use of four twisted-pair lines between nodes, with the data transmission making use of three pairs in one direction at a time.

For all of the 100BASE-T options, the topology is similar to that of 10BASE-T, namely a star-wire topology.

A traditional Ethernet is half duplex: A station can either transmit or receive a frame, but it cannot do both simultaneously. With full-duplex operation, a station can transmit and receive simultaneously. If a 100-Mbps Ethernet ran in full duplex mode, the theoretical transfer rate becomes 200 Mbps.

Several changes are needed to operate in full-duplex mode. The attached stations must have full-duplex rather than half-duplex adapter cards. The central point is a switch. In this case, each station constitutes a separate collision domain. In fact, there are no collisions and the CSMA/CD algorithm is no longer needed. However, the same 802.3 MAC frame format is used and the attached stations can continue to execute the CSMA/CD algorithm, even though no collisions can ever be detected.

Gigabit Ethernet

The strategy for Gigabit Ethernet is the same as that for Fast Ethernet. While defining a new medium and transmission specification, Gigabit Ethernet retains the CSMA/CD protocol and frame format of its 10-Mbps and 100-Mbps predecessors. It is compatible with 100BASE-T and 10BASE-T, preserving a smooth migration path. As more organizations move to 100BASE-T, putting huge traffic loads on backbone networks, demand for Gigabit Ethernet has intensified.

Figure 10.8 shows a typical application of Gigabit Ethernet. A 1-Gbps LAN switch provides backbone connectivity for central servers and high-speed workgroup switches.

Figure 10.8 Example Gigabit Ethernet Configuration

Figure 10.9 Gigabit Ethernet Medium Options (log scale)

Each workgroup LAN switch supports both 1-Gbps links, to connect to the backbone LAN switch and to support high-performance workgroup servers, and 100-Mbps links, to support high-performance workstations, servers, and 100-Mbps LAN switches.

The current 1-Gbps specification for IEEE 802.3 includes the following physical layer alternatives (Figure 10.9):

- **1000BASE-LX:** This long-wavelength option supports duplex links of up to 550 m of 62.5-μm or 50-μm multimode fiber or up to 5 km of 10-μm single-mode fiber. Wavelengths are in the range of 1270 to 1355 nm.

- **1000BASE-SX:** This short-wavelength option supports duplex links of up to 275 m using 62.5-μm multimode or up to 550 m using 50-μm multimode fiber. Wavelengths are in the range of 770 to 860 nm.

- **1000BASE-CX:** This option supports 1-Gbps links among devices located within a single room or equipment rack, using copper jumpers (specialized shielded twisted pair cable that spans no more than 25 m). Each link is composed of a separate shielded twisted pair running in each direction.

- **1000BASE-T:** This option makes use of four pairs of Category 5 unshielded twisted pair to support devices over a range of up to 100 m.

10–Gbps Ethernet

In recent years, 10-Gbps Ethernet switches have made considerable inroads in the LAN market. The principal driving requirement for 10 Gigabit Ethernet is the increase in Internet and intranet traffic. A number of factors contribute to the explosive growth in both Internet and intranet traffic:

- An increase in the number of network connections
- An increase in the connection speed of each end-station (e.g., 10-Mbps users moving to 100 Mbps, analog 56-kbps users moving to DSL and cable modems)

- An increase in the deployment of bandwidth-intensive applications such as high-quality video
- An increase in Web hosting and application hosting traffic

Initially, network managers are using 10-Gbps Ethernet to provide high-speed, local backbone interconnection between large-capacity switches. As the demand for bandwidth increases, 10-Gbps Ethernet will be deployed throughout the entire network and will include server farm, backbone, and campuswide connectivity. This technology enables Internet service providers (ISPs) and network service providers (NSPs) to create very high-speed links at a low cost, between co-located, carrier-class switches and routers.

The technology also allows the construction of metropolitan area networks (MANs) and WANs that connect geographically dispersed LANs between campuses or points of presence (PoPs). Thus, Ethernet begins to compete with ATM and other wide area transmission/networking technologies. In most cases where the customer requirement is data and TCP/IP transport, 10-Gbps Ethernet provides substantial value over ATM transport for both network end users and service providers:

- No expensive, bandwidth-consuming conversion between Ethernet packets and ATM cells is required; the network is Ethernet, end to end.
- The combination of IP and Ethernet offers quality of service and traffic policing capabilities that approach those provided by ATM, so that advanced traffic engineering technologies are available to users and providers.
- A wide variety of standard optical interfaces (wavelengths and link distances) have been specified for 10-Gbps Ethernet, optimizing its operation and cost for LAN, MAN, or WAN applications.

The goal for maximum link distances cover a range of applications: from 300 m to 40 km. The links operate in full-duplex mode only, using a variety of optical fiber physical media.

Four physical layer options are defined for 10-Gbps Ethernet (Figure 10.10):

- **10GBASE-S (short):** Designed for 850-nm transmission on multimode fiber. This medium can achieve distances up to 300 m.
- **10GBASE-L (long):** Designed for 1310-nm transmission on single-mode fiber. This medium can achieve distances up to 10 km.
- **10GBASE-E (extended):** Designed for 1550-nm transmission on single-mode fiber. This medium can achieve distances up to 40 km.
- **10GBASE-LX4:** Designed for 1310-nm transmission on single-mode or multimode fiber. This medium can achieve distances up to 10 km. This medium uses wavelength-division multiplexing (WDM) to multiplex the bit stream across four light waves.

100–Gbps Ethernet

Ethernet is widely deployed and is the preferred technology for wired local area networking. Ethernet dominates enterprise LANs, broadband access, data center networking, and has also become popular for communication across metropolitan and

Figure 10.10 10-Gbps Ethernet Distance Options (log scale)

even wide area networks. Further, it is now the preferred carrier wire line vehicle for bridging wireless technologies, such as WiFi and WiMAX, into local Ethernet networks.

This popularity of Ethernet technology is due to the availability of cost-effective, reliable, and interoperable networking products from a variety of vendors. Over the years, a number of industry consortiums have participated in the development of ever-faster versions of Ethernet, including the Fast Ethernet Alliance (100 Mbps), the Gigabit Ethernet Alliance, the 10 Gigabit Ethernet Alliance, the Ethernet Alliance, and the Road to 100G Alliance. As a testament to the continuing evolution of Ethernet, the first three of the alliances just mentioned no longer exist. The Ethernet Alliance is devoted to promoting the development of Ethernet, whatever the speed. The Road to 100G Alliance is focused on the development of standards and technologies for 100-Gbps Ethernet.

As this alliance evolution reflects, the development of converged and unified communications, the evolution of massive server farms, and the continuing expansion of VoIP, TVoIP, and Web 2.0 applications have driven the need for ever faster Ethernet switches. [HUFF06] lists the following market drivers for 100-Gbps Ethernet:

- **Data center/Internet media providers:** To support the growth of Internet multimedia content and Web applications, content providers have been expanding data centers, pushing 10-Gbps Ethernet to its limits. Likely to be high-volume early adopters of 100-Gbps Ethernet.

- **Metro-video/service providers:** Video on demand has been driving a new generation of 10-Gbps Ethernet metropolitan/core network buildouts. Likely to be high-volume adopters in the medium term.

- **Enterprise LANs:** Continuing growth in convergence of voice/video/data and in unified communications is driving up network switch demands. However, most enterprises still rely on 1-Gbps or a mix of 1-Gbps and 10-Gbps Ethernet, and adoption of 100-Gbps Ethernet is likely to be slow.

Table 10.4 Proposed High-Speed Ethernet Media Performance

	40 Gbps	100 Gbps
1m backplane	✓	
10 m copper	✓	✓
100 m multimode fiber	✓	✓
10 km single mode fiber	✓	✓
40 km single mode fiber		✓

- **Internet exchanges/ISP (Internet Service Provider) core routing:** With the massive amount of traffic flowing through these nodes, these installations are likely to be early adopters of 100-Gbps Ethernet.

In 2007, the IEEE 802.3 working group authorized the *IEEE P802.3ba 40Gb/s and 100Gb/s Ethernet Task Force*. Table 10.4 indicates the physical layer objectives for this task force. As can be seen, these high-speed switches will be standardized to operate at distances from 1 m to 40 km over a variety of physical media.

An example of the application of 100-Gbps Ethernet is shown in Figure 10.11, taken from [NOWE07]. The trend at large data centers, with substantial banks of blade servers,[2] is the deployment of 10-Gbps ports on individual servers to handle the massive multimedia traffic provided by these servers. Such arrangements are

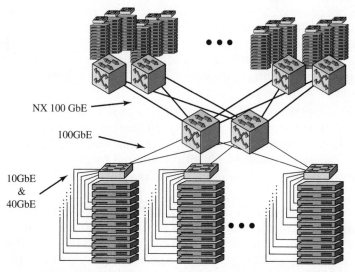

Figure 10.11 Example 100-Gbps Ethernet Configuration for Massive Blade Server Site

---

[2]A blade server is a server architecture that houses multiple server modules ("blades") in a single chassis. It is widely used in data centers to save space and improve system management. Either self-standing or rack mounted, the chassis provides the power supply, and each blade has its own CPU, memory, and hard disk. (definition from pcmag.com encyclopedia).

stressing the on-site switches needed to interconnect large numbers of servers. A 100GbE rate was proposed to provide the bandwidth required to handle the increased traffic load. It is expected that 100GbE will be deployed in switch uplinks inside the data center as well as providing interbuilding, intercampus, MAN, and WAN connections for enterprise networks.

The success of Fast Ethernet, Gigabit Ethernet, and 10-Gbps Ethernet highlights the importance of network management concerns in choosing a network technology. Both ATM and Fiber Channel, explored subsequently, may be technically superior choices for a high-speed backbone, because of their flexibility and scalability. However, the Ethernet alternatives offer compatibility with existing installed LANs, network management software, and applications. This compatibility has accounted for the survival of 30-year-old technology in today's fast-evolving network environment.

APPLICATION NOTE

Networking with Ethernet

Over the past two decades there have been a number of local area network protocols, but most of them are no longer in use. The vast majority of networks currently deployed are based on faster forms of Ethernet such as 10/100baseTX, 100baseFX, Gigabit, and even 10Gbps Ethernet. Today, and for the foreseeable future, Ethernet is the dominant local area network protocol. It is even beginning to make inroads into the last mile market. The strength of Ethernet lies in its backward compatibility, industry support and simplicity. Setting up an Ethernet network is nearly as simple as taking the equipment out of the box and plugging it in. In addition, common Ethernet components are becoming very inexpensive. In contrast, maintaining or installing any of the less popular, legacy systems can be very costly.

While the "under the hood" operation of Ethernet makes for good engineering reading, there are some very practical aspects of Ethernet that good to know in order to get the most out of the network. An organization must analyze its communication requirements and decide how much bandwidth is required for present and future use, what applications will be running over the network architecture, and how much money will be spent.

For the last couple of years, most networking equipment sold had 10/100 Ethernet ports. This means that the equipment port and the network interface card (NIC) in the computer will "auto-sense" the network conditions and determine what speed is available. With the advance in technology, many equipment vendors are now offering ports that are capable of gigabit speeds. These ports are also called 10/100/1000 or 1000baseT ports. Yet computer bus speeds and operating system delays represent barriers to actually making use of a network running at gigabit speeds. In addition, there are not very many computers that need to send that much data. For standard machines, the 100-Mbps or 10/100 cards are usually sufficient, and this is not likely to change in the near future. Even without gigabit capability, network cards and devices can be set for full duplex operation, which increases the two-way throughput to 200 Mbps. Even some 10-Mbps links can be set for 20 Mbps at full duplex.

For new installations or during planned network upgrades, the purchase of gigabit equipment may certainly be justified. This is especially true with the growth that many networks can expect. However, the cost per port for enterprise level equipment can still be expensive, and for many applications, the cost of this high-speed equipment may not justify itself outside of these situations. Gigabit, and even 10-Gbps Ethernet, is well suited to fiber backbone connections such as those between wiring closets, connections going off site, and to hard working servers. Of course fiber adds to the cost of any implementation.

While virtually no new networks will be installed at 10 Mbps, older networks may run at these slower speeds and have a mix of technologies. Any new equipment that is purchased should be of the 10/100 models to ensure compatibility with both the old system and any newer equipment purchased. However, new equipment will only transmit as fast as is permitted by the wiring. Old Category 3 wiring will not facilitate 100-Mbps speeds. Even Category 5 wiring may not support the higher speeds depending on distance. The problem is that while replacing equipment represents a certain fixed cost, when the cable plant itself must be replaced the cost can increase dramatically.

Hubs are another item that seem destined for extinction. Not too long ago, the cost per port for bridges and switches made the transition to them painfully expensive. However, in the last few years the cost reduction of these components more than justifies their purchase. The advanced features offered by switches over hubs can add significant management and security for the price. For example, many switches come with built-in statistics, virtual local area networks, and firewall filtering. Lastly, switches offer filtering and fault isolation as part of their standard operation.

For any new installation the shopping list should include the best-quality UTP cabling, network cards capable of 10/100 full duplex operation, and switches with ports capable of 10/100/1000 full duplex operation. When upgrading the old system, network administrators should follow these guidelines with the understanding that for best performance the equipment should be matched with the appropriate cabling infrastructure.

10.4 SUMMARY

High-speed LANs have emerged as a critical element of corporate information systems. Such LANs are needed not only to provide an on-premises backbone for linking departmental LANs, but also to support the high-performance requirements of graphics-based client/server and intranet applications.

For most applications, Fast Ethernet and the emerging Gigabit Ethernet technologies dominate corporate high-speed LAN choices. These systems involve the least risk and cost for managers for a number of reasons, including compatibility with the existing large Ethernet installed base, maturity of the basic technology, and compatibility with existing network management and configuration software.

In most cases, an organization will have multiple LANs that need to be interconnected. The simplest approach to meeting this requirement is the bridge.

10.5 RECOMMENDED READING AND WEB SITES

[SPUR00] provides a concise but thorough overview of all of the 10-Mbps through 1-Gbps 802.3 systems, including configuration guidelines for a single segment of each media type, as well as guidelines for building multisegment Ethernets using a variety of media types. [NORR03] provides a good overview of Gigabit Ethernet, with an extended discussion of applications of the technology. Two somewhat more technical treatments of both 100-Mbps and Gigabit Ethernet are [SEIF98] and [KADA98]. A good survey article on Gigabit Ethernet is [FRAZ99]. [10GE02] is a white paper providing a useful introduction to 10-Gbps Ethernet.

10GE02 10 Gigabit Ethernet Alliance. *10 Gigabit Ethernet Technology Overview.* White paper, May 2002. ethernetalliance.org/technology/white_papers

FRAZ99 Frazier, H., and Johnson, H. "Gigabit Ethernet: From 100 to 1,000 Mbps." *IEEE Internet Computing,* January/February 1999.

KADA98 Kadambi, J.; Crayford, I.; and Kalkunte, M. *Gigabit Ethernet.* Upper Saddle River, NJ: Prentice Hall, 1998.

NORR03 Norris, M. *Gigabit Ethernet Technology and Applications.* Norwood, MA: Artech House, 2003.

SEIF98 Seifert, R. *Gigabit Ethernet.* Reading, MA: Addison-Wesley, 1998.

SPUR00 Spurgeon, C. *Ethernet: The Definitive Guide.* Cambridge, MA: O'Reilly and Associates, 2000.

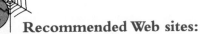

Recommended Web sites:

- **Interoperability Lab:** University of New Hampshire site for equipment testing for high-speed LANs.
- **Charles Spurgeon's Ethernet Web Site:** Provides extensive information about Ethernet, including links and documents.
- **Ethernet Alliance:** This consortium promotes Ethernet technology and products. Site includes numerous white papers.
- **Road to 100G Alliance:** Consortium of vendors and service providers promoting 100-Gbps Ethernet. Site includes white papers and resource links.

10.6 KEY TERMS, REVIEW QUESTIONS, AND PROBLEMS

Key Terms

bridge	Ethernet	layer 3 switch
carrier sense multiple access	Fast Ethernet	store-and-forward switch
with collision detection	frame	switch
(CSMA/CD)	frame check sequence (FCS)	
cut-through switch	Fibre Channel	
cyclic redundancy check	Hub	
(CRC)	layer 2 switch	

Review Questions

10.1 What is a server farm?

10.2 Explain why a data rate of 10 Mbps on all LAN segments is increasingly inadequate for many businesses.

10.3 What is CSMA/CD?

10.4 What functions are performed by a bridge?

10.5 What is the difference between a hub and a layer 2 switch?

10.6 What is the difference between a store-and-forward switch and a cut-through switch?

10.7 What are the differences between a bridge and a switch?

10.8 What is meant by the phrase *flat address space?*

10.9 What are the transmission medium options for Fast Ethernet?

10.10 What are the transmission medium options for Gigabit Ethernet?

10.11 What are the transmission medium options for 10-Gbps Ethernet?

Problems

10.1 Can you determine the type of network interface card installed in your computer? Describe this card in terms of the speed, layer 2 protocol and the type of medium you are using (for example, 10Mbps Ethernet over UTP).

10.2 Using capture programs such as Ethereal and built in programs like ping, nslookup, and ipconfig, can you find the following information?
  a. With ipconfig or ifconfig, find your MAC address.
  b. Capture traffic from your own computer and examine your MAC address—does it match the previous question?
  c. Can you determine the code value for IP in the frames you have been captured? This can be found in the control field of the Ethernet frame.

10.3 An argument that has been ongoing for some time now involves the question as to whether ATM or Gigabit Ethernet is the best choice for a high speed networking solution. Compare these two technologies and formulate a position paper outlining a potential scenario for each technology where it might constitute the optimal solution.

10.4 Broadband Integrated Services Digital Network (BISDN) is an optical broadband version of ISDN (which provides digital transmission over POTS). BISDN services incorporate several technologies, including Asynchronous Transfer Mode (ATM) and

Synchronous Optical Network (SONET). Provide a basic overview of SONET. Can SONET be used to extend the reach of the Fibre Channel data center protocol for international data traffic?

10.5   Token-Ring is an alternative (but largely considered obsolete) technology to Ethernet. Provide a basic overview of Token-Ring and explain why it has largely been effaced by Ethernet as a LAN technology alternative. RIC

10.6   When a collision occurs, IEEE 802.3 systems use an algorithm called *binary exponential backoff* to calculate the random amount of time the sender must wait before attempting to retransmit the frame. For each of the retransmissions, the algorithm doubles the range of the random delay. Thus, after n collisions, the system will wait for a random amount of time, in the range from 0 to $2^n - 1$ units of time before attempting to retransmit the frame. Analyze the advantages of this design decision.

10.7   Analyze the advantages of having the FCS field of IEEE 802.3 frames in the trailer of the frame rather than in the header of the frame.

CARLSON COMPANIES

Carlson Companies is one of the largest privately held companies in the United States, with more than 180,000 employees in more than 140 countries. Carlson enterprises include a presence in marketing, business and leisure travel, and hospitality industries.

Its Information Technology (IT) division, Carlson Shared Services, acts as a service provider to its internal clients and consequently must support a spectrum of user applications and services. The IT division uses a centralized data processing model to meet business operational requirements. The central computing environment includes an IBM mainframe and over 50 networked Hewlett-Packard and Sun servers [KRAN04, CLAR02, HIGG02]. The mainframe supports a wide range of applications, including Oracle financial database, e-mail, Microsoft Exchange, Web, PeopleSoft, and a data warehouse application.

In 2002, the IT division established six goals for assuring that IT services continued to meet the needs of a growing company with heavy reliance on data and applications:

1. Implement an enterprise data warehouse.
2. Build a global network.
3. Move to enterprise-wide architecture.
4. Established six-sigma quality for Carlson clients.
5. Facilitate outsourcing and exchange.
6. Leverage existing technology and resource.

The key to meeting these goals was to implement a storage area network (SAN) with a consolidated, centralized database to support mainframe and server applications. Carlson needed a SAN and data center approach that provided a reliable, highly scalable facility to accommodate the increasing demand of its users.

STORAGE REQUIREMENTS

Until recently, the central DP shop included separate disc storage for each server, plus that of the mainframe. This dispersed data storage scheme had the advantage of responsiveness; that is, the access time from a server to its data was minimal. However, the data management cost was high. There had to be backup procedures for the storage on each server, as well as management controls to reconcile data distributed throughout the system. The mainframe included an efficient disaster recovery plan to preserve data in the event of major system crashes or other incidents and to get data back online with little or no disruption to the users. No comparable plan existed for the many servers.

As Carlson's databases grow beyond 10 terabytes (TB) of business-critical data, the IT team determined that a comprehensive network storage strategy would be required to manage future growth.

SOLUTION CONCEPT

The existing Carlson server complex made use of Fibre Channel links to achieve communication and backup capabilities among servers. Carlson considered extending this capability to a full-blown Fibre Channel SAN that would encompass the server, the mainframe, and massive centralized storage facilities. The IT team concluded that further expansion using Fibre Channel technologies alone would be difficult and costly to manage. At the same time, in supporting the many offsite client systems that accessed data center server, the IT shop already had a substantial investment in IP network products and staff training. Accordingly, Carlson sought a solution that would leverage this IP investment, provide scalability as additional local and remote services are added, and require minimal traffic engineering of the storage transport network.

Thus, Carlson settled on a solution based on a core IP SAN that would meet both data-center and wide-area storage requirements and seamlessly integrate new storage technologies.

THE CARLSON SAN

The core of the Carlson SAN is an IP-based scheme in which Gigabit Ethernet switches carry IP traffic among servers and between servers and the central storage. Attached to the Gigabit switches are Nishan IP Storage switches, which provide a Fibre Channel interface for the servers and storage and an IP traffic switch into the Ethernet core (Figure IV.1). The Ethernet switches enjoy a considerable cost advantage over comparable Fibre Channel switches and require lower-cost management and maintenance.

For redundancy, servers are dual-homed to the IP storage switches, which in turn connect to redundant Ethernet switches. The ratio of servers to storage interconnect is determined by the throughput requirements of each server group. Similarly, multiple IP storage switches connect the Ethernet switch core to the SAN storage system. This configuration can be scaled to support additional servers and storage arrays by adding additional IP storage switches. The network core of Ethernet switches also expands easily by adding additional switches.

The focus of the Carlson SAN is a 13-TB HP Storage Works Disc array. A major consideration in planning the transition was the migration of data from the mainframe's storage to the central storage. The mainframe hosts several mission-critical applications in a round-the-clock fashion. Thus, an offline data migration was not feasible. The migration of all common data to this array proceeded in two phases. In the first phase, each server was taken offline and a simple copy was performed to transfer the

Fibre Channel domain   IP/IFCP domain   Fibre Channel domain

Figure IV.1   Carlson's Data Center SAN

application data on the server systems to the new storage system. The second phase involved the transfer of 1.2 TB of data from the mainframe's legacy storage to the new storage system. Carlson contracted this task out to HP storage experts who made use of proprietary data migration and network management tools to enable the transfer to occur during production processing hours. End users were unaffected during the migration.

Carlson's IP SAN helps reduce the ongoing administration and management of storage networking by taking advantage of well-established and well-understood IP networking technologies. In addition, putting storage data over IP facilitates integration of more efficient storage services for Carlson's enterprise-wide network, including centralized backup of remote sites to the data center SAN.

Discussion Questions

1. Discuss how the Carlson SAN approach addresses the IT goals the company is trying to achieve.

2. Discuss the pros and cons of consolidating data on a SAN central data facility versus the dispersed arrangement it replaces.

3. The Carlson SAN mixes equipment from a number of vendors. What problems does this raise and what are some management options for dealing with them?

CHAPTER 11

WIRELESS LANS

11.1 Overview
Wireless LAN Applications
Wireless LAN Requirements
Wireless LAN Technology

11.2 Wi-Fi Architecture and Services
The Wi-Fi Alliance
IEEE 802.11 Architecture
IEEE 802.11 Services

11.3 IEEE 802.11 Mac and Physical Layer Standards
IEEE 802.11 Medium Access Control
IEEE 802.11 Physical Layer

11.4 IEEE 802.11 Security Considerations
Access and Privacy Services
Wireless LAN Security Standards

11.5 Summary

11.6 Recommended Reading and Web Sites

11.7 Key Terms, Review Questions, and Problems

Chapter Objectives

After reading this chapter, you should be able to

♦ Discuss the importance of wireless LANs.

♦ Describe the various approaches to wireless local networking.

♦ Explain the key elements of the IEEE 802.11 wireless LAN architecture.

♦ Describe the services provided by IEEE 802.11.

♦ Discuss the functionality provided at each level of the IEEE 802.11 protocol architecture.

In just the past few years, wireless LANs have become a significant segment of the LAN market. Increasingly, organizations are finding that wireless LANs are an indispensable adjunct to traditional wired LANs, to satisfy requirements for mobility, relocation, ad hoc networking, and coverage of locations difficult to wire.

This chapter provides a survey of wireless LANs. We begin with an overview that looks at the motivations for using wireless LANs and summarizes the various approaches in current use. Then, the most widely used wireless LAN schemes, IEEE 802.11, also known as Wi-Fi, is examined. Appendix H examines another popular scheme known as Bluetooth.

11.1 OVERVIEW

As the name suggests, a wireless LAN is one that makes use of a wireless transmission medium. Until relatively recently, wireless LANs were little used. The reasons for this included high prices, low data rates, occupational safety concerns, and licensing requirements. As these problems have been addressed, the popularity of wireless LANs has grown rapidly.

Wireless LAN Applications

[PAHL95] lists four application areas for wireless LANs: LAN extension, cross-building interconnect, nomadic access, and ad hoc networks. Let us consider each of these in turn.

LAN EXTENSION   Early wireless LAN products, introduced in the late 1980s, were marketed as substitutes for traditional wired LANs. A wireless LAN saves the cost of the installation of LAN cabling and eases the task of relocation and other modifications to network structure. However, this motivation for wireless LANs was overtaken by events. First, as awareness of the need for LANs became greater, architects designed new buildings to include extensive prewiring for data applications. Second, with advances in data transmission technology, there is an increasing reliance on twisted-pair cabling for LANs and, in particular, Category 3 and Category 5 unshielded twisted pair. Most older buildings are already wired with an abundance of Category 3 cable, and many newer buildings are prewired with Category 5. Thus, the use of a wireless LAN simply to replace wired LANs has not happened to any great extent.

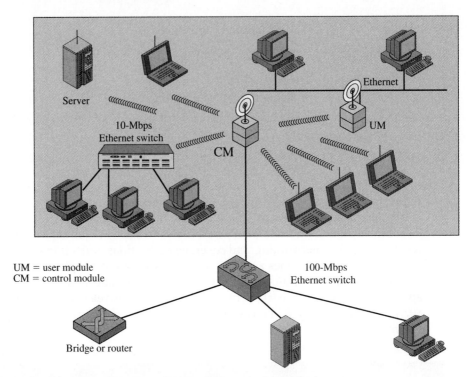

UM = user module
CM = control module

Figure 11.1   Example Single-Cell Wireless LAN Configuration

However, in a number of environments, there is a role for the wireless LAN as an alternative to a wired LAN. Examples include buildings with large open areas, such as manufacturing plants, stock exchange trading floors, and warehouses; historical buildings with insufficient twisted pair and where drilling holes for new wiring is prohibited; and small offices where installation and maintenance of wired LANs is not economical. In all of these cases, a wireless LAN provides an effective and more attractive alternative. In most of these cases, an organization will also have a wired LAN to support servers and some stationary workstations. For example, a manufacturing facility typically has an office area that is separate from the factory floor but that must be linked to it for networking purposes. Therefore, typically, a wireless LAN will be linked into a wired LAN on the same premises. Thus, this application area is referred to as LAN extension.

Figure 11.1 indicates a simple wireless LAN configuration that is typical of many environments. There is a backbone wired LAN, such as Ethernet, that supports servers, workstations, and one or more bridges or routers to link with other networks. In addition, there is a control module (CM) that acts as an interface to a wireless LAN. The control module includes either bridge or router functionality to link the wireless LAN to the backbone. It includes some sort of access control logic, such as a polling or token-passing scheme, to regulate the access from the end systems. Note that some of the end systems are standalone devices, such as a workstation or a server. Hubs or other user modules (UMs) that control a number of stations off a wired LAN may also be part of the wireless LAN configuration.

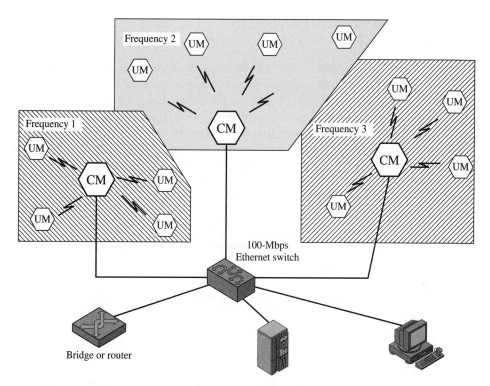

Figure 11.2   Example Multiple-Cell Wireless LAN Configuration

The configuration of Figure 11.1 can be referred to as a single-cell wireless LAN; all of the wireless end systems are within range of a single control module. Another common configuration, suggested by Figure 11.2, is a multiple-cell wireless LAN. In this case, there are multiple control modules interconnected by a wired LAN. Each control module supports a number of wireless end systems within its transmission range. For example, with an infrared LAN, transmission is limited to a single room; therefore, one cell is needed for each room in an office building that requires wireless support.

CROSS-BUILDING INTERCONNECT   Another use of wireless LAN technology is to connect LANs in nearby buildings, be they wired or wireless LANs. In this case, a point-to-point wireless link is used between two buildings. For example two microwave or infrared transmitter/receiver units can be placed on the rooftops of two buildings within the line of sight of each other. The devices so connected are typically bridges or routers. This single point-to-point link is not a LAN per se, but it is usual to include this application under the heading of wireless LAN.

NOMADIC ACCESS   Nomadic access provides a wireless link between a LAN hub and a mobile data terminal equipped with an antenna, such as a laptop computer or notepad computer. One example of the utility of such a connection is to enable an employee returning from a trip to transfer data from a personal portable computer to a server in the office. Nomadic access is also useful in an extended environment such as a campus or a business operating out of a cluster of buildings. In both of these cases, users may move around with their portable computers and may wish access to the servers on a wired LAN from various locations. Finally, even a usually stationary user in an office environment may rely on a laptop and need wireless access.

AD HOC NETWORKING   An ad hoc network is a peer-to-peer network (no centralized server) set up temporarily to meet some immediate need. For example, a group of employees, each with a laptop or palmtop computer, may convene in a conference room for a business or classroom meeting. The employees link their computers in a temporary network just for the duration of the meeting.

Figure 11.3 suggests the differences between a wireless LAN that supports LAN extension and nomadic access requirements and an ad hoc wireless LAN. In the former case, the wireless LAN forms a stationary infrastructure consisting of one or more cells with a control module for each cell. Within a cell, there may be a number of stationary

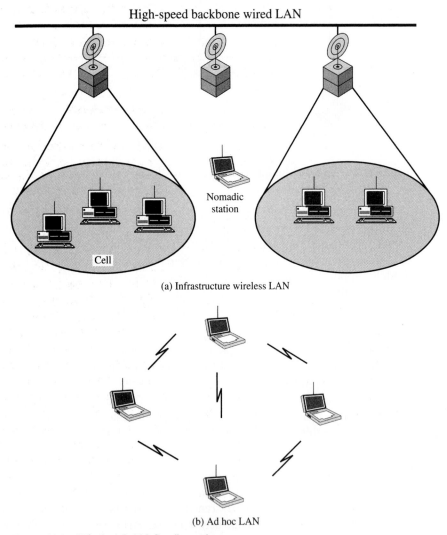

High-speed backbone wired LAN

Nomadic
station

Cell

(a) Infrastructure wireless LAN

(b) Ad hoc LAN

Figure 11.3   Wireless LAN Configurations

Wireless LAN Technology

Wireless LANs are generally categorized according to the transmission technique that is used. All current wireless LAN products fall into one of the following categories:

- **Spread spectrum LANs:** This type of LAN makes use of spread spectrum transmission technology. In most cases, these LANs operate in the ISM (industrial, scientific, and medical) 2.4-GHz microwave bands so that no Federal Communications Commission (FCC) licensing is required for their use in the United States.

- **OFDM LANs:** For higher speeds, a technology known as orthogonal frequency division multiplexing is superior to spread spectrum, and products with this technology are now common. These LANs typically operate in either the 2.4-GHz band or the 5-GHz band.

- **Infrared (IR) LANs:** An individual cell of an IR LAN is limited to a single room, because infrared light does not penetrate opaque walls.

11.2 WI-FI ARCHITECTURE AND SERVICES

In 1990, the IEEE 802 Committee formed a new working group, IEEE 802.11, specifically devoted to wireless LANs, with a charter to develop a MAC protocol and physical medium specification. Since that time, the demand for WLANs, at different frequencies and data rates, has exploded. Keeping pace with this demand, the IEEE 802.11 working group has issued an ever-expanding list of standards (Table 11.1). Table 11.2 briefly defines key terms used in the IEEE 802.11 standard.

The Wi-Fi Alliance

The first 802.11 standard to gain broad industry acceptance was 802.11b. Although 802.11b products are all based on the same standard, there is always a concern whether products from different vendors will successfully interoperate. To meet this concern, the Wireless Ethernet Compatibility Alliance (WECA), an industry consortium, was formed in 1999. This organization, subsequently renamed the Wi-Fi (Wireless Fidelity) Alliance, created a test suite to certify interoperability for 802.11b products. The term used for certified 802.11b products is *Wi-Fi*. Wi-Fi certification has been extended to 802.11g products,. The Wi-Fi Alliance has also developed a certification process for 802.11a products, called *Wi-Fi5*. The Wi-Fi Alliance is concerned with a range of market areas for WLANs, including enterprise, home, and hot spots.

IEEE 802.11 Architecture

Figure 11.4 illustrates the model developed by the 802.11 working group. The smallest building block of a wireless LAN is a **basic service set (BSS)**, which consists of some number of stations executing the same MAC protocol and competing for access to the same shared wireless medium. A BSS may be isolated or it may connect to a backbone **distribution system (DS)** through an **access point (AP)**. The AP functions as a bridge and a relay point. In a BSS, client stations do not communicate end systems. Nomadic stations can move from one cell to another. In contrast, there is no infrastructure for an ad hoc network. Rather, a peer collection of stations within range of each other may dynamically configure themselves into a temporary network.

Wireless LAN Requirements

A wireless LAN must meet the same sort of requirements typical of any LAN, including high capacity, ability to cover short distances, full connectivity among attached stations, and broadcast capability. In addition, there are a number of requirements specific to the wireless LAN environment. The following are among the most important requirements for wireless LANs:

- **Throughput:** The medium access control protocol should make as efficient use as possible of the wireless medium to maximize capacity.

- **Number of nodes:** Wireless LANs may need to support hundreds of nodes across multiple cells.

- **Connection to backbone LAN:** In most cases, interconnection with stations on a wired backbone LAN is required. For infrastructure wireless LANs, this is easily accomplished through the use of control modules that connect to both types of LANs. There may also need to be accommodation for mobile users and ad hoc wireless networks.

- **Service area:** A typical coverage area for a wireless LAN has a diameter of 100 to 300 m.

- **Battery power consumption:** Mobile workers use battery-powered workstations that need to have a long battery life when used with wireless adapters. This suggests that a MAC protocol that requires mobile nodes to monitor access points constantly or engage in frequent handshakes with a base station is inappropriate. Typical wireless LAN implementations have features to reduce power consumption while not using the network, such as a sleep mode.

- **Transmission robustness and security:** Unless properly designed, a wireless LAN may be interference prone and easily eavesdropped. The design of a wireless LAN must permit reliable transmission even in a noisy environment and should provide some level of security from eavesdropping.

- **Collocated network operation:** As wireless LANs become more popular, it is quite likely for two or more wireless LANs to operate in the same area or in some area where interference between the LANs is possible. Such interference may thwart the normal operation of a MAC algorithm and may allow unauthorized access to a particular LAN.

- **License-free operation:** Users would prefer to buy and operate wireless LAN products without having to secure a license for the frequency band used by the LAN.

- **Handoff/roaming:** The MAC protocol used in the wireless LAN should enable mobile stations to move from one cell to another.

- **Dynamic configuration:** The MAC addressing and network management aspects of the LAN should permit dynamic and automated addition, deletion, and relocation of end systems without disruption to other users.

Table 11.1 IEEE 802.11 Standards

Standard	Scope
IEEE 802.11	Medium access control (MAC): One common MAC for WLAN applications
	Physical layer: Infrared at 1 and 2 Mbps
	Physical layer: 2.4-GHz FHSS at 1 and 2 Mbps
	Physical layer: 2.4-GHz DSSS at 1 and 2 Mbps
IEEE 802.11a	Physical layer: 5-GHz OFDM at rates from 6 to 54 Mbps
IEEE 802.11b	Physical layer: 2.4-GHz DSSS at 5.5 and 11 Mbps
IEEE 802.11c	Bridge operation at 802.11 MAC layer
IEEE 802.11d	Physical layer: Extend operation of 802.11 WLANs to new regulatory domains (countries)
IEEE 802.11e	MAC: Enhance to improve quality of service and enhance security mechanisms
IEEE 802.11f	Recommended practices for multivendor access point interoperability
IEEE 802.11g	Physical layer: Extend 802.11b to data rates >20 Mbps
IEEE 802.11h	Physical/MAC: Enhance IEEE 802.11a to add indoor and outdoor channel selection and to improve spectrum and transmit power management
IEEE 802.11i	MAC: Enhance security and authentication mechanisms
IEEE 802.11j	Physical: Enhance IEEE 802.11a to conform to Japanese requirements
IEEE 802.11k	Radio resource measurement enhancements to provide interface to higher layers for radio and network measurements
IEEE 802.11m	Maintenance of IEEE 802.11-1999 standard with technical and editorial corrections
IEEE 802.11n	Physical/MAC: Enhancements to enable higher throughput
IEEE 802.11p	Physical/MAC: Wireless access in vehicular environments
IEEE 802.11r	Physical/MAC: Fast roaming (fast BSS transition)
IEEE 802.11s	Physical/MAC: ESS mesh networking
IEEE 802.11T	Recommended practice for the evaluation of 802.11 wireless performance
IEEE 802.11u	Physical/MAC: Interworking with external networks
IEEE 802.11w	MAC: data integrity, data origin authenticity, replay protection, and data confidentiality for MAC management frames
IEEE 802.11y	PHY: Extend 802.11a to include 3650-3700 MHz band
IEEE 802.11z	MAC: Amendment to define a new Direct Link Setup (DLS) mechanism to allow operation with non-DLS capable access points

directly with one another. Rather, if one station in the BSS wants to communicate with another station in the same BSS, the MAC frame is first sent from the originating station to the AP, and then from the AP to the destination station. Similarly, a MAC frame from a station in the BSS to a remote station is sent from the local station to the AP and then relayed by the AP over the DS on its way to the destination station. The BSS generally corresponds to what is referred to as a cell in the literature. The DS can be a switch, a wired network, or a wireless network.

When all the stations in the BSS are mobile stations, with no connection to other BSSs, the BSS is called an **independent BSS (IBSS)**. An IBSS is typically an ad hoc network. In an IBSS, the stations all communicate directly, and no AP is involved.

Table 11.2 IEEE 802.11 Terminology

Access point (AP)	Any entity that has station functionality and provides access to the distribution system via the wireless medium for associated stations
Basic service set (BSS)	A set of stations controlled by a single coordination function
Coordination function	The logical function that determines when a station operating within a BSS is permitted to transmit and may be able to receive PDUs
Distribution system (DS)	A system used to interconnect a set of BSSs and integrated LANs to create an ESS
Extended service set (ESS)	A set of one or more interconnected BSSs and integrated LANs that appear as a single BSS to the LLC layer at any station associated with one of these BSSs
MAC protocol data unit (MPDU)	The unit of data exchanged between two peer MAC entites using the services of the physical layer
MAC service data unit (MSDU)	Information that is delivered as a unit between MAC users
Station	Any device that contains an IEEE 802.11 conformant MAC and physical layer

A simple configuration is shown in Figure 11.4, in which each station belongs to a single BSS; that is, each station is within wireless range only of other stations within the same BSS. It is also possible for two BSSs to overlap geographically, so that a single station could participate in more than one BSS. Further, the association between a station and a BSS is dynamic. Stations may turn off, come within range, and go out of range.

An **extended service set (ESS)** consists of two or more basic service sets interconnected by a distribution system. Typically, the distribution system is a wired backbone LAN but can be any communications network. The extended service set appears as a single logical LAN to the logical link control (LLC) level.

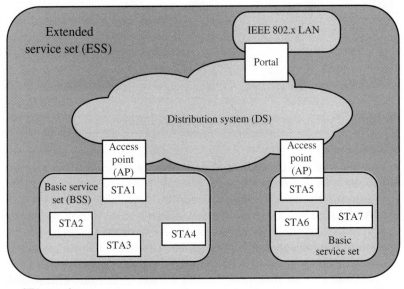

STA = station

Figure 11.4 IEEE 802.11 Architecture

Table 11.3 IEEE 802.11 Services

Service	Provider	Used to support
Association	Distribution system	MSDU delivery
Authentication	Station	LAN access and security
Deauthentication	Station	LAN access and security
Dissassociation	Distribution system	MSDU delivery
Distribution	Distribution system	MSDU delivery
Integration	Distribution system	MSDU delivery
MSDU delivery	Station	MSDU delivery
Privacy	Station	LAN access and security
Reassocation	Distribution system	MSDU delivery

Figure 11.4 indicates that an AP is implemented as part of a station; the AP is the logic within a station that provides access to the DS by providing DS services in addition to acting as a station. To integrate the IEEE 802.11 architecture with a traditional wired LAN, a **portal** is used. The portal logic is implemented in a device, such as a bridge or router, that is part of the wired LAN and that is attached to the DS.

IEEE 802.11 Services

IEEE 802.11 defines nine services that need to be provided by the wireless LAN to achieve functionality equivalent to that which is inherent to wired LANs. Table 11.3 lists the services and indicates two ways of categorizing them.

1. The service provider can be either the station or the DS. Station services are implemented in every 802.11 station, including AP stations. Distribution services are provided between BSSs; these services may be implemented in an AP or in another special-purpose device attached to the distribution system.

2. Three of the services are used to control IEEE 802.11 LAN access and confidentiality. Six of the services are used to support delivery of MAC service data units (MSDUs) between stations. The MSDU is a block of data passed down from the MAC user to the MAC layer; typically this is a LLC PDU. If the MSDU is too large to be transmitted in a single MAC frame, it may be fragmented and transmitted in a series of MAC frames.

Following the IEEE 802.11 document, we next discuss the services in an order designed to clarify the operation of an IEEE 802.11 ESS network. **MSDU delivery**, which is the basic service, has already been mentioned. Services related to security are introduced in Section 11.4 and discussed in Chapter 19.

DISTRIBUTION OF MESSAGES WITHIN A DS The two services involved with the distribution of messages within a DS are distribution and integration. **Distribution** is the primary service used by stations to exchange MAC frames when the frame must traverse the DS to get from a station in one BSS to a station in another BSS. For example, suppose a frame is to be sent from station 2 (STA 2) to STA 7 in Figure 11.4. The frame is sent from STA 2 to STA 1, which is the AP for this BSS. The AP gives the frame to the

DS, which has the job of directing the frame to the AP associated with STA 5 in the target BSS. STA 5 receives the frame and forwards it to STA 7. How the message is transported through the DS is beyond the scope of the IEEE 802.11 standard.

If the two stations that are communicating are within the same BSS, then the distribution service logically goes through the single AP of that BSS.

The **integration** service enables transfer of data between a station on an IEEE 802.11 LAN and a station on an integrated IEEE 802.x LAN. The term *integrated* refers to a wired LAN that is physically connected to the DS and whose stations may be logically connected to an IEEE 802.11 LAN via the integration service. The integration service takes care of any address translation and media conversion logic required for the exchange of data.

ASSOCIATION-RELATED SERVICES   The primary purpose of the MAC layer is to transfer MSDUs between MAC entities; this purpose is fulfilled by the distribution service. For that service to function, it requires information about stations within the ESS that is provided by the association-related services. Before the distribution service can deliver data to or accept data from a station, that station must be *associated*. Before looking at the concept of association, we need to describe the concept of mobility. The standard defines three transition types, based on mobility:

- **No transition:** A station of this type is either stationary or moves only within the direct communication range of the communicating stations of a single BSS.
- **BSS transition:** This is defined as a station movement from one BSS to another BSS within the same ESS. In this case, delivery of data to the station requires that the addressing capability be able to recognize the new location of the station.
- **ESS transition:** This is defined as a station movement from a BSS in one ESS to a BSS within another ESS. This case is supported only in the sense that the station can move. Maintenance of upper-layer connections supported by 802.11 cannot be guaranteed. In fact, disruption of service is likely to occur.

To deliver a message within a DS, the distribution service needs to know where the destination station is located. Specifically, the DS needs to know the identity of the AP to which the message should be delivered in order for that message to reach the destination station. To meet this requirement, a station must maintain an association with the AP within its current BSS. Three services relate to this requirement:

- **Association:** Establishes an initial association between a station and an AP. Before a station can transmit or receive frames on a wireless LAN, its identity and address must be known. For this purpose, a station must establish an association with an AP within a particular BSS. The AP can then communicate this information to other APs within the ESS to facilitate routing and delivery of addressed frames.
- **Reassociation:** Enables an established association to be transferred from one AP to another, allowing a mobile station to move from one BSS to another.
- **Disassociation:** A notification from either a station or an AP that an existing association is terminated. A station should give this notification before leaving an ESS or shutting down. However, the MAC management facility protects itself against stations that disappear without notification.

11.3 IEEE 802.11 MAC AND PHYSICAL LAYER STANDARDS

IEEE 802.11 Medium Access Control

The IEEE 802.11 MAC layer covers three functional areas: reliable data delivery, access control, and security. In this section we examine reliable data delivery and access control. Security is covered in the Section 11.4.

RELIABLE DATA DELIVERY   As with any wireless network, a wireless LAN using the IEEE 802.11 physical and MAC layers is subject to considerable unreliability. Noise, interference, and other propagation effects may result in the loss of a significant number of frames. Even with error-correction codes, a number of MAC frames may not successfully be received. This situation can be dealt with by reliability mechanisms at a higher layer, such as TCP. However, timers used for retransmission at higher layers are typically on the order of seconds. It is therefore more efficient to deal with errors at the MAC level. For this purpose, IEEE 802.11 includes a frame exchange protocol. When a station receives a data frame from another station, it returns an acknowledgment (ACK) frame to the source station. This exchange is treated as an atomic unit, not to be interrupted by a transmission from any other station. If the source does not receive an ACK within a short period of time, either because its data frame was damaged or because the returning ACK was damaged, the source retransmits the frame.

Thus, the basic data transfer mechanism in IEEE 802.11 involves an exchange of two frames. To further enhance reliability, a four-frame exchange may be used. In this scheme, a source first issues a Request to Send (RTS) frame to the destination. The destination then responds with a Clear to Send (CTS). After receiving the CTS, the source transmits the data frame, and the destination responds with an ACK. The RTS alerts all stations that are within reception range of the source that an exchange is under way; these stations refrain from transmission in order to avoid a collision between two frames transmitted at the same time. Similarly, the CTS alerts all stations that are within reception range of the destination that an exchange is under way. The RTS/CTS portion of the exchange is a required function of the MAC but may be disabled.

ACCESS CONTROL   The 802.11 working group considered two types of proposals for a MAC algorithm: distributed access protocols, which, like Ethernet, distribute the decision to transmit among all the nodes using a carrier-sense mechanism; and centralized access protocols, which involve regulation of transmission by a centralized decision maker. A distributed access protocol makes sense for an ad hoc network of peer workstations and may also be attractive in other wireless LAN configurations that consist primarily of bursty traffic. A centralized access protocol is natural for configurations in which a number of wireless stations are interconnected with each other and some sort of base station that attaches to a backbone wired LAN; it is especially useful if some of the data are time sensitive or high priority.

The end result for 802.11 is a MAC algorithm called DFWMAC (distributed foundation wireless MAC) that provides a distributed access control mechanism

Figure 11.5   IEEE 802.11 Protocol Architecture

with an optional centralized control built on top of that. Figure 11.5 illustrates the architecture. The lower sublayer of the MAC layer is the distributed coordination function (DCF). DCF uses an Ethernet-style contention algorithm to provide access to all traffic. Ordinary asynchronous traffic directly uses DCF. The point coordination function (PCF) is a centralized MAC algorithm used to provide contention-free service; this is done by polling stations in turn. Higher-priority traffic, or traffic with greater timing requirements, makes use of the PCF. PCF is built on top of DCF and exploits features of DCF to assure access for its users. Finally, the logical link control (LLC) layer provides an interface to higher layers and performs basic link layer functions such as error control.

IEEE 802.11 Physical Layer

The physical layer for IEEE 802.11 has been issued in five stages. The first part, simply called **IEEE 802.11**, includes the MAC layer and three physical layer specifications, two in the 2.4-GHz band (ISM) and one in the infrared, all operating at 1 and 2 Mbps. **IEEE 802.11a** operates in the 5-GHz band at data rates up to 54 Mbps. **IEEE 802.11b** operates in the 2.4-GHz band at 5.5 and 11 Mbps. **IEEE 802.11g** also operates in the 2.4-GHz band, at data rates up to 54 Mbps. Finally, IEEE 802.11n operates in either the 2.4-GHz band or the 5-GHz band with data rates in the hundreds of Gbps. Table 11.4 provides some details. We look at each of these in turn.

Table 11.4 IEEE 802.11 Physical Layer Standards

	802.11a	802.11b	802.11g	802.11n
Peak data throughput*	23 Mbps	6 Mbps	23 Mbps	60 Mbps (20 MHz channel) 90 Mbps (40 MHz channel)
Peak signalling rate	54 Mbps	11 Mbps	54 Mbps	124 Mbps (20 MHz channel) 248 Mbps (40 MHz channel)
RF band	5 GHz	2.4 GHz	2.4 GHz	2.4 GHz or 5 GHz
Channel width	20 MHz	20 MHz	20 Mhz	20 MHz or 40 MHz
Number of spatial streams	1	1	1	1, 2, 3, or 4

*This is the actual data throughput you get with real equipment under ideal conditions. Real-world performance is lower than this due to noise. This is also shared capacity among wireless clients. When two devices use the same access point, the capacity is typically divided in two, though it's possible some clients will use more of the capacity than others. *Source:* [OU07].

ORIGINAL *IEEE 802.11*   Three physical media are defined in the original 802.11 standard:

- Direct-sequence spread spectrum (DSSS) operating in the 2.4 GHz ISM band, at data rates of 1 Mbps and 2 Mbps
- Frequency-hopping spread spectrum (FHSS) operating in the 2.4 GHz ISM band, at data rates of 1 Mbps and 2 Mbps
- Infrared at 1 Mbps and 2 Mbps, operating at a wavelength between 850 and 950 nm

The infrared option never gained market support. The other two schemes use spread spectrum approaches. In essence, spread spectrum involves the use of a much wider bandwidth than is actually necessary to support a given data rate. The purpose of using a wider bandwidth is to minimize interference and drastically reduce the error rate. In the case of FHSS, spread spectrum is achieved by frequently jumping from one carrier frequency to another; thus, if there is interference or performance degradation at a given frequency, it only affects a small fraction of the transmission. DSSS effectively increases the data rate of a signal by mapping each data bit into a string of bits, with one string used for binary 1 and another used for binary 0. The higher data rate uses a greater bandwidth. The effect is to spread each bit out over time, which minimizes the effects of interference and degradation. FHSS, which is simpler, was employed in most early 802.11 networks. Products using DSSS, which is more effective in the 802.11 scheme, followed. However, all of the original 802.11 products were of limited utility because of the low data rates.

IEEE 802.11b   IEEE 802.11b is an extension of the IEEE 802.11 DSSS scheme, providing data rates of 5.5 and 11 Mbps within the 2.4 GHz band. A higher data rate is achieved by using a more complex modulation technique. The 802.11b specification quickly led to product offerings, including chipsets, PC cards, access points, and systems. Apple Computer was the first company to offer 802.11b products, with its iBook portable computer using the AirPort wireless network option. Other companies, including Cisco, 3Com, and Dell, have followed. Although these new products are all based on the same standard, there is always a concern whether products from different vendors will successfully interoperate. To meet this concern, the Wireless Ethernet Compatibility Alliance (now called The Wi-Fi Alliance) created a test suite to certify interoperability for 802.11b products. Interoperability tests have been conducted, and a number of products have achieved certification.

One other concern for both the original 802.11 and the 802.11b products is interference with other systems that operate in the 2.4-GHz band, such as Bluetooth, HomeRF, and many other devices that use the same portion of the spectrum (including baby monitors and garage door openers). A coexistence study group (IEEE 802.15) is examining this issue and so far the prospects are encouraging.

IEEE 802.11a   Although 802.11b achieved a certain level of success, its limited data rate results in limited appeal. To meet the needs for a truly high-speed LAN, **IEEE 802.11a** was developed. IEEE 802.11a makes use of the frequency band called the Universal Networking Information Infrastructure (UNNI), which is divided into three parts. The UNNI-1 band (5.15 to 5.25 GHz) is intended for indoor use; the UNNI-2 band (5.25 to 5.35 GHz) can be used either indoor or outdoor, and the UNNI-3 band (5.725 to 5.825 GHz) is for outdoor use.

Unlike the 2.4-GHz specifications, IEEE 802.11a does not use a spread spectrum scheme but rather uses **orthogonal frequency division multiplexing (OFDM)**. OFDM, also called *multicarrier modulation*, uses multiple carrier signals (up to 52) at different frequencies, sending some of the bits on each channel. The possible data rates for IEEE 802.11a are 6, 9, 12, 18, 24, 36, 48, and 54 Mbps.

At high data rates, OFDM is particularly effective in dealing with a major problem with wireless networks known as **multipath interference**. The essence of the problem is that in a transmission from one antenna to another, multiple copies of the signal may be received, one by a direct line of sight and other copies of the signal by reflection off objects in the vicinity. Because these signals travel different paths of different lengths, they arrive at slightly different times, causing interference. The higher the data rate, the more damaging the interference. With OFDM, instead of sending a single data stream at a high data rate over a given channel, the channel is broken up into many subchannels and a portion or the data stream is sent on each subchannel. Thus, roughly speaking, if there are 10 subchannels, each carries a portion of the data stream at a data rate of only 1/10 of the original data rate. For a more detailed discussion of multipath interference and OFDM, see Appendix I.

IEEE 802.11g   Although 802.11a offered higher data rates than 802.11b, acceptance of this new scheme was limiteds. This is because the equipment was relatively expensive and the scheme is not compatible with either the original 802.11 or 802.11b. Instead manufacturers and customers turned to a more recent standard, IEEE 802.11g.

Table 11.5 Estimated Distance (m) Versus Data Rate

Data Rate (Mbps)	802.11b	802.11a	802.11g
1	90+	—	90 +
2	75	—	75
5.5(b)/6(a/g)	60	60+	65
9	—	50	55
11(b)/12(a/g)	50	45	50
18	—	40	50
24	—	30	45
36	—	25	35
48	—	15	25
54	—	10	20

IEEE 802.11g is a higher-speed extension to IEEE 802.11b, providing data rates up to 54 Mbps, matching IEEE 802.11a. Like 802.11b, 802.11g operates in the 2.4-GHz range and thus the two are compatible. The standard is designed so that 802.11b devices will work when connected to an 802.11g AP, and 802.11g devices will work when connected to an 802.11b AP, in both cases using the lower 802.11b data rate.

IEEE 802.11g offers a wider array of data rate and modulation scheme options. At higher data rates, 802.11g adopts the 802.11a OFDM scheme, adapted for the 2.4 GHz rate; this is referred to as ERP-OFDM, with ERP standing for extended rate physical layer.

The IEEE 802.11 standards do not include a specification of speed versus distance objectives. Different vendors will give different values, depending on environment. Table 11.5, based on [LAYL04] gives estimated values for a typical office environment.

IEEE 802.11n With increasing demands being placed on wireless LANs, the 802.11 committee looked for ways to increase the data throughput and overall capacity of 802.11 networks. The goal of this effort is to not just increase the bit rate of the transmitting antennas but to increase the effective throughput of the network. Increasing effective throughput involves not only looking at the signal encoding scheme, but also at the antenna architecture and the MAC frame structure. The result of these efforts is a package of improvements and enhancements embodied in IEEE 802.11n. This standard is defined to operate in both the 2.4-GHz and the 5-GHz bands and can therefore be made upwardly compatible with either 802.11a or 802.11b/g.

IEEE 802.11n embodies changes in three general areas: use of MIMO, enhancements in radio transmission, and MAC enhancements. We briefly examine each of these.

Multiple-input-multiple-output (MIMO) antenna architecture is the most important of the enhancements provided by 802.11n. A discussion of MIMO is beyond our scope, so we content ourselves with a brief overview (see Figure 11.6). In a

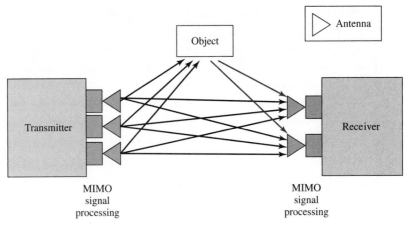

Figure 11.6 MIMO Scheme

MIMO scheme, the transmitter employs multiple antennas. The source data stream is divided into *n* substreams, one for each of the *n* transmitting antennas. The individual substreams are the input to the transmitting antennas (multiple input). At the receiving end, *m* antennas receive the transmissions from the *n* source antennas via a combination of line-of-sight transmission and multipath. The outputs from the *m* receiving antennas (multiple output) are combined with the signals from the other receive radios. With a lot of complex math, the result is a much better receive signal than can be achieved with either a single antenna802.11n defines a number of different combinations for the number of transmitters and the number of receivers, from 2 × 1 to 4 × 4. Each additional transmitter or receiver in the system increases the SNR (signal-to-noise ratio). However, the incremental gains from each additional transmitter or receiver diminish rapidly. The gain in SNR is large for each step from 2 × 1 to 2 × 2 and to 3 × 2, but the improvement with 3 × 3 and beyond is relatively small [CISC07].

In addition to MIMO, 802.11n makes a number of changes in the **radio transmission scheme** to increase capacity. The most significant of these techniques, known as channel bonding, combines two 20-MHz channels to create a 40-MHz channel. Using OFDM, this allows for twice as many subchannels, doubling the transmission rate.

Finally, 802.11 provides some **MAC enhancements**. The most significant change is to aggregate multiple MAC frames into a single block for transmission. Once a station acquires the medium for transmission, it can transmit long packets without significant delays between transmissions. The receiver sends a single block acknowledgement. Frame aggregation can result in significantly improved efficiency in the use of the transmission capacity.

Figure 11.7 gives an indication of the effectiveness of 802.11n compared to 802.11g [DEBE07]. The chart shows the average throughput per user on a shared system. As expected, the more active users competing for the wireless capacity, the smaller the average throughput per user. IEEE 802.11n provides a significant improvement, especially for networks in which a small number of users are actively competing for transmission time.

Figure 11.7   Average Throughput per User

11.4 IEEE 802.11 SECURITY CONSIDERATIONS

There are two characteristics of a wired LAN that are not inherent in a wireless LAN.

1. In order to transmit over a wired LAN, a station must be physically connected to the LAN. On the other hand, with a wireless LAN, any station within radio range of the other devices on the LAN can transmit. In a sense, there is a form of authentication with a wired LAN, in that it requires some positive and presumably observable action to connect a station to a wired LAN.

2. Similarly, in order to receive a transmission from a station that is part of a wired LAN, the receiving station must also be attached to the wired LAN. On the other hand, with a wireless LAN, any station within radio range can receive. Thus, a wired LAN provides a degree of privacy, limiting reception of data to stations connected to the LAN.

Access and Privacy Services

IEEE 802.11 defines three services that provide a wireless LAN with the two features just mentioned:

- **Authentication:** Used to establish the identity of stations to each other. In a wired LAN, it is generally assumed that access to a physical connection conveys authority to connect to the LAN. This is not a valid assumption for a wireless LAN, in which connectivity is achieved simply by having an attached antenna that is properly tuned. The authentication service is used by stations to establish their identity with stations they wish to communicate with. IEEE 802.11 supports several authentication schemes and allows for expansion of the functionality of these schemes. The standard does not mandate any particular authentication scheme, which could range from relatively unsecure handshaking to public-key encryption schemes. However, IEEE 802.11 requires mutually acceptable, successful authentication before a station can establish an association with an AP.

- **Deauthentication:** This service is invoked whenever an existing authentication is to be terminated.

- **Privacy:** Used to prevent the contents of messages from being read by other than the intended recipient. The standard provides for the optional use of encryption to assure privacy.

Wireless LAN Security Standards

The original 802.11 specification included a set of security features for privacy and authentication that, unfortunately, were quite weak. For **privacy**, 802.11 defined the Wired Equivalent Privacy (WEP) algorithm. The privacy portion of the 802.11 standard contained major weaknesses. Subsequent to the development of WEP, the 802.11i task group has developed a set of capabilities to address the WLAN security issues. In order to accelerate the introduction of strong security into WLANs, the Wi-Fi Alliance promulgated **Wi-Fi Protected Access (WPA)** as a Wi-Fi standard. WPA is a set of security mechanisms that eliminates most 802.11 security issues and was based on the current state of the 802.11i standard. As 802.11i evolves, WPA will evolve to maintain compatibility.

WPA is examined in Chapter 19.

APPLICATION NOTE

Deploying Wireless LANs

Many organizations are faced with the problem of deciding whether or not to deploy a wireless local area network or WLAN This problem is exacerbated by several issues regarding WLANs, such as security, management of deployed devices, and a confusing array of standards. Finally, deployment of a WLAN increases the responsibility of the support staff without necessarily providing them with the training or expertise to manage it. That said, there are a few reasons for deploying a wireless LAN: mobility, reduction in the cost of an installation, speed of deployment, ad hoc networking, and ability to connect to geographically remote nodes. The first thing that an organization should probably ask itself is if a WLAN is a requirement or simply something that would be nice to have. Many companies decide not to deploy a WLAN because of the security hole that the wireless network represents. It is understandable that it may simply be too much of a risk or a management nightmare to deploy. This approach comes with some danger, especially if the company also decides not to bother with wireless training. Most end user equipment has built-in wireless capability. In addition, employees, students, and visitors will deploy wireless equipment without company approval. This is not usually done to attack the company network; it is simply because more and more devices come equipped with wireless capability. Laptops are a very good example of this. Wireless devices also have the annoying ability to find connections automatically. This is made worse with operating systems like Windows XP, which handles many wireless issues transparently and has the functionality of connection sharing. Connection sharing will allow multiple users to access the network through a single computer's network connection. Further, the Windows wireless networking client does not provide very many control features. If you decide not to deploy a wireless network, you still should prepare for someone else deploying one within your organization.

Choosing the right standard can be very difficult. The 802.11 family has had several generations, with 802.11b being the most successful. However, there have been significant problems with the 802.11b standard, including relatively low bandwidth, a small number of access points able to operate in an area, and interference from other devices sharing the 2.4-GHz portion of the spectrum.

The next generation standards, 802.11a and 802.11g, both attempt to address these problems, with 802.11a being the more successful at avoiding interference because it has moved up to 5 GHz. This introduces the problem of smaller coverage areas; the higher frequencies do not propagate as far. If you already have a wireless network, then your decision may be slightly different than if you are deploying one from scratch. In order to be compatible with an existing 802.11b network, you may opt for 802.11g, which has higher data capacity but still can communicate directly with 802.11b nodes. 802.11g has been the choice for most businesses. Depending on the intended use, new installations may decide on one of the new standards exclusively. Remember that there is a tremendous amount of pre-existing 802.11b equipment so a decision must be made about its support. For many, 802.11a will be the best choice because of its high data rates, low interference and the number of available channels. The strength of 802.11a is also its weakness. A basic rule of thumb for radio based communication is that the higher the frequency, the shorter the transmission distance. Thus, because it uses higher frequencies, 802.11a has a shorter range than 802.11b. Another rule of thumb it that as the frequency increases, the easier it is to disrupt the signal. This last problem is highly dependent on your operating environment. For these reasons, 802.11g may be the best choice as it closely matches the model for 802.11b.

Our last discussion point will be about security. While there is never a silver bullet regarding security measures, there are some basic practices that will help reduce exposure and vulnerability. These include the following:

Place access points outside the company firewall to ensure that company data are not broadcast.

Turn on WEP or WPA-PSK. They do have their problems, but they will stop most casual eavesdroppers and bandwidth hogs.

Run access points back to switches instead of hubs, to provide increased traffic filtering. Complete a wireless site survey to determine your level of exposure.

Use a VPN for wireless nodes.

Deploy some basic layer 2 or 3 filters for securing access.

When in doubt, use encryption on your data.

Understand that most problems (both malicious and accidental) do not come from external hackers, but from internal users.

(Continued)

The real problem with wireless communication is that very few network administrators have spent much time with it. As a result, there is a tremendous lack of understanding and experience with the issues. While this short discussion is not meant to be the ultimate guide to wireless networking, it should help you understand some of the larger problems and thought processes associated with WLANs.

11.5 SUMMARY

In recent years, a whole new class of local area networks has arrived to provide an alternative to LANs based on twisted pair, coaxial cable, and optical fiber: wireless LANs. The key advantages of the wireless LAN are that it eliminates the wiring cost, which is often the most costly component of a LAN, and that it accommodates mobile workstations.

Wireless LANs use one of three transmission techniques: spread spectrum, narrowband microwave, and infrared. The most significant set of standards defining wireless LANs are those defined by the IEEE 802.11 committee.

11.6 RECOMMENDED READING AND WEB SITES

[ROSH04] provides a technical treatment of IEEE 802.11. Another useful book is [BING02]. [SHOE02] provides an overview of IEEE 802.11g. [CISC07] is a detailed treatment of IEEE 802.11n. [SKOR08] is a thorough examination of the 802.11n MAC frame aggregation scheme.

BING02 Bing, B. *Wireless Local Area Networks*. New York: Wiley, 2002.

CISC07 Cisco Systems, Inc. " 802.11n: The Next Generation of Wireless Performance." Cisco White Paper, 2007. cisco.com

ROSH04 Roshan, P., and Leary, J. *802.11 Wireless LAN Fundamentals*. Indianapolis: Cisco Press, 2004.

SHOE02 Shoemaker, M. "IEEE 802.11g Jells as Applications Mount." *Communications System Design*, April 2002. (www.commsdesign.com)

SKOR08 Skordoulis, D., et al. "IEEE 802.11n MAC Frame Aggregation Mechanisms for Next-Generation High-Throughput WLANs." *IEEE Wireless Communications*, February 2008.

Recommended Web sites:

- **Wireless LAN Association:** Gives an introduction to the technology, including a discussion of implementation considerations and case studies from users. Links to related sites.

- **The IEEE 802.11 Wireless LAN Working Group:** Contains working group documents plus discussion archives.
- **Wi-Fi Alliance:** An industry group promoting the interoperability of 802.11 products with each other and with Ethernet.

11.7 KEY TERMS, REVIEW QUESTIONS, AND PROBLEMS

Key Terms

access point (AP)	MIMO	service area
ad hoc networking	narrowband microwave LAN	spread spectrum LAN
IEEE 802.11	nomadic access	wireless LAN
infrared LAN	OFDM	

Review Questions

11.1 List and briefly define four application areas for wireless LANs.

11.2 List and briefly define key requirements for wireless LANs.

11.3 What is the difference between a single-cell and a multiple-cell wireless LAN?

11.4 What is the basic building block of an 802.11 WLAN?

11.5 Define an extended service set.

11.6 List and briefly define IEEE 802.11 services.

11.7 What is the difference between an access point and a portal?

11.8 Is a distribution system a wireless network?

11.9 How is the concept of an association related to that of mobility?

11.10 In general terms, what application areas are supported by Bluetooth?

11.11 What is the difference between a core specification and a profile specification?

11.12 What is a usage model?

Problems

Answer the following questions about your wireless network:

11.1 How much do you know about your wireless network?
  a. What is the SSID?
  b. Who is the equipment vendor?
  c. What standard are you using?
  d. What is the size of the network?

11.2 Using what you know about wired and wireless networks, draw the topology of your network.

11.3 There are many free tools and applications available for helping decipher wireless networks. One of the most popular is Netstumbler. Obtain the software at www.netstumbler.com and follow the links for downloads. The site has a list of supported wireless cards. Using the Netstumbler software, determine the following:
  a. How many access points in your network have the same SSID?
  b. What is your signal strength to your access point?
  c. How many other wireless networks and access points can you find?

11.4 Most wireless cards come with a small set of applications that can perform tasks similar to Netstumbler. Using your own client software, determine the same items you did with Netstumbler. Do they agree?

11.5 Try this experiment: How far can you go and still be connected to your network? This will depend to a large extent on your physical environment.

11.6 Compare and contrast wired and wireless LANs. What unique concerns must be addressed by the designer of a wireless LAN network? RIC

11.7 Two documents related to safety concerns associated with wireless media are the FCC OET-65 Bulletin and the ANSI/IEEE C95.1-1999. Briefly describe the purpose of these documents and briefly outline the safety concerns associated with wireless LAN technology. RIC

St. Luke's Episcopal Hospital

Hospitals have been some of the earliest adopters of wireless local area networks (WLANs). The user population is typically mobile and spread out across a number of buildings, with a need to enter and access data in real time. St. Luke's Episcopal Hospital in Houston, Texas is a good example of a hospital that has made effective use of a WLAN. Their wireless network is distributed throughout several hospital buildings and used in many different applications. Examples include the following:

- **Diagnosing patients and charting their progress:** Doctors and nurses use carts equipped with wireless laptops for instant access to an application that manages patient data.

- **Prescriptions:** Medications are dispensed from a cart that is wheeled from room to room. Clinician uses a wireless scanner to scan the patient's ID bracelet, the clinician's own ID, and the bar code on the medicine. If a prescription order has been changed or cancelled, the clinician will know immediately because the mobile device displays current patient data.

- **Critical care units:** These areas use the WLAN because running hard wires would mean moving ceiling panels. The dust and microbes that such work stirs up would pose a threat to patients.

- **Case management:** The case managers in the Utilization Management Department use the WLAN to document patient reviews, insurance calls/authorization information, and denial information. The wireless session enables real time access to information that ensures the correct level of care for a patient and/or timely discharge.

- **Blood pressure carts:** These carts are moved from one patient to another as the hospital staff collects and records blood pressure information.

- **Nutrition and diet:** Dietary service representatives collect patient menus at each nursing unit and enter them as they go. This allows more menus to be submitted before the cutoff time, giving more patients more choice. The dietitian can also see current patient information, such as supplement or tube feeding data, and view what the patient actually received for a certain meal.

The hospital spans three buildings and treats over 500,000 patients each year.

ORIGINAL WLAN

St. Luke's first WLAN was deployed in January 1998 in a single building using access points (APs) made by Proxim (www.proxim.com). The AP is a standalone device that functions as an interface between a local IEEE 802.11 cell (basic service set) and other cells, conforming to the IEEE 802.11 architecture of Figure 11.4. A principal goal of this initial installation was to improve efficiency. However, it sometimes had the opposite effect. The main problem was dropped connections. As a user moved about the building, there was a tendency for the WLAN to drop the connection rather than performing the desired handoff to another access point. As a result, a user had to reestablish the connection, log into the application again, and reenter whatever data might have been lost.

There were physical problems as well. The walls in part of the building were constructed around chicken wire, which interfered with radio waves. Some patients' rooms were located in pockets with weak radio signals. For these rooms, a nurse or doctor would sometimes lose a connection and have to step out into the hallway to reconnect. Microwave ovens in the kitchenettes on each floor were also a source of interference.

Finally, as more users were added to the system, the Proxim APs, with a capacity of 1.2 Mbps, became increasingly inadequate, causing ongoing performance issues.

ENHANCED LAN

To overcome the problems with their original WLAN and reap the potential benefits listed earlier in this case study, St. Luke's made two changes [CONR03, NETM03]. First, the hospital phased out the Proxim APs and replaced them with Cisco Aironet (www.aironet.com) APs. The Cisco APs, using IEEE 802.11b, operate at 11 Mbps. Also, the Cisco APs use direct sequence spread spectrum (DSSS), which is more reliable than the frequency-hopping technique used in the Proxim APs.

The second measure taken by St Luke's was to acquire a software solution from NetMotion Wireless (netmotionwireless.com) called Mobility. The basic layout of the Mobility solution is shown in Figure V.1. Mobility software is installed in each wireless client device (typically a laptop or handheld) and in two NetMotion servers whose task is to maintain connections. The two servers provide a backup capability in case one server fails. The Mobility software maintains the state of an application even if a wireless device moves out of range, experiences interference, or switches to standby mode. When a user comes back into range or switches into active mode, the user's application resumes where it left off.

In essence, Mobility works as follows: Upon connecting, each Mobility client is assigned a virtual IP address by the Mobility server on the wired network. The Mobility server manages network traffic on behalf of the client, intercepting packets destined for the client's virtual address and forwarding them to the client's current POP (point of presence) address. While the POP address may change when the device moves to a different subnet, from one coverage area to another, or even from one network to another, the virtual address remains constant while any connections

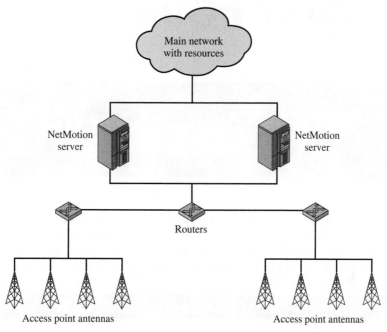

Figure V.1 St. Luke's Wireless LAN

are active. Thus, the Mobility server is a proxy device inserted between a client device and an application server.

As of early 2003, about one-third of the patient care area (21 floors) is covered by the WLAN, consisting of approximately 270 wireless devices. The other floors are still using paper charts. The transition to a wireless, paperless operation has taken longer than expected. One reason is simply a matter of staff members accepting a more computerized working environment and training them to use the devices properly.

Discussion Questions

1. Visit the NetMotion Web site and learn more about the technical approach of the Mobility architecture. Discuss how this approach provides the mobility features of the product.

2. Discuss potential problems that can occur in a WLAN environment at St. Luke's.

PART FOUR

Wide Area Networks

Part Four examines the internal mechanisms and user-network interfaces that have been developed to support voice, data, and multimedia communications over long-distance networks. The traditional technologies of packet switching and circuit switching are examined, as well as the more recent ATM and wireless WANs.

ROAD MAP FOR PART FOUR

Chapter 12 Circuit Switching and Packet Switching

Chapter 12 introduces the concept of network switching techniques. The chapter then introduces the two traditional approaches to wide area networking: circuit switching and packet switching. With circuit switching, a key design issue is that of control signaling, and this area is explored. The remainder of Chapter 12 introduces packet-switching technology. The chapter covers the basic principles of packet switching and analyzes datagram and virtual circuit approaches.

Chapter 13 Frame Relay and ATM

Frame relay is in essence a packet-switching technology, but it is more streamlined and efficient than traditional packet switching and is designed to support higher data rates. ATM, also known as cell relay, is also a packet-switching technology; it is even more streamlined than frame relay and is designed for very high data rates. Chapter 13 looks at the protocols and design issues involved in both frame relay and ATM.

Chapter 14 Wireless WANs

Chapter 14 begins with a discussion of the important design issues related to cellular wireless networks. The chapter then looks at issues of multiple access, with a special emphasis on code-division multiple access (CDMA), which is becoming the dominant cellular transmission technology. Chapter 14 next looks at issues related to third-generation cellular networks. The remainder of Chapter 14 deals with satellite communications.

CIRCUIT SWITCHING AND PACKET SWITCHING

12.1 Switching Techniques

12.2 Circuit-Switching Networks
Basic Operation
Control Signaling
Softswitch Architecture

12.3 Packet-Switching Networks
Basic Operation
Switching Technique

12.4 Traditional Wide Area Network Alternatives
Wide Area Networks for Voice
Wide Area Networks for Data

12.5 Summary

12.6 Recommended Reading and Web Sites

12.7 Key Terms, Review Questions, and Problems

Chapter Objectives

After reading this chapter, you should be able to

♦ Explain the need for a communications network for wide area voice and data communications.

♦ Define circuit switching and describe the key elements of circuit-switching networks.

♦ Discuss the important applications of circuit switching, including public networks, private networks, and software-defined networks.

♦ Define packet switching and describe the key elements of packet-switching technology.

♦ Discuss the important applications of packet switching, including public and private networks.

♦ Discuss the relative merits of circuit switching and packet switching and analyze the circumstances for which each is most appropriate.

This chapter begins with a general discussion of switched communications networks. The remainder of the chapter focuses on wide area networks and, in particular, on traditional approaches to wide area network design: circuit switching and packet switching.

12.1 SWITCHING TECHNIQUES

For transmission of data[1] beyond a local area, communication is typically achieved by transmitting data from source to destination through a network of intermediate switching nodes; this switched network design is typically used to implement LANs as well. The switching nodes are not concerned with the content of the data; rather, their purpose is to provide a switching facility that will move the data from node to node until they reach their destination. Figure 12.1 illustrates a simple network. The end devices that wish to communicate may be referred to as *stations*. The stations may be computers, terminals, telephones, or other communicating devices. We shall refer to the switching devices whose purpose is to provide communication as *nodes*. The nodes are connected to one another in some topology by transmission links. Each station attaches to a node, and the collection of nodes is referred to as a *communications network*.

In a *switched communication network*, data entering the network from a station are routed to the destination by being switched from node to node. For example, in Figure 12.1, data from station A intended for station F are sent to node 4. They may then be routed via nodes 5 and 6 or nodes 7 and 6 to the destination. Several observations are in order:

1. Some nodes connect only to other nodes (e.g., 5 and 7). Their sole task is the internal (to the network) switching of data. Other nodes have one or more

---

[1]We use this term here in a very general sense, to include audio, image, and video, as well as ordinary data (e.g., numerical, text).

path between two stations. That path is a connected sequence of links between network nodes. On each physical link, a channel is dedicated to the connection. The most common example of circuit switching is the telephone network.

Communication via circuit switching involves three phases, which can be explained with reference to Figure 12.1.

1. **Circuit establishment.** Before any signals can be transmitted, an end-to-end (station-to-station) circuit must be established. For example, station A sends a request to node 4 requesting a connection to station E. Typically, the link from A to 4 is a dedicated line, so that part of the connection already exists. Node 4 must find the next leg in a route leading to E. Based on routing information and measures of availability and perhaps cost, node 4 selects the link to node 5, allocates a free channel (using FDM or TDM) on that link and sends a message requesting connection to E. So far, a dedicated path has been established from A through 4 to 5. Because a number of stations may attach to 4, it must be able to establish internal paths from multiple stations to multiple nodes. How this is done is discussed later in this section. The remainder of the process proceeds similarly. Node 5 allocates a channel to node 6 and internally ties that channel to the channel from node 4. Node 6 completes the connection to E. In completing the connection, a test is made to determine if E is busy or is prepared to accept the connection.

2. **Data transfer.** Data can now be transmitted from A through the network to E. The transmission may be analog voice, digitized voice, or binary data, depending on the nature of the network. As the carriers evolve to fully integrated digital networks, the use of digital (binary) transmission for both voice and data is becoming the dominant method. The path is as follows: A-4 link, internal switching through 4, 4-5 channel, internal switching through 5, 5-6 channel, internal switching through 6, 6-E link. Generally, the connection is full duplex, and signals may be transmitted in both directions simultaneously.

3. **Circuit disconnect.** After some period of data transfer, the connection is terminated, usually by the action of one of the two stations. Signals must be propagated to nodes 4, 5, and 6 to deallocate the dedicated resources.

Note that the connection path is established before data transmission begins. Thus, channel capacity must be reserved between each pair of nodes in the path and each node must have available internal switching capacity to handle the requested connection. The switches must have the intelligence to make these allocations and to devise a route through the network.

Circuit switching can be rather inefficient. Channel capacity is dedicated for the duration of a connection, even if no data are being transferred. For a voice connection, utilization may be rather high, but it still does not approach 100%. For a client/server connection, the capacity may be idle during most of the time of the connection. In terms of performance, there is a delay prior to signal transfer for call establishment. However, once the circuit is established, the network is effectively transparent to the users. Information is transmitted at a fixed data rate with no delay other than the propagation delay through the transmission links. The delay at each node is negligible.

Figure 12.1 Simple Switching Network

stations attached as well; in addition to their switching functions, such
accept data from and deliver data to the attached stations.

2. Node-station links are generally dedicated point-to-point links. Node-nod
are usually multiplexed links, using either frequency division multip
(FDM) or some form of time division multiplexing (TDM).

3. Usually, the network is not fully connected; that is, there is not a direc
tween every possible pair of nodes. However, it is always desirab
more than one possible path through the network for each pair
This enhances the reliability of the network.

Two different technologies are used in wide area switched n
switching and packet switching. These two technologies differ in t'
switch information from one link to another on the way from sou
In the remainder of this chapter, we look at the details of both o'

12.2 CIRCUIT-SWITCHING NETWORKS

Basic Operation

Circuit switching is still the dominant technology for
although the volume of packet-based voice commun'
munication via circuit switching implies that there

Table 12.1 Applications of Circuit Switching and Packet Switching

Circuit Switching	Packet Switching
Public Telephone Network Provide interconnection for two-way voice exchange between attached telephones. Calls can be placed between any two subscribers on a national and international basis. This type of network handles an increasing volume of data traffic.	**Public Data Network (PDN)/Value-Added Network (VAN)** Provide a wide area data communications facility for computers and terminals. The network is a shared resource, owned by a provider who sells the capacity to others. Thus, it functions as a utility service for a number of subscriber communities.
Private Branch Exchange Provide a telephone and data exchange capability within a single building or cluster of buildings. Calls can be placed between any two subscribers within the local site; interconnection is also provided to public or private wide area circuit-switched networks.	**Private Packet-Switching Network** Provide a shared resource for one organization's computers and terminals. A private packet-switching network is justified if there are a substantial number of devices with a substantial amount of traffic in one organization.
Private Wide Area Network Provide interconnection among a number of sites. Generally used to interconnect PBXs that are part of the same organization.	
Data Switch Provide for the interconnection of terminals and computers within a local site.	

Circuit switching was developed to handle voice traffic but is now also used for data traffic. Some of the key applications of circuit switching are summarized in Table 12.1. The best-known example of a circuit-switching network is the public telephone network (Figure 12.2). This is actually a collection of national networks interconnected to form the international service. Although originally designed and implemented to service analog telephone subscribers, it handles substantial data traffic via

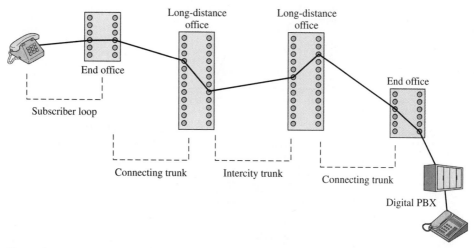

Figure 12.2 Example Connection over a Public Circuit-Switching Network

modem and is now primarily a digital network. Another well-known application of circuit switching is the private branch exchange (PBX), used to interconnect telephones within a building or office. Circuit switching is also used in private networks. Typically, such a network is set up by a corporation or other large organization to interconnect its various sites. Such a network usually consists of PBX systems at each site interconnected by dedicated, leased lines obtained from a carrier, such as AT&T.

A public telecommunications network can be described using four generic architectural components:

- **Subscribers:** The devices that attach to the network. It is still the case that most subscriber devices to public telecommunications networks are telephones, but the percentage of data traffic increases year by year.

- **Subscriber line:** The link between the subscriber and the network, also referred to as the *subscriber loop* or *local loop*. Almost all local loop connections use twisted-pair wire. The length of a local loop is typically in a range from a few kilometers to a few tens of kilometers.

- **Exchanges:** The switching centers in the network. A switching center that directly supports subscribers is known as an end office. Typically, an end office will support many thousands of subscribers in a localized area. There are over 19,000 end offices in the United States, so it is clearly impractical for each end office to have a direct link to each of the other end offices; this would require on the order of 2×10^8 links. Rather, intermediate switching nodes are used.

- **Trunks:** The branches between exchanges. Trunks carry multiple voice-frequency circuits using either FDM or synchronous TDM. These are also referred to as *carrier systems*.

Subscribers connect directly to an end office, which switches traffic between subscribers and between a subscriber and other exchanges. The other exchanges are responsible for routing and switching traffic between end offices. This distinction is shown in Figure 12.3. To connect two subscribers attached to the same end office, a

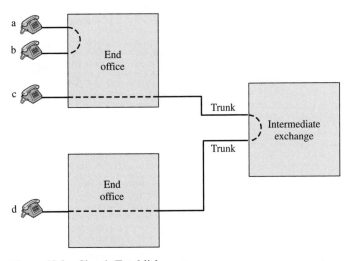

Figure 12.3 Circuit Establishment

circuit is set up between them in the same fashion as described before. If two subscribers connect to different end offices, a circuit between them consists of a chain of circuits through one or more intermediate offices. In the figure, a connection is established between lines a and b by simply setting up the connection through the end office. The connection between c and d is more complex. In c's end office, a connection is established between line c and one channel on a TDM trunk to the intermediate switch. In the intermediate switch, that channel is connected to a channel on a TDM trunk to d's end office. In that end office, the channel is connected to line d.

Circuit-switching technology has been driven by its use to carry voice traffic. One of the key requirements for voice traffic is that there must be virtually no transmission delay and certainly no variation in delay. A constant signal transmission rate must be maintained, because transmission and reception occur at the same signal rate. These requirements are necessary to allow normal human conversation. Further, the quality of the received signal must be sufficiently high to provide, at a minimum, intelligibility.

Circuit switching achieved its widespread, dominant position because it is well suited to the analog transmission of voice signals. In today's digital world, its inefficiencies are more apparent. However, despite the inefficiency, circuit switching is and will remain an attractive choice for both local area and wide area networking. One of its key strengths is that it is transparent. Once a circuit is established, it appears like a direct connection to the two attached stations; no special networking logic is needed at the station.

Control Signaling

Control signals are the means by which the network is managed and by which calls are established, maintained, and terminated. Both call management and overall network management require that information be exchanged between subscriber and switch, among switches, and between switch and network management center. For a large public telecommunications network, a relatively complex control signaling scheme is required.

SIGNALING FUNCTIONS Control signals affect many aspects of network behavior, including both network services visible to the subscriber and internal mechanisms. As networks become more complex, the number of functions performed by control signaling necessarily grows. The following functions are among the most important:

1. Audible communication with the subscriber, including dial tone, ringing tone, busy signal, and so on.
2. Transmission of the number dialed to switching offices that will attempt to complete a connection.
3. Transmission of information between switches indicating that a call cannot be completed.
4. Transmission of information between switches indicating that a call has ended and that the path can be disconnected.
5. A signal to make a telephone ring.

6. Transmission of information used for billing purposes.

7. Transmission of information giving the status of equipment or trunks in the network. This information may be used for routing and maintenance purposes.

8. Transmission of information used in diagnosing and isolating system failures.

9. Control of special equipment such as satellite channel equipment.

As an example of the use of control signaling, consider a typical telephone connection sequence from one line to another in the same central office:

1. Prior to the call, both telephones are not in use (on-hook). The call begins when one subscriber lifts the receiver (off-hook); this action is automatically signaled to the end office switch.

2. The switch responds with an audible dial tone, signaling the subscriber that a number may be dialed.

3. The caller dials a number, which is communicated as a called address to the switch.

4. If the called subscriber is not busy, the switch alerts that subscriber to an incoming call by sending a ringing signal, which causes the telephone to ring.

5. Feedback is provided to the calling subscriber by the switch:

   a. If the called subscriber is not busy, the switch returns an audible ringing tone to the caller while the ringing signal is being sent to the called subscriber.

   b. If the called subscriber is busy, the switch sends an audible busy signal to the caller.

   c. If the call cannot be completed through the switch, the switch sends an audible "reorder" message to the caller.

6. The called party accepts the call by lifting the receiver (off-hook), which is automatically signaled to the switch.

7. The switch terminates the ringing signal and the audible ringing tone, and establishes a connection between the two subscribers.

8. The connection is released when either subscriber hangs up.

When the called subscriber is attached to a different switch than the calling subscriber, the following switch-to-switch trunk signaling functions are required:

1. The originating switch seizes an idle interswitch trunk and sends an off-hook indication on the trunk so that the address may be communicated.

2. The terminating switch sends an off-hook followed by an on-hook signal, known as a "wink." This indicates a register-ready status.

3. The originating switch sends the address digits to the terminating switch.

This example illustrates some of the functions performed using control signals. Signaling can also be classified functionally as supervisory, address, call information, and network management.

The term **supervisory** is generally used to refer to control functions that have a binary character (true/false; on/off), such as request for service, answer, alerting, and return to idle. They deal with the availability of the called subscriber and of the needed network resources. Supervisory control signals are used to determine if a needed resource is available and, if so, to seize it. They are also used to communicate the status of requested resources.

Address signals identify a subscriber. Initially, an address signal is generated by a calling subscriber when dialing a telephone number. The resulting address may be propagated through the network to support the routing function and to locate and ring the called subscriber's phone.

The term **call information** refers to those signals that provide information to the subscriber about the status of a call. This is in contrast to internal control signals between switches used in call establishment and termination. Such internal signals are analog or digital electrical messages. In contrast, call information signals are audible tones that can be heard by the caller or an operator with the proper phone set.

Supervisory, address, and call information control signals are directly involved in the establishment and termination of a call. **Network management** signals are used for the maintenance, troubleshooting, and overall operation of the network. Such signals may be in the form of messages, such as a list of preplanned routes being sent to a station to update its routing tables. These signals cover a broad scope, and it is this category that will expand most with the increasing complexity of switched networks.

LOCATION OF SIGNALING   Control signaling needs to be considered in two contexts: signaling between a subscriber and the network, and signaling within the network. Typically, signaling operates differently within these two contexts.

Signaling between a telephone or other subscriber device and the switching office to which it attaches is, to a large extent, determined by the characteristics of the subscriber device and the needs of the human user. Signals within the network are entirely computer-to-computer. Internal signaling is concerned not only with the management of subscriber calls but also with the management of the network itself. Thus, for internal signaling, a more complex repertoire of commands, responses, and set of parameters is needed.

Because two different signaling techniques are used, the local switching office to which the subscriber is attached must provide a mapping between the relatively less complex signaling technique used by the subscriber and the more complex technique used within the network. For intranetwork signaling, Signaling System Number 7 (SS7) is used on most digital networks.

COMMON CHANNEL SIGNALING   Traditional control signaling in circuit-switching networks has been on a per-trunk or **inchannel** basis. With inchannel signaling, the same channel is used to carry control signals as is used to carry the call to which the control signals relate. Such signaling begins at the originating subscriber and follows the same path as the call itself. This has the merit that no additional transmission facilities are needed for signaling; the facilities for voice transmission are shared with control signaling.

As public telecommunications networks become more complex and provide a richer set of services, the drawbacks of inchannel signaling become more apparent. The information transfer rate is quite limited with inchannel signaling because the same capacity is shared with the information being transmitted. With such limits, it is difficult to accommodate, in a timely fashion, any but the simplest form of control messages. To take advantage of the potential services and to cope with the increasing complexity of evolving network technology, a richer and more powerful control signal repertoire is needed.

A second drawback of inchannel signaling is the amount of delay from the time a subscriber enters an address (dials a number) and the connection is established. The requirement to reduce this delay is becoming more important as the network is used in new ways. For example, computer-controlled calls, such as with transaction processing, use relatively short messages; therefore, the call setup time represents an appreciable part of the total transaction time.

Both of these problems can be addressed with common channel signaling, in which control signals are carried over paths completely independent of the voice channels. One independent control signal path can carry the signals for a number of subscriber channels and hence is a common control channel for these subscriber channels.

Internal to the network, common channel signals are transmitted on paths that are logically distinct from those that carry the subscriber information. In some cases, these may be physically distinct transmission facilities; in other cases, separate logical channels on shared trunks are used. The common channel can be configured with the bandwidth required to carry control signals for a rich variety of functions. Thus, both the signaling protocol and the network architecture to support that protocol are more complex than inchannel signaling. However, the continuing drop in computer hardware costs makes common channel signaling increasingly attractive. The control signals are messages that are passed between switches and between a switch and the network management center. Thus, the control signaling portion of the network is in effect a distributed computer network carrying short messages.

With inchannel signaling, control signals from one switch are originated by a control processor and switched onto the outgoing channel. On the receiving end, the control signals must be switched from the voice channel into the control processor. With common channel signaling, the control signals are transferred directly from one control processor to another, without being tied to a voice signal. This is a simpler procedure and one that is less susceptible to accidental or intentional interference between subscriber and control signals. This is one of the main motivations for common channel signaling. Another key motivation for common channel signaling is that call setup time is reduced. Consider the sequence of events for call setup with inchannel signaling when more than one switch is involved. A control signal will be sent from one switch to the next in the intended path. At each switch, the control signal cannot be transferred through the switch to the next leg of the route until the associated circuit is established through that switch. With common channel signaling, forwarding of control information can overlap the circuit-setup process.

Common channel techniques can also be used external to the network, at the interface between the subscriber and the network. This is the case with ISDN (Integrated Digital Services Network) and many other digital networks. For external signaling, a logically distinct channel on the subscriber-network link is devoted to control signaling, used for setting up and tearing down connections on other logical channels on that link. Thus, a multiplexed link is controlled by a single channel over that link.

Softswitch Architecture

The latest trend in the development of circuit-switching technology is generally referred to as the softswitch. In essence, a softswitch is a general-purpose computer running specialized software that turns it into a smart phone switch. Softswitches cost significantly less than traditional circuit switches and can provide more functionality. In particular, in addition to handling the traditional circuit-switching functions, a softswitch can convert a stream of digitized voice bits into packets. This opens up a number of options for transmission, including the increasingly popular voice over IP (Internet Protocol) approach (VoIP).

In any telephone network switch, the most complex element is the software that controls call processing. This software performs call routing and implements call-processing logic for hundreds of custom calling features. Typically, this software runs on a proprietary processor that is integrated with the physical circuit-switching hardware. A more flexible approach is to physically separate the call processing function from the hardware switching function. In softswitch terminology, the physical switching function is performed by a **media gateway** (MG) and the call processing logic resides is a **media gateway controller** (MGC). Often, these are combined in to a single gateway module.

Figure 12.4, based on [COFF04], contrasts the architecture of a traditional PBX circuit switch with the softswitch architecture. The traditional digital PBX can

(a) Traditional PBX architecture

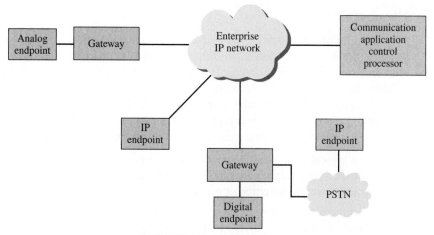

(b) IP-PBX (softswitch) architecture

Figure 12.4 Comparison between Traditional Circuit Switching and Softswitch accommodate both analog and digital endpoints. The most common endpoints are telephones; other endpoints are fax machines, modems, PDAs, and telephony applications running on laptop computers. The other typical components of a digital PBX include the following:

- **Control processor:** To run the software that operates the system features.
- **Modules:** House interface cards that provide endpoint interfaces to the switch. In the case of analog endpoints, the module interface converts between analog and digital.
- **Inter-module switching:** Allows the interconnection of ports in different modules, using circuit switching.

One module provides an interface to the public switched telephone network (PSTN).

Figure 12.4b illustrates, in general terms, the softswitch PBX architecture. The control processor is often an off-the-shelf server that runs communications application software on a standard operating system. The system can accommodate traditional analog and digital telephones as well as IP phones.

12.3 PACKET-SWITCHING NETWORKS

Around 1970, research began on a new form of architecture for long-distance digital data communications: **packet switching**. Although the technology of packet switching has evolved substantially since that time, it is remarkable that (1) the basic technology of packet switching is fundamentally the same today as it was in the early-1970s networks, and (2) packet switching remains one of the few effective technologies for long-distance data communications. The two newest WAN technologies, frame relay and ATM, are essentially variations on the basic packet-switching approach. In this chapter, we provide an overview of traditional packet switching, which is still in use; frame relay and ATM are discussed in Chapter 13.

Basic Operation

The long-haul circuit-switching telecommunications network was originally designed to handle voice traffic, and the majority of traffic on these networks continues to be voice. A key characteristic of circuit-switching networks is that resources within the network are dedicated to particular calls. For voice connections, the resulting circuit will enjoy a high percentage of utilization because, most of the time, one party or the other is talking. However, as the circuit-switching network began to be used increasingly for data connections, two shortcomings became apparent:

- In a typical user/host data connection (e.g., personal computer user logged on to a database server), much of the time the line is idle. Thus, with data connections, a circuit-switching approach is inefficient.
- In a circuit-switching network, the connection provides for transmission at a constant data rate. Thus, each of the two devices that are connected must transmit and receive at the same data rate as the other. This limits the utility of the network in interconnecting a variety of host computers and workstations.

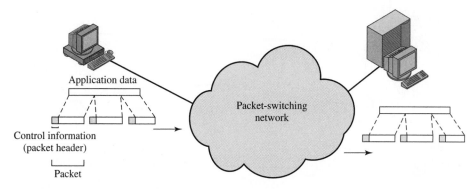

Figure 12.5 The Use of Packets

To understand how packet switching addresses these problems, let us briefly summarize packet-switching operation. Data are transmitted in short packets. A typical upper bound on packet length is approximately 1500 octets (bytes). If a source has a longer message to send, the message is broken up into a series of packets (Figure 12.5). Each packet contains a portion (or all for a short message) of the user's data plus some control information. The control information, at a minimum, includes the information that the network requires to be able to route the packet through the network and deliver it to the intended destination. At each node en route, the packet is received, stored briefly, and passed on to the next node.

Figure 12.6 illustrates the basic operation. A transmitting computer or other device sends a message as a sequence of packets (a). Each packet includes control information indicating the destination station (computer, terminal, etc.). The packets are initially sent to the node to which the sending station attaches. As each packet arrives at this node, it stores the packet briefly, determines the next leg of the route, and queues the packet to go out on that link. When the link is available, each packet is transmitted to the next node (b). All of the packets eventually work their way through the network and are delivered to the intended destination.

The packet-switching approach has a number of advantages over circuit switching:

- Line efficiency is greater, because a single node-to-node link can be dynamically shared by many packets over time. The packets are queued up and transmitted as rapidly as possible over the link. By contrast, with circuit switching, time on a node-to-node link is preallocated using synchronous time division multiplexing. Much of the time, such a link may be idle because a portion of its time is dedicated to a connection that is idle.

- A packet-switching network can carry out data-rate conversion. Two stations of different data rates can exchange packets, because each connects to its node at its proper data rate.

- When traffic becomes heavy on a circuit-switching network, some calls are blocked; that is, the network refuses to accept additional connection requests until the load on the network decreases. On a packet-switching network, packets are still accepted, but delivery delay increases.

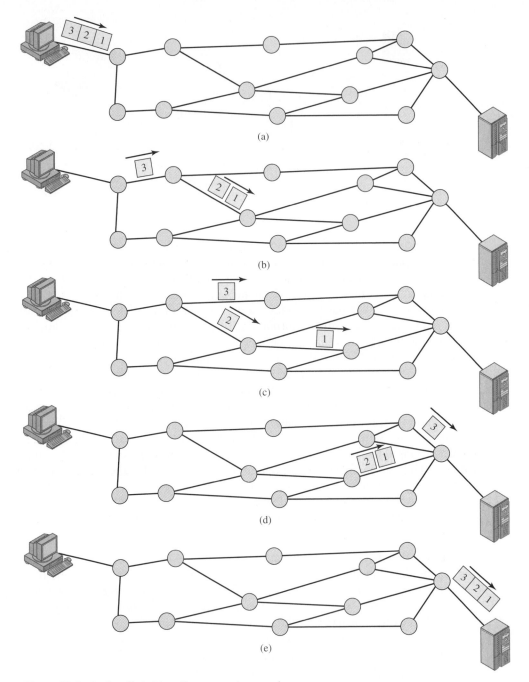

Figure 12.6 Packet Switching: Datagram Approach

- Priorities can be used. If a node has a number of packets queued for transmission, it can transmit the higher-priority packets first. These packets will therefore experience less delay than lower-priority packets.

Packet switching also has disadvantages relative to circuit switching:

- When a packet passes through a packet-switching node, it incurs a delay not experienced in circuit switching. At a minimum, it incurs a transmission delay equal to the length of the packet in bits divided by the incoming channel rate in bits per second; this is the time it takes to absorb the packet into an internal buffer. In addition, there may be a variable delay due to processing and queuing in the node.

- Because the packets between a given source and destination may vary in length, may take different routes, and may be subject to varying delay in the switches they encounter, the overall packet delay can vary substantially. This phenomenon, called **jitter**, may not be desirable for some applications (for example, in real-time applications including telephone voice and real-time video).

- To route packets through the network, overhead information including the address of the destination and often sequencing information must be added to each packet, which reduces the communication capacity available for carrying user data. This is not needed in circuit switching once the circuit is set up.

- More processing is involved in the transfer of information using packet switching than in circuit switching at each node. In the case of circuit switching, there is virtually no processing at each switch once the circuit is set up.

Switching Technique

A station has a message to send through a packet-switching network that is of greater length than the maximum packet size. It therefore breaks the message into packets and sends these packets, one at a time, to the network. A question arises as to how the network will handle this stream of packets as it attempts to route them through the network and deliver them to the intended destination. Two approaches are used in contemporary networks: datagram and virtual circuit.

In the **datagram** approach, each packet is treated independently, with no reference to packets that have gone before. This approach is illustrated in Figure 12.6. Each node chooses the next node on a packet's path, taking into account information received from neighboring nodes on traffic, line failures, and so on. So the packets, each with the same destination address, do not all follow the same route, and they may arrive out of sequence at the exit point. In this example, the exit node restores the packets to their original order before delivering them to the destination. In some datagram networks, it is up to the destination rather than the exit node to do the reordering. Also, it is possible for a packet to be damaged in the network. For example, if a packet-switching node crashes momentarily, all of its queued packets may be lost. Again, it is up to either the exit node or the destination to detect the loss of a packet and decide how to recover it. In this technique, each packet, treated independently, is referred to as a datagram.

In the **virtual circuit** approach, a preplanned route is established before any packets are sent. Once the route is established, all the packets between a pair of communicating parties follow this same route through the network. This is illustrated in Figure 12.7. Because the route is fixed for the duration of the logical

Figure 12.7 Packet Switching: Virtual-Circuit Approach

connection, it is somewhat similar to a circuit in a circuit-switching network and is referred to as a virtual circuit. Each packet now contains a virtual circuit identifier as well as data. Each node on the preestablished route knows where to direct such packets; no routing decisions are required. At any time, each station can have more than one virtual circuit to any other station and can have virtual circuits to more than one station.

So the main characteristic of the virtual-circuit technique is that a route between stations is set up prior to data transfer. Note that this does not mean that this is a dedicated path, as in circuit switching. A packet is still buffered at each node and queued for output over a line. The difference from the datagram approach is that, with virtual circuits, the node need not make a routing decision for each packet. It is made only once for all packets using that virtual circuit.

If two stations wish to exchange data over an extended period of time, there are certain advantages to virtual circuits. First, the network may provide services related to the virtual circuit, including sequencing and error control. Sequencing refers to the fact that, because all packets follow the same route, they arrive in the original order. Error control is a service that assures not only that packets arrive in proper sequence but also that all packets arrive correctly. For example, if a packet in a sequence from node 4 to node 6 fails to arrive at node 6, or arrives with an error, node 6 can request a retransmission of that packet from node 4. Another advantage is that packets should transit the network more rapidly with a virtual circuit; it is not necessary to make a routing decision for each packet at each node.

One advantage of the datagram approach is that the call setup phase is avoided. Thus, if a station wishes to send only one or a few packets, datagram delivery will be quicker. Another advantage of the datagram service is that, because it is more primitive, it is more flexible. For example, if congestion develops in one part of the network, incoming datagrams can be routed away from the congestion. With the use of virtual circuits, packets follow a predefined route, and thus it is more difficult for the network to adapt to congestion. A third advantage is that datagram delivery is inherently more reliable. With the use of virtual circuits, if a node fails, all virtual circuits that pass through that node are lost. With datagram delivery, if a node fails, subsequent packets may find an alternate route that bypasses that node.

12.4 TRADITIONAL WIDE AREA NETWORK ALTERNATIVES

As Table 12.1 indicates, packet switching adds several new alternatives for wide area networking, in addition to those that can be provided using circuit-switching technology. Just as there are public and private circuit-switching networks, there are also public and private packet-switching networks. A public packet-switching network works much like a public telephone network. In this case, the network provides a packet transmission service to a variety of subscribers. Typically, the network provider owns a set of packet-switching nodes and links these together with leased lines provided by a carrier such as AT&T. Such a network is called a **value-added network** (VAN), reflecting the fact that the network adds value to the underlying transmission facilities. In a number of countries, there is a single public network owned or controlled by the government and referred to as a **public data network** (PDN). The other packet-switching alternative is a network dedicated to the needs of a single organization. The organization may own the packet-switching nodes or lease an entire dedicated packet-switching network from a network provider. In either case, the links between nodes are again leased telecommunications lines.

Thus, a business is faced with an array of choices for meeting wide area networking needs. These choices include a number of high-speed options, such as frame relay and ATM. In this section, we explore the various traditional WAN options, to get some feel for the types of tradeoffs involved. The issues are revisited in Chapter 13.

Before beginning our evaluation of these alternatives, it is useful to consider the overview of circuit switching and packet switching provided in Table 12.2. While both circuit switching and packet switching can be used for data transmission, each has its particular strengths and weaknesses for a given application.

Table 12.2   Relative Merits of Circuit Switching and Packet Switching of Data

Circuit Switching	
Advantages	**Disadvantages**
Compatible with voice. Economies of scale can be realized by using the same network for voice and data. Commonality of calling procedures for voice and data. No special user training or communication protocols are needed to handle data traffic. Predictable, constant rate for data traffic.	Subject to blocking. This makes it difficult to size the network properly. The problem is less severe with the use of dynamic nonhierarchical routing techniques. Requires subscriber compatibility. The devices at each end of a circuit must be compatible in terms of protocol and data rate, since the circuit is a transparent connection. Large processing and signal burden. For transaction-type applications, data calls are of short duration and need to be set up rapidly. This proportionally increases the overhead burden on the network.
Packet Switching	
Advantages	**Disadvantages**
Provides speed conversion. Two attached devices with different data rates may exchange data; the network buffers the data and delivers them at the appropriate data rate. Appears nonblocking. As the network load increases, the delay increases, but new exchanges are usually permitted. Efficient utilization. Switches and trunks are used on demand rather than dedicating capacity to a particular call. Logical multiplexing. A host system can have simultaneous conversations with a number of terminals over a single line.	Complex routing and control. To achieve efficiency and resilience, a packet-switched network must employ a complex set of routing and control algorithms. Delay. Delay is a function of load. It can be long and it is variable.

Wide Area Networks for Voice

Traditionally, the preferred business alternatives for wide area voice communications all employ circuit switching. With the increasing competition and advancing technology of recent years, this still leaves the manager with many choices, including private networks, software-defined networks, ordinary telephone service, and a variety of special services such as toll-free numbers. Further complicating the choice is the introduction of services related to ISDN.

With all of these choices, and with the constantly changing prices attached to the various choices, it is difficult to generalize. What can be said is that business relies heavily on the public telephone networks and related services. Private networks are appropriate for an organization with a number of sites and with a substantial amount of voice traffic between them.

A new entry in the competition is voice over IP (VoIP), mentioned in Chapter 6. VoIP uses a packet transmission approach over Internets and intranets. VoIP is enjoying gradually growing acceptance as an alternative.

Wide Area Networks for Data

For data traffic, the number of wide area networking choices is even broader. Roughly, we can list the following categories as alternatives:

- **Public packet-switching networks:** There are a number of such networks in the United States and at least one in most industrialized countries. Typically, the user must lease a line from the user's computing equipment to the nearest packet-switching node.
- **Private packet-switching networks:** In this case, the user owns or leases the packet-switching nodes, which are generally collocated with the user's data processing equipment. Leased lines, typically 56 or 64 kbps digital lines, interconnect the nodes.
- **Private leased lines:** Dedicated lines can be used between sites. No switching is involved, so a leased line is needed between any pair of sites that wish to exchange data.
- **Public circuit-switching networks:** With the use of modems or switched digital service, the user can employ dial-up telephone lines for data communications.
- **Private circuit-switching networks:** If the user has an interconnected set of digital PBXs, either by leased 56-kbps lines or T-1 lines, then this network can carry data as well as voice.
- **ISDN:** ISDN offers both packet switching and traditional circuit switching in an integrated service.

The last two alternatives are likely to be justified on the basis of the voice traffic, with data traffic being a sort of bonus that comes with the network. Because this approach is therefore not directly comparable to the others, we do not consider it further in this chapter

As with voice, the choice of approach for data networking is complex and depends on current prices. In comparing the alternatives for wide area data networks, we look first at the cost and performance considerations, which are more easily quantified and analyzed. Then we consider some other issues that are also important in selecting a network.

COST/PERFORMANCE CONSIDERATIONS Data communications traffic can be roughly classified into two categories: stream and bursty. Stream traffic is characterized by lengthy and fairly continuous transmission. Examples are file transfer, telemetry, other sorts of batch data processing applications, and digitized voice communication. Bursty traffic is characterized by short, sporadic transmissions. Interactive client/server traffic, such as transaction processing, data entry, and time sharing, fits this description. Facsimile transmission is also bursty.

The public circuit-switching network approach makes use of dial-up lines. The cost is based on data rate, connection time, and distance. As we have said, this is quite inefficient for bursty traffic. However, for occasional stream-oriented requirements, this may be the most appropriate choice. For example, a corporation may have distributed offices. At the close of the day, each office transfers a file to headquarters summarizing the activities for that day. A dial-up line used for the single transfer from each office appears to be the most cost-effective solution. When there is a high volume of stream traffic among a few sites, the most economical solution is to obtain dedicated circuits among sites. These circuits, also known as leased lines or semipermanent circuits, may be leased from a telecommunications provider, such as a telephone company, or from a satellite provider. The dedicated circuit carries a constant fixed cost based on data rate and, in some cases, distance. If the traffic volume is high enough, then the utilization will be high enough to make this approach the most attractive.

On the other hand, if the traffic is primarily bursty, then packet switching has the advantage. Furthermore, packet switching permits terminals and computer ports of various data rates to be interconnected. If the traffic is primarily bursty but is of relatively modest volume for an organization, a public packet-switching network provides the best solution. In this case, the network provides a packet transmission service to a variety of subscribers, each of which has moderate traffic requirements. If there is a number of different subscribers, the total traffic should be great enough to result in high utilization. Hence, the public network is cost effective from the provider's point of view. The subscriber gets the advantages of packet switching without the fixed cost of implementing and maintaining the network. The cost to the subscriber is based on both connection time and traffic volume but not distance.

If the volume of an organization's bursty traffic is high and is concentrated among a small number of sites, a private packet-switching network is the best solution. With a lot of bursty traffic among sites, the private packet-switching network provides much better utilization and hence lower cost than using circuit switching or simple dedicated lines. The cost of a private network (other than the initial fixed cost of the packet switching nodes and the dedicated lines) is based solely on distance. Thus, it combines the efficiencies of public packet switching with the time and volume independence of dedicated circuits.

OTHER CONSIDERATIONS In addition to the issues of cost and performance, the choice of network should also take into account control, reliability, and security.

An organization large enough to need a wide area data network will come to rely heavily on that network. Accordingly, it is vital that management be able to maintain proper control of the network to provide an efficient and effective service to users. We will explore this topic at some length in Chapter 19. For our purposes here, we can say that three aspects of control are significant in comparing various network approaches: strategic control, growth control, and day-to-day operation of the network.

Strategic control involves the process of designing and implementing the network to meet the organization's unique requirements. With public packet switching, the subscriber has virtually no strategic control over service levels, reliability, or maintenance. The network is intended as a public utility to serve the average customer. With either dedicated lines or a private packet-switching network, the user organization can decide on the capacity and level of redundancy that it is willing to pay for. **Growth control** allows users to plan for network expansion and modifications arising as their needs change. A private packet-switching network provides the most flexibility in accommodating needs for growth. Additional packet switching nodes, more trunks, and higher-capacity trunks can be added as needed. These raise the overall capacity and reliability of the network. Although the user has control over the number and capacity of lines in a dedicated-line design, there is less flexibility for incrementally expanding the network. Again, with a public packet-switching network, the user has no control over growth. The user's needs are satisfied only if they happen to be within the capabilities of the public network. With respect to **day-to-day operation**, the user is concerned with accommodating peaks of traffic and with quickly diagnosing and repairing faults. Packet-switching networks can be designed with effective centralized network control that allows the network to be adjusted to changing conditions. Of course, in the case of the public network, the user is dependent on the network provider. As in any public utility, such as a transportation system, there tend to be "rush hours" in public networks when service levels decline. Day-to-day control is more difficult to automate in the case of dedicated lines; available tools are comparatively few and crude because we are not dealing with a unified network.

The inherent reliability of a packet-switching network is higher than that of a collection of dedicated lines. The network consists of a set of shared facilities and is equipped with centralized, automated network control facilities. Faults can be easily located and isolated and the traffic shifted to the healthy part of the network. A public network may be able to afford a greater investment in redundancy and control tools, because the cost is spread over many users. Further, the user is relieved of the burden of developing the expertise required to keep a large data communications network operational.

Finally, data security is vital to most corporations. We explore this topic in detail in Chapter 18. For purposes of the present discussion, we can say that use of a private network or dedicated lines will clearly afford greater security than a public packet-switching network. Public networks can use various access control mechanisms to limit the ways in which users can obtain data across the network. Those same control mechanisms are useful in private networks, because an organization may wish to segregate various communities of users.

Table 12.3 summarizes the difference among the various communications approaches.

Table 12.3 Features of Wide Area Networks

Feature	Dedicated (leased lines)	Public Packet	Private Packet
Strategic control	Network design, service, and maintenance can be given priority and controlled by user.	Service limited to that which suits average customer.	Network design, service, and maintenance can be given priority and controlled by user.
Growth control and operation control	Not integrated; decentralized fault detection may be expensive.	Provided by service supplier to satisfy average requirements.	Integrated into all equipment; centralized fault isolation and detection.
Reliability	Manual and user-visible recovery from failure.	Transparent and automatic recovery from failure.	Transparent and automatic recovery from failure.
Security	Private users only.	Public users, network access control.	Private users only, network access control.

APPLICATION NOTE

Switching

Discussions about switching can be confusing because there are so many protocols, different possible layers of networking models, and different types of switches. For many organizations, the type of switching used to send data from the local site to external destinations can be a complete mystery due to the complexity of wide area networks and a reduced level of local control. Once the data leave the home network, there may be little that a local network administrator can do to affect its travel. Usually the influence of the local network staff is limited to the customer premises equipment and the type of connection going offsite.

To make things more difficult, next generation networks will make use of multilayer switching techniques such as layer 3 switching (layer 2 routing), optical switching, and application layer switching. In the next couple of paragraphs we will try to provide some guidance into the switching terms that a typical network administrator is likely to run into and some of the terms used to describe external connectivity.

Almost all local area networks run the Internet Protocol (IP) over some form of Ethernet. Ethernet nodes are usually connected to each other via a layer 2 switch that examines layer 2 addresses in the frame prior to forwarding. The traffic encapsulated within the Ethernet frame is the IP-based data. The IP packet header includes all the information necessary for getting the packet from source to destination. This means that we are using a datagram approach. While upper-layer protocols like the Transmission Control Protocol (TCP) can control the flow of data to a certain extent, they do not change the type of switching/routing used. If we include the idea that any routers involved are processing the IP packets flowing between networks, we could classify this type of transmission as a packet-switching network with a datagram approach. Alternately, we might say that we used Ethernet switching and IP-based routers (packet switches) to move the traffic along. Both packet switching and its counterpart, circuit switching, are described in this chapter.

When traffic must travel offsite, it will be transferred to the network of the Internet service provider (ISP) for processing. Essentially, this is the beginning of the Internet. The Internet is actually a huge collection of networks. Web sites or Web servers are also attached to these networks. The ISP networks can vary quite a bit in terms of protocols used, speeds available, and the type of switching when compared to the local area networks of their customers. One consistent item is that all networks attached to the Internet transmit and receive IP packets. As a packet travels from source to destination, it will likely cross several different network types before arriving.

Upon entering the ISP network, routing decisions must be made. If the network utilizes a datagram approach, no further action is taken as the IP packets contain all of the necessary information and no circuit is required. However, if the network utilizes virtual circuits for establishing a pathway from one end of the ISP network to the other, this circuit must be established before any data can be forwarded. Examples of protocols utilizing virtual circuits are frame relay and asynchronous transfer mode, (ATM). Note that Ethernet rarely survives past the customer connection to the Internet.

Once the circuit has been established, the data are forwarded, with each network node making forwarding decisions based on the connection setup. Thus, a routing decision (typically layer 3) is made upon entrance to the network and then lower-layer switching decisions are made as the data cross the network. This virtual circuit is only valid to the border of the provider's network. All packets heading for the same destination follow the same path. At the edge, another routing decision must be made and a hand-off completed to the following network. At this point, the process starts again for each network until the destination is reached. The primary reason we process traffic in this fashion is for an improvement in speed. The advantage is that we do not have to process layer 3 IP addresses for the packets. Switching data at layer 2 is almost always faster than routing data at layer 3, no matter what kind of network you are on. Since these virtual circuit connections have a setup and teardown procedure and the circuit is allocated to that connection, this type of forwarding is called circuit switching.

In another example of circuit switching, a dial-up user initially connects to an ISP with a telephone call from a modem and the data are handled in the exact same fashion—circuit switching. The only difference is that instead of voice, the data started out as digital from the computer. Once the circuit-switched telephone call to the ISP is made, data can be transferred. The packets all follow the same path to the ISP. Internally, the ISP will have a standard IP network running over Ethernet that simply forwards the data to the correct router output interface. This interface may subsequently be connected to another, larger ISP using T carriers, a frame relay or an ATM network—but they all will carry IP packets as their payload. The packet passes through a router and is forwarded to the next network link. Note that at no time are the contents of the layer 3 IP datagrams manipulated. They are simply being carried over a different layer 2 network.

The term *switching* has many meanings, but all of them usually refer to the process of forwarding traffic between locations. The type of external switching that an organization selects is a decision that is often dependent upon factors such as bandwidth requirements, cost, and availability. There are a large number of protocols that can be used for connecting to the outside world, but choosing the correct type requires a survey of available products and an understanding of local requirements.

12.5 SUMMARY

The use of a direct point-to-point link for information communications is impractical for all but the most limited requirements. For cost-effective, practical information communications, some sort of communications network is needed. For communications outside the range of a single building or a cluster of buildings, a wide area network (WAN) is employed. Two basic technologies are employed: circuit switching and packet switching.

Circuit switching is used in public telephone networks and is the basis for private networks built on leased lines and using on-site circuit switches. Circuit switching was developed to handle voice traffic but can also handle digital data, although this latter use is often inefficient. With circuit switching, a dedicated path is established between two stations for communication. Switching and transmission resources within the network are reserved for the exclusive use of the circuit for the duration of the connection. The connection is transparent: Once it is established, it appears to attached devices as if there were a direct connection.

Packet switching is employed to provide an efficient means of using the shared facilities in a data communications network. With packet switching, a station transmits data in small blocks, called packets. Each packet contains some portion of the user data plus control information needed for proper functioning of the network. Public packet-switching networks are available, to be shared by a number of separate subscriber communities. The technology may also be employed to build a private packet-switching network.

The choice between circuit and packet switching depends on a host of considerations, including cost, performance, reliability, and flexibility. Both technologies will continue to be important in wide area networking.

12.6 RECOMMENDED READING AND WEB SITES

As befits its age, circuit switching has inspired a voluminous literature. Two good books on the subject are [BELL00] and [FREE04].

The literature on packet switching is also enormous. Books with good treatments of this subject include [SPOH02] and [BERT92]. [ROBE78] is a classic paper on how packet switching technology evolved. [BARA02] and [HEGG84] are also interesting.

BARA02 Baran, P. "The Beginnings of Packet Switching: Some Underlying Concepts." *IEEE Communications Magazine*, July 2002.

BELL00 Bellamy, J. *Digital Telephony.* New York: Wiley, 2000.

BERT92 Bertsekas, D., and Gallager, R. *Data Networks.* Englewood Cliffs, NJ: Prentice Hall, 1992.

FREE04 Freeman, R. *Telecommunication System Engineering.* New York: Wiley, 2004.

HEGG84 Heggestad, H. "An Overview of Packet Switching Communications." *IEEE Communications Magazine*, April 1984.

ROBE78 Roberts, L. "The Evolution of Packet Switching." *Proceedings of the IEEE*, November 1978.

SPOH02 Spohn, D. *Data Network Design.* New York: McGraw-Hill, 2002.

Recommended Web sites:

- **IP Multimedia Subsystems Forum:** News, technical information, and vendor information on Voice over IP and softswitch technology and products

12.7 KEY TERMS, REVIEW QUESTIONS, AND PROBLEMS

Key Terms

circuit switching	local loop	trunk
common channel signaling	packet	value-added network (VAN)
control signaling	packet switching	virtual circuit
datagram	public data network (PDN)	
exchange	softswitch	
inchannel signaling	subscriber	
integrated services digital network (ISDN)	subscriber line	
	subscriber loop	

Review Questions

12.1 Why is it useful to have more than one possible path through a network for each pair of stations?

12.2 Concerning a switched communications network, answer the following as either true or false.

  a. All switching nodes are connected to every other node.
  b. Links between switching nodes utilize some sort of multiplexing technique.
  c. Switching nodes provide connectivity for a single end station.

12.3 What are the four generic architectural components of a public communications network? Define each term.

12.4 Answer the following as either true or false regarding circuit switching.

  a. A complete connection from end to end must be completed before data transmission can occur.
  b. There are three basic stages; connection setup, data transfer, and connection termination.
  c. Circuit switching is very efficient.

12.5 What is the principal application that has driven the design of circuit-switching networks?

12.6 Distinguish between static and alternate routing in a circuit-switching network.

12.7 What is the difference between inchannel and common channel signaling?

12.8 The control signals used in the public switched telephone network are part of what architecture?

12.9 Explain the difference between datagram and virtual circuit operation.

12.10 What are some advantages of private networks?

12.11   What are some of the limitations of using a circuit-switching network for data transmission?

12.12   What is a value-added network (VAN)?

12.13   Why is packet switching impractical for digital voice transmission?

Problems

12.1   How far away from your local switching center is your business or home?

12.2   In the public switched telephone network, your call is set up and switched based on the numbers that you dial. These numbers actually provide different frequency sounds or tones to the switching center. What is this signaling called?

12.3   Define the following parameters for a switching network:

N = number of hops between two given end systems

L = message length in bits

B = data rate, in bits per second (bps), on all links

P = fixed packet size, in bits

H = overhead (header) bits per packet

S = call setup time (circuit switching or virtual circuit) in seconds

D = propagation delay per hop in seconds

   a.   For $N = 4, L = 3200, B = 9600, P = 1024, H = 16, S = 0.2, D = 0.001$, compute the end-to-end delay for circuit switching, virtual circuit packet switching, and datagram packet switching. Assume that there are no acknowledgments. Ignore processing delay at the nodes.

   b.   Derive general expressions for the three techniques of part (a), taken two at a time (three expressions in all), showing the conditions under which the delays are equal.

12.4   Consider a simple telephone network consisting of two end offices and one intermediate switch with a 1-MHz full-duplex trunk between each end office and the intermediate switch. The average telephone is used to make four calls per 8-hour workday, with a mean call duration of six minutes. Ten percent of the calls are long distance. What is the maximum number of telephones an end office can support?

12.5   Explain the flaw in the following reasoning: Packet switching requires control and address bits to be added to each packet. This introduces considerable overhead in packet switching. In circuit switching, a transparent circuit is established. No extra bits are needed.

   a.   Therefore, there is no overhead in circuit switching.

   b.   Because there is no overhead in circuit switching, line utilization must be more efficient than in packet switching.

12.6   Assuming no malfunction in any of the stations or nodes of a network, is it possible for a packet to be delivered to the wrong destination?

12.7   Consider a packet-switching network of N nodes, connected by the following topologies:

   a.   Star: One central node with no attached station; all other nodes attach to the central node.

   b.   Loop: Each node connects to two other nodes to form a closed loop.

   c.   Fully connected: Each node is directly connected to all other nodes.

   For each case, give the average number of hops between stations.

CHAPTER 13

FRAME RELAY AND ATM

13.1 Wide Area Networking Alternatives
    WAN Offerings
    Evolution of WAN Architectures

13.2 Frame Relay
    Background
    Frame Relay Protocol Architecture
    User Data Transfer
    Frame Relay Call Control
    Congestion Control

13.3 Asynchronous Transfer Mode (ATM)
    Virtual Channels and Virtual Paths
    ATM Cells
    ATM Service Categories

13.4 Summary

13.5 Recommended Reading and Web Sites

13.6 Key Terms, Review Questions, and Problems

Chapter Objectives

After reading this chapter, you should be able to

♦ Discuss the reasons for the growing interest in and availability of high-speed alternatives for wide area networking.

♦ Describe the features and characteristics of frame relay networks.

♦ Describe the features and characteristics of ATM networks.

♦ Assess the pros and cons of alternative high-speed services.

As the speed and number of local area networks (LANs) continue their relentless growth, increasing demand is placed on wide area packet-switching networks to support the tremendous throughput generated by these LANs. In the early days of wide area networking, X.25 was designed to support direct connection of terminals and computers over long distances. At speeds of up to 64 kbps, X.25 copes well with these demands. As LANs have come to play an increasing role in the local environment, X.25, with its substantial overhead, is an inadequate tool for wide area networking. Fortunately, several new generations of high-speed switched services for wide area networking have moved rapidly from the research lab and the draft standard stage to the commercially available, standardized-product stage. There are a number of such high-speed WAN services available.

Indeed, the network manager may now be faced with too many choices for solving capacity problems. In this chapter, we begin with an overview of various wide area networking alternatives, and show where the strengths and weaknesses lie. We then focus on perhaps the two most important WAN technologies: frame relay and ATM.

One approach that is not addressed in this chapter is the use of the Internet. The Internet is often used as a secondary or even primary WAN infrastructure for connecting computers at multiple sites. This topic, as well as the related topics of intranets, extranets, and virtual private networks, is best addressed separately and is dealt with elsewhere in this book.

13.1 WIDE AREA NETWORKING ALTERNATIVES

In considering wide area networking strategies for business and other organizations, two distinct but related trends need to be analyzed. The first is the distributed processing architecture used to support applications and to meet an organization's needs, and the second is the wide area networking technologies and services available to meet those needs.

WAN Offerings

To meet the demands of the new corporate computing paradigm, service and equipment providers have developed a variety of high-speed services. These include faster

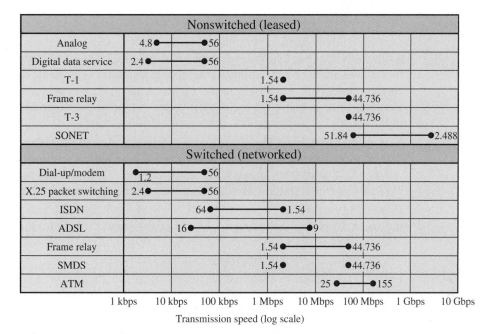

Nonswitched (leased)								
Analog	4.8●——————●56							
Digital data service	2.4●——————●56							
T-1			1.54●					
Frame relay			1.54●——————●44.736					
T-3				●44.736				
SONET					51.84●——————●2.488			
Switched (networked)								
Dial-up/modem	●1.2——————●56							
X.25 packet switching	2.4●——————●56							
ISDN	64●——————●1.54							
ADSL	16●——————●9							
Frame relay			1.54●——————●44.736					
SMDS			1.54●	●44.736				
ATM					25●——————●155			

1 kbps   10 kbps   100 kbps   1 Mbps   10 Mbps   100 Mbps   1 Gbps   10 Gbps

Transmission speed (log scale)

Figure 13.1   U.S. Carriers' Communications Services

multiplexed line schemes, such as T-3 and SONET/SDH, as well as faster switched networks schemes, including frame relay and ATM.

Figure 13.1 lays out the primary alternatives available from public U.S. carriers; a similar mix is available in other countries. A nonswitched, or dedicated, line is a transmission link leased for a fixed price. Such lines can be leased from a carrier and used to link offices of an organization. Common offerings include the following:

- **Analog:** The least expensive option is to lease a twisted-pair analog link. With dedicated private line modems, data rates of 4.8 to 56 kbps are common.

- **Digital data service:** High-quality digital lines that require digital signaling units rather than modems are more expensive but can be leased at higher data rates.

- **T-1, T-3:** For many years, the most common leased line for high-traffic voice and data needs was the T-1 line, which is still quite popular. For greater needs, the T-3 is widely available.

- **Frame relay:** Although frame relay is a switched network technology, the frame relay protocol can be used over a dedicated line to provide a convenient and flexible multiplexing technique. Frame relay devices are required at the customer's premises for this approach.

- **SONET:** The highest-speed leased lines that are available use SONET/SDH, discussed in Chapter 17.

Public switched services include the following:

- **Dial-up/modem:** Modems connected to the public telephone network provide a relatively inexpensive way to obtain low-speed data services. The modems themselves are inexpensive, and the telephone rates are reasonable for modest connect times. This is the near-universal access technique for residential users. In organizations, many LANs and PBXs are equipped with modem banks to provide low-cost, supplemental data transmission service.

- **X.25 packet switching:** This elderly standby is still used to provide a switched data transfer service. With the increasing use of graphic and multimedia applications, X.25 at its traditional data rates is becoming increasingly inadequate. Typically, network charges are based on the volume of data transferred.

- **ISDN:** The Integrated Services Digital Network provides both circuit switching and X.25 packet switching over 64-kbps B channels. Higher data rates are also achievable. Typically, network charges are based on the duration of the call regardless of the amount of data transferred.

- **Frame relay:** Provides switched capability at speeds equivalent to the leased T-1 rate and, in some offerings, higher rates up to T-3. Its low overhead makes it suitable for interconnecting LANs and high-speed standalone systems.

- **ATM:** Asynchronous transfer mode is widely viewed as a universal networking technology, destined to replace many of the current offerings.

Choosing among the various leased and switched alternatives is no easy task, and the proliferation of alternatives has increased the difficulty. Table 13.1 indicates common pricing practices in the United States; comparable practices are used in other countries. As can be seen, the pricing structures of the various services are not directly comparable. This is one complication. Other issues that complicate the selection process include the difficulty of forecasting future traffic volumes by organizations with wide area networking requirements, and difficulty in forecasting traffic distributions given the flexibility of applications and the mobility of users.

Evolution of WAN Architectures

Figure 13.2a shows the type of architecture that was dominant in business networks until recently and continues to be a popular model. In a typical configuration, all the

Table 13.1   WAN Alternatives (U.S. pricing)

Service	Usage Rate	Distance Rate
Leased line	Fixed price per month for a specific capacity (e.g., T-1 or T-3) and no additional fee for usage.	More for greater distance.
ISDN	Fixed price per month for service plus a usage charge based on amount of connect time.	Long-distance charges apply.
Frame relay	Fixed price per month for a port connection and a flat rate for a permanent virtual circuit (PVC) based on the capacity of the link.	Not distance sensitive.
ATM	Pricing policies vary.	Not distance sensitive.

(a) Integrated network access using dedicated channels

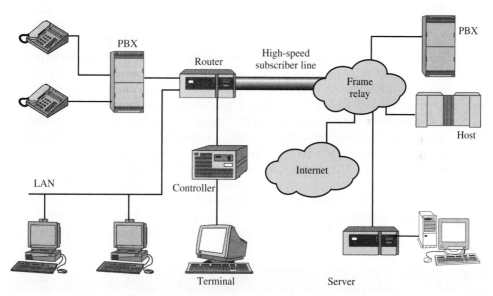

(b) Integrated network access using public switched WAN

Figure 13.2 Integrated Network Strategies

devices at a customer's premises are fed through a synchronous time division multiplexer onto a high-speed subscriber line to a carrier. This includes a PBX that controls phone and fax machines for voice and fax traffic as well as an interface to a LAN. Typically, the LAN is interfaced by means of a router, discussed in Chapter 4. There may also be a number of dumb terminals connected to a controller that interfaces to the multiplexer. The line itself can be either T-1 or T-3; as demand rises, SONET links will become more common.

At the carrier end, the multiplexed traffic can be split up into a number of leased circuits. These enable the creation of a private network linking to PBXs, LANs, and mainframe hosts at other locations for this customer. In addition, for data traffic, the carrier can provide an interface to a public high-speed switched network. Most commonly today, that network is frame relay, but ATM networks are also offered. Finally, a link to the Internet may be provided.

The configuration of Figure 13.2a is an attractive one. It integrates all of the customer's voice and data traffic onto a single external line, which simplifies network management and configuration. One drawback is its relative lack of flexibility. The capacity on the synchronous TDM line is divided into fixed partitions allocated to the various elements at the customer site, such as PBX, LAN, and terminal controller. This makes it difficult if not impossible to allocate capacity dynamically as needed.

With the advent of faster and faster public switched networks, a more flexible solution is now possible, an example of which is shown in Figure 13.2b. In this arrangement, the high-speed external line connects directly to a public switched network, such as frame relay or ATM. Although frame relay was initially offered as a data network, some recent offerings have sufficient capacity to handle voice as well, and ATM is quite capable of handling voice traffic. Thus, it is possible to link all of the site equipment onto this single line into the switched network. Virtual connections can be used to set up temporary "pipes" to various destinations. In addition, most frame relay and ATM suppliers offer what are called permanent virtual connections; these provide the equivalent of dedicated synchronous TDM channels and can be used to set up private networks. However, the permanent virtual connections can be changed from time to time to alter capacity. For maximum flexibility, the customer can rely on switched virtual connections that are set up and torn down dynamically. Each time a connection is set up, the customer can configure that connection to carry a particular capacity of traffic. Thus, as the mix of traffic into and out of the site changes, the customer can dynamically change the capacity mix to provide optimum performance.

For high-speed wide area networking, the frame relay and ATM offerings have become increasingly the methods of choice. Although ATM is considered technically superior, frame relay has a greater market share because it has been available for longer, allowing the development of a large installed base [WEXL03].

13.2 FRAME RELAY

Frame relay is designed to provide a more efficient transmission scheme than traditional packet switching. The standards for frame relay matured earlier than those for ATM, and commercial products also arrived earlier. Accordingly, there is a large installed base of frame relay products.

Background

The traditional approach to packet switching makes use of a protocol between the user and the network known as X.25. X.25 not only determines the user-network interface but also influences the internal design of the network. Several key features of the X.25 approach are as follows:

- Call control packets, used for setting up and terminating virtual circuits, are carried on the same channel and same virtual circuit as data packets. In effect, inband signaling is used.
- Multiplexing of virtual circuits takes place at layer 3.
- Both layer 2 and layer 3 include flow control and error control mechanisms.

The X.25 approach results in considerable overhead. At each hop through the network, the data link control protocol involves the exchange of a data frame and an acknowledgment frame. Furthermore, at each intermediate node, state tables must be maintained for each virtual circuit to deal with the call management and flow control/error control aspects of the X.25 protocol. All of this overhead may be justified when there is a significant probability of error on any of the links in the network. This approach is not suitable for modern digital communication facilities. Today's networks employ reliable digital transmission technology over high-quality, reliable transmission links, many of which are optical fiber. In addition, with the use of optical fiber and digital transmission, high data rates can be achieved. In this environment, the overhead of X.25 is not only unnecessary but degrades the effective utilization of the available high data rates.

Frame relay is designed to eliminate much of the overhead that X.25 imposes on end user systems and on the packet-switching network. The key differences between frame relaying and a conventional X.25 packet-switching service are as follows:

- Call control signaling, which is information needed to set up and manage a connection, is carried on a separate logical connection from user data. Thus, intermediate nodes need not maintain state tables or process messages relating to call control on an individual per-connection basis.
- Multiplexing and switching of logical connections takes place at layer 2 instead of layer 3, eliminating one entire layer of processing.
- There is no hop-by-hop flow control and error control. End-to-end flow control and error control are the responsibility of a higher layer, if they are employed at all.

Thus, with frame relay, a single user data frame is sent from source to destination, and an acknowledgment, generated at a higher layer, may be carried back in a frame. There are no hop-by-hop exchanges of data frames and acknowledgments.

Let us consider the advantages and disadvantages of this approach. The principal potential disadvantage of frame relaying, compared to X.25, is that we have lost the ability to do link-by-link flow and error control. (Although frame relay does not provide end-to-end flow and error control, this is easily provided at a higher layer.) In X.25, multiple virtual circuits are carried on a single physical link, and the link-layer protocol provides reliable transmission from the source to the packet-switching network and from the packet-switching network to the destination. In addition, at each hop through the network, the link control protocol can be used for reliability. With the use of frame relaying, this hop-by-hop link control is lost. However, with the increasing reliability of transmission and switching facilities, this is not a major disadvantage.

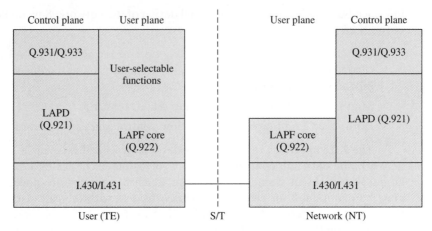

Figure 13.3   Frame Relay User–Network Interface Protocaol Architecture

The advantage of frame relaying is that we have streamlined the communications process. The protocol functionality required at the user–network interface is reduced, as is the internal network processing. As a result, lower delay and higher throughput can be expected. Studies indicate an improvement in throughput using frame relay, compared to X.25, of an order of magnitude or more [HARB92]. The ITU-T Recommendation I.233 indicates that frame relay is to be used at access speeds up to 2 Mbps. However, frame relay service at even higher data rates is now available, and frame relay continues to be a popular offering [BELL02].

Frame Relay Protocol Architecture

Figure 13.3 depicts the protocol architecture to support the frame relay. We need to consider two separate planes of operation: a control (C) plane, which is involved in the establishment and termination of logical connections, and a user (U) plane, which is responsible for the transfer of user data between subscribers. Thus, C-plane protocols are between a subscriber and the network, while U-plane protocols provide end-to-end functionality.

CONTROL PLANE   The control plane for frame relay is similar to that for common channel signaling for circuit-switching services, in that a separate logical channel is used for control information. At the data link layer, LAPD (Q.921) provides a reliable data link control service, with error control and flow control, between user (TE) and network (NT). This data link service is used for the exchange of Q.933 control signaling messages.

USER PLANE   For the actual transfer of information between end users, the user-plane protocol is LAPF (Link Access Procedure for Frame Mode Bearer Services), which is defined in Q.922. Only the core functions of LAPF are used for frame relay:

- Frame delimiting, alignment, and transparency
- Frame multiplexing/demultiplexing using the address field
- Inspection of the frame to ensure that it consists of an integral number of octets prior to zero bit insertion or following zero bit extraction

- Inspection of the frame to ensure that it is neither too long nor too short
- Detection of transmission errors
- Congestion control functions

The last function listed is new to LAPF. The remaining functions listed are also functions of LAPD.

The core functions of LAPF in the user plane constitute a sublayer of the data link layer. This provides the bare service of transferring data link frames from one subscriber to another, with no flow control or error control. Above this, the user may choose to select additional data link or network-layer end-to-end functions. These are not part of the frame relay service. Based on the core functions, a network offers frame relaying as a connection-oriented link layer service with the following properties:

- Preservation of the order of frame transfer from one edge of the network to the other
- A small probability of frame loss

As with X.25, frame relay involves the use of logical connections, in this case called data link connections rather than virtual circuits. Figure 13.4 emphasizes that the frames transmitted over these data link connections are not protected by a data link control pipe with flow and error control.

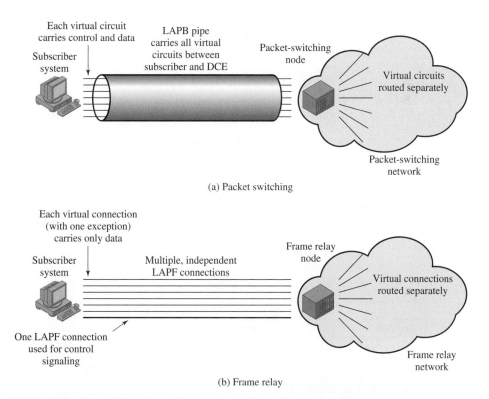

(a) Packet switching

(b) Frame relay

Figure 13.4   Virtual Circuits and Frame Relay Virtual Connections

Another difference between X.25 and frame relay is that the latter devotes a separate data link connection to call control. The setting up and tearing down of data link connections is done over this permanent control-oriented data link connection.

The frame relay architecture significantly reduces the amount of work required of the network. User data are transmitted in frames with virtually no processing by the intermediate network nodes, other than to check for errors and to route based on connection number. A frame in error is simply discarded, leaving error recovery to higher layers.

User Data Transfer

The operation of frame relay for user data transfer is best explained by beginning with the frame format, illustrated in Figure 13.5. The format is similar to that of other data link control protocols, such as HDLC (described in Chapter 17), with one omission: There is no Control field. In traditional data link control protocols, the Control field is used for the following functions:

- Part of the Control field identifies the frame type. In addition to a frame for carrying user data, there are various control frames. These carry no user data but are used for various protocol control functions, such as setting up and tearing down logical connections.

- The Control field for user data frames includes send and receive sequence numbers. The send sequence number is used to sequentially number each transmitted frame. The receive sequence number is used to provide a positive or negative acknowledgment to incoming frames. The use of sequence numbers allows the receiver to control the rate of incoming frames (flow control) and to report missing or damaged frames, which can then be retransmitted (error control).

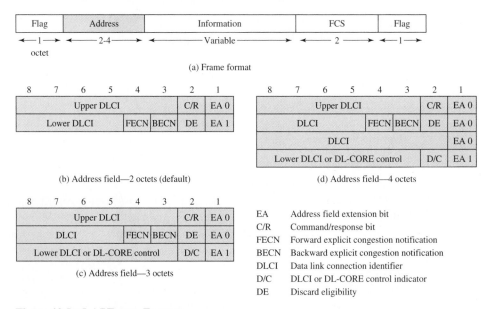

Figure 13.5 LAPE-core Formats

The lack of a Control field in the frame relay format means that the process of setting up and tearing down connections must be carried out on a separate channel at a higher layer of software. It also means that it is not possible to perform flow control and error control at the data link layer.

The Flag and Frame Check Sequence (FCS) fields function as in HDLC. The Flag field is a unique pattern that delimits the start and end of the frame. The FCS field is used for error detection. On transmission, the FCS checksum is calculated and stored in the FCS field. On reception, the checksum is again calculated and compared to the value stored in the incoming FCS field. If there is a mismatch, then the frame is assumed to be in error and is discarded.

The information field carries higher-layer data. The higher-layer data may be either user data or call control messages, as explained later.

The address field has a default length of 2 octets and may be extended to 3 or 4 octets. It carries a data link connection identifier (DLCI) of 10, 16, or 23 bits. The DLCI allows multiple logical frame relay connections to be multiplexed over a single channel.

The length of the address field, and hence of the DLCI, is determined by the address field extension (EA) bits. The C/R bit is application specific and is not used by the standard frame relay protocol. The remaining bits in the address field have to do with congestion control and are explained later.

Frame Relay Call Control

The actual details of the call control procedure for frame relay depend on the context of its use. Here, we summarize the essential elements of frame relay call control.

Frame relay supports multiple connections over a single link, and each has a locally unique DLCI. Data transfer involves the following stages:

1. Establish a logical connection between two endpoints, and assign a unique DLCI to the connection.
2. Exchange information in data frames. Each frame includes a DLCI field to identify the connection.
3. Release the logical connection.

The establishment and release of a logical connection is accomplished by the exchange of messages over a connection dedicated to call control, with DLCI = 0. A frame with DLCI = 0 contains a call control message in the information field. At a minimum, four message types are needed: SETUP, CONNECT, RELEASE, and RELEASE COMPLETE.

Either side may request the establishment of a logical connection by sending a SETUP message. The other side, upon receiving the SETUP message, must reply with a CONNECT message if it accepts the connection; otherwise it responds with a RELEASE COMPLETE message. The side sending the SETUP message may assign the DLCI by choosing an unused value and including this value in the SETUP message. Otherwise, the DLCI value is assigned by the accepting side in the CONNECT message.

Either side may request to clear a logical connection by sending a RELEASE message. The other side, upon receipt of this message, must respond with a RELEASE COMPLETE message.

Congestion Control

Congestion control for a frame relay network is challenging because of the limited tools available to the frame handlers. The frame relay protocol has been streamlined to maximize throughput and efficiency. A consequence of this is that a frame handler cannot control the flow of frames coming from a subscriber or an adjacent node using the typical flow control mechanism of other data link control protocols.

Congestion control is the joint responsibility of the network and the end users. The network (i.e., the collection of frame handling nodes) is in the best position to monitor the degree of congestion, while the end users are in the best position to control congestion by limiting the flow of traffic. With this in mind, two general congestion control strategies are supported in frame relay: congestion avoidance and congestion recovery.

Congestion avoidance procedures are used at the onset of congestion to minimize the effect on the network. At a point at which the network detects a build-up of queue lengths and the danger of congestion, there would be little evidence available to end users that congestion is increasing. Thus, there must be some explicit signaling mechanism from the network that will trigger the congestion avoidance.

Congestion recovery procedures are used to prevent network collapse in the face of severe congestion. These procedures are typically initiated when the network has begun to drop frames due to congestion. Such dropped frames will be reported by some higher layer of software, and serve as an implicit signaling mechanism.

For explicit signaling, two bits in the address field of each frame are provided. Either bit may be set by the frame handler that detects congestion. If a frame handler forwards a frame in which one or both of these bits are set, it must not clear the bits. Thus, the bits constitute signals from the network to the end user. The two bits are as follows:

- **Backward explicit congestion notification (BECN):** Notifies the user that congestion avoidance procedures should be initiated where applicable for traffic in the opposite direction of the received frame. It indicates that the frames that the user transmits on this logical connection may encounter congested resources.

- **Forward explicit congestion notification (FECN):** Notifies the user that congestion avoidance procedures should be initiated where applicable for traffic in the same direction as the received frame. It indicates that this frame, on this logical connection, has encountered congested resources.

Implicit signaling occurs when the network discards a frame, and this fact is detected by the end user at a higher layer. The network role, of course, is to discard frames as necessary. One bit in the address field of each frame can be used to provide guidance:

- **Discard eligibility (DE):** - Indicates a request that a frame should be discarded instead of other frames in which this bit is not set, when it is necessary to discard frames

The DE capability makes it possible for the user temporarily to send more frames than it is allowed to on average. In this case, the user sets the DE bit on the excess frames. The network will forward these frames if it has the capacity to do so.

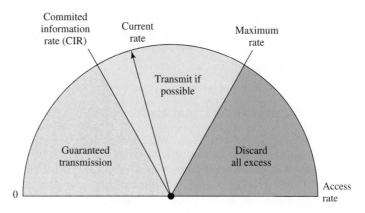

Figure 13.6 Operation of the CIR

The DE bit also can be set by a frame handler. The network can monitor the influx of frames from the user and use the DE bit to protect the network. That is, if the frame handler to which the user is directly connected decides that the input is potentially excessive, it sets the DE bit on each frame and then forwards it further into the network.

The DE bit can be used in such a way as to provide guidance for the discard decision and at the same time as a tool for providing a guaranteed level of service. This tool can be used on a per data link connection basis to ensure that heavy users can get the throughput they need without penalizing lighter users. The mechanism works as follows: Each user can negotiate a **committed information rate** (CIR) (in bits per second) at connection setup time. The requested CIR represents the user's estimate of its "normal" traffic during a busy period; the granted CIR, which is less than or equal to the requested CIR, is the network's commitment to deliver data at that rate in the absence of errors. The frame handler to which the user's station attaches then performs a metering function (Figure 13.6). If the user is sending data at less than the CIR, the incoming frame handler does not alter the DE bit. If the rate exceeds the CIR, the incoming frame handler will set the DE bit on the excess frames and then forward them; such frames may get through or may be discarded if congestion is encountered. Finally, a maximum rate is defined, such that any frames above the maximum are discarded at the entry frame handler.

13.3 ASYNCHRONOUS TRANSFER MODE (ATM)

Frame relay is designed to support access speeds up to 2 Mbps. But now, even the streamlined design of frame relay is faltering in the face of a requirement for wide area access speeds in the tens and hundreds of megabits per second. To accommodate these gargantuan requirements, a new technology has emerged: **asynchronous transfer mode** (ATM), also known as **cell relay**.

Cell relay is similar in concept to frame relay. Both frame relay and cell relay take advantage of the reliability and fidelity of modern digital facilities to provide faster packet switching than X.25. Cell relay is even more streamlined than frame relay in its functionality and can support data rates several orders of magnitude greater than frame relay.

Virtual Channels and Virtual Paths

ATM is a packet-oriented transfer mode. Like frame relay and X.25, it allows multiple logical connections to be multiplexed over a single physical interface. The information flow on each logical connection is organized into fixed-size packets, called **cells**. As with frame relay, there is no link-by-link error control or flow control.

Logical connections in ATM are referred to as **virtual channels**. A virtual channel is analogous to a virtual circuit in X.25 or a frame relay data link connection. It is the basic unit of switching in an ATM network. A virtual channel is set up between two end users through the network, and a variable-rate, full-duplex flow of fixed-size cells is exchanged over the connection. Virtual channels are also used for user-network exchange (control signaling) and network-network exchange (network management and routing).

For ATM, a second sublayer of processing has been introduced that creates and manages virtual paths (Figure 13.7). A **virtual path** is a bundle of virtual channels that have the same endpoints. Thus, all of the cells flowing over all of the virtual channels in a single virtual path are switched together.

Several advantages can be listed for the use of virtual paths:

- **Simplified network architecture:** Network transport functions can be separated into those related to an individual logical connection (virtual channel) and those related to a group of logical connections (virtual path).

- **Increased network performance and reliability:** The network deals with fewer, aggregated entities.

- **Reduced processing and short connection setup time:** Much of the work is done when the virtual path is set up. The addition of new virtual channels to an existing virtual path involves minimal processing.

- **Enhanced network services:** The virtual path is used internal to the network but is also visible to the end user. Thus, the user may define closed user groups or closed networks of virtual-channel bundles.

Figure 13.7 ATM Connection Relationships

VIRTUAL PATH/VIRTUAL CHANNEL CHARACTERISTICS   ITU-T Recommendation I.150 lists the following as characteristics of virtual channel connections:

- **Quality of service:** A user of a virtual channel is provided with a quality of service specified by parameters such as cell loss ratio (ratio of cells lost to cells transmitted) and cell delay variation.

- **Switched and semipermanent virtual channel connections:** Both switched connections, which require call-control signaling, and dedicated channels, called semipermanent, can be provided.

- **Cell sequence integrity:** The sequence of transmitted cells within a virtual channel is preserved.

- **Traffic parameter negotiation and usage monitoring:** Traffic parameters can be negotiated between a user and the network for each virtual channel. The input of cells to the virtual channel is monitored by the network to ensure that the negotiated parameters are not violated.

The types of traffic parameters that can be negotiated include average rate, peak rate, burstiness, and peak duration. The network may need a number of strategies to deal with congestion and to manage existing and requested virtual channels. At the crudest level, the network may simply deny new requests for virtual channels to prevent congestion. Additionally, cells may be discarded if negotiated parameters are violated or if congestion becomes severe. In an extreme situation, existing connections might be terminated.

I.150 also lists characteristics of virtual paths. The first four characteristics listed are identical to those for virtual channels. That is, quality of service, switched and semipermanent virtual paths, cell sequence integrity, and traffic parameter negotiation and usage monitoring are all characteristics of a virtual path. There are a number of reasons for this duplication. First, this provides some flexibility in how the network manages the requirements placed upon it. Second, the network must be concerned with the overall requirements for a virtual path, and within a virtual path may negotiate the establishment of virtual circuits with given characteristics. Finally, once a virtual path is set up, it is possible for the end users to negotiate the creation of new virtual channels. The virtual path characteristics impose a discipline on the choices that the end users may make.

In addition, a fifth characteristic is listed for virtual paths:

- **Virtual channel identifier restriction within a virtual path:** - One or more virtual channel identifiers, or numbers, may not be available to the user of the virtual path but may be reserved for network use. Examples would be virtual channels used for network management.

CONTROL SIGNALING   In ATM, a mechanism is needed for the establishment and release of virtual paths and virtual channels. The exchange of information involved in this process is referred to as control signaling and takes place on separate connections from those that are being managed.

For virtual channels, I.150 specifies four methods for providing an establishment/release facility. One or a combination of these methods will be used in any particular network:

1. **Semipermanent virtual channels** may be used for user-to-user exchange. In this case, no control signaling is required.

2. If there is no preestablished call control signaling channel, one must be set up. For that purpose, a control signaling exchange must take place between the user and the network on some channel. Hence we need a permanent channel, probably of low data rate, that can be used to set up a virtual channel that can be used for call control. Such a channel is called a **meta-signaling channel**, because the channel is used to set up signaling channels.

3. The meta-signaling channel can be used to set up a virtual channel between the user and the network for call control signaling. This user-to-network signaling virtual channel can than be used to set up virtual channels to carry user data.

4. The meta-signaling channel can also be used to set up a user-to-user signaling virtual channel. Such a channel must be set up within a preestablished virtual path. It can then be used to allow the two end users, without network intervention, to establish and release user-to-user virtual channels to carry user data.

For virtual paths, three methods are defined in I.150:

1. A virtual path can be established on a **semipermanent** basis by prior agreement. In this case, no control signaling is required.

2. Virtual path establishment/release may be **customer controlled**. In this case, the customer uses a signaling virtual channel to request the virtual path from the network.

3. Virtual path establishment/release may be **network controlled**. In this case, the network establishes a virtual path for its own convenience. The path may be network to network, user to network, or user to user.

ATM Cells

The asynchronous transfer mode makes use of fixed-size cells, consisting of a 5-octet header and a 48-octet information field. There are several advantages to the use of small, fixed-size cells. First, the use of small cells may reduce queuing delay for a high-priority cell, because it waits less if it arrives slightly behind a lower-priority cell that has gained access to a resource (e.g., the transmitter). Second, it appears that fixed-size cells can be switched more efficiently, which is important for the very high data rates of ATM. With fixed-size cells, it is easier to implement the switching mechanism in hardware.

Figure 13.8 shows the header format at the user-network interface. Figure 13.8b shows the cell header format internal to the network.

The **Generic Flow Control** (GFC) field does not appear in the cell header internal to the network, but only at the user–network interface. Hence, it can be used for control of cell flow only at the local user–network interface. The field could be used to assist the customer in controlling the flow of traffic for different qualities of service. In any case, the GFC mechanism is used to alleviate short-term overload conditions in the network.

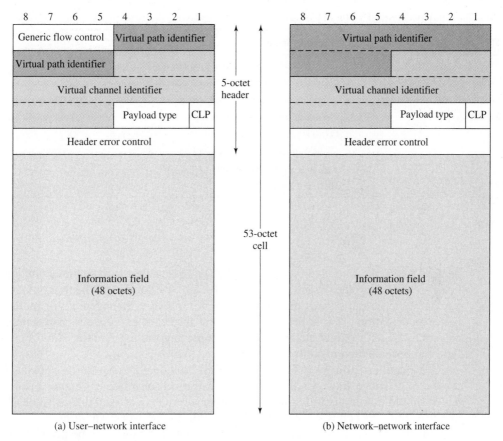

Figure 13.8 ATM Cell Format

I.150 lists as a requirement for the GFC mechanism that all terminals be able to get access to their assured capacities. This includes all constant-bit-rate (CBR) terminals as well as the variable-bit-rate (VBR) terminals that have an element of guaranteed capacity (CBR and VBR are explained subsequently).

The **Virtual Path Identifier** (VPI) field constitutes a routing field for the network. It is 8 bits at the user–network interface and 12 bits at the network–network interface, allowing for more virtual paths to be supported within the network. The **Virtual Channel Identifier** (VCI) field is used for routing to and from the end user. Thus, it functions much as a service access point.

The **Payload Type (PT)** field indicates the type of information in the information field. Table 13.2 shows the interpretation of the PT bits. A value of 0 in the first bit indicates user information (that is, information from the next higher layer). In this case, the second bit indicates whether congestion has been experienced; the third bit, known as the service data unit (SDU)[1] type bit, is a one-bit field that can

---

[1]This is the term used in ATM Forum documents. In ITU-T documents, this bit is referred to as the ATM-user-to-ATM-user (AAU) indication bit. The meaning is the same.

Table 13.2 Payload Type (PT) Field Coding

PT Coding	Interpretation	
0 0 0	User data cell, congestion not experienced	SDU-type = 0
0 0 1	User data cell, congestion not experienced	SDU-type = 1
0 1 0	User data cell, congestion experienced	SDU-type = 0
0 1 1	User data cell, congestion experienced	SDU-type = 1
1 0 0	OAM segment associated cell	
1 0 1	OAM end-to-end associated cell	
1 1 0	Resource management cell	
1 1 1	Reserved for future function	

SDU = Service data unit

OAM = Operations, administration, and maintenance

be used to discriminate two types of ATM SDUs associated with a connection. The term *SDU* refers to the 48-octet payload of the cell. A value of 1 in the first bit of the payload type field indicates that this cell carries network management or maintenance information. This indication allows the insertion of network-management cells onto a user's virtual channel without impacting the user's data. Thus, the PT field can provide inband control information.

The **cell loss priority** (CLP) bit is used to provide guidance to the network in the event of congestion. A value of 0 indicates a cell of relatively higher priority, which should not be discarded unless no other alternative is available. A value of 1 indicates that this cell is subject to discard within the network. The user might employ this field so that extra cells (beyond the negotiated rate) may be inserted into the network, with a CLP of 1, and delivered to the destination if the network is not congested. The network may set this field to 1 for any data cell that is in violation of the agreement concerning traffic parameters between the user and the network. In this case, the switch that does the setting realizes that the cell exceeds the agreed traffic parameters but that the switch is capable of handling the cell. At a later point in the network, if congestion is encountered, this cell has been marked for discard in preference to cells that fall within agreed traffic limits.

The **Header Error Control** (HEC) field is an 8-bit error code that can be used to correct single-bit errors in the header and to detect double-bit errors. In the case of most existing data link layer protocols, such as LAPD and HDLC, the data field that serves as input to the error code calculation is in general much longer than the size of the resulting error code. This allows for error detection. In the case of ATM, the input to the calculation is only 32 bits, compared to 8 bits for the code. The fact that the input is relatively short allows the code to be used not only for error detection but also, in some cases, for actual error correction. This is because there is sufficient redundancy in the code to recover from certain error patterns.

The error protection function provides both recovery from single-bit header errors and a low probability of the delivery of cells with errored headers under bursty error conditions. The error characteristics of fiber-based transmission systems appear to be a mix of single-bit errors and relatively large burst errors. For some transmission systems, the error correction capability, which is more time-consuming, might not be invoked.

ATM Service Categories

An ATM network is designed to be able to transfer many different types of traffic simultaneously, including real-time flows such as voice, video, and bursty TCP flows. Although each such traffic flow is handled as a stream of 53-octet cells traveling through a virtual channel, the way in which each data flow is handled within the network depends on the characteristics of the traffic flow and the QoS requirements of the application. For example, real-time video traffic must be delivered within minimum variation in delay.

In this subsection, we summarize ATM service categories, which are used by an end system to identify the type of service required. The following service categories have been defined by the ATM Forum:

- **Real-Time Service**
  - Constant bit rate (CBR)
  - Real-time variable bit rate (rt-VBR)
- **Non-Real-Time Service**
  - Non-real-time variable bit rate (nrt-VBR)
  - Available bit rate (ABR)
  - Unspecified bit rate (UBR)
  - Guaranteed frame rate (GFR)

REAL-TIME SERVICES The most important distinction among applications concerns the amount of delay and the variability of delay, referred to as jitter, that the application can tolerate. Real-time applications typically involve a flow of information to a user that is intended to reproduce that flow at a source. For example, a user expects a flow of audio or video information to be presented in a continuous, smooth fashion. A lack of continuity or excessive loss results in significant loss of quality. Applications that involve interaction between people have tight constraints on delay. Typically, any delay above a few hundred milliseconds becomes noticeable and annoying. Accordingly, the demands in the ATM network for switching and delivery of real-time data are high.

The **Constant Bit Rate (CBR)** service is perhaps the simplest service to define. It is used by applications that require a fixed data rate that is continuously available during the connection lifetime and a relatively tight upper bound on transfer delay. CBR is commonly used for uncompressed audio and video information. Example of CBR applications include the following:

- Videoconferencing
- Interactive audio (e.g., telephony)
- Audio/video distribution (e.g., television, distance learning, pay per view)
- Audio/video retrieval (e.g., video on demand, audio library)

The **Real-Time Variable Bit Rate (rt-VBR)** category is intended for time-sensitive applications; that is, those requiring tightly constrained delay and delay variation. The principal difference between applications appropriate for rt-VBR and those appropriate for CBR is that rt-VBR applications transmit at a rate that varies with time. Equivalently, an rt-VBR source can be characterized as somewhat bursty. For example, the standard approach to video compression results in a sequence of image frames of varying sizes. Because real-time video requires a uniform frame transmission rate, the actual data rate varies.

The rt-VBR service allows the network more flexibility than CBR. The network is able to statistically multiplex a number of connections over the same dedicated capacity and still provide the required service to each connection.

NON-REAL-TIME SERVICES   Non-real-time services are intended for applications that have bursty traffic characteristics and do not have tight constraints on delay and delay variation. Accordingly, the network has greater flexibility in handling such traffic flows and can make greater use of statistical multiplexing to increase network efficiency.

For some non-real-time applications, it is possible to characterize the expected traffic flow so that the network can provide substantially improved quality of service (QoS) in the areas of loss and delay. Such applications can use the **Non-Real-Time Variable Bit Rate (nrt-VBR)** service. With this service, the end system specifies a peak cell rate, a sustainable or average cell rate, and a measure of how bursty or clumped the cells may be. With this information, the network can allocate resources to provide relatively low delay and minimal cell loss.

The nrt-VBR service can be used for data transfers that have critical response-time requirements. Examples include airline reservations, banking transactions, and process monitoring.

At any given time, a certain amount of the capacity of an ATM network is consumed in carrying CBR and the two types of VBR traffic. Additional capacity is available for one or both of the following reasons: (1) Not all of the total resources have been committed to CBR and VBR traffic, and (2) the bursty nature of VBR traffic means that at some times less than the committed capacity is being used. All of this unused capacity could be made available for the **Unspecified Bit Rate (UBR)** service. This service is suitable for applications that can tolerate variable delays and some cell losses, which is typically true of TCP-based traffic. With UBR, cells are forwarded on a first-in, first-out (FIFO) basis using the capacity not consumed by other services; both delays and variable losses are possible. No initial commitment is made to a UBR source and no feedback concerning congestion is provided; this is referred to as a **best-effort service**. Examples of UBR applications include the following:

- Text/data/image transfer, messaging, distribution, retrieval
- Remote terminal (e.g., telecommuting)

Bursty applications that use a reliable end-to-end protocol such as TCP can detect congestion in a network by means of increased round-trip delays and packet discarding. However, TCP has no mechanism for causing the resources within the network to be shared fairly among many TCP connections. Further, TCP does not minimize congestion as efficiently as is possible using explicit information from congested nodes within the network.

To improve the service provided to bursty sources that would otherwise use UBR, the **Available Bit Rate (ABR)** service has been defined. An application using ABR specifies a peak cell rate (PCR) that it will use and a minimum cell rate (MCR) that it requires. The network allocates resources so that all ABR applications receive at least their MCR capacity. Any unused capacity is then shared in a fair and controlled fashion among all ABR sources. The ABR mechanism uses explicit feedback to sources to assure that capacity is fairly allocated. Any capacity not used by ABR sources remains available for UBR traffic.

An example of an application using ABR is LAN interconnection. In this case, the end systems attached to the ATM network are routers.

The most recent addition to the set of ATM service categories is **Guaranteed Frame Rate (GFR)**, which is designed specifically to support IP backbone subnetworks. GFR provides better service than UBR for frame-based traffic, including IP and Ethernet. A major goal of GFR is to optimize the handling of frame-based traffic that passes from a LAN through a router onto an ATM backbone network. Such ATM networks are increasingly being used in large enterprise, carrier, and Internet service provider networks to consolidate and extend IP services over the wide area. While ABR is also an ATM service meant to provide a greater measure of guaranteed packet performance over ATM backbones, ABR is relatively difficult to implement between routers over an ATM network. With the increased emphasis on using ATM to support IP-based traffic, especially traffic that originates on Ethernet LANs, GFR may offer the most attractive alternative for providing ATM service.

One of the techniques used by GFR to provide improved performance compared to UBR is to require that network elements be aware of frame or packet boundaries. Thus, when congestion requires the discard of cells, network elements must discard all of the cells that comprise a single frame. GFR also allows a user to reserve capacity for each GFR VC. The user is guaranteed that this minimum capacity will be supported. Additional frames may be transmitted if the network is not congested.

APPLICATION NOTE

Offsite Connectivity Solutions

There was a rule of thumb called the 80/20 rule which described where data were headed. There are actually several of these rules, but this one stated that about 80% of your network data would be local and 20% was going to head offsite. This is referred to as your "locality of reference." Increasingly we see organizations turning this rule on its head and sending/receiving 80% of their data to offsite locations as part of their normal business routine. As a result, traditional solutions will not be sufficient to handle the load. In addition to the protocols and services already mentioned in this chapter, there are other transport systems that have emerged as robust connectivity alternatives. Originally viewed as solutions for the home, cable and digital subscriber line systems (DSL) have proven themselves to be appropriate for businesses and so should be part of any site evaluation.

(Continued)

Like ATM and Frame Relay, cable and DSL can be "throttled." This means that the data transmission rate can be modified to suit a particular need. As you will see in the chapter problems, DSL also has several different types of service available. Cable has also come up with different service plans for businesses.

As with most services, there is the question of regional availability. Geographic offerings vary quite a bit. The pricing from area to area can also be significantly different. For example, in the Northeast, frame relay was very popular while ISDN and ATM remain available but expensive solutions. In the same region, cable and DSL services are both available and in fact directly compete with each other in advertising campaigns.

Cable simply means that the data are being sent down the same cabling infrastructure that provides cable television. Another channel (like the television channels) is allocated for this transmission. All of the channels are allocated 6MHz, and the data channel is no different. The upstream and downstream data transmissions are provided with different carriers, and the modems simply modulate or demodulate the signal. Cable is capable of long-range transmission because of the coaxial cable. This medium serves to protect the signal from outside interference.

The problem that most people complain about with cable is the number of users that may be on a particular segment. Cable distribution is a shared media, and because of this, all of the users in a neighborhood or building are often on the same line, fighting for bandwidth. Because of this, cable often starts to behave like shared Ethernet: The higher the number of users, the lower the bandwidth allocated to each individual. Even with this drawback, cable offers a high-speed alternative worth considering.

DSL runs over the same line that your telephone uses. Like cable, DSL providers advertise that you can use your telephone while transmitting data. While cable transmissions use a completely different system, DSL requires a mechanism for "stepping around" a telephone conversation. DSL data transmissions use different frequencies than that of voice. Voice output is low frequency, and DSL modems transmit at frequencies above this to prevent interference. It is interesting to note that cable and DSL use the same modulation technique—quadrature amplitude modulation (QAM).

Unlike cable, DSL users do not share a line with others. However, DSL has other restrictions. The most prominent problem is distance. This, coupled with the quality of the copper connecting a site to the central office, can eliminate DSL as a viable solution for some areas. DSL does not perform well beyond a few miles, and the farther the distance, the greater the noise and therefore the lower the data rate. Even with the best UTP, the maximum distance is limited to about 18,000 feet.

While neither cable nor DSL are currently capable of very high-speed connections (100 Mbps), they represent successful alternatives to traditional services. Companies providing these solutions are constantly adding bandwidth to make themselves more competitive. In addition, services are often bundled, which may make them very attractive. Depending on the organization needs and service availability, cable and DSL are definitely worth considering.

This discussion wouldn't be complete without noting another last-mile connectivity solution—Ethernet, both gigabit and 10 gigabit. Targeted specifically for this particular market, it leverages a well-known technology (Ethernet) and runs over fiber. The result is an extremely high-speed alternative to other services that is able to transmit over long distances. To compare, a high data transfer site like a university that might purchase an expensive OC-3 at 155Mbps could get a 10-gigabit connection that is up to 60 times faster. However, the equipment is still quite expensive and the service may not be available. The list of offsite connectivity solutions is already quite long, and we keep adding different technologies. Yet it won't be too long before several of the older technologies simply will not be able to keep up with bandwidth demands as companies push more and more data over their external links.

13.4 SUMMARY

A major change has occurred in the provision of wide area telecommunications services. The increasing capacity requirements of distributed computing systems, coupled with the introduction of transmission facilities of high speed and high reliability, have led to the introduction of a variety of WAN services that far outstrip the capabilities of traditional packet-switching networks.

The most widely available such service is frame relay. Frame relay is offered by a wide variety of providers for both public and private network configurations. Frame relay makes use of variable-sized packets, called frames, and a processing scheme that is considerably simpler than traditional packet-switching networks. Data rates of up to 2 Mbps are readily achievable.

Asynchronous transfer mode (ATM) is even more streamlined than frame relay and is intended to provide capacity in the 100s of Mbps and into the Gbps range. ATM technology is finding use in a wide variety of offerings for both wide area and local area networking.

13.5 RECOMMENDED READING AND WEB SITES

A more in-depth treatment of frame relay can be found in [STAL99]. An excellent book-length treatment is [BUCK00]. [MCDY99] and [BLAC99] provide good coverage of ATM.

BLAC99 Black, U. *ATM Volume I: Foundation for Broadband Networks.* Upper Saddle River, NJ: Prentice Hall, 1992.

BUCK00 Buckwalter, J. *Frame Relay: Technology and Practice.* Reading, MA: Addison-Wesley, 2000.

MCDY99 McDysan, D., and Spohn, D. *ATM: Theory and Application.* New York: McGraw-Hill, 1999.

STAL99 Stallings, W. *ISDN and Broadband ISDN, with Frame Relay and ATM.* Upper Saddle River, NJ: Prentice Hall, 1999.

Recommended Web sites:

- **Frame Relay Resource Center:** Good source of information on frame relay
- **ATM Hot Links:** Excellent collection of white papers and links maintained by the University of Minnesota
- **Cell Relay Retreat:** Contains archives of the cell-relay mailing list, links to numerous ATM-related documents, and links to many ATM-related Web sites

13.6 KEY TERMS, REVIEW QUESTIONS, AND PROBLEMS

Key Terms

asynchronous transfer mode (ATM)	guaranteed frame rate (GFR)	unspecified bit rate (UBR)
available bit rate (ABR)	integrated services digital network (ISDN)	variable bit rate (VBR)
cell	SONET	virtual channel
constant bit rate (CBR)	T-1	virtual path
frame relay	T-3	wide area network (WAN)

Review Questions

13.1 What are the key high-speed networking services available for wide area networking?

13.2 How does frame relay differ from packet switching?

13.3 What are the relative advantages and disadvantages of frame relay compared to packet switching?

13.4 Why is all of the error checking used by an X.25 system not required on modern communication facilities?

13.5 How is congestion control handled in a frame relay network?

13.6 How does ATM differ from frame relay?

13.7 What are the relative advantages and disadvantages of ATM compared to frame relay?

13.8 What is the difference between a virtual channel and a virtual path?

13.9 What are the advantages of using virtual paths?

13.10 What are the characteristics of a virtual channel?

13.11 What are the characteristics of a virtual path?

13.12 List and briefly explain the fields in an ATM cell.

13.13 List and briefly define the ATM service categories.

Problems

13.1 In every area of the country, the services available from carriers can vary. Determine the following for your area:

    a. What types of service are the most prevalent?

    b. What would be the cost of these services for 256 kbps? 512 kbps? 1 Mbps?

    c. In addition to the cost of the service, what other costs might be incurred?

13.2 List all 16 possible values of the GFC field and the interpretation of each value (some values are illegal).

13.3 One key design decision for ATM was whether to use fixed- or variable-length cells. Let us consider this decision from the point of view of efficiency. We can define transmission efficiency as

$$N = \frac{\text{Number of information octets}}{\text{Number of information octets } + \text{ Number of overhead octets}}$$

a. Consider the use of fixed length packets. In this case the overhead consists of the header octets. Define

L = Data field size of the cell in octet

H = Header size of the cell in octets

X = Number of information octets to be transmitted as a single message

Derive an expression for N. *Hint:* The expression will need to use the operator $[\bullet]$, where $[Y]$ = the smallest integer greater than or equal to Y.

b. If cells have variable length, then overhead is determined by the header, plus the flags to delimit the cells or an additional length field in the header. Let Hv = additional overhead octets required to enable the use of variable-length cells. Derive an expression for N in terms of X, H, and Hv.

c. Let $L = 48$, $H = 5$, and $Hv = 2$. Plot N versus message size for fixed- and variable-length cells. Comment on the results.

13.4 Another key design decision for ATM is the size of the data field for fixed-size cells. Let us consider this decision from the point of view of efficiency and delay.

a. Assume that an extended transmission takes place, so that all cells are completely filled. Derive an expression for the efficiency N as a function of H and L.

b. Packetization delay is the delay introduced into a transmission stream by the need to buffer bits until an entire packet is filled before transmission. Derive an expression for this delay as a function of L and the data rate R of the source.

c. Common data rates for voice coding are 32 kbps and 64 kbps. Plot packetization delay as a function of L for these two data rates; use a left-hand y-axis with a maximum value of 2 ms. On the same graph, plot transmission efficiency as a function of L; use a right-hand y axis with a maximum value of 100%. Comment on the results.

13.5 Consider the following applications. In each case indicate whether you would use X.25, frame relay, or ATM facilities. Assume that the facilities are available and "competitively" priced (i.e., determine, in each case, whether the functional characteristics of the service offering match well the requirements of the application). Explain in each case the reasons for your choice.

a. You have a large number of locations in a metropolitan area. At each location there is a large number of real-time data transactions processed. Information about the transactions must be sent independently and more or less randomly among the locations. That is, the transaction are not batched or do not occur in bunches. Performance requirements are such that the delay must be short. Volumes at each location are modest but in total range up to few megabits per second in total.

b. You now have a national WAN with about a half dozen locations in relatively remote areas. The transmission facilities are varied and include radio links, satellite links, and phone links using modems. The data rates are relatively modest.

c. In this case, you have multimedia applications. These include image communication and significant real-time video and audio services. These are interspersed with a multitude of other data services. The number of locations is small, but with the image and video applications, the volume is quite large, nearing gigabit per second ranges. There is also a large number of users and applications involved so that a large number of virtual circuits are needed even though the number of locations is small.

13.6 Consider compressed video transmission in an ATM network. Suppose standard ATM cells must be transmitted through 5 switches. The data rate is 43 Mbps.

a. What is the transmission time for one cell through one switch?

b. Each switch may be transmitting a cell from other traffic all of which we assume to have lower (non-preemptive for the cell) priority. If the switch is busy transmitting a cell, our cell has to wait until the other cell completes transmission. If the switch is free, our cell is transmitted immediately. What is the maximum time from when a typical video cell arrives at the first switch (and possibly waits) until it is finished being transmitted by the fifth and last one? Assume that you can ignore propagation time, switching time, and everything else but the transmission time and the time spent waiting for another cell to clear a switch.

c. Now suppose we know that each switch is utilized 60% of the time with the other low-priority traffic. By this we mean that with probability 0.6 when we look at a switch it is busy. Suppose that if there is a cell being transmitted by a switch, the average delay spent waiting for a cell to finish transmission is one-half a cell transmission time. What is the average time from the input of the first switch to clearing the fifth?

d. The measure of most interest is not delay, but jitter, which is the variability in the delay. Use parts (b) and (c) to calculate the maximum and average variability, respectively, in the delay.

In all cases assume that the various random events are independent of one another; for example, we ignore the burstiness typical of such traffic.

13.7 A widely used set of standards employed in local ATM environments is called ATM LAN Emulation (LANE). Provide a basic overview of LANE and describe its place in an organization's network strategy.

13.8 In order to support IP service over an ATM network, IP datagrams must first be segmented into a number of ATM cells before sending them over the ATM network. As ATM does not provide cell loss recovery, the loss of any of these cells will result in the loss of the entire IP packet. Given

PC = cell loss rate in the ATM network

n = number of cells required to transmit a single IP datagram

PP = IP-packet loss rate

a. Derive an expression for PP, and comment on the resulting expression.

b. What ATM service would you use to get the best possible performance?

FLORIDA DEPARTMENT OF MANAGEMENT SERVICES—PART TWO

Case Study II examined the evolution of a statewide information systems network that serves Florida state government agencies in 10 regional sites and connects these to the data center in Tallahassee. Up to the early 1990s, the network was based on the use of the proprietary Systems Network Architecture (SNA) from IBM and a mainframe at the data center that housed most of the applications. Over the course of 30 months, DMS built a statewide TCP/IP network, began offering Internet services to local and state agencies, and created a suite of Internet applications that will ultimately move personnel, accounting, and billing systems online.

In 2007, the DMS network went through another major overhaul and was renamed MyFloridaNet (MFN). This new network retains the fundamental TCP/IP and networking architecture with many upgrades. We examine MFN in this case study.

Figure VI.1 illustrates the core network of MFN. Each network node consists of at least two high-capacity, high-performance routers interconnected for redundancy and equipped with performance monitoring and network management equipment. These links between nodes use dedicated optical fiber links operating at 622 Mbps and 2.4 Gbps, with a high degree of redundancy. The core is thus a high-speed, redundant, private Internet.

Various state agencies can access the core network by means of the following core access methods:

- **Frame relay network:** DMS provides private frame relay network access at speeds from 64 kbps to 45 Mbps.

- **Metropolitan Ethernet network:** This option is available in some metropolitan area networks.

- **ATM network:** ATM service is available at speeds ranging from 1.536 Mbps to 622 Mbps.

- **Dedicated line to a core node:** Available at 64 kbps to 155 Mbps.

- **DSL line to a core node:** Available at 1.5 Mbps.

The core network and access methods are provided by a single vendor, Bell-South, replacing the multivendor contract of the preceding network architecture. Strong contract penalties provide Florida with stringent performance standards.

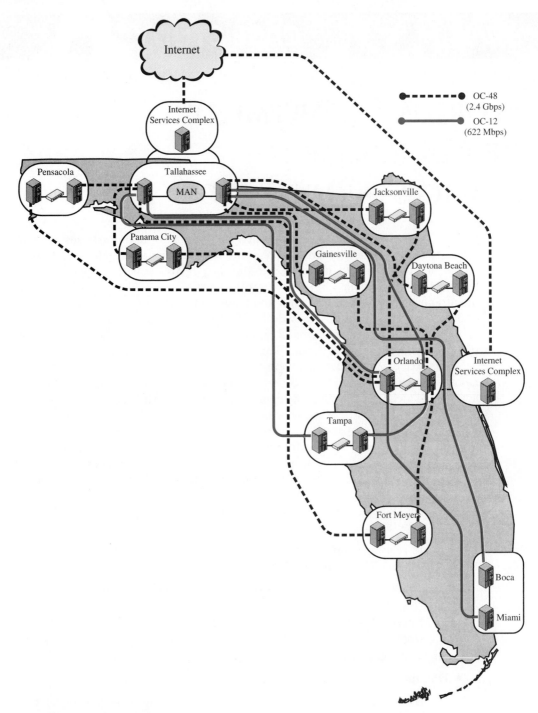

Figure VI.1 MYFloridaNet Core

Table VI.1 MyFloridaNet Core Service Levels

Service Level	Performance Target	Liquidated Damages	Measurement
Core network (PE-PE Failure)	Based on restoral & outage hours specified under liquidated damages	25% MRC of Service if outage > 60 seconds	Measured & calculated per incident based on the operational tools provided.
		50% MRC of Service if outage > 1 hour	
		100% MRC of Service if outage > 2 hours	
Latency	< (or equal to) 55 ms round trip: PE-PE Router	15% MRC of Service if performance target is unmet > 4 hours. 25% MRC of Service if performance target is unmet > 8 hours.	Use a 1400 byte packet size. Measured per incident every 5 minutes on the 3 most recent polls.
Jitter	< (or equal to) 20 ms round trip: PE-PE Router		
Packet loss	< (or equal to) 0.5% PE router to PE Router		

PE = Proveder edge
MRC of Service = MRC (or Monthly Recurring) of (Core Port + CPE + Access) for each site

This ensures that Florida's most critical communication systems, including the state's law enforcement officers' systems, are available in emergencies. The service levels provided by MFN are based upon guaranteed response times and other performance measurements, with associated user credits for service provider noncompliance. The MFN service levels are designed to ensure required performance and delivery expectations are met.

Table VI.1 defines the service levels provided for the MFN core. Service levels are also defined for core access and operational performance. These are shown in Table VI.2 and VI.3.

As an example of the cost benefit provided by this new system consider the migration of WAN services to MFN by the Florida Department of Highway Safety and Motor Vehicles (DHSMV). DHSMV's Information Systems Administration (ISA) has completed the migration of Driver License and Motor Vehicle field locations to the MFN. DHSMV coordinated with each office to replace the existing WAN network connection in all Driver License and Motor Vehicle field locations. The team migrated 40 offices per week starting in August of 2007 and completed the last office in early December of 2007 for a total of 416 offices migrated. It will also save a significant amount of funding each year, and it topped the list of budget reduction items for returning one of the largest funding amounts to the State during a recent budget reduction exercise [DHSM08].

Based on early experience with the new system and anticipated usage, DSM lists the following benefits for MFN:

- **Substantial savings:** A common platform for all state agencies and departments with standardized interfaces yields substantial savings. In contrast with today's environment, Internet access, firewall features, VPN services, network

Table VI.2 Access and Customer Premise Equipment (CPE) Service Levels

Service Level	Performance Target	Liquidated Damages	Measurement
Access & CPE failure	Based on restoral & outage hours specified under liquidated damages	15% MRC of Service if outage > 4 hours 100% MRC of Service if outage > 8 hours	Measured & calculated per incident based on the operational tools provided.
Latency	< (or equal to) 75 ms round trip for > (or equal to) TI speed & 420 ms round trip for 56kbps speed for both CE router to PE router and CE router to Internet gateway	15% MRC of Service if performance target is unmet > 4 hours. 25% MRC of Service if performance target is unmet > 8 hours.	Use a 1400 byte packet size. with link utilization < 65%. Measured per incident every 5 minutes on the 3 most recent polls.
Jitter	< (or equal to) 30 ms round trip for both CE-CE router and CE-Internet gateway		
Packet loss	< (or equal to) 1% for both CE-CE router and CE-Internet gateway		

CE = customer edge
PE = provider edge

management, configuration management, stringent SLAs, and full telephony bandwidth are all included in each MFN connection.

- **Any-to-any connectivity:** MFN provides fully meshed connectivity among all sites. Customers are able to order new sites without ever having to make router configuration changes at any of their other locations.

- **Web-based network management tools:** MFN provides Web-based tools so that customer agencies can monitor their own traffic and the performance of virtual private networks carried over the core network.

- **End-to-end quality of service:** MFN commits to providing the QoS thresholds defined in Tables VI.l through VI.3.

- **Integrated security:** The MFN service includes the deployment of firewalls and intrusion detection systems to protect connected agency networks.

- **Simple pricing structure:** MFN features simple, flat rate, packaged pricing statewide.

- **Access and core redundancy:** MFN features redundancy at multiple levels. Starting at the customer edge of the network, MyFloridaNet provides redundant Layer 3 connectivity between the customer location and the MFN core by connecting each customer site to both Core routers at the access point (Figure VI.l). Each core node consists of redundant routers complete with redundant aggregation circuits. In the unlikely event one of the core nodes either partially or completely fails, the other core router will continue to provide undegraded service. Each of the redundant core routers is connected with redundant circuits and redundant bandwidth provided almost entirely on private redundant optical fiber facilities.

Table VI.3   Operational Service Levels

Service Level	Performance Target	Liquidated Damages	Measurement
Install, moves, adds changes	64kbps to TI = 25 business days >TI to 45Mbps = 40 business days >45Mbps = 90 business days	25% MRC of Service if performance target not met.	Measured & calculated per incident based on the operational tools provided. The Install, Moves, Adds and Changes set of installation SLAs apply only after the 18-month migration.
CPE configuration changes	<(or equal to) 2 hours	10% MRC of Service	Measured & calculated per incident based on the operational tools provided. Changes can be made during or after working hours.
Service outage notification	15 minutes	10% MRC of Service	Measured & calculated per incident based on the operational tools provided.
Service degradation notification	30 minutes	10% MRC of Service	Measured & calculated per incident based on the operational tools provided.
Initial problem identification	2 hours	10% MRC of Service	Measured & calculated per incident based on the operational tools provided.

TI = 1.544 Mbps

SLA = service level aggrement

MFN is now the sole, integrated statewide private data transport service for voice, data, and video. By the end of 2008, all agencies and departments using the older DMS network had migrated to the new core network.

Discussion Questions

1. Visit the DMS MFN Web site to fully understand the elements of the service level elements of Tables VI.1 through VI.3 and discuss the adequacy and benefits of these service levels.

2. Discuss how the MFN strategy might be adopted and adapted by a large corporation for its own internal network needs.

GUARDIAN LIFE INSURANCE

One of the largest mutual life insurance firms in the United States, Guardian has more than 5500 employees and over 2800 financial representatives in 94 agencies. Guardian and its subsidiaries provide almost three million people with life and disability income insurance, retirement services, and investment products such as mutual funds, securities, variable life insurance, and variable annuities. The company also supplies employee benefits programs to five million participants, including life, health, and dental insurance, as well as qualified pension plans. In addition to regional home offices in New York City; Bethlehem, Pennsylvania; Spokane, Washington; and Appleton, Wisconsin, the company has 55 remote sales offices and 80 remote agency offices.

In the aftermath of the September 11, 2001 terrorist attacks, Guardian became concerned about business continuity issues. Guardian had four significant data centers, at its four home offices, but the primary data center was in New York City. Guardian performed an assessment of its data centers to provide a basis for planning on the location of data processing resources. One surprising outcome of this assessment had to do with utilization. The assessment revealed that the four data centers had about 1000 UNIX and NT servers, with an average capacity utilization of 10%. Even at peak demand, only 25% of the processing power of the servers was being used [CLAR03, MUS102]. Guardian responded to this assessment with a plan that included the following objectives:

1. Move the primary data center from New York City to Bethlehem, Pennsylvania.

2. Improve the efficiency of its data centers, including server and storage utilization. Specifically, Guardian set a goal of reducing the number of servers supporting Guardian's applications and databases by 40% and reducing the server support staff by 60%.

3. Ensure a smooth transition to the new primary data center.

Although it has considerable IT (information technology) expertise, Guardian felt that it needed outside assistance for such a massive undertaking. Warren Jones, vice president of IT operations, cited two reasons for seeking outside assistance:

1. Partnering gives you the ability to address a standalone project and get it done in a specific time from without being influenced by day-to-day activities.

2. Partnering brings in an outside perspective. The partner provides an independent assessment of the strengths and weaknesses of the plan.

The company chose IT consulting firm Greenwich Technology Partners (GTP) to help it design and carry out the transition. Four of the nine bids submitted for the outsourcing contract were financially competitive with GTP's. Guardian decided on GTP because of its promptness in responding to the RFP, its track record of flexibility on difficult jobs, and its commitment to supply any resources required to execute the project, without any hidden costs.

GTP began with an assessment of the company's IT environment and looked at the impact of moving the data center from New York to Bethlehem. A major issue related to the move was that the largest number of data center users was located in the New York area. Thus, the new deployment needed to provide for sufficient data transmission capacity to meet users' needs. Fortunately, the network infrastructure already in place was fairly standard and easily scalable (Figure VII.1). An ATM WAN backbone links the four regional home offices. Frame relay connections link the remote sales offices and remote agency offices, and 100-Mbps and 1-Gbps Ethernet LANs provide connectivity within campuses. The Cisco Catalyst 5500 and 7200 series routers provide Ethernet support combined with a modular, easily scalable design. The Cisco IGX 8400 ATM switches can be scaled to support an ATM network service at any desired capacity. With three widely used networking technologies in place, some of the problems that might have been encountered in a more convoluted networking environment are avoided.

Figure VII.1 Guardian's Network Infrastructure

GTP also looked at the application and database patterns. They determined which servers were application, database, and file and print servers, and analyzed the data in each. In addition to traditional applications such as file and print services, PeopleSoft, and Lotus Notes, Guardian also uses a collection of applications to support its intranet Web site. The site includes marketing materials and sales tools for the firm's agents, account profiling, and customer data. The company had also invested in a number of financial services applications, including applications for supporting its trading and securities functions. Due to their complexity and the amount of resource required to support them, many of Guardian's applications require dedicated servers.

The transition team, consisting of Guardian and GTP personnel, did extensive validation work and benchmarking to make sure the data they had gathered during the initial assessment were accurate. They measured network utilization at granular levels and modeled various consolidation scenarios for reducing server hardware.

From this analysis, GTP proceeded to develop a plan for consolidating the servers, looking at both business and technology issues. For example, the team considered the criticality of the applications supported by the servers, as well as which business units they belonged to. Some servers were good candidates for consolidation; others were not; and others were out of warranty, which made them too expensive to keep. After the migration plan was devised and the new architecture developed, more testing was conducted to ensure their viability.

The team devoted much thought and analysis to the migration to the new architecture, so as not to disrupt day-to-day operations. The plan targeted the least complex opportunities first, starting with file and print services. Guardian initially had more than 30 servers providing file and print services. These were consolidated into just two servers clustered in a high-availability, fault-tolerant configuration. For more complex parts of the plan, the team opted to do some of the consolidation in New York, and only then move the servers to Bethlehem after the consolidation had settled down.

The ongoing consolidation and relocation project has yielded tangible benefits to Guardian in terms of reduced hardware and personnel requirements. But the benefits extend beyond these initial objectives. The mindset of solving new problems efficiently and in the context of the existing infrastructure has taken hold. Guardian no longer automatically takes orders for new servers, as most of the operations and infrastructure world did throughout the 1990s. Instead, Guardian analyzes each new application requirement and attempts to support it with the existing hardware/software suite or with minimal upgrades and extensions.

The total cost of the project is $4.5 million, with GTP's services making up about 40% of the total. But the company saved more than $3 million in 2002, offsetting much of that cost. The company projects annual savings of over $5 million over the next two years.

Discussion Questions

1. Guardian initially decided to tackle the two key elements of its project simultaneously, namely the consolidation of its servers and the relocation of the primary data center. The alternatives would have been first to consolidate and then relocate, or first to relocate and then consolidate. As the preceding discussion indicates, Guardian ended up using a mix of the first and second strategies. Discuss the pros and cons of all three alternatives.
2. Discuss the pros and cons of outsourcing Guardian's project.

CHAPTER 14

WIRELESS WANS

14.1 Cellular Wireless Networks
Cellular Network Organization
Operation of Cellular Systems

14.2 Multiple Access
Code Division Multiple Access (CDMA)
Which Access Method to Use

14.3 Third-Generation Wireless Communication
Wireless Application Protocol (WAP)
The WAP Programming Model
The Wireless Markup Language (WML)
The Microbrowser
Wireless Telephony Applications (WTAs)
A Sample Configuration

14.4 Satellite Communications
Satellite Orbits
Satellite Network Configurations
Applications

14.5 Summary

14.6 Recommended Reading and Web Sites

14.7 Key Terms, Review Questions, and Problems

Chapter Objectives

After reading this chapter, you should be able to

♦ Identify the advantages and disadvantages of unguided (wireless communication) relative to guided communication.

♦ Distinguish among three generations of mobile telephony.

♦ Understand the relative merits of time division multiple access (TDMA) and code division multiple access (CDMA) approaches to mobile telephony.

♦ Describe the possibilities of personal communications systems (PCSs).

♦ Understand the properties and applications of LEOS, MEOS, and GEOS satellites.

Electronic information systems affect every aspect of our lives, and it becomes increasingly bothersome to be tethered to these systems by wires. Wireless communications offers us mobility and much else. Wireless communications should be considered when

- Mobile communication is needed.
- Communication must take place in a hostile or difficult terrain that makes wired communication difficult or impossible.
- A communication system must be deployed quickly.
- Communication facilities must be installed at low initial cost.
- The same information must be broadcast to many locations.

On the other hand, wireless communication has disadvantages compared to guided media such as twisted pair, coaxial cable, or optical fiber:

- Wireless communication operates in a less controlled environment and is therefore more susceptible to interference, signal loss, noise, and eavesdropping.
- Generally, wireless facilities have lower data rates than guided facilities.
- Frequencies can be more easily reused with guided media than with wireless media.

In this chapter we consider wide area wireless systems, including mobile telephony, third-generation wireless systems, and satellite communications. Wireless LANs are discussed in Chapter 11.

14.1 CELLULAR WIRELESS NETWORKS

Of all the tremendous advances in data communications and telecommunications, perhaps the most revolutionary is the development of cellular networks. Cellular technology is the foundation of mobile wireless communications and supports users in locations that are not easily served by wired networks. Cellular technology is the underlying technology for mobile telephones, personal communications systems, wireless Internet and wireless Web applications, and much more.

Cellular radio is a technique that was developed to increase the capacity available for mobile radio telephone service. Prior to the introduction of cellular radio, mobile radio telephone service was only provided by a high-power transmitter/receiver. A typical system would support about 25 channels with an effective radius of about 80 km. The way to increase the capacity of the system is to use lower-power transmitters with shorter radius and to use numerous transmitters/receivers.

Cellular Network Organization

The essence of a cellular network is the use of multiple low-power transmitters, on the order of 100 W or less. Because the range of such a transmitter is small, an area can be divided into cells, each one served by its own antenna. Each cell is allocated a band of frequencies and is served by a **base station**, consisting of transmitter, receiver, and control unit. Adjacent cells are assigned different frequencies to avoid interference or crosstalk. However, cells sufficiently distant from each other can use the same frequency band.

The first design decision to make is the shape of cells to cover an area. A matrix of square cells would be the simplest layout to define (Figure 14.1). However, this geometry is not ideal. If the width of a square cell is d, then a cell has four neighbors at a distance d and four neighbors at a distance $\sqrt{2}d$. As a mobile user within a cell moves toward the cell's boundaries, it is best if all of the adjacent antennas are equidistant. This simplifies the task of determining when to switch the user to an adjacent antenna and which antenna to choose. A hexagonal pattern provides for equidistant antennas (Figure 14.1b). The radius of a hexagon is defined to be the radius of the circle that circumscribes it (equivalently, the distance from the center to each vertex; also equal to the length of a side of a hexagon). For a cell radius R, the distance between the cell center and each adjacent cell center is $d = \sqrt{3}R$.

In practice, a precise hexagonal pattern is not used. Variations from the ideal are due to topographical limitations, local signal propagation conditions, and practical limitations on siting antennas.

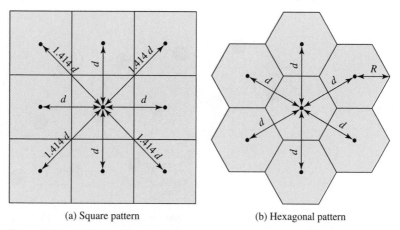

(a) Square pattern   (b) Hexagonal pattern

Figure 14.1   Cellular Geometries

A wireless cellular system limits the opportunity to use the same frequency for different communications because the signals, not being constrained, can interfere with one another even if geographically separated. Systems supporting a large number of communications simultaneously need mechanisms to conserve spectrum.

FREQUENCY REUSE   In a cellular system, each cell has a base transceiver. The transmission power is carefully controlled (to the extent that it is possible in the highly variable mobile communication environment) to allow communication within the cell using a given frequency while limiting the power at that frequency that escapes the cell into adjacent ones. The objective is to use the same frequency in other nearby (but not adjacent) cells, thus allowing the frequency to be used for multiple simultaneous conversations. Generally, 10 to 50 frequencies are assigned to each cell, depending on the traffic expected.

The essential issue is to determine how many cells must intervene between two cells using the same frequency so that the two cells do not interfere with each other. Various patterns of frequency reuse are possible. Figure 14.2 shows some

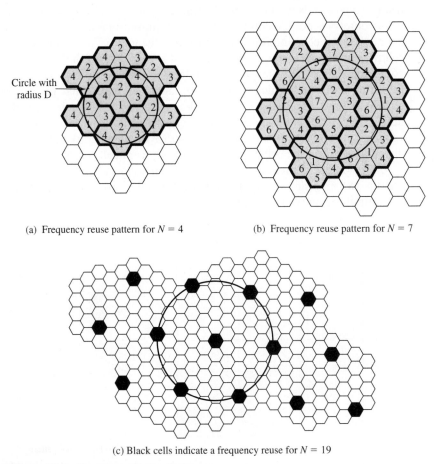

(a) Frequency reuse pattern for $N = 4$ (b) Frequency reuse pattern for $N = 7$

(c) Black cells indicate a frequency reuse for $N = 19$

Figure 14.2   Frequency Reuse Patterns

examples. If the pattern consists of N cells and each cell is assigned the same number of frequencies, each cell can have K/N frequencies, where K is the total number of frequencies allotted to the system. For AMPS (Advanced Mobile Phone Service, a widely used first-generation cellular scheme), $K = 395$, and $N = 7$ is the smallest pattern that can provide sufficient isolation between two uses of the same frequency. This implies that there can be at most 57 frequencies per cell on average.

In characterizing frequency reuse, the following parameters are commonly used:

D = minimum distance between centers of cells that use the same band of frequencies (called cochannels)

R = radius of a cell

d = distance between centers of adjacent cells ($d = \sqrt{3}R$)

N = number of cells in a repetitious pattern (each cell in the pattern uses a unique band of frequencies), termed the **reuse factor**

In a hexagonal cell pattern, only the following values of N are possible:

$$N = I^2 + J^2 + (I \times J), \quad I, J = 0, 1, 2, 3, \ldots$$

Hence, possible values of N are 1, 3, 4, 7, 9, 12, 13, 16, 19, 21, and so on. The following relationship holds:

$$\frac{D}{R} = \sqrt{3N}$$

This can also be expressed as $D/d = \sqrt{N}$.

INCREASING CAPACITY   In time, as more customers use the system, traffic may build up so that there are not enough frequencies assigned to a cell to handle its calls. A number of approaches have been used to cope with this situation, including the following:

- **Adding new channels:** Typically, when a system is set up in a region, not all of the channels are used, and growth and expansion can be managed in an orderly fashion by adding new channels.

- **Frequency borrowing:** In the simplest case, frequencies are taken from adjacent cells by congested cells. The frequencies can also be assigned to cells dynamically.

- **Cell splitting:** In practice, the distribution of traffic and topographic features is not uniform, and this presents opportunities for capacity increase. Cells in areas of high usage can be split into smaller cells. Generally, the original cells are about 6.5 to 13 km in size. The smaller cells can themselves be split; however, 1.5-km cells are close to the practical minimum size as a general solution (but see the subsequent discussion of microcells). To use a smaller cell, the power level used must be reduced to keep the signal within the cell. Also, as the mobile units move, they pass from cell to cell, which requires transferring of the call from one base transceiver to another. This process is called a *handoff*. As the cells get smaller, these handoffs become more frequent.

Table 14.1 Typical Parameters for Macrocells and Microcells

	Macrocell	**Microcell**
Cell radius	1 to 20 km	0.1 to 1 km
Transmission power	1 to 10 W	0.1 to 1 W
Average delay spread	0.1 to 10 μs	10 to 100 ns
Maximum bit rate	0.3 Mbps	1 Mbps

A radius reduction by a factor of F reduces the coverage area and increases the required number of base stations by a factor of F^2.

- **Cell sectoring:** With cell sectoring, a cell is divided into a number of wedge-shaped sectors, each with its own set of channels, typically three or six sectors per cell. Each sector is assigned a separate subset of the cell's channels, and directional antennas at the base station are used to focus on each sector.

- **Microcells:** As cells become smaller, antennas move from the tops of tall buildings or hills, to the tops of small buildings or the sides of large buildings, and finally to lamp posts, where they form microcells. Each decrease in cell size is accompanied by a reduction in the radiated power levels from the base stations and the mobile units. Microcells are useful in city streets, in congested areas along highways, and inside large public buildings.

Table 14.1 suggests typical parameters for traditional cells, called macrocells, and microcells with current technology. The average delay spread refers to multipath delay spread (i.e., the same signal follows different paths and there is a time delay between the earliest and latest arrival of the signal at the receiver). As indicated, the use of smaller cells enables the use of lower power and provides superior propagation conditions.

Example Assume a system of 32 cells with a cell radius of 1.6 km, a total of 32 cells, a total frequency bandwidth that supports 336 traffic channels, and a reuse factor of $N = 7$. If there are 32 total cells, what geographic area is covered, how many channels are there per cell, and what is the total number of concurrent calls that can be handled? Repeat for a cell radius of 0.8 km and 128 cells.

Figure 14.3a shows an approximately square pattern. The area of a hexagon of radius R is $1.5R^2\sqrt{3}$. A hexagon of radius 1.6 km has an area of 6.65 km^2, and the total area covered is $6.65 \times 32 = 213$ km^2. For $N = 7$, the number of channels per cell is 336/7 = 48, for a total channel capacity of $48 \times 32 = 1536$ channels. For the layout of Figure 14.3b, the area covered is $1.66 \times 128 = 213$ km^2. The number of channels per cell is 336/7 = 48, for a total channel capacity of $48 \times 128 = 6144$ channels.

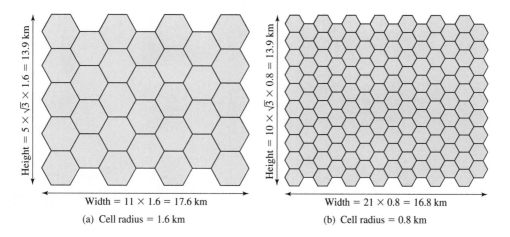

(a) Cell radius = 1.6 km

(b) Cell radius = 0.8 km

Operation of Cellular Systems

Figure 14.4 shows the principal elements of a cellular system. In the approximate center of each cell is a base station (BS). The BS includes an antenna, a controller, and a number of transceivers, all of which are used for communicating on the channels assigned to that cell. The controller is used to handle the call process between the mobile unit and the rest of the network. At any time, a number of mobile user units may be active and moving about within a cell, communicating with the BS. Each BS is connected to a mobile telecommunications switching office (MTSO), with one MTSO serving multiple BSs. Typically, the link between an MTSO and a BS is by a wire line, although a wireless link is also possible. The MTSO connects calls between mobile units. The MTSO is also connected to the public telephone or telecommunications network and can make a connection between a fixed subscriber to the public network and a mobile subscriber to the cellular network. The MTSO assigns the voice channel to each call, performs handoffs, and monitors the call for billing information.

The use of a cellular system is fully automated and requires no action on the part of the user other than placing or answering a call. Two types of channels are available between the mobile unit and the base station (BS): control channels and traffic channels. **Control channels** are used to exchange information having to do with setting up and maintaining calls and with establishing a relationship between a mobile unit and the nearest BS. **Traffic channels** carry a voice or data connection between users. Figure 14.5 illustrates the steps in a typical call between two mobile users within an area controlled by a single MTSO:

- **Mobile unit initialization:** When the mobile unit is turned on, it scans and selects the strongest setup control channel used for this system (Figure 14.6a). Cells with different frequency bands repetitively broadcast on different setup channels. The receiver selects the strongest setup channel and monitors that channel. The effect of this procedure is that the mobile unit has automatically

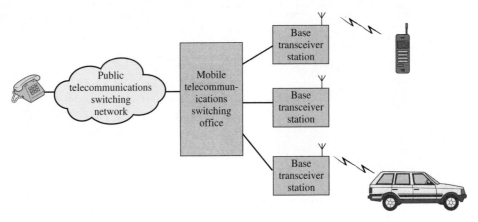

Figure 14.4 Overview of Cellular System

selected the BS antenna of the cell within which it will operate.[1] Then a handshake takes place between the mobile unit and the MTSO controlling this cell, through the BS in this cell. The handshake is used to identify the user and register its location. As long as the mobile unit is on, this scanning procedure is repeated periodically to account for the motion of the unit. If the unit enters a new cell, then a new BS is selected. In addition, the mobile unit is monitoring for pages, discussed subsequently.

- **Mobile-originated call:** A mobile unit originates a call by sending the number of the called unit on the preselected setup channel (Figure 14.5b). The receiver at the mobile unit first checks that the setup channel is idle by examining information in the forward (from the BS) channel. When an idle is detected, the mobile may transmit on the corresponding reverse (to BS) channel. The BS sends the request to the MTSO.

- **Paging:** The MTSO then attempts to complete the connection to the called unit. The MTSO sends a paging message to certain BSs depending on the called mobile number (Figure 14.5c). Each BS transmits the paging signal on its own assigned setup channel.

- **Call accepted:** The called mobile unit recognizes its number on the setup channel being monitored and responds to that BS, which sends the response to the MTSO. The MTSO sets up a circuit between the calling and called BSs. At the same time, the MTSO selects an available traffic channel within each BS's cell and notifies each BS, which in turn notifies its mobile unit (Figure 14.5d). The two mobile units tune to their respective assigned channels.

- **Ongoing call:** While the connection is maintained, the two mobile units exchange voice or data signals, going through their respective BSs and the MTSO (Figure 14.5e).

---

[1]Usually, but not always, the antenna and therefore the base station selected is the closest one to the mobile unit. However, because of propagation anomalies, this is not always the case.

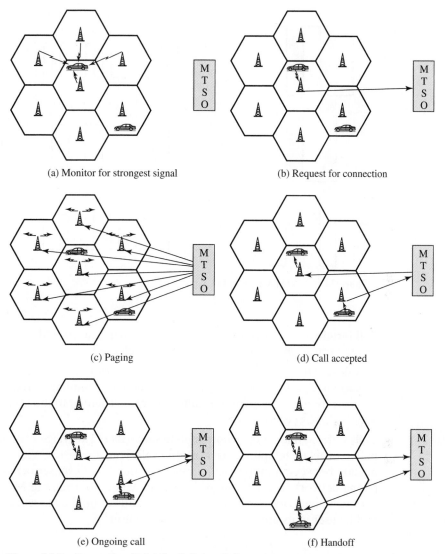

(a) Monitor for strongest signal

(b) Request for connection

(c) Paging

(d) Call accepted

(e) Ongoing call

(f) Handoff

Figure 14.5   Example of Mobile Cellular Call

- **Handoff:** If a mobile unit moves out of range of one cell and into the range of another during a connection, the traffic channel has to change to one assigned to the BS in the new cell (Figure 14.5f). The system makes this change without either interrupting the call or alerting the user.

Other functions performed by the system but not illustrated in Figure 14.5 include the following:

- **Call blocking:** During the mobile-initiated call stage, if all the traffic channels assigned to the nearest BS are busy, then the mobile unit makes a preconfigured number of repeated attempts. After a certain number of failed tries, a busy tone is returned to the user.

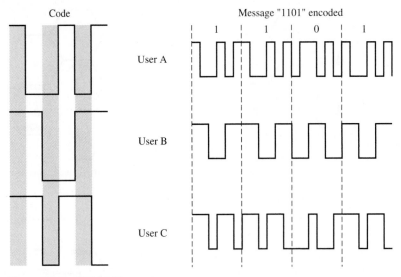

Figure 14.6 CDMA Example

- **Call termination:** When one of the two users hangs up, the MTSO is informed and the traffic channels at the two BSs are released.

- **Call drop:** During a connection, because of interference or weak signal spots in certain areas, if the BS cannot maintain the minimum required signal strength for a certain period of time, the traffic channel to the user is dropped and the MTSO is informed.

- **Calls to/from fixed and remote mobile subscriber:** The MTSO connects to the public switched telephone network (PSTN). Thus, the MTSO can set up a connection between a mobile user in its area and a fixed subscriber via the telephone network. Further, the MTSO can connect to a remote MTSO via the telephone network or via dedicated lines and set up a connection between a mobile user in its area and a remote mobile user.

14.2 MULTIPLE ACCESS

One can categorize mobile telephone systems into generations. The first-generation systems are based on analog voice communication using frequency modulation. A widely used first-generation system was the Advanced Mobile Phone System (AMPS), which is used in North and South America, Australia, and China. Due to the overwhelming popularity of the first-generation systems, systems that use the spectrum more efficiently became necessary to reduce congestion. This requirement was addressed by the second generation, which uses digital techniques and time division multiple access (TDMA) or code division multiple access (CDMA) for channel access. Advanced call processing features are present as well. The third generation is evolving from a number of second-generation wireless systems.

In this section, we describe the basic concept of multiple access, which is a key design element of any cellular system.

The primary motivation for the transition from the first-generation cellular telephones to the second was the need to conserve spectrum. The first-generation systems were extremely successful and the number of subscribers had been growing exponentially for years. However, use (and profit) is constrained by spectrum capacity. Hence there is a premium on the efficient use of spectrum. In the United States this interest has not been decreased by the recent policy of the Federal Communications Commission (FCC) to auction spectrum (for very large sums of money) rather than give it away. For these reasons, it is of interest to examine how the spectrum is divided among users in current and planned systems. There are basically four ways to divide the spectrum among active users: frequency division multiple access (FDMA), time division multiple access (TDMA), code division multiple access (CDMA), and space division multiple access (SDMA).[2] The first two types are discussed in Chapter 17; the remaining two we treat here.

Space division multiplexing is simply the idea of using the same spectral band in two physically disjoint places. A simple example is the idea of frequency reuse in cells, as discussed in this chapter. The same frequency can be used in two different cells as long as the cells are sufficiently far apart so that their signals do not interfere. Another form of space division that has been proposed for cellular telephony is to use highly directional antennas so that the same frequency may be used for two communications. This idea can be carried further by using steered beam antennas; these antennas can actually be aimed electronically and dynamically at a specific user. The ideas behind code division multiplexing are a little more complex, but because of their importance, we discuss them next.

Code Division Multiple Access (CDMA)

CDMA is based on direct sequence spread spectrum (DSSS). DSSS, which was briefly introduced in Chapter 11, is based on the following rather counterintuitive notion. We take a signal that we wish to communicate that has a data rate of, say, D bits per second and we convert it for transmission into a longer message and transmit it at a higher rate say, kD, where k is called the *spreading factor*. It might be about 100. Several things can be gained from this apparent waste of spectrum. For example, we can gain immunity from various kinds of noise and multipath distortion. The earliest applications of spread spectrum were military, where it was used for its immunity to jamming. It can also be used for hiding and encrypting signals. However, of interest to us is that several users can independently use the same (higher) bandwidth with very little interference.

Let us sketch how this works. We start with a data signal with rate D, which we call the bit data rate. We break each bit into k *chips* according to a fixed pattern that is specific to each user, called the user's code. The new channel has a chip data rate of kD chips per second. As an illustration we consider a simple example[3] with $k = 6$. It is

---

[2]The terms *FDMA*, *TDMA*, *CDMA*, and *SDMA* are essentially equivalent to the terms *FDM*, *TDM*, *CDM*, and *SDM*, respectively. The phrase *multiple access* emphasizes that a single channel is being shared (accessed by) multiple users.

[3]This example was provided by Professor Richard Van Slyke of the Polytechnic University of Brooklyn.

simplest to characterize a code as a sequence of 1s and -1s. Figure 14.6 shows the codes for three users, A, B, and C, each of which is communicating with the same base station receiver, R. Thus, the code for user A is $c_A = (1, -1, -1, 1, -1, 1)$. Similarly, user B has code $c_B = (1, 1, -1, -1, 1, 1)$, and user C has $c_C = (1, 1, 1, -1, 1, 1, -1)$.

Consider the case of user A communicating with the base station. The base station is assumed to know A's code. For simplicity, assume that communication is already synchronized so that the base station knows when to look for codes. If A wants to send a 1 bit, A transmits its code as a chip pattern $(1, -1, -1, 1, -1, 1)$. To send a 0 bit, A transmits the complement (1s and –1s reversed) of its code, $(-1, 1, 1, -1, 1, -1)$. At the base station the receiver decodes the chip patterns. If the receiver R receives a chip pattern $d = (d1, d2, d3, d4, d5, d6)$, and the receiver is seeking to communicate with a user u so that it has at hand u's code, $(c1, c2, c3, c4, c5, c6)$, the receiver performs the following decoding function:

$$S_u(d) = d1 \times c1 + d2 \times c2 + d3 \times c3 + d4 \times c4 + d5 \times c5 + d6 \times c6$$

The subscript u on S simply indicates that u is the user that we are interested in. Let's suppose the user u is actually A and see what happens. If A sends a 1 bit, then d is $(1, -1, -1, 1, -1, 1)$ and the preceding computation using S_A becomes

$$S_A(1, -1, -1, 1, -1, 1) = 1 \times 1 + (-1) \times (-1) + (-1) \times (-1) \\ + 1 \times 1 + (-1) \times (-1) + 1 \times 1 = 6$$

If A sends a 0 bit that corresponds to $d = (-1, 1, 1, -1, 1, -1)$, we get

$$S_A(-1, 1, 1, -1, 1, -1) = -1 \times 1 + 1 \times (-1) + 1 \times (-1) \\ + (-1) \times 1 + 1 \times (-1) + (-1) \times 1 = -6$$

Note that it is always the case that $-6 \leq S_A(d) \leq 6$ no matter what sequence of -1s and 1s that d is, and that the only d's resulting in the extreme values of 6 and -6 are A's code and its complement, respectively. So if S_A produces a $+6$, we say that we have received a 1 bit from A; if S_A produces a -6, we say that we have received a 0 bit from user A; otherwise, we assume that someone else is sending information or there is an error. So why go through all this? The reason becomes clear if we see what happens if user B is sending and we try to receive it with S_A, that is, we are decoding with the wrong code, A's. If B sends a 1 bit, then $d = (1, 1, -1, -1, 1, 1)$. Then

$$S_A(1, 1, -1, -1, 1, 1) = 1 \times 1 + 1 \times (-1) + (-1) \\ \times (-1) + (-1) \times 1 + 1 \times (-1) + 1 \times 1 = 0$$

Thus, the unwanted signal (from B) does not show up at all. You can easily verify that if B had sent a 0 bit, the decoder would produce a value of 0 for S_A again. This means that if the decoder is linear and if A and B transmit signals S_A and S_B, respectively, at the same time, then $S_A(S_A + S_B) = S_A(S_A) + S_A(S_B) = S_A(S_A)$ since the decoder ignores B when it is using A's code. The codes of A and B that have the property that $S_A(C_B) = S_B(C_A) = 0$ are called *orthogonal*. Such codes are very nice to have, but there are not many of them. More common is the case when $S_X(C_Y)$ is small in absolute value when $X \neq Y$. Then it is easy to distinguish between the two cases when $X = Y$ and when $X \neq Y$ In our example $S_A(c_C) = S_C(c_A) = 0$, but $S_B(c_C) = S_C(c_B) = 2$. In the latter case the C signal would make a small contribution to the decoded signal instead of 0. Using the decoder, S_u, the receiver can sort out transmission from u even when there may be other users broadcasting in the same cell.

In practice, the CDMA receiver can filter out the contribution from unwanted users or they appear as low-level noise. However, if there are many users competing for the channel with the user the receiver is trying to listen to, or if the signal power of one or more competing signals is too high, perhaps because it is very near the receiver (the "near/far" problem), the system breaks down. The coding gain we get, which is 6 in our simple example, may be greater than 100 in practical systems, so that the ability of our decoder to filter out unwanted codes can be quite effective.

Which Access Method to Use

Figure 14.7 illustrates the differences among FDMA, TDMA, and CDMA. In summary, with FDMA, each user communicates with the base station on its own narrow frequency band. For TDMA, the users share a wider frequency band and take turns communicating with the base station. For CDMA, many users can simultaneously use the same wide frequency band. Each user's signal is scrambled using a unique code so that it resembles random background noise to other users. The base station uses the same codes to unscramble the different user signals. CDMA allows more users to share a given bandwidth than does FDMA or TDMA.

(a) FDMA

(b) TDMA

(c) CDMA

Figure 14.7 Cellular Multiple Access Schemes

Besides the pure forms of splitting the channel (FDMA, TDMA, CDMA, SDMA), hybrids are also possible. For example, the second-generation system known as GSM uses FDM to divide the allotted spectrum into 124 carriers. Each carrier is then split in up to eight parts using TDMA. The number of potential users in any one cell is potentially enormalous. Any subscriber in the area could enter the cell; in addition, a whole world of roamers could show up. Fortunately, the number of customers who are in a given cell at one time and are using their units for calls is usually quite modest. The problem is how to determine which users are active in a cell and how to assign them to vacant subchannels. Mobiles/subscribers entering a cell by a handoff can be allocated a channel directly through the mobile switching office. The question remains what to do about mobiles/subscribers that are just becoming active. A common answer is to use a random access channel, in which any user can transmit at any time. If two users transmit at approximately the same time, their signals interfere and each must retransmit. Since the message from a mobile/subscriber announcing its presence is quite short and infrequent, the poor utilization that is characteristic of random access channels is not a problem. Similarly, control information originating from a mobile/subscriber can be carried in the same random access mode. One control message is to assign the mobile/subscriber a dedicated channel when a conversation or data transfer is necessary.

So the assignment of channels and other control functions that are relatively short and rare can be initiated using a random access method, while the higher-traffic activities can be carried out in dedicated conversation subchannels derived by a multiple access scheme.

The primary multiple access schemes used in cellular telephony (and satellite communications as well) are FDMA (e.g., the first-generation system AMPS), TDMA (e.g., Digital AMPS, the digital successor to AMPS, and GSM, which also uses FDM), and CDMA, pioneered by Qualcomm. This listing is in order of increasing complexity of implementation and also of increasing spectral efficiency. In Digital AMPS the 30-kHz channels of AMPS are divided into subchannels using TDM, giving about a 3 : 1 improvement in spectrum utilization. Qualcom claims a tenfold improvement for CDMA systems over AMPS. CDMA uses *soft handoff*, wherein the power from the codes in the old and new cells is summed by the mobile. In the other direction, the two signals received by the two base transceivers can be compared to make better communication.

In the United States there has been debate over the access method to use. FDMA is clearly too wasteful of spectrum for contemporary systems. Moreover, with the development of inexpensive, high-performance digital signal processing chips, FDMA is no longer necessarily easier to implement than TDMA. But the choice between TDMA and CDMA is a matter debated. Adherents of TDMA argue that the theoretical advantages of the CDMA scheme are hard to realize in practice and that there is a lot more successful experience with TDMA. CDMA proponents argue that the theoretical advantages can be realized and that CDMA offers additional features as well, such as increased range. The TDMA systems have achieved an early lead in actual implementations worldwide. But large wireless providers are beginning to sign up with CDMA vendors, and CDMA seems to be the access method of choice for third-generation systems.

14.3 THIRD-GENERATION WIRELESS COMMUNICATION

The objective of the third generation of wireless communication is to provide fairly high speed wireless communications to support multimedia, data, and video in addition to voice. The ITU's International Mobile Telecommunications for the year 2000 (IMT-2000) initiative has defined the ITU's view of third-generation capabilities as follows:

- Voice quality comparable to the public switched telephone network
- 144 kbps data rate available to users in high-speed motor vehicles over large areas
- 384 kbps available to pedestrians standing or moving slowly over small areas
- Support (to be phased in) for 2.048 Mbps for office use
- Support for both packet switched and circuit switched data services
- An adaptive interface to the Internet to reflect efficiently the common asymmetry between inbound and outbound traffic
- More efficient use of the available spectrum in general
- Support for a wide variety of mobile equipment
- Flexibility to allow the introduction of new services and technologies

More generally, one of the driving forces of modern communication technology is the trend toward universal personal telecommunications and universal communications access. The first concept refers to the ability of a person to identify himself or herself easily and use conveniently any communication system in an entire country, over a continent, or even globally, in terms of a single account. The second refers to the capability of using one's terminal in a wide variety of environments to connect to information services (e.g., to have a portable terminal that will work in the office, on the street, and on airplanes equally well). This revolution in personal computing will obviously involve wireless communication in a fundamental way. The GSM cellular telephony with its subscriber identity module, for example, is a large step toward these goals.

Personal communications services (PCSs) and personal communication networks (PCNs) are names attached to these concepts of global wireless communications, and they also form objectives for third-generation wireless.

Generally, the technology planned is digital using time division multiple access or code division multiple access to provide efficient use of the spectrum and high capacity.

PCS handsets are designed to be low power and relatively small and light. Efforts are being made internationally to allow the same terminals to be used worldwide. Worldwide frequency allocations have been made for second-generation cordless telephones (CT-2) in the 800-MHz region and for more advanced personal communications in the 1.7- to 2.2-GHz band of the spectrum.

The 1992 World Administrative Radio Conference (WARC 92) resulted in worldwide allocations for future public land mobile telecommunications systems (FPLMTS). This concept includes both terrestrial and satellite-based services. In addition, allocations were made for low-earth-orbiting (LEO) satellite services that can be used to support personal communications.

Some proposed technologies that come under the umbrella of PCS are American Digital Cellular System, Japanese Digital Cellular System, second-generation cordless telephones (CT-2), the European Community's Global System for Mobile communications (GSM) for digital cellular service, and Digital European Cordless Telephone (DECT). These involve advanced wireless telephony, which may be supported by LEO satellites and geostationary satellites, as well as by terrestrial antennas. The technology is developing rapidly. One desirable third-generation capability is mobile telephone and mobile terminals that can access Web services.

Wireless Application Protocol (WAP)

The Wireless Application Protocol (WAP) is a universal, open standard developed by the WAP Forum to provide mobile users of wireless phones and other wireless terminals such as pagers and personal digital assistants (PDAs) access to telephony and information services, including the Internet and the Web. WAP is designed to work with all wireless network technologies (e.g., GSM, CDMA, and TDMA). It is also based on existing Internet standards, such as IP, XML, HTML, and HTTP, as much as possible. It also includes security facilities. Ericsson, Motorola, Nokia, and Phone.com established the WAP Forum in 1997, which now has several hundred members. The WAP Forum released v1.1 of WAP in June 1999.

Strongly affecting the use of mobile phones and terminals for data services are the significant limitations of the devices and the networks that connect them. The devices have limited processors, memory, and battery life. The user interface is also limited, and the displays small. The wireless networks are characterized by relatively low bandwidth, high latency, and unpredictable availability and stability compared to wired connections. Moreover, all these features vary widely from terminal device to terminal device and from network to network. Finally, mobile, wireless users have different expectations and needs from other information systems users. For instance, mobile terminals must be extremely easy to use, much easier than workstations and personal computers. WAP is designed to deal with these challenges.

The WAP specification includes the following:

- A programming model based on the WWW Programming Model
- A markup language, the Wireless Markup Language, adhering to XML
- A specification of a small browser suitable for a mobile, wireless terminal
- A lightweight communications protocol stack
- A framework for wireless telephony applications (WTAs)

The WAP Programming Model

The WAP Programming Model is based on three elements: the *client*, the *gateway*, and the *original server* (Figure 14.8). HTTP is used between the gateway and the original server to transfer content. The gateway acts as a proxy server for the wireless domain. Its processor(s) provide services that offload the limited capabilities of the hand-held, mobile, wireless terminals. For example, the gateway provides

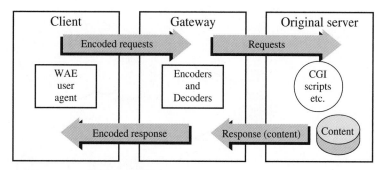

Figure 14.8   The WAP Programming Model

DNS services, converts between WAP protocol stack and the WWW stack (HTTP and TCP/IP), encodes information from the Web into a more compact form that minimizes wireless communication, and, in the other direction, decodes the compacted form into standard Web communication conventions. The gateway also caches frequently requested information.

The Wireless Markup Language (WML)

WML does not assume a standard keyboard or a mouse as an input device. It is designed to work with telephone keypads, styluses, and other input devices common to mobile, wireless communication. WML documents are subdivided into small, well-defined units of user interaction called *cards*. Users navigate by moving back and forth between cards. WML uses a small set of markup tags appropriate to telephony-based systems.

The Microbrowser

The microbrowser is based on a user interface model appropriate for mobile, wireless devices. A traditional 12-key phone keypad is used to enter alphanumeric characters. Users navigate among the WML cards using up and down scroll keys rather than a mouse. Navigation features familiar from the Web (e.g., Back, Home, and Bookmark) are provided as well.

Wireless Telephony Applications (WTAs)

WTA provides an interface to the local and wide area telephone systems. Thus, using WTA, applications developers can use the microbrowser to originate telephone calls and to respond to events from the telephone network.

A Sample Configuration

Figure 14.9 represents schematically a possible WAP configuration. There are three networks: the Internet (excluding the wireless net), the public switched telephone network (PSTN), and a wireless network based on, for example, GSM. The client could be a hand-held, mobile terminal in the wireless network. It communicates, in this example, with two gateways; one is the WAP Proxy to the Internet. The WAP Proxy communicates on the terminal's behalf with servers on the Internet. The Proxy translates HTML information to WML and sends it to the terminal. Material

Client

The Internet

WAP proxy

The public switched
telephone network
(PSTN)

WTA server

Figure 14.9 WAP Network Schematic

on the Internet already in WML format is passed directly to the terminal without translation. The other gateway, the WTA Server, is a gateway to the PSTN so that the WAP terminal can access telephony-based functionality such as call control, phone book access, and messaging through the microbrowser.

14.4 SATELLITE COMMUNICATIONS

Satellite communications is comparable in importance to optical fiber in the evolution of telecommunications and data communications.

The heart of a satellite communications system is a satellite-based antenna in a stable orbit above the earth. In a satellite communications system, two or more stations on or near the earth communicate via one or more satellites that serve as relay stations in space. The antenna systems on or near the earth are referred to as **earth stations**. A transmission from an earth station to the satellite is referred to as **uplink**, whereas transmissions from the satellite to the earth station are **downlink**. The electronics in the satellite that takes an uplink signal and converts it to a downlink signal is called a **transponder**.

Satellite Orbits

GEOSTATIONARY SATELLITES   The most common type of communications satellite today is the geostationary (GEO) satellite, first proposed by the science fiction author Arthur C. Clarke in 1945. If the satellite is in a circular orbit 35,863 km above the earth's surface and rotates in the equatorial plane of the earth, it will rotate at exactly the same angular speed as the earth and will remain above the same spot on the equator as the earth rotates. [4] Figure 14.10 depicts the GEO orbit in scale with

---

[4]The term *geosynchronous* is often used in place of *geostationary*. For purists, the difference is that a geosynchronous orbit is any circular orbit at an altitude of 35,863 km, and a geostationary orbit is a geosynchronous orbit with zero inclination, so the satellite hovers over one spot on the earth's equator.

Orbit: 35,863 km
over the equator

○ = Satellite

Figure 14.10   Geostationary Earth Orbit (GEO)

the size of the earth; the satellite symbols are intended to suggest that there are many satellites in GEO orbit, some of which are quite close to each other.

The GEO orbit has several advantages to recommend it:

- Because the satellite is stationary relative to the earth, there is no problem with frequency changes due to the relative motion of the satellite and antennas on earth (Doppler effect).

- Tracking of the satellite by its earth stations is simplified.

- At 35,863 km above the earth the satellite can communicate with roughly a fourth of the earth; three satellites in geostationary orbit separated by 120° cover most of the inhabited portions of the entire earth excluding only the areas near the north and south poles.

422 CHAPTER 14 / WIRELESS WANS

On the other hand, there are problems:

- The signal can get quite weak after traveling over 35,000 km.
- The polar regions and the far northern and southern hemispheres are poorly served by geostationary satellites.
- Even at the speed of light, about 300,000 km/s, the delay in sending a signal from a point on the equator beneath the satellite to the satellite and back is substantial.

The delay of communication between two locations on earth directly under the satellite is in fact $(2 \times 35{,}863)/300{,}000 \approx 0.24$ s. For other locations not directly under the satellite, the delay is even longer. If the satellite link is used for telephone communication, the added delay between when one person speaks and the other responds is increased twofold, to almost 0.5 s. This is definitely noticeable. Another feature of geostationary satellites is that they use their assigned frequencies over a very large area. For point-to-multipoint applications such as broadcasting TV programs, this can be desirable, but for point-to-point communications it is very wasteful of spectrum. Special spot and steered beam antennas, which restrict the area covered by the satellite's signal, can be used to control the "footprint" or signaling area. To solve some of these problems, orbits other than geostationary have been designed for satellites. *Low-earth-orbiting satellites (LEOSs)* and *medium-earth-orbiting satellites (MEOS)* are important for third-generation personal communications.

LEO SATELLITES   LEOSs (Figure 14.11) have the following characteristics:

- Circular or slightly elliptical orbit at less than 2000 km. Proposed and actual systems are in the range 500 to 1500 km.
- The orbit period is in the range of 1.5 to 2 hours.
- The diameter of coverage is about 8000 km.
- Round-trip signal propagation delay is less than 20 ms.
- The maximum time that the satellite is visible from a fixed point on earth (above the radio horizon) is up to 20 minutes.
- Because the motion of the satellite relative to a fixed point on earth is high, the system must be able to cope with large Doppler shifts, which change the frequency of the signal.
- The atmospheric drag on a LEO satellite is significant, resulting in gradual orbital deterioration.

Practical use of this system requires that multiple orbital planes be used, each with multiple satellites in orbit. Communication between two earth stations typically will involve handing off the signal from one satellite to another.

LEO satellites have a number of advantages over GEO satellites. In addition to the reduced propagation delay mentioned previously, a received LEOS signal is much stronger than that of GEOS signals for the same transmission power. LEOS coverage can be better localized so that spectrum can be better conserved. For this reason, this technology is currently being proposed for communicating with mobile terminals and with personal terminals that need stronger signals to function. On the other hand, to provide broad coverage over 24 hours, many satellites are needed.

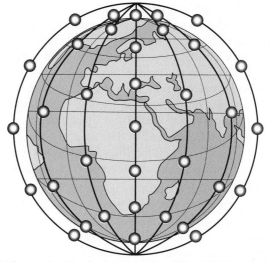

(a) Low earth orbit: often in polar orbit at 500 to 1500 km altitude

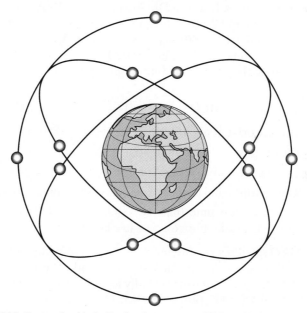

(b) Medium earth orbit: inclined to the equator, at 5000 to 12,000 km altitude

Figure 14.11   LEO and MEO Orbits

A number of commercial proposals have been made to use clusters of LEOSs to provide communications services. These proposals can be divided into two categories:

- **Little LEOS:** Intended to work at communication frequencies below 1 GHz using no more than 5 MHz of bandwidth and supporting data rates up to 10 kbps. These systems are aimed at paging, tracking, and low-rate messaging.

Orbcomm is an example of such a satellite system. It was the first (little) LEOS in operation; its first two satellites were launched in April of 1995. It is designed for paging and burst communication and is optimized for handling small bursts of data from 6 to 250 bytes in length. It is used by businesses to track trailers, railcars, heavy equipment, and other remote and mobile assets. It can also be used to monitor remote utility meters, oil and gas storage tanks, wells, and pipelines. It can be used to stay in touch with remote workers anywhere in the world as well. It uses frequencies in the range of 148.00 to 150.05 MHz to the satellites, and in the range of 137.00 to 138.00 MHz from the satellites. It has well over 30 satellites in low earth orbit. It supports subscriber data rates of 2.4 kbps to the satellite and 4.8 kbps down.

- **Big LEOS:** Work at frequencies above 1 GHz and support data rates up to a few megabits per second. These systems tend to offer the same services as those of the small LEOS, with the addition of voice and positioning services. Globalstar is one example of a Big LEO system. Its satellites are fairly rudimentary. Unlike some of the little LEOS systems, it has no onboard processing or communications between satellites. Most processing is done by the system's earth stations. It uses CDMA as in the CDMA cellular standard. It uses the S-Band (about 2 GHz) for the downlink to mobile users. Globalstar is tightly integrated with traditional voice carriers. All calls must be processed through earth stations. The satellite constellation consists of 48 operating satellites and 8 spares. They are in 1413-km-high orbits.

MEO SATELLITES   MEOSs (Figure 14.11b) have the following characteristics:

- Circular orbit at an altitude in the range 5000 to 12,000 km.
- The orbit period is about 6 hours.
- The diameter of coverage is from 10,000 to 15,000 km.
- Round-trip signal propagation delay is less than 50 ms.
- The maximum time that the satellite is visible from a fixed point on earth (above the radio horizon) is a few hours.

MEO satellites require much fewer handoffs than LEO satellites. While propagation delay to earth from such satellites and the power required are greater than for LEOSs, they are still substantially less than for GEO satellites. New ICO, established in January 1995, proposed a MEOS system. Launches began in 2000. Twelve satellites, including two spares, are planned in 10,400-km-high orbits. The satellites will be divided equally between two planes tilted 45° to the equator. Proposed applications are digital voice, data, facsimile, high-penetration notification, and messaging services.

Satellite Network Configurations

Figure 14.12 depicts in a general way two common configurations for satellite communication. In the first, the satellite is being used to provide a point-to-point link between two distant ground-based antennas. In the second, the satellite provides communications between one ground-based transmitter and a number of ground-based receivers.

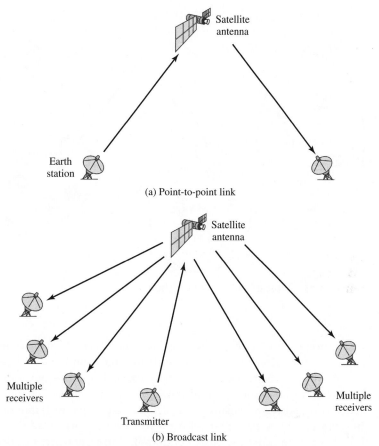

Figure 14.12   Satellite Communication Configurations

Applications

The communications satellite is a technological revolution as important as fiber optics. Among the most important applications for satellites are the following:

- Television distribution
- Long-distance telephone transmission
- Private business networks

Because of their broadcast nature, satellites are well suited to television distribution and are being used extensively for this purpose in the United States and throughout the world. In its traditional use, a network provides programming from a central location. Programs are transmitted to the satellite and then broadcast down to a number of stations, which then distribute the programs to individual viewers. A more recent application of satellite technology to television distribution is direct broadcast satellite (DBS), in which satellite video signals are transmitted directly to the home user.

Satellite transmission is also used for point-to-point trunks between telephone exchange offices in public telephone networks. It is a useful medium for high-usage

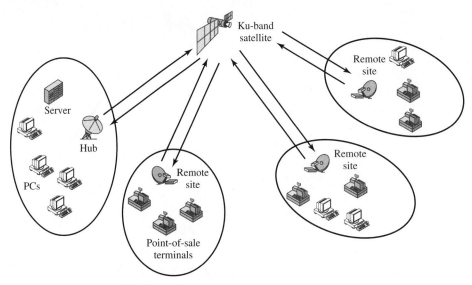

Figure 14.13   Typical VSAT Configuration

international trunks and is competitive with terrestrial systems for many long-distance intranational links, particularly in remote and undeveloped areas.

Finally, there are a number of business data applications for satellite. The satellite provider can divide the total capacity into a number of channels and lease these channels to individual business users. A user equipped with antennas at a number of sites can use a satellite channel for a private network. Traditionally, such applications have been quite expensive and limited to larger organizations with high-volume requirements. Today, the very small aperture terminal (VSAT) system provides a low-cost alternative. Figure 14.13 depicts a typical VSAT configuration. A number of subscriber stations are equipped with low-cost VSAT antennas. Using some discipline, these stations share a satellite transmission capacity for transmission to a hub station. The hub station can exchange messages with each of the subscribers and can relay messages between subscribers.

APPLICATION NOTE

PDAs, Cell Phones, and Laptops

Businesses are faced with several questions regarding computing resources. While it is common for an organization to purchase dozens or even hundreds of desktop computers, increasingly organizations must also make mobile computing decisions. The choices really depend on the application or use for which the device is intended. More than one company has stretched its budget by buying devices that are overpowered for the application or the devices may be left to gather dust because they are unsatisfactory for the defined tasks. In order to make the right decision, some analysis for the right tools must be undertaken.

Laptops are probably the first option that comes to mind when we think of mobile devices. Laptops have a great deal of processing power, memory, and hard drive capacity. They come equipped with built-in wireless connectivity that makes them very attractive because there is no need to purchase the wireless network cards. Combined with a docking station, this type of computer can double as a desktop station. As attractive as they are, laptops do have a darker side. Laptops are sometimes more difficult to use because of the keyboard style and type of built-in mouse. Many users opt to have larger monitors, extended keyboards, and an extra mouse when working in desktop mode. Another downside to laptop purchases, if the laptop is actually used as a mobile station, is that batteries rarely behave as advertised. Every activity drains the battery further, and the true mobile user must become familiar with power-saving settings or have a second battery on hand. Yet for a user that requires the processing power, large storage capacity, and easy access to all of his/her files when moving from home to the office, the laptop may represent the best solution.

Handhelds or personal data assistants (PDAs) are another solution to mobile connectivity. Palm Pilots, iPAQs, Blackberries, and even some cellular phones are among the most popular. All handhelds-boast a wide variety of tools, including e-mail, image viewing, and calendaring. General-use PDA applications seem to pop up daily in addition to those developed locally by an organization. Connectivity for a PDA is usually accomplished via a packet radio system (which runs over a local cellular provider network) like the general packet radio service or GPRS. Some also use 802.11 networks.

PDAs represent a compact, highly portable data access device that can upload data from or download data to a computer. They can be a solid asset where a limited number of applications are needed and document generation is not required. A good example is the legal industry, where lawyers previously outfitted with laptops had them replaced with handheld devices. This was a good match because the attorneys did not need to generate their own documents. Their real requirement was staying in contact with the office via e-mail. As a result, the firms realized significant savings and the attorneys were not burdened with the heavier laptop.

A PDA is not a replacement for a laptop as it does not have the processing capability or the storage capacity. While this is improving, there is also the question of usability. Working with a stylus or miniature keyboard can be a frustrating experience. However, for the determined PDA user, folding keyboards are also available. In fact, PDAs can be equipped with an impressive array of add-on devices, including wireless or wired local area network connection modules.

Cell phones are our third mobile connectivity option and provide some value-added services, such as messaging or two-way radio. While the services offered in the United States are not at the level of those offered in some other countries, they are improving. The real strength of the cell phone lies in its anywhere, anytime voice connectivity. While a PDA can connect over the same network, the packet data service is not always available and support for voice is not at its best. The same is true for laptop voice (soft phone) support. In addition to the value-added services, cell phones are also beginning to show signs of applications for the end user. However, these applications seem to be more geared toward entertainment than a business model. Examples of additional cell phone capabilities include games, video, still images, and push technologies such as sporting news and weather.

(Continued)

Lastly, laptop cards that connect the laptop to the cellular data network are available. There was a time when the bandwidth one could expect for the data connection was very small. This is changing for the good as more and more demands are placed on data connections. Thus, for a monthly fee and the cost of the card, the portability of the cell phone and some PDAs can be extended to the laptop via a cellular network.

As is often the case, we must first ask ourselves, "What are we trying to do?" or "What do we need to do?" Once these questions are answered, it is usually easier to find a solution that fits the needs of the organization. PDAs and cell phones, while often considered necessary tools, are not usually a replacement for a laptop or desktop computer. For sheer portability, it is often much more feasible to carry around a wallet-sized device rather than a tablet-sized one. On the other hand, there is a big difference between wanting and needing, especially where the bottom line is concerned. Companies would be well advised to look at usage patterns before and after PDA or cell phone purchases to determine if they are indeed necessary. Even if the power of a laptop is currently the best solution, improvements in cell phones and PDAs can have us struggling to decide which device is best for the next generation of connectivity as the lines between them are no longer well defined.

14.5 SUMMARY

Cellular wireless networks have traditionally supported mobile telephony but now also support wireless Internet access and other wireless data networking applications. Cellular networks are becoming pervasive worldwide and carry an increasing portion of long-distance voice and data traffic. A cellular system is based on the principle of using a large number of relatively small geographic areas, called cells, to cover a large area. Each cell is allocated a band of frequencies and is served by a base station, consisting of transmitter, receiver, and control unit. Adjacent cells are assigned different frequencies to avoid interference or crosstalk. However, cells sufficiently distant from each other can use the same frequency band.

The capacity available within each cell is shared among a number of users by means of some sort of multiple access scheme. For a given system, multiple access is based on TDMA, FDMA, CDMA, or some combination of these.

Another important form of wireless communications is satellite communications. The bulk of satellite traffic has traditionally been carried by geostationary satellites. Recently, networks using LEO and MEO satellites have been introduced.

14.6 RECOMMENDED READING AND WEB SITES

The topics in this chapter are covered in greater depth in [STAL05]. An excellent survey text is [RAPP02]. For a detailed technical treatment of wireless transmission and communications, see [FREE97].

FREE97 Freeman, R. *Radio System Design for Telecommunications.* New York: Wiley, 1997.

RAPP02 Rappaport, T., *Wireless Communications: Principles and Practice.* Upper Saddle River, NJ: Prentice Hall, 2002.

STAL05 Stallings, W. *Wireless Communications and Networks.* Upper Saddle River, NJ: Prentice Hall, 2005.

Recommended Web sites:

- **CDMA Development Group:** A consortium of wireless companies active in CDMA wireless systems around the world.

- **Cellular Telecommunications and Internet Association:** An industry consortium that provides information on successful applications of wireless technology.

- **3G Americas:** A trade group of Western Hemisphere companies supporting a variety of second and third-generation schemes. Includes industry news, white papers, and other technical information.

- **Open Mobile Alliance:** Concerned with a range of standards for mobile communications. Includes WAP technical specifications and industry links.

- **Lloyd Wood's satellite Web page:** An excellent overview of satellite communications, with lots of links.

- **Satellite Industry Association:** Trade organization representing U.S. space and communications companies in the commercial satellite arena. Lots of links.

14.7 KEY TERMS, REVIEW QUESTIONS, AND PROBLEMS

Key Terms

base station	frequency division multiple access (FDMA)	space division multiple access (SDMA)
cell sectoring	frequency reuse	time division multiple access (TDMA)
cell splitting	geostationary satellite	transponder
cellular wireless network	low-earth-orbiting (LEO) satellite	uplink
code division multiple access (CDMA)	medium-earth-orbiting (MEO) satellite	wireless application protocol (WAP)
communications satellite	microcells	wireless markup language (WML)
direct sequence spread spectrum (DSSS)	multiple access	
downlink	reuse factor	
earth station		

Review Questions

14.1 What geometric shape is used in cellular system design?

14.2 What is the principle of frequency reuse in the context of a cellular network?

14.3 List five ways of increasing the capacity of a cellular system.

14.4 Explain the paging function of a cellular system.

14.5 What is cellular handoff?

14.6 For a cellular system, describe the function of the following: control channels and traffic channels.

14.7 Describe what is meant by the term *multiple access* as it applies to cellular communication.

14.8 Briefly explain the principle behind CDMA.

14.9 What is the wireless application protocol (WAP)?

14.10 Explain what GEOS, LEOS, and MEOS satellites are (including what the acronyms stand for). Compare the three types with respect to factors such as size and shape of orbits, signal power, frequency reuse, propagation delay, number of satellites for global coverage, and handoff frequency.

14.11 Under what circumstances would you use GEOS, LEOS, and MEOS, respectively?

Problems

14.1 There are many cellular providers serving each geographic area, and each one may use a different technology.

    a. Who are the providers in your area and what are the multiple access technologies used?

    b. What are the technologies behind the cellular phones you or your family and friends use?

14.2 Consider four different cellular systems that share the following characteristics. The frequency bands are 825 to 845 MHz for mobile unit transmission and 870 to 890 MHz for base station transmission. A duplex circuit consists of one 30-kHz channel in each direction. The systems are distinguished by the reuse factor, which is 4, 7, 12, and 19, respectively.

    a. Suppose that in each of the systems, the cluster of cells (4, 7, 12, 19) is duplicated 16 times. Find the number of simultaneous communications that can be supported by each system.

    b. Find the number of simultaneous communications that can be supported by a single cell in each system.

    c. What is the area covered, in cells, by each system?

    d. Suppose the cell size is the same in all four systems and a fixed area of 100 cells is covered by each system. Find the number of simultaneous communications that can be supported by each system.

14.3 Describe a sequence of events similar to that of Figure 14.5 for

    a. a call from a mobile unit to a fixed subscriber

    b. a call from a fixed subscriber to a mobile unit

14.4 An analog cellular system has a total of 33 MHz of bandwidth and uses two 25-kHz simplex (one-way) channels to provide full duplex voice and control channels.

    a. What is the number of channels available per cell for a frequency reuse factor of (1) 4 cells, (2) 7 cells, and (3) 12 cells?

    b. Assume that 1 MHz is dedicated to control channels but that only one control channel is needed per cell. Determine a reasonable distribution of control channels and voice channels in each cell for the three frequency reuse factors of part (a).

14.5 A cellular system uses FDMA with a spectrum allocation of 12.5 MHz in each direction, a guard band at the edge of the allocated spectrum of 10 kHz, and a channel bandwidth of 30 kHz. What is the number of available channels?

14.6 For a cellular system, FDMA spectral efficiency is defined as $\eta_a = \dfrac{B c N_T}{B_w}$, where

B_c = channel bandwidth
B_w = total bandwidth in one direction
N_T = total number of voice channels in the covered area
What is an upper bound on η_a

14.7 Global System for Mobile communications (GSM) is an international standard for digital cellular communication. Provide a basic overview of GSM, focusing on the three primary functional entities of a GSM network. Is the GSM strategy a superior or inferior alternative to CDMA? Support your answer.

14.8 Some concern has been expressed regarding potential health hazards related to cellular phone use. Discuss potential health risks related to cellular phone technology. What precautions can be taken to minimize potential dangers involved in cell phone use?

CHOICE HOTELS INTERNATIONAL

Within the hospitality industry, there has traditionally been a division between networks that serve guest functions and those that serve operations and administration, both with respect to data transmission and voice transmission. In recent years, most hotel and motel chains have moved in the direction of consolidating multiple functions on networks that used to be dedicated to one use. Tighter integration of voice and data and of guest and operations/administration networking is a fast-growing trend. Choice Hotels International is a good example of this trend.

Choice Hotels International is the world's second largest hotel franchise, with enough beds for about a million people. The company franchises more than 5000 hotels, inns, all-suite hotels, and resorts open and under development in 48 countries under the Comfort Inn, Comfort Suites, Quality, Clarion, Sleep Inn, Rodeway Inn, Econo Lodge, and MainStay Suites brands.

IN-HOUSE NETWORKING FUNCTIONS

Choice supports two distinct networking functions. A central Web site enables customers to reserve rooms at any Choice franchise accommodation. The central reservation system, known as Profit Manager, automatically finds the most appropriate hotel based on location, price range, or standard. Individual hotels also take bookings, so there needs to be a way for hotels and the central system to remain synchronized.

Choice networks also support its franchisees. Choice is in fact a relatively small company in terms of personnel (about 2000 employees) and does not own or operate any hotels. All of the establishments under its brand names are independently owned and pay Choice licensing fees and a royalty on all sales. In return, they receive a variety of services, including marketing, quality control, and inventory management. Many of these services are offered via network, such as allowing managers to order supplies online and check booking status. This support network is similar to a corporate intranet but has a higher reliability requirement. The 5000 hotel managers are, in effect, Choice's customers, not employees. Thus, the standards for reliability and performance of the network are high.

In the late 1990s, Choice began to focus on providing a state-of-the-art global reservation system. At this point, the synchronization of local and online reservations was done manually. Each hotel provided Choice with a fixed block of inventory to sell over the central reservation system, with an average of 30% of capacity. Once that 30% was sold, Profit Manager listed the hotel as fully booked, even though there might be plenty of rooms available from the other 70%. The reverse problem also occurred: If the local reservation system had sold all available rooms except those assigned to Choice, the local staff had to refuse additional customers or overbook. Thus, the system was inherently inefficient.

Around this time, Choice moved from a purely telephone-based central reservation system to a Web-based system. Choice found, as did many companies, that letting customers serve themselves online saved time and money. Further, unlike many industries burned in the move to e-commerce, the travel sector is an ideal match for Web-based services. Booking a hotel room has always been done remotely, via telephone. There are none of the fulfillment problems that have plagued the online mail-order business, because there are no shipping costs and no shipping and delivery hassles. And the benefits are striking. Customers can get an instant list of every room available with their chosen criteria. They can also view the hotel and, in some cases, the individual room. In addition, hotel rooms are a typical example of "distressed" products; like airline seats and theater tickets, they can't be stockpiled if left unsold. Thus, they are ideal for using last-minute special offers and promotions, which can be posted online or e-mailed to interested customers.

But all of these benefits require full integration between local reservation systems and the central reservation system. Choice decided to implement a franchise-wide IP network that provided every American hotel with a permanent connection to the central Profit Manager database. The most important criteria for this network were coverage and reliability. The network needed to reach every franchise and needed to be highly available. Capacity was not a particular concern, because updates and reservations use little capacity.

To meet its needs, Choice decided to go with a satellite network [HARL02, DORN01, UHLA00]. Even within the United States, reliable universal coverage requires expensive leased lines or dependence on switched networks that may not always deliver. The situation is far worse internationally. Satellite networks provide the universal coverage and are in fact more reliable than the competition. Satellites that use fixed dishes are a mature, dependable technology. Downtime averages only minutes each year.

For its initial effort, Choice went to Hughes Network Systems, which set up a dedicated IP network using two geostationary satellites based at separate hubs (Figure VIII.1). The hub is a ground-based control center that includes a number of switches and routers. At the hub, Hughes separates Choice's traffic from that of its other customers and routes it accordingly. The Los Angeles hub covers the entire United States via a broad-beam satellite service. The Germantown hub controls a number of narrower spot beams that service Alaska and Hawaii and provides extra capacity for major cities. Each hotel is equipped with a VSAT (very small aperture terminal) dish.

The satellite system has worked well, and Choice has gradually transitioned operational and administrative functions to the network. For example, data for settling accounts with travel agents and tracking the Choice Privilege frequent-stayer program are sent on the satellite network.

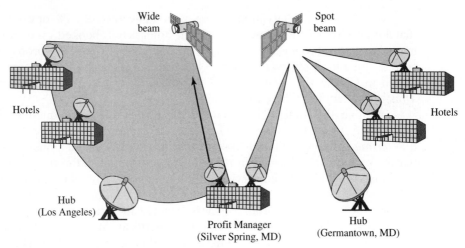

Figure VIII.1 Choice Hotels U.S. Network

Guest Internet Access

In 2004, choice began implementing free high-speed Internet access for all guests in its Clarion Hotels and Comfort Suites, using 3Com equipment. The implementation uses an efficient combination of wireless and wired access within each hotel [3COM04, 3COM06].

To be able to affordably provide Internet service, hotels have traditionally invested in expensive and disruptive construction, including the installation of additional cabling and forcing the closing of income-producing rooms. To recover their costs, hotels normally surcharge by the minute for Internet access—which is exactly the situation Choice Hotels wished to avoid. To allow its franchises to affordably fulfill its mandate, Choice Hotels needed a powerful, low-cost network solution that could be installed quickly and easily.

Access is provided in wireless and wired modes. For wireless access, each hotel implements Wi-Fi that serves all guest rooms. Using the 3Com Wi-Fi network, guests are able to check e-mail, exchange files, and browse the Web at speeds up to 54 Mbps. Built-in encryption and support for multiple security options help safeguard data as they travel over the wireless network. With each access point supporting up to 256 users, setting up conference room connectivity requires no additional wiring or IT assistance to provide ample bandwidth even to large groups.

Users without wireless capabilities will be able to plug their laptops into 3Com wireless LAN workgroup bridges in guest rooms and hotel data centers for immediate connectivity.

Discussion Questions

1. Perhaps the major drawback to a satellite-based system is latency. The delays can be noticeable on some online applications. Discuss what issues this might raise for the Choice suite of applications.

2. What issues would you expect to arise as Choice moves to expand the network to full global reach?

PART FIVE

Data Communications

T he material in Part Five deals with fundamental aspects of communications technology. In a business context it is important to have at least a modest level of understanding of these technologies to be able to assess various products and services. However, in most cases, the choices facing the decision maker do not boil down to a simple selection of a technology but rather to a product or service that exploits a variety of technologies. Thus, it is only in other chapters (Part Four onward) of this book that we are able to relate effectively the concepts being discussed to the needs of the business.

ROAD MAP FOR PART FIVE

Chapter 15 Data Transmission

The principles of data transmission underlie all of the concepts and techniques presented in this book. To understand the need for encoding, multiplexing, switching, error control, and so on, the reader should understand the behavior of data signals propagated through a transmission medium. Chapter 15 discusses the distinction between digital and analog data and digital and analog transmission. Concepts of **attenuation** and **noise** are also examined.

Chapter 16 Data Communication Fundamentals

The transmission of information across a transmission medium involves more than simply inserting a signal on the medium. Chapter 16 discusses a number of data communications concepts, including analog versus digital transmission, data encoding techniques, and the distinction between asynchronous and synchronous transmission. This chapter also deals with the topic of error detection.

Chapter 17 Data Link Control and Multiplexing

True cooperative exchange of digital data between two devices requires some form of data link control. Chapter 17 examines the fundamental techniques common to all data link control protocols, including flow control and error control, and then

435

examines the most commonly used protocol, HDLC. Chapter 17 discusses the two most common types of multiplexing techniques. The first, frequency division multiplexing (FDM), is the most widespread and is familiar to anyone who has ever used a radio or television set. The second is a particular case of time division multiplexing (TDM) often known as synchronous TDM. This is commonly used for multiplexing digitized voice streams.

CHAPTER 15

DATA TRANSMISSION

15.1 Signals for Conveying Information
Electromagnetic Signals
Analog Signals
Digital Signals

15.2 Transmission Impairments and Channel Capacity
Guided Media
Unguided Media
Channel Capacity

15.3 Summary

15.4 Recommended Reading and Web Sites

15.5 Key Terms, Review Questions, and Problems

Chapter Objectives

After reading this chapter, you should be able to

◆ Explain the various ways in which audio, data, image, and video can be represented by electromagnetic signals.

◆ Discuss the various transmission impairments that affect the quality and transfer rate of information.

◆ Explain the concept of channel capacity.

In this book we are concerned with one particular means for communicating information: the transmission of electromagnetic waves. All of the forms of information that we have discussed (audio, data, image, video) can be represented by electromagnetic signals and transmitted over a suitable transmission medium.

We first look at the types of electromagnetic signals that are used to convey information. In doing so we describe the most straightforward way in which each of the four types of information can be represented. Then we discuss the sad fact that such transmission is subject to impairments that can introduce errors and inefficiencies. Following this discussion, we can arrive at an understanding of the concept of channel capacity.

15.1 SIGNALS FOR CONVEYING INFORMATION

Electromagnetic Signals

Information is transmitted by means of electromagnetic signals. An electromagnetic signal is a function of time, but it can also be expressed as a function of frequency; that is, the signal consists of components of different frequencies. It turns out that the frequency domain view of a signal is far more important to an understanding of data transmission than a time domain view. Both views are introduced here.

TIME DOMAIN CONCEPTS   Viewed as a function of time, an electromagnetic signal can be either analog or digital. An **analog signal** is one in which the signal intensity varies in a smooth fashion over time. In other words, there are no breaks or discontinuities in the signal. A **digital signal** is one in which the signal intensity maintains a constant level for some period of time and then changes to another constant level. Figure 15.1 shows examples of both kinds of signals. The analog signal might represent speech, and the digital signal might represent binary 1s and 0s.

The simplest sort of signal is a **periodic signal**, in which the same signal pattern repeats over time. Figure 15.2 shows an example of a periodic analog signal (**sine wave**) and a periodic digital signal (**square wave**). The sine wave is the fundamental analog signal. A general sine wave can be represented by three parameters: peak amplitude (A), frequency (f), and phase (ϕ). The **peak amplitude** is the maximum value or strength of the signal over time; typically, this value is measured in volts. The **frequency** is the rate [in cycles per second, or hertz (Hz)] at which the signal

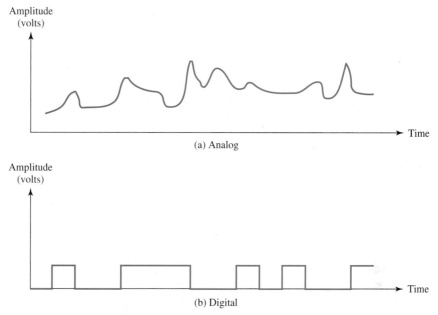

Figure 15.1 Analog and Digital Waveforms

repeats. An equivalent parameter is the **period** (T) of a signal, which is the amount of time it takes for one repetition; therefore, $T = 1/f$. **Phase** is a measure of the relative position in time within a single period of a signal, as illustrated later.

The general sine wave can be written

$$s(t) = A \sin(2\pi ft + \phi)$$

Figure 15.3 shows the effect of varying each of the three parameters. In part (a) of the figure, the frequency is 1 Hz; thus the period is $T = 1$ second. Part (b) has the same frequency and phase but a peak amplitude of 0.5. In part (c) we have $f = 2$, which is equivalent to $T = 1/2$. Finally, part (d) shows the effect of a phase shift of $\pi/4$ radians, which is 45 degrees (2π radians = $360° = 1$ period).

In Figure 15.3 the horizontal axis is time; the graphs display the value of a signal at a given point in space as a function of time. These same graphs, with a change of scale, can apply with horizontal axes in space. In this case the graphs display the value of a signal at a given point in time as a function of distance. For example, for a sinusoidal transmission (say, an electromagnetic radio wave some distance from a radio antenna or a sound some distance from loudspeaker) at a particular instant of time, the intensity of the signal varies in a sinusoidal way as a function of distance from the source.

There is a simple relationship between the two sine waves, one in time and one in space. The **wavelength** (λ) of a signal is defined as the distance occupied by a single cycle, or, put another way, the distance between two points of corresponding phase of two consecutive cycles. Assume that the signal is traveling with a velocity v. Then the wavelength is related to the period as follows: $\lambda = vT$. Equivalently, $\lambda f = v$.

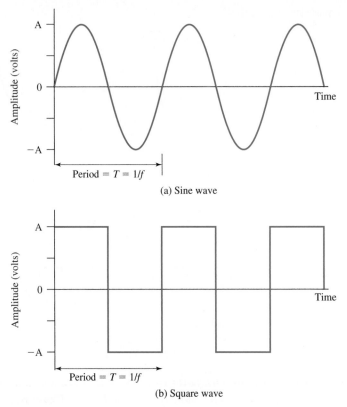

Figure 15.2 Examples of Periodic Signals

Of particular relevance to this discussion is the case where $v = c$, the speed of light in free space, which is approximately 3×10^8 m/s.

FREQUENCY DOMAIN CONCEPTS In practice, an electromagnetic signal will be made up of many frequencies. For example, the signal

$$s(t) = (4/\pi) \times (\sin(2\pi ft) + (1/3)\sin(2\pi(3f)t))$$

is shown in Figure 15.4c. The components of this signal are just sine waves of frequencies f and $3f$; parts (a) and (b) of the figure show these individual components. Two interesting points can be made about this figure:

- The second frequency is an integer multiple of the first frequency. When all of the frequency components of a signal are integer multiples of one frequency, the latter frequency is referred to as the **fundamental frequency**.
- The period of the total signal is equal to the period of the fundamental frequency. The period of the component $\sin(2\pi ft)$ is $T = 1/f$, and the period of $s(t)$ is also T, as can be seen from Figure 15.4c.

By adding together enough sinusoidal signals, each with the appropriate amplitude, frequency, and phase, any electromagnetic signal can be constructed. Put

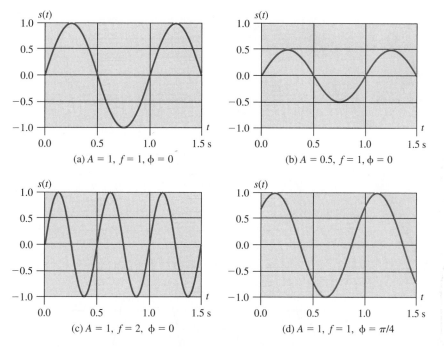

Figure 15.3 $s(t) = A \sin (2\pi ft + \Phi)$

another way, any electromagnetic signal can be shown to consist of a collection of periodic analog signals (sine waves) at different amplitudes, frequencies, and phases. The importance of being able to look at a signal from the frequency perspective (frequency domain) rather than a time perspective (time domain) should become clear as the discussion proceeds.

The **spectrum** of a signal is the range of frequencies that it contains. For the signal of Figure 15.4c, the spectrum extends from f to $3f$. The absolute bandwidth of a signal is the width of the spectrum. In the case of Figure 15.4c, the bandwidth is $3f - f = 2f$. Many signals have an infinite bandwidth. However, most of the energy in the signal is contained in a relatively narrow band of frequencies. This band is referred to as the effective bandwidth, or just **bandwidth**.

There is a direct relationship between the information-carrying capacity of a signal and its bandwidth: The greater the bandwidth, the higher the information-carrying capacity. As a very simple example, consider the square wave of Figure 15.2b. Suppose that we let a positive pulse represent binary 0 and a negative pulse represent binary 1. Then the waveform represents the binary stream 0101.... The duration of each pulse is $1/(2f)$; thus the data rate is $2f$ bits per second (bps). What are the frequency components of this signal? To answer this question, consider again Figure 15.4. By adding together sine waves at frequencies f and $3f$, we get a waveform that begins to resemble the original square wave. Let us continue this process by adding a sine wave of frequency $5f$, as shown in Figure 15.5a, and then adding a sine wave of frequency $7f$, as shown in Figure 15.5b. As we add additional odd multiples of f, suitably scaled, the resulting waveform approaches that of a square wave more and more closely.

Figure 15.4 Addition of Frequency Components ($T = 1/f$)

Indeed, it can be shown that the frequency components of the square wave with amplitudes A and $-A$ can be expressed as follows:

$$s(t) = A \times \frac{4}{\pi} \times \sum_{k\,\text{odd},\,k=1}^{\infty} \frac{\sin(2\pi k f t)}{k}$$

Thus, this waveform has an infinite number of frequency components and hence an infinite bandwidth. However, the peak amplitude of the kth frequency component, kf, is only $1/k$, so most of the energy in this waveform is in the first few frequency components. What happens if we limit the bandwidth to just the first three frequency components? We have already seen the answer, in Figure 15.5a. As we can see, the shape of the resulting waveform is reasonably close to that of the original square wave.

We can use Figures 15.4 and 15.5 to illustrate the relationship between data rate and bandwidth. Suppose that we are using a digital transmission system that is capable of transmitting signals with a bandwidth of 4 MHz. Let us attempt to transmit a sequence of alternating 1s and 0s as the square wave of Figure 15.5c. What data rate can be achieved? We look at three cases.

Case I. Let us approximate our square wave with the waveform of Figure 15.5a. Although this waveform is a "distorted" square wave, it is sufficiently close to

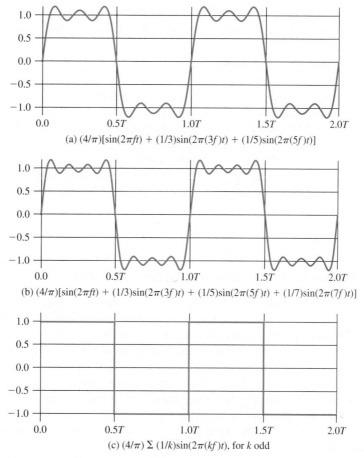

(a) $(4/\pi)[\sin(2\pi ft) + (1/3)\sin(2\pi(3f)t) + (1/5)\sin(2\pi(5f)t)]$

(b) $(4/\pi)[\sin(2\pi ft) + (1/3)\sin(2\pi(3f)t) + (1/5)\sin(2\pi(5f)t) + (1/7)\sin(2\pi(7f)t)]$

(c) $(4/\pi)\ \Sigma\ (1/k)\sin(2\pi(kf)t)$, for k odd

Figure 15.5   Frequency Components of Square Wave $(T = 1/f)$

the square wave that a receiver should be able to discriminate between a binary 0 and a binary 1. If we let $f = 10^6$ cycles/second = 1 MHz, then the bandwidth of the signal

$$s(t) = \frac{4}{\pi} \times \left[\sin\left((2\pi \times 10^6)t\right) + \frac{1}{3}\sin\left((2\pi \times 3 \times 10^6)t\right) \right.$$
$$\left. + \frac{1}{5}\sin\left((2\pi \times 5 \times 10^6)t\right) \right]$$

is $(5 \times 10^6) - 10^6 = 4$ MHz. Note that for $f = 1$ MHz, the period of the fundamental frequency is T $= 1/10^6 = 10^{-6} = 1$ μs. If we treat this waveform as a bit string of 1s and 0s, one bit occurs every 0.5 μs, for a data rate of $2 \times 10^6 = 2$ Mbps. Thus, for a bandwidth of 4 MHz, a data rate of 2 Mbps is achieved.

Case II. Now suppose that we have a bandwidth of 8 MHz. Let us look again at Figure 15.5a, but now with $f = 2$ MHz. Using the same line of reasoning as before, the bandwidth of the signal is $(5 \times 2 \times 10^6) - (2 \times 10^6) = 8$ MHz. But in this case $T = 1/f = 0.5$ μs. As a result, one bit occurs every 0.25 μs for a data rate of 4 Mbps. Thus, other things being equal, by doubling the bandwidth, we double the potential data rate.

Case III. Now suppose that the waveform of Figure 15.4c is considered adequate for approximating a square wave. That is, the difference between a positive and negative pulse in Figure 15.4c is sufficiently distinct that the waveform can be successfully used to represent a sequence of 1s and 0s. Assume as in Case II that $f = 2$ MHz and $T = 1/f = 0.5$ μs, so that one bit occurs every 0.25 μs for a data rate of 4 Mbps. Using the waveform of Figure 15.4c, the bandwidth of the signal is $(3 \times 2 \times 10^6) - (2 \times 10^6) = 4$ MHz. Thus, a given bandwidth can support various data rates depending on the ability of the receiver to discern the difference between 0 and 1 in the presence of noise and other impairments.

To summarize,

- **Case I:** Bandwidth = 4 MHz; data rate = 2 Mbps
- **Case II:** Bandwidth = 8 MHz; data rate = 4 Mbps
- **Case III:** Bandwidth = 4 MHz; data rate = 4 Mbps

We can draw the following conclusions from the preceding discussion. In general, any digital waveform will have infinite bandwidth. If we attempt to transmit this waveform as a signal over any medium, the transmission system will limit the bandwidth that can be transmitted. Furthermore, for any given medium, the greater the bandwidth transmitted, the greater the cost. Thus, on the one hand, economic and practical reasons dictate that digital information be approximated by a signal of limited bandwidth. On the other hand, limiting the bandwidth creates distortions, which makes the task of interpreting the received signal more difficult. The more limited the bandwidth, the greater the distortion and the greater the potential for error by the receiver.

Analog Signals

AUDIO SIGNALS Just as an analog signal is one whose value varies in a continuous fashion, we can say that analog information is information that takes on continuous values. The most familiar example of analog information is audio, or acoustic, information, which, in the form of sound waves, can be perceived directly by human beings. One form of acoustic information, of course, is human speech, which has frequency components in the range 20 Hz to 20 kHz. This form of information is easily converted to an electromagnetic signal for transmission (Figure 15.6). In essence, all of the sound frequencies, whose amplitude is measured in terms of loudness, are converted into electromagnetic frequencies, whose amplitude is measured in volts. The telephone handset contains a simple mechanism for making such a conversion.

Thus, the voice sound wave can be represented directly by an electromagnetic signal occupying the same spectrum. However, there is a need to compromise between the fidelity of the sound as transmitted electromagnetically and the cost of transmission, which increases with increasing bandwidth. Although, as mentioned, human speech has a spectrum of 20 Hz to 20 kHz, tests have shown that a much narrower bandwidth, the range 300 to 3400 Hz, will produce acceptable

In this graph of a typical analog signal, the variations in amplitude and frequency convey the gradations of loudness and pitch in speech or music. Similar signals are used to transmit television pictures, but at much higher frequencies.

Figure 15.6   Conversion of Voice Input to Analog Signal

voice reproduction. That is, if the frequency components outside that range are subtracted, the remainder sounds quite natural. For this reason, telephone networks are able to use communication facilities that limit the transmission of sound to that narrower bandwidth (Figure 15.7). This reduction in the capacity requirement for the transmission of speech results in a corresponding reduction in the cost of the facility.

Note from Figure 15.7 that the actual bandwidth used by the telephone transmission facility is 4 kHz, not 3.1 kHz. The extra bandwidth serves the purpose of isolating the audio signal from interference from signals in adjacent bandwidths.[1] For transmission, then, the telephone handset converts the incoming voice-produced sound wave into an analog electromagnetic signal over the range 300 to 3400 Hz. This signal is then transmitted over the telephone system to a telephone receiver, which reproduces a sound wave from the incoming electromagnetic signal.

VIDEO SIGNALS   To produce a video signal, a TV camera, which performs similar functions to the TV receiver, is used. One component of the camera is a photosensitive plate, upon which a scene is optically focused. An electron beam sweeps across the plate from left to right and top to bottom, in the same fashion as depicted in

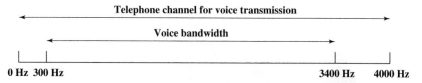

The human voice creates waves of many frequencies, but natural-sounding speech can be limited to a frequency range, or band, of 300 to 3400 Hz. Telephone equipment allows voice a bandwidth of 4000 Hz, which includes a guardband at each end of the frequency range to prevent interference from adjacent voice channels when a number of voice channels are multiplexed.

Figure 15.7   The Voice Band

---

[1]We show in Chapter 17 that it is common to have a number of signals occupy the same transmission medium at different portions of the spectrum, a process known as multiplexing. The extra bandwidth, or guardbands, prevents adjacent signals from interfering with one another.

Figure 2.5 for the receiver. As the beam sweeps, an analog electric signal is developed proportional to the brightness of the scene at a particular spot. A total of 483 lines are scanned at a rate of 30 complete scans per second. This is an approximate number taking into account the time lost during the vertical retrace interval. The actual U.S. standard is 525 lines, but of these about 42 are lost during vertical retrace. Thus the horizontal scanning frequency is (525 lines) $\times$ (30 scan/s) = 15,750 lines per second, or 63.5 μs/line. Of this 63.5 μs, about 11 μs are allowed for horizontal retrace, leaving a total of 52.5 μs per video line.

To transmit analog video information at the necessary rate, a bandwidth of about 4 MHz is needed. As with voice transmission over the telephone network, video signaling over cable TV or via broadcast involves the use of extra bandwidth or guardbands to isolate video signals. With these guardbands, the standard bandwidth for color video signaling is 6 MHz.

Digital Signals

The term *digital signaling* usually refers to the transmission of electromagnetic pulses that represent the two binary digits, 1 and 0. For example, a constant positive voltage pulse could represent binary 0 and a constant negative voltage pulse could represent binary 1. Another alternative is to have one binary digit represented by a constant voltage pulse and the other represented by the absence of any voltage. In either case, what is being represented is binary information. Binary information is generated by terminals, computers, and other data processing equipment and then converted into digital voltage pulses for transmission, as illustrated in Figure 15.8. In the context of this book, the data in which we are interested are in the form of numbers or text. In either case, we must convert this information into binary form; in binary form, it can then be converted into a digital signal.

For humans, numbers are represented in decimal form. In the decimal system, 10 different digits are used to represent numbers. The position of each digit in a number determines its value. Thus, the decimal number 83 means eight tens plus three:

$$83 = (8 \times 10) + 3$$

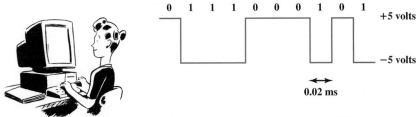

User input at a PC is converted into a stream of binary digits (1s and 0s). In this graph of a typical digital signal, binary one is represented by −5 volts and binary zero is represented by +5 volts. The signal for each bit has a duration of 0.02 ms, giving a data rate of 50,000 bits per second (50 kbps).

Figure 15.8 Conversion of PC Input to Digital Signal

and the number 4728 means

$$4728 = (4 \times 1000) + (7 \times 100) + (2 \times 10) + 8$$

The decimal system is said to have a base of 10. This means that each digit in the number is multiplied by 10 raised to a power corresponding to that digit's position. Thus,

$$83 = (8 \times 10^1) + 3$$
$$4728 = (4 \times 10^3) + (7 \times 10^2) + (2 \times 10^1) + 8$$

In the binary system, we have only two digits, 1 and 0. Thus, numbers in the binary system are represented to the base 2. As with decimal notation, each digit in a binary number has a value depending on its position:

$$10 = (1 \times 2) + 0 = \text{decimal } 2$$
$$11 = (1 \times 2) + 1 = \text{decimal } 3$$
$$100 = (1 \times 2^2) + (0 \times 2) + 0 = \text{decimal } 4$$

where the first number on each line is a binary number. The binary notation can be extended to represent fractional values and negative numbers. The details are not of concern here.

15.2 TRANSMISSION IMPAIRMENTS AND CHANNEL CAPACITY

With any communications system, the signal that is received will differ from the signal that is transmitted, due to various transmission impairments. For analog signals, these impairments introduce various random modifications that degrade the signal quality. For digital signals, bit errors are introduced: A binary 1 is transformed into a binary 0, and vice versa. In this section we examine the various impairments and comment on their effect on the information-carrying capacity of a communications link; Chapter 16 looks at measures that can be taken to compensate for these impairments.

For guided media such as twisted pair, coaxial cable, and optical fiber, the most significant impairments are

- Attenuation and attenuation distortion
- Delay distortion
- Noise

  With wireless transmission, the concerns are

- Free-space loss
- Atmospheric absorption
- Multipath
- Refraction
- Thermal noise

Guided Media

ATTENUATION When an electromagnetic signal is transmitted along any medium, it gradually becomes weaker at greater distances; this is referred to as attenuation. Attenuation introduces three considerations for the transmission engineer:

1. A received signal must have sufficient strength so that the electronic circuitry in the receiver can detect and interpret the signal.
2. The signal must maintain a level sufficiently higher than noise to be received without error.
3. Attenuation is greater at higher frequencies, and this causes distortion.

The first and second considerations are dealt with by attention to signal strength and the use of amplifiers or repeaters. In the simplest sort of link between transmitter and receiver, data transmission occurs between a *transmitter* and a *receiver* over a *transmission medium*. For a very short link, no measures may need to be taken to compensate for attenuation. For distances at which the attenuation becomes significant, one or more intermediate devices may be used to compensate. In the case of analog signals, an amplifier is used; the amplifier boosts the amplitude, or strength, of the signal. In the ideal case, the amplifier will not alter the information content of the signal. In practice, however, the amplifier will introduce some distortion to the signal. This distortion will be cumulative if multiple amplifiers are used along the path between the transmitter and receiver. In the case of digital signals, the intermediate devices are one or more repeaters. The repeater receives the incoming signal on one side, recovers the binary data, and transmits a new digital signal on the other side (Figure 15.9). Thus, there is not an accumulation of distortion. However, any error made in recovering the binary data from the incoming signal persists for the remainder of the transmission path.

The third consideration, known as attenuation distortion, is particularly noticeable for analog signals. Because attenuation is different for different frequencies, and the signal is made up of a number of components at different

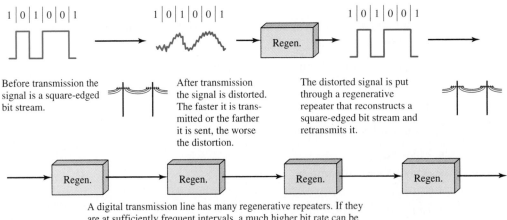

Figure 15.9 Regenerative Repeaters

frequencies, the received signal is not only reduced in strength but is also distorted. To overcome this problem, techniques are available for equalizing attenuation across a band of frequencies. This is commonly done for telephone lines by using loading coils that change the electrical properties of the line to smooth out attenuation effects.

Digital signals are also made up of a number of frequencies. However, most of the energy in a digital signal is concentrated in a reasonably narrow band. Hence, attenuation distortion is less of a problem than it is for analog signals.

DELAY DISTORTION   Delay distortion is a phenomenon that occurs in transmission cables (such as twisted pair, coaxial cable, and optical fiber); it does not occur when signals are transmitted through the air by means of antennas. Delay distortion is caused by the fact that the velocity of propagation of a signal through a cable is different for different frequencies. For a signal with a given bandwidth, the velocity tends to be highest near the center frequency of the signal and to fall off toward the two edges of the band. Thus, various components of a signal will arrive at the receiver at different times.

This effect is referred to as delay distortion because the received signal is distorted due to a variable delay in its frequency components. Delay distortion is particularly critical for digital data. Because of delay distortion, some of the signal energy in one bit position will spill over into other bit positions, which may cause errors on reception; this is a major limitation to the data rate for digital data.

NOISE   When information is transmitted in the form of an electromagnetic signal, the received signal will consist of the transmitted signal, modified by attenuation and the various distortions imposed by the transmission system, plus the addition of unwanted electromagnetic energy that is inserted somewhere between transmitter and receiver. The latter, undesired signals are referred to as **noise**. It is noise that is the major limiting factor in communications system performance.

Noise may be divided into four categories:

- Thermal noise
- Intermodulation noise
- Crosstalk
- Impulse noise

Thermal noise is due to thermal agitation of electrons in a conductor. It is present in all electronic devices and transmission media and is a function of temperature. Thermal noise is uniformly distributed across the frequency spectrum and hence is often referred to as **white noise**. Thermal noise cannot be eliminated and therefore places an upper bound on communications system performance.

When signals of different frequencies share the same transmission medium, the result may be *intermodulation noise*. The effect of intermodulation noise is to produce signals at a frequency that is the sum or difference of the two original frequencies or multiples of those frequencies. For example, if two signals, one at 4000 Hz and one at 8000 Hz, share the same transmission facility, they might produce energy at 12,000 Hz. This noise could interfere with an intended signal at 12,000 Hz.

Intermodulation noise is produced when there is some nonlinearity in the transmitter, receiver, or intervening transmission system. Normally, these components behave as linear systems; that is, the output is equal to the input times a constant. In a nonlinear system, the output is a more complex function of the input. Such nonlinearity can be caused by component malfunction or the use of excessive signal strength. It is under these circumstances that the sum and difference terms occur.

Crosstalk has been experienced by anyone who, while having a telephone conversation, has been able to hear another telephone conversation; it is an unwanted coupling between signal paths. It can occur by electrical coupling between nearby cables or by the overlap of signals transmitted by antennas. Typically, crosstalk is of the same order of magnitude as, or less than, thermal noise.

All of the types of noise discussed so far have reasonably predictable and reasonably constant magnitudes. Thus, it is possible to engineer a transmission system to cope with them. *Impulse noise*, however, is noncontinuous, consisting of irregular pulses or noise spikes of short duration and of relatively high amplitude. It is generated from a variety of causes, including external electromagnetic disturbances, such as lightning, and faults and flaws in the communications system.

Impulse noise is generally only a minor annoyance for analog data. For example, voice transmission may be corrupted by short clicks and crackles with no loss of intelligibility. However, impulse noise is the primary source of error in digital data communication. For example, a sharp spike of energy of 0.01 s duration would not destroy any voice information but would wash out about 500 bits of data being transmitted at 56 kbps. Figure 15.10 is an example of the effect on a digital signal. Here the noise consists of a relatively modest level of thermal noise plus occasional spikes of impulse noise. The digital data are recovered from the signal by sampling the received waveform once per bit time. As can be seen, the noise is occasionally sufficient to change a 1 to a 0 or a 0 to a 1.

Unguided Media

FREE-SPACE LOSS For any type of wireless communication, the signal disperses with distance. Therefore, an antenna with a fixed area will receive less signal power the farther it is from the transmitting antenna. For satellite communication this is the primary mode of signal loss. Under idealized conditions, the ratio of the power P_r received by the antenna to the radiated power P_t is given by

$$\frac{P_r}{P_t} = \frac{A_r A_t f^2}{(cd)^2}$$

where A_r is the area of the receiving antenna, A_t the area of the transmitting antenna, d the distance between the antennas, f the carrier frequency, $\lambda = c/f$ the wavelength, and c = 300,000 km/s the speed of the electromagnetic wave. Thus, for the same antenna dimensions and separation, the higher the carrier frequency f, the lower is the free-space path loss.

ATMOSPHERIC ABSORPTION An additional loss between the transmitting and receiving antennas is atmospheric absorption. Water vapor and oxygen contribute most to attenuation. A peak attenuation occurs in the vicinity of 22 GHz due to water vapor. At frequencies below 15 GHz, the attenuation is less. The presence of oxygen results in an absorption peak in the vicinity of 60 GHz but contributes less at frequencies below 30 GHz. Rain and fog (suspended water droplets) cause scatter-

Figure 15.10 Effect of Noise on Digital Signal

ing of radio waves that results in attenuation. This can be a major cause of signal loss. Thus, in areas of significant precipitation, either path lengths have to be kept short or lower-frequency bands should be used.

MULTIPATH For wireless facilities where there is a relatively free choice of where antennas are to be located, they can be placed so that if there are no nearby interfering obstacles, there is a direct line-of-sight path from transmitter to receiver. This is generally the case for many satellite facilities and for point-to-point microwave. In other cases, such as mobile telephony, there are obstacles in abundance. The signal can be reflected by such obstacles so that multiple copies of the signal with varying delays can be received. In fact, in extreme cases, there may be no direct signal. Depending on the differences in the path lengths of the direct and reflected waves, the composite signal can be either larger or smaller than the direct signal. Reinforcement and cancellation of the signal resulting from the signal following multiple paths can be controlled for communication between fixed, well-sited antennas, and between satellites and fixed ground stations, but for mobile telephony and communication to antennas that are not well sited, multipath considerations can be paramount.

REFRACTION Radio waves are refracted (or bent) when they propagate through the atmosphere. The refraction is caused by changes in the speed of the signal with altitude or by other spatial changes in the atmospheric conditions. Normally, the speed of the signal increases with altitude, causing radio waves to bend downward. However, on occasion, weather conditions may lead to variations in speed with height that differ significantly from the typical variations. This may result in a situation in which only a fraction or no part of the line-of-sight wave reaches the receiving antenna.

THERMAL NOISE Thermal or white noise is inescapable. It arises from the thermal activity of the devices and media of the communication system. Because of the weakness of the signal received by satellite earth stations, thermal noise is particularly important for satellite communication.

Channel Capacity

We have seen that there are a variety of impairments that distort or corrupt a signal. For digital data, the question that then arises is to what extent these impairments limit the data rate that can be achieved. The rate at which data can be transmitted over a given communication path, or channel, under given conditions, is referred to as the **channel capacity**.

There are four concepts here that we are trying to relate to one another:

- **Data rate:** This is the rate, in bits per second (bps), at which data can be communicated.

- **Bandwidth:** This is the bandwidth of the transmitted signal as constrained by the transmitter and the nature of the transmission medium, expressed in cycles per second, or Hertz.

- **Noise:** This is the average level of noise over the communications path.

- **Error rate:** This is the rate at which errors occur, where an error is the reception of a 1 when a 0 was transmitted or the reception of a 0 when a 1 was transmitted.

The problem we are addressing is this: Communications facilities are expensive, and, in general, the greater the bandwidth of a facility, the greater the cost. Furthermore, all transmission channels of any practical interest are of limited bandwidth. The limitations arise from the physical properties of the transmission medium or from deliberate limitations at the transmitter on the bandwidth to prevent interference from other sources. Accordingly, we would like to make as efficient use as possible of a given bandwidth. For digital data, this means that we would like to get as high a data rate as possible at a particular limit of error rate for a given bandwidth. The main constraint on achieving this efficiency is noise.

We have already shown the relationship between bandwidth and data rate in Figure 15.4. All other things being equal, doubling the bandwidth doubles the data rate. Now consider the relationship among data rate, noise, and error rate. This can be explained intuitively by again considering Figure 15.10. The presence of noise can corrupt one or more bits. If the data rate is increased, the bits become "shorter," so that more bits are affected by a given pattern of noise. Thus, at a given noise level, the higher the data rate, the higher the error rate.

All of these concepts can be tied together neatly in a formula developed by the mathematician Claude Shannon. As we have just illustrated, the higher the data rate, the more damage that unwanted noise can do. For a given level of noise, we would expect that a greater signal strength would improve the ability to receive data correctly in the presence of noise. The key parameter involved in this reasoning is the signal-to-noise ratio (SNR, or S/N), which is the ratio of the power in a signal to the power contained in the noise that is present at a particular point in the transmission. Typically, this ratio is measured at a receiver, because it is at this point that an attempt is made to process the signal and eliminate the unwanted noise. The signal-to-noise ratio is important in the transmission of digital data because it sets the upper bound on the achievable data rate. Shannon's result is that the maximum channel capacity, in bits per second, obeys the equation

$$C = B \log_2(1 + \text{SNR})$$

where C is the capacity of the channel in bits per second and B is the bandwidth of the channel in Hertz. The Shannon formula represents the theoretical maximum that can be achieved. In practice, however, lower rates are achieved. One reason for this is that the formula assumes white noise (thermal noise). Impulse noise is not accounted for, nor are attenuation distortion or delay distortion.

Several observations concerning the Shannon equation can be made. The measure of efficiency of a digital transmission is the ratio C/B, which is the bps per hertz value that is achieved. For a given level of noise, it would appear that the data rate could be increased by increasing the signal strength or bandwidth. However, as the signal strength increases, so do nonlinearities in the system, leading to an increase in intermodulation noise. Note also that because noise is assumed to be white, the wider the bandwidth, the more noise is admitted to the system. Thus, as B increases, SNR decreases.

APPLICATION NOTE

Analog Signals

We are surrounded by signals from a wide variety of sources. Understanding these signals can often help us get through basic problems with communications equipment. For example, cellular telephone users often learn to stand by windows to improve their reception. When we are responsible for communications systems, understanding the signals around us can be the difference between reliable and spotty connectivity.

It is interesting to note the differences between digital and analog signals. Analog communications, based largely on the modulation of a sine wave, have certainly been around for a much longer period of time. With the digital revolution in the 1970s and 1980s, analog systems were believed to be inferior. And now with advances in cellular technology

(*Continued*)

and other communications systems, we all want digital communication. What is interesting is that all communication is, in fact, still analog. What is really meant by the terms *digital cellular communication* or *digital subscriber lines* is that we are converting digital information for conveyance over an analog network.

Communication in many systems, and especially communication through the air, requires an analog carrier. Even high-speed communications over fiber optics use analog-based signals. Digital cellular phones still use an analog carrier to carry the digitally encoded messages from one place to another. Even digital local area network signals can be broken down into their component analog parts.

For this reason, understanding analog signals, environmental effects, and the infrastructure type can be extremely beneficial to an organization. Appreciation for the issues makes us better able to make appropriate choices during design phases and facilitates troubleshooting should problems occur after installation.

For guided media, problems are easier to track down and eliminate. As we discussed in previous chapters, the best defense against communication problems in guided media systems is a solid installation. This is true not only for copper-based systems like Ethernet over UTP, but for fiber as well. For wireless systems, even the finest quality system can be rendered inoperable by uncontrollable, outside forces. These forces do not have to be significant events like hurricanes. Even small changes to the environment can create problems. Cellular telephone providers know this only too well, as they have experienced the difference even a tree can make depending on whether or not it is wet. Local construction of a new building or fountain can create reflections or even eliminate line of sight between source and destination.

In addition to obvious problems like skyscrapers are unseen obstacles such as other sources of electromagnetic radiation. Cellular towers, radio stations, police and fire channels, XM radio, and many others can, individually or together, create problems for a local wireless system. In the case of wireless optical communications, radio interference is not a problem, but line of sight and weather conditions certainly are. Probably the worst problem in terms of weather is mist or fog, but other problems, such as heating/cooling of the transceiver platform, wind, dust, and even large trucks, can cause misalignment problems or reduce performance.

XM radio presents an interesting case of radio interference. XM radio is a satellite-based service offering primarily music and news channels over the satellite frequencies. The frequencies happen to be very close to those used by WiFi or wireless local area networks. Wireless "hotspots" have been installed in increasing numbers and these hotspots cause interference with the XM radio receivers. Because the XM radio providers paid for the license to operate in this portion of the spectrum, it was felt that their signals were improperly interfered with from an unlicensed source. Unfortunately, the vast proliferation of wireless networking equipment makes this problem difficult to fix.

The problems experienced by wired and wireless analog systems are many and varied. Even though people clamor for digital information, the reality is that we continue to rely heavily on analog transmission. Understanding how analog signals propagate, their interaction, and the effect of local conditions can vastly improve our chances for successful and robust communications. It is intriguing that what we are learning about analog wired and wireless communications, amateur radio operators have known for years.

15.3 SUMMARY

All of the forms of information that are discussed in this book (audio, data, image, video) can be represented by electromagnetic signals and transmitted over a suitable transmission medium. Depending on the transmission medium and the communications environment, either analog or digital signals can be used to convey information. Any electromagnetic signal, analog or digital, is made up of a number of constituent frequencies. A key parameter that characterizes the signal is bandwidth, which is the width of the range of frequencies that comprise the signal. In general, the greater the bandwidth of the signal, the greater its information-carrying capacity.

A major problem in designing a communications facility is transmission impairment. The most significant impairments are attenuation, attenuation distortion, delay distortion, and the various types of noise. The various forms of noise include thermal noise, intermodulation noise, crosstalk, and impulse noise. For analog signals, transmission impairments introduce random modifications that degrade the quality of the received information and may affect intelligibility. For digital signals, transmission impairments may cause bit errors.

The designer of a communications facility must deal with four factors: the bandwidth of the signal, the data rate that is used for digital information, the amount of noise and other impairments, and the level of error rate that is acceptable. The bandwidth is limited by the transmission medium and the desire to avoid interference with other nearby signals. Because bandwidth is a scarce resource, we would like to maximize the data rate that is achieved in a given bandwidth. The data rate is limited by the bandwidth, the presence of impairments, and the error rate that is acceptable. The efficiency of a transmission system is measured by the ratio of data rate (in bps) to bandwidth (in Hz). Efficiencies of between 1 and 5 bps/Hz are considered good.

15.4 RECOMMENDED READING AND WEB SITES

[STAL07] covers all of the topics in this chapter in greater detail. [FREE05] is also a readable and rigorous treatment of the topics of this chapter. An excellent survey book is [HELD00]. A thorough treatment of both analog and digital communication is provided in [COUC07].

COUC07 Couch, L. *Digital and Analog Communication Systems.* Upper Saddle River, NJ: Prentice Hall, 2007.

FREE05 Freeman, R. *Fundamentals of Telecommunications.* New York: Wiley, 2005.

HELD00 Held, G. *Understanding Data Communications: from Fundamentals to Networking.* New York: Wiley, 2000.

STAL07 Stallings, W. *Data and Computer Communications, Eighth Edition.* Upper Saddle River: NJ: Prentice Hall, 2007.

Recommended Web sites:

- **Siemon Company:** Good collection of technical articles on cabling, plus information about cabling standards
- **Wireless Developer Network:** News, tutorials, and discussions on wireless topics

15.5 KEY TERMS, REVIEW QUESTIONS, AND PROBLEMS

Key Terms

amplitude	frequency	phase
analog signal	fundamental frequency	radian
attenuation	Hertz	sine wave
bandwidth	noise	spectrum
channel capacity	peak amplitude	square wave
delay distortion	period	wavelength
digital signal	periodic signal	white noise

Review Questions

15.1   Differentiate between an analog and a digital electromagnetic signal.

15.2   What are three important characteristics of a periodic signal?

15.3   How many radians are there in a complete circle of 360 degrees?

15.4   What is the relationship between the wavelength and frequency of a sine wave?

15.5   Define fundamental frequency.

15.6   What is the relationship between a signal's spectrum and its bandwidth?

15.7   How can telephone networks use communication facilities that limit the transmission of sound to a narrow bandwidth?

15.8   What is attenuation?

15.9   How does delay distortion place a limitation on the data rate for digital data?

15.10   What is noise?

15.11   What is white noise?

15.12   Why does thermal noise place an upper bound on communication system performance?

15.13   What is intermodulation noise?

15.14   Describe the phenomenon known as multipath.

15.15   Define channel capacity.

15.16   What key factors affect channel capacity?

Problems

15.1 A signal has a fundamental frequency of 1000 Hz. What is its period?

15.2 Express the following in the simplest form you can:
   a. $\sin(2\pi ft - \pi) + \sin(2\pi ft + \pi)$
   b. $\sin 2\pi ft + \sin(2\pi ft - \pi)$

15.3 Sound may be modeled as sinusoidal functions. Compare the relative frequency and wavelength of musical notes. Use 330 m/s as the speed of sound and the following frequencies for the musical scale.

Note	C	D	E	F	G	A	B	C
Frequency	264	297	330	352	396	440	495	528

15.4 If the solid curve in Figure 15.11 represents $\sin(2\pi t)$, what does the dotted curve represent? That is, the dotted curve can be written in the form $A \sin(2\pi ft + \phi)$; what are A, f, and ϕ?

15.5 Decompose the signal $(1 + 0.1 \cos 5t) \cos 100t$ into a linear combination of sinusoidal functions, and find the amplitude, frequency, and phase of each component. *Hint:* Use the identity for $\cos a \cos b$.

15.6 Find the period of the function $f(t) = (10 \cos t)^2$.

15.7 Figure 15.4 shows the effect of eliminating higher-harmonic components of a square wave and retaining only a few lower harmonic components. What would the signal look like in the opposite case; that is, retaining all higher harmonics and eliminating a few lower harmonics?

15.8 Given the narrow (usable) audio bandwidth of a telephone transmission facility, a nominal SNR of 56dB (400,000), and a distortion level of <0.2%,
   a. What is the theoretical maximum channel capacity (Kbps) of traditional telephone lines (POTS)?
   b. What is the actual maximum channel capacity?

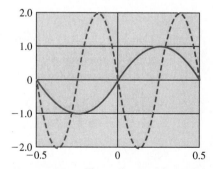

Figure 15.11 Figure for Problem 15.4

CHAPTER 16

DATA COMMUNICATION FUNDAMENTALS

16.1 Analog and Digital Data Communications

16.2 Data Encoding Techniques
  Analog Encoding of Digital Information
  Digital Encoding of Analog Information
  Digital Encoding of Digital Data
  Analog Encoding of Analog Information

16.3 Asynchronous and Synchronous Transmission
  Asynchronous Transmission
  Synchronous Transmission

16.4 Error Detection
  The Need for Error Control
  Parity Checks
  Cyclic Redundancy Check

16.5 Summary

16.6 Recommended Reading and Web Sites

16.7 Key Terms, Review Questions, and Problems

Chapter Objectives

After reading this chapter, you should be able to

♦ Explain the differences between analog and digital transmission.

♦ Describe how digital data can be encoded by means of a modem so that they can be transmitted over analog telephone lines.

♦ Describe how analog data, such as voice, can be encoded by means of a codec so that it can be transmitted over digital facilities.

♦ Explain the differences between asynchronous and synchronous transmission and when each technique is used.

♦ Describe the process of error detection.

The transmission of data across a transmission medium involves more than simply inserting a signal on the medium. A considerable degree of cooperation between the two sides is needed. This chapter and the next explore the essential mechanisms involved in the successful transmission of data between two devices across a transmission medium. First, we discuss the distinction between analog and digital transmission. Then we discuss the ways in which signals can be encoded for effective and efficient communication. Next, we look at the issue of synchronization: The receiver, to interpret correctly the incoming signal, must know when each arriving bit begins and ends so that it can keep pace with the transmitter. Several common techniques for synchronizing the receiver with the transmitter are described. Finally, this chapter introduces the concept of error detection.

16.1 ANALOG AND DIGITAL DATA COMMUNICATIONS

Electromagnetic signals, which are capable of propagation on a variety of transmission media, can be used to convey data. The exact way in which these signals are encoded to convey data will determine the efficiency and reliability of the transmission. This section introduces some basic concepts that are essential to the discussion.

The terms *analog* and *digital* correspond, roughly, to *continuous* and *discrete*, respectively. These two terms are frequently used in data communications in at least three contexts: data, signaling, and transmission.

The use of these terms in different contexts is often the source of confusion in articles and books. In this section, we clarify the various uses of these two terms. Briefly, we define **data** as entities that convey meaning, or information. **Signals** are electric or electromagnetic representations of data. **Signaling** is the physical propagation of the signal along a suitable medium. **Transmission** is the communication of data by the propagation and processing of signals.

We have already had occasion to use these terms in the first two contexts. **Analog data** take on continuous values on some interval. For example, voice and video are continuously varying patterns of intensity. Most data collected by sensors, such as temperature and pressure, are continuous valued. **Digital data** take on discrete values; examples are text, integers, and binary data.

In a communications system, data are propagated from one point to another by means of electromagnetic signals. An **analog signal** is a continuously varying electromagnetic wave that may be transmitted over a variety of media, depending on frequency. A **digital signal** is a sequence of voltage pulses that may be transmitted over a wire medium; for example, a constant positive voltage may represent binary 0, and a constant negative value may represent binary 1. The principal advantages of digital signaling are that it is generally cheaper than analog signaling and is less susceptible to noise interference. The principal disadvantage is that digital signals suffer more from attenuation than do analog signals. Note that digital signaling is possible only on copper media and cannot be used on optical fiber or wireless media.

Both analog and digital data can be represented, and hence propagated, by either analog or digital signals; this is illustrated in Figure 16.1. Generally, analog data are a function of time and occupy a limited frequency spectrum. Such data can

Figure 16.1 Analog and Digital Signaling of Analog and Digital Data

be directly represented by an electromagnetic signal occupying the same spectrum (e.g., voice data in the telephone voice band). In addition, we shall see that various forms of encoding can be used to provide an analog signal at a different portion of the spectrum. This is done to improve signal quality or transmission efficiency.

Digital data can also be represented by analog signals, by use of a **modem** (modulator/demodulator). The modem converts a series of binary voltage pulses into an analog signal by modulating a *carrier frequency*. The resulting signal occupies a certain spectrum of frequency centered about the carrier and may be propagated across a medium suitable for that carrier. The most common modems represent digital data in the voice spectrum and hence enable digital data to be propagated over ordinary voice-grade telephone lines. At the other end of the line, a modem demodulates the signal to recover the original data. Various modulation techniques are discussed in this section.

In an operation very similar to that performed by a modem, analog data can be represented by a digital signal. The device that performs this function is a **codec** (coder/decoder). In essence, the codec takes an analog signal that directly represents the voice data and approximates that signal by a bit stream. At the other end of a line, the bit stream is used to reconstruct the analog data.

Finally, digital data can be represented directly, in binary form, by two voltage levels. To improve propagation characteristics, however, the binary data are often encoded, as explained subsequently.

Each of the four combinations just described is in widespread use. The reasons for choosing a particular combination for any given communications task vary. We list here some representative reasons:

- **Digital data, digital signal:** In general, the equipment for encoding digital data into a digital signal is less complex and less expensive than digital-to-analog equipment.

- **Analog data, digital signal:** Conversion of analog data to digital form permits the use of modern digital transmission and switching equipment.

- **Digital data, analog signal:** Some transmission media, such as optical fiber and satellite, will only propagate analog signals.

- **Analog data, analog signal:** Analog data are easily converted to an analog signal.

A final distinction remains to be made. Both analog and digital signals may be transmitted on suitable transmission media. The way these signals are treated is a function of the transmission system. Table 16.1 summarizes the methods of transmission. **Analog transmission** is a means of transmitting analog signals without regard to their content; the signals may represent analog data (such as voice) or digital data (such as data that pass through a modem). In either case, the analog signal will suffer attenuation, which limits the length of the transmission link. To achieve longer distances, the analog transmission system includes amplifiers that boost the energy in the signal. Unfortunately, the amplifier also boosts the noise components. With amplifiers cascaded to achieve long distance, the signal becomes more and more distorted. For analog data, such as voice, quite a bit of distortion can be tolerated and the data remain intelligible. However, for digital data transmitted as analog signals, cascaded amplifiers will increase the number of errors.

Table 16.1 Analog and Digital Transmission

(a) Data and Signals

	Analog Signal	Digital Signal
Analog Data	Two alternatives: (1) signal occupies the same spectrum as the analog data; (2) analog data are encoded to occupy a different portion of spectrum.	Analog data are encoded using a codec to produce a digital bit stream.
Digital Data	Digital data are encoded using a modem to produce analog signal.	Two alternatives: (1) signal consists of a two voltage levels to represent the two binary values; (2) digital data are encoded to produce a digital signal with desired properties.

(b) Treatment of Signals

	Analog Transmission	Digital Transmission
Analog Signal	Is propagated through amplifiers; same treatment whether signal is used to represent analog data or digital data.	Assumes that the analog signal represents digital data. Signal is propagated through repeaters; at each repeater, digital data are recovered from inbound signal and used to generate a new analog outbound signal.
Digital Signal	Not used	Digital signal represents a stream of 1s and 0s, which may represent digital data or may be an encoding of analog data. Signal is propagated through repeaters; at each repeater, stream of 1s and 0s is recovered from inbound signal and used to generate a new digital outbound signal.

Digital transmission, in contrast, is concerned with the content of the signal. We have mentioned that a digital signal can be propagated only a limited distance before attenuation endangers the integrity of the data. To achieve greater distances, repeaters are used. A repeater receives the digital signal, recovers the pattern of ones and zeros, and retransmits a new signal. Thus the attenuation is overcome.

The same technique may be used with an analog signal if it is assumed that the signal carries digital data. At appropriately spaced points, the transmission system has retransmission devices rather than amplifiers. The retransmission device recovers the digital data from the analog signal and generates a new, clean analog signal. Thus noise is not cumulative.

The question naturally arises as to which is the preferred method of transmission. The answer being supplied by the telecommunications industry and its customers is digital, this despite an enormous investment in analog communications facilities. Both long-haul telecommunication facilities and intrabuilding services are gradually being converted to digital transmission and, where possible, digital signaling techniques. The most important reasons for this are summarized in Table 16.2.

We now turn to an examination of each of the four signal encoding options.

Table 16.2   Advantages of Digital Transmission

Cost
The advent of large-scale integration (LSI) and very-large-scale integration (VLSI) has caused a continuing drop in the cost and size of digital circuitry. Analog equipment has not shown a similar drop. Further, maintenance costs for digital circuitry are a fraction of those for analog circuitry.

Data Integrity
With the use of digital repeaters rather than analog amplifiers, the effects of noise and other signal impairments are not cumulative. Thus it is possible to transmit data longer distances and over lesser-quality lines by digital means while maintaining the integrity of the data.

Capacity Utilization
It has become economical to build transmission links of very high bandwidth, including satellite channels and optical fiber. A high degree of multiplexing is needed to effectively utilize such capacity, and this is more easily and cheaply achieved with digital (time division) rather than analog (frequency division) techniques (see Chapter 17).

Security and Privacy
Encryption techniques can be readily applied to digital data and to analog data that have been digitized.

Integration
By treating both analog and digital information digitally, all signals have the same form and can be treated similarly. Thus economies of scale and convenience can be achieved by integrating voice, video, image, and digital data.

16.2 DATA ENCODING TECHNIQUES

As we have pointed out, data, either analog or digital, must be converted into a signal for purposes of transmission.

In the case of digital data, different signal elements are used to represent binary 1 and binary 0. The mapping from binary digits to signal elements is the *encoding scheme* for transmission. Encoding schemes are designed to minimize errors in determining the start and end of each bit and errors in determining whether each bit is a 1 or a 0.

For analog data, the encoding scheme is designed to enhance the quality, or fidelity, of transmission. That is, we would like the received analog data to be as close as possible to the transmitted data.

Analog Encoding of Digital Information

The basis for analog encoding is a continuous constant-frequency signal known as the *carrier signal*. Digital information is encoded by means of a **modem** that modulates one of the three characteristics of the carrier: amplitude, frequency, or phase, or some combination of these. Figure 16.2 illustrates the three basic forms of modulation of analog signals for digital data:

- Amplitude shift keying
- Frequency shift keying
- Phase shift keying

In all these cases, the resulting signal contains a range of frequencies on both sides of the carrier frequency; this range is the bandwidth of the signal.

In **amplitude shift keying (ASK)**, the two binary values are represented by two different amplitudes of the carrier frequency. In some cases, one of the amplitudes

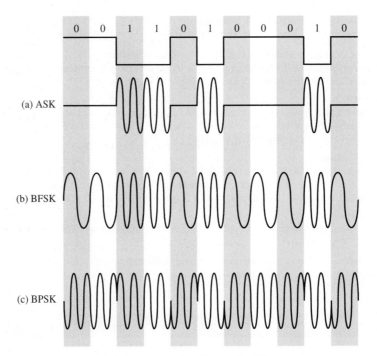

Figure 16.2 Modulation of Analog Signals for Digital Data

is zero; that is, one binary digit is represented by the presence, at constant amplitude, of the carrier, the other by the absence of the carrier. ASK is susceptible to sudden gain changes and is a rather inefficient modulation technique. On voice-grade lines, it is typically used only up to 1200 bps.

The ASK technique is also commonly used to transmit digital data over optical fiber. For LED transmitters, binary 1 is represented by a short pulse of light and binary 0 by the absence of light. Laser transmitters normally have a fixed "bias" current that causes the device to emit a low light level. This low level represents binary 0, while a higher-amplitude lightwave represents binary 1.

In **frequency shift keying (FSK)**, the two binary values are represented by two different frequencies near the carrier frequency. This scheme is less susceptible to error than ASK. On voice-grade lines, it is typically used up to 1200 bps. It is also commonly used for high-frequency (4 to 30 MHz) radio transmission.

In **phase shift keying (PSK)**, the phase of the carrier signal is shifted to encode data. Figure 16.2c is an example of a two-phase system. In this system, a 0 is represented by sending a signal burst of the same phase as the preceding signal burst sent. A 1 is represented by sending a signal burst of opposite phase to the preceding one. Phase-shift keying can use more then two phase shifts. A four-phase system would encode two bits with each signal burst. The phase-shift keying technique is more noise resistant and efficient than FSK; on a voice-grade line, rates up to 9600 bps are achieved.

Finally, the techniques just discussed may be combined. A common combination is PSK and ASK, where some or all of the phase shifts may occur at one or two amplitudes. These techniques are referred to as *multilevel* signaling because each signal element represents multiple bits. Note that four-phase phase-shift keying also falls into this category.

DATA RATE AND SIGNALING RATE   With multilevel signaling, we must distinguish between data rate, which is the rate, in bits per second, that bits are transmitted, and modulation rate, or signaling rate, which is the rate at which signal elements are transmitted. This latter rate is expressed in *baud,* or signal elements per second.

Four-phase PSK illustrates the difference between the data rate R (in bps) and the modulation rate D (in baud) of a signal. Let us assume that this scheme is being employed with digital input in which each bit is represented by a constant voltage pulse, one level for binary one and one level for binary zero. The data rate is $R = 1/T_b$, where T_b is the duration of one bit. However, the encoded signal contains $L = 4$ bits in each signal element using $M = 16$ different combinations of amplitude and phase. The modulation rate can be seen to be $R/4$, because each change of signal element communicates four bits. Thus the line signaling speed is 2400 baud, but the data rate is 9600 bps. This is the reason that higher bit rates can be achieved over voice-grade lines by employing more complex modulation schemes.

In general,

$$D = \frac{R}{L} = \frac{R}{\log_2 M}$$

where

D = modulation rate, baud
R = data rate, bps
M = number of different signal elements = 2^L
L = number of bits per signal element

MODEMS   Although both public and private telecommunications facilities are becoming increasingly digital, the use of analog facilities for data transmission will be substantial for many years to come. Thus, the modem is one of the most widely used pieces of communications gear.

Modems are offered in several different forms for use in different applications. Standalone modems, for instance, are self-contained, with internal power supplies, and are used with separate information products. Where a number of circuits come together—as at the interface to a large computer system—rack-mounted modems are often used, sharing power supplies and packaging. Modems can also be packaged inside another system (such as personal computer). Such integrated modems usually lower overall cost but increase the complexity of the information product and the cost of designing it. Integrated modems are usually offered as an option, because to standardize on a particular modem type with a product might restrict the usefulness of the product. In this subsection, we provide a brief introduction to three popular types of modems: voice-grade, cable, and ADSL.

Voice-grade modems are designed for the transmission of digital data over ordinary telephone lines. Thus, the modems make use of the same 4-kHz bandwidth available for voice signals. Because modems are used in pairs for communications, and because this use often occurs over the public telephone network, allowing many different modems to be paired, standards are essential. Table 16.3 lists the most

Table 16.3 Modem Specifications

ITU-T Recommendation	Data Rate (bps)	Dial-Up	Half-Duplex	Full-Duplex
V.29	9600		X	X
V.32	9600	X		X
V.32bis	14,400	X		X
V.33	14,400			X
V.34	33,600	X	X	X
V.90	33,600 (send) 56,000 (receive)	X	X	X

popular voice-grade modem types, as designated by the ITU-T Recommendation that defines them.[1]

The **cable modem** permits Internet access over cable television networks. The cable television industry has been the early leader in providing high-speed access to the home. Figure 16.3 shows a typical layout for cable delivery. At the cable central location, or linked by a high-speed line, is the Internet service provider (ISP). Typically, the cable company offers its own ISP but may also provide links to other ISPs. From the central location, the cable company lays out a network of underground fiber and coaxial cable lines that can reach every home and office in its region of

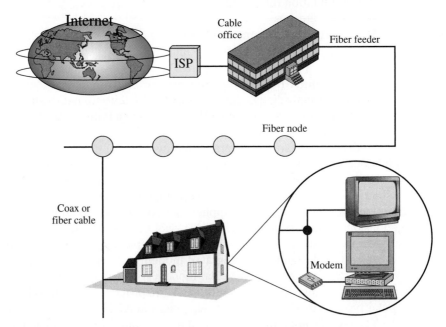

Figure 16.3 Cable Modem Application

---

[1]A discussion of ITU-T and other standards bodies is contained in a supporting document at this book's Web site.

operation. Traditionally, this system has been used to deliver one-way transmission of television channels, using 6 MHz per channel. The same cable layout, with appropriate electronics at both ends, can also be used to deliver a data channel to the subscriber and to provide a reverse channel from subscriber to the central location. Both upstream and downstream channels used for data transmission are shared among a number of subscribers, using a time-division multiplexing technique, described in Chapter 17. Within the subscriber's home or office, a splitter is employed to direct ordinary television signals to a television and the data channel to a cable modem, which can serve one or a network of PCs.

In the implementation and deployment of a high-speed wide area public digital network, the most challenging part is the link between subscriber and network: the digital subscriber line. With billions of potential endpoints worldwide, the prospect of installing new cable for each new customer is daunting. Instead, network designers have sought ways of exploiting the installed base of twisted-pair wire that links virtually all residential and business customers to telephone networks. These links were installed to carry voice-grade signals in a bandwidth from 0 to 4 kHz. However, the wires are capable of transmitting signals over a far broader spectrum— 1 MHz or more. The **asymmetric digital subscriber line (ADSL)** is the most widely publicized of a family of new modem technologies designed to provide high-speed digital data transmission over ordinary telephone wire. ADSL is now being offered by a number of carriers.

Figure 16.4 depicts the ADSL configuration for Internet access. The telephone central office can provide support for a number of ISPs, each of which must support

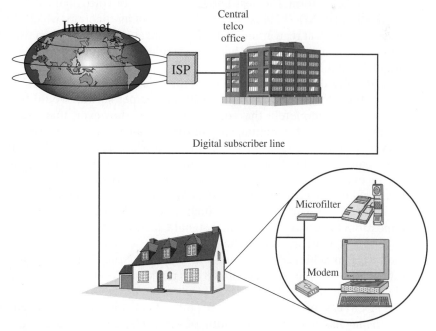

Figure 16.4 ADSL Modem Application

Table 16.4 Speeds for Internet Access Methods

Access Method	Upload Speed	Download Speed	Download Time (10 megabit file)
Dial-up modem	33.6 kbps	56 kbps	3 minutes
ISDN basic rate (two channels)	128 kbps	128 kbps	1.3 minutes
ADSL	16 to 640 kbps	1.5 to 9 Mbps	1.1 to 6.7 seconds
Cable modem	400 kbps	10 to 30 Mbps	0.3 to 1 second

the ADSL modem technology. At the central office, the ISP data signal is combined with a voice signal from the ordinary telephone voice switch. The combined signal can then be transmitted to/from a local subscriber over the subscriber line. At the subscriber's site, the twisted pair is split and routed to both a PC and a telephone. At the PC, an ADSL modem demodulates the data signal for the PC. At the telephone, a microfilter passes the 4-kHz voice signal. The data and voice signals are combined on the twisted pair line using frequency division multiplexing techniques, as described in Chapter 17.

Table 16.4 compares the performance of the various modems we have discussed with each other and with ISDN access, which uses a digital signaling technique.

Digital Encoding of Analog Information

The evolution of public telecommunications networks and private branch exchanges to digital transmission and switching requires that voice data be represented in digital form. The best-known technique for voice digitization is **pulse-code modulation** (PCM). PCM is based on the sampling theorem, which states that if a signal is sampled at regular intervals of time and at a rate higher than twice the highest significant signal frequency, then the samples contain all the information of the original signal.

If voice data were limited to frequencies below 4000 Hz, as is done in the analog telephone network, then 8000 samples per second would be sufficient to characterize completely the voice signal. Note, however, that these are analog samples. To convert to digital, each of these analog samples must be assigned a binary code. Figure 16.5 shows an example in which the original signal is assumed to be bandlimited with a bandwidth of B. Analog samples are taken at a rate of $2B$, or once every $Ts = 1/2B$ seconds. Each analog sample is approximated by being *quantized* into one of 16 different levels. Each sample can then be represented by 4 bits. But because the quantized values are only approximations, it is impossible to recover the original signal exactly. By using an 8-bit sample, which allows 256 quantizing levels, the quality of the recovered voice signal is comparable with that achieved via analog transmission. Note that this implies that a data rate of 8000 samples per second × 8 bits per sample = 64 kbps is needed for a single voice signal.

PCM can, of course, be used for other than voice signals. For example, a color TV signal has a useful bandwidth of 4.6 MHz, and reasonable quality can be achieved with 10-bit samples, for a data rate of 92 Mbps.

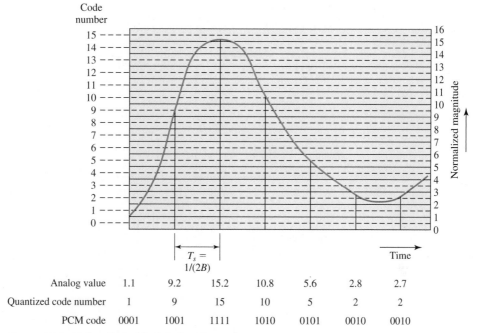

Figure 16.5   Pulse-Code Modulation Example

In recent times, variations on the PCM technique, as well as other encoding techniques, have been used to reduce the digital data rate required to carry voice. Good-quality voice transmission can be achieved with a data rate of 8 kbps. With video, advantage can be taken of the fact that from frame to frame most picture elements will not change. Interframe coding techniques should allow the video requirement to be reduced to about 15 Mbps, and for slowly changing scenes, such as those in a video teleconference, down to 1.5 Mbps or less. Indeed, recent advances have resulted in commercial videoconference products with data rates as low as 64 kbps.

Digital Encoding of Digital Data

The most common, and easiest, way to transmit digital signals is to use two different voltage levels for the two binary digits. Typically, a negative voltage represents binary 1 and a positive voltage represents binary 0 (Figure 16.6a). This code is known as **Nonreturn-to-Zero-Level (NRZ-L)** (meaning the signal never returns to zero voltage, and the value during a bit time is a level voltage). NRZ-L is often used for very short connections, such as between a personal computer and an external modem or a terminal and a nearby computer.

A variation of NRZ is **NRZI (NRZ, Invert on Ones)**. As with NRZ-L, NRZI maintains a constant-voltage pulse for the duration of a bit time. The data themselves are encoded as the presence or absence of a signal transition at the beginning of the bit time. A transition (low to high or high to low) at the beginning of a bit time

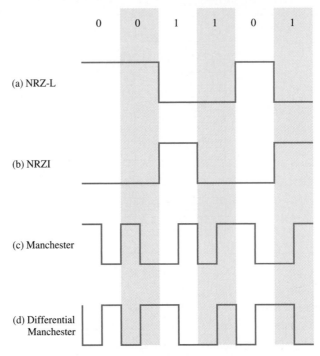

Figure 16.6 Example of Digital Signal Encoding Schemes

denotes a binary 1 for that bit time; no transition indicates a binary 0 (Figure 16.6b). NRZI is used on low-speed (64 kbps) ISDN connections.

NRZI is an example of *differential encoding*. In differential encoding, the signal is decoded by comparing the polarity of adjacent signal elements rather than determining the absolute value of a signal element. One benefit of this scheme is that it may be more reliable to detect a transition in the presence of noise than to compare a value to a threshold. Another benefit is that, with a complex cabling layout, it is easy to lose the sense of the polarity of the signal. For example, if the leads from an attached device to a twisted-pair cable are accidentally inverted, all ones and zeros will be inverted for NRZ-L. This does not happen with differential encoding.

A significant disadvantage of NRZ transmission is that it is difficult to determine where one bit ends and another begins. To picture the problem, consider that with a long string of ones or zeros for NRZ-L, the output is a constant voltage over a long period of time. Under these circumstances, any drift between the timing of transmitter and receiver will result in the loss of synchronization between the two.

There is a set of alternative coding techniques, grouped under the term *biphase,* that overcomes this problem. Two of these techniques, Manchester and differential Manchester, are in common use. All of the biphase techniques require at least one transition per bit time and may have as many as two transitions. Thus, the maximum modulation rate is twice that for NRZ; this means that the bandwidth required is correspondingly greater. To compensate for this, the biphase schemes have two advantages:

- **Synchronization:** Because there is a predictable transition during each bit time, the receiver can synchronize on that transition. For this reason, the biphase codes are known as self-clocking codes.

- **Error detection:** The absence of an expected transition can be used to detect errors. Noise on the line would have to invert both the signal before and after the expected transition to cause an undetected error.

In the **Manchester** code (Figure 16.6c), there is a transition at the middle of each bit period. The midbit transition serves as a clocking mechanism and also as data: A high-to-low transition represents a 0, and a low-to-high transition represents a 1. Manchester coding is used in Ethernet and a number of other local area networks (LANs). In **differential Manchester** (Figure 16.6d), the midbit transition is used only to provide clocking. The encoding of a 0 is represented by the presence of a transition at the beginning of a bit period, and a 1 is represented by the absence of a transition at the beginning of a bit period. Differential Manchester is used in token ring LANs. Differential Manchester has the added advantage of employing differential encoding.

Analog Encoding of Analog Information

Analog information can be converted directly into an analog signal that occupies the same bandwidth. The best example of this is voice. Voice-generated sound wave in the range of 300 to 3400 Hz can be represented by an electromagnetic signal with the same frequency components. This signal can then be directly transmitted on a voice-grade telephone line.

It is also possible to use an analog signal to modulate a carrier to produce a new analog signal that conveys the same information but occupies a different frequency band. There are two principal reasons for doing this:

- A higher frequency may be needed for effective transmission. For unguided media, it is virtually impossible to transmit low-frequency signals; the required antennas would be many kilometers in diameter. Guided media also have constraints on frequency range. Optical fiber, for example, requires that the frequency be on the order of 1014 Hz.

- Analog-to-analog modulation permits frequency-division multiplexing, an important technique explored in Chapter 17.

As with digital-to-analog modulation, analog-to-analog modulation involves an information source that is used to modulate one of the three principal characteristics of a carrier signal: amplitude, frequency, or phase.

Figure 16.7 illustrates the three possibilities. With amplitude modulation (AM), the amplitude of the carrier varies with the pattern of the modulating signal. Similarly, frequency modulation (FM) and phase modulation (PM) modulate the frequency and phase of a carrier, respectively.

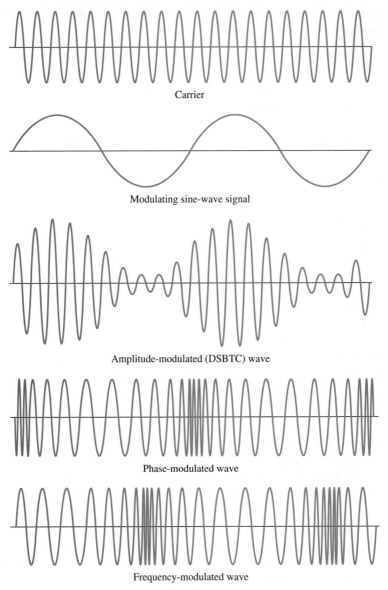

Carrier

Modulating sine-wave signal

Amplitude-modulated (DSBTC) wave

Phase-modulated wave

Frequency-modulated wave

Figure 16.7 Amplitude, Phase, and Frequency Modulation of a Sine-Wave Carrier by a Sine-Wave Signal

16.3 ASYNCHRONOUS AND SYNCHRONOUS TRANSMISSION

Recall from Figure 15.10 that the reception of digital data involves sampling the incoming signal once per bit time to determine the binary value. One of the difficulties encountered in such a process is that various transmission impairments will corrupt the signal so that occasional errors will occur. This problem is compounded by a timing difficulty: In order for the receiver to sample the incoming bits properly, it must know the arrival time and duration of each bit that it receives.

Suppose that the sender simply transmits a stream of data bits. The sender has a clock that governs the timing of the transmitted bits. For example, if data are to be transmitted at one million bits per second (1 Mbps), then one bit will be transmitted every $1/10^6 = 1$ microsecond (μs), as measured by the sender's clock. Typically, the receiver will attempt to sample the medium at the center of each bit time. The receiver will time its samples at intervals of one bit time. In our example, the sampling would occur once every 1 μs. If the receiver times its samples based on its own clock, then there will be a problem if the transmitter's and receiver's clocks are not precisely aligned. If there is a drift of 1% (the receiver's clock is 1% faster or slower than the transmitter's clock), then the first sampling will be 0.01 of a bit time (0.01 μs) away from the center of the bit (center of bit is 0.5 μs from beginning and end of bit). After 50 or more samples, the receiver may be in error because it is sampling in the wrong bit time ($50 \times .01 = 0.5$ μs). For smaller timing differences, the error would occur later, but eventually the receiver will be out of step with the transmitter if the transmitter sends a sufficiently long stream of bits and if no steps are taken to synchronize the transmitter and receiver.

Asynchronous Transmission

Two approaches are common for achieving the desired synchronization. The first is called, oddly enough, **asynchronous transmission**. The strategy with this scheme is to avoid the timing problem by not sending long, uninterrupted streams of bits. Instead, data are transmitted one character at a time, where each character is 5 to 8 bits in length.[2] Timing or synchronization must only be maintained within each character; the receiver has the opportunity to resynchronize at the beginning of each new character.

Figure 16.8 illustrates this technique. When no character is being transmitted, the line between transmitter and receiver is in an *idle* state. The definition of *idle* is equivalent to the signaling element for binary 1. Thus, for NRZ-L signaling (see Figure 16.6), which is common for asynchronous transmission, idle would be the presence of a negative voltage on the line. The beginning of a character is signaled by a *start bit* with a value of binary 0. This is followed by the 5 to 8 bits that actually make up the character. The bits of the character are transmitted beginning with the least significant bit. For example, for IRA characters, the data bits are usually followed by a parity bit, which therefore is in the most significant bit position. The parity bit is set by the transmitter such that the total number of ones in the character, including the parity bit, is even (even parity) or odd (odd parity), depending on the convention being used. This bit is used by the receiver for error detection, as discussed in Section 16.4. The final element is a *stop element*, which is a binary 1. A minimum length for the stop element is specified, and this is usually 1, 1.5, or 2 times the duration of an ordinary bit. No maximum value is specified. Because the stop element is the same as the idle state, the transmitter will continue to transmit the stop element until it is ready to send the next character.

---

[2]The number of bits that comprise a character depends on the code used. We have already seen one common example, the IRA code, which uses 7 bits per character (Chapter 2). Another common code is the Extended Binary Coded Decimal Interchange Code (EBCDIC), which is an 8-bit character code used on all IBM machines except for IBM's personal computers.

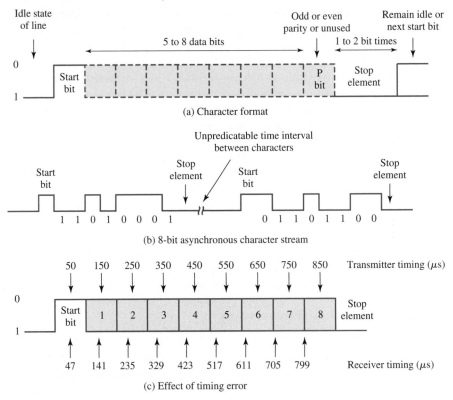

Figure 16.8 Asynchronous Transmission

If a steady stream of characters is sent, the interval between two characters is uniform and equal to the stop element. For example, if the stop element is one bit time and the IRA characters ABC are sent (with even parity bit), the pattern is 01000001010010000101011000011111...111.[3] The start bit (0) starts the timing sequence for the next nine elements, which are the 7-bit IRA code, the parity bit, and the stop element. In the idle state, the receiver looks for a transition from 1 to 0 to signal the beginning of the next character and then samples the input signal at 1-bit intervals for seven intervals. It then looks for the next 1-to-0 transition, which will occur no sooner than one more bit time.

The timing requirements for this scheme are modest. For example, IRA characters are typically sent as 8-bit units, including the parity bit. If the receiver is 5% slower or faster than the transmitter, the sampling of the eighth character bit will be displaced by 45% and still be correctly sampled. Figure 16.8c shows the effects of a timing error of sufficient magnitude to cause an error in reception. In this example we assume a data rate of 10,000 bits per second (10 kbps); therefore, each bit is of 0.1 millisecond (ms), or 100 μs, duration. Assume that the receiver is fast by 6%, or 6 μs per bit time. Thus, the receiver samples the incoming character every 94 μs (based on the transmitter's clock). As can be seen, the last sample is erroneous.

---

[3] In the text, the transmission is shown from left (first bit transmitted) to right (last bit transmitted).

Asynchronous transmission is simple and cheap but requires an overhead of 2 to 3 bits per character. For example, for an 8-bit character with no parity bit, using a 1-bit-long stop element, 2 out of every 10 bits convey no information but are there merely for synchronization; thus the overhead is 20%. Of course, the percentage overhead could be reduced by sending larger blocks of bits between the start bit and stop element. However, as Figure 16.8c suggests, the larger the block of bits, the greater the cumulative timing error. To achieve greater efficiency, a different form of synchronization, known as synchronous transmission, is used.

Synchronous Transmission

With **synchronous transmission**, a block of bits is transmitted in a steady stream without start and stop codes. The block may be many characters in length. To prevent timing drift between transmitter and receiver, their clocks must somehow be synchronized. One possibility is to provide a separate clock line between transmitter and receiver. One side (transmitter or receiver) pulses the line regularly with one short pulse per bit time. The other side uses these regular pulses as a clock. This technique works well over short distances, but over longer distances the clock pulses are subject to the same impairments as the data signal, and timing errors can occur. The other alternative is to embed the clocking information in the data signal. For digital signals, this can be accomplished with Manchester or differential Manchester encoding, as explained in Section 16.2. For analog signals, a number of techniques can be used; for example, the carrier frequency itself can be used to synchronize the receiver based on the phase of the carrier.

With synchronous transmission, there is another level of synchronization required, to allow the receiver to determine the beginning and end of a block of data. To achieve this, each block begins with a *preamble* bit pattern and generally ends with a *postamble* bit pattern. In addition, other bits added to the block convey control information used in the data link control procedures discussed in Chapter 17. The data plus preamble, postamble, and control information are called a **frame**. The exact format of the frame depends on which data link control procedure is being used.

For sizable blocks of data, synchronous transmission is far more efficient than asynchronous. Asynchronous transmission requires 20% or more overhead. The control information, preamble, and postamble in synchronous transmission are typically less than 100 bits. For example, one of the more common schemes, HDLC, contains 48 bits of control, preamble, and postamble. Thus, for a 1000-character block of data, each frame consists of 48 bits of overhead and $1000 \times 8 = 8,000$ bits of data, for a percentage overhead of only $48/8048 = 100\% = 0.6\%$.

For applications involving low-speed terminals or personal computers, asynchronous transmission is the most common technique. The technique is inexpensive, and its inefficiency is not a problem in most interactive applications, where more time is spent in looking at the screen and thinking than in transmission. However, the overhead of asynchronous transmission would be a heavy price to pay in more communications-intensive applications.

For large systems and computer networks, the efficiency of synchronous transmission is needed, even though it introduces the technical problem of synchronizing the clocks of transmitter and receiver.

In addition to the requirement for efficiency, large transfers introduce a requirement for error checking. The interactive user checks his or her own input and output for errors by looking at the screen and rekeying or asking for retransmission of portions that contain errors. Such a procedure is clearly impractical for long file transfers that occur at fast rates and often without an operator present. As we will see, synchronous transmission involves the use of a data link control procedure, which will automatically detect transmission errors and cause a frame in error to be retransmitted.

16.4 ERROR DETECTION

The Need for Error Control

As discussed in Chapter 15, any transmission facility has the potential of introducing errors. The ability to control those errors is an increasingly important task of a data communications system. This is partly because the issue of data integrity is becoming increasingly important. There is downward pressure on the allowable error rates for communication and mass storage systems as bandwidths and volumes of data increase. Certain data cannot be wrong; for example, consider the effect of an undetected data error on an electronic funds transfer. More generally, in any system that handles large amounts of data, uncorrected and undetected errors can degrade performance, response time, and possibly increase the need for intervention by human operators.

The process of **error control** involves two elements:

- **Error detection:** Redundancy is introduced into the data stream so that the occurrence of an error will be detected.

- **Error correction:** Once an error is detected by the receiver, the receiver and the transmitter cooperate to cause the frames in error to be retransmitted.

In this section, we look at the error detection process. We examine error correction in Chapter 17.

Parity Checks

The simplest approach to error detection is to append a parity bit to the end of a block of data. A typical example is IRA transmission, in which a parity bit is attached to each 7-bit IRA character. The value of this bit is selected so that the character has an even number of 1s (even parity) or an odd number of 1s (odd parity). So, for example, if the transmitter is transmitting the character G (1110001) and using odd parity, it will append a 1 and transmit 11100011. The receiver examines the received character and, if the total number of 1s is odd, assumes that no error has occurred. If one bit (or any odd number of bits) is erroneously inverted during transmission (for example, 11000011), then the receiver will detect an error. Note, however, that if two (or any even number of) bits are inverted due to error, an undetected error occurs. Typically, even parity is used for synchronous transmission and odd parity for asynchronous transmission.

The use of the parity bit is not foolproof, because noise impulses are often long enough to destroy more than one bit, particularly at high data rates.

Cyclic Redundancy Check

When synchronous transmission is used, it is possible to employ an error detection technique that is both more efficient (lower percentage of overhead bits) and more powerful (more errors detected) than the simple parity bit. This technique requires the addition of a **frame check sequence (FCS)**, or **error-detecting code**, to each synchronous frame. The use of an FCS is illustrated in Figure 16.9, using the CRC code described in this subsection. On transmission, a calculation is performed on the bits of the frame to be transmitted; the result is inserted as an additional field in the frame. On reception, the same calculation is performed on the received bits and the calculated result is compared to the value stored in the incoming frame. If there is a discrepancy, the receiver assumes that an error has occurred.

One of the most common, and one of the most powerful, of the error-detecting codes is the **cyclic redundancy check (CRC)**. For this technique, the message to be transmitted is treated as one long binary number. This number is divided by a unique prime binary number (a number divisible only by itself and 1), and the remainder is attached to the frame to be transmitted. When the frame is received, the receiver performs the same division, using the same divisor, and compares the calculated remainder with the remainder received in the frame. The most commonly used divisors are a 17-bit divisor, which produces a 16-bit remainder, and a 33-bit divisor, which produces a 32-bit remainder.

The measure of effectiveness of any error-detecting code is what percentage of errors it detects. For a CRC of length N, the rate of undetected errors is on the order of 2^{-N} (see [STAL04] for details). In summary, the CRC is a very powerful means of error detection and requires very little overhead. As an example, if a 16-bit FCS is used with frames of 1000 bits, then the overhead is only 1.6%. With a 32-bit FCS, the overhead is 3.2%.

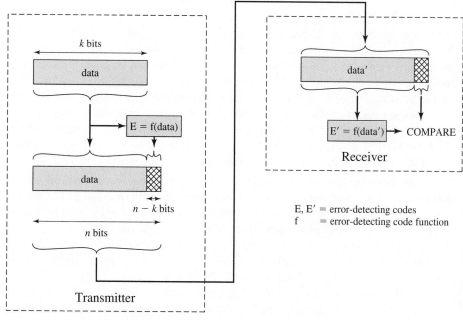

Figure 16.9 Error Detection Process

APPLICATION NOTE

Devices, Encoding, Communication Parameters, and Protocols

Encoding schemes, protocols, and errors are not normally a part of our everyday networking experience. From an end user perspective, all we know is whether or not the network (or computer) is working. Even if we directly interact with the various communication systems, we do not often have to give these things much thought. However, during installation, maintenance, and troubleshooting, insight into the mechanisms used by data transmission equipment and the standards involved can make a big difference.

Today's computers have a number of methods they can use to communicate with other machines. USB, EIA232 (A.K.A. COM or serial port), Firewire, network cards, video, and interfaces for mice and keyboards all represent some form of data transmission. What adds to the confusion is that organizations often wind up with several different computing platforms. As a result, the protocols and encoding schemes used by one device can be markedly different from the next. As an example, a company may have a variety or Macintosh computers alongside Windows-based machines. This can create an environment wherein peripherals must be purchased for both Firewire and USB. In addition, the network protocols can be different or require additional support.

Terminal emulation programs can also be a source of difficulty. Computers connected via a serial connection must be configured to "speak the same language." This amounts to determining the speed of the link, the number of data bits used, and the parity. This is a manual configuration that must be done on both ends of the link. The most common application for these programs is to configure routers and access points via a console port. However, networking protocols such as those connecting us to the WAN may require some additional serial- based configuration. If any one of these is incorrect, the communication cannot proceed.

Operating systems and device drivers can create problems because they expose settings that users can change. An example can be found in Ethernet-speed configurations. Ports on network equipment and the network interface card can be configured for a particular speed and full or half duplex. While normally left to "auto sense" the network, manually changing these can limit or even stop network connectivity. In this case, different settings will make it impossible for the two ends to understand each other because not only are the speeds different, but the encoding schemes have completely changed. Another example is the type of wireless network that you are connecting to. Simply changing from one 802.11 standard to another can disconnect you from the network.

Part of every successful transmission is error control. Error control can mean error detection or error detection *and* correction. Contemporary networks have extremely low error rates. Having a single bit in error for a billion bits transmitted would be excessive. The most common forms of error detection today are single parity bits, cyclical redundancy checks, and checksums. These are used primarily by lower-layer protocols and file systems. Some lower-layer protocols have many error-checking and testing functions built in. Protocols like the Point-to-Point Protocol (PPP) have provided extra tools, although they are not often used today. Supplementing these mechanisms are those used in the upper-layer protocols such as the sequence numbers and retransmission in TCP.

With the advent of wireless networks, the error rates have increased and additional problems such as lost connections can occur. Generally, the throughput of wireless local area networks is less than that of wired networks. This because the wireless network is a shared medium and the nodes must contend with each other for bandwidth. The access method used is similar to Ethernet but can take even longer. Finally, each frame in a wireless LAN is acknowledged (ACK), which further slows things down. While some of this delay will be alleviated with the newer, faster wireless standards, the media will remain shared and still require ACKs. For these reasons it may be necessary to modify communication parameters (e. g., preamble length, load sharing, channels) to ensure the successful completion of wireless transmissions.

End users or network administrators cannot modify all of the parameters in a communication system. For example, no one will change the encoding used by 100baseT Ethernet. However, understanding the interrelated nature of encoding schemes, settings, and protocol operation can help improve efficiency, speed troubleshooting efforts, and assist in the design phases so that many problems can be avoided. It is the wise network administrator who understands what settings end users can (and will) change. In many cases, getting back to basics is the only way to solve a problem.

16.5 SUMMARY

Both analog and digital information can be encoded as either analog or digital signals. The particular encoding that is chosen depends on the specific requirements to be met and the media and communications facilities available. For example, to transmit digital information over an analog telephone line, a modem is used to convert the digital data into analog form. Similarly, there is an increasing use of digital facilities, and voice information must be encoded in digital form to be transmitted on these digital facilities.

The transmission of a stream of bits from one device to another across a transmission link involves a great deal of cooperation and agreement between the two sides. One of the most fundamental requirements is **synchronization**. The receiver must know the rate at which bits are being received so that it can sample the line at regular intervals to determine the value of each received bit. Two techniques are in common use for this purpose. In asynchronous transmission, each character of data is treated independently. Each byte begins with a start bit that alerts the receiver that a character is arriving. The receiver samples each bit in the character and then looks for the beginning of the next character. This technique would not work well for long blocks of data because the receiver's clock might eventually drift out of synchronization with the transmitter's clock. However, sending data in large blocks is more efficient than sending data one character at a time. For large blocks, synchronous transmission is used. Each block of data is formatted as a frame that includes a starting and ending flag. Some form of synchronization, such as the use of Manchester encoding, is employed to maintain synchronization.

Error detection techniques are an important part of data transmission. The most widely used algorithm for error detection is the cyclic redundancy check.

16.6 RECOMMENDED READING AND WEB SITES

[STAL07] covers the topics of this chapter in greater detail. Another comprehensive treatment is [FREE05].

FREE05 Freeman, R. *Fundamentals of Telecommunications.* New York: Wiley, 2005.

STAL07 Stallings, W. *Data and Computer Communications, Seventh Edition.* Upper Saddle River, NJ: Prentice Hall, 2007.

Recommended Web sites:

- **Broadband Forum:** Includes a FAQ and technical information on DSL technologies and standards. Forum specifications
- **Cable Digital News:** Good collection of information on cable modems

16.7 KEY TERMS, REVIEW QUESTIONS, AND PROBLEMS

Key Terms

amplitude modulation	cyclic redundancy check	frequency shift keying
amplitude shift keying	(CRC)	modem
analog data	digital data	parity bit
analog signal	digital signal	phase modulation
analog transmission	digital transmission	phase shift keying
asynchronous transmission	error-detecting code	pulse-code modulation (PCM)
baud	error detection	synchronous transmission
codec	frequency modulation	

Review Questions

16.1 Distinguish among analog data, analog signaling, and analog transmission.

16.2 Distinguish among digital data, digital signaling, and digital transmission.

16.3 What is the difference between amplification and retransmission?

16.4 What is differential encoding?

16.5 What function does a modem perform?

16.6 Are the modem and the codec functional inverses (i.e., could an inverted modem function as a codec, or vice versa)?

16.7 Indicate three major advantages of digital transmission over analog transmission.

16.8 How are binary values represented in amplitude shift keying, and what is the limitation of this approach?

16.9 Indicate the major categories into which modems may be classified based on their data rates.

16.10   What is NRZ-L? What is a major disadvantage of this data encoding approach?

16.11   Match the device or system with the correct type of signal and data.

Device/System	Data/Signal
Modem transmissions	A. Digital data/digital encoding
Ethernet	B. Digital data/analog encoding
AM/FM radio	C. Analog data/digital encoding
PCM	D. Analog data/analog encoding

16.12   How is the transmission of a single character differentiated from the transmission of the next character in asynchronous transmission?

16.13   What is a major disadvantage of asynchronous transmission?

Problems

16.1   Given the bit pattern 01100, encode this data using ASK, BFSK, and BPSK.

16.2   Using Manchester encoding, encode the bit pattern 01001110.

16.3   Suppose a file of 10,000 bytes is to be sent over a line at 2400 bps.
   a.   Calculate the overhead in bits and time in using asynchronous communication. Assume one start bit and a stop element of length one bit, and 8 bits to send the byte itself for each character. The 8-bit character consists of all data bits, with no parity bit.
   b.   Calculate the overhead in bits and time using synchronous communication. Assume that the data are sent in frames. Each frame consists of 1000 characters = 8000 bits and an overhead of 48 control bits per frame.
   c.   What would the answers to parts (a) and (b) be for a file of 100,000 characters?
   d.   What would the answers to parts (a) and (b) be for the original file of 10,000 characters except at a data rate of 9600 bps?

16.4   A data source produces 7-bit IRA characters. Derive an expression of the maximum effective data rate (rate of IRA data bits) over a x-bps line for the following:
   a.   Asynchronous transmission, with a 1.5-unit stop element and a parity bit.
   b.   Synchronous transmission, with a frame consisting of 48 control bits and 128 information bits. The information field contains 8-bit (parity included) IRA characters.
   c.   Same as part (b), except that the information field is 1024 bits.

16.5   Demonstrate by example (write down a few dozen arbitrary bit patterns; assume one start bit and a stop element of length 1 bit) that a receiver that suffers a framing error on asynchronous transmission will eventually become realigned.

16.6   Suppose that a sender and receiver use asynchronous transmission and agree not to use any stop elements. Could this work? If so, explain any necessary conditions.

16.7   An asynchronous transmission scheme uses 8 data bits, an even parity bit, and a stop element of length 2 bits. What percentage of clock inaccuracy can be tolerated at the receiver with respect to the framing error? Assume that the bit samples are taken at the middle of the clock period. Also assume that at the beginning of the start bit the clock and incoming bits are in phase.

16.8   Suppose that a synchronous serial data transmission is clocked by two clocks (one at the sender and one at the receiver) that each has a drift of 1 minute in one year. How long a sequence of bits can be sent before possible clock drift could cause a problem? Assume that a bit waveform will be good if it is sampled within 40% of its center and that the sender and receiver are resynchronized at the beginning of each frame. Note that the transmission rate is not a factor, as both the bit period and the absolute timing error decrease proportionately at higher transmission rates.

16.9 When President Franklin Delano Roosevelt gave his first inaugural speech—"the only thing we have to fear is fear itself..."—it lasted about 23 minutes. In printed form it takes about 4 pages. The part that is printed on a page is about 4 1/2 inches wide and 7 3/8 inches vertically. There are about 77 characters per line, and there are about 5 1/3 lines per vertical inch. Suppose you wished to represent the speech in a CD-ROM encyclopedia.

a. How many 8-bit bytes would it take to store a recording of FDR giving the speech using PCM without compression assuming a bandwidth of 22,000 Hz, monaural? Ignore any overhead. You wish to pick a sample discretization that can encode about 64,000 amplitude levels. Use the minimum sampling rate implied by the sampling theorem.

b. Suppose the speech was stored as text, one text character per byte without compression. How much space, in bytes, is on the CD-ROM now?

c. Suppose the speech was stored as an image of the text as specified previously. That is, you only scan the area with text. Suppose the image is scanned at 1200 pixels per inch in both the horizontal and vertical directions, and that the image is stored as black and white (no color or gray scale). Again ignore overhead and assume no compression. How much CD-ROM storage in bytes is needed for this representation?

Note: The relative size of the results of (a), (b), and (c) make qualitative sense. The reading carries the most information, including inflection and pacing, in addition to the text itself. This representation takes the most space. The image carries more information than the text, such as fonts and page layout, but less information than the reading. The text as an ASCII string carries no additional information beyond the text itself but is the most compact.

16.10 Two communicating devices are using a single-bit even parity check for error detection. The transmitter sends the byte 10101010 and, because of channel noise, the receiver gets the byte 10011010. Will the receiver detect the error? Why or why not?

CHAPTER 17

DATA LINK CONTROL AND MULTIPLEXING

17.1 Flow Control and Error Control
Flow Control
Error Control

17.2 High-Level Data Link Control
HDLC Frame Structure
HDLC Operation

17.3 Motivation for Multiplexing

17.4 Frequency Division Multiplexing
Wavelength Division Multiplexing
ADSL

17.5 Synchronous Time Division Multiplexing
The TDM Mechanism
Digital Carrier Systems
T-1 Facilities
SONET/SDH

17.6 Summary

17.7 Recommended Reading and Web Sites

17.8 Key Terms, Review Questions, and Problems

Chapter Objectives

After reading this chapter, you should be able to

♦ Explain the need for a data link control protocol.

♦ Describe the basic operation of a data link control protocol such as the widely used HDLC.

♦ Explain the need for transmission efficiency and list the two major approaches used to achieve efficiency.

♦ Discuss the use of frequency division multiplexing in video distribution and in voice networks.

♦ Describe the use of multiplexing in digital carrier systems.

♦ Discuss the T-1 service and describe its importance and the applications that are using it.

♦ Discuss the SONET standard and its significance for wide area networking.

This chapter examines two important data communications concepts: data link control and multiplexing.

A data link control protocol includes techniques for regulating the flow of data over a communications link and for compensating for transmission errors. We first examine the concepts of flow control and error control and then illustrate their use in the data link control protocol HDLC. This protocol is one of the most commonly used ones, and it illustrates the techniques used in such protocols.

A major source of expense in any distributed or networked environment is transmission cost. Because of the critical nature of transmission in such environments and their potentially high cost, it is important to maximize the amount of information that can be carried over a given resource or, alternatively, to minimize the transmission capacity needed to satisfy a given business information communications requirement. The latter part of the chapter looks at key approach to achieving transmission efficiency: multiplexing.

17.1 FLOW CONTROL AND ERROR CONTROL

Physical interface standards provide a means by which a stream of data can be transmitted, either synchronously or asynchronously, onto a transmission medium. However, these interfaces do not include all of the required functions for data communication. Among the most important items lacking are flow control and error control.

To provide these needed functions, a data link control protocol is used. Such protocols are generally only used for synchronous transmission. The basic scheme is as follows. The data to be transmitted by an application are sent to the data link module, which organizes the data into a set of frames. Each frame is supplemented with control bits that allow the two sides to cooperate to deliver the data reliably. The control bits are added by the sender of the frame. When the frame arrives, the receiver examines the control bits and, if the data arrive successfully, strips off the

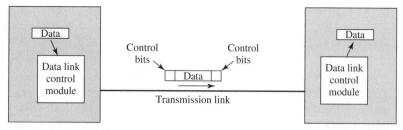

Figure 17.1 Operation of a Data Link Control Module

control bits and then delivers the pure data to the intended destination point within the system. Figure 17.1 illustrates the process.

With the use of control bits, a number of functions can be performed, including flow control and error control. In this section, we introduce these functions. The next section looks specifically at one data link control protocol, known as HDLC (High-Level Data Link Control).

Flow Control

Suppose that we wish to write a program, called a printer driver, to pass data from a computer to a printer. We connect the two with the appropriate cable to a port on the host machine. The host port is programmable to match the peripheral device. In this case, let us say that the printer is set up for IRA 7-bit characters, odd parity, a stop of 1-bit length, and a data rate of 9600 bps. We use these parameters on the host port, write the program, and try to send a page of text to the printer. The result is that, after the first few lines of text, there are a number of missing characters; in fact, more missing characters than are printed.

What is the problem? First, let's calculate the character transfer rate. We have 7 bits for the character, 1 for the start bit, 1 for parity, and 1 for stop, for a total of 10 bits per character. Because the computer is transmitting at 9600 bps, the character rate is 960 characters per second. Checking the printer manual, we find that the printer can print at a maximum rate of 80 characters per second. This means that we are sending 12 times as much data as the printer can accept. No wonder that data are lost.

It may seem odd that the printer is equipped with a higher data rate capability than printing capability, but this is common. The printer includes a small buffer (perhaps 200 characters) so that it can accept characters in a burst of speed, print those characters, and then accept another burst. This allows the printer to be used on a shared line that is running at a sufficiently high speed to service a number of printers and terminals. For example, a 9600-bps line could easily accommodate 5 or 10 such printers. However, because the data rate is higher than the printing rate, it is possible for the overrun condition previously described to occur.

Flow control is a technique for assuring that a transmitting entity does not overwhelm a receiving entity with data. In the case of an electromagnetic device, such as a printer or disk drive, a fixed buffer is provided, as described previously. In the case of data being transmitted to a computer, it is typically destined for some application or system program. The receiving computer allocates a data buffer of some maximum length for that application or system program. When data are received, the computer must do a certain amount of processing before passing the data to the higher-level software. In the absence of flow control, the receiver's buffer may fill up and overflow while it is processing old data.

For data link control protocols, flow control is achieved by numbering each frame sequentially (e.g., 0, 1, 2, ...). Initially, a buffer is allocated at the receiver of an agreed size. As frames arrive and are processed, the receiver returns an acknowledgment indicating which frames have been received and implicitly indicating that more frames may be sent. This should be clearer when HDLC is discussed subsequently.

Error Control

In Chapter 16, we discussed techniques that enable a receiver to detect errors that occur in the transmission and reception process. To correct these errors, data link control provides mechanisms by which the two sides cooperate in the retransmission of frames that suffer from errors on the first try. These mechanisms extend the flow control techniques discussed previously. Again, data are sent as a sequence of frames. In addition, we consider two types of errors:

- **Lost frame:** A frame fails to arrive at the other side. In the case of a network, the network may simply fail to deliver a frame. In the case of a direct point-to-point data link, a noise burst may damage a frame to the extent that the receiver is not aware that a frame has been transmitted.

- **Damaged frame:** A recognizable frame does arrive, but some of the bits are in error (have been altered during transmission).

The most common techniques for error control are based on some or all of the following ingredients:

- **Error detection:** The destination detects frames that are in error, using the techniques described in the preceding chapter, and discards those frames.

- **Positive acknowledgment:** The destination returns a positive acknowledgment to successfully received, error-free frames.

- **Retransmission after timeout:** The source retransmits a frame that has not been acknowledged after a predetermined amount of time.

- **Negative acknowledgment and retransmission:** The destination returns a negative acknowledgment to frames in which an error is detected. The source retransmits such frames.

Collectively, these mechanisms are all referred to as **automatic repeat request** (ARQ). The effect of ARQ is to turn a potentially unreliable data link into a reliable one. The precise mechanism of ARQ is described in the next section as part of our discussion of HDLC.

17.2 HIGH-LEVEL DATA LINK CONTROL

The most important data link control protocol is HDLC. HDLC is widely used and is the basis for many other important data link control protocols, which use the same or similar formats and the same mechanisms as employed in HDLC.

HDLC Frame Structure

Perhaps the best way to begin an explanation of HDLC is to look at the frame structure. The operation of HDLC involves the exchange of two sorts of information between the two connected stations. First, HDLC accepts user data from some higher layer of software and delivers that user data across the link to the other side. On the other side, HDLC accepts the user data and delivers it to a higher layer of software on that side. Second, the two HDLC modules exchange control information to provide for flow control, error control, and other control functions. The method by which this is done is to format the information that is exchanged into a **frame**. A frame is a predefined structure that provides a specific location for various kinds of control information and for user data.

Figure 17.2 depicts the format of the HDLC frame. The frame has the following fields:

- **Flag:** Used for synchronization. It appears at the beginning and end of the frame and always contains the pattern 01111110.

- **Address:** Indicates the secondary station for this transmission. It is needed in the case of a multidrop line, where a primary may send data to one of a number of secondaries, and one of a number of secondaries may send data to the primary. This field is usually 8 bits long but can be extended (Figure 17.2b).

- **Control:** Identifies the purpose and functions of the frame. It is described later in this subsection.

- **Information:** Contains the user data to be transmitted.

- **Frame Check Sequence:** Contains a 16- or 32-bit cyclic redundancy check, used for error detection.

HDLC defines three types of frames, each with a different control field format. Information frames (I frames) carry the user data to be transmitted for the station. Additionally, the information frames contain control information for flow control and error control. Supervisory frames (S frames) provide another means of exercising flow control and error control. Unnumbered frames (U frames) provide supplemental link control functions.

The first one or two bits of the control field serve to identify the frame type. The remaining bit positions are organized into subfields, as indicated in Figures 17.2c and 17.2d. Their use is explained in the discussion of HDLC operation, which follows. Note that the basic control field for S and I frames uses 3-bit sequence numbers. With the appropriate set-mode commands, an extended control field can be used that employs 7-bit sequence numbers.

All of the control field formats contain the poll/final (P/F) bit. Its use depends on context. Typically, in command frames, it is referred to as the P bit and is set to 1 to solicit (poll) a response frame from the peer HDLC entity. In response frames, it is referred to as the F bit and is set to 1 to indicate the response frame transmitted as a result of a soliciting command.

HDLC Operation

HDLC operation consists of the exchange of I frames, S frames, and U frames between two stations. The various commands and responses defined for these frame

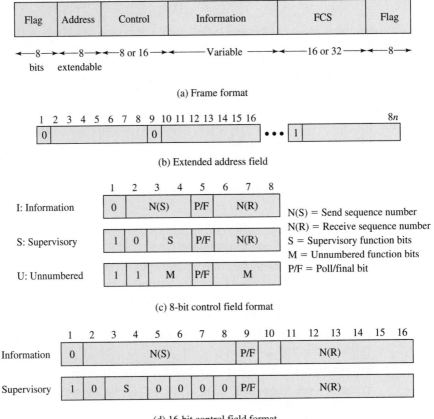

Figure 17.2   HDLC Frame Structure

types are listed in Table 17.1 In describing HDLC operation, we will discuss these three types of frames.

The operation of HDLC involves three phases. First, one side or another initializes the data link so that frames may be exchanged in an orderly fashion. During this phase, the options that are to be used are agreed upon. After initialization, the two sides exchange user data and the control information to exercise flow and error control. Finally, one of the two sides signals the termination of the operation.

INITIALIZATION   Either side may request initialization by issuing one of the six set-mode commands. This command serves three purposes:

1. It signals the other side that initialization is requested.

2. It specifies which of three modes is requested; these modes have to do with whether one side acts as a primary and controls the exchange or whether the two sides are peers and cooperate in the exchange.

3. It specifies whether 3- or 7-bit sequence numbers are to be used.

Table 17.1   HDLC Commands and Responses

Name	Command/Response	Description
Information (I)	C/R	Exchange user data
Supervisory (S)		
Receive ready (RR)	C/R	Positive acknowledgment; ready to receive I frame
Receive not ready (RNR)	C/R	Positive acknowledgment; not ready to receive
Reject (REJ)	C/R	Negative acknowledgment; go back N
Selective reject (SREJ)	C/R	Negative acknowledgment; selective reject
Unnumbered (U)		
Set normal response/extended mode (SNRM/SNRME)	C	Set mode; extended = 7-bit sequence numbers
Set asynchronous response/extended mode (SARM/SARME)	C	Set mode; extended = 7-bit sequence numbers
Set asynchronous balanced/extended mode (SABM, SABME)	C	Set mode; extended = 7-bit sequence numbers
Set initialization mode (SIM)	C	Initialize link control functions in addressed station
Disconnect (DISC)	C	Terminate logical link connection
Unnumbered acknowledgment (UA)	R	Acknowledge acceptance of one of the set-mode commands
Disconnected mode (DM)	R	Responder is in disconnected mode
Request disconnect (RD)	R	Request for DISC command
Request initialization mode (RIM)	R	Initialization needed; request for SIM command
Unnumbered information (UI)	C/R	Used to exchange control information
Unnumbered poll (UP)	C	Used to solicit control information
Reset (RSET)	C	Used for recovery; resets $N(R), N(S)$
Exchange identification (XID)	C/R	Used to request/report status
Test (TEST)	C/R	Exchange identical information fields for testing
Frame reject (FRMR)	R	Report receipt of unacceptable frame

If the other side accepts this request, then the HDLC module on that end transmits an Unnumbered Acknowledgement (UA) frame back to the initiating side. If the request is rejected, then a Disconnected Mode (DM) frame is sent.

DATA TRANSFER   When initialization has been requested and accepted, a logical connection is established. Both sides may begin to send user data in I frames, starting with sequence number 0. The N(S) and N(R) fields of the I frame are sequence numbers that support flow control and error control. An HDLC module sending a sequence of I frames will number them sequentially, modulo 8 or 128, depending on whether 3- or 7-bit sequence numbers are used, and place the sequence number in N(S). N(R) is the acknowledgment for I frames received; it enables the HDLC module to indicate which number I frame it expects to receive next.

S frames are also used for flow control and error control. The Receive Ready (RR) frame is used to acknowledge the last I frame received by indicating the next I frame expected. The RR is used when there is no reverse user data traffic (I frames) to carry an acknowledgment. Receive Not Ready (RNR) acknowledges an I frame, as with RR, but also asks the peer entity to suspend transmission of I frames. When the entity that issued RNR is again ready, it sends an RR. REJ initiates the go-back-N ARQ. It indicates that the last I frame received has been rejected and that retransmission of all I frames beginning with number N(R) is required. Selective reject (SREJ) is used to request retransmission of a single frame.

DISCONNECT   Either HDLC module can initiate a disconnect, either on its own initiative if there is some sort of fault or at the request of its higher-layer user. HDLC issues a disconnect by sending a Disconnect (DISC) frame. The other side must accept the disconnect by replying with a UA.

EXAMPLES OF OPERATION   To better understand HDLC operation, several examples are presented in Figure 17.3. In the example diagrams, each arrow includes a legend that specifies the frame type, the setting of the P/F bit, and, where appropriate, the values of N(R) and N(S). The setting of the P or F bit is 1 if the designation is present and 0 if absent.

Figure 17.3a shows the frames involved in link setup and disconnect. The HDLC entity for one side issues an SABM command[1] to the other side and starts a timer. The other side, upon receiving the SABM, returns a UA response and sets local variables and counters to their initial values. The initiating entity receives the UA response, sets its variables and counters, and stops the timer. The logical connection is now active, and both sides may begin transmitting frames. Should the timer expire without a response, the originator will repeat the SABM, as illustrated. This would be repeated until a UA or DM is received or until, after a given number of tries, the entity attempting initiation gives up and reports failure to a management entity. In such a case, higher-layer intervention is necessary. The same figure (Figure 17.3a) shows the disconnect procedure. One side issues a DISC command, and the other responds with a UA response.

Figure 17.3b illustrates the full-duplex exchange of I frames. When an entity sends a number of I frames in a row with no incoming data, then the receive sequence number, N(R), is simply repeated (e.g., I,1,1; I,2, 1 in the A-to-B direction). When an entity receives a number of I frames in a row with no outgoing frames, then the receive sequence number in the next outgoing frame must reflect the cumulative activity (e.g., I,1, 3 in the B-to-A direction). Note that, in addition to I frames, data exchange may involve supervisory frames.

Figure 17.3c shows an operation involving a busy condition. Such a condition may arise because an HDLC entity is not able to process I frames as fast as they are

---

[1]This stands for Set Asynchronous Mode Balanced. The SABM command is a request to start an exchange. The ABM part of the acronym refers to the mode of transfer, a detail that need not concern us here.

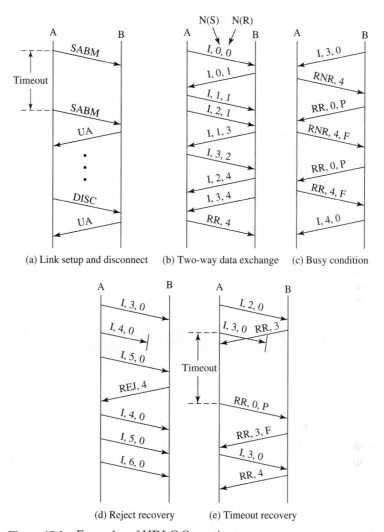

Figure 17.3 Examples of HDLC Operation

arriving, or the intended user is not able to accept data as fast as they arrive in I frames. In either case, the entity's receive buffer fills up and it must halt the incoming flow of I frames, using an RNR command. In this example, station A issues an RNR, which requires the other side to halt transmission of I frames. The station receiving the RNR will usually poll the busy station at some periodic interval by sending an RR with the P bit set. This requires the other side to respond with either an RR or an RNR. When the busy condition has cleared, A returns an RR, and I frame transmission from B can resume.

An example of error recovery using the REJ command is shown in Figure 17.3d. In this example, A transmits I frames numbered 3, 4, and 5. Frame 4 suffers an error. B detects the error and discards the frame. When B receives I frame 5, it discards this frame because it is out of order and sends an REJ with an N(R) of 4. This causes A to initiate retransmission of all I frames sent, beginning with frame 4. It may continue to send additional frames after the retransmitted frames.

An example of error recovery using a timeout is shown in Figure 17.3e. In this example, A transmits I frame number 3 as the last in a sequence of I frames. The frame suffers an error. B detects the error and discards it. However, B cannot send an REJ. This is because there is no way to know if this was an I frame. If an error is detected in a frame, all of the bits of that frame are suspect, and the receiver has no way to act upon it. A, however, started a timer as the frame was transmitted. This timer has a duration long enough to span the expected response time. When the timer expires, A initiates recovery action. This is usually done by polling the other side with an RR command with the P bit set, to determine the status of the other side. Because the poll demands a response, the entity will receive a frame containing an N(R) field and be able to proceed. In this case, the response indicates that frame 3 was lost, which A retransmits.

These examples are not exhaustive. However, they should give the reader a good feel for the behavior of HDLC.

17.3 MOTIVATION FOR MULTIPLEXING

Typically, two communicating stations will not utilize the full capacity of a data link. For efficiency, it should be possible to share that capacity. A generic term for such sharing is *multiplexing*.

A common application of multiplexing is in long-haul communications. Trunks on long-haul networks are high-capacity fiber, coaxial, or microwave links. These links can carry large numbers of voice and data transmissions simultaneously using multiplexing.

Figure 17.4 depicts the multiplexing function in its simplest form. There are *n* inputs to a multiplexer. The multiplexer is connected by a single data link to a demultiplexer. The link is able to carry *n* separate channels of data. The multiplexer combines (multiplexes) data from the *n* input lines and transmits over a higher-capacity data link. The demultiplexer accepts the multiplexed data stream, separates (demultiplexes) the data according to channel, and delivers them to the appropriate output lines.

Figure 17.4 Multiplexing

The widespread use of multiplexing in data communications can be explained by the following:

- The higher the data rate, the more cost-effective the transmission facility. That is, for a given application and over a given distance, the cost per kbps declines with an increase in the data rate of the transmission facility. Similarly, the cost of transmission and receiving equipment, per kbps, declines with increasing data rate.

- Most individual data communicating devices require relatively modest data rate support. For example, for many terminal and personal computer applications that do not involve Web access or intensive graphics, a data rate of between 9600 bps and 64 kbps is generally adequate.

The preceding statements were phrased in terms of data communicating devices. Similar statements apply to voice communications. That is, the greater the capacity of a transmission facility, in terms of voice channels, the less the cost per individual voice channel, and the capacity required for a single voice channel is modest.

The remainder of this chapter concentrates on two types of multiplexing techniques. The first, frequency division multiplexing (FDM), is the most heavily used and is familiar to anyone who has ever used a radio or television set. The second is a particular case of time division multiplexing (TDM) known as synchronous TDM. This is commonly used for multiplexing digitized voice streams and data streams.

17.4 FREQUENCY DIVISION MULTIPLEXING

Frequency division multiplexing (FDM) is a familiar and widely used form of multiplexing. A simple example is its use in cable TV systems, which carry multiple video channels on a single cable. FDM is possible when the useful bandwidth of the transmission medium exceeds the required bandwidth of signals to be transmitted. A number of signals can be carried simultaneously if each signal is modulated onto a different carrier frequency and the carrier frequencies are sufficiently separated that the bandwidths of the signals do not overlap. A general case of FDM is shown in Figure 17.5a. Six signal sources are fed into a multiplexer, which modulates each signal onto a different frequency $(f_1, \ldots, f_6)$. Each modulated signal requires a certain bandwidth centered on its carrier frequency, referred to as a *channel*. To prevent interference, the channels are separated by guard bands, which are unused portions of the spectrum.

The composite signal transmitted across the medium is analog. Note, however, that the input signals may be either digital or analog. In the case of digital input, the input signals must be passed through modems to be converted to analog. In either case, each analog input signal must then be modulated to move it to the appropriate frequency band.

A simple example of FDM is illustrated in Figure 17.6, which shows the transmission of three voice signals simultaneously over a transmission medium.

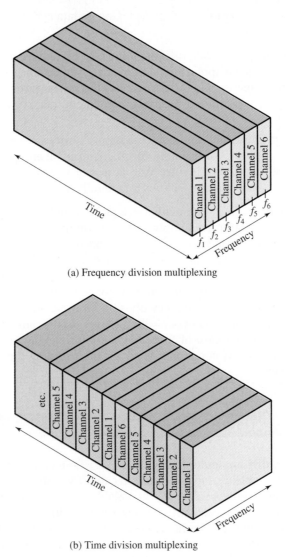

(a) Frequency division multiplexing

(b) Time division multiplexing

Figure 17.5 FDM and TDM

As was mentioned, the bandwidth of a voice signal is generally taken to be 4 kHz, with an effective spectrum of 300 to 3400 Hz (Figure 17.6a). If such a signal is used to amplitude modulate a 64-kHz carrier, the spectrum of Figure 17.6b results. The modulated signal has a bandwidth of 8 kHz, extending from 60 to 68 kHz. To make efficient use of bandwidth, we elect to transmit only the lower half of the spectrum, called the lower sideband. Similarly, the two other voice signals can be modulated to fit into the ranges 64 to 68 kHz and 68 to 72 kHz, respectively. These signals are then combined in the multiplexer to produce a single signal with a range of 60 to 72 kHz. At the receiving end, the demultiplexing process involves splitting the received signal into three frequency bands and then demodulating

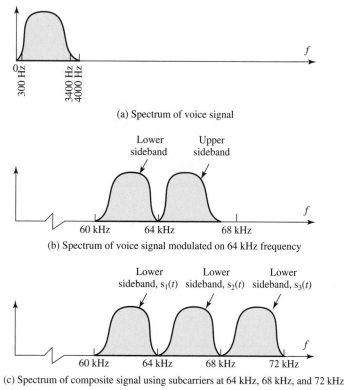

(a) Spectrum of voice signal

(b) Spectrum of voice signal modulated on 64 kHz frequency

(c) Spectrum of composite signal using subcarriers at 64 kHz, 68 kHz, and 72 kHz

Figure 17.6 FDM of Three Voiceband Signals

each signal back to the original voice band (0 to 4 kHz). Note that there is only a minor amount of overlap between the multiplexed signals. Because the effective bandwidth of each signal is actually less than 4 kHz, no noticeable interference results.

FDM was the mainstay of telephone transmission for many years; it is actually more efficient in terms of bandwidth than digital systems. The problem is that noise is amplified along with the voice signal. This fact, and the great decrease in the cost of digital electronics, has led to the widespread replacement of FDM systems with TDM systems in telephone networks.

Although the use of FDM for voice transmission is declining rapidly, it is still used almost exclusively for television distribution systems, including broadcast television and cable TV. The analog television signal discussed in Chapter 2 fits comfortably into a 6-MHz bandwidth. Figure 17.7 depicts the transmitted video signal and its bandwidth. The black-and-white video signal is amplitude modulated on a carrier signal. The resulting signal has a bandwidth of about 5 MHz, most of which is above the carrier signal. A separate color subcarrier is used to transmit color information. This is spaced far enough from the main carrier that there is essentially no interference. Finally, the audio portion of the signal is modulated on a third carrier, outside the effective bandwidth of the other two signals. The composite signal fits into a 6-MHz

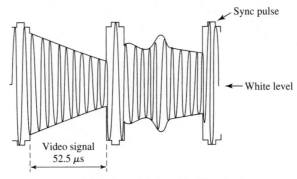

(a) Amplitude modulation with video signal

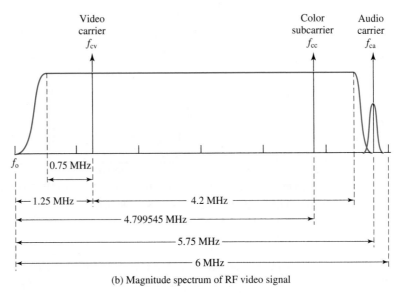

(b) Magnitude spectrum of RF video signal

Figure 17.7 Transmitted TV Signal

bandwidth with the video, color, and audio signal carriers at 1.25 MHz, 4.799545 MHz, and 5.75 MHz above the lower edge of the band, respectively. Thus, multiple TV signals can be frequency division multiplexed on a cable, each with a bandwidth of 6 MHz. Given the enormous bandwidth of coaxial cable (as much a 500 MHz), dozens of video signals can be simultaneously carried using FDM.

Wavelength Division Multiplexing

The true potential of optical fiber is fully exploited when multiple beams of light at different frequencies are transmitted on the same fiber. This is a form of frequency division multiplexing (FDM) but is commonly called wavelength division multiplexing (WDM). With WDM, the light streaming through the fiber consists of many colors, or wavelengths, each carrying a separate channel of data. In 1997, a landmark was reached when Bell Laboratories was able to demonstrate a WDM system with 100 beams each operating at 10 Gbps, for a total data rate of 1 trillion bits per second (also referred to as 1 terabit per second or 1 Tbps). Commercial systems with 160 channels of 10 Gbps are now available. In a lab environment, Alcatel has carried 256 channels at 39.8 Gbps each, a total of 10.1 Tbps, over a 100-km span.

A typical WDM system has the same general architecture as other FDM systems. A number of sources generate a laser beam at different wavelengths. These are sent to a multiplexer, which consolidates the sources for transmission over a single fiber line. Optical amplifiers, typically spaced tens of kilometers apart, amplify all of the wavelengths simultaneously. Finally, the composite signal arrives at a demultiplexer, where the component channels are separated and sent to receivers at the destination point.

Most WDM systems operate in the 1550-nm range. In early systems, 200 GHz was allocated to each channel, but today most WDM systems use 50-GHz spacing. The channel spacing defined in ITU-T G.692, which accommodates 80 50-GHz channels, is summarized in Table 17.2

The term **dense wavelength division multiplexing** (DWDM) is often seen in the literature. There is no official or standard definition of this term. The term connotes the use of more channels, more closely spaced, than ordinary WDM. In general, a channel spacing of 200 GHz or less could be considered dense.

ADSL

The asymmetric digital subscriber line provides an interesting example of the use of FDM. In this section, we provide a brief overview of the method.

ADSL DESIGN   The term *asymmetric* is used because ADSL provides more capacity downstream (from the carrier's central office to the customer's site) than upstream (from customer to carrier). ADSL was originally targeted at the expected need for video on demand and related services. This application has not

Table 17.2   ITU WDM Channel Spacing (G.692)

Frequency (THz)	Wavelength in Vacuum (nm)	50 GHz	100 GHz	200 GHz
196.10	1528.77	X	X	X
196.05	1529.16	X		
196.00	1529.55	X	X	
195.95	1529.94	X		
195.90	1530.33	X	X	X
195.85	1530.72	X		
195.80	1531.12	X	X	
195.75	1531.51	X		
195.70	1531.90	X	X	X
195.65	1532.29	X		
195.60	1532.68	X	X	
...	...			
192.10	1560.61	X	X	X

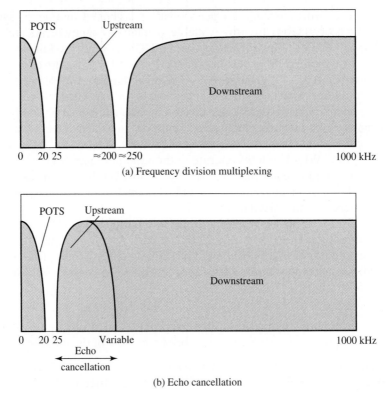

(a) Frequency division multiplexing

(b) Echo cancellation

Figure 17.8 ADSL Channel Configuration

materialized. However, since the introduction of ADSL technology, the demand for high-speed access to the Internet has grown. Typically, the user requires far higher capacity for downstream than for upstream transmission. Most user transmissions are in the form of keyboard strokes or transmission of short e-mail messages, whereas incoming traffic, especially Web traffic, can involve large amounts of data and include images or even video. Thus, ADSL provides a perfect fit for the Internet requirement.

ADSL uses frequency division modulation (FDM) in a novel way to exploit the 1-MHz capacity of twisted pair. There are three elements of the ADSL strategy (Figure 17.8):

- Reserve lowest 25 kHz for voice, known as POTS (plain old telephone service). The voice is carried only in the 0- to 4-kHz band; the additional bandwidth is to prevent crosstalk between the voice and data channels.
- Use either echo cancellation[2] or FDM to allocate two bands, a smaller upstream band and a larger downstream band.

---

[2]Echo cancellation is a signal processing technique that allows transmission of signals in both directions in the same frequency band on a single transmission line simultaneously. In essence, a transmitter must subtract the echo of its own transmission from the incoming signal to recover the signal sent by the other side.

- Use FDM within the upstream and downstream bands. In this case, a single bit stream is split into multiple parallel bit streams and each portion is carried in a separate frequency band. A commonly used technique is known as discrete multitone, explained subsequently.

When echo cancellation is used, the entire frequency band for the upstream channel overlaps the lower portion of the downstream channel. This has two advantages compared to the use of distinct frequency bands for upstream and downstream.

- The higher the frequency, the greater the attenuation. With the use of echo cancellation, more of the downstream bandwidth is in the "good" part of the spectrum.
- The echo cancellation design is more flexible for changing upstream capacity. The upstream channel can be extended upward without running into the downstream; instead, the area of overlap is extended.

The disadvantage of the use of echo cancellation is the need for echo cancellation logic on both ends of the line.

The ADSL scheme provides a range of up to 5.5 km, depending on the diameter of the cable and its quality. This is sufficient to cover about 95% of all U.S. subscriber lines and should provide comparable coverage in other nations.

DISCRETE MULTITONE Discrete multitone (DMT) uses multiple carrier signals at different frequencies, sending some of the bits on each channel. The available transmission band (upstream or downstream) is divided into a number of 4-kHz subchannels. On initialization, the DMT modem sends out test signals on each subchannel to determine the signal-to-noise ratio. The modem then assigns more bits to channels with better signal transmission qualities and less bits to channels with poorer signal transmission qualities. Figure 17.9 illustrates this process. Each subchannel can carry a data rate of from 0 to 60 kbps. The figure shows a typical situation in which there is increasing attenuation and hence decreasing signal-to-noise ratio at higher frequencies. As a result, the higher-frequency subchannels carry less of the load.

Present ADSL/DMT designs employ 256 downstream subchannels. In theory, with each 4-kHz subchannel carrying 60 kbps, it would be possible to transmit at a rate of 15.36 Mbps. In practice, transmission impairments prevent attainment of this data rate. Current implementations operate at from 1.5 to 9 Mbps, depending on line distance and quality.

Figure 17.9 DMT Bits per Channel Allocation

17.5 SYNCHRONOUS TIME DIVISION MULTIPLEXING

The TDM Mechanism

The other major form of multiplexing is **time division multiplexing** (TDM). In this section we examine **synchronous TDM**, which is often simply referred to as TDM.

Time division multiplexing is possible when the data rate of the transmission medium exceeds the required data rate of signals to be transmitted. A number of digital signals, or analog signals carrying digital data, can be carried simultaneously by interleaving portions of each signal in time. A general case of TDM is shown in Figure 17.5b. Six signal sources are fed into a multiplexer, which interleaves the bits from each signal by taking turns transmitting bits from each of the signals in a round-robin fashion. For example, the multiplexer in Figure 17.5b has six inputs that might be, say, 9.6 kbps each. A single line with a capacity of at least 57.6 kbps accommodates all six sources.

A simple example of TDM is illustrated in Figure 17.10, which shows the transmission of three data signals simultaneously over a transmission medium. In this example, each source operates at 64 kbps. The output from each source is briefly buffered. Each buffer is typically one bit or one character in length. The buffers are scanned in round-robin fashion to form a composite digital data stream. The scan operations are sufficiently rapid so that each buffer is emptied before more data can arrive. The scanned data are combined by the multiplexer into a composite data stream. Thus, the data rate transmitted by the multiplexer must at least equal the sum of the data rates of the three inputs (3 × 64 = 192 kbps). The digital signal produced by the multiplexer may be transmitted digitally or passed through a modem so that an analog signal is transmitted. In either case, transmission is typically synchronous (as opposed to asynchronous). At the receiving end,

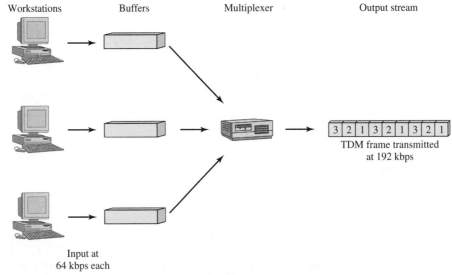

Figure 17.10   Synchronous TDM of Three Data Channels

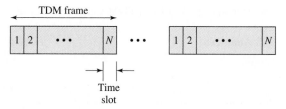

Figure 17.11 TDM Frame Structure

the demultiplexing process involves distributing the incoming data among three destination buffers.

The data transmitted by a synchronous TDM system have a format like that of Figure 17.11. The data are organized into **frames**, each of which contains a cycle of time slots. In each frame, one or more slots are dedicated to each data source. Transmission consists of the transmission of a sequence of frames. The set of time slots dedicated to one source, from frame to frame, is called a **channel**. Note that this is the same term used for FDM. The two uses of the term *channel* are logically equivalent. In both cases, a portion of the transmission capacity is dedicated to signals from a single source; that source sees a constant-data-rate or constant-bandwidth channel for transmission.

The slot length equals the transmitter buffer length, typically a bit or a byte (character). The byte-interleaving technique is used with both asynchronous and synchronous sources. Each time slot contains one byte of data. Typically, the start and stop bits of each character are eliminated before transmission and reinserted by the receiver, thus improving efficiency. The bit-interleaving technique is used with synchronous sources.

Synchronous TDM is called synchronous not because synchronous transmission is used but because the time slots are preassigned to sources and are fixed. The time slots for a given source are transmitted whether or not the source has data to send. This is, of course, also the case with FDM: A frequency band is dedicated to a particular source whether or not the source is transmitting at any given time. In both cases, capacity is wasted to achieve simplicity of implementation. Even when fixed assignment is used, however, it is possible for a synchronous TDM device to handle sources of different data rates. For example, the slowest input devices could be assigned one slot per frame, while faster devices are assigned multiple slots per frame.

Digital Carrier Systems

The long-distance carrier system provided in the United States and throughout the world was designed to transmit voice signals over high-capacity transmission links, such as optical fiber, coaxial cable, and microwave. Part of the evolution of these telecommunications networks to digital technology has been the adoption of synchronous TDM transmission structures. In the United States, AT&T developed a hierarchy of TDM structures of various capacities; this structure is used in Canada and Japan as well as the United States. A similar, but unfortunately not identical, hierarchy has been adopted internationally under the auspices of ITU-T (Table 17.3).

Table 17.3 North American and International TDM Carrier Standards

North American			International (ITU-T)		
Designation	**Number of Voice Channels**	**Data Rate (Mbps)**	**Level**	**Number of Voice Channels**	**Data Rate (Mbps)**
DS-1	24	1.544	1	30	2.048
DS-1C	48	3.152	2	120	8.448
DS-2	96	6.312	3	480	34.368
DS-3	672	44.736	4	1920	139.264
DS-4	4032	274.176	5	7680	565.148

The basis of the TDM hierarchy (in North America and Japan) is the DS-1 transmission format (Figure 17.12), which multiplexes 24 channels. Each frame contains 8 bits per channel plus a framing bit for a total of $24 \times 8 + 1 = 193$ bits. For voice transmission, the following rules apply. Each channel contains one word of digitized voice data. The original analog voice signal is digitized using pulse-code modulation (PCM) at a rate of 8000 samples per second. Therefore, each channel slot and hence each frame must repeat 8000 times per second. With a frame length of 193 bits, we have a data rate of $8000 \times 193 = 1.544$ Mbps. For five of every six frames, 8-bit PCM samples are used. For every sixth frame, each channel contains a 7-bit PCM word plus a signaling bit. The signaling bits form a stream for each voice channel that contains network control and routing information. For example, control signals are used to establish a connection or terminate a call.

The same DS-1 format is used to provide digital data service. For compatibility with voice, the same 1.544-Mbps data rate is used. In this case, 23 channels of data

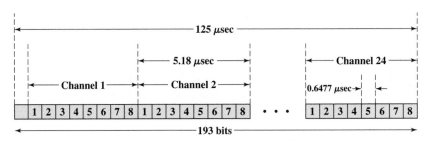

Notes:

1. The first bit is a framing bit, used for synchronization.
2. Voice channels:
   • 8-bit PCM used on five of six frames.
   • 7-bit PCM used on every sixth frame; bit 8 of each channel is a signaling bit.
3. Data channels:
   • Channel 24 is used for signaling only in some schemes.
   • Bits 1–7 used for 56 kbps service
   • Bits 2–7 used for 9.6, 4.8, and 2.4 kbps service.

Figure 17.12 DS-1 Transmmission Format

are provided. The twenty-fourth channel position is reserved for a special sync byte, which allows faster and more reliable reframing following a framing error. Within each channel, 7 bits per frame are used for data, with the eighth bit used to indicate whether the channel, for that frame, contains user data or system control data. With 7 bits per channel, and because each frame is repeated 8000 times per second, a data rate of 56 kbps can be provided per channel. Lower data rates are provided using a technique known as subrate multiplexing. For this technique, an additional bit is robbed from each channel to indicate which subrate multiplexing rate is being provided. This leaves a total capacity per channel of $6 \times 8000 = 48$ kbps. This capacity is used to multiplex five 9.6-kbps channels, ten 4.8-kbps channels, or twenty 2.4-kbps channels. For example, if channel 2 is used to provide 9.6-kbps service, then up to five data subchannels share this channel. The data for each subchannel appear as six bits in channel 2 every fifth frame.

Finally, the DS-1 format can be used to carry a mixture of voice and data channels. In this case, all 24 channels are utilized; no sync byte is provided.

Above this basic data rate of 1.544 Mbps, higher-level multiplexing is achieved by interleaving bits from DS-1 inputs. For example, the DS-2 transmission system combines four DS-1 inputs into a 6.312-Mbps stream. Data from the four sources are interleaved 12 bits at a time. Note that $1.544 \times 4 = 6.176$ Mbps. The remaining capacity is used for framing and control bits.

The designations DS-1, DS-1C, and so on refer to the multiplexing scheme used for carrying information. AT&T and other carriers supply transmission facilities that support these various multiplexed signals, referred to as carrier systems. These are designated with a "T" label. Thus, the T-1 carrier provides a data rate of 1.544 Mbps and is thus capable of supporting the DS-1 multiplex format, and so on for higher data rates.

T-1 Facilities

The T-1 facility is widely used by companies as a way of supporting networking capability and controlling costs. The most common external use (not part of the telephone network) of T-1 facilities is for leased dedicated transmission between customer premises. These facilities allow the customer to set up private networks to carry traffic throughout an organization. Examples of applications for such private networks are as follows:

- **Private voice networks:** When there is a substantial amount of intersite voice traffic, a leased private network can provide significant savings over using dialup facilities.

- **Private data networks:** Similarly, high data volumes between two or more sites can be supported by T-1 lines.

- **Video teleconferencing:** Allows high-quality video to be transmitted. As the bandwidth requirement for video declines, private video conferencing links can share T-1 facilities with other applications.

- **High-speed digital facsimile:** Permits rapid transmission of facsimile images and, depending on the facsimile load, may be able to share the T-1 link with other applications.

- **Internet access:** If a high volume of traffic between the site and the Internet is anticipated, then a high-capacity access line to the local Internet service provider is needed.

For users with substantial data transmission needs, the use of private T-1 networking is attractive for two reasons. First, T-1 permits simpler configurations than the use of a mix of lower-speed offerings, and second, T-1 transmission services are less expensive.

Another popular use of T-1 is to provide high-speed access from the customer's premises to the telephone network. In this application, a local area network or telephone exchange on the customer's premises supports a number of devices that generate sufficient off-site traffic to require the use of a T-1 access line to the public network.

SONET/SDH

SONET (Synchronous Optical Network) is an optical transmission interface originally proposed by BellCore and standardized by ANSI. A compatible version, referred to as Synchronous Digital Hierarchy (SDH), has been published by ITU-T in Recommendations G.707, G.708, and G.709.[3] SONET is intended to provide a specification for taking advantage of the high-speed digital transmission capability of optical fiber.

SIGNAL HIERARCHY   The SONET specification defines a hierarchy of standardized digital data rates (Table 17.4). The lowest level, referred to as STS-1 (Synchronous Transport Signal level 1) or OC-1 (Optical Carrier level 1),[4] is 51.84 Mbps. This rate can be used to carry a single DS-3 signal or a group of lower-rate signals, such as DS1, DS1C, DS2, plus ITU-T rates (e.g., 2.048 Mbps).

Multiple STS-1 signals can be combined to form an STS-N signal. The signal is created by interleaving bytes from *N* STS-1 signals that are mutually synchronized. For the ITU-T Synchronous Digital Hierarchy, the lowest rate is 155.52 Mbps, which is designated STM-1. This corresponds to SONET STS-3.

FRAME FORMAT   The basic SONET building block is the STS-1 frame, which consists of 810 octets and is transmitted once every 125 μs, for an overall data rate of 51.84 Mbps (Figure 17.13a). The frame can logically be viewed as a matrix of 9 rows of 90 octets each, with transmission being one row at a time, from left to right and top to bottom.

The first three columns (3 octets × 9 rows = 27 octets) of the frame are devoted to overhead octets, called section overhead and line overhead, which relate to

---

[3] In what follows, we will use the term *SONET* to refer to both specifications. Where differences exist, these will be addressed.

[4] An OC-N rate is the optical equivalent of an STS-N electrical signal. End user devices transmit and receive electrical signals; these must be converted to and from optical signals for transmission over optical fiber.

Table 17.4   SONET/SDH Signal Hierarchy

SONET Designation	ITU-T Designation	Data Rate	Payload Rate (Mbps)
STS-1/OC-1	STM-0	51.84 Mbps	50.112 Mbps
STS-3/OC-3	STM-1	155.52 Mbps	150.336 Mbps
STS-9/OC-9		466.56 Mbps	451.008 Mbps
STS-12/OC-12	STM-4	622.08 Mbps	601.344 Mbps
STS-18/OC-18		933.12 Mbps	902.016 Mbps
STS-24/OC-24		1.24416 Gbps	1.202688 Gbps
STS-36/OC-36		1.86624 Gbps	1.804032 Gbps
STS-48/OC-48	STM-16	2.48832 Gbps	2.405376 Gbps
STS-96/OC-96		4.87664 Gbps	4.810752 Gbps
STS-192/OC-192	STM-64	9.95328 Gbps	9.621504 Gbps
STS-768	STM-256	39.81312 Gbps	38.486016 Gbps
STS-3072		159.25248 Gbps	1.53944064 Gbps

different levels of detail in describing a SONET transmission. These octets convey not only synchronization information but network management information.

The remainder of the frame is payload, which is provided by the logical layer of SONET called the path layer. The payload includes a column of path overhead, which is not necessarily in the first available column position; the line overhead contains a pointer that indicates where the path overhead starts.

Figure 17.13b shows the general format for higher-rate frames, using the ITU-T designation.

(a) STS-1 frame format

(b) STM-N frame format

Figure 17.13   SONET/SDH Frame Formats

APPLICATION NOTE

Changing Communications

It is interesting to follow data communications mechanisms as they change. Of special interest is how data gets from place to place compared to how it did ten or even five years ago. Like anything else, techniques put in place to ensure successful transmissions go out of date, only to be replaced by other fault eliminating tools. These changes are not always a result of advances in technology; many of them come about because of changes in what we communicate and with whom.

Technology certainly does advance and create new ways to get things done. When we examine wide area networks, and in particular the protocols used, we see many changes to the quality and speed of the connections. For example, X.25 was a popular protocol used to connect sites to the WAN. It has several functions built in to ensure-error free connectivity. All of the nodes that were part of the network performed these checks. With improvements in data transmission, both in the transmitting equipment and the media used, this amount of error checking is no longer necessary and is considered wasted overhead.

However, this overhead may not have been an issue had it not been for the huge demand for offsite connectivity. At one time, individual nodes did not require much in the way of external resources. With the advent of distributed processing, secure connections between business sites, Web sites, hotmail, search engines, and significant research resources available online, this rule has been almost completely reversed. Increasingly, we see people and organizations sending data to sites "beyond the horizon."

We make demands for increases in speed and accuracy to prevent clogging the outgoing lines with retransmissions. New applications can add to this need for external connectivity. The gaming industry is spending tremendous sums of money developing powerful virtual worlds that are engaging enough to secure their percentage of users moving online. Online games such as World of Warcraft and *Halo3* are perfect examples of this trend. We have seen migrations from X.25 to Frame Relay, T carriers and ATM, which were followed by SONET. The next generation may accomplish all information transfer via 10 Gigabit Ethernet links or something even faster.

Universities are potentially the best illustration of organizations affected by this trend. Universities compete for a position on various "most wired" lists such as can be seen in *PC Magazine* and the older the Yahoo! Internet Life reports. Constant upgrades to improve desktop link speeds, router capability, protocol support, mobility, and offsite connectivity are all part of this drive to be super-wired. These goals also include a host of new policies for acceptable use and security for campus networks. Students can place very high demands on the infrastructure. Most network administrators and professors would probably agree that anytime there are new tools or techniques to communicate and share files over the network, students implement them.

But links to the external world are not the only changes to the way we swap information. Wireless communication is another area of demand for both educational and noneducational networks that certainly reflects change to our communication needs. It is difficult to imagine a world without wireless networking. Wireless has wide ranging effects in terms of support, security, and management. People now want to be connected on the go and wherever they happen to be. So this means that the applications will require what is called persistence. Persistence refers to a connection's ability to weather changes to topology, protocol, and speed as a user moves. The most obvious technology is 802.11, but the list must also include MobileIP (to ensure roaming connectivity) and IPv6 to accommodate the larger number of users and the quality of service they will expect. Major changes to telephony will also be part of this migration as we move to a more IP-based existence.

Moving to wireless also means increased performance difficulties as users familiar with dedicated 10- or 100-Mbps connections must share slower, more error-prone links. This places demands on the providers to ensure some level of quality, increasing levels of access for individual nodes and radio interference control.

As we move from one architecture to the next and from one set of protocols to another, the methods of flow and error control may change, but the goals remain the same. Links must be managed to reduce errors and ensure connectivity. In addition understanding the new protocols, it is important for providers to follow the flow of information as users take different pathways and change system requirements.

17.6 SUMMARY

Because of the possibility of transmission errors, and because the receiver of data may need to regulate the rate at which data arrive, the synchronization and interfacing techniques are insufficient by themselves. It is necessary to impose a layer of control in each communicating device that provides functions such as flow control, error detection, and error control. This layer of control is known as a **data link control protocol**. The most common of these is HDLC. Other similar data link control protocols are also in use.

Transmission costs are the most substantial portion of most data communications and voice communications budgets. Organizations that are faced with increasing needs for business information communications must exploit techniques for increasing transmission efficiency. Two complementary approaches are in common use. Multiplexing allows several transmission sources to share a larger transmission capacity. This allows the user to realize the economies of scale of using fewer higher-capacity lines compared to many lower-capacity lines. Compression is used to reduce the capacity required for a given transmission source. This allows more sources to share a given transmission capacity or allows less capacity to be used to support a single source. Multiplexing and compression can be combined to provide even greater improvements in efficiency.

Frequency division multiplexing can used with analog signals. A number of signals can be carried simultaneously on the same medium by allocating each signal a different frequency band. Modulation equipment is needed to move each signal to the required frequency band, and multiplexing equipment is needed to combine the modulated signals. This technique is used in both broadcast and cable TV video distribution systems. It has also been widely used in telephone networks to multiplex voice signals. However, this latter use is being displaced by synchronous time division multiplexing techniques as telephone networks convert to digital operation.

Synchronous time division multiplexing can be used with digital signals or analog signals carrying digital data. In this form of multiplexing, data from various sources are carried in repetitive frames. Each frame consists of a set of time slots, and each source is assigned one or more time slots per frame. The effect is to interleave bits of data from the various sources. This technique is widely used in digital telephone networks and in data communications facilities within organizations. One of the most popular forms of synchronous TDM is known as T-1. This refers to a leased transmission facility of 1.544 Mbps available from various sources and the specific multiplex format used on this facility. T-1 is popular for constructing private networks within geographically dispersed organizations and is increasingly used to provide business-user access to public telephone networks.

Statistical time division multiplexing provides a generally more efficient service than synchronous TDM for the support of terminals. With statistical TDM, time slots are not pre-assigned to particular data sources. Rather, user data are buffered and transmitted as rapidly as possible using available time slots. Statistical TDM has largely supplanted synchronous TDM for terminal networking applications.

17.7 RECOMMENDED READING AND WEB SITES

A discussion of FDM and TDM carrier systems can be found in [FREE05] and [CARN99]. SONET is treated in greater depth in [STAL07].

CARN99 Carne, E. *Telecommunications Primer: Data, Voice, and Video Communications.* Upper Saddle River, NJ: Prentice Hall, 1999.
FREE05 Freeman, R. *Fundamentals of Telecommunications.* New York: Wiley, 2005.
STAL07 Stallings, W. *Data and Computer Communications, Seventh Edition.* Upper Saddle River, NJ: Prentice Hall, 2007.

Recommended Web site:

- **SONET Home Page:** Useful links, tutorials, white papers, FAQ

17.8 KEY TERMS, REVIEW QUESTIONS, AND PROBLEMS

Key Terms

asymmetric digital subscriber line (ADSL)	flow control	synchronous optical network (SONET)
automatic repeat request (ARQ)	frame	synchronous TDM
data link control protocol	frequency division multiplexing (FDM)	TDM channel
dense wavelength division multiplexing (DWDM)	High-Level Data Link Control (HDLC)	TDM frame
digital subscriber line (DSL)	Multiplexing	time division multiplexing (TDM)
discrete multitone (DMT)	synchronous digital hierarchy (SDH)	wavelength division multiplexing (WDM)
error control		

Review Questions

17.1   Define *flow control*.

17.2   Define *error control*.

17.3   List common ingredients for error control for a link control protocol.

17.4   What is the purpose of the flag field in HDLC?

17.5   What type of error detection is used in the HDLC frame check sequence field?

17.6   What are the three frame types supported by HDLC? Describe each.

17.7   What is multiplexing?

17.8   The set of time slots or the frequency allocated to a single source is called what?

17.9   Why is multiplexing so cost-effective?

17.10   How is interference avoided by using frequency division multiplexing?

17.11   What is echo cancellation?

17.12   Define *upstream* and *downstream* with respect to subscriber lines.

17.13   Explain how synchronous time division multiplexing (TDM) works.

17.14   What are some of the major uses of T-1 lines?

17.15   Why is the use of private T-1 lines attractive to companies?

Problems

17.1   In HDLC, flag fields delimit the frame at both ends with the unique pattern 01111110. A single flag may be used as the closing flag for one frame and the opening flag for the next. On both sides of the user–network interface, receivers are continuously hunting for the flag sequence to synchronize on the start of a frame. While receiving a frame, a station continues to hunt for that sequence to determine the end of the frame. Because the protocol allows the presence of arbitrary bit patterns (i.e., there are no restrictions on the content of the various fields imposed by the link protocol), there is no assurance that the pattern 01111110 will not appear somewhere inside the frame, thus destroying synchronization. To avoid this problem, a procedure known as **bit stuffing** is used. For all bits between the starting and ending flags, the transmitter inserts an extra 0 bit after each occurrence of five 1s in the frame. After detecting a starting flag, the receiver monitors the bit stream. When a pattern of five 1s appears, the sixth bit is examined. If this bit is 0, it is deleted. If the sixth bit is a 1 and the seventh bit is a 0, the combination is accepted as a flag. If the sixth and seventh bits are both 1, the sender is indicating an abort condition. With the use of bit stuffing, arbitrary bit patterns can be inserted into the data field of the frame. This property is known as **data transparency**.

    a. Apply bit stuffing to the following bit string: 111111111111011111101111110.

    b. In which instances of bit stuffing for this string is the extra 0 is not strictly necessary for avoiding a flag pattern but necessary for the operation of the algorithm?

17.2 It is clear that bit stuffing is needed for the Address, Data, and FCS fields of an HDLC frame. Is it needed for the Control field?

17.3 Because of the provision that a single flag can be used as both an ending and a starting flag, a single bit error can cause problems.

    a. Explain how a single bit error can merge two frames into one.

    b. Explain how a single bit error can split a single frame into two frames.

17.4 Suggest improvements to the bit stuffing algorithm to overcome the problems of single-bit errors described in the preceding problem.

17.5 Using the example bit string of Problem 17.1a, show the signal pattern on the line using NRZ-L coding. Does this suggest a side benefit of bit stuffing?

17.6 Consider that several physical links connect two stations. We would like to use a "multi-link HDLC" that makes efficient use of these links by sending frames on a FIFO (first-in, first-out) basis on the next available link. What enhancements to HDLC are needed?

17.7 How do we achieve a data rate of 56 kbps in 23 channels using a DS-1 format?

17.8 To get some indication of the relative demands of voice and data traffic, consider the following:

    a. Calculate the number of bits used to send a 3-minute telephone call using standard PCM.

    b. How many pages of IRA text with an average of 65 characters a line and 55 lines a page corresponds to one 3-minute telephone call?

    c. How many pages of facsimile at standard resolution, that is, 200 dpi (dots per inch) horizontally and 100 dpi vertically, correspond to one 3-minute phone call? Assume that the effective page is 8 inches wide and 10.5 inches long. Moreover, assume an effective compression ratio of 10 to 1.

17.9 Recently a new scanner was announced that provided 1200 dpi resolution and over 1 billion colors.

    a. How much memory in bytes would it take to store a bit map of an 8×10 inch monochrome picture at 1200 dpi with a 10-bit gray scale?

    b. Suppose the colors are represented as a combination of three colors — red, blue, green — each with n bits to represent its intensity. What is the least value of n that will provide over 1 billion colors?

    c. How long would it take to send a gray scale representation of an 8×10 inch picture at 1200 dpi over a T-1 line (1.544 Mbps)?

17.10 To paraphrase Lincoln, all of the channel some of the time, some of the channel all of the time. Refer to Figure 17.5 and relate the preceding to the figure.

17.11 Assume that you are to design a TDM carrier, which we will call T-489, to support 30 voice channels using 6 bit samples and a structure similar to T-1. Determine the required bit rate.

17.12 Statistical (or asynchronous) TDM is an alternative to synchronous TDM. Describe how STDM is different from (synchronous) TDM. What advantages and disadvantages does STDM exhibit? RIC

17.13 T-3 and OC-3 lines are alternatives to the T-1 line. What are the maximum data rates for these two media? Describe a scenario where each media (T-1, T-3, and OC-3) would constitute an optimal solution. Consider capacity and cost considerations in your response.

HAUKELAND UNIVERSITY HOSPITAL

Haukeland University Hospital is one of the largest hospitals in Norway. The hospital offers almost every form of medical diagnosis and treatment. Haukeland University Hospital is the regional hospital for the Western Area Health Region, offering services to the region's 900,000 inhabitants. With 200 admissions and 1000 outpatients a day, it is one of the busiest hospitals in Scandinavia. With its total of 6000 employees, the hospital is also the largest employer in Western Norway. More than 500 physicians and 2000 nurses provide round-the-clock health services to more than 67,000 inpatients and 314,000 outpatients a year. The hospital has 1100 beds. Haukeland University Hospital is a teaching hospital with close links to the University of Bergen. Every year, 180 medical students receive their clinical training at the hospital, which is also an important teaching and training center for other groups of health care practitioners and other students. At the hospital's own training center, more than 100 nurses a year specialize in intensive care, anesthesia, pediatrics, and theater nursing. The hospital also offers 100 nursing specialists additional education every year.

Haukeland is the principal member of a health care network of treatment centers, local hospitals, psychiatric institutions, and dental facilities throughout southwestern Norway; the network is known as iHelse.net. The sparse population density and mountainous terrain make this region an ideal candidate for telemedicine. The hospital recognized a need to create a network and image transfer infrastructure such that location did not limit the availability of medical specialists. Without such an infrastructure, specialists have to travel to look at every individual patient, wasting valuable time traveling throughout the region. Thus, a telemedicine facility significantly enhances specialist productivity. Further, if patients move from one hospital to another, their treatment isn't delayed, because the hospital they choose can immediately access the patient's medical history, including past radiology scans. Finally, doctors working at any location have access to all the records and information services as at the central hospital because of the computer interconnections.

Central to the hospital's telemedicine strategy was the installation of the Picture Archiving and Communications System (PACS), which can produce digital images of radiology scans and other medical documents. PACS requires considerable storage and, equally important, the support of a high-capacity WAN that could serve the hospital's region [KIRB01].

When Haukeland decided to develop PACS, a key part of the planning was to look at the current WAN infrastructure that served iHelse.net. At the time, iHelse.net relied on a 256-kbps frame relay network, at a cost of $600 per month per connection. The iHelse.net WAN served 70 locations in the region, with 10,000 users and over 5000 workstations. While the coverage of the WAN was satisfactory for the then-current day-to-day operations, it could not support PACS. The hospital needed to significantly increase capacity, and initially project leaders set their sights on upgrading the WAN to 10 Mbps or 100 Mbps using frame relay or ATM.

To their surprise and delight, the hospital administrators found that they could do better than they had hoped, and save money in the bargain. The reason for this concerns the economics of providing long-distance fiber links. Competitive local exchange carriers (CLECs) typically install fiber optic cable with enormous amounts of capacity. The principal costs in long-distance fiber installation are land costs and labor; the fiber itself is an incidental expense. Thus, the strategy is to put down lots of cable while you've got the dirt excavated and the trench open, and make back the investment selling low-cost capacity. With such capacity available, Haukeland was able to put together a deal that involved not just 100-Mbps but 1-Gbps connection capacity at a price of $500 per month per connection. This is today's economics in long-distance capacity: Haukeland got a 400,000% increase in connection capacity at a reduced price.

The networking technology used to support this WAN service was Gigabit Ethernet. Although Ethernet is generally thought of as a LAN technology, it has in fact become a competitive player for modest distances in the WAN market—a niche often called metropolitan area network (MAN). For Gigabit Ethernet, links between Ethernet switches, using single-mode fiber, on the order of tens of kilometers

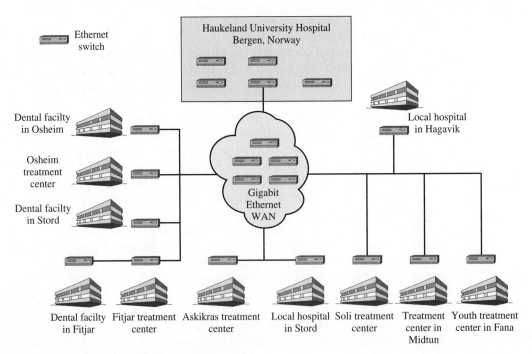

Figure IX.1   Haukeland Network Configuration

are feasible. With a diameter of about 200 km, the hospital's region lends itself to a switched Ethernet MAN.

One of the most attractive features of the Ethernet solution for the hospital is that it already was using Gigabit Ethernet on its LAN. Thus, the hospital's IT staff required no training to incorporate the Ethernet MAN into the facility. Figure IX.1 gives an overview of the current configuration.

Discussion Questions

1. Research current offerings for frame relay, ATM, and Ethernet MANs, and discuss the relative advantages of each.
2. What transition issues would you expect Haukeland to face in going from the frame relay WAN to the Ethernet WAN?

PART SIX

Management Issues

A s the networks used in an organization and the distributed applications they support grow in scale and complexity, management issues become increasingly difficult and important. In this final part, we look at the issues involved in including the Internet in the corporate computing environment and the operational management of computer networks.

Note: Chapters 20 and 21 are available online at williamstallings.com/BDC/BDC6e.html.

ROAD MAP FOR PART SIX

Chapter 18 Computer and Network Security Threats

Chapter 18 begins with an overview of computer security concepts. Then the chapter provides a survey of the threats to computer security. The bulk of the chapter is devoted to a discussion of intrusion and malicious software.

Chapter 19 Computer and Network Security Techniques

Chapter 19 surveys important techniques used to counter computer security threats. These include access control, intrusion detection, and defenses against malicious software. Chapter 19 also discusses SSL and the set of IP security standards.

Chapter 20 Network Management

A vital element for any business network is network management. Chapter 20 lays out the requirements for network management and then looks at the key elements of network management systems. The important Simple Network Management Protocol (SNMP) is examined in detail.

Chapter 21 Network Planning Design

Chapter 21 looks first at the larger issues of how organizational strategy, culture, and policies affect planning and designing of data communication systems. Next, the chapter looks at systematic methods for planning and design. The final section is an overview of design algorithms and tools.

514

CHAPTER 18

COMPUTER AND NETWORK SECURITY THREATS

18.1 Computer Security Concepts

18.2 Threats, Attacks, and Assets
Threats and Attacks
Threats and Assets

18.3 Intruders
Intruder Behavior Patterns
Intrusion Techniques

18.4 Malicious Software Overview
Backdoor
Logic Bomb
Trojan Horse
Mobile Code
Multiple-Threat Malware

18.5 Viruses, Worms, and Bots
Viruses
Worms
Bots

18.6 Recommended Reading and Web Sites

18.7 Key Terms, Review Questions, and Problems

Chapter Objectives

After reading this chapter, you should be able to

♦ Describe the key security requirements of confidentiality, integrity, and availability.

♦ Describe the major categories of threats to computers and networks.

♦ Discuss the types of intruders and the techniques used by intruders to access computer systems.

♦ Discuss the types of malicious software.

The area of computer and network security is a broad one and encompasses physical and administrative controls as well as automated controls. In this chapter, we confine ourselves to consideration of automated security tools. Following an overview of computer security concepts and computer security threats, the remainder of the chapter deals with the two broad categories of threat: intruders and malicious software.

Encryption plays a role both in computer security threats and computer security techniques. Appendix J provides an overview of encryption.

18.1 COMPUTER SECURITY CONCEPTS

The NIST *Computer Security Handbook* [NIST95] defines the term *computer security* as follows:

Computer Security: The protection afforded to an automated information system in order to attain the applicable objectives of preserving the integrity, availability, and confidentiality of information system resources (includes hardware, software, firmware, information/data, and telecommunications)

This definition introduces three key objectives that are at the heart of computer security:

- **Confidentiality:** This term covers two related concepts:
  - **Data[1] confidentiality:** Assures that private or confidential information is not made available or disclosed to unauthorized individuals
  - **Privacy:** Assures that individuals control or influence what information related to them may be collected and stored and by whom and to whom that information may be disclosed

---

[1]RFC 2828 (*Internet Security Glossary*) defines *information* as "facts and ideas, which can be represented (encoded) as various forms of data," and *data* as "information in a specific physical representation, usually a sequence of symbols that have meaning; especially a representation of information that can be processed or produced by a computer." Security literature typically does not make much of a distinction; nor does this chapter.

- **Integrity:** This term covers two related concepts:
  - —**Data integrity:** Assures that information and programs are changed only in a specified and authorized manner
  - —**System integrity:** Assures that a system performs its intended function in an unimpaired manner, free from deliberate or inadvertent unauthorized manipulation of the system
- **Availability:** Assures that systems work promptly and service is not denied to authorized users

These three concepts form what is often referred to as the **CIA triad** (Figure 18.1). The three concepts embody the fundamental security objectives for both data and for information and computing services. For example, the NIST standard FIPS 199 (*Standards for Security Categorization of Federal Information and Information Systems*) lists confidentiality, integrity, and availability as the three security objectives for information and for information systems. FIPS PUB 199 provides a useful characterization of these three objectives in terms of requirements and the definition of a loss of security in each category:

- **Confidentiality:** Preserving authorized restrictions on information access and disclosure, including means for protecting personal privacy and proprietary information. A loss of confidentiality is the unauthorized disclosure of information.
- **Integrity:** Guarding against improper information modification or destruction, including ensuring information nonrepudiation and authenticity. A loss of integrity is the unauthorized modification or destruction of information.
- **Availability:** Ensuring timely and reliable access to and use of information. A loss of availability is the disruption of access to or use of information or an information system.

Although the use of the CIA triad to define security objectives is well established, some in the security field feel that additional concepts are needed to present a complete picture. Two of the most commonly mentioned are as follows:

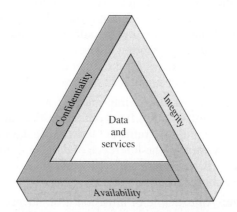

Figure 18.1 The Security Requirements Triad

- **Authenticity:** The property of being genuine and being able to be verified and trusted; confidence in the validity of a transmission, a message, or message originator. This means verifying that users are who they say they are and that each input arriving at the system came from a trusted source.

- **Accountability:** The security goal that generates the requirement for actions of an entity to be traced uniquely to that entity. This supports nonrepudiation, deterrence, fault isolation, intrusion detection and prevention, and after-action recovery and legal action. Because truly secure systems aren't yet an achievable goal, we must be able to trace a security breach to a responsible party. Systems must keep records of their activities to permit later forensic analysis to trace security breaches or to aid in transaction disputes.

Note that FIPS PUB 199 includes authenticity under integrity.

18.2 THREATS, ATTACKS, AND ASSETS

We turn now to a look at threats, attacks, and assets as related to computer security.

Threats and Attacks

Table 18.1, based on RFC 2828, describes four kinds of threat consequences and lists the kinds of attacks that result in each consequence.

Unauthorized disclosure is a threat to confidentiality. The following types of attacks can result in this threat consequence:

- **Exposure:** This can be deliberate, as when an insider intentionally releases sensitive information, such as credit card numbers, to an outsider. It can also be the result of a human, hardware, or software error, which results in an entity gaining unauthorized knowledge of sensitive data. There have been numerous instances of this, such as universities accidentally posting student confidential information on the Web.

- **Interception:** Interception is a common attack in the context of communications. On a shared local area network (LAN), such as a wireless LAN or a broadcast Ethernet, any device attached to the LAN can receive a copy of packets intended for another device. On the Internet, a determined hacker can gain access to e-mail traffic and other data transfers. All of these situations create the potential for unauthorized access to data.

- **Inference:** An example of inference is traffic analysis, in which an adversary is able to gain information from observing the pattern of traffic on a network, such as the amount of traffic between particular pairs of hosts on the network. Another example is the inference of detailed information from a database by a user who has only limited access; this is accomplished by repeated queries whose combined results enable inference.

- **Intrusion:** An example of intrusion is an adversary gaining unauthorized access to sensitive data by overcoming the system's access control protections.

Table 18.1   Threat Consequences, and the Types of Threat Actions That Cause Each Consequence. (Based on RFC 2828)

Threat Consequence	Threat Action (attack)
Unauthorized Disclosure A circumstance or event whereby an entity gains access to data for which the entity is not authorized.	**Exposure:** Sensitive data are directly released to an unauthorized entity. **Interception:** An unauthorized entity directly accesses sensitive data traveling between authorized sources and destinations. **Inference:** A threat action whereby an unauthorized entity indirectly accesses sensitive data (but not necessarily the data contained in the communication) by reasoning from characteristics or byproducts of communications. **Intrusion:** An unauthorized entity gains access to sensitive data by circumventing a system's security protections.
Deception A circumstance or event that may result in an authorized entity receiving false data and believing it to be true.	**Masquerade:** An unauthorized entity gains access to a system or performs a malicious act by posing as an authorized entity. **Falsification:** False data deceive an authorized entity. **Repudiation:** An entity deceives another by falsely denying responsibility for an act.
Disruption A circumstance or event that interrupts or prevents the correct operation of system services and functions.	**Incapacitation:** Prevents or interrupts system operation by disabling a system component. **Corruption:** Undesirably alters system operation by adversely modifying system functions or data. **Obstruction:** A threat action that interrupts delivery of system services by hindering system operation.
Usurpation A circumstance or event that results in control of system services or functions by an unauthorized entity.	**Misappropriation:** An entity assumes unauthorized logical or physical control of a system resource. **Misuse:** Causes a system component to perform a function or service that is detrimental to system security.

Deception is a threat to either system integrity or data integrity. The following types of attacks can result in this threat consequence:

- **Masquerade:** One example of masquerade is an attempt by an unauthorized user to gain access to a system by posing as an authorized user; this could happen if the unauthorized user has learned another user's logon ID and password. Another example is malicious logic, such as a Trojan horse, that appears to perform a useful or desirable function but actually gains unauthorized access to system resources or tricks a user into executing other malicious logic.

- **Falsification:** This refers to the altering or replacing of valid data or the introduction of false data into a file or database. For example, a student my alter his or her grades on a school database.

- **Repudiation:** In this case, a user either denies sending data or a user denies receiving or possessing the data.

Disruption is a threat to availability or system integrity. The following types of attacks can result in this threat consequence:

- **Incapacitation:** This is an attack on system availability. This could occur as a result of physical destruction of or damage to system hardware. More typically, malicious software, such as Trojan horses, viruses, or worms, could operate in such a way as to disable a system or some of its services.

- **Corruption:** This is an attack on system integrity. Malicious software in this context could operate in such a way that system resources or services function in an unintended manner. Or a user could gain unauthorized access to a system and modify some of its functions. An example of the latter is a user placing backdoor logic in the system to provide subsequent access to a system and its resources by other than the usual procedure.

- **Obstruction:** One way to obstruct system operation is to interfere with communications by disabling communication links or altering communication control information. Another way is to overload the system by placing excess burden on communication traffic or processing resources.

Usurpation is a threat to system integrity. The following types of attacks can result in this threat consequence:

- **Misappropriation:** This can include theft of service. An example is an a distributed denial of service attack, when malicious software is installed on a number of hosts to be used as platforms to launch traffic at a target host. In this case, the malicious software makes unauthorized use of processor and operating system resources.

- **Misuse:** Misuse can occur either by means of malicious logic or a hacker that has gained unauthorized access to a system. In either case, security functions can be disabled or thwarted.

Threats and Assets

The assets of a computer system can be categorized as hardware, software, data, and communication lines and networks. In this subsection, we briefly describe these four categories and relate these to the concepts of integrity, confidentiality, and availability introduced in Section 18.1 (see Figure 18.2 and Table 18.2).

HARDWARE   A major threat to computer system hardware is the threat to availability. Hardware is the most vulnerable to attack and the least susceptible to automated controls. Threats include accidental and deliberate damage to equipment as well as theft. The proliferation of personal computers and workstations and the widespread use of LANs increase the potential for losses in this area. Theft of CD-ROMs and DVDs can lead to loss of confidentiality. Physical and administrative security measures are needed to deal with these threats.

SOFTWARE   Software includes the operating system, utilities, and application programs. A key threat to software is an attack on availability. Software, especially application software, is often easy to delete. Software can also be altered or damaged to render it useless. Careful software configuration management, which includes making backups of the most recent version of software, can maintain high availability. A more difficult problem to deal with is software modification that results in a

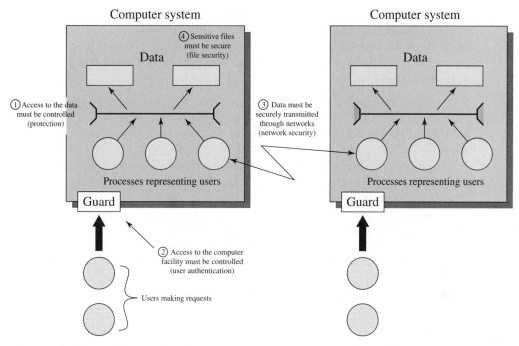

Figure 18.2 Scope of System Security

Table 18.2 Computer and Network Assets, with Examples of Threats

	Availability	Confidentiality	Integrity
Hardware	Equipment is stolen or disabled, thus denying service.		
Software	Programs are deleted, denying access to users.	An unauthorized copy of software is made.	A working program is modified, either to cause it to fail during execution or to cause it to do some unintended task.
Data	Files are deleted, denying access to users.	An unauthorized read of data is performed. An analysis of statistical data reveals underlying data.	Existing files are modified or new files are fabricated.
Communication Lines	Messages are destroyed or deleted. Communication lines or networks are rendered unavailable.	Messages are read. The traffic pattern of messages is observed.	Messages are modified, delayed, reordered, or duplicated. False messages are fabricated.

program that still functions but that behaves differently than before, which is a threat to integrity/authenticity. Computer viruses and related attacks fall into this category. A final problem is protection against software piracy. Although certain countermeasures are available, by and large the problem of unauthorized copying of software has not been solved.

DATA   Hardware and software security are typically concerns of computing center professionals or individual concerns of personal computer users. A much more widespread problem is data security, which involves files and other forms of data controlled by individuals, groups, and business organizations.

Security concerns with respect to data are broad, encompassing availability, secrecy, and integrity. In the case of availability, the concern is with the destruction of data files, which can occur either accidentally or maliciously.

The obvious concern with secrecy is the unauthorized reading of data files or databases, and this area has been the subject of perhaps more research and effort than any other area of computer security. A less obvious threat to secrecy involves the analysis of data and manifests itself in the use of so-called statistical databases, which provide summary or aggregate information. Presumably, the existence of aggregate information does not threaten the privacy of the individuals involved. However, as the use of statistical databases grows, there is an increasing potential for disclosure of personal information. In essence, characteristics of constituent individuals may be identified through careful analysis. For example, if one table records the aggregate of the incomes of respondents A, B, C, and D and another records the aggregate of the incomes of A, B, C, D, and E, the difference between the two aggregates would be the income of E. This problem is exacerbated by the increasing desire to combine data sets. In many cases, matching several sets of data for consistency at different levels of aggregation requires access to individual units. Thus, the individual units, which are the subject of privacy concerns, are available at various stages in the processing of data sets.

Finally, data integrity is a major concern in most installations. Modifications to data files can have consequences ranging from minor to disastrous.

COMMUNICATION LINES AND NETWORKS   Network security attacks can be classified as *passive attacks* and *active attacks*. A passive attack attempts to learn or make use of information from the system but does not affect system resources. An active attack attempts to alter system resources or affect their operation.

Passive attacks are in the nature of eavesdropping on, or monitoring of, transmissions. The goal of the attacker is to obtain information that is being transmitted. Two types of passive attacks are release of message contents and traffic analysis.

The **release of message contents** is easily understood. A telephone conversation, an electronic mail message, and a transferred file may contain sensitive or confidential information. We would like to prevent an opponent from learning the contents of these transmissions.

A second type of passive attack, **traffic analysis**, is subtler. Suppose that we had a way of masking the contents of messages or other information traffic so that opponents, even if they captured the message, could not extract the information from the message. The common technique for masking contents is encryption. If we had encryption protection in place, an opponent might still be able to observe the pattern of these messages. The opponent could determine the location and identity of communicating hosts and could observe the frequency and length of messages being exchanged. This information might be useful in guessing the nature of the communication that was taking place.

Passive attacks are very difficult to detect because they do not involve any alteration of the data. Typically, the message traffic is sent and received in an apparently normal fashion and neither the sender nor receiver is aware that a third party has read the messages or observed the traffic pattern. However, it is feasible to prevent the success of these attacks, usually by means of encryption. Thus, the emphasis in dealing with passive attacks is on prevention rather than detection.

Active attacks involve some modification of the data stream or the creation of a false stream and can be subdivided into four categories: replay, masquerade, modification of messages, and denial of service.

Replay involves the passive capture of a data unit and its subsequent retransmission to produce an unauthorized effect.

A **masquerade** takes place when one entity pretends to be a different entity. A masquerade attack usually includes one of the other forms of active attack. For example, authentication sequences can be captured and replayed after a valid authentication sequence has taken place, thus enabling an authorized entity with few privileges to obtain extra privileges by impersonating an entity that has those privileges.

Modification of messages simply means that some portion of a legitimate message is altered, or that messages are delayed or reordered, to produce an unauthorized effect. For example, a message stating "Allow John Smith to read confidential file accounts" is modified to say "Allow Fred Brown to read confidential file accounts."

The **denial of service** prevents or inhibits the normal use or management of communications facilities. This attack may have a specific target; for example, an entity may suppress all messages directed to a particular destination (e.g., the security audit service). Another form of service denial is the disruption of an entire network, either by disabling the network or by overloading it with messages so as to degrade performance.

Active attacks present the opposite characteristics of passive attacks. Whereas passive attacks are difficult to detect, measures are available to prevent their success. On the other hand, it is quite difficult to prevent active attacks absolutely, because to do so would require physical protection of all communications facilities and paths at all times. Instead, the goal is to detect them and to recover from any disruption or delays caused by them. Because the detection has a deterrent effect, it may also contribute to prevention.

18.3 INTRUDERS

One of the two most publicized threats to security is the intruder (the other is viruses), often referred to as a hacker or cracker. In an important early study of intrusion, Anderson [ANDE80] identified three classes of intruders:

- **Masquerader:** An individual who is not authorized to use the computer and who penetrates a system's access controls to exploit a legitimate user's account
- **Misfeasor:** A legitimate user who accesses data, programs, or resources for which such access is not authorized, or who is authorized for such access but misuses his or her privileges
- **Clandestine user:** An individual who seizes supervisory control of the system and uses this control to evade auditing and access controls or to suppress audit collection

The masquerader is likely to be an outsider; the misfeasor generally is an insider; and the clandestine user can be either an outsider or an insider.

Intruder attacks range from the benign to the serious. At the benign end of the scale, there are many people who simply wish to explore internets and see what is out there. At the serious end are individuals who are attempting to read privileged data, perform unauthorized modifications to data, or disrupt the system.

[GRAN04] lists the following examples of intrusion:

- Performing a remote root compromise of an e-mail server
- Defacing a Web server
- Guessing and cracking passwords
- Copying a database containing credit card numbers
- Viewing sensitive data, including payroll records and medical information, without authorization
- Running a packet sniffer on a workstation to capture usernames and passwords
- Using a permission error on an anonymous FTP server to distribute pirated software and music files
- Dialing into an unsecured modem and gaining internal network access
- Posing as an executive, calling the help desk, resetting the executive's e-mail password, and learning the new password
- Using an unattended, logged-in workstation without permission

Intruder Behavior Patterns

The techniques and behavior patterns of intruders are constantly shifting, to exploit newly discovered weaknesses and to evade detection and countermeasures. Even so, intruders typically follow one of a number of recognizable behavior patterns, and these patterns typically differ from those of ordinary users. In the following, we look at three broad examples of intruder behavior patterns to give the reader some feel for the challenge facing the security administrator. Table 18.3, based on [RADC04], summarizes the behavior.

HACKERS Traditionally, those who hack into computers do so for the thrill of it or for status. The hacking community is a strong meritocracy in which status is determined by level of competence. Thus, attackers often look for targets of opportunity and then share the information with others. A typical example is a break-in at a large financial institution reported in [RADC04]. The intruder took advantage of

Table 18.3 Some Examples of Intruder Patterns of Behavior

(a) Hacker

1. Select the target using IP lookup tools such as NSLookup, Dig, and others.
2. Map network for accessible services using tools such as NMAP.
3. Identify potentially vulnerable services (in this case, pcAnywhere).
4. Brute force (guess) pcAnywhere password.
5. Install remote administration tool called DameWare.
6. Wait for administrator to log on and capture his password.
7. Use that password to access remainder of network.

(b) Criminal Enterprise

1. Act quickly and precisely to make their activities harder to detect.
2. Exploit perimeter through vulnerable ports.
3. Use Trojan horses (hidden software) to leave backdoors for reentry.
4. Use sniffers to capture passwords.
5. Do not stick around until noticed.
6. Make few or no mistakes.

(c) Internal Threat

1. Create network accounts for themselves and their friends.
2. Access accounts and applications they wouldn't normally use for their daily jobs.
3. E-mail former and prospective employers.
4. Conduct furtive instant-messaging chats.
5. Visit Web sites that cater to disgruntled employees, such as f'dcompany.com.
6. Perform large downloads and file copying.
7. Access the network during off hours.

the fact that the corporate network was running unprotected services, some of which were not even needed. In this case, the key to the break-in was the pcAnywhere application. The manufacturer, Symantec, advertises this program as a remote control solution that enables secure connection to remote devices. But the attacker had an easy time gaining access to pcAnywhere; the administrator used the same three-letter username and password for the program. In this case, there was no intrusion detection system on the 700-node corporate network. The intruder was only discovered when a vice president walked into her office and saw the cursor moving files around on her Windows workstation.

Benign intruders might be tolerable, although they do consume resources and may slow performance for legitimate users. However, there is no way in advance to know whether an intruder will be benign or malign. Consequently, even for systems with no particularly sensitive resources, there is a motivation to control this problem.

Intrusion detection systems (IDSs) and intrusion prevention systems (IPSs), of the type described in this Chapter 19, are designed to counter this type of hacker threat. In addition to using such systems, organizations can consider restricting remote logons to specific IP addresses and/or use virtual private network technology.

One of the results of the growing awareness of the intruder problem has been the establishment of a number of computer emergency response teams (CERTs). These cooperative ventures collect information about system vulnerabilities and disseminate it to systems managers. Hackers also routinely read CERT reports. Thus, it is important for system administrators to quickly insert all software patches to discovered vulnerabilities. Unfortunately, given the complexity of many IT systems and the rate at which patches are released, this is increasingly difficult to achieve without automated updating. Even then, there are problems caused by incompatibilities resulting from the updated software (hence the need for multiple layers of defense in managing security threats to IT systems).

CRIMINALS   Organized groups of hackers have become a widespread and common threat to Internet-based systems. These groups can be in the employ of a corporation or government but often are loosely affiliated gangs of hackers. Typically, these gangs are young, often Eastern European, Russian, or southeast Asian hackers who do business on the Web [ANTE06]. They meet in underground forums with names like DarkMarket.org and theftservices.com to trade tips and data and coordinate attacks. A common target is a credit card file at an e-commerce server. Attackers attempt to gain root access. The card numbers are used by organized crime gangs to purchase expensive items and are then posted to carder sites, where others can access and use the account numbers; this obscures usage patterns and complicates investigation.

Whereas traditional hackers look for targets of opportunity, criminal hackers usually have specific targets, or at least classes of targets in mind. Once a site is penetrated, the attacker acts quickly, scooping up as much valuable information as possible and exiting.

IDSs and IPSs can also be used for these types of attackers but may be less effective because of the quick in-and-out nature of the attack. For e-commerce sites, database encryption should be used for sensitive customer information, especially credit cards. For hosted e-commerce sites (provided by an outsider service), the e-commerce organization should make use of a dedicated server (not used to support multiple customers) and closely monitor the provider's security services.

INSIDER ATTACKS   Insider attacks are among the most difficult to detect and prevent. Employees already have access to and knowledge of the structure and content of corporate databases. Insider attacks can be motivated by revenge or simply a feeling of entitlement. An example of the former is the case of Kenneth Patterson, fired from his position as data communications manager for American Eagle Outfitters. Patterson disabled the company's ability to process credit card purchases during five days of the holiday season of 2002. As for a sense of entitlement, there have always been many employees who felt entitled to take extra office supplies for home use, but this now extends to corporate data. An example is that of a vice president of sales for a stock analysis firm who quit to go to a competitor. Before she left, she copied the customer database to take with her. The offender reported feeling no animus toward her former employee; she simply wanted the data because it would be useful to her.

Although IDS and IPS facilities can be useful in countering insider attacks, other more direct approaches are of higher priority. Examples include the following:

- Enforce least privilege, only allowing access to the resources employees need to do their job.
- Set logs to see what users access and what commands they are entering.
- Protect sensitive resources with strong authentication.
- Upon termination, delete employee's computer and network access.
- Upon termination, make a mirror image of employee's hard drive before reissuing it. That evidence might be needed if your company information turns up at a competitor.

Intrusion Techniques

The objective of the intruder is to gain access to a system or to increase the range of privileges accessible on a system. Most initial attacks use system or software vulnerabilities that allow a user to execute code that opens a back door into the system. Intruders can get access to a system by exploiting attacks such as buffer overflows on a program that runs with certain privileges.

Alternatively, the intruder attempts to acquire information that should have been protected. In some cases, this information is in the form of a user password. With knowledge of some other user's password, an intruder can log in to a system and exercise all the privileges accorded to the legitimate user.

18.4 MALICIOUS SOFTWARE OVERVIEW

Perhaps the most sophisticated types of threats to computer systems are presented by programs that exploit vulnerabilities in computing systems. Such threats are referred to as **malicious software**, or **malware**. In this context, we are concerned with application programs as well as utility programs, such as editors and compilers. Malware is software designed to cause damage to or use up the resources of a target computer. It is frequently concealed within or masquerades as legitimate software. In some cases, it spreads itself to other computers via e-mail or infected floppy disks.

The terminology in this area presents problems because of a lack of universal agreement on all of the terms and because some of the categories overlap. Table 18.4 is a useful guide.

Malicious software can be divided into two categories: those that need a host program, and those that are independent. The former, referred to as **parasitic**, are essentially fragments of programs that cannot exist independently of some actual application program, utility, or system program. Viruses, logic bombs, and backdoors are examples. The latter are self-contained programs that can be scheduled and run by the operating system. Worms and bot programs are examples.

Table 18.4 Terminology of Malicious Programs

Name	Description
Virus	Malware that, when executed, tries to replicate itself into other executable code; when it succeeds the code is said to be infected. When the infected code is executed, the virus also executes.
Worm	A computer program that can run independently and can propagate a complete working version of itself onto other hosts on a network.
Logic bomb	A program inserted into software by an intruder. A logic bomb lies dormant until a predefined condition is met; the program then triggers an unauthorized act.
Trojan horse	A computer program that appears to have a useful function, but also has a hidden and potentially malicious function that evades security mechanisms, sometimes by exploiting legitimate authorizations of a system entity that invokes the Trojan horse program.
Backdoor (trapdoor)	Any mechanisms that bypasses a normal security check; it may allow unauthorized access to functionality.
Mobile code	Software (e.g., script, macro, or other portable instruction) that can be shipped unchanged to a heterogeneous collection of platforms and execute with identical semantics.
Exploits	Code specific to a single vulnerability or set of vulnerabilities.
Downloaders	Program that installs other items on a machine that is under attack. Usually, a downloader is sent in an e-mail.
Auto-rooter	Malicious hacker tools used to break into new machines remotely.
Kit (virus generator)	Set of tools for generating new viruses automatically.
Spammer programs	Used to send large volumes of unwanted e-mail.
Flooders	Used to attack networked computer systems with a large volume of traffic to carry out a denial-of-service (DoS) attack.
Keyloggers	Captures keystrokes on a compromised system.
Rootkit	Set of hacker tools used after attacker has broken into a computer system and gained root-level access.
Zombie, bot	Program activated on an infected machine that is activated to launch attacks on other machines.
Spyware	Software that collects information from a computer and transmits it to another system.
Adware	Advertising that is integrated into software. It can result in pop-up ads or redirection of a browser to a commercial site.

We can also differentiate between those software threats that do not replicate and those that do. The former are programs or fragments of programs that are activated by a trigger. Examples are logic bombs, backdoors, and bot programs. The latter consist of either a program fragment or an independent program that, when executed, may produce one or more copies of itself to be activated later on the same system or some other system. Viruses and worms are examples.

In the remainder of this section, we briefly survey some of the key categories of malicious software, deferring discussion on the key topics of viruses, worms, and bots until the following section.

Backdoor

A **backdoor**, also known as a **trapdoor**, is a secret entry point into a program that allows someone who is aware of the backdoor to gain access without going through the usual security access procedures. Programmers have used backdoors legitimately for many years to debug and test programs; such a backdoor is called a **maintenance hook**. This usually is done when the programmer is developing an application that has an authentication procedure, or a long setup, requiring the user to enter many different values to run the application. To debug the program, the developer may wish to gain special privileges or to avoid all the necessary setup and authentication. The programmer may also want to ensure that there is a method of activating the program should something be wrong with the authentication procedure that is being built into the application. The backdoor is code that recognizes some special sequence of input or is triggered by being run from a certain user ID or by an unlikely sequence of events.

Backdoors become threats when unscrupulous programmers use them to gain unauthorized access. The backdoor was the basic idea for the vulnerability portrayed in the movie *War Games*. Another example is that during the development of Multics, penetration tests were conducted by an Air Force "tiger team" (simulating adversaries). One tactic employed was to send a bogus operating system update to a site running Multics. The update contained a Trojan horse (described later) that could be activated by a backdoor and that allowed the tiger team to gain access. The threat was so well implemented that the Multics developers could not find it, even after they were informed of its presence [ENGE80].

It is difficult to implement operating system controls for backdoors. Security measures must focus on the program development and software update activities.

Logic Bomb

One of the oldest types of program threat, predating viruses and worms, is the logic bomb. The logic bomb is code embedded in some legitimate program that is set to "explode" when certain conditions are met. Examples of conditions that can be used as triggers for a logic bomb are the presence or absence of certain files, a particular day of the week or date, or a particular user running the application. Once triggered, a bomb may alter or delete data or entire files, cause a machine halt, or do some other damage. A striking example of how logic bombs can be employed was the case of Tim Lloyd, who was convicted of setting a logic bomb that cost his employer, Omega Engineering, more than $10 million, derailed its corporate growth strategy, and eventually led to the layoff of 80 workers [GAUD00]. Ultimately, Lloyd was sentenced to 41 months in prison and ordered to pay $2 million in restitution.

Trojan Horse

A Trojan horse [2] is a useful, or apparently useful, program or command procedure containing hidden code that, when invoked, performs some unwanted or harmful function.

Trojan horse programs can be used to accomplish functions indirectly that an unauthorized user could not accomplish directly. For example, to gain access to the files of another user on a shared system, a user could create a Trojan horse program that, when executed, changes the invoking user's file permissions so that the files are readable by any user. The author could then induce users to run the program by placing it in a common directory and naming it such that it appears to be a useful utility program or application. An example is a program that ostensibly produces a listing of the user's files in a desirable format. After another user has run the program, the author of the program can then access the information in the user's files. An example of a Trojan horse program that would be difficult to detect is a compiler that has been modified to insert additional code into certain programs as they are compiled, such as a system login program [THOM84]. The code creates a backdoor in the login program that permits the author to log on to the system using a special password. This Trojan horse can never be discovered by reading the source code of the login program.

Another common motivation for the Trojan horse is data destruction. The program appears to be performing a useful function (e.g., a calculator program), but it may also be quietly deleting the user's files. For example, a CBS executive was victimized by a Trojan horse that destroyed all information contained in his computer's memory [TIME90]. The Trojan horse was implanted in a graphics routine offered on an electronic bulletin board system.

Trojan horses fit into one of three models:

- Continuing to perform the function of the original program and additionally performing a separate malicious activity
- Continuing to perform the function of the original program but modifying the function to perform malicious activity (e.g., a Trojan horse version of a login program that collects passwords) or to disguise other malicious activity (e.g., a Trojan horse version of a process listing program that does not display certain processes that are malicious)
- Performing a malicious function that completely replaces the function of the original program

Mobile Code

Mobile code refers to programs (e.g., script, macro, or other portable instruction) that can be shipped unchanged to a heterogeneous collection of platforms and execute with identical semantics [JANS01]. The term also applies to situations involving a large homogeneous collection of platforms (e.g., Microsoft Windows).

---

[2] In Greek mythology, the Greeks used the Trojan horse during their siege of Troy. Epeios constructed a giant hollow wooden horse in which thirty of the most valiant Greek heroes concealed themselves. The rest of the Greeks burned their encampment and pretended to sail away but actually hid nearby. The Trojans, convinced the horse was a gift and the siege over, dragged the horse into the city. That night, the Greeks emerged from the horse and opened the city gates to the Greek army. A bloodbath ensued, resulting in the destruction of Troy and the death or enslavement of all its citizens.

Mobile code is transmitted from a remote system to a local system and then executed on the local system without the user's explicit instruction. Mobile code often acts as a mechanism for a virus, worm, or Trojan horse to be transmitted to the user's workstation. In other cases, mobile code takes advantage of vulnerabilities to perform its own exploits, such as unauthorized data access or root compromise. Popular vehicles for mobile code include Java applets, ActiveX, JavaScript, and VBScript. The most common ways of using mobile code for malicious operations on local system are cross-site scripting, interactive and dynamic Web sites, e-mail attachments, and downloads from untrusted sites or of untrusted software.

Multiple Threat Malware

Viruses and other malware may operate in multiple ways. The terminology is far from uniform; this subsection gives a brief introduction to several related concepts that could be considered multiple-threat malware.

A **multipartite** virus infects in multiple ways. Typically, the multipartite virus is capable of infecting multiple types of files, so that virus eradication must deal with all of the possible sites of infection.

A **blended attack** uses multiple methods of infection or transmission, to maximize the speed of contagion and the severity of the attack. Some writers characterize a blended attack as a package that includes multiple types of malware. An example of a blended attack is the Nimda attack, erroneously referred to as simply a worm. Nimda uses four distribution methods:

- **E-mail:** A user on a vulnerable host opens an infected e-mail attachment; Nimda looks for e-mail addresses on the host and then sends copies of itself to those addresses.

- **Windows shares:** Nimda scans hosts for unsecured Windows file shares; it can then use NetBIOS86 as a transport mechanism to infect files on that host in the hopes that a user will run an infected file, which will activate Nimda on that host.

- **Web servers:** Nimda scans Web servers, looking for known vulnerabilities in Microsoft IIS. If it finds a vulnerable server, it attempts to transfer a copy of itself to the server and infect it and its files.

- **Web clients:** If a vulnerable Web client visits a Web server that has been infected by Nimda, the client's workstation will become infected.

Thus, Nimda has worm, virus, and mobile code characteristics. Blended attacks may also spread through other services, such as instant messaging and peer-to-peer file sharing.

18.5 VIRUSES, WORMS, AND BOTS

Viruses

A computer virus is a piece of software that can "infect" other programs by modifying them; the modification includes injecting the original program with a routine to make copies of the virus program, which can then go on to infect other programs.

Biological viruses are tiny scraps of genetic code—DNA or RNA—that can take over the machinery of a living cell and trick it into making thousands of flawless replicas of the original virus. Like its biological counterpart, a computer virus carries in its instructional code the recipe for making perfect copies of itself. The typical virus becomes embedded in a program on a computer. Then, whenever the infected computer comes into contact with an uninfected piece of software, a fresh copy of the virus passes into the new program. Thus, the infection can be spread from computer to computer by unsuspecting users who either swap disks or send programs to one another over a network. In a network environment, the ability to access applications and system services on other computers provides a perfect culture for the spread of a virus.

THE NATURE OF VIRUSES   A virus can do anything that other programs do. The only difference is that it attaches itself to another program and executes secretly when the host program is run. Once a virus is executing, it can perform any function that is allowed by the privileges of the current user, such as erasing files and programs.

A computer virus has three parts [AYCO06]:

- **Infection mechanism:** The means by which a virus spreads, enabling it to replicate. The mechanism is also referred to as the **infection vector**.
- **Trigger:** The event or condition that determines when the payload is activated or delivered.
- **Payload:** What the virus does, besides spreading. The payload may involve damage or may involve benign but noticeable activity.

During its lifetime, a typical virus goes through the following four phases:

- **Dormant phase:** The virus is idle. The virus will eventually be activated by some event, such as a date, the presence of another program or file, or the capacity of the disk exceeding some limit. Not all viruses have this stage.
- **Propagation phase:** The virus places an identical copy of itself into other programs or into certain system areas on the disk. Each infected program will now contain a clone of the virus, which will itself enter a propagation phase.
- **Triggering phase:** The virus is activated to perform the function for which it was intended. As with the dormant phase, the triggering phase can be caused by a variety of system events, including a count of the number of times that this copy of the virus has made copies of itself.
- **Execution phase:** The function is performed. The function may be harmless, such as a message on the screen, or damaging, such as the destruction of programs and data files.

Most viruses carry out their work in a manner that is specific to a particular operating system and, in some cases, specific to a particular hardware platform. Thus, they are designed to take advantage of the details and weaknesses of particular systems.

VIRUS STRUCTURE   A virus can be prepended or postpended to an executable program, or it can be embedded in some other fashion. The key to its operation is that

```
        program V :=
{goto main;
    1234567;

    subroutine infect-executable :=
        {loop:
        file := get-random-executable-file;
        if (first-line-of-file = 1234567)
            then goto loop
            else prepend V to file; }

    subroutine do-damage :=
        {whatever damage is to be done}

    subroutine trigger-pulled :=
        {return true if some condition holds}

main: main-program :=
        {infect-executable;
        if trigger-pulled then do-damage;
        goto next;}

next:

}
```

Figure 18.3   A Simple Virus

the infected program, when invoked, will first execute the virus code and then execute the original code of the program.

A very general depiction of virus structure is shown in Figure 18.3 (based on [COHE94]). In this case, the virus code, V, is prepended to infected programs, and it is assumed that the entry point to the program, when invoked, is the first line of the program.

The infected program begins with the virus code and works as follows. The first line of code is a jump to the main virus program. The second line is a special marker that is used by the virus to determine whether or not a potential victim program has already been infected with this virus. When the program is invoked, control is immediately transferred to the main virus program. The virus program may first seeks out uninfected executable files and infect them. Next, the virus may perform some action, usually detrimental to the system. This action could be performed every time the program is invoked, or it could be a logic bomb that triggers only under certain conditions. Finally, the virus transfers control to the original program. If the infection phase of the program is reasonably rapid, a user is unlikely to notice any difference between the execution of an infected and an uninfected program.

A virus such as the one just described is easily detected because an infected version of a program is longer than the corresponding uninfected one. A way to thwart

```
    program CV :=

{goto main;
    01234567;

    subroutine infect-executable :=
        {loop:
            file := get-random-executable-file;
        if (first-line-of-file = 01234567) then goto loop;
    (1)     compress file;
    (2)     prepend CV to file;
    }

main: main-program :=
            {if ask-permission then infect-executable;
    (3)     uncompress rest-of-file;
    (4)     run uncompressed file;}
    }
```

Figure 18.4   Logic for a Compression Virus

such a simple means of detecting a virus is to compress the executable file so that both the infected and uninfected versions are of identical length. Figure 18.4 [COHE94] shows in general terms the logic required. The important lines in this virus are numbered. We assume that program P_1 is infected with the virus CV. When this program is invoked, control passes to its virus, which performs the following steps:

1. For each uninfected file P_2' that is found, the virus first compresses that file to produce , P_2' which is shorter than the original program by the size of the virus.
2. A copy of the virus is prepended to the compressed program.
3. The compressed version of the original infected program, P_1', is uncompressed.
4. The uncompressed original program is executed.

In this example, the virus does nothing other than propagate. As previously mentioned, the virus may include a logic bomb.

INITIAL INFECTION   Once a virus has gained entry to a system by infecting a single program, it is in a position to potentially infect some or all other executable files on that system when the infected program executes. Thus, viral infection can be completely prevented by preventing the virus from gaining entry in the first place. Unfortunately, prevention is extraordinarily difficult because a virus can be part of any program outside a system. Thus, unless one is content to take an absolutely bare piece of iron and write all one's own system and application programs, one is vulnerable. Many forms of infection can also be blocked by denying normal users the right to modify programs on the system.

The lack of access controls on early PCs is a key reason why traditional machine code-based viruses spread rapidly on these systems. In contrast, while it is easy enough to write a machine code virus for UNIX systems, they were almost never seen in practice because the existence of access controls on these systems prevented effective propagation of the virus. Traditional machine code-based viruses are now less prevalent, because modern PC operating systems have more effective access controls. However, virus creators have found other avenues, such as macro and e-mail viruses, as discussed subsequently.

VIRUSES CLASSIFICATION   There has been a continuous arms race between virus writers and writers of antivirus software since viruses first appeared. As effective countermeasures are developed for existing types of viruses, newer types are developed. There is no simple or universally agreed upon classification scheme for viruses. In this section, we follow [AYCO06] and classify viruses along two orthogonal axes: the type of target the virus tries to infect and the method the virus uses to conceal itself from detection by users and antivirus software.

A virus **classification by target** includes the following categories:

- **Boot sector infector:** Infects a master boot record or boot record and spreads when a system is booted from the disk containing the virus
- **File infector:** Infects files that the operating system or shell consider to be executable
- **Macro virus:** Infects files with macro code that is interpreted by an application

A virus classification by concealment strategy includes the following categories:

- **Encrypted virus:** A typical approach is as follows: A portion of the virus creates a random encryption key and encrypts the remainder of the virus. The key is stored with the virus. When an infected program is invoked, the virus uses the stored random key to decrypt the virus. When the virus replicates, a different random key is selected. Because the bulk of the virus is encrypted with a different key for each instance, there is no constant bit pattern to observe.
- **Stealth virus:** A form of virus explicitly designed to hide itself from detection by antivirus software. Thus, the entire virus, not just a payload is hidden.
- **Polymorphic virus:** A virus that mutates with every infection, making detection by the "signature" of the virus impossible.
- **Metamorphic virus:** As with a polymorphic virus, a metamorphic virus mutates with every infection. The difference is that a metamorphic virus rewrites itself completely at each iteration, increasing the difficulty of detection. Metamorphic viruses may change their behavior as well as their appearance.

One example of a **stealth virus** was discussed earlier: a virus that uses compression so that the infected program is exactly the same length as an uninfected version. Far more sophisticated techniques are possible. For example, a virus can place intercept logic in disk I/O routines, so that when there is an attempt to read suspected portions of the disk using these routines, the virus will present back the original, uninfected program. Thus, *stealth* is not a term that applies to a virus as such but, rather, refers to a technique used by a virus to evade detection.

A **polymorphic virus** creates copies during replication that are functionally equivalent but have distinctly different bit patterns. As with a stealth virus, the purpose is to defeat programs that scan for viruses. In this case, the "signature" of the virus will vary with each copy. To achieve this variation, the virus may randomly insert superfluous instructions or interchange the order of independent instructions. A more effective approach is to use encryption. The strategy of the encryption virus is followed. The portion of the virus that is responsible for generating keys and performing encryption/decryption is referred to as the *mutation engine*. The mutation engine itself is altered with each use.

VIRUS KITS   Another weapon in the virus writers' armory is the virus-creation toolkit. Such a toolkit enables a relative novice to quickly create a number of different viruses. Although viruses created with toolkits tend to be less sophisticated than viruses designed from scratch, the sheer number of new viruses that can be generated using a toolkit creates a problem for antivirus schemes.

MACRO VIRUSES   In the mid-1990s, macro viruses became by far the most prevalent type of virus. Macro viruses are particularly threatening for a number of reasons:

1. A macro virus is platform independent. Many macro viruses infect Microsoft Word documents or other Microsoft Office documents. Any hardware platform and operating system that supports these applications can be infected.

2. Macro viruses infect documents, not executable portions of code. Most of the information introduced onto a computer system is in the form of a document rather than a program.

3. Macro viruses are easily spread. A very common method is by electronic mail.

4. Because macro viruses infect user documents rather than system programs, traditional file system access controls are of limited use in preventing their spread.

Macro viruses take advantage of a feature found in Word and other office applications such as Microsoft Excel—namely, the macro. In essence, a macro is an executable program embedded in a word processing document or other type of file. Typically, users employ macros to automate repetitive tasks and thereby save keystrokes. The macro language is usually some form of the Basic programming language. A user might define a sequence of keystrokes in a macro and set it up so that the macro is invoked when a function key or special short combination of keys is input.

Successive releases of MS Office products provide increased protection against macro viruses. For example, Microsoft offers an optional Macro Virus Protection tool that detects suspicious Word files and alerts the customer to the potential risk of opening a file with macros. Various antivirus product vendors have also developed tools to detect and correct macro viruses. As in other types of viruses, the arms race continues in the field of macro viruses, but they no longer are the predominant virus threat.

E-MAIL VIRUSES   A more recent development in malicious software is the e-mail virus. The first rapidly spreading e-mail viruses, such as Melissa, made use of a Microsoft Word macro embedded in an attachment. If the recipient opens the e-mail attachment, the Word macro is activated. Then

1. The e-mail virus sends itself to everyone on the mailing list in the user's e-mail package.

2. The virus does local damage on the user's system.

In 1999, a more powerful version of the e-mail virus appeared. This newer version can be activated merely by opening an e-mail that contains the virus rather than opening an attachment. The virus uses the Visual Basic scripting language supported by the e-mail package.

Thus we see a new generation of malware that arrives via e-mail and uses e-mail software features to replicate itself across the Internet. The virus propagates itself as soon as it is activated (either by opening an e-mail attachment or by opening the e-mail) to all of the e-mail addresses known to the infected host. As a result, whereas viruses used to take months or years to propagate, they now do so in hours. This makes it very difficult for antivirus software to respond before much damage is done. Ultimately, a greater degree of security must be built into Internet utility and application software on PCs to counter the growing threat.

Worms

A worm is a program that can replicate itself and send copies from computer to computer across network connections. Upon arrival, the worm may be activated to replicate and propagate again. In addition to propagation, the worm usually performs some unwanted function. An e-mail virus has some of the characteristics of a worm because it propagates itself from system to system. However, we can still classify it as a virus because it uses a document modified to contain viral macro content and requires human action. A worm actively seeks out more machines to infect, and each machine that is infected serves as an automated launching pad for attacks on other machines.

Network worm programs use network connections to spread from system to system. Once active within a system, a network worm can behave as a computer virus or bacteria, or it could implant Trojan horse programs or perform any number of disruptive or destructive actions.

To replicate itself, a network worm uses some sort of network vehicle. Examples include the following:

- **Electronic mail facility:** A worm mails a copy of itself to other systems, so that its code is run when the e-mail or an attachment is received or viewed.

- **Remote execution capability:** A worm executes a copy of itself on another system, either using an explicit remote execution facility or by exploiting a program flaw in a network service to subvert its operations.

- **Remote login capability:** A worm logs onto a remote system as a user and then uses commands to copy itself from one system to the other, where it then executes.

The new copy of the worm program is then run on the remote system, where, in addition to any functions that it performs at that system, it continues to spread in the same fashion.

A network worm exhibits the same characteristics as a computer virus: a dormant phase, a propagation phase, a triggering phase, and an execution phase. The propagation phase generally performs the following functions:

1. Search for other systems to infect by examining host tables or similar repositories of remote system addresses.

2. Establish a connection with a remote system.

3. Copy itself to the remote system and cause the copy to be run.

The network worm may also attempt to determine whether a system has previously been infected before copying itself to the system. In a multiprogramming system, it may also disguise its presence by naming itself as a system process or using some other name that may not be noticed by a system operator.

As with viruses, network worms are difficult to counter.

WORM PROPAGATION MODEL   [ZOU05] describes a model for worm propagation based on an analysis of recent worm attacks. The speed of propagation and the total number of hosts infected depend on a number of factors, including the mode of propagation, the vulnerability or vulnerabilities exploited, and the degree of similarity to preceding attacks. For the latter factor, an attack that is a variation of a recent previous attack may be countered more effectively than a more novel attack. Figure 18.5 shows the dynamics for one typical set of parameters. Propagation proceeds through three phases. In the initial phase, the number of hosts increases exponentially. To see that this is so, consider a simplified case in which a worm is launched from a single host and infects two nearby hosts. Each of these hosts infects two more hosts, and so on. This results in exponential growth. After a time, infecting hosts waste some time attacking already infected hosts, which reduces the rate of infection. During this middle phase, growth is approximately linear, but the rate of infection is rapid. When most vulnerable computers have been infected, the attack enters a slow finish phase as the worm seeks out those remaining hosts that are difficult to identify.

Clearly, the objective in countering a worm is to catch the worm in its slow start phase, at a time when few hosts have been infected.

Figure 18.5   Worm Propagation Model

STATE OF WORM TECHNOLOGY   The state of the art in worm technology includes the following:

- **Multiplatform:** Newer worms are not limited to Windows machines but can attack a variety of platforms, especially the popular varieties of UNIX.

- **Multiexploit:** New worms penetrate systems in a variety of ways, using exploits against Web servers, browsers, e-mail, file sharing, and other network-based applications.

- **Ultrafast spreading:** One technique to accelerate the spread of a worm is to conduct a prior Internet scan to accumulate Internet addresses of vulnerable machines.

- **Polymorphic:** To evade detection, skip past filters, and foil real-time analysis, worms adopt the virus polymorphic technique. Each copy of the worm has new code generated on the fly using functionally equivalent instructions and encryption techniques.

- **Metamorphic:** In addition to changing their appearance, metamorphic worms have a repertoire of behavior patterns that are unleashed at different stages of propagation.

- **Transport vehicles:** Because worms can rapidly compromise a large number of systems, they are ideal for spreading other distributed attack tools, such as distributed denial-of-service bots.

- **Zero-day exploit:** To achieve maximum surprise and distribution, a worm should exploit an unknown vulnerability that is only discovered by the general network community when the worm is launched.

Bots

A bot (robot), also known as a zombie or drone, is a program that secretly takes over another Internet-attached computer and then uses that computer to launch attacks that are difficult to trace to the bot's creator. The bot is typically planted on hundreds or thousands of computers belonging to unsuspecting third parties. The collection of bots often is capable of acting in a coordinated manner; such a collection is referred to as a **botnet**.

A botnet exhibits three characteristics: the bot functionality, a remote control facility, and a spreading mechanism to propagate the bots and construct the botnet. We examine each of these characteristics in turn.

USES OF BOTS   [HONE05] lists the following uses of bots:

- **Distributed denial-of-service attacks:** A DDoS attack is an attack on a computer system or network that causes a loss of service to users.

- **Spamming:** With the help of a botnet and thousands of bots, an attacker is able to send massive amounts of bulk e-mail (spam).

- **Sniffing traffic:** Bots can also use a packet sniffer to watch for interesting clear-text data passing by a compromised machine. The sniffers are mostly used to retrieve sensitive information like usernames and passwords.

- **Keylogging:** If the compromised machine uses encrypted communication channels (e.g. HTTPS or POP3S), then just sniffing the network packets on the victim's computer is useless because the appropriate key to decrypt the packets is missing. But by using a keylogger, which captures keystrokes on the infected machine, an attacker can retrieve sensitive information. An implemented filtering mechanism (e.g., "I am only interested in key sequences near the keyword 'paypal.com'") further helps in stealing secret data.

- **Spreading new malware:** Botnets are used to spread new bots. This is very easy since all bots implement mechanisms to download and execute a file via HTTP or FTP. A botnet with 10,000 hosts that acts as the start base for a worm or mail virus allows very fast spreading and thus causes more harm.

- **Installing advertisement add-ons and browser helper objects (BHOs):** Botnets can also be used to gain financial advantages. This works by setting up a fake Web site with some advertisements: The operator of this Web site negotiates a deal with some hosting companies that pay for clicks on ads. With the help of a botnet, these clicks can be "automated" so that instantly a few thousand bots click on the pop-ups. This process can be further enhanced if the bot hijacks the start page of a compromised machine so that the "clicks" are executed each time the victim uses the browser.

- **Attacking IRC chat networks:** Botnets are also used for attacks against Internet relay chat (IRC) networks. Popular among attackers is especially the so-called clone attack: In this kind of attack, the controller orders each bot to connect a large number of clones to the victim IRC network. The victim is flooded by service requests from thousands of bots or thousands of channel-joins by these cloned bots. In this way, the victim IRC network is brought down, similar to a DDoS attack.

- **Manipulating online polls/games:** Online polls/games are getting more and more attention, and it is rather easy to manipulate them with botnets. Since every bot has a distinct IP address, every vote will have the same credibility as a vote cast by a real person. Online games can be manipulated in a similar way.

REMOTE CONTROL FACILITY   The remote control facility is what distinguishes a bot from a worm. A worm propagates itself and activates itself, whereas a bot is controlled from some central facility, at least initially.

A typical means of implementing the remote control facility is on an IRC server. All bots join a specific channel on this server and treat incoming messages as commands. More recent botnets tend to avoid IRC mechanisms and use covert communication channels via protocols such as HTTP. Distributed control mechanisms are also used, to avoid a single point of failure.

Once a communications path is established between a control module and the bots, the control module can activate the bots. In its simplest form, the control module simply issues command to the bot that causes the bot to execute routines that are already implemented in the bot. For greater flexibility, the control module can issue update commands that instruct the bots to download a file from some Internet location and execute it. The bot in this latter case becomes a more general-purpose tool that can be used for multiple attacks.

CONSTRUCTING THE ATTACK NETWORK   The first step in a botnet attack is for the attacker to infect a number of machines with bot software that will ultimately be used to carry out the attack. The essential ingredients in this phase of the attack are the following:

1. Software that can carry out the attack. The software must be able to run on a large number of machines, must be able to conceal its existence, must be able to communicate with the attacker or have some sort of time-triggered mechanism, and must be able to launch the intended attack toward the target.

2. A vulnerability in a large number of systems. The attacker must become aware of a vulnerability that many system administrators and individual users have failed to patch and that enables the attacker to install the bot software.

3. A strategy for locating and identifying vulnerable machines, a process known as **scanning** or **fingerprinting**.

In the scanning process, the attacker first seeks out a number of vulnerable machines and infects them. Then, typically, the bot software that is installed in the infected machines repeats the same scanning process, until a large distributed network of infected machines is created. [MIRK04] lists the following types of scanning strategies:

- **Random:** Each compromised host probes random addresses in the IP address space, using a different seed. This technique produces a high volume of Internet traffic, which may cause generalized disruption even before the actual attack is launched.

- **Hit list:** The attacker first compiles a long list of potential vulnerable machines. This can be a slow process done over a long period to avoid detection that an attack is underway. Once the list is compiled, the attacker begins infecting machines on the list. Each infected machine is provided with a portion of the list to scan. This strategy results in a very short scanning period, which may make it difficult to detect that infection is taking place.

- **Topological:** This method uses information contained on an infected victim machine to find more hosts to scan.

- **Local subnet:** If a host can be infected behind a firewall, that host then looks for targets in its own local network. The host uses the subnet address structure to find other hosts that would otherwise be protected by the firewall.

18.6 RECOMMENDED READING AND WEB SITES

The topics in this chapter are covered in more detail in [STAL08].

STAL08 Stallings, W., and Brown L. *Computer Security: Principles and Practice.* Upper Saddle River, NJ: Prentice Hall, 2008.

Recommended Web sites:

- **Computer Security Resource Center:** Maintained by the National Institute on Standards and Technology (NIST). Contains a broad range of information on security threats, technology, and standards.
- **CERT Coordination Center:** The organization that grew from the computer emergency response team formed by the Defense Advanced Research Projects Agency. Site provides good information on Internet security threats, vulnerabilities, and attack statistics.
- **Vmyths:** Dedicated to exposing virus hoaxes and dispelling misconceptions about real viruses.

18.7 KEY TERMS, REVIEW QUESTIONS, AND PROBLEMS

Key Terms

accountability	falsification	passive attack
active attack	e-mail virus	privacy
asset	hacker	replay
attack	insider attack	repudiation
authenticity	integrity	system integrity
availability	interception	threat
backdoor	intruder	traffic analysis
confidentiality	intrusion	trap door
data integrity	logic bomb	Trojan horse
deception	macro virus	usurpation
denial of service	malicious software	virus
disruption	malware	virus kit
exposure	masquerade	worm

Review Questions

18.1 Define *computer security*.

18.2 What are the fundamental requirements addressed by computer security?

18.3 What is the difference between passive and active security threats?

18.4 List and briefly define three classes of intruders.

18.5 List and briefly define three intruder behavior patterns.

18.6 What is the role of compression in the operation of a virus?

18.7 What is the role of encryption in the operation of a virus?

18.8 What are typical phases of operation of a virus or worm?

18.9 In general terms, how does a worm propagate?

Problems

18.1 Consider an automated tell machine (ATM) in which users provide a personal identification number (PIN) and a card for account access. Give examples of confidentiality, integrity, and availability requirements associated with the system and, in each case, indicate the degree of importance of the requirement.

18.2   Repeat Problem 1.1 for a telephone switching system that routes calls through a switching network based on the telephone number requested by the caller.

18.3   Consider a desktop publishing system used to produce documents for various organizations.

   a. Give an example of a type of publication for which confidentiality of the stored data is the most important requirement.

   b. Give an example of a type of publication in which data integrity is the most important requirement.

   c. Give an example in which system availability is the most important requirement.

18.4   For each of the following assets, assign a low, moderate, or high impact level for the loss of confidentiality, availability, and integrity, respectively. Justify your answers.

   a. An organization managing public information on its Web server.

   b. A law enforcement organization managing extremely sensitive investigative information.

   c. A financial organization managing routine administrative information (not privacy-related information).

   d. An information system used for large acquisitions in a contracting organization contains both sensitive, presolicitation phase contract information and routine administrative information. Assess the impact for the two data sets separately and the information system as a whole.

   e. A power plant contains a SCADA (supervisory control and data acquisition) system controlling the distribution of electric power for a large military installation. The SCADA system contains both real-time sensor data and routine administrative information. Assess the impact for the two data sets separately and the information system as a whole.

18.5   Assume that passwords are selected from four-character combinations of 26 alphabetic characters. Assume that an adversary is able to attempt passwords at a rate of one per second.

   a. Assuming no feedback to the adversary until each attempt has been completed, what is the expected time to discover the correct password?

   b. Assuming feedback to the adversary flagging an error as each incorrect character is entered, what is the expected time to discover the correct password?

18.6   There is a flaw in the virus program of Figure 18.3. What is it?

18.7   The question arises as to whether it is possible to develop a program that can analyze a piece of software to determine if it is a virus. Consider that we have a program D that is supposed to be able to do that. That is, for any program P, if we run D(P), the result returned is TRUE (P is a virus) or FALSE (P is not a virus). Now consider the following program:

```
Program CV :=
   { . . .
   main-program :=
      {if D(CV) then goto next:
      else infect-executable;
      }
next:
   }
```

In the preceding program, infect-executable is a module that scans memory for executable programs and replicates itself in those programs. Determine if D can correctly decide whether CV is a virus.

18.8 The point of this problem is to demonstrate the type of puzzles that must be solved in the design of malicious code and therefore, the type of mindset that one wishing to counter such attacks must adopt.

a. Consider the following C program:

```
begin
    print (*begin print (); end.*);
end
```

What do you think the program was intended to do? Does it work?

b. Answer the same questions for the following program:

```
char [] = {'0', ' ', '}', ';', 'm', 'a', 'i', 'n', '(',
            ')', '{',
and so on... 't', ')', '0'};
main ()
  {
    int I;
    printf(*char t[] = (*);
    for (i=0; t[i]!=0; i=i+1)
            printf("%d, ", t[i]);
    printf("%s", t);
  }
```

c. What is the specific relevance of this problem to this chapter?

18.9 Consider the following fragment:

```
legitimate code
if data is Friday the 13th;
    crash_computer();
legitimate code
```

What type of malicious software is this?

18.10 Consider the following fragment in an authentication program:

```
username = read_username();
password = read_password();
if username is "133t h4ck0r"
    return ALLOW_LOGIN;
if username and password are valid
    return ALLOW_LOGIN;
else return DENY_LOGIN
```

What type of malicious software is this?

18.11 The following code fragments show a sequence of virus instructions and a polymorphic version of the virus. Describe the effect produced by the metamorphic code.

Original Code	Metamorphic Code

mov eax, 5
add eax, ebx
call [eax]
	mov eax, 5
	push ecx
	pop ecx
	add eax, ebx
	swap eax, ebx
	swap ebx, eax
	call [eax]
	nop

CHAPTER 19

COMPUTER AND NETWORK SECURITY TECHNIQUES

19.1 Virtual Private Networks and IPSEC
 IPSec Functions
 Transport and Tunnel Modes
 Key Management
 IPSec and VPNs

19.2 SSL and TLS
 SSL Architecture
 SSL Record Protocol
 Change Cipher Spec Protocol
 Alert Protocol
 Handshake Protocol

19.3 Wi-Fi Protected Access
 Access Control
 Privacy with Message Integrity

19.4 Intrusion Detection
 Basic Principles
 Host-Based Intrusion Detection Techniques

19.5 Firewalls
 Firewall Characteristics
 Types of Firewalls

19.6 Malware Defense
 Antivirus Approaches
 Worm Countermeasures
 Bot Countermeasures

19.7 Recommended Reading and Web Sites

19.8 Key Terms, Review Questions, and Problems

Chapter Objectives

After reading this chapter, you should be able to

♦ Discuss the use of IPSec to create a virtual private network.

♦ Discuss the role of SSL in Web security and describe its basic functionality.

♦ Explain the use of Wi-Fi Protected Access in an 802.11 network.

♦ Understand the basic principles and techniques of intrusion detection systems.

♦ Explain the characteristics and types of firewalls.

♦ Assess the approaches for defending against the various types of malicious software.

This chapter introduces common measures and protocols used to counter the security threats discussed in Chapter 18.

19.1 VIRTUAL PRIVATE NETWORKS AND IPSEC

Virtual private networks (VPNs) and IPSec (Internet Protocol Security) were introduced in Chapter 5, where we looked at the applications and benefits of IPSec. This section provides some of the technical details.

IPSec Functions

IPSec provides three main facilities: an authentication-only function referred to as Authentication Header (AH), a combined authentication/encryption function called Encapsulating Security Payload (ESP), and a key exchange function. For VPNs, both authentication and encryption are generally desired, because it is important both to (1) assure that unauthorized users do not penetrate the virtual private network, and (2) assure that eavesdroppers on the Internet cannot read messages sent over the virtual private network. Because both features are generally desirable, most implementations are likely to use ESP rather than AH. The key exchange function allows for manual exchange of keys as well as an automated scheme.

The current specification requires that IPSec support the Data Encryption Standard (DES) for encryption, but a variety of other encryption algorithms may also be used. Because of concern about the strength of DES, it is likely that other algorithms, such as triple DES, will be widely used. For authentication, a relatively new scheme, known as HMAC, is required.

Transport and Tunnel Modes

ESP supports two modes of use: transport and tunnel mode.

Transport mode provides protection primarily for upper-layer protocols. That is, transport mode protection extends to the payload of an IP packet. Typically, transport mode is used for end-to-end communication between two hosts (e.g., a client and a server, or two workstations). ESP in transport mode encrypts and optionally authenticates the IP payload but not the IP header (Figure 19.1b). This configuration

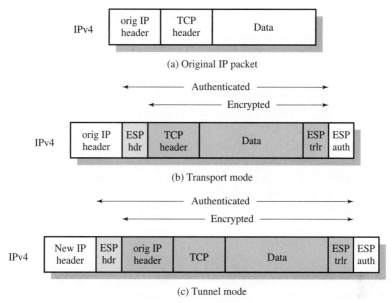

Figure 19.1   Scope of ESP Encryption and Authentication

is useful for relatively small networks, in which each host and server is equipped with IPSec. However, for a full-blown VPN, tunnel mode is far more efficient.

Tunnel mode provides protection to the entire IP packet. To achieve this, after the ESP fields are added to the IP packet, the entire packet plus security fields is treated as the payload of new "outer" IP packet with a new outer IP header. The entire original, or inner, packet travels through a "tunnel" from one point of an IP network to another; no routers along the way are able to examine the inner IP header. Because the original packet is encapsulated, the new, larger packet may have totally different source and destination addresses, adding to the security. Tunnel mode is used when at least on of the two ends is a security gateway, such as a firewall or router that implements IPSec. With tunnel mode, a number of hosts on networks behind firewalls may engage in secure communications without implementing IPSec. The unprotected packets generated by such hosts are tunneled through external networks by using tunnel mode, set up by the IPSec software in the firewall or secure router at the boundary of the local network.

Here is an example of how tunnel-mode IPSec operates. Host A on a network generates an IP packet with the destination address of host B on another network. This packet is routed from the originating host to a firewall or secure router at the boundary of A's network. The firewall filters all outgoing packets to determine the need for IPSec processing. If this packet from A to B requires IPSec, the firewall performs IPSec processing and encapsulates the packet in an outer IP header. The source IP address of this outer IP packet is this firewall, and the destination address may be a firewall that forms the boundary to B's local network. This packet is now routed to B's firewall, with intermediate routers examining only the outer IP header. At B's firewall, the outer IP header is stripped off, and the inner packet is delivered to B.

ESP in tunnel mode encrypts and optionally authenticates the entire inner IP packet, including the inner IP header.

Key Management

The key management portion of IPSec involves the determination and distribution of secret keys. The IPSec Architecture document mandates support for two types of key management:

- **Manual:** A system administrator (SA) manually configures each system with its own keys and with the keys of other communicating systems. This is practical for small, relatively static environments.
- **Automated:** An automated system enables the on-demand creation of keys and facilitates the use of keys in a large distributed system with an evolving configuration. An automated system is the most flexible but requires more effort to configure and requires more software, so smaller installations are likely to opt for manual key management.

IPSec and VPNs

The driving force for the acceptance and deployment of secure IP is the need for business and government users to connect their private WAN/LAN infrastructure to the Internet for (1) access to Internet services, and (2) use of the Internet as a component of the WAN transport system. Users need to secure their networks and at the same time send and receive traffic over the Internet. The authentication and privacy mechanisms of secure IP provide the basis for a security strategy.

Because IP security mechanisms have been defined independent of their use with either the current IP or IPv6, deployment of these mechanisms does not depend on deployment of IPv6. Indeed, it is likely that we will see widespread use of secure IP features long before IPv6 becomes popular, because the need for IP-level security is greater than the need for the added functions that IPv6 provides compared to the current IP.

With the arrival of IPSec, managers have a standardized means of implementing security for VPNs. Further, all of the encryption and authentication algorithms, and security protocols, used in IPSec are well studied and have survived years of scrutiny. As a result, the user can be confident that the IPSec facility indeed provides strong security.

IPSec can be implemented in routers or firewalls owned and operated by the organization. This gives the network manager complete control over security aspects of the VPN, which is much to be desired. However, IPSec is a complex set of functions and modules and the management and configuration responsibility is formidable. The alternative is to seek a solution from a service provider. A service provider can simplify the job of planning, implementing, and maintaining Internet-based VPNs for secure access to network resources and secure communication between sites.

19.2 SSL AND TLS

Chapter 7 introduced the Secure Sockets Layer (SSL) and the follow-on Internet standard known as Transport Layer Security (TLS). This section provides some of the technical details.

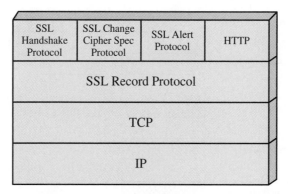

Figure 19.2 SSL Protocol Stack

SSL Architecture

SSL is designed to make use of TCP to provide a reliable end-to-end secure service. SSL is not a single protocol but rather two layers of protocols, as illustrated in Figure 19.2.

The SSL Record Protocol provides basic security services to various higher-layer protocols. In particular, the Hypertext Transfer Protocol (HTTP), which provides the transfer service for Web client/server interaction, can operate on top of SSL. Three higher-layer protocols are defined as part of SSL: the Handshake Protocol, the Change Cipher Spec Protocol, and the Alert Protocol. These SSL-specific protocols are used in the management of SSL exchanges and are examined later in this section.

Two important SSL concepts are the SSL session and the SSL connection, which are defined in the specification as follows:

- **Connection:** A connection is a transport (in the OSI layering model definition) that provides a suitable type of service. For SSL, such connections are peer-to-peer relationships. The connections are transient. Every connection is associated with one session.

- **Session:** An SSL session is an association between a client and a server. Sessions are created by the Handshake Protocol. Sessions define a set of cryptographic security parameters, which can be shared among multiple connections. Sessions are used to avoid the expensive negotiation of new security parameters for each connection.

Between any pair of parties (applications such as HTTP on client and server), there may be multiple secure connections. In theory, there may also be multiple simultaneous sessions between parties, but this feature is not used in practice.

SSL Record Protocol

The SSL Record Protocol provides two services for SSL connections:

- **Confidentiality:** The Handshake Protocol defines a shared secret key that is used for symmetric encryption of SSL payloads.

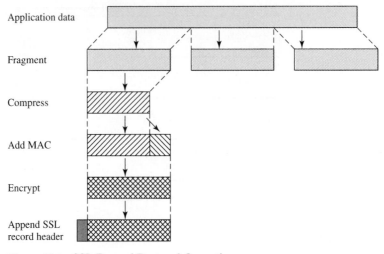

Figure 19.3   SSL Record Protocol Operation

- **Message integrity:** The Handshake Protocol also defines a shared secret key that is used to form a message authentication code (MAC).

Figure 19.3 indicates the overall operation of the SSL Record Protocol. The first step is **fragmentation**. Each upper-layer message is fragmented into blocks of 2^{14} bytes (16,384 bytes) or less. Next, **compression** is optionally applied. The next step in processing is to compute a **message authentication code** over the compressed data. Next, the compressed message plus the MAC are **encrypted** using symmetric encryption.[1]

The final step of SSL Record Protocol processing is to prepend a header, consisting of the following fields:

- **Content Type (8 bits):** The higher-layer protocol used to process the enclosed fragment.

- **Major Version (8 bits):** Indicates major version of SSL in use. For SSLv3, the value is 3.

- **Minor Version (8 bits):** Indicates minor version in use. For SSLv3, the value is 0.

- **Compressed Length (16 bits):** The length in bytes of the plaintext fragment (or compressed fragment if compression is used). The maximum value is 2^{14} + 2048.

The content types that have been defined are change_cipher_spec, alert, handshake, and application_data. The first three are the SSL-specific protocols, discussed next. Note that no distinction is made among the various applications (e.g., HTTP) that might use SSL; the content of the data created by such applications is opaque to SSL.

---

[1]The cryptographic concepts referenced in this chapter are discussed in Appendix J.

The Record Protocol then transmits the resulting unit in a TCP segment. Received data are decrypted, verified, decompressed, and reassembled, and then delivered to higher-level users.

Change Cipher Spec Protocol

The Change Cipher Spec Protocol is one of the three SSL-specific protocols that use the SSL Record Protocol, and it is the simplest. This protocol consists of a single message, which consists of a single byte with the value 1. The sole purpose of this message is to cause the pending state to be copied into the current state, which updates the cipher suite to be used on this connection.

Alert Protocol

The Alert Protocol is used to convey SSL-related alerts to the peer entity. As with other applications that use SSL, alert messages are compressed and encrypted, as specified by the current state.

Each message in this protocol consists of two bytes. The first byte takes the value warning(1) or fatal(2) to convey the severity of the message. If the level is fatal, SSL immediately terminates the connection. Other connections on the same session may continue, but no new connections on this session may be established. The second byte contains a code that indicates the specific alert. An example of a fatal alert is an incorrect MAC. An example of a nonfatal alert is a close_notify message, which notifies the recipient that the sender will not send any more messages on this connection.

Handshake Protocol

The most complex part of SSL is the Handshake Protocol. This protocol allows the server and client to authenticate each other and to negotiate an encryption and MAC algorithm and cryptographic keys to be used to protect data sent in an SSL record. The Handshake Protocol is used before any application data are transmitted.

The Handshake Protocol consists of a series of messages exchanged by client and server. The exchange can be viewed as having four phases.

Phase 1 is used to initiate a logical connection and to establish the security capabilities that will be associated with it. The exchange is initiated by the client, which sends a client_hello message with the following parameters:

- **Version:** The highest SSL version understood by the client.
- **Random:** A client-generated random structure, consisting of a 32-bit timestamp and 28 bytes generated by a secure random number generator. These values are used during key exchange to prevent replay attacks.
- **Session ID:** A variable-length session identifier. A nonzero value indicates that the client wishes to update the parameters of an existing connection or create a new connection on this session. A zero value indicates that the client wishes to establish a new connection on a new session.
- **CipherSuite:** This is a list that contains the combinations of cryptographic algorithms supported by the client, in decreasing order of preference. Each

element of the list (each cipher suite) defines both a key exchange algorithm and a CipherSpec.

- **Compression Method:** This is a list of the compression methods the client supports.

After sending the client_hello message, the client waits for the server_hello message, which contains the same parameters as the client_hello message.

The details of **phase 2** depend on the underlying public-key encryption scheme that is used. In some cases, the server passes a certificate to the client, possibly additional key information, and a request for a certificate from the client.

The final message in phase 2, and one that is always required, is the server_done message, which is sent by the server to indicate the end of the server hello and associated messages. After sending this message, the server will wait for a client response.

In **phase 3**, upon receipt of the server_done message, the client should verify that the server provided a valid certificate if required and check that the server_hello parameters are acceptable. If all is satisfactory, the client sends one or more messages back to the server, depending on the underlying public-key scheme.

Phase 4 completes the setting up of a secure connection. The client sends a change_cipher_spec message and copies the pending CipherSpec into the current CipherSpec. Note that this message is not considered part of the Handshake Protocol but is sent using the Change Cipher Spec Protocol. The client then immediately sends the finished message under the new algorithms, keys, and secrets. The finished message verifies that the key exchange and authentication processes were successful.

In response to these two messages, the server sends its own change_cipher_spec message, transfers the pending to the current CipherSpec, and sends its finished message. At this point the handshake is complete and the client and server may begin to exchange application layer data.

19.3 WI-FI PROTECTED ACCESS

As discussed in Chapter 11, the 802.11i task group has developed a set of capabilities to address the WLAN security issues. In order to accelerate the introduction of strong security into WLANs, the Wi-Fi Alliance promulgated **Wi-Fi Protected Access (WPA)** as a Wi-Fi standard. WPA is a set of security mechanisms that eliminates most 802.11 security issues and was based on the current state of the 802.11i standard. As 802.11i evolves, WPA will evolve to maintain compatibility.

IEEE 802.11i addresses three main security areas: authentication, key management, and data transfer privacy. To improve authentication, 802.11i requires the use of an authentication server (AS) and defines a more robust authentication protocol. The AS also plays a role in key distribution. For privacy, 802.11i provides three different encryption schemes. The scheme that provides a long-term solution makes use of the Advanced Encryption Standard (AES) with 128-bit keys. However, because the use of AES would require expensive upgrades to existing equipment, alternative schemes based on 104-bit RC4 are also defined.

Figure 19.4 802.11i Operational Phases

Figure 19.4 gives a general overview of 802.11i operation. First, an exchange between a station and an AP enables the two to agree on a set of security capabilities to be used. Then, an exchange involving the AS and the station provides for secure authentication. The AS is responsible for key distribution to the AP, which in turn manages and distributes keys to stations. Finally, strong encryption is used to protect data transfer between the station and the AP.

The 802.11i architecture consists of three main ingredients:

- **Authentication:** A protocol is used to define an exchange between a user and an AS that provides mutual authentication and generates temporary keys to be used between the client and the AP over the wireless link.

- **Access control:** This function enforces the use of the authentication function, routes the messages properly, and facilitates key exchange. It can work with a variety of authentication protocols.

- **Privacy with message integrity:** MAC-level data (e.g., an LLC PDU) are encrypted, along with a message integrity code that ensures that the data have not been altered.

Authentication operates at a level above the LLC and MAC protocols and is considered beyond the scope of 802.11. There are a number of popular authentication protocols in use, including the Extensible Authentication Protocol (EAP) and the Remote Authentication Dial-In User Service (RADIUS). These are not covered in this book. The remainder of this section examines access control and privacy with message integrity.

Access Control

IEEE 802.11i makes use of another standard that was designed to provide access control functions for LANs. The standard is IEEE 802.1X, Port-Based Network

Access Control. IEEE 802.1X uses the terms *supplicant, authenticator,* and *authentication server* (AS). In the context of an 802.11 WLAN, the first two terms correspond to the wireless station and the AP. The AS is typically a separate device on the wired side of the network (i.e., accessible over the DS) but could also reside directly on the authenticator.

Before a supplicant is authenticated by the AS, using an authentication protocol, the authenticator only passes control or authentication messages between the supplicant and the AS; the 802.1X control channel is unblocked but the 802.11 data channel is blocked. Once a supplicant is authenticated and keys are provided, the authenticator can forward data from the supplicant, subject to predefined access control limitations for the supplicant to the network. Under these circumstances, the data channel is unblocked.

As indicated in Figure 19.5, 802.1X uses the concepts of controlled and uncontrolled ports. Ports are logical entities defined within the authenticator and refer to physical network connections. For a WLAN, the authenticator (the AP) may have only two physical ports, one connecting to the DS and one for wireless communication within its BSS. Each logical port is mapped to one of these two physical ports. An uncontrolled port allows the exchange of PDUs between the supplicant and other the AS regardless of the authentication state of the supplicant. A controlled port allows the exchange of PDUs between a supplicant and other systems on the LAN only if the current state of the supplicant authorizes such an exchange.

The 802.1X framework, with an upper-layer authentication protocol, fits nicely with a BSS architecture that includes a number of wireless stations and an AP. However, for an IBSS, there is no AP. For an IBSS, 802.11i provides a more complex solution that, in essence, involves pairwise authentication between stations on the IBSS.

Figure 19.5   802.11i Access Control

Privacy with Message Integrity

IEEE 802.11i defines two schemes for protecting data transmitted in 802.11 MAC PDUs. The first scheme is known as the Temporal Key Integrity Protocol (TKIP) or WPA-1. TKIP is designed to require only software changes to devices that are implemented with an older wireless LAN security approach called Wired Equivalent Privacy (WEP); it uses the same RC4 stream encryption algorithm as WEP. The second scheme is known as Counter Mode-CBC MAC Protocol (CCMP) or WPA-2. CCMP makes use of the Advanced Encryption Standard (AES) encryption protocol.[2]

Both TKIP and WPA-2 add a message integrity code (MIC) to the 802.11 MAC frame after the data field. The MIC is generated by an algorithm, called Michael, that computes a 64-bit value calculated using the source and destination MAC address values and the Data field. This value is then encrypted using a separate key from that used for encrypting the Data fields. Thus, both the data and MIC fields are encrypted. The use of a more complex algorithm, a separate encryption key, and a 64-bit length, all make the MIC and substantially stronger message authentication feature than the ICV. The MIC serves the purpose of message authentication.

19.4 INTRUSION DETECTION

The following definitions from RFC 2828 (Internet Security Glossary) are relevant to our discussion:

Security Intrusion: A security event, or a combination of multiple security events, that constitutes a security incident in which an intruder gains, or attempts to gain, access to a system (or system resource) without having authorization to do so

Intrusion Detection: A security service that monitors and analyzes system events for the purpose of finding, and providing real-time or near-real-time warning of, attempts to access system resources in an unauthorized manner

---

Intrusion detection systems (IDSs) can be classified as follows:

- **Host-based IDS:** Monitors the characteristics of a single host and the events occurring within that host for suspicious activity
- **Network-based IDS:** Monitors network traffic for particular network segments or devices and analyzes network, transport, and application protocols to identify suspicious activity

An IDS comprises three logical components:

- **Sensors:** Sensors are responsible for collecting data. The input for a sensor may be any part of a system that could contain evidence of an intrusion. Types of input to a sensor include network packets, log files, and system call traces. Sensors collect and forward this information to the analyzer.

---

[2]The AES algorithm is described in detail in [STAL06] and [STAL02].

- **Analyzers:** Analyzers receive input from one or more sensors or from other analyzers. The analyzer is responsible for determining if an intrusion has occurred. The output of this component is an indication that an intrusion has occurred. The output may include evidence supporting the conclusion that an intrusion occurred. The analyzer may provide guidance about what actions to take as a result of the intrusion.

- **User interface:** The user interface to an IDS enables a user to view output from the system or control the behavior of the system. In some systems, the user interface may equate to a manager, director, or console component.

Basic Principles

Authentication facilities, access control facilities, and firewalls all play a role in countering intrusions. Another line of defense is intrusion detection, and this has been the focus of much research in recent years. This interest is motivated by a number of considerations, including the following:

1. If an intrusion is detected quickly enough, the intruder can be identified and ejected from the system before any damage is done or any data are compromised. Even if the detection is not sufficiently timely to preempt the intruder, the sooner that the intrusion is detected, the less the amount of damage and the more quickly that recovery can be achieved.

2. An effective IDS can serve as a deterrent, thus acting to prevent intrusions.

3. Intrusion detection enables the collection of information about intrusion techniques that can be used to strengthen intrusion prevention measures.

Intrusion detection is based on the assumption that the behavior of the intruder differs from that of a legitimate user in ways that can be quantified. Of course, we cannot expect that there will be a crisp, exact distinction between an attack by an intruder and the normal use of resources by an authorized user. Rather, we must expect that there will be some overlap.

Figure 19.6 suggests, in abstract terms, the nature of the task confronting the designer of an IDS. Although the typical behavior of an intruder differs from the typical behavior of an authorized user, there is an overlap in these behaviors. Thus, a loose interpretation of intruder behavior, which will catch more intruders, will also lead to a number of **false positives**, or authorized users identified as intruders. On the other hand, an attempt to limit false positives by a tight interpretation of intruder behavior will lead to an increase in **false negatives**, or intruders not identified as intruders. Thus, there is an element of compromise and art in the practice of intrusion detection.

In Anderson's study [ANDE80], it was postulated that one could, with reasonable confidence, distinguish between a masquerader and a legitimate user. Patterns of legitimate user behavior can be established by observing past history, and significant deviation from such patterns can be detected. Anderson suggests that the task of detecting a misfeasor (legitimate user performing in an unauthorized fashion) is more difficult, in that the distinction between abnormal and normal behavior may be small. Anderson concluded that such violations would be undetectable solely through the search for anomalous behavior. However, misfeasor behavior might

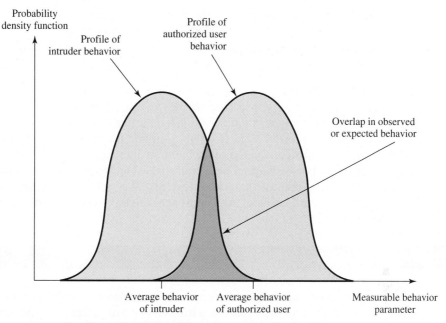

Figure 19.6 Profiles of Behavior of Intruders and Authorized Users

nevertheless be detectable by intelligent definition of the class of conditions that suggest unauthorized use. Finally, the detection of the clandestine user was felt to be beyond the scope of purely automated techniques. These observations, which were made in 1980, remain true today.

For the remainder of this section, we concentrate on host-based intrusion detection.

Host–Based Intrusion Detection Techniques

Host-based IDSs add a specialized layer of security software to vulnerable or sensitive systems; examples include database servers and administrative systems. The host-based IDS monitors activity on the system in a variety of ways to detect suspicious behavior. In some cases, an IDS can halt an attack before any damage is done, but its primary purpose is to detect intrusions, log suspicious events, and send alerts.

The primary benefit of a host-based IDS is that it can detect both external and internal intrusions, something that is not possible either with network-based IDSs or firewalls.

Host-based IDSs follow one of two general approaches to intrusion detection:

1. **Anomaly detection:** Involves the collection of data relating to the behavior of legitimate users over a period of time. Then statistical tests are applied to observed behavior to determine with a high level of confidence whether that behavior is not legitimate user behavior. The following are two approaches to statistical anomaly detection:

   a. *Threshold detection:* This approach involves defining thresholds, independent of user, for the frequency of occurrence of various events.

    b. *Profile based:* A profile of the activity of each user is developed and used to detect changes in the behavior of individual accounts.

2. **Signature detection:** Involves an attempt to define a set of rules or attack patterns that can be used to decide that a given behavior is that of an intruder.

In essence, anomaly approaches attempt to define normal, or expected, behavior, whereas signature-based approaches attempt to define proper behavior.

In terms of the types of attackers listed earlier, anomaly detection is effective against masqueraders, who are unlikely to mimic the behavior patterns of the accounts they appropriate. On the other hand, such techniques may be unable to deal with misfeasors. For such attacks, signature-based approaches may be able to recognize events and sequences that, in context, reveal penetration. In practice, a system may employ a combination of both approaches to be effective against a broad range of attacks.

19.5 FIREWALLS

The firewall is an important complement to host-based security services such as intrusion detection systems. Typically, a firewall is inserted between the premises network and the Internet to establish a controlled link and to erect an outer security wall or perimeter. The aim of this perimeter is to protect the premises network from Internet-based attacks and to provide a single choke point where security and auditing can be imposed.

The firewall provides an additional layer of defense, insulating the internal systems from external networks. This follows the classic military doctrine of "defense in depth," which is just as applicable to IT security.

Firewall Characteristics

[BELL94] lists the following design goals for a firewall:

1. All traffic from inside to outside, and vice versa, must pass through the firewall. This is achieved by physically blocking all access to the local network except via the firewall. Various configurations are possible, as explained later in this chapter.

2. Only authorized traffic, as defined by the local security policy, will be allowed to pass. Various types of firewalls are used, which implement various types of security policies, as explained later in this chapter.

3. The firewall itself is immune to penetration. This implies the use of a hardened system with a secured operating system. Trusted computer systems are suitable for hosting a firewall and often required in government applications.

[SMIT97] lists four general techniques that firewalls use to control access and enforce the site's security policy. Originally, firewalls focused primarily on service control, but they have since evolved to provide all four:

• **Service control:** Determines the types of Internet services that can be accessed, inbound or outbound. The firewall may filter traffic on the basis of IP address, protocol, or port number; may provide proxy software that receives and interprets each service request before passing it on; or may host the server software itself, such as a Web or mail service.

- **Direction control:** Determines the direction in which particular service requests may be initiated and allowed to flow through the firewall.

- **User control:** Controls access to a service according to which user is attempting to access it. This feature is typically applied to users inside the firewall perimeter (local users). It may also be applied to incoming traffic from external users; the latter requires some form of secure authentication technology, such as is provided in IPSec.

- **Behavior control:** Controls how particular services are used. For example, the firewall may filter e-mail to eliminate spam, or it may enable external access to only a portion of the information on a local Web server.

Before proceeding to the details of firewall types and configurations, it is best to summarize what one can expect from a firewall. The following capabilities are within the scope of a firewall:

1. A firewall defines a single choke point that keeps unauthorized users out of the protected network, prohibits potentially vulnerable services from entering or leaving the network, and provides protection from various kinds of IP spoofing and routing attacks. The use of a single choke point simplifies security management because security capabilities are consolidated on a single system or set of systems.

2. A firewall provides a location for monitoring security-related events. Audits and alarms can be implemented on the firewall system.

3. A firewall is a convenient platform for several Internet functions that are not security related. These include a network address translator, which maps local addresses to Internet addresses, and a network management function that audits or logs Internet usage.

4. A firewall can serve as the platform for IPSec. Using the tunnel mode capability described in Section 19.1, the firewall can be used to implement virtual private networks.

Firewalls have their limitations, including the following:

1. The firewall cannot protect against attacks that bypass the firewall. Internal systems may have dial-out capability to connect to an ISP. An internal LAN may support a modem pool that provides dial-in capability for traveling employees and telecommuters.

2. The firewall may not protect fully against internal threats, such as a disgruntled employee or an employee who unwittingly cooperates with an external attacker.

3. An improperly secured wireless LAN may be accessed from outside the organization. An internal firewall that separates portions of an enterprise network cannot guard against wireless communications between local systems on different sides of the internal firewall.

4. A laptop, PDA, or portable storage device may be used and infected outside the corporate network, and then attached and used internally.

Types of Firewalls

A firewall may act as a packet filter. It can operate as a positive filter, allowing to pass only packets that meet specific criteria, or as a negative filter, rejecting any packet that meets certain criteria. Depending on the type of firewall, it may examine one or more protocol headers in each packet, the payload of each packet, or the pattern generated by a sequence of packets. In this section, we look at the principal types of firewalls.

PACKET FILTERING FIREWALL   A **packet filtering firewall** applies a set of rules to each incoming and outgoing IP packet and then forwards or discards the packet (Figure 19.7b). The firewall is typically configured to filter packets going in both directions (from and to the internal network). Filtering rules are based on information contained in a network packet:

- **Source IP address:** The IP address of the system that originated the IP packet (e.g., 192.178.1.1)
- **Destination IP address:** The IP address of the system the IP packet is trying to reach (e.g., 192.168.1.2)
- **Source and destination transport-level address:** The transport-level (e.g., TCP or UDP) port number, which defines applications such as SNMP or TELNET
- **IP protocol field:** Defines the transport protocol
- **Interface:** For a firewall with three or more ports, which interface of the firewall the packet came from or which interface of the firewall the packet is destined for

The packet filter is typically set up as a list of rules based on matches to fields in the IP or TCP header. If there is a match to one of the rules, that rule is invoked to determine whether to forward or discard the packet. If there is no match to any rule, then a default action is taken. Two default policies are possible:

- **Default = discard:** That which is not expressly permitted is prohibited.
- **Default = forward:** That which is not expressly prohibited is permitted.

The default = discard policy is more conservative. Initially, everything is blocked, and services must be added on a case-by-case basis. This policy is more visible to users, who are more likely to see the firewall as a hindrance. However, this is the policy likely to be preferred by businesses and government organizations. Further, visibility to users diminishes as rules are created. The default = forward policy increases ease of use for end users but provides reduced security; the security administrator must, in essence, react to each new security threat as it becomes known. This policy may be used by generally more open organizations, such as universities.

Table 19.1, from [BELL94], gives some examples of packet filtering rule sets. In each set, the rules are applied top to bottom. The "*" in a field is a wildcard designator that matches everything. We assume that the default = discard policy is in force.

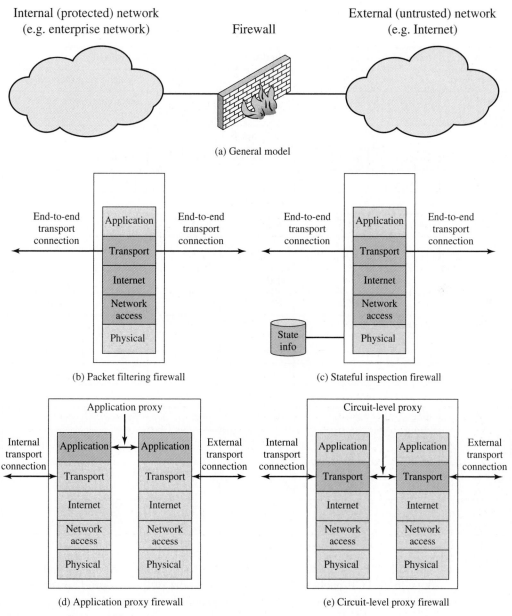

Internal (protected) network
(e.g. enterprise network)

Firewall

External (untrusted) network
(e.g. Internet)

(a) General model

(b) Packet filtering firewall

(c) Stateful inspection firewall

(d) Application proxy firewall

(e) Circuit-level proxy firewall

Figure 19.7 Types of Firewalls

A. Inbound mail is allowed (port 25 is for SMTP incoming), but only to a gateway host. However, packets from a particular external host, SPIGOT, are blocked because that host has a history of sending massive files in e-mail messages.

B. This is an explicit statement of the default policy. All rule sets include this rule implicitly as the last rule.

Table 19.1 Packet-Filtering Examples

Rule Set A

action	ourhost	port	theirhost	port	comment
block	*	*	SPIGOT	*	we don't trust these people
allow	OUR-GW	25	*	*	connection to our SMTP port

Rule Set B

action	ourhost	port	theirhost	port	comment
block	*	*	*	*	default

Rule Set C

action	ourhost	port	theirhost	port	comment
allow	*	*	*	25	connection to their SMTP port

Rule Set D

action	src	port	dest	port	flags	comment
allow	{our hosts}	*	*	25		our packets to their SMTP port
allow	*	25	*	*	ACK	their replies

Rule Set E

action	src	port	dest	port	flags	comment
allow	{our hosts}	*	*	*		our outgoing calls
allow	*	*	*	*	ACK	replies to our calls
allow	*	*	*	>1024		traffic to non-servers

C. This rule set is intended to specify that any inside host can send mail to the outside. A TCP packet with a destination port of 25 is routed to the SMTP server on the destination machine. The problem with this rule is that the use of port 25 for SMTP receipt is only a default; an outside machine could be configured to have some other application linked to port 25. As this rule is written, an attacker could gain access to internal machines by sending packets with a TCP source port number of 25.

D. This rule set achieves the intended result that was not achieved in C. The rules take advantage of a feature of TCP connections. Once a connection is set up, the ACK flag of a TCP segment is set to acknowledge segments sent from the other side. Thus, this rule set states that it allows IP packets where the source IP address is one of a list of designated internal hosts and the destination TCP port number is 25. It also allows incoming packets with a source port number of 25 that include the ACK flag in the TCP segment. Note that we explicitly designate source and destination systems to define these rules explicitly.

E. This rule set is one approach to handling FTP connections. With FTP, two TCP connections are used: a control connection to set up the file transfer and a data connection for the actual file transfer. The data connection uses a different port number that is dynamically assigned for the transfer. Most servers, and hence most attack targets, use low-numbered ports; most outgoing calls tend to use a higher-numbered port, typically above 1023. Thus, this rule set allows

—Packets that originate internally

—Reply packets to a connection initiated by an internal machine

—Packets destined for a high-numbered port on an internal machine

This scheme requires that the systems be configured so that only the appropriate port numbers are in use.

Rule set E points out the difficulty in dealing with applications at the packet filtering level. Another way to deal with FTP and similar applications is either stateful packet filters or an application-level gateway, both described subsequently in this section.

One advantage of a packet filtering firewall is its simplicity. Also, packet filters typically are transparent to users and are very fast. [WACK02] lists the following weaknesses of packet filter firewalls:

- Because packet filter firewalls do not examine upper-layer data, they cannot prevent attacks that employ application-specific vulnerabilities or functions. For example, a packet filter firewall cannot block specific application commands; if a packet filter firewall allows a given application, all functions available within that application will be permitted.

- Because of the limited information available to the firewall, the logging functionality present in packet filter firewalls is limited. Packet filter logs normally contain the same information used to make access control decisions (source address, destination address, and traffic type).

- Most packet filter firewalls do not support advanced user authentication schemes. Once again, this limitation is mostly due to the lack of upper-layer functionality by the firewall.

- Packet filter firewalls are generally vulnerable to attacks and exploits that take advantage of problems within the TCP/IP specification and protocol stack, such as *network layer address spoofing*. Many packet filter firewalls cannot detect a network packet in which the OSI Layer 3 addressing information has been altered. Spoofing attacks are generally employed by intruders to bypass the security controls implemented in a firewall platform.

- Finally, due to the small number of variables used in access control decisions, packet filter firewalls are susceptible to security breaches caused by improper configurations. In other words, it is easy to accidentally configure a packet filter firewall to allow traffic types, sources, and destinations that should be denied based on an organization's information security policy.

Some of the attacks that can be made on packet filtering firewalls and the appropriate countermeasures are the following:

- **IP address spoofing:** The intruder transmits packets from the outside with a source IP address field containing an address of an internal host. The attacker hopes that the use of a spoofed address will allow penetration of systems that employ simple source address security, in which packets from specific trusted internal hosts are accepted. The countermeasure is to discard packets with an inside source address if the packet arrives on an external interface. In fact, this countermeasure is often implemented at the router external to the firewall.

- **Source routing attacks:** The source station specifies the route that a packet should take as it crosses the Internet, in the hopes that this will bypass security measures that do not analyze the source routing information. The countermeasure is to discard all packets that use this option.

- **Tiny fragment attacks:** The intruder uses the IP fragmentation option to create extremely small fragments and force the TCP header information into a separate packet fragment. This attack is designed to circumvent filtering rules that depend on TCP header information. Typically, a packet filter will make a filtering decision on the first fragment of a packet. All subsequent fragments of that packet are filtered out solely on the basis that they are part of the packet whose first fragment was rejected. The attacker hopes that the filtering firewall examines only the first fragment and that the remaining fragments are passed through. A tiny fragment attack can be defeated by enforcing a rule that the first fragment of a packet must contain a predefined minimum amount of the transport header. If the first fragment is rejected, the filter can remember the packet and discard all subsequent fragments.

STATEFUL INSPECTION FIREWALLS   A traditional packet filter makes filtering decisions on an individual packet basis and does not take into consideration any higher layer context. To understand what is meant by *context* and why a traditional packet filter is limited with regard to context, a little background is needed. Most standardized applications that run on top of TCP follow a client/server model. For example, for the Simple Mail Transfer Protocol (SMTP), e-mail is transmitted from a client system to a server system. The client system generates new e-mail messages, typically from user input. The server system accepts incoming e-mail messages and places them in the appropriate user mailboxes. SMTP operates by setting up a TCP connection between client and server, in which the TCP server port number, which identifies the SMTP server application, is 25. The TCP port number for the SMTP client is a number between 1024 and 65535 that is generated by the SMTP client.

In general, when an application that uses TCP creates a session with a remote host, it creates a TCP connection in which the TCP port number for the remote (server) application is a number less than 1024 and the TCP port number for the local (client) application is a number between 1024 and 65535. The numbers less than 1024 are the "well-known" port numbers and are assigned permanently to particular applications (e.g., 25 for server SMTP). The numbers between 1024 and 65535 are generated dynamically and have temporary significance only for the lifetime of a TCP connection.

Table 19.2   Example Stateful Firewall Connection State Table

Source Address	Source Port	Destination Address	Destination Port	Connection State
192.168.1.100	1030	210.9.88.29	80	Established
192.168.1.102	1031	216.32.42.123	80	Established
192.168.1.101	1033	173.66.32.122	25	Established
192.168.1.106	1035	177.231.32.12	79	Established
223.43.21.231	1990	192.168.1.6	80	Established
219.22.123.32	2112	192.168.1.6	80	Established
210.99.212.18	3321	192.168.1.6	80	Established
24.102.32.23	1025	192.168.1.6	80	Established
223.21.22.12	1046	192.168.1.6	80	Established

A simple packet filtering firewall must permit inbound network traffic on all these high-numbered ports for TCP-based traffic to occur. This creates a vulnerability that can be exploited by unauthorized users.

A stateful inspection packet firewall tightens up the rules for TCP traffic by creating a directory of outbound TCP connections, as shown in Table 19.2. There is an entry for each currently established connection. The packet filter will now allow incoming traffic to high-numbered ports only for those packets that fit the profile of one of the entries in this directory.

A stateful packet inspection firewall reviews the same packet information as a packet filtering firewall, but also records information about TCP connections (Figure 19.7c). Some stateful firewalls also keep track of TCP sequence numbers to prevent attacks that depend on the sequence number, such as session hijacking. Some even inspect limited amounts of application data for some well-known protocols like FTP, IM and SIPS commands, in order to identify and track related connections.

APPLICATION-LEVEL GATEWAY   An application-level gateway, also called an **application proxy**, acts as a relay of application-level traffic (Figure 19.7d). The user contacts the gateway using a TCP/IP application, such as Telnet or FTP, and the gateway asks the user for the name of the remote host to be accessed. When the user responds and provides a valid user ID and authentication information, the gateway contacts the application on the remote host and relays TCP segments containing the application data between the two endpoints. If the gateway does not implement the proxy code for a specific application, the service is not supported and cannot be forwarded across the firewall. Further, the gateway can be configured to support only specific features of an application that the network administrator considers acceptable while denying all other features.

Application-level gateways tend to be more secure than packet filters. Rather than trying to deal with the numerous possible combinations that are to be allowed and forbidden at the TCP and IP level, the application-level gateway need only scrutinize a few allowable applications. In addition, it is easy to log and audit all incoming traffic at the application level.

A prime disadvantage of this type of gateway is the additional processing overhead on each connection. In effect, there are two spliced connections between the end users, with the gateway at the splice point, and the gateway must examine and forward all traffic in both directions.

CIRCUIT-LEVEL GATEWAY A fourth type of firewall is the circuit-level gateway or **circuit-level proxy** (Figure 19.7e). This can be a stand-alone system or it can be a specialized function performed by an application-level gateway for certain applications. As with an application gateway, a circuit-level gateway does not permit an end-to-end TCP connection; rather, the gateway sets up two TCP connections, one between itself and a TCP user on an inner host and one between itself and a TCP user on an outside host. Once the two connections are established, the gateway typically relays TCP segments from one connection to the other without examining the contents. The security function consists of determining which connections will be allowed.

A typical use of circuit-level gateways is a situation in which the system administrator trusts the internal users. The gateway can be configured to support application-level or proxy service on inbound connections and circuit-level functions for outbound connections. In this configuration, the gateway can incur the processing overhead of examining incoming application data for forbidden functions but does not incur that overhead on outgoing data.

19.6 MALWARE DEFENSE

Antivirus Approaches

The ideal solution to the threat of viruses is prevention: Do not allow a virus to get into the system in the first place. This goal is, in general, impossible to achieve, although prevention can reduce the number of successful viral attacks. The next best approach is to be able to do the following:

- **Detection:** Once the infection has occurred, determine that it has occurred and locate the virus.
- **Identification:** Once detection has been achieved, identify the specific virus that has infected a program.
- **Removal:** Once the specific virus has been identified, remove all traces of the virus from the infected program and restore it to its original state. Remove the virus from all infected systems so that the disease cannot spread further.

If detection succeeds but either identification or removal is not possible, then the alternative is to discard the infected program and reload a clean backup version. Advances in virus and antivirus technology go hand in hand. Early viruses were relatively simple code fragments and could be identified and purged with relatively simple antivirus software packages. As the virus arms race has evolved, both viruses and, necessarily, antivirus software have grown more complex and sophisticated. Increasingly sophisticated antivirus approaches and products continue to appear. In this subsection, we highlight two of the most important.

GENERIC DECRYPTION Generic decryption (GD) technology enables the antivirus program to easily detect even the most complex polymorphic viruses while maintaining fast scanning speeds [NACH97]. Recall that when a file containing a polymorphic virus is executed, the virus must decrypt itself to activate. In order to detect such a structure, executable files are run through a GD scanner, which contains the following elements:

- **CPU emulator:** A software-based virtual computer. Instructions in an executable file are interpreted by the emulator rather than executed on the underlying processor. The emulator includes software versions of all registers and other processor hardware, so that the underlying processor is unaffected by programs interpreted on the emulator.
- **Virus signature scanner:** A module that scans the target code looking for known virus signatures.
- **Emulation control module:** Controls the execution of the target code.

At the start of each simulation, the emulator begins interpreting instructions in the target code, one at a time. Thus, if the code includes a decryption routine that decrypts and hence exposes the virus, that code is interpreted. In effect, the virus does the work for the antivirus program by exposing the virus. Periodically, the control module interrupts interpretation to scan the target code for virus signatures.

During interpretation, the target code can cause no damage to the actual personal computer environment, because it is being interpreted in a completely controlled environment.

The most difficult design issue with a GD scanner is to determine how long to run each interpretation. Typically, virus elements are activated soon after a program begins executing, but this need not be the case. The longer the scanner emulates a particular program, the more likely it is to catch any hidden viruses. However, the antivirus program can take up only a limited amount of time and resources before users complain of degraded system performance.

DIGITAL IMMUNE SYSTEM The digital immune system is a comprehensive approach to virus protection developed by IBM [KEPH97a, KEPH97b, WHIT99] and subsequently refined by Symantec [SYMA01]. The motivation for this development has been the rising threat of Internet-based virus propagation. We first say a few words about this threat and then summarize IBM's approach.

Traditionally, the virus threat was characterized by the relatively slow spread of new viruses and new mutations. Antivirus software was typically updated on a monthly basis, and this was sufficient to control the problem. Also traditionally, the Internet played a comparatively small role in the spread of viruses. But as [CHES97] points out, two major trends in Internet technology have had an increasing impact on the rate of virus propagation in recent years:

- **Integrated mail systems:** Systems such as Lotus Notes and Microsoft Outlook make it very simple to send anything to anyone and to work with objects that are received.
- **Mobile-program systems:** Capabilities such as Java and ActiveX allow programs to move on their own from one system to another.

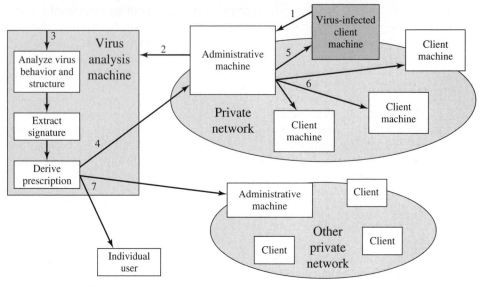

Figure 19.8 Digital Immune System

In response to the threat posed by these Internet-based capabilities, IBM has developed a prototype digital immune system. This system expands on the use of program emulation discussed in the preceding subsection and provides a general-purpose emulation and virus-detection system. The objective of this system is to provide rapid response time so that viruses can be stamped out almost as soon as they are introduced. When a new virus enters an organization, the immune system automatically captures it, analyzes it, adds detection and shielding for it, removes it, and passes information about that virus to systems running IBM AntiVirus so that it can be detected before it is allowed to run elsewhere.

Figure 19.8 illustrates the typical steps in digital immune system operation:

1. A monitoring program on each PC uses a variety of heuristics based on system behavior, suspicious changes to programs, or family signature to infer that a virus may be present. The monitoring program forwards a copy of any program thought to be infected to an administrative machine within the organization.

2. The administrative machine encrypts the sample and sends it to a central virus analysis machine.

3. This machine creates an environment in which the infected program can be safely run for analysis. Techniques used for this purpose include emulation, or the creation of a protected environment within which the suspect program can be executed and monitored. The virus analysis machine then produces a prescription for identifying and removing the virus.

4. The resulting prescription is sent back to the administrative machine.

5. The administrative machine forwards the prescription to the infected client.

6. The prescription is also forwarded to other clients in the organization.

7. Subscribers around the world receive regular antivirus updates that protect them from the new virus.

The success of the digital immune system depends on the ability of the virus analysis machine to detect new and innovative virus strains. By constantly analyzing and monitoring the viruses found in the wild, it should be possible to continually update the digital immune software to keep up with the threat.

BEHAVIOR-BLOCKING SOFTWARE Unlike heuristics or fingerprint-based scanners, behavior-blocking software integrates with the operating system of a host computer and monitors program behavior in real time for malicious actions [CONR02, NACH02]. The behavior-blocking software then blocks potentially malicious actions before they have a chance to affect the system. Monitored behaviors can include

- Attempts to open, view, delete, and/or modify files;
- Attempts to format disk drives and other unrecoverable disk operations;
- Modifications to the logic of executable files or macros;
- Modification of critical system settings, such as start-up settings;
- Scripting of e-mail and instant messaging clients to send executable content; and
- Initiation of network communications.

Figure 19.9 illustrates the operation of a behavior blocker. Behavior-blocking software runs on server and desktop computers and is instructed through policies set by the network administrator to let benign actions take place but to intercede

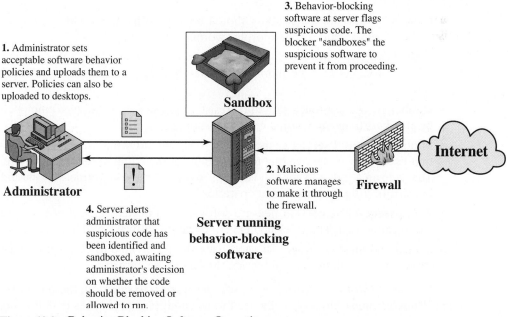

Figure 19.9   Behavior-Blocking Software Operation

when unauthorized or suspicious actions occur. The module blocks any suspicious software from executing. A blocker isolates the code in a sandbox, which restricts the code's access to various OS resources and applications. The blocker then sends an alert.

Because a behavior blocker can block suspicious software in real time, it has an advantage over such established antivirus detection techniques as fingerprinting or heuristics. While there are literally trillions of different ways to obfuscate and re-arrange the instructions of a virus or worm, many of which will evade detection by a fingerprint scanner or heuristic, eventually malicious code must make a well-defined request to the operating system. Given that the behavior blocker can intercept all such requests, it can identify and block malicious actions regardless of how obfuscated the program logic appears to be.

Behavior blocking alone has limitations. Because the malicious code must run on the target machine before all its behaviors can be identified, it can cause harm before it has been detected and blocked. For example, a new virus might shuffle a number of seemingly unimportant files around the hard drive before infecting a single file and being blocked. Even though the actual infection was blocked, the user may be unable to locate his or her files, causing a loss to productivity or possibly worse.

Worm Countermeasures

There is considerable overlap in techniques for dealing with viruses and worms. Once a worm is resident on a machine, antivirus software can be used to detect it. In addition, because worm propagation generates considerable network activity, network activity and usage monitoring can form the basis of a worm defense.

To begin, let us consider the requirements for an effective worm countermeasure scheme:

- **Generality:** The approach taken should be able to handle a wide variety of worm attacks, including polymorphic worms.
- **Timeliness:** The approach should respond quickly so as to limit the number infected systems and the number of generated transmissions from infected systems.
- **Resiliency:** The approach should be resistant to evasion techniques employed by attackers to evade worm countermeasures.
- **Minimal denial-of-service costs:** The approach should result in minimal reduction in capacity or service due to the actions of the countermeasure software. That is, in an attempt to contain worm propagation, the countermeasure should not significantly disrupt normal operation.
- **Transparency:** The countermeasure software and devices should not require modification to existing (legacy) OSs, application software, and hardware.
- **Global and local coverage:** The approach should be able to deal with attack sources both from outside and inside the enterprise network.

No existing worm countermeasure scheme appears to satisfy all these requirements. Thus, administrators typically need to use multiple approaches in defending against worm attacks.

Following [JHI07], we list six classes of worm defense:

A. **Signature-based worm scan filtering:** This type of approach generates a worm signature, which is then used to prevent worm scans from entering/leaving a network/host. Typically, this approach involves identifying suspicious flows and generating a worm signature. This approach is vulnerable to the use of polymorphic worms: Either the detection software misses the worm or, if it is sufficiently sophisticated to deal with polymorphic worms, the scheme may take a long time to react.

B. **Filter-based worm containment:** This approach is similar to class A but focuses on worm content rather than a scan signature. The filter checks a message to determine if it contains worm code. This approach can be quite effective but requires efficient detection algorithms and rapid alert dissemination.

C. **Payload-classification-based worm containment:** These network-based techniques examine packets to see if they contain a worm. Various anomaly detection techniques can be used, but care is needed to avoid high levels of false positives or negatives. This approach does not generate signatures based on byte patterns but rather looks for control and data flow structures that suggest an exploit.

D. **Threshold random walk (TRW) scan detection:** TRW exploits randomness in picking destinations to connect to as a way of detecting if a scanner is in operation. TRW is suitable for deployment in high-speed, low-cost network devices. It is effective against the common behavior seen in worm scans.

E. **Rate limiting:** This class limits the rate of scanlike traffic from an infected host. Various strategies can be used, including limiting the number of new machines a host can connect to in a window of time, detecting a high connection failure rate, and limiting the number of unique IP addresses a host can scan in a window of time. This class of countermeasures may introduce longer delays for normal traffic. This class is also not suited for slow, stealthy worms that spread slowly to avoid detection based on activity level.

F. **Rate halting:** This approach immediately blocks outgoing traffic when a threshold is exceeded either in outgoing connection rate or diversity of connection attempts [JHI07]. The approach must include measures to quickly unblock mistakenly blocked hosts in a transparent way. Rate halting can integrate with a signature- or filter-based approach so that once a signature or filter is generated, every blocked host can be unblocked. Rate halting appears to offer a very effective countermeasure. As with rate limiting, rate halting techniques are not suitable for slow, stealthy worms.

Bot Countermeasures

A number of the countermeasures discussed in this chapter make sense against **bots**, including IDSs and digital immune systems. Once bots are activated and an attack is underway, these countermeasures can be used to detect the attack. But the primary objective is to try to detect and disable the botnet during its construction phase.

APPLICATION NOTE

Security Layers

Security regarding computers and networks can be very confusing. In addition to the large number of threats, the wide variety of systems and technologies that need to be protected can make the job of security guru seem all but impossible. It can be helpful to divide up the tasks or areas and find the best security approach. One method is to divide the domain into system and network security groups. Another might be to secure different areas of the network perimeter.

Perhaps one of the first rules of security, no matter what area you are focusing on, is to understand the nature of the threat. Companies spend millions of dollars on equipment and personnel in order to protect things that don't need protection. Most organizations agree that their own users, whether accidentally or with intent, become their worst security problem. The range of difficulties can include downloaded viruses, improper use of company resources, and poor control of their own passwords and the passwords of others. One recent experiment showed that people were willing to give up their passwords for a free cup of coffee. But the cracker burrowing through corporate firewalls in order to steal valuable company research isn't the typical case. From the outside, the bad guys are usually trying to shut things down with some sort of denial-of-service attack or use company resources. Another common problem is simply that unauthorized computers are getting a free ride using your bandwidth.

When working with system security, the network administrators are usually focused on servers and end user computers. These are the most common devices to be compromised. Examine any recent attack and you see that most problems end up being solved or blocked with a variety of upgrades, system patches, or personal firewalls. Every time a server or service is brought online, it must be up to date regarding the operating system and only the required communication ports opened. Other ports must be disabled.

With network security, we are trying to prevent unauthorized traffic. The problem is that there are dozens of protocols used today and there are a myriad of services open. Thus, blocking a certain type of traffic may cause a valid service to be disrupted. As a result, network administrators must have a deep understanding of not only initial configuration, but how protocols operate as well. It is also important to protect your network devices from attack just as you protect the servers.

Often we refer to the programs and techniques used in security as our toolbox. For the network security analyst, one of the easiest ways to think of this toolbox is as a series of layers that correspond to the layers of the TCP/IP or OSI networking models. A sample of the tools for TCP/IP layers follows:

1. **Physical:** The problem is with the actual signal and so the approaches are very straightforward—locking doors, minimizing access to ports, selecting antenna locations, and using low-level encryption such as AES, 3DES, or WPA. Encryption of this type includes protection for layer 2.

2. **Network:** Moving up the stack, we are now dealing with increased intelligence in the networking devices and can start to apply low-level firewalls such as MAC address–based filters. Additional tools include VLANs and 802.1x.

3. **Internetwork:** At layer 3 the IP header is exposed and so filtering or firewalls can be applied to IP addresses. Other valuable methods include VPNs and NAT.

4. **Transport:** The TCP and UDP ports are the main focus and so our filters now target particular streams of communication such as http or ftp. Filters are sometimes referred to as standard or extended access control lists.

5. **Application:** The tools available to us here are usually focused at the user with passwords and authentication. These can be combined with other tools mentioned earlier, like 802.1x and VPNs. In addition, other forms of encryption exist, like those used in SSH and SSL.

This is only a partial list, and no single approach can be said to work against all threats. In fact, most security techniques can be defeated if they are applied individually. However, taken together as a layered approach, they represent a formidable barrier to would be interlopers.

Whatever your area of focus, system or network, of great importance is a policy regarding safe and acceptable use. Education for users is also very important. Many times users defeat security practices unintentionally by going around them; viruses provide an excellent example. Policies and some basic education for best practices can go a long way toward protecting the network and system assets.

19.7 RECOMMENDED READING AND WEB SITES

The topics in this chapter are covered in greater detail in [STAL06].

STAL06 Stallings, W. *Cryptography and Network Security: Principles and Practice, Fourth Edition*. Upper Saddle River, NJ: Prentice Hall, 2006.

Recommended Web sites:

- **AntiVirus Online:** IBM's site on virus information
- **VirusList:** Site maintained by commercial antivirus software provider. Good collection of useful information

19.8 KEY TERMS, REVIEW QUESTIONS, AND PROBLEMS

Key Terms

antivirus	intrusion detection	stateful inspection firewall
bot	intrusion detections system	Transport Layer Security
digital immune system	(IDS)	(TLS)
firewall	malware	Wi-Fi Protected Access
host-based IDS	packet filtering firewall Secure	(WPA)
IP security (IPSec)	Sockets Layer (SSL)	worm

Review Questions

19.1 What services are provided by IPSec?

19.2 What protocols comprise SSL?

19.3 What is the difference between and SSL connection and an SSL session?

19.4 What services are provided by the SSL Record Protocol?

19.5 What security areas are addressed by IEEE 802.11i?

19.6 Explain the difference between anomaly intrusion detection and signature intrusion detection.

19.7 List three design goals for a firewall.

19.8 List four techniques used by firewalls to control access and enforce a security policy.

19.9 What information is used by a typical packet-filtering router?

19.10 What are some weaknesses of a packet-filtering router?

19.11 What is the difference between a packet-filtering router and a stateful inspection firewall?

19.12 What is a digital immune system?

19.13 How does behavior-blocking software work?

19.14 Describe some worm countermeasures.

Problems

19.1 The authentication header (AH) in IPSec includes a message authentication code (MAC), which is calculated over all of the fields of the IPSec packet except IP header fields that either do not change in transit (immutable) or that are predictable in value upon arrival at the endpoint for the AH SA. Fields that may change in transit and whose value on arrival are unpredictable are set to zero for purposes of calculation at both source and destination.
   a. For each of the fields in the IPv4 header, indicate whether the field is immutable, mutable but predictable, or mutable.
   b. Do the same for the IPv6 header.
   In each case, justify your decision for each field.

19.2 In SSL and TLS, why is there a separate Change Cipher Spec Protocol rather than including a change_cipher_spec message in the Handshake Protocol?

19.3 In the context of an IDS, we define a false positive to be an alarm generated by an IDS in which the IDS alerts to a condition that is actually benign. A false negative occurs when an IDS fails to generate an alarm when an alert-worthy condition is in effect. Using the following diagram, depict two curves that roughly indicate false positives and false negatives, respectively.

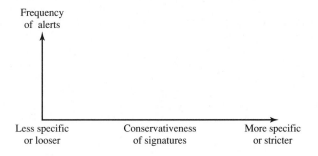

19.4   The overlapping area of the two probability density functions of Figure 19.6 represents the region in which there is the potential for false positives and false negatives. Further, Figure 19.6 is an idealized and not necessarily representative depiction of the relative shapes of the two density functions. Suppose there is 1 actual intrusion for every 1000 authorized users, and the overlapping area covers 1% of the authorized users and 50% of the intruders.

    a. Sketch such a set of density functions and argue that this is not an unreasonable depiction.

    b. What is the probability that an event that occurs in this region is that of an authorized user? Keep in mind that 50% of all intrusions fall in this region.

19.5   An example of a host-based intrusion detection tool is the tripwire program. This is a file integrity checking tool that scans files and directories on the system on a regular basis and notifies the administrator of any changes. It uses a protected database of cryptographic checksums for each file checked and compares this value with that recomputed on each file as it is scanned. It must be configured with a list of files and directories to check, and what changes, if any, are permissible to each. It can allow, for example, log files to have new entries appended, but not for existing entries to be changed. What are the advantages and disadvantages of using such a tool? Consider the problem of determining which files should only change rarely, which files may change more often and how, and which change frequently and hence cannot be checked. Consider the amount of work in both the configuration of the program and on the system administrator monitoring the responses generated.

19.6   Test the vulnerability of a machine at the following site: http://grc.com/default.htm. Follow the ShieldsUP! link for a series of free tests listed midway down the page.

19.7   As was mentioned in Section 19.5, one approach to defeating the tiny fragment attack is to enforce a minimum length of the transport header that must be contained in the first fragment of an IP packet. If the first fragment is rejected, all subsequent fragments can be rejected. However, the nature of IP is such that fragments may arrive out of order. Thus, an intermediate fragment may pass through the filter before the initial fragment is rejected. How can this situation be handled?

19.8   In an IPv4 packet, the size of the payload in the first fragment, in octets, is equal to Total Length $-$ ($4 \times$ IHL). If this value is less than the required minimum (8 octets for TCP), then this fragment and the entire packet are rejected. Suggest an alternative method of achieving the same result using only the Fragment Offset field.

19.9   RFC 791, the IPv4 protocol specification, describes a reassembly algorithm that results in new fragments overwriting any overlapped portions of previously received fragments. Given such a reassembly implementation, an attacker could construct a series of packets in which the lowest (zero-offset) fragment would contain innocuous data (and thereby be passed by administrative packet filters), and in which some subsequent packet having a nonzero offset would overlap TCP header information (destination port, for instance) and cause it to be modified. The second packet would be passed through most filter implementations because it does not have a zero fragment offset. Suggest a method that could be used by a packet filter to counter this attack.

THE HACKER IN ALL OF US[1]

"How do you spell pillage?" asks Fred Norwood, manager of information infrastructure technology at El Paso Energy Corp. in Houston. Twelve of us had just hacked Microsoft Corp.'s crown jewel—a Windows NT box—and were copying passwords to our hard drives. From across the room, a quick-witted Sam Gerard, data security manager at Motorola Inc., spells out the answer for us: "F-U-N!" Thus goes Day 2 of Extreme Hacking, a course taught by security whiz kids at Ernst and Young LLP's towering Houston offices.

For four days, network managers, auditors and security specialists from companies such as Motorola, Electronic Data Systems Corp. and State Farm Insurance switched to the dark side. In so doing, they learned just what they're up against in their fight to keep crackers out of their networks.

The truth is, hacking is easy. And, well, fun. We pushed open server doors and helped ourselves to whatever data we wanted—all without any feeling of culpability.

"This course gives me a lot more insight into the mentality and capability of attackers," says John McGraw, a security technology planner at a large computing services company. "We know all these vulnerabilities, but there are probably so many more that no one knows about."

So fun was it that I was sorry to leave the capture-the-flag game at the end of Day 3. But my cab to the airport was waiting 20 floors below. By then, I had leapfrogged to the fourth and final victim Unix server and was closing in on that flag. But I had a plane to catch.

DAY 1: FINDING THE GOODS

On Day 1, we case out our victim. Our instructor, Stuart McClure, prefers the more sanitized term "discovery." We begin discovery by finding publicly available information on the Internet. McClure talks about searching the Securities and Exchange Commission (SEC) Web site to get a thumbnail sketch of a company and its affiliates, laboratories and acquisitions. We could use this information to break in to a company by hacking its acquisitions or subsidiaries because those subnetworks aren't usually as well monitored or secure as networks at the home office. But for expediency's sake we bypass the SEC and go straight to the InterNic Registrar, the service that assigns domain names. By querying InterNic with a simple "whois" command, we get all the IP addresses of our victim's Web servers—along with company nicknames—

[1]Reprinted with permission from *ComputerWorld*, October 11, 1999, by Deborah Radcliff.

and auxiliary domain name servers (DNS) in affiliates and laboratories. We even find out what type of servers they are (the main DNS is a Sun-3/180 running Unix), along with the names and phone numbers of the server administrators.

I flash to the infamous cracker, Kevin Mitnick, who loved this little InterNic feature. He'd call those network administrators and try to "social engineer" (sweet-talk) them out of network information. "It's amazing the amount of information you can get from the Internet. You don't realize you're hanging out there as exposed as you are," says El Paso Energy's Norwood.

We deploy a few common network-troubleshooting tools (like zone transfers—normally used to correlate data between the backup and primary servers, and Name Service lookup—a utility used to look up the IP address of a name like www.microsoft.com) against some of the IP addresses we've just gleaned. We soon have a list of domain names and IP addresses of all the machines connected to our victim network.

Next, we use traceroute (another administrative tool, which traces the route between a source and destination) to view the network topology and identify potential access control devices like routers and firewalls, which we'll steer clear of.

Time to rattle some doors and look in some windows. McClure calls this "port-scanning"—using administration and downloadable hacking tools to find out what ports are open and what services are running on those ports. I'm particularly taken with the stealthy Nmap, a utility for network mapping available for free off the Web. We deploy Nmap against our primary target to get a road map of open ports, along with the network protocols and application services they support. At the top of our list, for example, we see: "Port 7: Open; protocol TCP; service Telnet." And so it goes for 10 other open ports on that machine alone. The classroom buzzes with excitement.

I realize how removed I feel from the victim. It's chilling to think that there are hundreds, nay thousands, of other crackers from underground groups such as Global Hell who probably feel the same way.

DAY 2: THE NT ROOT DANCE

We're introduced to Eric Schultze, affectionately called a "Hoover" by his cronies. A Hoover can really suck the guts out of a victim machine, and Schultze, 31, proves he's worthy of his name. We start by picking our target. Test servers are notorious for lax password controls and monitoring. Or we could sniff the mail server for user names and passwords. We decide to go for the backup domain controller—a separate physical server—where user names are stored and security is often forgotten because it's a backup.

We establish a null session (a Microsoft utility that allows services to communicate with one another without a user identification) with the victim server. I feel like a ghost inside someone else's house. I can see everything—network services, password files, user accounts, even payroll. But I can't touch anything because null is only designed for interprocess communication.

For the victim, "the sad thing about Microsoft is it doesn't log any of this," Schultze explains.

We're itching to gain root access (the most privileged level of access). But first, we must log off and then back on as legitimate users in order to grab the password hashes (encoded passwords) and submit them to our ace password-cracking tools. We get back in under the user name "backup" by guessing the password (which is also "backup"). "Command completed successfully," the machine responds.

I ask Schultze whether raised awareness has pushed administrators to better monitor passwords. No, he says. Most networks are still chock-full of such easy-to-guess passwords.

Once in, we copy user files and encrypted password hashes onto our hard drive. We log off and hit the hashes with L0phtcrack and the even faster John the Ripper. Available on the Web, both tools test passwords against a dictionary of common passwords until they break open. The tougher passwords may take a day, though, as they must be cracked one character at a time. Within minutes, we've got more than 70% of plain-text passwords in our greasy little paws.

Microsoft's LAN Manager hashes are the worst from a victim standpoint because LAN Manager splits passwords into seven-character halves and uses a known constant to encrypt each half, says Schultze. Our cracking tools are programmed for this, so they kick out passwords much faster than they would in Unix. And if the administrator disables LAN Manager, the NT box won't talk to any Windows 95 or 98 boxes, so it's a tough problem to solve.

Armed with our newfound passwords, we finally reach our goal for the day and hack back into the machine at administrator level and get root control of our machine. "What's the first thing you do when you gain root? You do the root dance," explains Ron Nguyen, another instructor. Push one arm up, jiggle your hips, put the other arm up, jiggle your hips and repeat until you get it out of your system.

For our reward, Nguyen hands out a red wallet card titled "18 Things to Do After You've Hacked Admin" (Table X.1). But for the final slap to our victims' faces, we hide our hacking tools in an alternate data stream behind a readme.txt file on the victim server. You could easily hide 10 Mbytes of hacker tools behind such a file without changing the file size, according to Schultze. The only way administrators can catch this is to set up audit logs that would alert them when disk space changes significantly.

DAY 3: CAPTURING THE UNIX FLAG

"Hacking root is a state of mind." Thus begins our syllabus for Day 3. And we really are getting into this "state." We arrive at the class rubbing our hands in anticipation of breaking the venerable Unix. Our instructor, former Air Force geek Chris Prosise, doesn't let us down.

We begin by repeating discovery and gaining entry in much the same way we did on NT. But Prosise wants to have a little fun. He's showing us how to corrupt the DNS server to reroute traffic to a phony IP address on an "evil.com" server where he can: a) grab information or b) reroute the message into oblivion.

He also shows us how to conduct common HTTP attacks like test Common Gateway Interface, which forces the victim to give up files and directories with a simple "get" command, and how to execute remote commands that would disable

Table X.1 Things to Do after You've Hacked Admin

1.	Disable auditing
2.	Grab the password file
3.	Create an "adminkit" (hacker tools)
4.	Enumerate server information
5.	Enumerate secrets of LSA (Windows NT's Local Security Authority in the registry where password hashes are kept)
6.	Dump registry info
7.	Use Nltest (a tool that queries NT servers remotely)
8.	Pilfer the box
9.	Add an administrator account
10.	Grab a remote command shell
11.	Hijack the graphical user interface
12.	Disable Passprop (NT's password policy settings)
13.	Install a back door
14.	Install Trojan horses and sniffers
15.	Repeat
16.	Hide the adminikit (so you can use the machine as a launch point to attack others)
17.	Enable auditing
18.	Eat a nice meal

access controls. We install Trojan horses (executable code to do our bidding remotely) and punch open back doors so we can get back in using a Telnet terminal session without needing identifications or passwords.

Then we play capture the flag by leapfrogging among four Unix boxes. And this, I'm afraid, is where I was so rudely interrupted by my awaiting taxi.

Suffice it to say, we learned our lessons. Network and security managers have a tough row to hoe. Bullet-proof security is a misnomer. And managing security risk is the best anyone can hope for. We also learned that there's a little bit of hacker in all of us. And by cultivating this hacker within, information security professionals can better fight the cracker without.

Discussion Points

1. How vulnerable do you think the typical computer site is?
2. What is the magnitude of the risk? That is, if security is compromised, what is the potential cost to the victim?
3. What policies and procedures can you suggest to counter the types of threats illustrated in this case study?

APPENDIX A

BUSINESS DATA COMMUNICATIONS PROJECTS

A.1   **Animations and Animation Projects**

A.2   **Practical Exercises**

A.3   **Wireshark Projects**

A.4   **Research Projects**

A.5   **Reading/Report Assignments**

A.6   **Writing Assignments**

Many instructors believe that research or implementation projects are crucial to the clear understanding of the concepts of data and computer communications. Without projects, it may be difficult for students to grasp some of the basic concepts and interactions among components. Projects reinforce the concepts introduced in the book, give the student a greater appreciation of the how protocols and transmission schemes work, and can motivate students and give them confidence that they have mastered the material.

In this text, I have tried to present the concepts as clearly as possible and have provided nearly 200 homework problems to reinforce those concepts. Many instructors will wish to supplement this material with projects. This appendix provides some guidance in that regard and describes support material available in the instructor's supplement. The support material covers six types of projects and other student exercises:

- Animations and animation projects
- Practical exercises
- Wireshark projects
- Research projects
- Reading/report assignments
- Writing assignments

A.1   ANIMATIONS AND ANIMATION PROJECTS

Animations provide a powerful tool for understanding the complex mechanisms of network protocols. A total of 12 Web-based animations are used to illustrate protocol behavior. Each animation allows the users to step through the operation of the protocol by selecting the next step at each point in the protocol exchange. Table A.1 lists the animations by chapter. At appropriate places in the textbook, the animations are indicated by an icon so that the student can invoke the animation at the proper point in studying the book. The animations will be made available to professors at the **Instructor's Resource Center** (**IRC**) for this book in such a way as to enable online access by students.

The animations can be used in two ways. In a **passive mode**, the student can click more or less randomly on the next step at each point in the animation and watch as the given concept or principle is illustrated. The **active mode** can be used for two types of assignments. First, the student can be given a specific set of steps to invoke and watch the animation and then be asked to analyze and comment on the results. Second, the student can be given a specific endpoint and required to devise a sequence of steps that achieve the desired result. The instructor's supplement includes a set of assignments for each of the animations, plus suggested solutions so that instructors can assess the student's work.

These animations were developed at the University of Stirling in Scotland by Iain Robin and Ken Turner, with contributions from Paul Johnson and Kenneth Whyte [TURN01]. Larry Tan of the University of Stirling developed the animation assignments.

Table A.1 Business Data Communications Animations by Chapter

Chapter 4—The Internet	
Boot Protocol Simulator	A simple connection-less protocol, typically used by a diskless workstation to discover its Internet address and/or the name of its bootstrap file.
Chapter 5—TCP/IP	
TCP Client/Server Simulator	The use of TCP to support client/server interaction.
TCP Peer-to-Peer Simulator	The use of TCP to support peer-to-peer interaction.
UDP Simulator	Demonstrates UDP operation.
IP Simulator	Demonstrates IP operation.
Trivial File Transfer Protocol Simulator	Demonstrates TFTP operation.
Chapter 7—Internet-Based Applications	
SMTP Simulator	Simulator deals with main commands: HELO, MAIL FROM, RCPT TO, DATA, QUIT.
HTTP Simulator	Simulator deals with main commands: GET, HEAD, POST, PUT.
Chapter 17—Data Link Control and Multiplexing	
Alternating Bit Protocol Simulator	A connection-less protocol for transferring messages in one direction between a pair of protocol entities. It is a simple form of the Sliding Window Protocol with a window size of 1.
Sliding Window Protocol (3-column Simulator)	Illustrates sliding-window operation without showing the end users.
Sliding Window Protocol (5-column Simulator)	Illustrates sliding-window operation showing the end users.
Abracadabra Protocol Simulator	A connection-oriented protocol that allows data to be sent in either direction using the Alternating Bit Protocol.

A.2 PRACTICAL EXERCISES

The instructor's supplement includes Web pages that provide a set of practical exercises for an introduction to the use of IP over a LAN. The exercises naturally follow one another and build on the experience of the previous exercises. They do not, however, need to be attempted one after another. The four exercises may more easily be done on four separate occasions. The practical exercises are designed to help the student understand the operation of an Ethernet LAN and an IP network. The exercises involve using simple network commands available on most computers. About an hour is needed to perform all four exercises. The exercises cover the following topics: your own network connection, computers on your LAN, computers on remote networks, and the Internet.

A.3 WIRESHARK PROJECTS

Wireshark, formerly known as Ethereal, is used by network professionals around the world for troubleshooting, analysis, software and protocol development, and education. It has all of the standard features you would expect in a protocol analyzer and several features not seen in any other product. Its open source license allows talented experts in the networking community to add enhancements. It runs on all popular computing platforms, including UNIX, Linux, Windows, and Mac OS X.

Wireshark is ideal for allowing students to study the behavior of protocols not only because of its many features and multiplatform capability but also because students may subsequently use Wireshark in their professional life.

The IRC includes a Student User's Manual and a set of project assignments for Wireshark created specifically for use with *Business Data Communications*. In addition, there is a very useful video tutorial that introduces the student to the use of Wireshark.

Michael Harris of Indiana University initially developed the Ethereal exercises and user's guide. Dave Bremer of Otago Polytechnic in New Zealand updated the material for the most recent Wireshark release; he also developed the online video tutorial.

A.4 RESEARCH PROJECTS

An effective way of reinforcing basic concepts from the course and for teaching students research skills is to assign a research project. Such a project could involve a literature search as well as a Web search of vendor products, research lab activities, and standardization efforts. Projects could be assigned to teams or, for smaller projects, to individuals. In any case, it is best to require some sort of project proposal early in the term, giving the instructor time to evaluate the proposal for appropriate topic and appropriate level of effort. Student handouts for research projects should include

- A format for the proposal
- A format for the final report
- A schedule with intermediate and final deadlines
- A list of possible project topics

The students can select one of the listed topics or devise their own comparable project. The instructor's supplement includes a suggested format for the proposal and final report plus a list of possible research topics.

A.5 READING/REPORT ASSIGNMENTS

Another excellent way to reinforce concepts from the course and to give students research experience is to assign papers from the literature to be read and analyzed. The IRC site includes a suggested list of papers to be assigned, organized by chapter.

The IRC provides a copy of each of the papers. The IRC also includes a suggested assignment wording.

A.6 WRITING ASSIGNMENTS

Writing assignments can have a powerful multiplier effect in the learning process in a technical discipline such as data communications and networking. Adherents of the Writing Across the Curriculum (WAC) movement (http://wac.colostate.edu/) report substantial benefits of writing assignments in facilitating learning. Writing assignments lead to more detailed and complete thinking about a particular topic. In addition, writing assignments help to overcome the tendency of students to pursue a subject with a minimum of personal engagement, just learning facts and problem-solving techniques without obtaining a deep understanding of the subject matter.

The IRC contains a number of suggested writing assignments, organized by chapter. Instructors may ultimately find that this is the most important part of their approach to teaching the material. I would greatly appreciate any feedback on this area and any suggestions for additional writing assignments.

GLOSSARY

amplitude   The size or magnitude of a voltage or current waveform.

amplitude-shift keying Modulation in which the two binary values are represented by two different amplitudes of the carrier frequency.

analog data   Data represented by a physical quantity that is considered to be continuously variable and whose magnitude is made directly proportional to the data or to a suitable function of the data.

analog signal   A continuously varying electromagnetic wave that may be propagated over a variety of media.

analog transmission   The transmission of analog signals without regard to content. The signal may be amplified, but there is no intermediate attempt to recover the data from the signal.

application layer Layer 7 of the OSI model. This layer determines the interface of the system with the user and provides useful application-oriented services.

asynchronous transfer mode (ATM) A form of packet switching in which fixed-size cells of 53 octets are used. There is no network layer and many of the basic functions have been streamlined or eliminated to provide for greater throughput.

asynchronous transmission Transmission in which each information character is individually synchronized, usually by the use of start elements and stop elements.

attenuation A decrease in magnitude of current, voltage, or power of a signal in transmission between points.

automatic repeat request (ARQ) A feature that automatically initiates a request for retransmission when an error in transmission is detected.

availability   The percentage of time that a particular function or application is available for users.

bandwidth The difference between the limiting frequencies of a continuous frequency band.

baud   A unit of signaling speed equal to the number of discrete conditions or signal events per second, or the reciprocal of the time of the shortest signal element.

best effort   A network or internet delivery technique that does not guarantee delivery of data and treats all packets equally. All packets are forwarded on a first-come-first-served basis. Preferential treatment based on priority or other concerns is not provided.

bit   Binary digit. A unit of information represented by either a zero or a one.

bridge   An internetworking device that connects two similar local area networks that use the same LAN protocols.

byte   A binary bit string operated on as a unit and usually eight bits long and capable of holding one character in the local character set.

cellular network   A wireless communications network in which fixed antennas are arranged in a hexagonal pattern and mobile stations communicate through nearby fixed antennas.

checksum   An error-detecting code based on a summation operation performed on the bits to be checked.

central office (CO) The place where telephone companies terminate customer lines and locate switching equipment to interconnect those lines with other networks.

ciphertext The output of an encryption algorithm; the encrypted form of a message or data.

circuit switching A method of communicating in which a dedicated communications path is established between two devices through one or more intermediate switching nodes. Unlike with packet switching, digital data are sent as a continuous stream of bits. Data rate is guaranteed, and delay is essentially limited to propagation time.

client/server A common form of distributed system in which software is split between server tasks and client tasks. A client sends requests to a server, according to some protocol, asking for information or action, and the server responds.

coaxial cable A cable consisting of one conductor, usually a small copper tube or wire, within and insulated from another conductor of larger diameter, usually copper tubing or copper braid.

code division multiple access A multiplexing technique used with spread spectrum.

codec Coder-decoder. Transforms analog data into a digital bit stream (coder) and digital signals into analog data (decoder).

common channel signaling Technique in which network control signals (e.g., call request) are separated from the associated voice or data path by placing the signaling from a group of voice or data paths on a separate channel dedicated to signaling only.

customer premises equipment (CPE) Telecommunications equipment that is located on the customer's premises (physical location) rather than on the provider's premises or in between.

cyclic redundancy check (CRC) An error-detecting code in which the code is the remainder resulting from dividing the bits to be checked by a predetermined binary number.

database A collection of interrelated data, often with controlled redundancy, organized to serve multiple applications. The data are stored so that they can be used by different programs without concern for the internal data structure or organization.

datagram In packet switching, a self-contained packet, independent of other packets, that carries information sufficient for routing from the originating data terminal equipment (DTE) to the destination DTE without relying on earlier exchanges between the DTEs and the network.

data link layer Layer 2 of the OSI model. Converts an unreliable transmission channel into a reliable one.

decibel A measure of the relative strength of two signals. The number of decibels is 10 times the log of the ratio of the power of two signals, or 20 times the log of the ratio of the voltage of two signals.

decryption The translation of encrypted text or data (called ciphertext) into original text or data (called plaintext). Also called deciphering.

differentiated services Functionality in the Internet and private internets to support specific QoS requirements for a group of users, all of whom use the same service label in IP packets.

digital data Data represented by discrete values or conditions.

digital signal A discrete or discontinuous signal, such as a sequence of voltage pulses.

digital signature An authentication mechanism that enables the creator of a message to attach a code that acts as a signature. The signature guarantees the source and integrity of the message.

digital transmission The transmission of digital data or analog data that have been digitized, using either an analog or digital signal, in which the digital content is recovered and repeated at intermediate points to reduce the effects of impairments, such as noise, distortion, and attenuation.

direct sequence spread spectrum A form of spread spectrum in which each bit in the original signal is represented by multiple bits in the transmitted signal, using a spreading code.

distributed database A database that is not stored in a single location but is dispersed over a network of interconnected computers.

distributed data processing Data processing in which some or all of the processing, storage, and control functions, in addition to input/output functions, are dispersed among data processing stations.

domain A group of networks that are part of the Internet and that are under the administrative control of a single entity, such as a company or government agency.

Domain Name System (DNS) A directory lookup service that provides a mapping between the name of a host on the Internet and its numerical address.

downlink The communications link from satellite to earth station.

electronic mail Correspondence in the form of messages transmitted between workstations over a network. The most common protocol used to support electronic mail is the Simple Mail Transfer Protocol (SMTP).

encryption To convert plain text or data into unintelligible form by means of a reversible mathematical computation.

error control A technique for detecting and correcting errors.

error detecting code A code in which each data signal conforms to specific rules of construction, so that departures from this construction in the received signal can be automatically detected.

extranet The extension of a company's intranet out onto the Internet to allow selected customers, suppliers, and mobile workers to access the company's private data and applications via the World Wide Web. This is in contrast to, and usually in addition to, the company's public Web site, which is accessible to everyone. The difference can be somewhat blurred, but generally an extranet implies real-time access through a firewall of some kind.

frame A group of bits that includes data plus one or more addresses and other protocol control information. Generally refers to a link layer (OSI layer 2) protocol data unit.

frame check sequence (FCS) An error-detecting code inserted as a field in a block of data to be transmitted. The code serves to check for errors upon reception of the data.

frame relay A form of packet switching based on the use of variable-length link layer frames. There is no network layer, and many of the basic functions have been streamlined or eliminated to provide for greater throughput.

frequency Rate of signal oscillation in cycles per second (Hertz).

Frequency division multiplexing (FDM) Division of a transmission facility into two or more channels by splitting the frequency band transmitted by the facility into narrower bands, each of which is used to constitute a distinct channel.

frequency shift keying Modulation in which the two binary values are represented by two different frequencies near the carrier frequency.

guided medium A transmission medium in which electromagnetic waves are guided along a solid medium, such as copper twisted pair, copper coaxial cable, or optical fiber.

header System-defined control information that precedes user data in a protocol data unit.

host Any end system, such as a PC, workstation, or server, that connects to the Internet.

Internet A worldwide internetwork based on TCP/IP that interconnects thousands of public and private networks and millions of users.

Internet Protocol (IP) A standardized protocol that executes in hosts and routers to interconnect a number of independent networks.

internetworking Communication among devices across multiple networks.

Internet service provider (ISP) A company that provides other companies or individuals with access to, or presence on, the Internet.

intranet A corporate internetwork that provides the key Internet applications, especially the World Wide Web. An intranet operates within the organization for internal purposes and can exist as an isolated, self-contained internet, or may have links to the Internet. The most common example is the use by a company of one or more World Wide Web servers on an internal TCP/IP network for distribution of information within the company.

local area network (LAN) A communications network that encompasses a small area, typically a single building or cluster of buildings, used to connect various data processing devices, including PCs, workstations, and servers.

local loop A transmission path, generally twisted pair, between the individual subscriber and the nearest switching center of a public telecommunications network. Also referred to as a subscriber loop.

Medium Access Control (MAC) For a communications network, the method of determining which station has access to the transmission medium at any time.

modem Modulator/demodulator. A device that converts digital data to an analog signal that can be transmitted on a telecommunication line and converts the received analog signal to digital data.

multiplexing In data transmission, a function that permits two or more data sources to share a common transmission medium such that each data source has its own channel.

network access point (NAP) In the United States, a network access point (NAP) is one of several major Internet interconnection points that serve to tie all the ISPs together.

network layer Layer 3 of the OSI model. Responsible for routing data through a communication network.

network service provider (NSP) A company that provides backbone services to an Internet service provider (ISP), the company that most Web users use for access to the Internet.

noise Unwanted signals that combine with and hence distort the signal intended for transmission and reception.

octet A group of eight adjacent bits, usually operated upon as a unit.

Open Systems Interconnection (OSI) reference model A model of communications between cooperating devices. It defines a seven-layer architecture of communication functions.

optical fiber A thin filament of glass or other transparent material through which a signal-encoded light beam may be transmitted by means of total internal reflection.

packet A group of bits that includes data plus control information. Generally refers to a network layer (OSI layer 3) protocol data unit.

packet switching A method of transmitting messages through a communications network, in which long messages are subdivided into short packets. Each packet is passed from source to destination through intermediate nodes. At each node, the entire message is received, stored briefly, and then passed on to the next node.

parity bit A check bit appended to an array of binary digits to make the sum of all the binary digits, including the check bit, always odd or always even.

period The absolute value of the minimum interval after which the same characteristics of a periodic waveform recur.

periodic signal A signal $f(t)$ that satisfies $f(t) = f(t + nk)$ for all integers n, with k being a constant.

phase For a periodic signal $f(t)$, the fractional part t/P of the period P through which t has advanced relative to an arbitrary origin. The origin is usually taken at the last previous passage through zero from the negative to the positive direction.

phase shift keying Modulation in which the phase of the carrier signal is shifted to represent digital data.

physical layer Layer 1 of the OSI model. Concerned with the electrical, mechanical, and timing aspects of signal transmission over a medium.

plaintext The input to an encryption function or the output of a decryption function.

point of presence (POP) A site that has a collection of telecommunications equipment, usually refers to ISP or telephone company sites. An ISP POP is the edge of the ISP's network; connections from users are accepted and authenticated here. An Internet access provider may operate several POPs distributed throughout their area of operation to increase the chance that its subscribers will be able to reach one with a local telephone call.

point-to-point A configuration in which two and only two stations share a transmission path.

port A transport-layer address that identifies a user of a transport-layer protocol.

presentation layer Layer 6 of the OSI model. Concerned with data format and display.

protocol A set of semantic and syntactic rules that describe how to transmit data, especially across a network. Low-level protocols define the electrical and physical standards to be observed, bit- and byte-ordering, and the transmission and error detection and correction of the bit stream. High-level protocols deal with the data formatting, including the syntax of messages, the terminal to computer dialogue, character sets, and sequencing of messages.

protocol architecture The software structure that implements the communications function. Typically, the protocol architecture consists of a layered set of protocols, with one or more protocols at each layer.

protocol data unit (PDU) Information that is delivered as a unit between peer entities of a network. A PDU typically contains control information and address information in a header. The PDU may also contain data.

public-key encryption A form of cryptosystem in which encryption and decryption are performed using two different keys, one of which is referred to as the public key and one of which is referred to as the private key.

pulse code modulation (PCM) A process in which a signal is sampled, and the magnitude of each sample with respect to a fixed reference is quantized and converted by coding to a digital signal.

quality of service (QoS) A set of parameters that describe the quality (e.g., data rate, timeliness, buffer usage, priority) of a specific stream of data. The minimum QoS is best effort, which treats all packets equally on a first-come-first-served basis. QoS may dictate the path chosen for delivery by a router, the network service requested by the router of the next network on that path, and the order in which waiting packets are forwarded from the router.

router An internetworking device that connects two computer networks. It makes use of an internet protocol and assumes that all attached devices on the networks use the same protocol architecture at the internet layer and above.

routing The determination of a path that a data unit (frame, packet, message) will traverse from source to destination.

service access point (SAP) A means of identifying a user of the services of a protocol entity. A protocol entity provides one or more SAPs, for use by higher-level entities.

Service-oriented architecture (SOA) The modularization of business functions for greater flexibility and reusability. Instead of building monolithic applications for each department, an SOA organizes business software in a granular fashion so that common functions can be used interchangeably by different departments internally and by external business partners as well. The more granular the components (the more pieces), the more they can be reused.

session layer Layer 5 of the OSI model. Manages a logical connection (session) between two communicating processes or applications.

signal An electromagnetic wave used to convey information.

signaling The production of an electromagnetic signal that represents analog or digital data and its propagation along a transmission medium.

spectrum Refers to an absolute, contiguous range of frequencies.

symmetric encryption A form of cryptosystem in which encryption and decryption are performed using the same key. Also known as conventional encryption.

synchronous time division multiplexing A method of TDM in which time slots on a shared transmission line are assigned to devices on a fixed, predetermined basis.

synchronous transmission Data transmission in which the time of occurrence of each signal representing a bit is related to a fixed time frame.

time division multiplexing (TDM) The division of a transmission facility into two or more channels by allotting the common channel to several different information channels, one at a time.

transmission The communication of data by the propagation and processing of signals. In the case of digital signals or of analog signals that encode digital data, repeaters may be used. For analog signals, amplifiers may be used.

transmission medium The physical medium that conveys data between data stations.

transport layer Layer 4 of the OSI model. Provides reliable, sequenced transfer of data between endpoints.

twisted pair A transmission medium that consists of two insulated conductors twisted together to reduce noise.

unguided medium A transmission medium, such as the atmosphere or outer space, used for wireless transmission.

uplink The communications link from earth station to satellite.

virtual circuit A packet-switching mechanism in which a logical connection (virtual circuit) is established between two stations at the start of transmission. All packets follow the same route, need not carry a complete address, and arrive in sequence.

virtual private network (VPN) The use of encryption and authentication in the lower protocol layers to provide a secure connection through an otherwise insecure network, typically the Internet. VPNs are generally cheaper than real private networks using private lines but rely on having the same encryption and authentication system at both ends. The encryption may be performed by firewall software or possibly by routers.

white noise Noise that has a flat, or uniform, frequency spectrum in the frequency range of interest.

wireless transmission Electromagnetic transmission through air, vacuum, or water by means of an antenna.

World Wide Web (WWW) A networked, graphically oriented hypermedia system. Information is stored on servers, exchanged between servers and browsers, and displayed on browsers in the form of pages of text and images.

REFERENCES

ABBREVIATIONS

ACM   Association for Computing Machinery
IEEE   Institute of Electrical and Electronics Engineers

3COM04   3Com Corp. *Choice Hotels International Teams Up with 3Com to Offer Free Wireless Internet Access at Clarion Hotels and Comfort Suites.* 3Com Press Release, 18 February 2004. http://www.3com.com/

3COM06   3Com Corp. *Case Study: Choice Hotels International, Inc.,* US. 2006. http://www.3com.com/

10GE02   10 Gigabit Ethernet Alliance. *10 Gigabit Ethernet Technology Overview.* White paper, May 2002. ethernetalliance.org/technology/white_papers

ANDE80   Anderson, *J. Computer Security Threat Monitoring and Surveillance.* Fort Washington, PA: James P. Anderson Co., April 1980.

ANTE06   Ante, S., and Grow, B. "Meet the Hackers." *Business Week,* May 29, 2006.

ARMI00   Armitage, G. *Quality of Service in IP Networks.* Indianapolis, IN: Macmillan Technical Publishing, 2000.

AUDI04a   Audin, G. "Architectures for Convergence." *Business Communications Review,* October 2004.

AUDI04b   Audin, G. "A Roadmap to Convergence." *Business Communications Review,* October 2004.

AVAY04   Avaya, J. "Not Your Father's PBX?" ACM Queue, September 2004.

AYCO06   Aycock, J. *Computer Viruses and Malware.* New York: Springer, 2006.

BARA02   Baran, P. "The Beginnings of Packet Switching: Some Underlying Concepts." *IEEE Communications Magazine,* July 2002.

BARN04   Barnett, D.; Groth, D.; and McBee, J. *Cabling: The Complete Guide to Network Wiring.* San Francisco: Sybex, 2004.

BELL94   Bellovin, S., and Cheswick, W. "Network Firewalls." *IEEE Communications Magazine,* September 1994.

BELL00   Bellamy, J. *Digital Telephony.* New York: Wiley, 2000.

BELL02   Bellman, R. "Frame Relay: Good for Another 10 Years?" *Business Communications Review*, July 2002.

BERN96   Bernstein, P. "Middleware: A Model for Distributed System Services." *Communications of the ACM*, February 1996.

BERN98   Bernard, R. *The Corporate Intranet.* New York: Wiley, 1998.

BERS96   Berson, A. *Client/Server Architecture.* New York: McGraw-Hill, 1996.

BERT92   Bertsekas, D., and Gallager, R. *Data Networks.* Englewood Cliffs, NJ: Prentice Hall, 1992.

BIDG08a   Bidgoli, H., editor. *Handbook of Computer Networks.* New York: Wiley, 2008.

BIDG08b   Bidgoli, H., editor. "The Internet Fundamentals." In [BIDG08a].

BIEB05   Bieberstein, N., et al. "Impact of Service-Oriented Architecture on Enterprise Systems, Organizational Structures, and Individuals." " *IBM Systems Journal*, Vol. 44, No. 4, 2005.

BIH06   Bih, J. "Service Oriented Architecture (SOA): A New Paradigm to Implement Dynamic E-Business Solutions." *ACM Ubiquity*, August 2006; acm.org/ubiquity/views/v7i30_soa.html

BING02	Bing, B. *Wireless Local Area Networks.* New York: Wiley, 2002.
BISE07	Bisel, L. "The Role of SSL in Cybersecurity." *IT Pro*, March/April 2002.
BLAC99	Black, U. *ATM Volume I: Foundation for Broadband Networks.* Upper Saddle River, NJ: Prentice Hall, 1992.
BLAC00	Black, U. *IP Routing Protocols: RIP, OSPF, BGP, PNNI & Cisco Routing Protocols.* Upper Saddle River, NJ: Prentice Hall, 2000.
BORT02	Borthick, S. "SIP Services: Slowly Rolling Forward." *Business Communications Review*, June 2002.
BORT03	Borthick, S. "SIP for the Enterprise: Work in Progress." *Business Communications Review*, February 2003.
BRAG00	Bragg, A. "Which Network Design Tool Is Right for You?" *IT Pro*, September/October 2000.
BRIT04	Britton, C. *IT Architectures and Middleware.* Reading, MA: Addison-Wesley, 2004.
BUCK00	Buckwalter, J. *Frame Relay: Technology and Practice.* Reading, MA: Addison-Wesley, 2000.
BOUI02	Bouillet, E.; Mitra, D.; and Ramakrishnan, K. "The Structure and Management of Service Level Agreements in Networks." *IEEE Journal on Selected Areas in Communications*, May 2002.
BREY99	Breyer, R., and Riley, S. *Switched, Fast, and Gigabit Ethernet.* New York: Macmillan Technical Publishing, 1999.
BROW03	Brown, A.; Johnston, S.; and Kelly, K. *Using Service-Oriented Architecture and Component-Based Development to Build Web Service Applications. IBM Rational Software Technical Report*, 2003; ibm.com/developerworks/rational/library/510.html/
BRUN99	Bruno, L. " Extranet Indemnity." *Data Communications*, July 1999.
CAHN98	Cahn, R., *Wide Area Network Design.* San Francisco: Morgan-Kaufmann, 1998.
CAMP99	Campbell, A.; Coulson, G.; and Kounavis, M. "Managing Complexity: Middleware Explained." *IT Pro*, October 1999.
CARE08	Carey, M. "SOA What?" *IEEE Computer*, March 2008.
CERF74	Cerf, V., and Kahn, R. "A Protocol for Packet Network Interconnection." *IEEE Transactions on Communications*, May 1974.
CHEN02	Chen, T. "Internet Performance Monitoring." *Proceedings of the IEEE*, September 2002.
CHER05	Cherbacko, L., et al. "Impact of Service Orientation at the Business Level." *IBM Systems Journal*, Vol. 44, No. 4, 2005.
CHES97	Chess, D. "The Future of Viruses on the Internet." *Proceedings, Virus Bulletin International Conference*, October 1997.
CHOU02	Chou, W. "Inside SSL: The Secure Sockets Layer Protocol." *IT Pro*, July/August 2002.
CISC07	Cisco Systems, Inc. " 802.11n: The Next Generation of Wireless Performance." Cisco White Paper, 2007. cisco.com
CLAR02	Clark, E. "Carlson Companies Trades up to an IP SAN." *Network Magazine*, December 2002.
CLAR03	Clark, E. "Dallas County Plugs into eGovernment." *Network Magazine*, April 2003.

COFF04   Covvman, J. "Not Your Father's PBX?" *ACM Queue*, September 2004.

COHE94   Cohen, F. *A Short Course on Computer Viruses*. New York: Wiley, 1994.

COHE96   Cohen, J. "Rule Reversal: Old 80/20 LAN Traffic Model Is Getting Turned on Its Head." *Network World*, December 16, 1996.

COME07   Comer, D. *The Internet Book*. Upper Saddle River, NJ: Prentice Hall, 2007.

CONN99   Connor, D. "Data Replication Helps Prevent Potential Problems." *Network World*, December 13, 1999.

CONR02   Conry-Murray, A. "Behavior-Blocking Stops Unknown Malicious Code." *Network Magazine*, June 2002.

CONR03   Conery-Murray, A. "Hospital Cures Wireless LAN of Dropped Connections." *Network Magazine*, January 2003.

CORM01   Cormen, T.; Leiserson, C.; Rivest, R.; and Stein, C. *Introduction to Algorithms*. Cambridge, MA: MIT Press, 2001.

COUC07   Couch, L. *Digital and Analog Communication Systems*. Upper Saddle River, NJ: Prentice Hall, 2007.

COUL05   Coulouris, G.; Dollimore, J.; and Kindberg, T. *Distributed Systems: Concepts and Design*. Reading, MA: Addison-Wesley, 2005.

CROL00   Croll, A., and Packman, E. *Managing Bandwidth: Deploying QoS in Enterprise Networks*. Upper Saddle River, NJ: Prentice Hall, 2000.

DHSM08   Florida Department of Highway Safety and Motor Vehicles. "DHSMV Migrates Wide Area Network to New MyFloridaNet." *FDHSM Expressways*, Winter 2008.

DIAN02   Dianda, J.; Gurbani, V.; and Jones, M. "Session Initiation Protocol Services Architecture." *Bell Labs Technical Journal*, Vol. 7, No. 1, 2002.

DEBE07   Debeasi, P. "802.11n: Beyond the Hype." *Burton Group White Paper*, July 2007. www.burtongroup.com

DORN01   Dornan, A. "Hotel Chain Reserves Room on Space Network." *Network Magazine*, January 1001.

DWYE92   Dwyer, S., et al. "Teleradiology Using Switched Dialup Networks." *IEEE Journal on Selected Areas in Communications*, September 1992.

ECKE95   Eckerson, W. "Client Server Architecture." *Network World Collaboration*, Winter 1995.

ECKE96   Eckel, G. *Intranet Working*. Indianapolis, IN: New Riders, 1996.

ELLI08   Elliot, B. "The Value of Unified Communications." *Network World*, January 7, 2008.

ELSA02   El-Sayed, M., and Jaffe, J. "A View of Telecommunications Network Evolution." *IEEE Communications Magazine*, December 2002.

ENGE80   Enger, N., and Howerton, P. *Computer Security*. New York: Amacom, 1980.

EVAN96   Evans, T. *Building an Intranet*. Indianapolis, IN: Sams, 1996.

FLOY94   Floyd, S., and Jacobson, V. "The Synchronization of Periodic Routing Messages," *IEEE/ACM Transactions on Networking*, April 1994.

FRAZ99   Frazier, H., and Johnson, H. "Gigabit Ethernet: From 100 to 1,000 Mbps." *IEEE Internet Computing*, January/February 1999.

FREE97   Freeman, R. *Radio System Design for Telecommunications*. New York: Wiley, 1997.

FREE04   Freeman, R. *Telecommunication System Engineering*. New York: Wiley, 2004.

FREE05   Freeman, R. *Fundamentals of Telecommunications*. New York: Wiley, 2005.

GARF02   Garfinkel, S., and Spafford, G. *Web Security, Privacy & Commerce.* Sebastapol, CA: O'Reilly, 2002.

GAUD00   Gaudin, S. "The Omega Files." *Network World,* June 26, 2000.

GITT06   Gittlen, S. " A Dashboard That Unites E-Mail, Instant Messaging, Collaboration and More." *Network World,* November 11, 2006.

GOLI99   Golick, J. "Distributed Data Replication." *Network Magazine,* December 1999.

GOOD02   Goode, B. "Voice Over Internet Protocol (VoIP)." *Proceedings of the IEEE,* September 2002.

GOUR02   Gourley, D., et al. *HTTP: The Definitive Guide.* Sebastopol, CA: O'Reilly, 2002.

GRAN04   Grance, T.; Kent, K.; and Kim, B. *Computer Security Incident Handling Guide.* NIST Special Publication SP 800-61, January 2004.

GUYN88   Guynes, J. 1988. "Impact of System Response Time on State Anxiety." *Communications of the ACM,* March, 1988.

HAFN96   Hafner, K., and Lyon, M. *Where Wizards Stay Up Late.* New York: Simon and Schuster, 1996.

HARB92   Harbison, R. "Frame Relay: Technology for Our Time." *LAN Technology,* December 1992.

HARL02   Harler, C. "Bring It On!" *Hospitality Technology Magazine,* January/February 2002.

HEGG84   Heggestad, H. "An Overview of Packet Switching Communications." *IEEE Communications Magazine,* April 1984.

HELD00   Held, G. *Understanding Data Communications: from Fundamentals to Networking.* New York: Wiley, 2000.

HETT03   Hettick, L. "Building Blocks for Converged Applications." *Business Communications Review,* June 2003.

HIGG02   Higgins, K. "T.G.I. Friday's Owner Serves up an IP SAN." *Network Computing,* September 15, 2002.

HIGG03   Higgins, K. "Warehouse Data Earns its Keep." *Network Computing,* May 1, 2003.

HOFF00   Hoffman, P. "Overview of Internet Mail Standards." *The Internet Protocol Journal,* June 2000 (www.cisco.com/warp/public/759

HOFF02   Hoffer, J.; Prescott, M.; and McFadden, F. *Modern Database Management.* Upper Saddle River, NJ: Prentice Hall, 2002.

HONE05   Honeynet Project. *Knowing Your Enemy: Tracking Botnets.* Honeynet White Paper, March 2005. http://honeynet.org/papers/bots

HUFF06   Huff, D. "Perspective on 100 Gb/s Ethernet." *100 Gb/s Ethernet Workshop,* Optoelectronics Industry Development Association, September 2006. www.ethernetalliance.org/technology/presentations/

HUIT00   Huitema, C. *Routing in the Internet.* Upper Saddle River, NJ: Prentice Hall, 2000.

HUTC08   Hutchinson, J., et al. "Migrating to SOAs by Way of Hybrid Systems." *IT Pro,* January/February 2008.

IBM00   IBM Corp. "ING Life Develops Extranet Using Domino and Host On-Demand with VSE/ESA." *VM and VSE Solutions Journal,* July 2000.

JANS01   Jansen, W. *Guidelines on Active Content and Mobile Code.* NIST Special Publication SP 800-28, October 2001.

JHI07   Jhi, Y., et al. "Proactive Containment of Fast Scanning Worms through White Detection." *Proceedings of 3rd International Conference on Security and Privacy in Communication Networks*, September 2007.

JOHN96   Johnson, J. "Tech Team." *Data Communications*, February 1996.

KADA98   Kadambi, J.; Crayford, I.; and Kalkunte, M. *Gigabit Ethernet*. Upper Saddle River, NJ: Prentice Hall, 1998.

KANE98   Kanel, J.; Givler, J.; Leiba, B.; and Segmuller, W. "Internet Messaging Frameworks." *IBM Systems Journal*, No. 1, 1998.

KEPH97a   Kephart, J.; Sorkin, G.; Chess, D.; and White, S. "Fighting Computer Viruses." *Scientific American*, November 1997.

KEPH97b   Kephart, J.; Sorkin, G.; Swimmer, B.; and White, S. "Blueprint for a Computer Immune System." *Proceedings, Virus Bulletin International Conference*, October 1997.

KERR06   Kerravala, Z. *The Impact of Microsoft's Unified Communications Launch.* White Paper, Yankee Group, August 2006.

KESH98   Keshav, S., and Sharma, R. "Issues and Trends in Router Design." *IEEE Communications Magazine*, May 1998.

KIRB01   Kirby, R. "Telemedicine and the No-Brainer Bandwidth Bargain." *Network Magazine*, February 2001.

KLEI75   Kleinrock, L. *Queueing Systems, Vol. I: Theory*. New York: John Wiley, 1975.

KLEI08   Kleinrock, L. "History of the Internet and Its Flexible Future." *IEEE Wireless Communications*, February 2008.

KNAU05   Knauer, B. "Voice Goes Wireless." *Cisco Packet Magazine*, Third Quarter, 2005.

KRAN04   Kranz, G. "Strategic Storage: Eyeing IP Storage." *Searchstorage.com*, November 9, 2004.

KRIS01   Krishnamurthy, B., and Rexford, J. *Web Protocols and Practice: HTTP/1.1, Networking Protocols, Caching, and Traffic Measurement*. Upper Saddle River, NJ: Prentice Hall, 2001.

LAYL04   Layland, R. "Understanding Wi-Fi Performance." *Business Communications Review*, March 2004.

LAZA07   Laxar, I. "*Unified Communications: What, Why, and How?* Issue Paper, Nemertes Research, 2007.

LELA94   Leland, W.; Taqqu, M.; Willinger, W.; and Wilson, D. "On the Self-Similar Nature of Ethernet Traffic (Extended Version)." *IEEE/ACM Transactions on Networking*, February 1994.

LI04   Li, Z., and Drew, M. *Fundamentals of Multimedia*. Upper Saddle River, NJ: Prentice Hall, 2004.

MADA98   Madaus, J., and Webster, L. "Opening the Door to Distance Learning." *Computers in Libraries*, May 1998.

MART88   Martin, J., and Leban, *J. Principles of Data Communication*. Englewood Cliffs, NJ: Prentice Hall, 1988.

MART02   Martin, J., and Nilsson, A. "On Service Level Agreements for IP Networks." *Proceedings, IEEE INFOCOMM '02*, 2002.

MCAF06   McAfee, A. "Enterprise 2.0: The Dawn of Emergent Collaboration." *Sloan Management Review*, Spring 2006.

MCDY99   McDysan, D., and Spohn, D. *ATM: Theory and Application*. New York: McGraw-Hill, 1999.

MCFA08 McFarland, D., and Nicholson, D. "Client/Server Computing Basics." In [BIDG08a].

MELL07 Melle, S., et al. "Market Drivers and Implementation Options for 100-BgE Transport Over the WAN." *IEEE Applications and Practice*, November 2007.

MENA05 Menasce, D. "MOM vs. RPC: Communication Models for Distributed Applications." *IEEE Internet Computing*, March/April 2005.

MILL05 Miller, H.; Levine, H.; and Bates, S. "Welcome to Convergence." *IT Pro*, May/June 2005.

MILO00 Milonas, A. "Enterprise Networking for the New Millennium." *Bell Labs Technical Journal*, January–March 2000.

MIRK04 Mirkovic, J., and Relher, P. "A Taxonomy of DDoS Attack and DDoS Defense Mechanisms." *ACM SIGCOMM Computer Communications Review*, April 2004.

MURU07 Murugesan, S. "Understanding Web 2.0." *IT Pro, July/August 2007*.

MUSI02 Musich, P. "Project Gets Helping Hand." eWeek, November 25, 2002. www.eweek.com.

NACH97 Nachenberg, C. "Computer Virus-Antivirus Coevolution." *Communications of the ACM*, January 1997.

NACH02 Nachenberg, C. "Behavior Blocking: The Next Step in Anti-Virus Protection." *White Paper*, SecurityFocus.com, March 2002.

NETM03 Netmotion Wireless, Inc. " NetMotion Mobility: Curing the Wireless LAN at St. Luke's Episcopal Hospital." *Case Study*, 2003. netmotionwireless.com/resources/case_studies.aspx

NIST95 National Institute of Standards and Technology. *An Introduction to Computer Security: The NIST Handbook*. Special Publication 800-12. October 1995.

NORR03 Norris, M. *Gigabit Ethernet Technology and Applications*. Norwood, MA: Artech House, 2003.

NOWE07 Nowell, M.; Vusirikala, V.; and Hays, R. "Overview of Requirements and Applications for 40 Gigabit and 100 Gigabit Ethernet." *Ethernet Alliance White Paper*, August 2007.

OU07 Ou, G. "The Role of 802.11n in the Enterprise." *White Paper*, zdnet.com, July 2007.

OZSU99 Ozsu, M., and Valduriez, P. *Principles of Distributed Database Systems*. Upper Saddle River, NJ: Prentice Hall, 1999.

PAHL95 Pahlavan, K., Probert, T. and Chase, M. "Trends in Local Wireless Networks." *IEEE Communications Magazine*, March 1995.

PAXS94 Paxson, V., and S. Floyd, "Wide-Area Traffic: The Failure of Poisson Modeling," *Proc. SIGCOMM' 94*. 1994:

PARZ06 Parziale, L., et al. *TCP/IP Tutorial and Technical Overview*. IBM Redbook GG24-3376-07, 2006. http://www.redbooks.ibm.com/abstracts/gg243376.html

PAXS96 Paxson, V. "Toward a Framework for Defining Internet Performance Metrics." *Proceedings, INET' 96*, 1996. http://www-nrg.ee.lbl.gov

PERL00 Perlman, R. *Interconnections: Bridges, Routers, Switches, and Internetworking Protocols*. Reading, MA: Addison-Wesley, 2000.

PFAF98 Pfaffenberger, B. *Building a Strategic Extranet*. Foster City, CA: IDG Books, 1998.

POL07   Pol, C., and Russo, P. "Convergence: Worth the Journey" *Business Trends Quarterly,* Q1 2007.

RADC04   Radcliff, D. "What Are They Thinking?" *Network World*, March 1, 2004.

RAO02   Rao, K.; Bojkovic, Z.; and Milovanovic, D. *Multimedia Communication Systems: Techniques, Standards, and Networks.* Upper Saddle River, NJ: Prentice Hall, 2002.

RAPP02   Rappaport, T., *Wireless Communications: Principles and Practice.* Upper Saddle River, NJ: Prentice Hall, 2002.

REAG00a   Reagan, P. *Client/Server Computing.* Upper Saddle River, NJ: Prentice Hall, 2000.

REAG00b   Reagan, P. *Client/Server Network: Design, Operation, and Management.* Upper Saddle River, NJ: Prentice Hall, 2000.

REGA04   Regan, P. *Local Area Networks.* Upper Saddle River, NJ: Prentice Hall, 2004.

REGE96   Rege, J. "A New Face For Florida." *Oracle Magazine*, July/August 1996.

RENA96   Renaud, P. *An Introduction to Client/Server Systems.* New York: Wiley, 1996.

ROBE78   Roberts, L. "The Evolution of Packet Switching." *Proceedings of the IEEE*, November 1978.

ROSE98   Rose, M., and Strom, D. *Internet Messaging: From the Desktop to the Enterprise.* Upper Saddle River, NJ: Prentice Hall, 1998.

ROSH04   Roshan, P., and Leary, J. *802.11 Wireless LAN Fundamentals.* Indianapolis: Cisco Press, 2004.

ROTH93   Rothschild, M. "Coming Soon: Internal Markets." *Forbes ASAP*, June 7, 1993.

SCHU98   Schulzrinne, H. and Rosenberg, J. "The Session Initiation Protocol: Providing Advanced Telephony Access Across the Internet." *Bell Labs Technical Journal*, October-December 1998.

SCHU99   Schulzrinne, H., and Rosenberg, J. "The IETF Internet Telephony Architecture and Protocols." *IEEE Network*, May/June 1999.

SECR06   Secrist, M. *SOA Concepts.* Hewlett-Packard Technical Report, 2006. boston-technology.com/index-2.html

SEIF98   Seifert, R. *Gigabit Ethernet.* Reading, MA: Addison-Wesley, 1998.

SENS02   Sens, T. "Next Generation of Unified Communications for Enterprises." *Alcatel Telecommunications Review*, Fourth Quarter 2002.

SEVC96   Sevcik, P. "Designing a High-Performance Web Site." *Business Communications Review*, March 1996.

SEVC03   Sevcik, P. "How Fast Is Fast Enough?" *Business Communications Review,* March 2003.

SHEN95   Shenker, S. "Fundamental Design Issues for the Future Internet." *IEEE Journal on Selected Areas in Communications*, September 1995.

SHER04   Sherburne, P., and Fitzgerald, C. "You Don't Know Jack About VoIP." *ACM Queue*, September 2004.

SHNE84   Shneiderman, B. "Response Time and Display Rate in Human Performance with Computers." *ACM Computing Surveys*, September 1984.

SHOE02   Shoemaker, M. "IEEE 802.11g Jells as Applications Mount." *Communications System Design*, April 2002 (www.commsdesign.com)

SIMO95   Simon, A., and Wheeler, T. *Open Client/Server Computing and Middleware.* Chestnut Hill, MA: AP Professional Books, 1995.

SKOR08   Skordoulis, D., et al. "IEEE 802.11n MAC Frame Aggregation Mechanisms for Next-Generation High-Throughput WLANs." *IEEE Wireless Communications*, February 2008.

SMIT88   Smith, M. "A Model of Human Communication." *IEEE Communications Magazine*, February 1988.

SMIT97   Smith, R. *Internet Cryptography*. Reading, MA: Addison-Wesley, 1997.

SPAR07   Sparks, R., and Systems, E. "SIP—Basics and Beyond." *ACM Queue*, March 2007.

SPOH02   Spohn, D. *Data Network Design*. New York: McGraw-Hill, 2002.

SPOR03   Sportack, M. *IP Addressing Fundamentals*. Indianapolis, IN: Cisco Press, 2003.

SPUR00   Spurgeon, C. *Ethernet: The Definitive Guide*. Cambridge, MA: O'Reilly and Associates, 2000.

SRIR88   Sriram, K., and Whitt, W. "Characterizing Superposition Arrival Processes in Packet Multiplexers for Voice and Data." *IEEE Journal on Selected Areas in Communications*, September 1988.

STAL99a   Stallings, W. *SNMP, SNMPv2, SNMPv3, and RMON 1 and 2*. Reading, MA: Addison-Wesley, 1999.

STAL99b   Stallings, W. *ISDN and Broadband ISDN, with Frame Relay and ATM*. Upper Saddle River, NJ: Prentice Hall, 1999.

STAL00   Stallings, W. *Local and Metropolitan Area Networks, Sixth Edition*. Upper Saddle River, NJ: Prentice Hall, 2000.

STAL02   Stallings, W. "The Advanced Encryption Standard." *Cryptologia*, July 2002.

STAL05   Stallings, W. *Wireless Communications and Networks*. Upper Saddle River, NJ: Prentice Hall, 2005.

STAL06   Stallings, W. *Cryptography and Network Security: Principles and Practice, Fourth Edition*. Upper Saddle River, NJ: Prentice Hall, 2003.

STAL07   Stallings, W. *Data and Computer Communications, Seventh Edition*. Upper Saddle River, NJ: Prentice Hall, 2004.

STAL08   Stallings, W., and Brown L. *Computer Security: Principles and Practice*. Upper Saddle River, NJ: Prentice Hall, 2008.

STEI02a   Steinmetz, R., and Nahrstedt, K. *Multimedia Fundamentals, Volume 1: Media Coding and Content Processing*. Upper Saddle River, NJ: Prentice Hall, 2002.

STEI02b   Steinert-Threlkeld, T. "MasterCard Tools Up Data Handling." *Baseline Magazine*, June 17, 2002.

SUBR00   Subranamian, M. *Network Management: Principles and Practice*. Reading, MA: Addison-Wesley, 2000.

SYMA01   Symantec Corp. *The Digital Immune System*. Symantec Technical Brief, 2001.

TANE07   Tanenbaum, A., and Steen, M. *Distributed Systems: Principles and Paradigms*. Upper Saddle River, NJ: Prentice Hall, 2007.

TARL07   Tarleja, M.; Chandra, S.; and Tantzen, B. "UC: Adding to the Bottom and Top Lines Today." *Business Communications Review*, November 2007.

TEGE95   Teger, S. "Multimedia: From Vision to Reality." *AT & T Technical Journal*, September/October 1995.

THAD81   Thadhani, A. "Interactive User Productivity." IBM Systems Journal, No. 1, 1981.

THOM84   Thompson, K. "Reflections on Trusting Trust (Deliberate Software Bugs)." *Communications of the ACM*, August 1984.

TIME90   Time, Inc. *Computer Security, Understanding Computers Series.* Alexandria, VA: Time-Life Books, 1990.

TURE04   Turek, M. "The Future of Presence." *Business Communications Review,* May 2004.

TURN01   Turner, K., and Robin, I. "An Interactive Visual Protocol Simulator." *Computer Standards & Interfaces,* September 2001.

UHLA00   Uhland, V. "The Turbo-Charged Enterprise." *Satellite Broadband*, November 2001.

VANS74   Van Slyke, R.; Chou, W.; and Frank, H. "Avoiding Simulation in Simulating Computer Communication Networks." *Proceedings of the 1974 NCC*, AFIPS Press, RI, 1974.

VANS86   Van Slyke, R, "Computer Communication Networks." in Handbook of Modern Electronics and Electrical Engineering, Charles Belove (ed.), John Wiley and Sons, 1986.

VERM04   Verma, D. "Service Level Agreements on IP Networks." *Proceedings of the IEEE*, September 2004.

WACK02   Wack, J.; Cutler, K.; and Pole, J. *Guidelines on Firewalls and Firewall Policy.* NIST Special Publication SP 800-41, January 2002.

WEXL03   Wexler, J. "Irrepressible Frame Relay." *Business Communications Review*, July 2003.

WHET96   Whetzel, J. "Integrating the World Wide Web and Database Technology." *AT & T Technical Journal,* March/April 1996.

WHIT99   White, S. *Anatomy of a Commercial-Grade Immune System.* IBM Research White Paper, 1999.

XIAO99   Xiao, X., and Ni, L. "Internet QoS: A Big Picture." *IEEE Network,* March/April 1999.

ZOU05   Zou, C., et al. "The Monitoring and Early Detection of Internet Worms." *IEEE/ACM Transactions on Networking*, October 2005.

INDEX

Access point (AP), 322–324
ACK packet, 144
Acknowledgement number, 138–139
Active attacks, 523
Ad hoc networking, 320–321
Address signals, 351
Addresses, 89, 95–97, 227–230,
    253–254, 487–488
    domains and, 95–97
    dotted decimal notation for, 228, 229
    globally unique, 253–254
    HDLC, 487–488
    Internet Protocol (IP), 89, 227–228
    Internet Service Provider (ISP)
        assignment, 253–254
    network classes, 227–228
    subnets and subnet masks, 228–230
Advanced Encryption Standard
    (AES), 555
Advanced Mobile Phone System
    (AMPS), 412
Advanced Research Projects Agency
    (ARPA), 84
Alert Protocol, SSL, 551
Amplitude modulation (AM), 471–472
Amplitude shift keying (ASK), 463–464
Analog information, 33, 444–446,
    453–454, 459–462, 463–469,
    471–472
    applications of, 453–454
    data communication, 459–462,
        463–469, 471–472
    data transmission, 444–446, 453–454
    encoding, 463–468, 471–472
    signals, 444–446, 453–454, 459–462
Antivirus approaches, 566–570
Application layer, 111, 113, 115, 573
Application Programming Interface
    (API), 154, 165, 179
Application proxy firewall, 561,
    565–566
ARPA package-switching network
    (ARPANET), 84, 87–88
Association for Computer Machinery
    (ACM), 5
Asymmetric digital subcriber line
    (ADSL), 467–468, 497–499
Asynchronous transfer mode (ATM),
    2, 21, 24, 381–389
Asynchronous transmission, 473–475
Atmospheric absorption, 450–451
Attenuation, 448–449
Audio (voice) communication, 15–16,
    33–35, 444–445
Authentication header (AH), 132, 546
Automatic repeat request (ARQ), 486
Autonomous systems (AS), 231
Available Bit Rate (ABR), 389

Backbone LANs, 264
Backdoor (trapdoor) attacks, 529
Backend networks, 262–263
Backoff time, 291
Backward explicit congestion noti-
    fication (BECN), 380

Bandwidth, 34, 268, 441–442, 452,
    493–496
    audio quality, 34
    data transmission, 441–442, 452
    FDM channels, 493–496
Base station (BS), 405, 409
Basic service set (BSS), 322
Bit (b), 29–30, 36
Blade server, 307–308
Blended attacks, 531
Border Gateway Protocol (BGP),
    231–233
Bots (zombies), 539–541, 571
Bottom-up configuration, 266–267
Bridges, 121–122, 294–296
Broadcast storm. 300
Browsers, 9
Bus topology LAN, 290–291
Business requirements, 2, 15–17,
    32–62, 237–250
    audio (voice) communication,
        15–16, 33–35
    centralized compared to distrib-
        uted data processing, 53–62
    client/server architecture, 59–62
    data communication, 16, 36–37
    differentiated services (DS),
        242–249
    file sizes, 47–48
    image communication, 16, 37–40
    internet speed, 237–240
    performance measures, 42–48
    quality of service (QoS), 2, 240–242
    response time, 37, 43–46
    service level agreements (SLAs),
        249–250
    video communication, 16, 40–42
Byte (B), 29, 36

Cable modems, 466–467
Cables types of, 269–276, 281–282
Cache, HTTP, 201–204
Carrier sense multiple access with
    collision detection (CSMA/CD),
    290–292
Cell loss priority (CLP) bit, 386
Cell phones, 426–428
Cell relay, see Asynchronous transfer
    mode (ATM)
Cell splitting, 407–408
Cellular networks, 404–412
    frequency reuse, 406–407
    increasing capacity, 407–409
    mobile telecommunications switch-
        ing office (MTSO), 409–412
    organization, 405–409
Central office (CO), 92–93
Centralized data processing, 53–62
Centralized database, 67, 70
Centrex, 35
Change Cipher Spec Protocol, SSL, 551
Channels, 382–383, 385, 452–453,
    493–496, 409, 501
    capacity, 452–453
    cellular traffic control, 409

multiplexing bandwidth,
    493–496, 501
    virtual, 382–383, 385
Checksum, 113, 139, 141
Circuit-level proxy firewall, 561, 566
Circuit switching, 20, 84, 86, 345–354,
    359–364
    basic operation, 345–349
    control signaling, 349–352
    Internet messages and, 84, 86
    networks, 20, 84, 86, 345–345, 360–364
    packet switching, comparison with,
        359–364
    Private branch exchange (PBX),
        347–348, 353–354
    Public circuit-switching network,
        347–349
    softswitch architecture, 352–354
Clandestine users, 524
Clear to Send (CTS), 327
Client/server computing, 18–19,
    59–62, 153–162, 179–180
    Application Programming Inter-
        face (API), 154, 165, 179
    applications, 157–162
    architecture, 59–62, 157–158, 162,
        176–179
    classes, 160–162
    client applications, comparison of,
        179–180
    client-based processing, 160–161
    cooperative processing, 160–161
    data processing and, 59–62
    database applications, 158–160
    evolution of, 156–157
    extranets, 62, 174–176
    graphical user interfaces (GUIs)
        and, 158
    host-based processing, 160–161
    intranets, 62, 170–174
    middleware, 154, 163–170
    networks for, 154–155
    server-based processing, 160–161
    service-oriented architecture
        (SOA), 176–179
    Structural Query Language (SQL),
        154, 158–159, 163
    Web systems compared to, 173–174
Clients, 59, 153–154, 160–162,
    179–180, 209
Coaxial cable, 272
Code division multiple access, 412–416
Codepoints, 244
Collision of transmissions, 291
Commercial Information Exchange
    (CIX), 90
Committed information rate (CIT), 381
Common Object Request Broker Ar-
    chitecture (CORBA), 170, 176
Communication, see Data communica-
    tion; Information communication
Component Object Model (COM), 170
Compression, 25
Computer storage prefixes, 30
Constant Bit Rate (CBR), 385, 387

602

Control module (CM), 318
Control signaling, 349–352, 383–384
Convergence, 10–12, 14
Cooperative processing, 160–161
Counter Mode-CBC MAC Protocol (CCMP), 555
Criminal attacks, 525–526
Cross–building interconnect, 319
Customer premises equipment (CPE), 91–93
Cut–through switches, 299
Cyclic redundancy check (CRC), 280, 477

Damaged frame errors, 486
Data communication, 2, 8–10, 16, 36–37, 435–513, 581–585
  analog, 459–462, 463–469, 471–472
  animation projects, 582–583
  business requirements for, 16, 36–37
  data link protocol, 483–510
  digital, 460–463, 463–471
  drivers, 10–11
  encoding, 436–472, 478–479
  error control, 476–477, 478–479, 486
  flow control, 484–486
  high-level data link control (HDLC), 486–492
  multiplexing, 436, 492–505
  networking, 8–11, 37
  parameters and protocols, 478–479
  practical exercises, 583
  reading/report assignments, 584
  research projects, 584
  technological changes, 506–507
  transmission, 30, 437–457, 472–476
  trends, 8–10
  wireshark projects, 584
  writing assignments, 585
Data Encryption Standard (DES), 546
Data packet, 144
Data rate, 452–453, 465
Data transmission, 30, 437–457, 472–476
  analog signals, 444–446
  asynchronous, 473–475
  atmospheric absorption, 450–451
  attenuation, 448–449
  channel capacity, 452–453
  digital signals, 446–447
  electromagnetic signals, 438–444
  guided media, 448–450
  impairments, 447–452
  noise, 449–450, 452
  prefixes, 30
  synchronous, 475–476
  unguided media, 450–452
Databases, 65–70, 158–160, 172–173
  centralized, 67, 70
  client/server applications, 158–160
  distributed, 67, 70
  intranet Web applications, 172–173
  management systems (DBMS), 65–67, 70
  partitioned, 68–70
  replicated, 67–68, 70
  Structural Query Language (SQL), 66, 158–159
Datagram, IP, 117
Datagram approach, packet switching, 357

Deauthentication, 334
Decibels (dB), 285–287
Defense Advanced Research Projects Agency (DARPA), 114
Delay distortion, 449
Denial of service (DoS), 249, 423, 539
Differential Manchester code, 470–471
Differentiated services (DS), 242–249
  codepoints, 244
  configuration and operation of, 246–249
  domains, 243, 246
  field, 244–246
  performance parameters, 243–244
  per-hop behavior (pH), 246–247
  queuing discipline, 245–246
  token bucket scheme for, 248–249
Digital carrier systems, 501–503
Digital electronics, 239–240
Digital immune system, 567–569
Digital information, 33, 41–42, 446–447, 460–463, 463–471
  data communication, 460–463, 463–471
  data transmission, 446–447
  encoding, 468–471
  signals, 446–447, 460–463
  video, 41–42
Digital subscriber line, 22
Direct broadcast satellite, 425
Discard eligibility (DE), 380–381
Discrete multitone (DMT), 499
Distributed applications, 2, 17–19, 81–258
  client/server computing, 18–19, 153–162, 179–180
  differentiated services (DS), 242–249
  extranets, 121–122, 174–176
  Internet communication and, 17–19, 81–258
  Internet Protocol Security (IPSEC), 130–132
  Internet Protocols (IPs), 140–142
  internetworking, 121–125
  intranets, 18, 121–122, 170–174
  middleware, 163–170
  networking protocol choices, 133–134
  Open Systems Interconnection (OSI), 125–130
  protocol architecture, 107–114
  service level agreement (SLA), 249–250
  service-oriented architecture (SOA), 176–179
  Systems network Architecture (SNA), 17
  Transmission Control Protocol (TCP), 115, 117–118, 138–139
  Transmission Control Protocol/ Internet Protocol (TCP/IP), 18, 114–121
  Trivial File Transfer Protocol (TFTP), 142–146
  User Datagram Protocol (UDP), 117–118, 140
  virtual private networks (VPN), 130
Distributed coordination functions (DCF), 328
Distributed data processing (DDP), 17, 52–77

centralized data processing compared to, 53–62
database management systems (DBMS), 65–67, 70
horizontal partitioning, 64
networking implementations of, 71–72
partitioned database, 68–70
replicated database, 67–68, 70
support for, 73–74
vertical partitioning, 63–64
Distribution system (DS), 322–324, 325–326
Document formats, 39–40
Domain Name System (DNS), 88, 97–102
  databases, 97, 98
  internet names and addresses using, 95–97
  operation, 98–99
  root name servers, 99–101
  server hierarchy, 99–100
  structure of, 101–102
Domains, 95–97, 243, 246
Downlink transmissions, 420
Drivers, 10–11

Earth stations, 420
Elastic traffic, 240–241
Electromagnetic signals, 438–444
Electromagnetic spectrum of frequencies, 268–269
Electronic data interchange (EDI), 94
Electronic Industries Association (EIA) standards, 270–272, 275–276
Electronic mail (e-mail), 174, 186–200, 536–537
  internet applications, 186–200
  Internet Mail Access Protocol (IMAP), 189
  intranet applications, 174
  message facilities, 187
  message transfer agent (MTA), 189
  Multipurpose Internet Mail Extension (MIME), 189, 195–200
  Post Office Protocol (POP3), 189
  Simple Mail Transfer Protocol (SMTP), 189, 190–195
  single- and multiple-computer comparison, 186–190
  user agent (UA), 189
  viruses, 536–537
Encapsulating Security Payload (ESP), 132
Encoding, 436–472, 478–479
  amplitude modulation (AM), 471–472
  amplitude shift keying (ASK), 463–464
  analog, 463–468, 471–472
  asymmetric digital subscriber line (ADSL), 467–468
  differential Manchester code, 470–471
  digital, 468–471
  frequency modulation (FM), 471–472
  frequency shift keying (FSK), 464
  Manchester code, 470–471
  modem modulation, 463, 465–467
  multilevel signaling, 464–465

Encoding (*continued*)
  Nonreturn-to-Zero (NRZ) techniques, 469–470
  phase modulation (PM), 471–472
  phase shift keying (PSK), 464
  pulse-code modulation (PCM), 468–469
End systems (ES), 121–122
End-user programming applications, 59
Enterprise services, 11
Error control, 476–479, 486
  automatic repeat request (ARQ), 486
  correction, 476
  cyclic redundancy check (CRC), 477
  damaged frame errors, 486
  detection, 476–477
  frame-check sequence (FCS)
  lost frame errors, 486
  parity checks, 476
  protocols, 478–479
Error detection code, 113. *See also* Checksum
Error packet, 144
Error rate, 452–453
Ethernet, 8–9, 288–315
  bridges, 294–296
  bus topology LAN, 290–291
  carrier sense multiple access with collision detection (CSMA/CD), 290–292
  Case Study: Carlson Companies, 313–315
  Fast, 301–303
  frames, 290–291, 293
  Gigabit, 303–308
  high-speed, 301–308
  hubs, 296–297
  IEEE 802.3 options for, 293–294, 302–303
  medium access control (MAC), 291–294
  networking, 300–301, 308–309
  rates, 8–9
  switches, 297–301
Exchanges, 348
Extended service set (ESS), 324
Extensible Markup Language (XML), 176
Exterior router protocol (ERP), 231
Extranets, 62, 121–122, 174–176

Factory LANs, 264–265
Fast Ethernet, 301–303
Federal Information Processing Standards (FIPS), 28
Fiber-optic transmission, 24, 272–274
Fibre Channel, 289
File sizes, 47–48
File Transfer Protocol (FTP), 87, 120
Firewalls, 558–566
Flags, 138, 140, 487
Flow-based switches, 300
Flow control, 484–486
Forward explicit congestion notification (FECN), 380
Frame relay, 20–21, 374–381
  call control, 379
  congestion control, 380–381
  control plane, 376
  protocol architecture, 376–378
  user data transfer, 378–379

  user plane, 376–378
  X.25 approach, 374–376
Frame-check sequence (FCS), 280, 487
Frames, 278, 280, 290–291, 293, 475, 487–488, 501, 504–505
  bus topology, 290–291
  Ethernet, 290–291, 293
  high-level data link control (HDLC), 487–488
  information (I frames), 487–488
  local area networks (LANs), 278, 280
  medium access control (MAC), 278, 280, 293
  supervisory (S frames), 487–488
  synchronous data transmission, 475
  time division multiplexing (TDM), 501, 504–505
  unnumbered (U frames), 487–488
Free-space loss, 450
Frequency (f), 438–443
Frequency division multiplexing (FDM), 345, 413, 415–416, 436, 493–499
  asymmetric digital subscriber line (ADSL), 497–499
  channels, 493–496
  discrete multitone (DMT), 499
  multiple access (FDMA), 413, 415–416
  signal transmission, 493–496
  switching stations, 345
  wavelength division (WDM), 496–497
Frequency domain, electromagnetic signals in, 440–444
Frequency modulation (FM), 471–472
Frequency reuse, cellular networks, 406–407
Frequency shift keying (FSK), 464
Fundamental frequency, 440

Gateway, HTTP, 201–203
Generic decryption (GD), 567
Generic Flow Control (GFC) field, 384–385
Geostationary earth orbit (GEO), 420–422
Gigabit Ethernet, 303–308
Graphical user interfaces (GUIs), 158
Graphics Interchange Format (GIF), 39
Grayscale images, 38–39
Guaranteed Frame Rate (GFR), 389
Guided transmission media, 267–276, 448–450

Hackers, 524–526
Handoff, 407, 411
Handshake Protocol, SSL, 551–552
Header Error Control (HEC) field, 386–387
Header hub (HHUB), 296
Headers, 113, 117–119
High-level data link control (HDLC), 486–492
  data transfer, 489–490
  frame structure, 487–488
  initialization, 488–489
High-speed service, 237–240, 289, 301–308, 316–341
  digital electronics, 239–240

LANs, 237–238, 289–341
WANs, 238–239
Internet, 237–240
Ethernets, 289–315
wireless LANs, 289, 316–341
Fibre Channel, 289
Hop limit, 142
Horizontal partitioning, 64
Host-based intrusion detection, 555, 557–558
Host-based processing, 160–161
Host-to-host layer, 115
Hosts, 88–89
HTTPS (HTTP over SSL), 207–208
Hubs, Ethernet, 296–297
Hyperlinks, 90
Hypertext Markup Language (HTML), 90
Hypertext Transfer Protocol (HTTP), 91, 200–205

IEEE 802 reference model, 276–281, 290, 293–294, 302–303
  Ethernet 802.3 standards, 290, 293–294
  Fast Ethernet 802.3 standards, 302–303
  LAN protocol architecture, 276–278
  logical link control (LLC), 277–281
  medium access control (MAC) layer, 278, 280–281, 290–294
  physical layer functions, 276–278
IEEE 802.11 wireless model, 322–334
  access control, 327–328
  architecture, 322–325
  extensions, 330–333
  medium access control (MAC) layer, 325–328
  message distribution, 325–326
  multiple-input multiple-output (MIMO) architecture and, 331–332
  physical layer functions, 328–333
  reliable data delivery, 327
  security, 333–334
  services, 325–326, 333–334
  standards, 323, 328–329
  Wireless Fidelity (Wi-Fi), 322–326
Image communication, 16, 37–40
  document formats, 39–40
  networking implementations, 40
  representation, 38–39
  transmission time, 37–38
Impulse noise, 450
Independent BSS (IBSS), 323–324
Inelastic traffic, 241–242
Information communication, 1–5, 6–80. *See also* Data Transmission; Traffic
  asynchronous transfer mode (ATM) networks, 2, 21, 24
  business requirements, 2, 15–17, 32–51
  computer storage prefixes, 30
  convergence, 10–12
  data communication, 2, 8–10, 16
  distributed applications, 2, 17–19
  distributed data processing, 17, 52–77
  internet, 10, 7–19
  internet resources, 3–4
  local area networks (LANs), 2, 19–20, 21–22, 24

management issues, 2, 26–27
metropolitan area networks
    (MANs), 22
networking, 7–10
networks, 19–24
publications for, 4–5
quality of service (QoS), 2
reader's guide, 1–5
standards, 27–28
technology, 7–10
transmission of, 24–26, 30
unified communication (UC), 10,
    13–15
USENET newsgroups for, 4
Web sites for, 3–4
wide area networks (WANs), 2, 20–21
wireless networks, 2, 21–22
Infrared (IR) LANs, 322
Injection laser diode (ILD), 274
Insider attacks, 525–527
Institute of Electrical and Electronics
    Engineers (IEEE), 27–28
Interior router protocol (IRP), 231
Interlacing, 41
Intermediate hubs (IHUBs), 296
Intermediate system (IS), 121–122
International Reference Alphabet
    (IRA), 36
International Telecommunication
    Union (ITU), 27, 417
Internet Activities Board (IAB), 114
Internet Architecture Board (IAB),
    27, 130
Internet Assigned Numbers Authority
    (IANA), 96
Internet communication, 10, 17–19,
    81–258. *See also* Internet
    Protocols (IPs)
    addresses, 95–97, 227–230, 253–254
    applications, 185–222
    architecture, 91–95
    Border Gateway Protocol (BGP),
        231–233
    commercial use of, 94–95
    differentiated services (DS), 242–249
    distributed applications and, 17–19,
        81–258
    Domain Name System (DNS), 88,
        97–102
    domains, 95–102
    electronic mail, 174, 186–200
    extranets, 121–122, 174–176
    high-speed, 237–240
    history of, 84–91
    Hypertext Transfer Protocol
        (HTTP), 91, 200–205
    Internet Protocol Performance
        Metrics Working Group (IPPM),
        250–253
    Internet Protocol Security
        (IPSEC), 130–132
    internetworking, 121–125
    intranets, 18, 121–122, 170–174
    metropolitan area exchanges
        (MAEs), 90
    network access points (NAPs),
        89–90, 92–93
    Open Shortest Path First (OSPF)
        protocol, 233–237
    operation, 226–258
    Quality of Service (QoS), 240–242

routers, 89, 115, 121–123, 230–237
server system management, 218–219
service level agreement (SLA),
    249–250
Session Description Protocol
    (SDP), 209, 211, 217
Session Initiation Protocol (SIP),
    208–217
telephony, 208–217
Transmission Control Protocol/
    Internet Protocol (TCP/IP), 18,
    114–121
Web systems, 171–176
World Wide Web (WWW), 90–91,
    200–208, 218–219
Internet Corporation for Assigned
    Names and Numbers
    (ICANN), 96
Internet Engineering Task Force
    (IETF), 27, 118
Internet Mail Access Protocol
    (IMAP), 189
Internet Organization for Standard-
    ization (ISO), 27
Internet Protocol (IP), 12, 35,
    118–119, 140–142
    headers, 118–119
    IPv4 operation, 140–141
    IPv6 operation, 118, 141–142
    TCP/IP architecture using,
        118–119
    voice over (VoIP), 35
Internet Protocol Performance Metrics
    Working Group (IPPM), 250–253
Internet Protocol Security (IPSEC),
    130–132, 546–548
Internet relay chat (IRC) networks, 540
Internet resources, 3–4
Internet service provider (ISP),
    22–23, 91–92, 253–254
Internet Society (ISOC), 27
Internetworking, 121–125
Intranets, 62, 121–122, 170–174
    client/server architecture and, 62,
        170–174
    electronic mail, 174
    internetworking and, 121–122
    USENET, 174
    Web system applications, 171–174
Intruders, 523–527, 555–558
    criminals, 525–526
    detection systems (IDS), 555–558
    hackers, 525–526
    host-based IDS, 555, 557–558
    insider attacks, 525–527
    masqueraders, 523, 524
    network-based IDS, 555
    threats, 523–527

Jitter, 357
Joint Photographic Experts Group
    (JPEG), 39

Key management, IPSEC, 548
Keylogging, 540

Laptop computers, 426–428
Light-emitting diode (LED), 274
Local area networks (LANs), 2, 19–20,
    21–22, 24, 237–238, 259–341
    backbone, 264

backend networks, 262–263
cables, 269–276, 281–282
Ethernet, 288–315
factory, 264–265
guided transmission media,
    267–276
high-speed, 237–238, 263–264
IEEE 802 reference model,
    276–278, 293–294
logical link control (LLC), 277–279
medium access control (MAC),
    280–281
personal computer (PC), 261–262,
    265–266
protocol architecture, 276–281
server farms, 265
signal strength, 285–287
storage area networks (SAN), 263
tiered configuration, 265–267
wireless, 21–22, 289, 316–341
Location service, SIP, 209
Logic bombs, 529
Logical link control (LLC), 277–281
London Internet Exchange (LINX), 90
Lost frame errors, 486
Low-earth-orbiting (LEOS) satellites,
    422–424

Macro viruses, 536
Mainframes, LANs, 265–266
Malicious software, 527–544, 566–571
    antivirus approaches to, 566–570
    bots (zombies), 539–541, 571
    malware defense, 566–571
    threats, 527–541
    viruses, 531–537
    worms, 537–539, 570–571
Malware, *see* Malicious software
Management issues, 2, 26–27, 514–580
    availability, 514, 521
    computer security, 516–544
    confidentiality, 516–517, 521
    integrity, 517, 521
    network management, 26–27
    network security, 26, 515–576
    security techniques, 545–576
    threats to security, 515–544
Manchester code, 470–471
Masquerade, 519, 523, 524
Media gateway (MG), 353
Medium access control (MAC), 278,
    280–281, 290–294, 325–328
    carrier sense multiple access with
        collision detection (CSMA/CD),
        290–292
    Ethernet protocol architecture,
        290–294
    frame formats, 278, 280, 293
    IEEE 802 layer, 278, 280–281
    IEEE 802.11 layer standards,
        325–328
    IEEE 802.3 layer standards, 293–294
    LAN protocol architecture, 278,
        280–281
    protocol data unit (MPDU), 324
    service data unit (MSDU), 324, 325
    wireless LAN protocol architec-
        ture, 325–328
Medium-earth-orbiting satellites
    (MEOS), 422, 424
Message integrity code (MIC), 555

Message switching, 84–86
Message transfer agent (MTA), 189
Messages, 165–167, 187, 204–205,
    214–217, 325–326, 522–523
  electronic mail facilities, 187
  Hypertext Transfer Protocol
    (HTTP), 204–205
  IEEE 802.11 distribution, 325–326
  modification of, 523
  passing in middleware, 165–167
  release of contents, 522
  requests, 204–205, 214–216
  responses, 204–205, 216–217
  Session Initiation Protocol (SIP),
    214–217
Metropolitan area exchanges
    (MAEs), 90
Metropolitan area networks (MANs), 22
Microbrowser, 419
Microcells, 408
Middleware, 154, 163–170
  architecture, 163–165
  client/server computing, 154, 163–170
  message passing, 165–167
  remote procedure calls, 167–169
Structural Query Language (SQL)
    incompatibilities, 163
Misfeasor, 524
Mobile code, 530–531
Mobile telecommunications switching
    office (MTSO), 409–412
Modems, 463, 465–467
Modulation, 463, 465–472
Multilevel signaling, 464–465
Multipartite virus, 531
Multipath interference, 330, 451
Multiple access, 412–416
Multiple-input multiple-output
    (MIMO) architecture, 331–332
Multiplexing, 25, 436, 492–505
  asymmetric digital subcriber line
    (ADSL), 497–499
  channels, 493–496, 501
  digital carrier systems, 501–503
  frequency division (FDM), 436,
    493–499
  Synchronous Digital Hierarchy
    (SDH), 504–505
  Synchronous Optical Network
    (SONET), 504–505
  T-1 facilities, 503–504
  time division (TDM), 436, 500–505
  wavelength division (WDM),
    496–497
Multipurpose Internet Mail Exten-
    sion (MIME), 189, 195–200

National Institute of Standards and
    Technology (NIST), 28
National Science Foundation (NSF), 89
Neighbor acquisition and reachability,
    232–233
Network access layer, 111, 113, 115
Network access points (NAPs), 89–90,
    92–94
Network jitter, 250
Network management signals, 351
Network service providers (NSPs),
    92–94
Networking, 7–11, 34–35, 37, 40, 42,
    71–72, 133–134, 300–301, 308–309

audio (voice) communication, 34–35
data communication trends, 8–10, 37
distributed data processing (DDP),
    71–72
drivers, 10–11
Ethernet, 8–9, 300–301, 308–309
image communication, 40
information technology, 7–10
protocol choices, 133–134
switches used in, 300–301
video communication, 42
Networks, 19–24, 154–155, 237–239,
    259–341, 342–434, 424–425
  asynchronous transfer mode
    (ATM), 21, 24, 381–389
  circuit switching, 20, 345–354,
    359–364
  client/server computing, 154–155
  configuration of, 22–24, 265–267
  high–speed, 237–239, 263–264
  integration, 19–20
  local area (LANs), 19–20, 21–22,
    24, 237–238, 259–341
  metropolitan area (MANs), 22
  packet switching, 20, 354–364
  personal computer (PC), 261–262
  public data (PDN), 360
  satellite communications, 424–425
  storage area (SAN), 263
  synchronous optical (SONET), 23
  value-added (VAN), 359
  wide area (WANs), 20–21, 238–239,
    342–434
  wireless, 21–22, 289, 316–341, 403–434
Nodes, 344–345
Noise interference, 449–450, 452
Nomadic access, 319–320
Nonpersistant binding, 169
Nonreturn-to-Zero (NRZ), 469–470

Object Linking and Embedding
    (OLE), 170
Object-oriented mechanisms, middle-
    ware, 170
Off-the-shelf applications, 59
Offsite connectivity, WANs, 389–391
Open Shortest Path First (OSPF)
    protocol, 233–237
Open Systems Interconnection (OSI),
    125–130
Optical fiber, 272–274
Origin server, HTTP, 200–202
Orthogonal frequency division multi-
    plexing (OFDM), 322, 330

Packet-by-packet switches, 300
Packet delay variation metric, 252–253
Packet filtering firewalls, 560–564
Packet switching, 20, 85–89, 354–364
  basic operation, 354–357
  datagram approach, 357
  virtual-circuit approach, 358–359
  Internet messages and, 85–89
  networks, 20, 354–359, 360–364
  circuit switching, comparison with,
    359–364
Packets, 113, 143–145. *See also* Proto-
    col data unit (PDU)
Paging, 410
Parity bits, 36
Parity checks, 476

Partitioned database, 68–70
Passive attacks, 522–523
Payload Type (PT) field, 385–386
Peak amplitude (A), 438
Peer entities, 109–110
Performance metrics, 250–253
Per-hop behavior (PH), 246
Period (T) of a signal, 439
Periodic signals, 438–440
Persistent binding, 169
Personal computer (PC), 261–262,
    265–266
Personal digital assistants (PDAs),
    418, 426–428
Phase (φ), 438
Phase modulation (PM), 471–472
Phase of a signal, 439
Phase shift keying (PSK), 464
Physical layer, 115, 276–277, 328–333,
    572
Pixels, 38
Point coordination functions
    (PCF), 328
Point of presence (POP), 91–92
Polymorphic virus, 535–536
Portable Document Format (PDF),
    39–40
Portal, 325
Post Office Protocol (POP3), 189
Postscript documents, 4
Presence server, SIP, 210
Privacy, 334, 555
Private branch exchange (PBX), 35,
    347–348, 353–354
Protocol architecture, 107–114,
    114–115, 125–130, 142–146,
    276–281, 322–333, 367–378, 549
  distributed applications, 107–114
  frame relay, 376–378
  layers, 111, 113, 115
  local area networks (LANs), 276–281
  logical link control (LLC), 277–279
  medium access control (MAC),
    280–281, 325–328
  Open Systems Interconnection
    (OSI), 125–130
  packets, 113, 143–145
  peer entities, 109–110
  physical layer, 115, 276–277, 328–333
  Secure Sockets Layer (SSL), 549
  TCP/IP, 114–115
  TFTP, 142–146
  three-layer model of, 110–114
  timing, 108, 146
wireless LAN, 322–333
  Protocol data unit (PDU), 113,
    128–129, 143–145, 278–280, 324
  Internet protocol packets, 113,
    143–145
  logical link control (LLC), 278–280
  medium access control (MPDU), 324
  Open Systems Interconnection
    (OSI), 128–129
Trivial File Transfer Protocol (TFTP)
    packets, 143–145
Proxy server, 201–203, 209
Public circuit-switching network,
    347–349
Public data network (PDN), 347, 360
Public switched telephone network
    (PSTN), 412, 419

Pulse-code modulation (PCM), 468–469

Quality of service (QoS), 2, 240–242
Quantization, 34
Queuing discipline, DS, 245–246

Raster graphics, 38
Real-time communications (RTC)
　dashboard, 13–14
Real-Time Transport Protocol (RTP),
　208, 211
Record Protocol, SSL, 549–551
Redirect servers, SIP, 209
Refraction, 452
Registrar, SIP, 209
Remote control facilities, 540–541
Remote procedure calls, 167–169
Replicated database, 67–68, 70
Request to Send (RTS), 327
Response time, 37, 43–46
RFC 822, 194–195
RGB color representation, 39
Routers, 89, 115, 121–123, 230–237
　Border Gateway Protocol (BGP),
　　231–233
　internet protocols, 230–237
　internetworking and, 121–123
　neighbor acquisition and reach-
　　ability, 232–233
　Open Shortest Path First (OSPF)
　　protocol, 233–237
RRQ packet, 143

Sample metric, IPPM, 251
Satellite communications, 87, 420–426
　applications, 425–426
　geostationary earth orbit (GEO),
　　420–422
　low-earth-orbiting (LEOS), 422–424
　medium-earth-orbiting (MEOS),
　　422, 424
　network configurations, 424–425
　networks (SATNET), 87
Secure Shell (SH), 120
Secure Sockets Layer (SSL), 206–207,
　548–552
　Alert Protocol, 551
　Change Cipher Spec Protocol, 551
　Handshake Protocol, 551–552
　network security, 548–552
　protocol architecture, 549
　Record Protocol, 549–551
　Web security, 206–207
Security, 26, 130–132, 205–208, 211,
　333–334, 515–580
　authentication, 333, 518
　availability, 514, 521
　computers, 515–544
　confidentiality, 516–517, 521
　deauthentication, 334
　Encapsulating Security Payload
　　(ESP), 132, 546–547
　firewalls, 558–566
　IEEE 802.11 services, 333–334
　integrity, 517, 521
　Internet Protocol (IPSEC),
　　130–132, 546–548
　intrusion detection systems (IDS),
　　555–558
　layers, 572–573
　network, 26, 545–580

　privacy, 334, 555
　Secure Sockets Layer (SSL), 548–552
　techniques, 545–576
　threats, 515–544
　Transport Layer Security (TLS),
　　211, 548
　virtual private networks (VPNs),
　　546–548
　Web, 205–208
　Wi-Fi Protected Access (WPA),
　　334, 552–555
　wireless LAN, 333–334
Segments, 113
Semantics, 108, 146
Sequence number, 138–139
Servers, 61, 99–101, 153–154, 209–210,
　265, 307–308
　based processing, 160–161
　blade, 307–308
　client/server architecture using, 61
　domain hierarchy, 99–100
　farms, LANs, 265
　presence, 210
　proxy, 209
　redirect, 209
　root name, 99–101
　SIP components, 209–210
Service access points (SAPs), 111
Service data unit (SDU) bit, 385–386
Service level agreements (SLAs),
　249–250
Service-oriented architecture (SOA),
　176–179
Session Description Protocol (SDP),
　209, 211, 217
Session Initiation Protocol (SIP),
　208–217
　components and protocols for,
　　209–211
　internet telephony (VoIP) using,
　　208–217
　messages, 214–217
　operation, 211–214
Shielded twisted pair (STP), 270
Signaling rate, 465
Signals, 285–287, 438–447, 459–463,
　504–505
　analog, 444–446, 459–462
　audio, 444–445
　data transmission, 438–447, 459–463
　digital, 446–447, 460–463
　electromagnetic, 438–444
　frequency (f), 438–443
　frequency domain concepts, 440–444
　periodic, 438–439
　SONET/SDH hierarchy, 504–505
　strength, 285–287
　time domain concepts, 438–440
　video, 445–446
Signal-to-noise ratio (SNR), 453
Simple Mail Transfer Protocol
　(SMTP), 119–120, 189, 190–195
　mail flow, 190–192
　mail transfer, 193–194
　RFC 822, 194–195
　TCP/IP, 119–120
Simple Network Management Proto-
　col (SNMP), 121
Singleton metric, IPPM, 251
Sniffing traffic, 539
Softswitch architecture, 352–354

Spamming, 539
Special Publications (SP), 28
Spectrums, 268–269, 441
Spread spectrum LANs, 322
Stateful inspection firewall, 561,
　564–565
Stateless protocol, 200
Stations, 344–345
Statistical metric, IPPM, 252
Stealth virus, 535
Storage area networks (SAN), 263
Store-and-forward switches, 299
Structural Query Language (SQL),
　154, 158–159, 163
Structured cabling, 274–276
Subnet masks, 228–229
Subnets, 228–230
Subnetworks, 121–122, 300
Subscribers, 348
Switches, 297–301
　Ethernet, 297–301
　layer 2, 297–299
　layer 3, 299–301
　networking using, 300–301
Switching techniques, 344–345,
　359–364, 364–365. *See also* Circuit
　switching; Packet switching
Synchronous Digital Hierarchy
　(SDH), 504–505
Synchronous Optical Network
　(SONET), 23, 504–505
Synchronous transmission, 475–476
Syntax, 108, 146
Systems Network Architecture
　(SNA), 17

T-1 facilities, 503–504
Temporal Key Integrity Protocol
　(TKIP), 555
Thermal noise, 452
Third generation wireless communi-
　cation, 417–420
Threats, 515–544
　active attacks, 523
　bots (zombies), 539–541
　communication lines, 521–523
　data, 521–522
　deception, 519
　disruption, 519–520
　hardware, 520–521
　intruders, 523–527
　malicious software (malware),
　　527–541
　passive attacks, 522–523
　software, 520–521
　unauthorized disclosure, 518–519
　usurpation, 519–520
　viruses, 531–537
　worms, 537–539
Three-tier architecture, 162
Throughput, 46
Time division multiplexing (TDM),
　345, 412–413, 415–416, 436, 500–505
　digital carrier systems, 501–503
　frames, 501, 504–505
　multiple access (TDMA), 412–413,
　　415–416
　signal hierarchy, 504–505
　Synchronous Digital Hierarchy
　　(SDH), 504–505
　synchronous mechanism, 500–505

Time division multiplexing (*continued*)
 Synchronous Optical Network (SONET), 504–505
 T-1 facilities, 503–504
Time domain, 438–440
Token bucket scheme, 248–249
Top-down configuration, 267
Traffic, 8, 206, 240–242, 247, 522–523, 409
 analysis threats, 522–523
 channels, 409
 conditioning functions, 247
 elastic, 240–241
 inelastic, 241–242
 quality of service (QoS) and, 240–242
 Web security approaches, 206
Transfer identifier (TID), 143
Transmission Control Protocol (TCP), 115, 117–118, 138–139
 operation, 138–139
 transfer (host-to-host) layer, 115
 User Datagram Protocol (UDP) and, 117–118
Transmission Control Protocol/Internet Protocol (TCP/IP), 18, 114–121
 applications, 119–120
 architecture, 114–121
 IP protocols for, 118–119
 layers, 114–115
 operation of, 115–117
 protocol interfaces, 120–121
 Simple Mail Transfer Protocol (SMTP) and, 119–120
 Transmission Control Protocol (TCP) and, 115, 117–118
 User Data Protocol (UDP) and, 117–118
Transmission systems, 24–26, 30, 37–38, 267–276, 277–281, 285–287, 290–294, 437–457, 472–476
 bandwidth, 268, 441–442, 452
 bus topology LAN, 290–291
 carrier sense multiple access with collision detection (CSMA/CD), 290–292
 coaxial cable, 272
 collision, 291
 data, 437–457, 472–476
 decibels (dB), 285–287
 efficiency, 25–26
 electromagnetic spectrum of frequencies for, 268–269
 Ethernet, 290–294
 fiber optic, 24, 272–274
 frames, 278, 280, 290–291, 293
 guided media, 267–276
 local area networks (LANs), 267–281
 logical link control (LLC), 277–279
 medium access control (MAC), 278, 280–281, 290–294
 prefixes, 30
 signal strength, 285–287
 structured cabling, 274–276
 time, image communication, 37–38
 twisted pair, 269–272
 wireless, 24–25, 267–276
Transponders, 420
Transport layer, 111, 113, 115
Transport Layer Security (TLS), *see* Secure Sockets Layer (SSL)

Transport mode, IPSEC, 546–547
Trivial File Transfer Protocol (TFTP), 142–146
Trojan horse, 530
Trunks, 348
Tunnel mode, 201–203, 547–548
Twisted pair, 269–272

U.S. Department of Defense (DoD), 96
Unguided media transmission, 267, 450–452
Unified communication (UC), 10, 13–15
Uniform Resource Identifier (URI), 211
Unshielded twisted pair (UTP), 270
Unspecified Bit Rate (UBR), 388–389
Uplink transmissions, 420
USENET newsgroups, 4, 174
User agent (UA), 189, 200–202, 209
User Datagram Protocol (UDP), 117–118, 140
User module (UM), 318

Value-added network (VAN), 347, 359
Variable Bit Rate (VBR), 385, 388
Vector graphics, 38
Vertical partitioning, 63–64
Very small aperture terminal (VSAT), 426
Video communication, 16, 40–42, 445–446
Virtual channels and paths, 382–383, 385
Virtual-circuit approach, packet switching, 358–359
Virtual private networks (VPNs), 130, 175–176, 546–548
Viruses, 531–537, 566–570
 antivirus approaches to, 566–570
 behavior blocking software, 569–570
 classifications, 535–536
 digital immune system protection from, 567–569
 e-mail, 536–537
 generic decryption (GD) for, 567
 infection, 534–535
 macro, 536
 polymorphic, 535–536
 stealth, 535
 structure of, 532–534
Voice-grade modems, 465–466
Voice Over Internet Protocol (VoIP), 35, 208–217
Voice switching, 347–349, 361

Wavelength (λ), 439–450
Wavelength division multiplexing (WDM), 8, 496–497
Web security, 205–208
Web site resources, 3–4
Web systems, 171–176
Web 2.0, 13
White noise, 449, 452
Wide area networks (WANs), 2, 20–21, 238–239, 342–434
 architecture, 372–374
 asynchronous transfer mode (ATM), 21, 381–389
 circuit switching, 20, 345–354, 359–364

data switching, 347–348, 361–364
 dedicated (leased) services, 371–374
 frame relay, 20–21, 374–381
 high-speed, 238–239
 offerings, 370–372
 offsite connectivity, 389–391
 packet switching, 20, 354–364
 private and public switching comparisons, 359–364
 public data network (PDN), 347, 360
 switched services, 372–374
 switching techniques, 344–345, 359–365
 traditional alternatives, 359–346
 value-added network (VAN), 347, 359
 voice switching, 347–349, 361
 wireless, 403–434
Wi-Fi Protected Access (WPA), 334, 552–555
Wired Equivalent Privacy (WEP), 555
Wireless application protocol (WAP), 418–420
Wireless Ethernet Compatibility Alliance (WCA), 322
Wireless Fidelity (Wi-Fi) Alliance, 322–326
Wireless LANs, 21–22, 289, 316–341
 ad hoc networking, 320–321
 applications, 317–321
 deploying, 334–336
 IEEE 802.11 model, 322–334
 nomadic access, 319–320
 orthogonal frequency division multiplexing (OFDM), 322, 330
 protocol architecture, 322–325
 requirements, 321
 security, 333–334
 technology, 322
 Wireless Fidelity (Wi-Fi), 322–326
Wireless markup language (WML), 419–420
Wireless telephony applications (WTAs), 419–420
Wireless WANs, 403–434
 business applications, 426–428
 cellular networks, 404–412
 multiple access, 412–416
 personal digital assistants (PDAs), 418, 426–428
 satellite communications, 420–426
 third generation, 417–420
Wiring closet, 275, 281
Workstations, LANs, 265–266
World Wide Web (WWW), 90–91, 200–208, 218–219
 access, 200–205
 history of, 90–91
 Hypertext Transfer Protocol (HTTP), 91, 200–205
 messages, 204–205
 security, 205–208
Worms, 537–539, 570–571
 countermeasures, 570–571
 network threats, 537–539
 propagation model, 538
 state-of-the-art technology, 539
WRQ packet, 143

X.25 approach for frame relay, 374–376